MW01609132

# IDEOLOGIES AND INSTITUTIONS

# IDEOLOGIES AND INSTITUTIONS

*American Conservative and Liberal*

*Governance Prescriptions since 1933*

J. Richard Piper

ROWMAN & LITTLEFIELD PUBLISHERS, INC.

*Lanham • New York • Boulder • Oxford*

ROWMAN & LITTLEFIELD PUBLISHERS, INC.

Published in the United States of America
by Rowman & Littlefield Publishers, Inc.
4720 Boston Way, Lanham, Maryland 20706

12 Hid's Copse Road
Cummor Hill, Oxford OX29JJ, England

British Library Cataloguing in Publication Information Available

**Library of Congress Cataloging-in-Publication Data**

Piper, J. Richard, 1946–
    Ideologies and institutions: American conservative and liberal
governance prescriptions since 1933 / J. Richard Piper.
        p.   cm.
    Includes bibliographical references and index.
    ISBN 0–8476–8458–X (cloth : alk. paper). — ISBN 0-8476-8459-8
(pbk. : alk. paper)
        1. Conservatism—United States.   2. Liberalism—United States.
            3. Political culture—United States..   I. Title.
JC573.2.U6P57   1997                                      96–51886
320.5'0973—dc21                                               CIP

ISBN 0–8476–8458–X (cloth : alk. paper)
ISBN 0–8476–8459–8 (pbk. : alk. paper)

Printed in the United States of America

⊖ ™   The paper used in this publication meets the minimum requirements of
American National Standard for Information Sciences—Permanence of Paper
for Printed Library Materials, ANSI Z39.48–1984.

# Contents

**1981–1993**

**Conclusion**

# Tables

# Preface

The ideas underlying this book began to take shape during my years as an undergraduate in the late 1960s, a period of particularly dramatic flux in patterns of ideological governance prescriptions. Though fascinated by such shifts as the widespread liberal abandonment of presidential government and the tentative conservative embrace of executive leadership, I eventually turned my attention to other research interests as I progressed through graduate school and into my college teaching career. Years later, I returned to focus on my early interest, nudged in that direction by an undergraduate honors program seminar on American liberalism and conservatism since the New Deal that I taught a few years ago at the University of Tampa. Student interest and excitement in that course encouraged me to put my ideas into writing and to undertake further research, which was facilitated by a semester-long sabbatical leave from the University of Tampa.

As for acknowledgments, I owe a primary debt to my parents, who started my education and always encouraged me to pursue my ideas and to write. I also wish to express my thanks to my students at the University of Tampa, who have provided invaluable feedback both inside and outside the classroom; to my wife and daughter, who tolerated my long hours in the study and the library; to the helpful library staffs at various libraries, but especially the Merl Kelce Library; to Brian Garman and Steve Hekkanen for educating me on computer use; to Bob Kerstein, who read and made helpful comments on an early draft of this work; and to Dean Jan Dargel and former Dean Terry Parssinen, who made possible my sabbatical leave. Finally, I owe special thanks to Stephen Wrinn, Cheryl Hoffman, Lawrence Paulson, the reviewers, and the other staff at Rowman & Littlefield Publishers, Inc. Having acknowledged the critical assistance of many, I should stress that the flaws of this book are entirely my own responsibility.

# 1

# Introduction

---

Author of *Conscience of a Conservative* and recognized leader of the conservative movement in the United States, Barry M. Goldwater spoke for most of his ideological supporters as he campaigned against a strong presidency in 1964 even while he sought the presidential office. Goldwater reserved special denunciation for those who "hail the display of Presidential strength simply because they approve of the result reached by the use of power. This is nothing less than the totalitarian philosophy that the ends justify the means." Seven years later, Goldwater declared: "I would put more faith in the judgment of the Office of the President at this time than I would of Congress." Moreover, Goldwater was now an enthusiastic supporter of *institutional* prescriptions giving the presidency the upper hand over Congress on such important matters as war powers and budgetary powers. Conservatives increasingly joined Goldwater in endorsing presidential primacy. Meanwhile, a shift at least equally dramatic was occurring among liberal Democrats—in the opposite direction![1]

In a contrasting picture of long-term consistency, most conservatives were to maintain at least the rhetoric of states' rights in their recommendations concerning federalism for more than six decades from the 1930s to the 1990s. Despite some shifts on federalist matters over time and from issue to issue, most conservatives tended to favor more decentralization of powers to the states than most liberals did throughout this long era.

What do these patterns indicate about American politics? That is the subject of this book.

❖

This book is about modern American political ideologies and government institutions. Following the lead of A. James Reichley and paralleling numerous other studies, it defines a political ideology as "a distinct and broadly coherent structure of values, beliefs, and attitudes with implications for social policy." However, in a departure from most previous analyses, it adds to that definition "and implications for governance." Since the inception of the Republic, most political ideologies in the United States have enunciated prescriptions not only for public policy but also for the "proper" structuring and functioning of the major institutions of American government: appropriate methods of constitutional interpretation, division of powers between the national government and the states, presidential-congressional relations, the roles of the federal judiciary (especially the Supreme Court), and, in modern times, the administrative state. This study will treat the ideologically based prescriptions for institutions as "governance theories" when they demonstrate high levels of coherence and persist over time, although James Ceaser, who coined the term "theory of governance," has employed it in a slightly different fashion.[2]

Soon after the Constitution went into effect, the United States witnessed one of many successive battles between ideological coalitions that articulated distinctive theories of governance. The early Jeffersonian Republicans fused advocacy of strict construction of the new Constitution, a states' rights conception of federalism, and congressionally centered checks and balances together with hostility to judicial activism to create a governance theory that distinguished them clearly, at least in their rhetoric, from the Hamiltonian Federalists. In contrast to the Republicans, the early Federalists called for flexible construction of the Constitution, centralized federalism, presidential government, and judicial activism. Eventually, each of these ideological movements made some adjustments—the Jeffersonians embracing a party-government model that bridged the legislative and executive branches during the Jefferson administration, the Federalists at the Hartford Convention of 1814 staking out a states' rights position, for example. Later in American history, Jacksonian Democrats and Whigs, Progressives and early-twentieth-century conservatives, and other ideological coalitions also demonstrated affinities for particular institutional prescriptions and at times for full-fledged theories of governance. Yet they, too, sometimes found adjustments over time to be appropriate. Although a full history of ideologically based institutional prescriptions would be a valuable project, it is beyond the scope of the present study. This book focuses only on the period since 1933 and examines "liberalism" and "conservatism" and their recommendations concerning the major institutions of American government.[3]

Like many overviews of modern American ideologies, this book employs the liberal-versus-conservative framework as a useful starting point for its analysis. Liberalism as it took shape during the New Deal and persisted into the 1990s has generally emphasized government action to enhance various social and socioeconomic rights for the "disadvantaged." Conservatism as it developed in reaction against the New Deal and its liberal successors has nearly always questioned the egalitarian and rationalistic assumptions of liberalism and stressed strong support for property rights. Of course, there have been internal divisions within both ideological camps, fluctuating areas of overlap between conservatism and liberalism, multiple right-left attitudinal/behavioral dimensions, partially altered meanings of conservatism and liberalism over the six decades between 1933 and today, and political responses to nonideological factors as well as to the major ideologies. Despite these qualifications, this study agrees with a wide array of authors that liberalism and conservatism have been critical to modern American political thought. Its greatest distinction from the other major works on modern American ideologies lies in its primary emphasis on the institutional prescriptions associated with liberalism and conservatism.[4]

In stressing the institutional recommendations of the intellectuals, politicians, and activists associated with the conservative and liberal movements or coalitions from the New Deal to the 1990s, this book always does so against the backdrop of the major assumptions, values, and public policy preferences of the ideological adherents. For insights into the prescriptions themselves and their relationships to one another and to other components of each ideology, this study draws heavily upon numerous insightful, but specifically focused, scholarly analyses. Most of these have centered on one set of institutional prescriptions or on one short time period. For instance, Timothy Conlan and David Robertson and Dennis Judd have given us invaluable works on federal relations. Sidney Milkis, Richard Nathan, James MacGregor Burns, and Arthur M. Schlesinger Jr. are among those who have shed valuable light on the administrative state and presidential government. Stephen Macedo, Christopher Wolfe, and C. Herman Pritchett have highlighted judicial prescriptions and constitutional interpretation issues. A. James Reichley has provided a model study of one time period (the Nixon-Ford years). To all of these, and others, the author of this book is deeply indebted.[5]

Yet none of these works aimed, as the present study does, at an overall synthesis. Therefore, a number of gaps among them had to be filled. This book has done so by focusing on the original writings of liberal and conservative intellectuals, politicians, and activists and on government documents and congressional and judicial voting records. By integrating these with the particular analyses of institutional recommendations and the

general studies of conservative and liberal assumptions, values, and public policies, this study aims to achieve a synthesis that will highlight the
factors giving rise to ideologically based governance prescriptions and
the impact of those prescriptions on various aspects of American politics.

Guiding this study are two major hypotheses, which blend a focus on
individual and group motivations with the "new institutionalism" that
has rejuvenated interest in government institutions in recent years. The
first hypothesis holds that distinct ideological coalitions or movements in
the United States have characteristically generated institutional prescriptions, and sometimes theories of governance, that fit their members'
underlying assumptions, basic values, and programmatic policy preferences and that comport well with the institutional power positions held
by movement political leaders inside the government. It treats such institutional recommendations as the norm, though governance theories may
be more fully developed and more coherent in certain periods than in
others. Rather than conceptualizing institutional prescriptions as mere
means toward power or public policy ends (an "instrumentalist" view),
as many analysts (such as Arthur M. Schlesinger Jr., Samuel H. Beer,
David Kairys, and William G. Andrews) have suggested, or as ends in
themselves, as some proponents (such as Barry Goldwater and C. P. Ives)
have claimed, this hypothesis posits a complex set of means-ends links
but holds that institutional prescriptions have usually been more instrumental means than ultimate ends for modern American conservatives
and liberals. It thus takes a middle position, albeit one considerably closer to the former view than to the latter. This study aims to test this
hypothesis in several ways. It analyzes the timing by which each institutional prescription has emerged and gained wide ideological support. It
also looks at the types of justifications that advocates have offered for
their institutional recommendations. Furthermore, it considers the extent
to which ideological movements have continued to support a prescription when alterations in the values/policy goals and/or the power positions of coalition leaders have undermined the compatibility of the prescription with these power positions and looks at gaps between rhetoric
and behavior.[6]

The second basic hypothesis steering this study is that ideologically
based institutional recommendations, whatever the motivating forces driving their proponents, have had consequences (albeit sometimes unintended ones) for government institutions and their operations, for other
aspects of the political process (including political parties, interest groups,
and popular attitudes), and for other components of the ideology, including future policy and institutional prescriptions. Sidney Milkis's treat-

ment of the impact of liberal presidential government on the American political party system and David Robertson and Dennis Judd's analysis of the effects of federalism compromises on future public policies are prototypes of the kinds of evidence most pertinent in this respect.[7]

The general format of this book employs the basic conservative-liberal dichotomy (with the modifications previously noted) and divides the years 1933–93 into four time periods: 1933–45, 1945–66, 1966–81, and 1981–93. The dividing lines among these are, of course, somewhat arbitrary but reflect the author's assessment of the degree of change evident in the components of the liberal and conservative ideologies and in their power bases within government institutions. They also reflect a decision not to split any presidential administration between two periods, except for the Johnson administration of the 1960s, when the degree of ideological change became so considerable that establishment of a dividing line about 1966 seemed advisable.

The period 1933–45 covered the twelve years of the Franklin D. Roosevelt administration. It was the time in which New Deal liberalism, distinctive in important ways from the previous "progressivism," emerged and gained ascendance, reshaping the basic agenda of American politics. Always strong throughout these years in the upper reaches of the executive branch, with the presidency as its chief focal point, the New Deal liberal coalition held considerable sway in Congress until the late 1930s but lost its power base there even as the Supreme Court shifted decisively toward liberalism. Conservatism, drawing upon two distinctive traditions, regrouped hesitantly and in a rather fragmented pattern in reaction against New Deal liberalism during this period. Yet it had assumed a number of long-term characteristics and had established strong bases of support in Congress and its committee system and in many of the states by the late 1930s. Meanwhile, enduring theories of governance had crystallized in each major ideological coalition and would last far beyond World War II. For the liberal coalition, the recommended institutional framework entailed a "living" Constitution and within it a centralized federalism, presidential government, an expanded administrative state, and judicial restraint in the socioeconomic domain. From conservatives, in contrast, came appeals to an allegedly immutable Constitution of the framers and prescriptions for states' rights, congressionally centered checks and balances, a highly restricted and congressionally oriented administrative state, and judicial activism in defense of private property rights.

The years 1945–66 included the Truman, Eisenhower, and Kennedy administrations and a portion of the Johnson administration. In terms of governance theories, this time was marked more by continuity than by change. However, the Cold War international environment and a domestic scene of rising economic affluence and increasing focus on African-American civil rights at first generated new pressures evoking a "vital center" overlap between liberalism and conservatism, or what some saw as an "end of ideology." Eventually, these factors helped to stimulate other forces that would feed a rebirth of sharpened ideological conflict, erode the governance theories of the two coalitions, and bring this period of relative ideological stability and consolidation to a close.

In the 1966–81 period, ideological patterns in the United States underwent their most dramatic changes since the early New Deal, though flux rather than coherent realignment characterized most of these years. Mainstream liberalism shifted in a generally leftward direction on certain key values and public policies and increasingly splintered. Mainstream conservatism gained neoconservative and "religious right" adherents and additional militancy from older business-oriented conservative proponents, as it shifted some of its emphases markedly. Meanwhile, conservative and liberal theories of governance suffered major ruptures and gave way to certain distinctly new institutional prescriptions, but prescriptions that were often poorly integrated with one another and lacking in durability.

The 1981–93 period, inaugurated by the Reagan presidency and extending through the Bush administration, brought a return to some stability with regard to most major components of the conservative and liberal ideologies and the coalitions that supported them. A near reversal of long-term liberal and conservative positions on presidential-congressional relations was just the most evident of several new shifts on governance questions. However, considerable continuity returned to the coalitions' institutional prescriptions after the turbulence of the preceding decade and a half. For the first time since 1933, conservatives more than liberals clearly dominated agenda-setting in American politics, though conservatives nonetheless suffered a number of setbacks on both their public policy and institutional recommendations. The 1992 elections brought a "New Democrat" to the White House, ending the clear conservative dominion over the executive branch that had characterized the Reagan-Bush years and threatening conservative control of the federal judiciary. The fact that Congress became staunchly conservative and Republican following the 1994 elections was yet another indicator of political change to suggest that another ideological time period had terminated. Whether an entire ideological era of conservative-liberal debate over values, public policies, and institutional prescriptions was also ending was a matter of considerable debate in the mid-1990s.

Within the framework of the liberal-conservative pattern and the divisions into historical time periods, this book follows a format designed to highlight its two central hypotheses: (1) the largely but not fully instrumental roles of institutional prescriptions and governance theories within the conservative and liberal coalitions; and (2) the importance of these prescriptions for shaping government institutions, future ideological choices, and political processes. To accomplish this goal, each of the four sections covering a particular time period (1933–45, 1945–66, 1966–81, and 1981–93) is divided into five parallel chapters.

The first chapter in each historical section seeks to determine which assumptions, values, and public policy prescriptions lay at the heart of liberalism and conservatism in that time period, which ones were peripheral but widely accepted, and which ones internally divided either coalition or both of them. Most of the evidence for these chapters is drawn from major overviews of modern American ideologies and studies of particular ideologies in particular periods. When necessary to fill gaps or resolve differences in interpretation, these are supplemented by original research delving into the writings of intellectuals or politicians and/or analyses of executive, legislative, or judicial behavior.

The second chapter in each section asks: Who were the liberals and conservatives of the period, and what were their bases of institutional strength within the government in particular? Evidence is drawn primarily from assessments of previous scholarly analyses, *Congressional Quarterly* studies (such as those on the conservative coalition), self-identification of participants, and common classifications made by contemporary activists (including *New Republic* and the *Nation* for the liberal coalition for almost all of the sixty-year era, and *National Review* and the *Chicago Tribune* for the conservative coalition for major portions of the era).[8]

The third and fourth chapters addressing each period emphasize the development of the institutional prescriptions that most conservatives and liberals advocated during those years. These chapters begin with brief overviews, look at chronological patterns, summarize those patterns for each ideological movement on the five major institutional issues, and draw conclusions about theories of governance. These chapters are usually the most heavily endnoted and contain the most original research.

The final chapter in each historical section examines how past institutional prescriptions affected those of the current period, the nature and extent of power and policy/values instrumentalism in motivating liberals' and conservatives' choices of institutional recommendations, and the impact of those choices on government institutions, parties, interest groups, and popular attitudes. In assessing motivations, each of these chapters analyzes timing, justifications, persistence of recommendations in the face of contradictory goals, and gaps between rhetoric and behavior.

The concluding chapter, "Retrospect and Prospect" (chapter 22), then takes an overview of modern American political ideologies and their distinctive institutional prescriptions, places modern American patterns in broad historical and comparative contexts, and raises issues for further investigation. It closes with a tentative exploration of future possible developments regarding American ideologies and institutions.

## Notes

1.  Barry M. Goldwater, "My Case for the Republican Party," *Saturday Review* 47 (17 October 1964): 23. The second quotation is cited by James L. Sundquist, *The Decline and Resurgence of Congress* (Washington: Brookings Institution, 1981), 292.

2.  A. James Reichley, *Conservatives in an Age of Change* (Washington: Brookings Institution, 1981), 3; James Ceaser, "The Theory of Governance of the Reagan Administration," in *The Reagan Presidency and the Governing of America*, ed. Lester Salamon and Michael S. Lund (Washington: Urban Institute Press, 1985), 57–87.

3.  Among the best studies addressing ideologically based governance prescriptions in the nineteenth century are Leonard D. White's series of "studies in administrative history," as he terms them: *The Federalists* (New York: Macmillan, 1948); *The Jeffersonians* (New York: Macmillan, 1951); *The Jacksonians* (New York: Macmillan, 1954); and *The Republican Era: 1869–1901* (New York: Macmillan, 1958).

4.  E. J. Dionne Jr., *Why Americans Hate Politics* (New York: Simon & Schuster, 1991); Kenneth M. Dolbeare and Linda J. Medcalf, *American Ideologies Today*, 2d ed. (New York: McGraw-Hill, 1993); Linda J. Medcalf and Kenneth M. Dolbeare, *Neopolitics: American Political Ideas in the 1980s* (New York: Random House, 1985); Kenneth M. Dolbeare and Patricia Dolbeare, *American Ideologies*, 2d ed. (Chicago: Markham, 1973); Paul Gottfried and Thomas Fleming, *The Conservative Movement* (Boston: Twayne, 1988); Alonzo L. Hamby, *Liberalism and Its Challengers: From F.D.R. to Bush*, 2d ed. (New York: Oxford University Press, 1992); Michael W. Miles, *The Odyssey of the American Right* (New York: Oxford University Press, 1980); Iwan W. Morgan, *Beyond the Liberal Consensus* (New York: St. Martin's Press, 1994); George H. Nash, *The Conservative Intellectual Movement in America since 1945* (New York: Basic Books, 1976); Vernon Van Dyke, *Ideology and Political Choice: The Search for Freedom, Justice, and Virtue* (Chatham, NJ: Chatham House, 1995).

5.  Timothy J. Conlan, *New Federalism: Intergovernmental Reform from Nixon to Reagan* (Washington: Brookings Institution, 1988); David B. Robertson and Dennis R. Judd, *The Development of American Public Policy* (Chicago: Scott, Foresman, 1988); Sidney M. Milkis, *The President and the Parties* (New York: Oxford University Press, 1993); Richard P. Nathan, *The Plot That Failed* (New York: Wiley, 1975); Richard P. Nathan, *The Administrative Presidency* (New York: Wiley, 1983); James MacGregor Burns, *Presidential Government* (Boston: Houghton Mifflin, 1965);

Arthur M. Schlesinger Jr., *The Imperial Presidency* (New York: Popular Library, 1974); Stephen Macedo, *The New Right v. the Constitution* (Washington: Cato Institute, 1987); Christopher Wolfe, *The Rise of Modern Judicial Review*, rev. ed. (Lanham, MD: Rowman and Littlefield, 1994); C. Herman Pritchett, *The Roosevelt Court* (Chicago: Quadrangle Books, 1948); Reichley, *Age of Change.*

6. On the "new institutionalism," see James G. March and Johan P. Olsen, "The New Institutionalism: Organizational Factors in Political Life," *American Political Science Review* 78 (September 1984): 734–749. Arthur M. Schlesinger Jr., in Schlesinger and Alfred de Grazia, *Congress and the Presidency* (Washington: American Enterprise Institute, 1967), 8–9, comments: "From the start, views of the proper distribution of power betwen the Congress and the President depended a good deal less on considerations of high principle than on preferences about the uses to which the power was put." Samuel H. Beer concurs with reference to federalism and separation of powers in his introduction to Conlan, *New Federalism.* David Kairys agrees concerning judicial activism and restraint, in his introduction to Kairys, ed., *The Politics of Law* (New York: Pantheon Press, 1990), 5. William G. Andrews, "The Presidency, Congress, and Constitutional Theory," in *Perspectives on the Presidency*, ed. Aaron Wildavsky (Boston: Little, Brown, 1975), 38. Goldwater, "My Case," denounced as "totalitarian" and anticonstitutional those (mainly liberals, in his view) who treat goverment institutions as means toward ends. C. P. Ives asserted that conservatives treat constitutional checks and balances as "the end which would legitimate and fortify all the other ends." Ives, "The Well-Intending Judges," *Modern Age* 13 (Summer 1969): 242.

7. Milkis, *The President and the Parties*; Robertson and Judd, *Development of American Public Policy.*

8. *National Review* began publication in 1955. The *Chicago Tribune*, while remaining generally conservative in its editorial policies throughout the sixty-year era, became less closely identified with the conservative movement by the late 1960s than it had been from 1933–34 until then.

# 1933–1945

# 2

# Liberal and Conservative Values and Programmatic Policies

A "new" liberalism, rooted in American "progressive" reform but also drawing upon British "new liberal" values associated with T. H. Green, John Maynard Keynes, and David Lloyd George, and focused more on economics and less on moral uplift than progressivism had been, was emerging in the United States even before the advent of the presidency of Franklin D. Roosevelt. Nonetheless, the political power of the liberal movement, its preferred programmatic public policies and theory of governance, and even some its basic assumptions and values reflected the influence of Roosevelt and his closest associates in government. In fact, they did so to such a degree that some analysts have described FDR as the founding father of modern American liberalism.[1]

There is some irony in Roosevelt's primacy in the later liberal pantheon. Many of the intellectuals who were developing the new liberalism before 1933 saw him as less than an inspiring leader. For instance, the editors of the *New Republic*, who styled it a journal of liberal opinion and had played a leading role in redefining liberalism along the new lines, found Roosevelt unworthy of an endorsement in the 1932 election campaign, frequently criticized him and his administration for insufficient liberalism, and supported his three reelection bids only with some reservations. FDR's personal belief system has often been described as nonideological; his policies often seemed experimental, jumbled, and even contradictory; and his inclination to compromise was legendary. However, the values that Roosevelt articulated on key occasions over the 1933–45 period, the public policy themes that he pursued, and the institutional prescriptions that he embraced proved central to the liberal political coalition and continued to do so long after his death. Therefore, the expressed values and the public policies of the Roosevelt administration are critical to an understanding of the liberal ideology that prevailed during the New Deal era and later.[2]

Even conservatism defined itself largely in response to Roosevelt and his New Deal. The conservatism of 1933–45 was an amalgam of elements, but the most evident tendency derived largely from John Locke's seventeenth-century ideas of classical liberalism, with a "Manchester" liberal twist, reflecting late-nineteenth-century social Darwinism associated with the rising industrialists of Manchester, England, and their American compatriots. The other major tendency emphasized tradition and order and drew in part upon ideas articulated by Edmund Burke in the eighteenth century. Even the label "conservative" was a matter of dispute. There was, of course, no conservative counterpart to FDR or the Roosevelt administration, or even to the liberal intellectual movement. The American Liberty League made an early stab at seizing leadership of conservatism between 1934 and 1936 but ultimately fell short; a cluster of conservative senators sought to enlist broad support for a conservative manifesto in 1937, but with only limited success; and a few writers such as Albert Jay Nock and Friedrich A. Hayek articulated intellectual values and premises that would eventually win wide conservative endorsement. Nevertheless, common conservative themes did emerge from the major struggles against "New Deal liberalism," and the conservative coalition was not without its victories.[3]

Outside the commonly defined boundaries of both liberal and conservative movements stood several populistic mass movements; a small coterie of fascists; various socialisms; and, despite their sometimes popular front with liberalism, the Communist movement. Because these had little impact on the contemporary or future government institutions central to this study, they will be treated only peripherally.

### Liberal Assumptions and Values

The predominant strands in the liberal thought of the New Deal era shared with progressivism and British new liberalism broadly egalitarian and rationalistic assumptions about humans' potential to shape their environment through a mix of government effort, backed by social scientific expertise, and private pursuits. Liberalism displayed a somewhat greater inclination than progressivism had to apply rationalism to collective economic endeavors, while still seeking to protect some individualistic private property rights. In spheres of free expression, however, its assumptions were highly individualistic and oriented toward notions of a "free marketplace of ideas," in a manner reminiscent of classical liberalism. As noted previously, it was both more materialistic and less moralistic than progressivism had been.[4]

Though a few analysts have seen equality as the highest value of liberal ideology in the New Deal era, equality of opportunity was much more commonly expressed as a value by leading liberals of the period than was "equality of results." Roosevelt often employed egalitarian symbols, but he was usually quite clear what he intended: "we do not destroy ambition, nor do we seek to divide our wealth into equal shares. . . . We continue to recognize the greater ability of some to earn more than others." New Deal policies and their effects certainly gave little evidence of aiming at equal outcomes. Most students of the subject have associated the mainstream of liberalism, as FDR did, with equality of opportunity.[5]

Also common to the worldview of liberalism was the value of positive freedom. First clearly articulated by T. H. Green, the British "new liberal" philosopher, in the late nineteenth century and popularized in the United States by John Dewey, this conception—in contrast to the "negative freedom" or "liberty" value of classical liberalism—stressed freedom, not as the absence of external constraint, but as "a positive power or capacity of doing or enjoying something worth doing or enjoying." Whereas negative freedom was commonly seen as freedom from government restrictions, positive freedom might well be enhanced by government action to raise the potential of humans to the fullest. Government programs to enhance equality of opportunity would likely promote positive freedom for those at lower socioeconomic levels, thus reconciling equality and freedom values as New Deal liberals defined them. Roosevelt's "freedom from want" and "freedom from fear" portions of his Four Freedoms reflected the positive freedom value, as did one of his favorite recurring themes in his speeches, an "economic bill of rights" to promote positive economic freedoms.[6]

At the same time, reflecting individualistic assumptions, liberals of the New Deal era continued to give high priority to negative freedom. In the economic realm, private property rights were to be respected, though modified, in the quest for equality of opportunity and positive freedom (and social security, another major value). In the area of free expression, however, many liberals—perhaps most—thought that liberty should prevail over most other considerations. The executive and legislative branches of the government that were to promote liberal economic opportunity, positive freedom, and social security might need constraints in the area of civil liberties—thus an evolving notion that certain negative freedoms were preferred. The main liberal rationale for this approach was that a minority group losing its free expression to a majority would be deprived of its basic means for becoming a majority or accomplishing its political goals, whereas a minority restricted in some of its property rights would still retain its ability to use free expression to effect a different outcome in the future. Some noted liberals, however, rejected the preferred-freedoms approach. Certainly, finding a way to mesh negative freedom with the other preeminent liberal values represented one of the greatest dilemmas for liberalism in this and in later periods.[7]

Although social security was in conception more collectivist than the other values, and some analysts view it as more central to New Deal liberalism than they, social security in fact integrated fairly easily with liberal interpretations of equality of opportunity and positive freedom. Roosevelt himself made the linkage explicitly in his 1944 and 1945 State of the Union addresses, in terms evocative of those that he had used years before in his Commonwealth Club speech during the 1932 election campaign. The 1944 address asserted: "We have accepted, so to speak, a second Bill of Rights under which a new basis of security and prosperity can be established for all, regardless of station, race, or creed." After listing a variety of positive freedoms, FDR added: "All of these rights spell security." The 1932 version stated: "As I see it, the task of government in its relation to business is to assist the development of an economic declaration of rights, an economic constitutional order. This is the common task of statesman and business man. It is the minimum requirement of a more permanently safe order of things."[8]

Reflecting their generally materialistic orientations and the obvious pressures generated by the Great Depression, New Deal liberals not surprisingly emphasized economic growth. This value they shared with most conservatives, though the two ideological movements differed sharply over how best to enlarge the gross national product. Liberal collectivism and rationalism pointed to much more reliance on the public sector than the conservatives, with their free-market faith, found appropriate or likely to succeed.

Outside the material realm, the value of popular sovereignty through a procedural but majoritarian democracy was high on the list of New Deal liberal priorities. Henry Wallace's conception that this was to be "the century of the common man" stirred widespread liberal enthusiasm. Max Lerner echoed many other liberals when he hailed the presidency as "the greatest majority-weapon our democracy has thus far shaped." Often liberal editorialists and commentators treated presidential election victories as policy "mandates." Yet no major efforts were made, apart from an abortive Senate liberal drive led by George Norris to replace the electoral college with direct popular vote, Roosevelt's brief stab at judicial restructuring in 1937, and liberal attacks on the poll tax during World War II, to alter the formal procedural rules of the game to enhance popular participation. Neither the progressive-era drive for primaries, initiatives, referendums, and recalls nor the 1960s-era demands for participatory democratic reforms characterized New Deal liberalism. Nevertheless, conservatives of the period often saw the liberals as dangerously plebiscitarian in their democratic values and interpretations.[9] Of the key liberal values between 1933 and 1945, the set least clearly integrated with the others and most likely to contradict them was negative freedom (liberty). The preferred-freedoms doctrine represented a serious effort at reconciliation but fell short of full success. Moreover, the liberal values concerning democracy tended toward vagueness and gave rise to few concrete public policies.

### Liberal Programmatic Public Policies

In light of liberal assumptions and values, it is unsurprising that liberal programmatic public policies centered in the socioeconomic realm, particularly in the 1930s. Sociocultural issues generally remained on the periphery. Black civil rights controversies were deliberately kept off the agenda most of the time by the Roosevelt administration, with only mild protestations from the bulk of the liberal coalition. Civil liberties issues captured some liberal enthusiasm, but only sporadically. Only international policy matters intruded seriously enough to distract attention from the domestic socioeconomic policy focus of liberalism, and they did not do so until late in 1939.

Within the domain of socioeconomic public policy, liberals displayed more unity on social welfare reform proposals than on government economic management matters, despite some differences in each area. Most liberals agreed that to maximize equality of opportunity, positive freedom, and social security, the government should undertake an array of social welfare reforms: relief efforts, including public works jobs programs whenever possible; a social security program encompassing unemployment compensation, old age and survivors' insurance, and aid to dependent children; rural electrification; and public housing, to name the major innovations. Although liberals sometimes bickered over precise means, these programmatic public policies won virtually unanimous liberal endorsement in broad outline. Moreover, most liberals responded enthusiastically to Roosevelt's 1944 and 1945 calls for postwar extension of social-economic government programs to include guaranteed rights to "a useful and remunerative job"; to an opportunity to "earn enough to provide adequate food and clothing and recreation"; to "adequate medical care and

the opportunity to achieve and enjoy good health"; and to "a good education." In fact, their chief concerns were that the Roosevelt administration
acted too slowly and too insufficiently in the promotion of social welfare.[10]

In the economic management policy domain, most of the pro–New
Deal liberal coalition distinguished themselves from conservatives to
their right and from communists and some socialists to their left by advocating public policies that would preserve a broadly capitalist economic
system but subject it to increased government regulation to enhance the
liberal values. However, there was little liberal consensus on particular
management policies or even on a general strategy. Dominant in the First
New Deal of 1933–34 was an approach stressing business-government
planning cooperation, with a subordinate position for organized labor, in
the National Recovery Administration (NRA), though policy experiments
with other approaches occurred simultaneously. The NRA, in particular,
aroused much liberal opposition in its implementation processes; both the
*New Republic* and the *Nation* found it increasingly unsatisfactory well
before its demise at the hands of the conservative-dominated, but (on this
issue) unanimous, Supreme Court in 1935. Although some liberals continued to advocate an NRA-type approach to government economic management, countervailing-powers strategies (such as the Wagner Act of
1935, during the Second New Deal); Keynesian-style indirect approaches,
and antitrust strategies all enjoyed considerable support within the liberal alliance. Eventually, during the World War II years, an emergent but
still partial liberal consensus came to center around Keynesianism. A
basic problem for liberalism was, of course, that the often contradictory
and confusing economic management policies of the Roosevelt administration never really produced the economic growth that was one of their
chief aims.[11]

If liberal agreement beyond a vague conception of a middle way
between state socialism and free-market capitalism was somewhat elu-
sive in the economic management area, the same was true of consensus
on black civil rights, civil liberties, and foreign policy. The Roosevelt
administration usually handled the first of these by ignoring civil rights
issues as much as possible and then dealing with them administratively
when action appeared unavoidable. The classic example of the administrative approach was FDR's issuance of his 1941 executive order (poorly
enforced) to make equal employment opportunity regardless of race a
condition of government defense contracts when he faced the threat of a
black march on Washington. Although the liberal intellectuals of the
*Nation* and the *New Republic,* as well as Eleanor Roosevelt, Harold Ickes,
and Henry Wallace, pushed for fuller application of equality of opportu-

nity, positive freedom, social security, economic growth, and democracy to black Americans, congressional liberals did little more than push unsuccessfully for antilynching and antipoll tax legislation.[12]

With regard to civil liberties policies, the American Civil Liberties Union and most liberal intellectuals associated with the *Nation* and the *New Republic* generally pursued a preferred-freedoms approach. On the Supreme Court, too, this strategy enjoyed the endorsement of some liberals. Justice Harlan Stone, in fact, had embodied it in a footnote in the *Carolene Products* case in 1938, though he himself was less prone to protect civil liberties through his actions than some of his colleagues were. However, the Roosevelt administration (most notably in its interning of Japanese-Americans during World War II) had a decidedly mixed policy record, leading James MacGregor Burns to conclude that "Roosevelt was not a strong civil libertarian." Congressional liberal devotion to civil liberties was also uneven—more evident when denouncing the Dies Committee and its unorthodox methods for probing "un-American" activities than in defending the liberties of Japanese-Americans or Jehovah's Witnesses.[13]

As noted at the outset of this section, foreign policy prescriptions increasingly came to the fore after 1939. Roosevelt's brand of internationalist liberal policy mixed Woodrow Wilson's multilateral global idealism with "realistic" power calculations of national interests and New Dealish "Four Freedoms" and "century of the common man" symbolism to muster fairly solid liberal support by 1940. Nevertheless, a small bloc of isolationist antiwar liberals, mostly drawn from Midwestern and Western "old progressive" ranks, and already worried about what they viewed as excessive presidential powers and centralization, resisted his approach with intensity, sometimes coming to identify with the conservative opposition even on domestic matters.[14]

## Conservative Assumptions and Values

Two sometimes conflicting strands of thought, both prevalent in American politics long before the depression, underlay conservative assumptions and values of the 1933–45 period. One, tracing its intellectual roots back at least to Adam Smith and John Locke, was usually described as classical liberalism. It tended toward rationalistic, individualistic, and materialistic assumptions about human nature. Its original egalitarianism had been rejected by Herbert Spencer and William Graham Sumner and their disciples in favor of a much less egalitarian conception of human nature, thus partially harmonizing it with the other major conservative strand in the United States. This one, a traditional conservatism reaching back at least to the ideas of Edmund Burke in the eighteenth century, believed that humans were unequal, often inclined to irrationality and mass political behavior, and in need of spiritual guidance to attain virtue. Though the former strand was more pronounced than the latter in most American conservative thought during the New Deal years, conservatism drew from both. The traditional strand often took the form that Michael Miles has termed "Americanism." One overall effect of the mingling was greater skepticism among conservatives than among liberals about the prospects for positive public-sector social engineering on the socioeconomic questions at the heart of depression-era politics.[15]

In contrast to the liberal quest for equal opportunity, conservatism usually posited no more than the value of formal, legal equality. The conservative *Saturday Evening Post* editorialized in early 1934: "Thomas Jefferson was not given to uttering nonsense. When he wrote into the Declaration of Independence his axiom that all men are created equal, he wrote as a statesman and not as a biologist. He referred to equality of civil liberties and not equality of natural endowments or of natural handicaps. He knew, as well as we, that the first law of Nature is inequality." Even those conservatives who sometimes used the term "equality of opportunity," as Herbert Hoover occasionally did, generally intended no more than a formal equality in legal terms. Some conservatives rejected the value of equality altogether. Frank Meyer, a leading fusionist between the two main intellectual wings of conservatism in the post–World War II period, doubtless spoke for many when he declared: "The freedom of the individual person from government, not the equality of individual persons, is the central theme of our constitutional arrangements. . . . Freedom and equality are opposites."[16]

Certainly, the conservative movement was virtually as one on the view that liberty conceived in negative terms, as freedom from external (mainly government) constraint, was a higher priority than equality. Positive freedom fostered by government was a chimera, likely to lead to socialism, communism, or fascism. As Albert Jay Nock put it in the title of his 1935 book, we must recognize "our enemy—the state." Of all the personal liberties, those pertaining to property rights and "liberty of contract" held the highest priority for conservatives. Judicial conservatives of the 1890–1937 period made this point repeatedly in speech and action and found widespread conservative assent. Friedrich A. Hayek, the Austrian emigré whose book *The Road to Serfdom* was a conservative sensation when it was published in 1944, made the case thus: "Economic control is not merely control of a sector of human life which can be separated from the rest; it is the control of the means to all of our ends." Here was the conservatives' response to the liberals' notion of preferred freedoms. Yet despite the high priority assigned to liberty in the conservative movement of the 1930s, most conservatives distinguished liberty from license; liberty needed to be vested within a stable social order.[17]

"Order," or "national security," or "Americanism" came more readily to conservative lips than did "social security." For traditional conservatives, order was a value of very high priority, often linked to nationalistic appeals and potentially overriding liberty. Classical liberals tended to conceive it as an essential collective good critical to protection of liberty within free markets of private-property exchange. Regardless, conservatism treated it as a more appropriate purpose of government than those posited by New Deal liberalism. State defense of order and private property at home and abroad usually won conservative endorsement, despite differences over mechanisms and rationales. However, when the quest for order and the preservation of liberty came into conflict, conservatism faced a dilemma, heightened by the different priorities of its competing strands of thought. Order and conservative republican principles also could potentially conflict; for the former often entailed more unrestrained government powers than the "constitutionalism" of republican principles indicated were appropriate.[18]

Conservatism, like liberalism and most other ideologies of the period, assigned a high value to economic growth. However, most conservatives agreed with the conservative manifesto of 1937, presented by Democratic Senator Josiah Bailey of North Carolina, that "private enterprise, properly fostered, carries the indispensable element of vigor." Capitalism, not government management, held the key to economic vitality.[19]

Finally, the majoritarian democracy of the liberal coalition, even if procedural and not participatory, was too "plebiscitary" for most conservatives' tastes. Human inequality and irrationality were too evident to make it an attractive prospect, nor did majoritarian democracy comport well with their widespread assumption that traditions should be changed only gradually, if at all. The American Constitution and its republican principles, emphasizing indirect representation, were preferable to popular mandates. Battles over the roles of judges, especially in the 1933–37 period, would bring this set of conservative values to the forefront. Most conservatives also fought against liberal efforts to replace the electoral college with direct popular voting for president.[20]

## Conservative Programmatic Public Policies

Conservative public policy prescriptions resembled liberal ones in one respect during the 1930s—they focused on socioeconomic issues. Of the ten planks in the conservative manifesto of 1937, for instance, nine dealt with matters in this domain (the other one focused on "states' rights, home rule, and local self-government"). Since the manifesto was the product of coordinated efforts among many segments of the conservative movement from both partiesand from elected officials and business leaders, its prescriptions offered a particularly accurate guide to conservative policy preferences. Tax cuts (with reductions in taxes on undistributed profits and capital gains heading the list); a balanced budget, achieved through "reduced public expenditures at every point practicable"; and an end to government competition with, or harm to, private enterprise—these were the primary conservative economic management recommendations. On social welfare policy, the manifesto was rather vague, stressing property rights, avoidance of competition with the private sector, and insistence that relief be only "temporary."[21]

A more complete picture of conservative social welfare policy positions is evident through analysis of congressional roll-call votes. There, conservatives registered opposition to liberal-backed policies on public works, labor-organizing rights, social security, public housing, wealth distribution, public housing, and labor standards. Successful conservative efforts to abolish the Civilian Conservation Corps, the National Youth Administration, the Works Progress Administration, and the National Resources Planning Board (which did the studies that supported FDR's Economic Bill of Rights proposals) indicated a continuation of the struggle during World War II, despite grudging conservative acceptance by then of some of the New Deal welfare state.[22]

In the domain of civil rights for African Americans, Northern and Western conservatives showed little difference from their liberal colleagues, though the conservatives generally were less likely than the liberals to take leading positions on either antilynching or anti–poll tax legislation. Civil liberties issues illustrated a sharper but still not entirely clear-cut contrast between conservatives and liberals. On the Supreme Court, judicial conservatives fairly consistently took a non-civil-libertarian position. The landmark case *Near v. Minnesota* (1931) had found all four Supreme Court judicial conservatives in opposition to the view that the First and Fourteenth Amendments forbade prior restraint of the press. In *Herndon v. Lowry* (1937), they again formed a solid bloc, this time favoring restriction of pro-Communist expression. A concern for sustaining

"Americanism" and combating Communists led conservatives in Congress and in the coalition generally to endorse the House of Representatives Special Committee on Un-American Activities and its hearings and to favor its establishment as a standing committee—actions anathema to most of the liberal movement.[23]

Foreign policy matters split the conservative movement more severely than they did the liberal coalition, at least between 1939 and the attack on Pearl Harbor on 7 December 1941. Southern conservatives generally and a significant number of Eastern big business conservatives supported Roosevelt's increasingly interventionist actions against the Axis powers. For the Southerners, the pull toward internationalism was in part due to Democratic party ties, in part due to strong military traditions. For Eastern big business, financial and business links to London played important roles. Nonetheless, the majority of the conservatives inclined toward an anti-European, "America-first" style of isolationism until Pearl Harbor. Even the interventionist conservatives were more inclined to view the global future in terms of Henry Luce's "American Century" than of Henry Wallace's "century of the common man." Unilateralism and distrust of liberal "idealism" about international relations ran deep in the conservative movement.[24]

### Liberal and Conservative Internal Conflicts

The two ideological coalitions of 1933–45 were far from monolithic. Even at the level of basic values, each ideological movement suffered some internal dissension. On some of the specific policy dimensions, such as foreign policy, disunity was even more evident, as previously discussed. A social democratic tendency within liberalism, strong in some unions of the Congress of Industrial Organizations and on the staffs of the *Nation* and the *New Republic*, showed inclinations to pursue equality of condition and rarely flinched at the label "socialism." White Southern liberalism was less inclined than the liberal mainstream to extend equal opportunity, positive freedom, social security, civil liberties, democratic procedures, and the benefits of economic growth to black as well as white Americans. Even as staunch a Southern liberal as Senator Claude Pepper of Florida publicly endorsed "white supremacy" in this period and insisted that a mild federal antilynching bill was "out of harmony with the New Deal. It runs counter to progressive democracy." However, aside from antilynching and anti–poll tax campaigns, most liberals showed no great urgency on civil rights, thus maintaining considerable North-South unity, at least until late in the period. Western "old progressives," such as Robert M. LaFollette, Jr., George Norris, and Burton K. Wheeler—unlike the liberal mainstream, centered more in the Republican party or third parties than in the Democratic party—tended to hold more moralistic assumptions, to take a rural perspective, and to fear international extensions of liberal ideology more than most others in the liberal movement did. Another liberal split, noted previously, concerned disputes over how and when to mesh negative liberty with the other liberal values.[25]

Among conservatives, a pronounced underlying difference between a Lockean classical liberal belief system and a Burkean traditional conservative set of values was not fully recognized but possessed the potential to split the movement. Moreover, much of business conservatism showed more propensity than other visions of conservatism to perceive that property rights required some "social security" in the form of tariffs, price-fixing, and other protections from competition. White Southern conservatives—housed, unlike most of their conservative contemporaries, mainly in the Democratic party—applied the assumptions about gradual change to local racial traditions in ways not always acceptable to other conservatives and resisted even formal, legal equality for Southern blacks. A final source of internal tension was that both Eastern big business and White Southern conservatives displayed more inclinations toward interventionism abroad than most of the rest of the movement did.[26]

### Beyond and between Liberalism and Conservatism

Beyond the boundaries of the liberal and conservative coalitions of the period lay other, smaller ideological movements, none of which was able to enjoy a major influence on government institutions. Communism and a variety of socialisms sometimes tugged liberalism in the direction of equality of results, as did such populist but nonsocialist movements as those led by Huey Long, Father Coughlin, and Francis Townsend. The populist values of the latter groups partially influenced liberalism, too, or at least its rhetoric, though the majoritarianism of the liberals was to be channeled almost entirely through the existing procedures and institutions. A small contingent of American fascist thinkers, the most notable being Lawrence Dennis, had even less impact on the mainstream than the leftists and populists did.[27]

More significant than the other ideological movements for the evolution of liberalism and conservatism during these years and in the future were "moderate" ideas and policy positions that bridged the gaps between the two coalitions. Party politics in the United States had been distinctly nonideological most of the time since the era of good feelings in the early nineteenth century; patronage and power considerations were often viewed by political leaders as far more critical than high principles. American interest groups, too, had tended to be more material or solidary than purposive in their emphasis. Although most analysts detected an increase in ideological (primarily liberal-conservative) politics during the realignment of the 1930s, previous patterns remained quite significant and served to moderate liberal and conservative tendencies in both partisan and interest-group arenas. Moreover, even many politicians and intellectuals who were concerned with principles staked out positions in the broad areas of overlap or gaps between the two major ideologies: the common desire for economic growth but with mixed methods of achieving it; the blurred lines between equality of opportunity and formal, legal equality; the mix of positive freedom and negative liberty; the overlapping types of security to be emphasized; and the gap between majoritarian procedural democracy and a constitutional republic.[28]

## Conclusions

By the end of the 1930s, both American conservatism and liberalism had taken distinctive forms that distinguished them from one another and from past ideological movements. Of course, tensions between social democrats and liberal capitalist reformers and difficulties in defining the boundaries between negative and positive freedom were among the fault lines challenging liberal unity. Traditional conservative versus classical liberal assumptions and values and the lack of a clear center for political or intellectual leadership continued to be problems for conservatism. Moderate or nonideological actors outside the two coalitions often exerted a significant impact on American politics. Nonetheless, the liberal and conservative movements gave political life in the United States an ideological tinge far beyond what most observers might have imagined just a few years before.

## Notes

1. On the mixture of American "progressive" and British "liberal" roots, see Ronald D. Rotunda, *The Politics of Language* (Iowa City: University of Iowa Press, 1986); and Vernon Van Dyke, *Ideology and Political Choice* (Chatham, NJ: Chatham

House, 1995), chaps. 1, 2. Richard Hoftstadter, *The Age of Reform* (New York: Alfred A. Knopf, 1972), 314–315, emphasizes the economic focus of liberalism in comparison with progressivism. Gary Gerstle ("The Protean Character of American Liberalism," *American Historical Review* 99 [October 1994]: 1043–1073) makes a strong case that a liberal economic focus had already become evident in the 1920s. Alonzo L. Hamby, *Liberalism and Its Challengers,* 2d ed. (New York: Oxford University Press, 1992), chap. 1, is one of several studies portraying FDR as the "founding father."

2. "Voting for a Party," *New Republic* 73 (26 October 1932): 272–273; "The Editors' Choice," *New Republic* 87 (23 September 1936): 207–208; "Reelect Roosevelt," *New Republic* 103 (22 July 1940): 102–103; "The Home Stretch," *New Republic* 111 (6 November 1944): 579–580.

3. Rotunda, *Politics of Language*, chap. 4, discusses the disputes over the conservative label. On the American Liberty League, see George Wolfskill, *The Revolt of the Conservatives* (Boston: Houghton Mifflin, 1962). A good account of the conservative manifesto of 1937 appears in James T. Patterson, *Congressional Conservatism and the New Deal* (Lexington, KY: University of Kentucky Press, 1967), 200–209. Albert Jay Nock and Friedrich A. Hayek are both discussed extensively by George H. Nash, *The Conservative Intellectual Movement in America Since 1945* (New York: Basic Books, 1976), chap. 1.

4. John G. Broesamle, *Reform and Reaction in Twentieth-Century American Politics* (New York: Greenwood Press, 1990), 30–32, provides a good review of the literature comparing and contrasting progressivism and liberalism. On the individualistic-collectivistic tensions within liberalism, see C. Herman Pritchett, *The Roosevelt Court* (Chicago: Quadrangle Books, 1948), 273–277; and Garry Wills, *Nixon Agonistes* (New York: New American Library, 1969), 490–506.

5. The Roosevelt quotation is cited by Van Dyke, *Ideology and Political Choice,* 39. Also see T. V. Smith, "Political Liberty Today: Is It Being Restricted or Enlarged by Economic Regulation?" *American Political Science Review* 31 (April 1937), 243–252. Among those tying New Deal liberalism to equality of opportunity are Van Dyke, *Ideology and Political Choice, 39–40*; and Linda J. Medcalf and Kenneth M. Dolbeare, *Neopolitics* (New York: Random House, 1985), chap. 2.

6. T. H. Green, *Works: Miscellanies and Memoir* (New York: Longmans, Green, 1906), 371–372; John Dewey, "The Future of Liberalism," reprinted in *Political Ideologies*, ed. James A. Gould and Willis H. Truitt (New York: Macmillan, 1973), 76–79; Andrew Heywood, *Political Ideologies: An Introduction* (New York: St. Martin's Press, 1992), 43–45; Van Dyke, *Ideology and Political Choice,* 81. For Roosevelt's Four Freedoms address and discussion of its relation to the Economic Bill of Rights theme, see James MacGregor Burns, *Roosevelt: Soldier of Freedom* (New York: Harcourt Brace Jovanovich, 1970), 33–35.

7. Pritchett, *Roosevelt Court,* 273–277; William E. Leuchtenburg, *The Supreme Court Reborn* (New York: Oxford University Press, 1995), 227–236.

8. In Fred X. Israel, ed., *The State of the Union Messages of the Presidents,* (New York: Chelsea House, 1967), 3:2881. For a full discussion of the background, see Burns, *Roosevelt: Soldier of Freedom,* 422–426. Alan Dawley, *Struggles for Justice* (Cambridge: Belknap Press of Harvard University Press, 1990), 370, stresses the

primacy of social security values. The Commonwealth Club Address quotation is from Howard Zinn, ed., *New Deal Thought* (Indianapolis: Bobbs-Merrill, 1966), 50.

9. Richard J. Walton, *Henry Wallace, Harry Truman, and the Cold War* (New York: Viking Press, 1976), 10–13, discusses Wallace's "century of the common man" theme. Max Lerner, *Ideas for the Ice Age* (New York: Viking Press, 1941), 390. "Will Roosevelt Go Left?" *Nation* 143 (7 November 1936), 535–536, typifies the policy mandate appraoch often taken by New Deal liberals. Theodore J. Lowi, *The Personal President:* (Ithaca, NY: Cornell University Press, 1985), 65, portrays FDR as a chief architect of the "plebiscitary" presidency.

10. The quotations are from Roosevelt in Israel, *State of the Union,* 2881–2883.

11. This section draws particularly from Alan Brinkley, "The New Deal and the Idea of the State," in *The Rise and Fall of the New Deal Order, 1930–1980,* ed. Steve Fraser and Gary Gerstle (Princeton: Princeton University Press, 1989), 85–121, Arthur M. Schlesinger Jr., *The Crisis of the Old Order* (Boston: Houghton Miffilin, 1957), chap. 23; Arthur M. Schlesinger Jr., *The Coming of the New Deal* (Boston: Houghton Mifflin, 1959), pts. 1–3; Arthur M. Schlesinger Jr., *The Politics of Upheaval* (Boston: Houghton Mifflin, 1960), chap. 21; and Hamby, *Liberalism and Its Challengers,* chap. 1.

12. Harvard A. Sitkoff, *A New Deal for Blacks* (New York: Oxford University Press, 1978); Robert A. Garson, *The Democratic Party and the Politics of Sectionalism, 1941–1948* (Baton Rouge: Louisiana State University Press, 1974), chaps. 1–4; and Leslie H. Fishel Jr., "A Case Study: The Negro and the New Deal," in *The New Deal,* ed. Alonzo L. Hamby, 2d ed. (New York: Longman, 1981), 177–187.

13. Pritchett, *Roosevelt Court,* chaps. 5, 10; Burns, *Roosevelt: Soldier of Freedom,* 216; Leuchtenburg, *Supreme Court Reborn,* 208.

14. Ronald L. Feinman, *Twilight of Progressivism* (Baltimore: Johns Hopkins University Press, 1981), chaps. 8–11; Ronald Radosh, *Prophets on the Right: Profiles of Conservative Critics of American Globalism* (New York: Simon & Schuster, 1975).

15. Michael W. Miles, *The Odyssey of the American Right* (New York: Oxford University Press, 1980), chaps. 1 and 2; Nash, *Conservative Intellectual Movement,* chaps. 1–3.

16. "The First Law of Nature," *Saturday Evening Post* 207 (31 March 1934): 22. William F. Russell, "So Concerned and So Dedicated," *Atlantic Monthly* (May 1935), 520, discusses Hoover's usage and its meaning. Meyer's quote is cited in Nash, *Conservative Intellectual Movement,* 224.

17. Albert Jay Nock, *Our Enemy, the State* (New York: William Morrow, 1935); Hayek's quote is from Nash, *Conservative Intellectual Movement,* 5.

18. Miles, *Odyssey,* chap. 2; Wills, *Nixon Agonistes,* 490–506.

19. Patterson, *Congressional Conservatism,* 205.

20. Miles, *Odyssey,* 18–19, discusses 1930s conservatism's antipathy to popular democracy. E. F. Albertsworth, "The New Constitutionalism," *American Bar Association Journal* 26 (November 1940): 865–869, offers a good example. Conservative views concerning the "crisis of the Constitution" are discussed by Schlesinger, *Politics of Upheaval,* 447–496. The electoral college debate and vote are in 78 *Cong. Record* (22 May 1934), 9243–9245.

21. Patterson, *Congressional Conservatism,* 200–209.

22. Patterson (*Congressional Conservatism*) covers the 1933–39 period. For the World War II picture, see Garson, *Politics of Sectionalism*, 31–36; *New Republic* voting records, 18 May 1942, 699–705, and 8 May 1944, 647–656; and Roland Young, *Congressional Politics in the Second World War* (New York: Columbia University Press, 1956), 24.

23. Pritchett, *Roosevelt Court*, 224; Leuchtenburg, *Supreme Court Reborn*, 231; David Caute, *The Great Fear* (New York: Simon & Schuster, 1978), 88–89; Miles, *Odyssey*, 36–37.

24. Miles, *Odyssey*, chaps. 4, 5; Leroy N. Rieselbach, *The Roots of Isolationism* (Indianapolis: Bobbs-Merrill, 1966).

25. On the social democratic tendency in liberalism, see Nelson Lichtenstein, "From Corporatism to Collective Bargaining: Organized Labor and the Eclipse of Social Democracy in the Postwar Era," in Fraser and Gerstle, *New Deal Order*, 122–152, (see note 11); Hofstadter, *Age of Reform*, 306; Miles, *Odyssey*, 13. Analysis of *Nation* and *New Republic* editorials by the author supports the stated conclusion about them. On "white supremacy," Pepper was quoted in the *New York Times*, 15 April 1944, cited by Garson, *Politics of Sectionalism*, 91. On antilynching, the quotation is from David B. Robertson and Dennis R. Judd, *The Development of American Public Policy* (Glenview, IL: Scott, Foresman, 1989), 179–180. On the Western "old progressives," see Ronald A. Mulder, *The Insurgent Progressives in the United States Senate and the New Deal* (New York: Garland Publishing, 1979); and Feinman, *Twilight of Progressivism*.

26. On the business quest for its own "social security," see Miles, *Odyssey*, 9, 14, 30–31; and Kim McQuaid, *Big Business and Presidential Power* (New York: William Morrow, 1982), chaps. 1–3.

27. Schlesinger, *Politics of Upheaval*, 15–207.

28. On the party system, see Sidney M. Milkis, *The President and the Parties* (New York: Oxford University Press, 1993), esp. chaps. 2–4. On interest groups, see Robert Salisbury, "An Exchange Theory of Interest Groups," *Midwest Journal of Political Science* 13 (February 1969): 1–32.

# 3

# Liberal and Conservative Power Bases

---

Over the years between 1933 and 1945, there existed considerable continuity, yet some significant change, in the institutional power centers of the liberal and conservative coalitions, as well as in their popular bases of support. Both ideologies enjoyed more coherence and consistency of expression at elite than at mass levels of politics, though many leaders took nonideological or moderate positions outside, or bridging the boundaries between, the alliances; and the liberal and conservative coalitions each won more popular support among some segments of the general population than among others. The power bases and support patterns of the ideological alliances reflected, and to some extent influenced, the content of their expressed values and programmatic policy prescriptions (chapter 2). Furthermore, the institutional power centers of each coalition were particularly critical to shaping their distinctive theories of governance (the subject of chapters 4, 5, and 6).[1]

## Government Institutions

Despite the misgivings that various members of the liberal movement expressed from time to time about President Franklin D. Roosevelt—particularly his opportunism and frequent willingness to make deals with conservatives—few doubted that his presidency was the major focal point for liberal success within the state structure. Certainly, most conservatives of the period harbored no illusions that "that man in the White House" was anything other than their most formidable political opponent. While vehement in their attacks on FDR, conservatives often reserved their most bitter vitriol for the "New Dealers" who they believed populated the upper reaches of the executive branch and the independent regulatory agencies.

29

In fact, the executive branch was not uniformly liberal. In the cabinet itself, Henry Wallace at Agriculture (and vice president, 1941–45), Harold Ickes at Interior, and Frances Perkins at Labor were long-term leaders of the liberal cause; and shorter-term Cabinet members such as Harry Hopkins, Frank Murphy, and Robert Jackson were also prominent liberals. However, the Cabinet also always included some moderate and even moderately conservative members: Henry Morgenthau at Treasury, Cordell Hull at State, Henry Stimson at War, Frank Knox at Navy, and Jesse Jones at Commerce were generally viewed as nonliberals. Moreover, department and agency officials were frequently more attached to interest triangles linking them to clientele groups and entrenched congressional committee oligarchs than to liberal ideology.[2]

Almost certainly the most important liberal power base inside government lay among those (mostly lawyers and academicians) who flocked to Washington as New Dealers to fill high- and midlevel positions in the executive branch and the independent regulatory agencies: people such as Thurman Arnold, Adolf Berle, Benjamin Cohen, Thomas Corcoran, William O. Douglas, Marriner Eccles, Jerome Frank, Alvin Hansen, Leon Henderson, James Landis, David Lilienthal, Rexford Tugwell, and Robert Weaver formed the heart of New Deal liberalism in government—a fact clearly recognized and sometimes exaggerated by their conservative critics. Many opponents of the New Deal saw the executive branch as a hierarchical liberal monolith run by New Dealers—the "burocracy" to the *Chicago Tribune.* It was not that, but clearly it was more liberal in orientation than Congress, the Supreme Court (until after 1940), or the state governments.[3]

Congress began the period with a receptiveness to executive leadership —liberal or otherwise—conditioned by the crisis of the depression, Roosevelt's charismatic personality and landslide victory in 1932, and enormous Democratic majorities eager to support a Democratic president and to receive patronage from him and his minions. As the "new" liberalism crystalized into its dominant form by 1935, both houses of Congress continued to provide large voting majorities for public policies that were generally dubbed "liberal." Conservatives constituted a distinct congressional minority from 1933 to 1937 and appeared threatened with oblivion for a time.[4]

James Patterson's analysis of congressional alignments in early 1937 counted only 110 conservatives (25.3 percent of the total) in the House of Representatives and 28 conservatives (29.2 percent of the total) in the Senate. However, the recession of 1937, along with Roosevelt administration miscues on its effort to enlarge the Supreme Court and reorganize the executive branch, altered attitudes in Congress (and the country) sufficiently to enable congressional conservatives to thwart many liberal legislative initiatives during 1937 and 1938. The 1938 elections greatly enhanced conservative power in Congress, and a pattern of growing congressional conservatism continued during the World War II years. By the Seventy-eighth Congress (1943–44), data on congressional rollcall votes gathered by the liberal *New Republic* and the Union for Democratic Action (UDA) showed that members with conservative voting records (defined as voting 67 percent or more times against *New Republic*/UDA positions on recorded votes) outnumbered liberals (voting 67 percent or more times for *New Republic*/UDA positions on recorded votes) by a margin of 201–135, with 88 moderates, in the House and 38–32, with 22 moderates, in the Senate (see table 3.1). If congressional conservatives lacked a clear majority, they nonetheless could virtually halt new liberal reform efforts, with the aid of even a few moderates in the House, and could sometimes even force retrenchment of liberal programs in the early 1940s.[5]

The Supreme Court witnessed a shift in liberal and conservative power that was nearly the reverse of the pattern in Congress. From 1933 through 1937, the usual lineup saw three liberals (Louis Brandeis, Benjamin Cardozo, and Harlan Stone) versus four conservatives (Pierce Butler, James McReynolds, George Sutherland, and Willis VanDevanter), with Chief Justice Charles Evans Hughes and Owen Roberts as key moderates who generally, but not always, voted with the conservatives. Occasionally, as in the *Schechter* ruling against the National Industrial Recovery Act in 1935, even the judicial liberals would join in opposing the New Deal, creating a general perception in the country that the Supreme Court was, indeed, the most conservative government institution in the United States. Certainly, the precedents set by the High Court since 1890 appeared to establish a framework inclining the institution to be even more conservative than its

Table 3.1
Congressional Liberals and Conservatives in the 78th Congress

| Ideological Group | House of Representatives | | Senate | |
|---|---|---|---|---|
| | N | % | N | % |
| Liberals | 135 | 31.8% | 32 | 34.8% |
| Moderates | 88 | 20.8 | 22 | 23.9 |
| Conservatives | 201 | 47.4 | 38 | 41.3 |
| TOTAL | 424 | 100.0 | 92 | 100.0 |

members' own political philosophies might incline them to be.[6]

Just how quickly and extensively the Supreme Court's position vis-à-vis the liberal and conservative movements could change became evident between 1937 and 1945. By 1944, the general assessment was that the Court consisted of eight liberals and one moderate conservative. However, the Court liberals almost immediately divided into two fairly contentious wings, with Frank Murphy, Wiley Rutledge, William O. Douglas, and Hugo Black raising the banner of activist civil libertarianism and Felix Frankfurter—often joined by Robert Jackson, Stanley Reed, and even Harlan Stone (the latter the author of the *Carolene Products* footnote articulating the "preferred freedoms" doctrine)—showing an inclination toward self-restraint on such matters. On socioeconomic questions, the liberals were more harmonious. Owen Roberts now stood alone among the justices on what had become the far right of the judicial spectrum.[7]

The state governments tended toward moderation or even conservatism during the years 1933–45. Though a few liberal governors, such as Herbert Lehman in New York, George Earle in Pennsylvania, Frank Murphy in Michigan, Philip LaFollette in Wisconsin, and Ellis Arnall in Georgia, carried the banner of liberalism into state politics, the major study of gubernatorial patterns in the New Deal era concludes that "most governors were nobodies—moderate, undramatic, yawn-inspiring men with legislative programs as pedestrian as they were unsuccessful." Some, such as Frank Fitzgerald of Michigan, Harry Nice of Maryland, Martin Davey of Ohio, Herman Talmadge of Georgia, and Harold Hoffman of New Jersey, were overtly and militantly conservative. State legislatures, many with constituency boundaries explicitly drawn to overrepresent usually conservative rural and small-town areas, others simply unredistricted after decennial censuses, were particular centers of conservative power. Probably even more than the values and policy inclinations of their leaders, the inherited constitutions and institutional structures of the states, their machine-oriented party organizations in many cases, and the competition among the states and localities to attract or retain desperately needed businesses in a time of economic distress, hampered the development of the new liberalism in state and local politics.[8]

## Political Parties

Overlapping the institutions of government, but also external to them, were the political parties: as parties in government operating caucuses in both houses of Congress, sometimes linked to the executive branch; as party organizations providing a base of power outside of government; and as parties in the electorate mobilizing popular voting support. The American Democratic and Republican parties that entered the New Deal era were mainly decentralized and patronage oriented. By 1945, they still possessed these characteristics to a high degree; but the Democratic party outside the South had become generally identified with liberalism, especially in national presidential politics; while the Republican party had become generally identified with conservatism, especially in national congressional politics.[9]

The Democratic "presidential party" was the primary center of liberalism in party politics from 1936 onward. A coalition of liberal interest groups and other liberal influentials gathered for each presidential campaign and increasingly coordinated their efforts to reelect Roosevelt in 1936, 1940, and 1944. Central to this effort by 1944 were the Congress of Industrial Organizations and its political action committee (CIO-PAC), the National Farmers Union (NFU), the Independent Voters Committee of the Arts, Sciences, and Professions (ICCASP), and the Union for Democratic Action. Important as these liberal activists were to the Democratic presidential party, however, they could not completely direct it, despite the South's loss of its veto over nominees in 1936, when the party abandoned its rule requiring a two-thirds majority for nomination. Party machines both North and South were well represented at Democratic national conventions and were sufficiently influential to compel Roosevelt in 1944 to replace the liberals' hero, Henry Wallace, as the vice presidential nominee with Harry Truman, a machine-backed senator with a generally liberal voting record but little emotional appeal to the liberal coalition.[10]

Liberalism was weaker in the Democratic congressional party and most state Democratic parties than in the Democratic presidential party arena. In the congressional Democratic caucuses, conservatives were a significant minority force, representing a variety of mainly but not entirely rural and small-town constituencies during the 1930s but concentrated increasingly in the South during the 1940s. Furthermore, the seniority system, awarding committee chairs to the longest-serving members of the majority party, placed many of these conservatives in charge of key standing committees, thus exaggerating conservative influence in the legislative process. By the 1943–44 sessions, a distinct North-South cleavage was evident among congressional Democrats (see table 3.2).[11]

State Democratic parties remained generally decentralized, patronage oriented, and nonideological, though some machine-style leaders such as Joseph Guffey in Pennsylvania, Ed Kelly in Chicago, and Edward J. Flynn in the Bronx displayed an affinity for liberalism.[12]

Table 3.2
Democratic Liberals and Conservatives in the 78th Congress

| Ideological Group | Northern Democrats | | Southern Democrats | | All Democrats | |
|---|---|---|---|---|---|---|
| | N | % | N | % | N | % |
| | House of Representatives | | | | | |
| Liberals | 90 | 90.9% | 37 | 32.5% | 127 | 59.6% |
| Moderates | 5 | 5.1 | 60 | 52.6 | 65 | 30.5 |
| Conservatives | 4 | 4.0 | 17 | 14.9 | 21 | 9.9 |
| TOTAL | 99 | 100.0 | 114 | 100.0 | 213 | 100.0 |
| | Senate | | | | | |
| Liberals | 22 | 71.0 | 5 | 20.0 | 27 | 48.2 |
| Moderates | 4 | 12.9 | 9 | 36.0 | 13 | 23.2 |
| Conservatives | 5 | 16.1 | 11 | 44.0 | 16 | 28.6 |
| TOTAL | 31 | 100.0 | 25 | 100.0 | 56 | 100.0 |

The Republican congressional party increasingly became a power center for conservatism as the years advanced. As early as 1933–34, the House Republicans were conservative led (by Bertrand Snell) and overwhelmingly conservative oriented in their voting. In the Senate, however, Republican leader Charles McNary was himself a Western "old progressive"; and the Senate Republican caucus was not clearly conservative dominated until the late 1930s, when most of the old progressives left the Senate, became independents, or shifted toward conservatism. By the Seventy-eighth Congress (1943–44), the conservatism uniting most congressional Republicans was evident, as table 3.3 indicates.[13]

The presidential Republican party, somewhat inchoate because of its inability to attain the presidency as a focal point of organization, was considerably less conservative than its congressional counterpart during this period. This was due partly to its chief aim: to win control of the presidency by wooing the national electorate and carrying the electoral votes of at least some large urban industrial states—states generally inhospitable in this period to the brand of conservatism that played well in the small towns and rural constituencies that predominated in the House of Representatives (owing especially to the rural bias of districting) and in the Senate (owing to the equal representation of states regard-

Table 3.3
Republican Liberals and Conservatives in the 78th Congress

| | House of Representatives | | Senate | |
|---|---|---|---|---|
| Ideological Group | N | % | N | % |
| Liberals | 4 | 1.9% | 4 | 11.4% |
| Moderates | 23 | 11.1 | 9 | 25.7 |
| Conservatives | 180 | 87.0 | 22 | 62.9 |
| TOTAL | 207 | 100.0 | 35 | 100.0 |

less of population). It was due partly to the prominent roles of Eastern-based financiers and industrialists and moderate governors in naming Republican presidential candidates. These leaders, especially by the early 1940s, had generally come to terms with the New Deal, however much they might dislike much of its liberalism and particularly its class-oriented popular appeals. A pragmatic desire to win and the willingness of many big businessmen and Republican governors to work within the prevailing power structure to attain their immediate material and power goals seemed to incline the presidential Republicans away from the increasingly focused conservatism of their partisan colleagues in Congress. Thus, Alfred M. Landon and Thomas E. Dewey, the Republican presidential nominees of 1936 and 1944, respectively, took generally moderate positions; and Wendell L. Willkie, the Republican candidate of 1940, was a former Democrat who even leaned toward moderate liberalism. Robert A. Taft, a hero to the conservative Republicans in Congress, where he emerged as their most effective leader and articulator of the conservative creed, would never be able to win control of the presidential Republican party, despite ultimately making three bids for the presidential nomination.[14]

The state Republican parties offered a mixed picture, as was true in the Democratic party. Patronage still often took precedence over policy and principles, but some of the state and local Republican parties were led by such conservatives as Charles D. Hilles and J. Henry Roraback, heads of the New York and Connecticut Republican parties, respectively, in the 1930s.[15]

More than in any previous era in American history since the rise of patronage-oriented mass parties, the New Deal period was one in which the major parties became increasingly imbued with ideology—liberalism for the Democrats, conservatism for the Republicans. Decentralization, patronage, and opportunistic electioneering often hindered this development. Moreover, in the Democratic party, a sharp regional cleavage proved a gigantic obstacle to a "responsible two-party system" based on liberal-conservative ideological differences.

## Interest Groups

The particularlistic claims of many interest groups led their leaders and activists to distance themselves from sweeping ideological commitments. Nevertheless, a number of interest groups became important power bases for each of the major ideological coalitions that emerged in the 1930s. Particularly important in this respect were the major peak associations for business, labor, and agriculture and some overtly purposive organizations that linked themselves to liberal or conservative values, policy prescriptions, and theories of governance.

Broad liberal purposive interest groups of the period included the Union for Democratic Action, the National Citizens Political Action Committee, and the Independent Voters Committee of the Arts, Sciences, and Professions. The latter two were primarily election oriented, while the UDA undertook a wide array of liberal causes despite its relatively small size. All of them drew support primarily from middle-class intellectuals and other professionals interested in liberal ideas. Purposive groups with specific focuses such as black civil rights (notably the National Association for the Advancement of Colored People and the Urban League) and civil liberties (the American Civil Liberties Union) also linked themselves frequently to the liberal coalition.[16]

Labor unions were a critical base of financial and organizational support for liberal political candidates and causes in the 1930s and 1940—more so than ever before or after. Not all union leaders were liberal in inclination. In fact, some of the older craft union heads in the American Federation of Labor were distinctly illiberal. However, many labor activists, especially in the industrial unions of the burgeoning new Congress of Industrial Organizations, took leading liberal roles, often coordinating their efforts with those of middle-class purposive groups. Labor liberals founded Labor's Non-Partisan League in 1936; and the CIO Political Action Committee, headed by Sidney Hillman, played a significant part in liberal efforts in the 1940s, including support for the National Citizens Political Action Committee.[17]

Strongest in the Western Plains and Mountain states and portraying itself as the legitimate heir of the populist movement and a spokesman for struggling small farmers, the National Farmers Union became another mainstay of the liberal coalition, after opposing the first Agricultural Adjustment Act that the Roosevelt administration had developed with the union's chief agricultural antagonist, the American Farm Bureau Federation, and supporting William Lemke's third-party bid for the presidency in 1936. Though smaller than the rival Farm Bureau, the Farmers Union was an important player in liberal politics after 1937, when it began to ally itself with Labor's Non-Partisan League and to support the liberal coalition on most major issues. By the 1940s, its influence extended well beyond agricultural issues, largely because of its dynamic head, James Patton.[18]

Conservative purposive groups included the American Liberty League, prominent in the battles against liberalism between 1934 and 1937. Backed largely by wealthy big businessmen, it also included several very prominent conservative Democratic politicians (most notably, Alfred E. Smith and John W. Davis, the presidential nominees of 1928 and 1924, respectively). However, despite its enormous financial resources and support from prominent figures, the Liberty League enjoyed little success and declined in importance after Roosevelt's landslide victory in the 1936 campaign, during which he had made the "economic royalists" of the league a major target. Another major conservative purposive group, one that emerged during the 1937–40 battles over the Supreme Court and executive reorganization, was the National Committee to Uphold Constitutional Government. Taking the conservative theory of governance as its central theme, this group, led by publisher Frank Gannett, also enlisted a few liberals during the Supreme Court battle of 1937 and spawned several other groups. But after some early successes, its influence waned.[19]

More durable than the conservative purposive groups were those based in business and the professions. Two business peak associations, which mobilized members across the United States for conservative pro-business policies, were the National Association of Manufacturers and the United States Chamber of Commerce. Usually less overtly conservative than these were a variety of business trade associations and the Business Council; the latter enjoyed direct access to Roosevelt, as it had to previous presidents and would to Roosevelt's successors. Although a few prominent big businessmen, such as Joseph P. Kennedy and Averell Harriman, actively supported the New Deal and others eventually sought accommodation with it, most of the organized business community was distinctly conservative. Indeed, many critics suspected that conservative ideology was little more than a smokescreen for business interests.[20]

The leadership of the American Bar Association (ABA) formed another power base for conservatism during most of the period. ABA roles often meshed with those of many state bar associations, particularly in efforts to challenge the liberal theory of governance and build support for conservative prescriptions for government institutions and the law. Even before the formation of the Liberty League and the crystalizing of conservative opposition to the New Deal, the ABA leaders were in the vanguard of conservative critics of the Roosevelt administration.[21]

Largest of the conservative-oriented interest groups and among the most durable was the American Farm Bureau Federation, an alliance of generally prosperous Southern and Midwestern agriculturalists that initially worked with the Roosevelt administration but eventually broke sharply with it and moved toward the conservative coalition. Drawing upon a larger and more affluent membership than the Farmers Union, the Farm Bureau often found areas of common ground with business groups, particularly after 1940, and helped them to extend their influence. Another agricultural interest group, the National Grange, less than half the size of the Farm Bureau and strongest in the Northeast, took a generally conservative, anti–New Deal approach throughout the period.[22]

Each ideological coalition drew significantly from 1933 to 1945 upon a distinctive array of interest groups that, in turn, shaped many of the features of the political ideology. Organized labor's strong support of liberalism made it a much more urban working class–oriented ideology than progressivism had been, for example. Business support focused conservatives' negative-freedom concerns at times almost single-mindedly on protection of private property.

### Wordsmiths

The power of words is an important resource in politics, and both liberals and conservatives drew upon particular sources of support among wordsmiths. In the intellectual world of academicians, journalists, and other writers, liberalism enjoyed such a distinct edge over conservatism between 1933 and 1945 that Albert Jay Nock, probably the leading conservative intellectual of the era, described his conservatives as "The Remnant." However, many intellectuals often tended to pursue their own independent ways outside conventional ideological boundaries. Men such as Walter Lippmann and Charles Beard, for example, defied easy classification.[23]

Important centers of liberal thought during the period were the *New*

*Republic* and the *Nation,* both of which sought through their editorials to guide the direction of the liberal movement and through their articles and book reviews to provide a forum for wide liberal intellectual discussion. Though both journals had circulations under forty-five thousand, they enjoyed wide influence on liberalism. Much more peripheral to the liberal coalition of the period was the *New York Times,* generally moderate to liberal in its editorial stances but usually about as far to the right of Roosevelt as the *Nation* and *New Republic* were to his left.[24]

The conservative movement lacked any equivalent of the *New Republic* or *Nation* during the period. However, most of the major newspapers of the country leaned strongly to conservatism in their editorial stances, as did the popular *Saturday Evening Post. Editor and Publisher* found that at least 60 percent of the daily newspapers opposed Roosevelt's reelection bid even in 1936, when he was at the peak of his popularity. The *Chicago Tribune* became widely known as the flagship for conservatism, but many others emulated its vehement attacks on liberal perfidy. Even the *Washington Post,* later to be regarded as a bastion of liberalism, was strongly conservative in its domestic policy prescriptions during this period. In fact, Felix Morley, soon to be one of the chief architects of the conservative intellectual movement, served as the *Post*'s editor from 1933 to 1940. Moreover, David Lawrence, Frank Kent, and Mark Sullivan headed a sizable list of popular columnists who regularly articulated conservative views.[25]

## Conclusions

Liberalism and conservatism, despite areas of overlap and shifting patterns over time, held distinctive power bases between 1933 and 1945. Liberals enjoyed strong support among intellectuals; in the ranks and leadership of organized labor; and throughout the Democratic party outside the South, particularly in the party's presidentially centered networks. Conservatism occupied a position of strength among most of the organized business community; prosperous agriculturalists of the Farm Bureau and the National Grange; the attorneys of the American Bar Association; the upper middle classes generally; and in the Republican Party, particularly the House of Representatives Republican conference (caucus).

Most pertinent to the theories of governance associated with the ideologies, liberalism and conservatism held different power bases within the institutions of government. The presidency and the upper reaches of the executive branch were the major centers for liberalism throughout the period, populated often but not always by New Dealers. Control of the federal judiciary changed dramatically from conservative to liberal. Congress became increasingly conservative. The states, despite a few notably liberal governors, displayed a propensity either to downplay ideology or to adopt conservative stances. These patterns, in conjunction with some inherent structural features that each set of government institutions possessed or was perceived to possess, helped to shape the liberal and conservative prescriptions for government institutions in significant ways.

## Notes

1.  That this elite-mass pattern is typical is suggested by Philip E. Converse, "The Nature of Belief Systems in Mass Publics," in *Ideology and Discontent*, ed. David E. Apter (New York: Free Press, 1964), 206–231.

2.  J. Lieper Freeman, *The Political Process*, rev. ed. (New York: Random House, 1965), and Richard J. Polenberg, *Reorganizing Roosevelt's Government: The Controversy over Executive Reorganization, 1936–1939* (Cambridge: Harvard University Press, 1966), esp. chap. 4, show the importance of interest triangles during the period. Jordan A. Schwartz, *The New Dealers* (New York: Alfred A. Knopf, 1993) treats such generally conservative figures as Jesse Jones as New Dealers, but most contemporary observers and later analysts support the distinctions noted here.

3.  For examples of the *Chicago Tribune*'s diatribes on the "burocracy" of the New Dealers, see "The Duration of the New Deal," 10 February 1934, 12; "The Dictatorship Exposed," 30 May 1935, 10; and "Proposed White House Staff," 19 March 1938, 12.

4.  James T. Patterson, *Congressional Conservatism and the New Deal* (Lexington: University of Kentucky Press, 1967), chap. 2.

5.  Patterson, *Congressional Conservatism*, 82. Votes taken from *New Republic*, 8 May 1944, 647–656. Figures do not include members who missed more than 60 percent of the recorded votes.

6.  Arthur M. Schlesinger Jr., *The Politics of Upheaval* (Boston: Houghton Mifflin, 1960), 458–464; C. Herman Pritchett, *The Roosevelt Court*, (Chicago: Quadrange Books, 1948), 239–249.

7.  Pritchett, *Roosevelt Court*, 249–263.

8.  James T. Patterson, *The New Deal and the States* (Westport, CT: Greenwood Press, 1969), 153, is the source of the quotation. Most of the classifications of the governors derive from Patterson, chap. 6. David B. Robertson and Dennis R. Judd, *The Development of American Public Policy* , (Glenview, IL: Scott, Foresman, 1988), chap. 4, explores some of the conservatizing effects of state politics in the period. James L. Sundquist, *Dynamics of the Party System*, rev. ed. (Washington: Brookings Institution, 1983), chap. 11, notes that the full impact of the New Deal on state politics was often delayed until a second stage after the 1930s.

9.  Sidney M. Milkis, *The President and the Parties* (New York: Oxford University Press, 1993), chaps. 2–4; Sundquist, *Dynamics of the Party System,* chap. 10.

10.  Alonzo L. Hamby, *Beyond the New Deal* (New York: Columbia University Press, 1973), 31–36.

11.  James MacGregor Burns, *The Deadlock of Democracy* (Englewood Cliffs, NJ: Prentice-Hall, 1963), 156–173 and chap. 10. Patterson, *Congressional Conservatism,* covers the 1933–39 period thoroughly. Robert A. Garson, *The Democratic Party and the Politics of Sectionalism, 1941–1948* (Baton Rouge: Louisiana State University Press, 1974), chaps. 1–4, discusses the growing concentration of Democratic conservatives in the South. Author's analysis of data from *New Republic,* 8 May 1944, 647–656; "liberals" voted with the *New Republic* recommendations at least 67 percent of the time, "conservatives" 33 percent or less of the time.

12.  Schlesinger, *Politics of Upheaval,* 442.

13.  Ronald A. Mulder, *The Insurgent Progressives in the United States Senate and the New Deal* (New York: Garland, 1979), chap. 8; Ronald L. Feinman, *Twilight of Progressivism* (Baltimore: Johns Hopkins University Press, 1981).

14.  Burns, *Deadlock of Democracy,* stresses the presidential Republican–congressional Republican distinction. Also see Nicol C. Rae, *The Decline and Fall of the Liberal Republicans from 1952 to the Present* (New York: Oxford University Press, 1989), 6–7.

15.  Arthur M. Schlesinger Jr., *The Coming of the New Deal* (Boston: Houghton Mifflin, 1959), 480.

16.  Schlesinger, *Politics of Upheaval,* 435–437, on the NAACP, and 91–92, on the ACLU. On the NAACP, see Harvard A. Sitkoff, *A New Deal for Blacks* (New York: Oxford University Press, 1978), esp. chap. 3. On the ACLU, also see William A. Donohue, *The Politics of the American Civil Liberties Union* (New Brunswick, NJ: Transaction Books, 1985), 38–52.

17.  David Brady, *In Labor's Cause* (New York: Oxford University Press, 1993), 65–69; Hamby, *Beyond the New Deal,* 33–38.

18.  John O. Crampton, *The National Farmers Union* (Lincoln: University of Nebraska Press, 1965). Basil Rauch, *The History of the New Deal, 1933–1938* (New York: Capricorn Books, 1944), 68, discusses the NFU's opposition to the first Agricultutral Adjustment Act. *New York Times,* 28 June 1936, 25, discusses its support of Lemke; 13 December 13, l, its new cooperation with Labor's Non-Partisan League.

19.  George Wolfskill, *The Revolt of the Conservatives* (Boston: Houghton Mifflin, 1962); Polenberg, *Reorganizing Roosevelt's Government,* chap. 3.

20.  Kim McQuaid, *Big Business and Presidential Power* (New York: William Morrow, 1982), chaps. 1–3; William E. Leuchtenburg, *Franklin D. Roosevelt and the New Deal, 1932–1940* (New York: Harper & Row, 1963), 147, 176–177; "A Program for Conservatives," *Nation* 143 (5 September 1936): 260–261.

21.  *New York Times,* 31 August 1933, 11; 1 September 1933, 9; 3 September 1933, 15; 28 August 1936, 5. "A Program for Conservatives," *Nation* 143 (5 September 1936): 260–261. Frank J. Hogan, "Important Shifts in Constitutional Doctrines," *American Bar Association Journal* 25 (July 1939): 629–638. Robert Stanley Rankin,

"The Presidency under the New Deal," *South Atlantic Quarterly* 33 (April 1934): 152–164.

22.  Grant McConnell, *The Decline of Agrarian Democracy* (Berkeley: University of California Press, 1959), 100–111, 118. V. O. Key Jr., *Politics, Parties, and Pressure Groups* , 5th ed. (New York: Thomas Y. Crowell, 1964), 32–37.

23.  On Nock, see George H. Nash, *The Conservative Intellectual Movement in America since 1945* (New York: Basic Books, 1976), 14–15; on Beard and Lippmann, see Schlesinger, *The Politics of Upheaval*, 151–154 and 399–400.

24.  Richard Pells, *The Liberal Mind in a Conservative Age* (New York: Harper & Row, 1985), 8–26. The *New York Times* endorsed Roosevelt in 1932, 1936, and 1944, but, concerned over the third-term issue in particular, it supported Willkie in 1940.

25.  Gary Dean Best, *The Critical Press and the New Deal* (Westport, CT: Praeger, 1993), 29; Lloyd Wendt, *Chicago Tribune* (Chicago: Rand McNally, 1979), 378–380; Michael W. Miles, *The Odyssey of the American Right* (New York: Oxford University Press, 1980), 33; Chalmers M. Roberts, *In the Shadow of Power* (Washington: Seven Locks Press, 1989), 194–199, 206–211, 231; "Blackout for the New Deal?" *New Republic* 106 (16 March 1942): 351.

# 4

# The Liberal Theory of Governance

The liberal coalition that adhered to a distinctive set of values and assumptions, advocated social welfare and regulatory programs, and occupied an institutional power base centered in the executive branch of the national government also developed a set of institutional prescriptions that, taken together, came to constitute a theory of governance during the 1933–45 period. Five components were central to the theory, though each should be conceptualized less as a single, fixed position than as a cluster of positions along a continuum or, in some instances, a set of related continuums.

The first and most general of these components concerned the nature of the Constitution and the constitutional framework within which all government institutions must operate. On a scale ranging from flexible permissiveness to rigid prescriptiveness, most liberal recommendations tended toward flexibility. Influenced by pragmatism and legal realism, the predominant liberal conception was of a "living" Constitution that had been, and should continue to be, adapted to changing circumstances, especially in the socioeconomic realm. Partially demurring, some liberals saw the Constitution as inherently too rigid in its present form to permit desirable reforms and called for formal constitutional amendments; but this became a distinctly minority view after 1937. In another variation, some saw certain aspects of the Constitution, particularly the First Amendment, as appropriately more fixed and specific than others. Nevertheless, most liberals were quite distinct from most conservatives in their inclination toward constitutional flexibility.

A second element in the liberal theory of governance was the advocacy of a national government–state government relationship more centralized than in the past and more centralized than most conservatives of the period favored. While liberals differed over whether this was to be centralized

43

or cooperative federalism (and a few even favored a shift to a centralized unitary relationship such as that in Britain and France), there was no question that liberals in general tended to gravitate toward the centralization end of the continuum on national-state relations.

Third, within the national government itself, liberals of the period usually advocated the development of an administrative-state bureaucracy, possessing the characteristics of professionalism and hierarchy that German sociologist Max Weber had described as essential features of modern bureaucracy, to replace either a "nightwatchman" limited state overseeing largely laissez-faire market relations or patronage-based, unprofessional, fragmented administration. Beyond that, most liberals favored lodging this administrative state clearly in the executive branch of the national government, subject to presidential direction, not to congressional micromanagement efforts.

A fourth, and closely related, element of the liberal model was presidential government. This encompassed strengthened presidential roles with regard to leadership and management in domestic and national security and foreign policy, but it also entailed presidential roles in actively promoting socioeconomic reform (including initiating programs and driving them through Congress) and in mobilizing popular majorities. The recommendations included somewhat diminished roles for Congress vis-à-vis the president in these spheres, though most liberals emphasized these ideas less than their presidential role prescriptions. Each of the prescribed roles occupied a position on a somewhat distinctive continuum of its own, and liberals differed a bit among themselves in their blending of these roles; but presidentialism became a distinguishing feature of the liberal theory of governance, certainly when compared with the conservative theory.

Finally, there were the liberal prescriptions concerning the Supreme Court and its proper relationships to the other institutions of government. Of all of the major components of liberal theory, this was the most subject to change and continuing dispute during the 1933–45 period. At first largely, but not fully, supportive of judicial restraint vis-à-vis majoritarian institutions (Congress, the president, elected state officials), liberals eventually found themselves unable to agree on a common denominator beyond the proposition that the Supreme Court should defer to the president and Congress when these elective institutions agreed on socioeconomic policy in areas where the Constitution was ambiguous.

Later in this chapter, we shall return to these five components and elucidate further some of the liberals' specific views and internal differences concerning them. First, however, it is appropriate to consider how and when the liberal institutional recommendations emerged, evolved, and became integrated into a general theory of governance between 1933 and 1945.

### The Roosevelt Administration Initiatives of 1933–1935

The approach taken by the Roosevelt administration to promote economic relief, recovery, and reform played an important part in shaping what became the dominant new liberal theory of governance in the 1930s and 1940s. Preferences and behavior patterns inherited from the Progressive Era of 1900–20, of course, helped to influence that approach, as well as to condition the responses of the liberal coalition to it.

The approach of the First New Deal of 1933 was typified by such major initiatives of the First Hundred Days as the Emergency Banking Act, the Economy Act, the Agricultural Adjustment Act, and the National Industrial Recovery Act. The national government, not the states, should take the primary responsibility for addressing the critical socioeconomic issues, though the states would often be involved cooperatively through matching grants-in-aid in areas such as the relief administered by the newly created Federal Emergency Relief Administration. Within the national government itself, Congress should delegate sweeping grants of unclearly defined authority to the president and a swelling administrative bureaucracy under his aegis. The president was also expected to take the lead in developing reforms and driving them through Congress and to assume a role as the "tribune" of a popular majority. The Constitution, it was thought, was flexible enough to permit these massive institutional changes without a constitutional amendment, though there was some concern that the Supreme Court, given its past track record, might not agree and might overturn New Deal initiatives. The Roosevelt administration, however, evinced little concern about possible judicial negation. Lifting high the blue-eagle standard of its newly created National Recovery Administration, it exhorted its supporters to follow where it led. Most new liberals did, though not without some qualms.

FDR's early actions were pragmatic, frankly experimental responses. But they did reflect the assumptions and attitudes of many who had risen to power in the Progressive Era and its wake. Probably the most common analogy that New Dealers drew was to the war crisis of 1917–18, when a centralized, presidentially directed, embryonic administrative state had taken control of government policy at home and abroad. Was not the depression a crisis of similar magnitude, demanding a similar response?

The nation, claimed FDR, must move "as a trained and loyal army willing to sacrifice for the good of a common discipline." What was needed was "broad Executive power to wage a war against the emergency, as great as the power that would be given to me if we were in fact invaded by a foreign foe." Some of the new institutions, such as the National Recovery Administration (NRA), drew directly upon World War I models.[1]

Beyond the wartime experience, however, lay other inheritances from progressivism. Rationalistic assumptions that governmental social engineering could lead to human social progress were an important carryover, though the liberals of the 1930s were much more inclined than the early progressives to eschew moral uplift in favor of socioeconomic betterment as the primary goal of their reform efforts. Presidential government and an administrative state had been advocated by both the Theodore Roosevelt and the Woodrow Wilson brands of progressivism, though each had developed its own distinctive model. Progressive jurists, such as Oliver Wendell Holmes and Louis Brandeis, had, usually in dissents, laid the ground work for developing liberal views on appropriate judicial roles and constitutional interpretation. In his 1908 book, *Constitutional Government in the United States,* Woodrow Wilson had stressed conceptions of constitutional flexibility, rooted in pragmatism as a philosophy; and FDR as governor of New York had termed the Constitution "the most marvelously elastic compilation of rules of government ever written." Even a move toward more centralized federalism had engaged considerable progressive support, as seen in the expansion of grant-in-aid programs during the Wilson administration and the centralization during World War I. But on this point, progressive thought was badly divided. Democratic party progressives, especially, had long employed the rhetoric of states' rights and Jeffersonian decentralism, as had some Republican progressives such as Senator William E. Borah. FDR himself had stressed the importance of states' rights and had linked them to democracy in a nationwide radio address as recently as 2 March 1930, concluding that "almost every new or old problem of government must be solved, if it is to be solved to the satisfaction of the people of the whole country, by each State in its own way."[2]

Much of the Roosevelt administration's approach to governance during the First New Deal was implicit rather than explicit, with more emphasis on programmatic policies or desired outcomes than on institutional reforms as such. Nonetheless, widespread awareness of major changes in institutions was evident almost immediately. The *New York Times* headlined an article "Roosevelt Gets Power of a Dictator" on 11 March 1933. In the *New Republic,* TRB noted on 22 March that "Mr. Roosevelt has, in some respects, more power than any other President under our Constitution ever had, except perhaps Mr. Wilson in wartime."[3]

Some of the new liberals of 1933, especially among intellectuals, favored much more dramatic and more explicit breaks with traditional American theories of governance than FDR was prepared to endorse. Among these, such men as Jerome Frank, Rexford Tugwell, and Luther Gulick had considerable impact on the administration and its behavior.

On the subject of constitutionalism, Frank was a leading proponent, along with Karl Llewellyn and Herman Oliphant, of a "legal realism" that viewed judicial interpretations of the Constitution as little more than lawmaking exercises. Not only was the Constitution "flexible," as most progressives had come to conclude, but its interpretation almost inevitably reflected the interpreters' own ideological propensities. Legal realism was part of a general revolt against formalism and conceptualism. Growing in importance from the 1920s onward, it had a profound effect on the new liberalism. Elizabeth Mensch summarized its implications: "There was *no such thing* as an objective legal methodology behind which judges could hide in order to evade responsibility for the social consequences of legal decision making. Every decision they made was a moral and political choice."[4]

Echoing the legal realists, Rexford Tugwell, already a New Deal architect as he addressed the Bar Association of Western New York in June 1933, declared: "'Constitutionality' is talked about as if it were a tangible fact, undeviating and precise. The wiser lawyers of my acquaintance agree with me in recognizing the folly of such a notion. Constitutional law, at any given time, is the then current theory of what ought and what ought not to be done under the Constitution, a legalistic expression of the prevailing political and economic philosophy."[5]

Gulick, professor of government at Columbia University and soon to be renowned for his work on the President's Committee on Administrative Management, advocated both a Weberian administrative state on the European model, headed by a presidency with enhanced powers, and a highly centralized federalism, with strong national power, perhaps modified by "some regional authority, to be set up by the national government," rather than by state sovereignty. Addressing the issue of federalism in June 1933, Gulick called for an institutional power shift extending far beyond that of the early New Deal: "All essential powers effecting [sic] economic planning and control must be taken from the states and given to the nation. These would seem to include all control over banking, insurance, credit, transportation and communications, social insurance, the creation of corporations, the regulation of utilities, the major highways, automobile licensing, all control of labor, prices, production and profits, and finally taxation, with the exception of real estate."[6]

If Frank, Tugwell, Gulick, and others like them were pushing beyond the early Roosevelt administration in the direction of flexible constitutional law, a highly centralized federal system, and a strong presidency directing an administrative state, other liberals and future liberals were fearful that the administration's initiatives were going too far—at least too far toward presidential dominance or centralization. For the most part, doubters focused on one or the other, but some expressed concern about both.

On the matter of presidential-congressional relations, the moderate-to-liberal *New York Times,* at the end of the Hundred Days, expressed pleasure with Roosevelt's thus far cautious use of his new authority but emphasized the emergency nature of the powers and voiced the hope that many of them would never be employed.[7]

Paul Y. Anderson, writing in the *Nation,* was less optimistic than the *New York Times* editors: "Worst of all, a dangerous precedent has been reaffirmed. . . . To the precise extent that Roosevelt Rex exercises his new powers with wisdom, restraint, and decency, will it be easier for some future Hoover to seize them."[8]

Like many other liberals, TRB in the *New Republic* took an explicitly intrumentalist approach of "wait and see." Noting that "Mr. Roosevelt is granted authority such as no President ever dreamed of asking before, but he is not directed to use that authority," he urged liberals to withhold their applause for the time being. Although "the progressive leaders have been enthusiastic over what they firmly believe is the convinced liberalism of the White House," TRB stressed, Roosevelt was continuing to consult with and reassure conservative political and business leaders. "Mr. Roosevelt, while acquiring power, has as yet to make a single decision, and both sides in the Senate are unclear as to his future course. I rather think he is uncertain himself."[9]

Sharing reservations about broad grants of powers for ill-defined purposes, or fearing that the purposes were illiberal in character, more than a third of those later identified as liberals in the House of Representatives on 11 March 1933 opposed the Roosevelt administration's Economy Bill. Two days previously, most of the small core of Senate opposition to the Emergency Banking Bill had also come from liberals or "old progressives." However, even on these votes, most congressional liberals sided with the administration; and subsequent augmentations of presidential and executive branch power such as those embodied in the National Industrial Recovery Act won almost unanimous congressional liberal endorsement.[10]

The national government's accumulation of powers also worried some liberals, though few expressed their concerns in terms of the states' rights arguments voiced by most conservative critics. Instead, most who hesitated or opposed Roosevelt's initiatives expressed fears of a big government–big business partnership. "*The New Republic* has been a consistent advocate of social-economic planning," wrote its editors in early May 1933, "but it has again and again pointed out that the objectives of planning, the methods, and the powers in control, are of crucial importance. There is a kind of 'planning' wanted by certain advanced business leaders, and now being urged upon the administration, which is wholly unsound." More than most other Roosevelt agencies, the NRA tapped these fears, as indicated by the ongoing criticisms of its policies by both the *Nation* and the *New Republic*. However, almost all congressional liberals (unlike many conservatives) voted for the National Industrial Recovery Act that established the NRA and enhanced national governmental as well as executive powers in a variety of ways.[11]

Among those who had been progressive supporters of states' rights in the previous era, virtually none joined the new liberal coalition, whether they were Western Republicans like Senator Borah or Wilsonian Democrats like Senator Carter Glass of Virginia. Glass almost immediately took a leading role in the conservative opposition to the New Deal and voted against the New Deal on 81 percent of the key votes analyzed by James Patterson, often on state sovereignty grounds—more than any other Democrat in the 1933–39 years. In contrast, Borah, a leading progressive Republican advocate of states' rights, ambled along a convoluted path toward the conservative camp but never fully joined it.[12]

Concerning constitutional flexibility, some liberals were more inclined than the legal realists or even the bulk of the Roosevelt administration to root their position in the language and "original intent" of the framers. Such liberals included Robert L. Stern, author of a highly influential article on the commerce clause in the *Harvard Law Review* in 1934—a piece later hailed as "the most notable attempt by a New Dealer to return to the framers for guidance on the commerce clause." Stern subsequently joined the administration on the solicitor general's staff. Throughout the New Deal, attorneys representing the government couched their legal arguments in terms that paid homage to constitutional language, original intent, and appropriate precedents to a greater degree than the legal realists and many other liberals believed necessary. Usually, they focused on the "general welfare," "necessary and proper," and "interstate commerce" clauses of the Constitution and harkened back to Hamiltonian and Marshall Court interpretations to bolster their arguments. Even the liberals who employed originalism, however, were generally far removed from what most conservatives claimed to be essential to good constitutional jurisprudence.[13]

## Liberal Views of the Supreme Court, 1933–1936

Although since 1890 populists, progressives, and labor unionists had put forward numerous—sometimes contradictory—prescriptions for altering Supreme Court roles and power, the Roosevelt administration, and most liberals, appeared relatively unconcerned about prescribing judicial roles in 1933 and 1934. As long as the Court took no steps to invalidate New Deal legislation or its modes of implementation, Roosevelt made no recommendations and took no action concerning the judiciary. During the first two years of the New Deal, hopes were high in the administration, and among liberals generally, that the majority of Supreme Court justices would indeed vote to uphold most of the new policies and institutional power arrangements. Thurman Arnold spoke for many when, in November 1933, he summarized in conventional legal arguments the liberals' case for the New Deal's constitutionality.[14]

As the New Deal programs and policies unfolded during 1933, 1934, and 1935, the intellectuals of the *New Republic* and the *Nation* increasingly endorsed the ideas of an administrative state headed by a strong presidency and a centralized form of federalism. With their votes, and often their voices, congressional liberals did likewise. Despite their continuing misgivings about some of Roosevelt's approaches, as on social insurance, for example, liberals' criticism was usually that his policies conceded too much to the states, not too little. As for the courts and the Constitution, while most urged judicial deference to lawmaking majorities (and often to the "will of the people") and flexible constitutional construction, there was no major drive to reform the Supreme Court or curb its powers. When the High Court moderates, Roberts and Hughes, joined the liberals in two major state cases in 1934 to hold that "neither property rights nor contract rights are absolute" and to defer to lawmaking majorities in cases of constitutional doubt, most liberals cheered, mistakenly perceiving these cases as harbingers of Court endorsement for the New Deal in the near future.[15]

January 1935 brought a decision that shook many liberals' confidence. By an 8–1 vote, the Supreme Court held unconstitutional the provision of the National Industrial Recovery Act (NIRA) that authorized the president to forbid the interstate shipment of "hot" oil (produced in violation of state quotas). Even then, however, the *New Republic* editors assured their readers, "The Court's conclusions by no means invalidate the rest of the N.I.R.A. or the other phases of the Roosevelt program."[16]

But the Supreme Court decisions of Black Monday, 27 May 1935, left little doubt on the matter. The justices unanimously overruled the NIRA not only on grounds of overly broad delegation of congressional lawmaking powers but also on states' rights grounds, giving a narrow definition (as often but not always in the past) of interstate commerce; unanimously rejected, on grounds that the president had intruded into a commission possessing functions that were not purely "executive" in nature, Roosevelt's removal of a Federal Trade Commissioner who had opposed administration policies; and unanimously overturned the Frazier-Lemke Act for the relief of farm mortgagors. More such decisions were to follow soon, though usually by close votes.[17]

Many liberals had been lukewarm or even hostile to the National Recovery Administration. Some, such as the *New Republic* editors, even welcomed its demise and were willing to concede that perhaps there had been overly broad delegations of powers to the executive. But the Court's return to a narrow definition of interstate commerce, the unanimity of the decisions of Black Monday, and the cumulative effects of the rulings unleashed a storm of liberal denunciations and demands for some means of "democratizing" the powers of the Supreme Court. The common element in the varied liberal prescriptions was that the Court should at least be restricted from overruling congressional lawmaking majorities on socioeconomic questions on which liberals believed the Constitution to be ambiguous. At this point, however, most liberals saw the Supreme Court, and the judiciary generally, as inherently undemocratic and in need of formal and fundamental restructuring or restraint. A torrent of proposed constitutional amendments to such effects gushed from multiple wellsprings throughout the liberal coalition in the weeks and months that followed. Two types of proposals predominated: those that would require Court unanimity or super-majorities to overrule statutes, and those that would make explicit the constitutional grants of power that were the subject of dispute. Ultimately, Roosevelt would opt for a third approach, but he decided to bide his time until after the 1936 elections.[18]

By focusing unprecedented public attention on the institutional issues of presidential power, the administrative state, the federal system and states' rights, the nature of constitutional interpretation and the Constitution itself, and the roles of the Supreme Court, the Court decisions of May 1935 and the next two years made theories of governance a very major and explicit topic for discussion in both ideological coalitions. As a result, the liberal movement clarified its commitment to a well-defined set of institutional prescriptions, some of which were to endure for more than a generation. Those who could not accept the general tenor of these, including Borah and a number of other old progressives, moved much further from the liberal camp than previously. Thus, the controversies swirling around the liberal and conservative theories of governance and the proposed modes for implementing them came to provoke significant ideological clarification and realignment.[19]

## The Third New Deal, 1937–1939

Claiming a mandate from the people in the 1936 elections, which returned Roosevelt to office with a record 60.4 percent of the popular vote and gave liberals what appeared to be clear majorities in both houses of Congress, the Roosevelt administration in January and February of 1937 unveiled its plans to implement a theory of governance based upon a flexible, living Constitution (no need for formal amendment), centralized or cooperative federalism, and a strong presidency heading a streamlined administrative state. The new Roosevelt institutional proposals between 1937 and 1939, and the controversies concerning them, have been dubbed the Third New Deal by some analysts, who compare and contrast them with the First New Deal of 1933 and the Second New Deal of 1935.[20]

The most controversial proposed mode for dealing with the Supreme Court was to try to persuade Congress, not to begin the formal amendment process, but to use its constitutional powers over the size of the Court to add one new justice to the Supreme Court for each sitting justice over the age of seventy, up to a total of fifteen (instead of the existing nine). This would allow Roosevelt, with Senate approval of his nominations, to appoint six new justices. Since most rulings unfavorable to the New Deal had been by 5-4 or 6-3 votes (not the unanimity of 27 May 1935), Roosevelt saw this mode, supplemented by measures to permit enlargement of other federal courts and to encourage judicial retirements, as the quickest and easiest way to achieve the "proper" constitutional jurisprudence. This method, while holding considerable promise of aiding liberal institutional and programmatic policy goals, was hatched in relative secrecy and clothed in a bogus argument about increasing judicial efficiency; it failed to address the basic structural problems of the Supreme Court in the eyes of many liberals who viewed the judiciary as inherently a vehicle for conservatism. As a result, it split the liberal coalition and gave the conservative opposition a rallying point that enabled it to make a number of new recruits.[21]

The moderate-to-liberal *New York Times,* previously quite supportive of the Roosevelt administration, was quick to announce its opposition to FDR's court proposals. The day after the president laid out publicly his ideas for reshaping the judiciary, the newspaper noted the "danger of political sharp practice" and stressed the need for "full and searching discussion of the subject." By the next day, it was ready to denounce the main proposal for the Supreme Court: "the consequences of this action will be to disturb profoundly the balance of power on which American democracy has been founded." While the *New York Times* was far from sympathetic to the conservatism of the Supreme Court and proclaimed its willingness to consider constitutional amendments for either compulsory retirement for justices reaching the age of seventy-five, or congressional power to overrule the Supreme Court by a two-thirds majority in "certain circumstances," it saw FDR's approach as creating too much presidential power and as lacking a clear mandate since it had not been discussed openly in the 1936 election campaign.[22]

As conservatives united in vehement opposition to the Roosevelt court proposals, a significant number of moderates and even liberals voiced concerns similar to those of the *New York Times* editorial writers. Almost no support came from outside the liberal camp, and liberals themselves often expressed misgivings. The American Civil Liberties Union decided to take no stand.[23]

However, quite a few liberals, especially in the labor movement, were highly enthusiastic proponents of the Roosevelt judicial reforms. The American Federation of Labor endorsed them, its president, William Green, going before the Senate Judiciary Committee to voice his strong support. Labor's Non-Partisan League backed the proposals and held rallies in twenty-four cities to mobilize popular support. A wide variety of individual unions also contributed their efforts. Outside the labor movement, James Patton and an array of state Farmers Union presidents and its national vice president defied the president of the organization to campaign on behalf of the Roosevelt proposals, signaling a significant movement within the NFU toward the liberal coalition—a movement that would crystallize into firm support later in the year. The Harlem Lawyers Association, taking a position sharply at odds with the New York State Bar and the American Bar Association, also gave its endorsement.[24]

Even though both the *Nation* and the *New Republic* had previously called for constitutional amendments to curb the judiciary, both journals were quick and enthusiastic in their praise for FDR's effort. The *Nation*'s editors hailed it as a "brilliant *tour de force*" by Roosevelt and declared that "it is the task of progressives to support the measure," though they believed that a constitutional amendment would still probably be needed also. The *New Republic*, proclaiming the need to register the popular majority's desire for change in judicial behavior, concluded: "'Packing the Court is as good a way to do this as any."[25]

Despite the efforts of much of the liberal coalition in behalf of the Roosevelt court proposals, Supreme Court decisions upholding New Deal legislation, including the Wagner Act, combined with strong conservative opposition and widespread misgivings elsewhere to kill FDR's plan in Congress. When the Senate voted on 22 July 1937 to return the main bill to the Judiciary Committee, everyone knew that the measure was dead. But even in defeat, the liberals were to attain some of their key goals. The Court-packing effort itself may have helped to persuade the two moderate justices, Hughes and Roberts, to shift toward positions upholding the constitutionality of New Deal programs (though the 1936 election results were apparently already having that effect). In any event, although Congress refused to adopt Roosevelt's Court-packing proposals, the altered Court voting patterns and the retirements of several justices in short order transformed the Court into one adopting behavior that met the standards of the liberal common denominator: it did not overrule presidential-congressional actions concerning socioeconomic questions on which the constitutional language was at all in doubt.[26]

The second Rooseveltian method for establishing his theory of governance as a firm and enduring foundation for American government was his plan for executive branch reorganization, drawn up in 1936 by a presidentially appointed committee consisting of Louis Brownlow, Luther Gulick, and Charles Merriam. This committee closely coordinated its plans with the president before Roosevelt presented the proposals publicly on 12 January 1937, three weeks before the unveiling of his Court plan. Though overshadowed for a time by the Court-packing controversy, the struggle over executive reorganization was to consume most of the next two years and come close to equaling the Court bill for the heat that it generated.

The *Report of the President's Committee on Administrative Management* outlined sweeping proposals to consolidate an administrative state and place the president firmly at its head. These included recommendations to "expand the White House staff," "strengthen and develop the managerial agencies of the government" as arms of the chief executive, extend civil service protection to most New Deal appointees, reorganize the civil service, "overhaul" the independent commissions and other independent agencies and place them within a reorganized set of departments reporting to the president, and "restore to the Executive complete responsibility of accounts and current transactions" (undermining the independent power of the uncooperative comptroller general).[27]

On this issue, Roosevelt enjoyed more unified liberal support than he had on his chosen method of court reform. Again, the *New Republic* and the *Nation* endorsed the bulk of the president's recommendations, but this time they were joined by an enthusiastic *New York Times*, which believed that they would "strengthen the processes of democratic government by drawing a clearer line between the responsibilities of the Executive and of Congress, and by creating authority within these fields which is commensurate with responsibility." Even the call to shift independent commissions and agencies into departments was "daring" but "essentially a sound one" according to the *Times*.[28]

By 1939, Roosevelt was able to obtain from Congress part of what he had requested, largely owing to liberal support. However, because of rising and vociferous opposition from conservatives, joined on some points by moderates and even a few liberals such as Senator Robert Wagner of New York, he was forced to retreat on some aspects of the report and compromise on others. FDR gained increased White House and other managerial staff and was able to create the Executive Office of the President by executive order without suffering a legislative veto from Congress. Most New Dealers in government were brought under the protective umbrella of the expanded civil service system, thus securing their dominant positions for a generation to come. However, independent commissions and other bodies and various interest triangles of congressional committee barons, bureaucrats, and interest group leaders continued to limit presidential powers in the administrative state. Moreover, Roosevelt was barely able to rally enough liberal support to sustain his veto of the Walter-Logan bill of 1940, which conservatives had pushed through Congress in an effort to permit the regular judicial process to impinge severely on the new administrative state.[29]

The third method adopted by Roosevelt to achieve his governance objectives was a purge of the congressional Democratic party, undertaken rather suddenly and haphazardly during the summer and fall of 1938. Here the aim was to displace conservative Democrats in Congress with liberal challengers. Had it succeeded, this effort would have fostered party realignment along liberal Democratic–conservative Republican lines and, in the short term at least, would have enhanced presidential government directly and other aspects of the liberal theory of governance at least indirectly. However, despite strong support from the *New Republic* and the *Nation* and many liberal interest groups, only the conservative chair of the House Rules Committee was defeated as a part of the purge; such Southern conservatives as Senators Walter George and "Cotton Ed" Smith returned in triumph, overcoming the liberals' efforts to elect their intraparty rivals.[30]

Most of the support that Roosevelt received in his three-pronged effort to advance his theory of governance during the Third New Deal came from liberals. Though on the specifics of the Court-packing approach, the liberals had split and some had opposed Roosevelt vigorously, virtually all were pleased by the new Supreme Court that had emerged by 1939. Most liberals in and out of Congress endorsed the broad goals of the executive reorganization and, despite some disagreements over certain of its complex aspects, enabled Roosevelt to obtain much of what he desired and to block the Walter-Logan attack on the new administrative state. Even the largely unsuccessful effort to replace conservative Democratic congressmen with liberals gave the liberals an incentive to develop further their organizational skills and their roles in future election campaigns. The liberal coalition that emerged from the Third New Deal was one reduced in size by old progressive and moderate defections and by lack of success in the 1938 elections, but it was now quite united around a theory of governance.

## World War II and the Liberal Theory

As World War II erupted overseas, debates over government institutions increasingly shifted to international matters, particularly to the presidential roles as commander-in-chief and chief diplomat. Already, liberals had shown an inclination to accept an expanded use of executive agreements by the administration; but most congressional liberals had joined their moderate and conservative colleagues in tying the president's hands with neutrality legislation during the 1930s, even as they welcomed the other aspects of presidential government.

Now most liberals—in and out of Congress—proved willing to modify the neutrality legislation, to acquiesce in the destroyer deal that FDR undertook on his own in 1940 with Britain, and then (in February and March 1941) to grant the president sweeping powers to produce or obtain "any defense article for the government of any country whose defense the President deems vital to the defense of the United States," to lend or lease or sell such, and to arrange terms for the appropriate deals. Despite vocal opposition from dissenting isolationist liberals, the key roll calls in Congress on the lend-lease bill found 88 percent of House liberals and 79 percent of Senate liberals voting to endorse the broad grant of authority to the president. The *Nation* and the *New Republic* on the left wing of liberalism and the *New York Times* on its moderate fringe joined in the general liberal endorsement of new presidential diplomatic and war powers during the events of 1940 and 1941. From this point onward through 1945, the liberal presidential government model fully encompassed both foreign and domestic roles, with liberals becoming even more supportive of presidential dominance over Congress than they previously had been.[31]

Table 4.1 shows the high levels of congressional liberal support for most liberal institutional prescriptions during the 1933–45 period; the 1937 Senate vote on the Court-packing bill was the sole exception to solid liberal backing on key roll calls. The gap between liberals' congressional voting patterns and those of their conservative colleagues was generally quite striking, particularly after the Hundred Days of 1933.

By 1940–45, presidential government, an administrative state, centralized (or at least cooperative) federalism, and a flexible Constitution had

Table 4.1
Congressional Ideological Divisions on Key Governance Roll Calls

| | | | % for "Liberal" Position | | |
|---|---|---|---|---|---|
| Bill | Date | Governance Issues | Libs. | Cons. | Lib.-Cons. Gap |
| House of Representatives | | | | | |
| Economy | 3/11/33 | Pres.-Cong. | 62.7% | 81.4% | -18.7% |
| NIRA | 5/26/33 | Pres.-Cong./Fed. | 96.5 | 59.6 | 36.9 |
| Exec. reorg. | 8/13/37 | Pres.-Cong./Adm. St. | 95.2 | 39.0 | 56.2 |
| Walter-Logan veto | 12/18/40 | Adm. St. | 94.6 | 1.8 | 92.8 |
| Lend-Lease | 2/6/41 | Pres.-Cong.. | 87.8 | 29.6 | 58.2 |
| Senate | | | | | |
| Emerg. banking | 3/9/33 | Pres.-Cong./Fed. | 88.2 | 95.7 | -7.5 |
| NIRA | 6/9/33 | Pres.-Cong./Fed. | 100.0 | 52.4 | 48.6 |
| Court-packing | 7/22/37 | Judicial | 46.9 | 0.0 | 46.9 |
| Exec. reorg. | 3/28/38 | Pres.-Cong./Adm. St. | 77.8 | 19.4 | 58.4 |
| Walter-Logan | 11/26/40 | Adm. St./Jud./Pres.-Cong. | 85.2 | 23.1 | 62.1 |
| Lend-Lease | 3/8/41 | Pres.-Cong. | 78.9 | 60.5 | 18.4 |

become hallmarks of American liberalism. On matters of court roles, considerable liberal disagreement remained, particularly concerning the appropriate degree of judicial activism or self-restraint vis-à-vis the elective institutions of government. Although most liberals agreed most of the time by the early 1940s on judicial restraint in socioeconomic matters, citing democratic arguments primarily in support of this proposition, liberals such as Henry Steele Commager, Felix Frankfurter, and Robert Jackson took positions favoring far more judicial restraint in general than did such liberals as Fred Rodell, William O. Douglas, and Frank Murphy. Not until the Warren Court period after 1954 did the liberal consensus shift decisively toward judicial activism on civil liberties, civil rights, and other matters.[32]

## Liberal Consensus and Discord

Each of the five major components of the liberal theory of governance won wide support from liberals, in contrast to the usual opposition of most conservatives to them. However, the liberal endorsement was broad and general, as it was on issues of values and programmatic public policies. It often consisted more of tendencies than of firm, coherent positions on institutional structure or specific modes of operation. And some liberals did dissent, sometimes vehemently, on particular matters. The nature of liberal consensus and discord on each component of the theory illustrated these patterns.

### A Flexible Constitution

The range of liberal prescriptions on the flexibility-rigidity continuum extended from the legal realists' position at the high flexibility pole to moderate positions maintaining strong links to constitutional language, original intent, and precedents. No liberals publicly embraced the rigid "mechanical jurisprudence" of the type expressed by Justice Owen Roberts and many conservatives. However, some, such as Hugo Black, did take the position that certain constitutional provisions—particularly those of the First Amendment—were to be treated as very strict restrictions on legislative or executive action.[33]

### Centralized or Cooperative Federalism

On the centralization-decentralization continuum, the liberal positions ranged from advocacy of the total abolition of the states by the *New*

*Republic* editors in June, 1935, through Luther Gulick's highly centralized federalism, to the cooperative federalism of most Roosevelt administration grant-in-aid programs. Few liberals advocated further decentralization to the states, though Southern liberals (with a few notable exceptions, such as Maury Maverick and sometimes Claude Pepper and Estes Kefauver) usually took extreme decentralist states' rights positions on matters of race relations. When threatened by the possibility of undesirable national governmental action, Northern liberals, too, occasionally resorted to states' rights arguments, as a few did concerning proposed national actions against sit-down strikes in 1937, for example. However, such instances were rare during this period. Most liberals most of the time favored centralized, or at least cooperative, federalism.[34]

*An Administrative State*

Here, too, liberals enjoyed considerable consensus, although at least two somewhat different continuums could be discerned. One pitted an administrative state against a "nightwatchman" state. Most liberals ranged from positions supporting a social democratic administrative state similar to that favored by British Labourites to those advocating a middle-of-the road capitalist administrative state relying on indirect Keynesian economic management tools. None publicly advocated the laissez-faire model of the nightwatchman state. The other continuum pitted a hierarchical, professionalized administrative state against a fragmented, spoils-system bureaucracy. On this scale, liberals ranged from extreme civil-service advocates to compromisers with patronage, like Roosevelt himself. A few full-fledged spoilsmen, such as Edward J. Flynn or Ed Kelly, were sometimes identified with the liberal coalition, but liberal attitudes generally rejected fully machine-style administration.

*Presidential Government*

This component entailed expansion of presidential power, often at the expense of congressional prerogatives. It included at least four different (but related) continuums. One posited more presidential than congressional direction of the domestic administrative state; another leaned toward advocacy of presidential rather than congressional agenda-setting initiatives in social-economic reform; a third saw the president rather than Congress as the spokesperson for a national popular majority; and the last posited presidential rather than congressional direction of defense and foreign policy. On the first three, liberals achieved considerable consensus by 1937, although they often differed over degree, as they did on some of the other components of the theory. Concerning the presidential-congressional roles in national security and foreign policy matters, liberals were deeply divided during the 1930s between internationalists, who favored presidential leadership in world affairs; and isolationists, who sought congressional control. Policy ends (global intervention versus nonintervention) intertwined with questions of presidential-congressional power questions to complicate matters on this scale. However, by the time of the lend-lease votes in 1941, most liberals had moved toward the presidential end of this continuum also. Pressures for consistency and links to the liberal coalition probably accelerated the movement to liberal consensus.

*Judicial Restraint or Deference*

During the 1933–37 period, most liberals harbored deep distrust of the judiciary and tended to take positions near the judicial restraint end of a restraint-activism continuum dealing with court deference (or lack thereof) to lawmaking majorities in the elected branches of government. Even then, some took the position, adumbrated by past judicial progressives such as Oliver Wendell Holmes, that judicial activism was more justified concerning civil liberties than it was in the socioeconomic realm. The attainment of a liberal majority on the Supreme Court and the sharp disagreement among judicial liberals over judicial activism to protect preferred freedoms, especially those of "discrete or insular minorities," split much liberal thought. In the 1937–45 period, as noted previously, it can probably be said only that the liberal coalition enjoyed considerable consensus on the proposition that the courts should show restraint on socioeconomic issues where the president and Congress were united and the Constitution was ambiguous.[35]

## Conclusions

The five main institutional prescriptions of the liberal theory of governance were in large part mutually supportive, or at least not directly contradictory to one another. Constitutional flexibility permitted (but did not require) centralized or cooperative federalism, an administrative state, presidential government, and judicial deference to presidential-congressional wishes on socioeconomic questions. An administrative state, more centralized government, and strong presidential leadership were compatible with one another—even conducive to one another. And judicial def-

erence to joint presidential-congressional actions on socioeconomic matters permitted (but did not require) presidential dominance of an administrative state within a federal system that added to previous national
government powers.

Beyond that, liberals who wrote or spoke publicly about the subject
usually described their perceptions of links between their institutional
prescriptions and their core values of equal opportunity, positive freedom, social security, majoritarian procedural democracy, and economic
growth. Certainly, their underlying, broadly egalitarian, rationalistic,
and materialistic assumptions played some part, too, shaping their core
values, programmatic public policy preferences, and institutional prescriptions.

After the next chapter discusses the theory of governance of the conservative opposition to the New Deal, we shall return to analyze the subject of linkages: To what extent did the liberals and conservatives of
1933–45 offer their institutional prescriptions as mere means toward
immediate power and public policy ends? What were their priorities
when their prescriptions clashed with one another or with other elements
of their ideology? Did their prescriptions in fact help the movements to
achieve their desired ends? What impact did the prescriptions have
(sometimes unintentionally) on the actual operations of the institutions of
government, the public policies of the American political system, such
other institutions as the political parties and interest groups, and the
nature of the ideologies themselves?

## Notes

1. William E. Leuchtenburg, *Franklin D. Roosevelt and the New Deal, 1932–1940*
(New York: Harper & Row, 1963), cites this quotation from the inaugural address
on p. 41; he notes the World War I model for the NRA on p. 57. The analogy to
World War I was echoed in Congress. See, for example, *Cong. Rec.*, 73rd Cong., 1st
sess. (11 March 1933), 201.

2. Richard Hofstadter, *The Age of Reform* (New York: Alfred A. Knopf, 1972),
314–315, on liberal-progressive similarities and differences. On Theodore Roosevelt and Wilson, James MacGregor Burns, *Presidential Government* (Boston:
Houghton Mifflin, 1965), 314–315; Wilfred E. Binkley, *Powers of the President: Problems of American Democracy* (Garden City, NY: Doubleday, Doran, 1937), chaps. 10
and 11; and Scot Zentner, "Liberalism and Executive Power: Woodrow Wilson and
the American Founders," *Polity* 26 (Summer 1994): 577–599. On judicial roles, see
Christopher Wolfe, *The Rise of Modern Judicial Review* , rev. ed. (Lanham, MD: Rowman & Littlefield, 1994), 3–10, 218–229; C. Herman Pritchett, *The Roosevelt Court*

(Chicago: Quadrangle Books, 1948). On constitutional flexibility, Barry Dean Karl (*Executive Reorganization and Reform in the New Deal* [Cambridge: Harvard University Press, 1963], 60) stresses the roots in pragmatism; Wolfe, *Modern Judicial Review,* 213–214, discusses Wilson's developing views on the subject; the Roosevelt quotation is from an address reprinted in Egbert Ray Nichols, ed., *Congress or the Supreme Court* (New York: Noble & Noble, 1938), 355. Democratic states' rights emphases combined with considerable centralization by the Wilson administration are discussed in the *New York Times,* 14 February 1934, 18; Barry Dean Karl, *The Uneasy State* (Chicago: University of Chicago Press, 1983), 17–18, stresses the progressives' ambiguity on federalism; on Borah, see Ronald L. Feinman, *Twilight of Progressivism* (Baltimore: Johns Hopkins University Press, 1981), 2–4. The final FDR quotation is reprinted in Nichols, *Congress or the Supreme Court,* 358.

3.  *New York Times,* 11 March 1933, 7; TRB, "Washington Notes," *New Republic* 74 (22 March 1933): 156.

4.  Arthur M. Schlesinger Jr., *The Politics of Upheaval* (Boston: Houghton Mifflin, 1960), 486–487; Elizabeth Mensch, "The History of Mainstream Legal Thought," in *The Politics of Law: A Progressive Critique,* ed. David Kairys (New York: Pantheon Books, 1990), 22.

5.  Rexford Tugwell, "Address to the Federation of Bar Associations of Western New York," reprinted in *Congressional Digest* 12 (November 1933): 270.

6.  *New York Times,* 28 June 1933, 11.

7.  "Permissive Powers," *New York Times,* 11 June 1933, sec. 4. p. 4.

8.  Paul Y. Anderson, "In Defense of Congress," *Nation* 136 (28 June 1933): 722.

9.  TRB, "Washington Notes," *New Republic* 75 (10 May 1933): 363–364.

10. Voting patterns on these and other key institutional roll calls are included in table 4.1. Liberals were defined as those voting for the *New Republic* / UDA positions at least 67 percent of the time on the 1937–41 roll calls; see *New Republic* (18 May 1942), 699–705.

11. "Roosevelt and Business: A Word of Warning," *New Republic* 75 (10 May 1933): 350–351.See also, "Business Hops Aboard," *Nation* 136 (28 June 1933): 712–713; "The Crisis of the N.R.A.," *New Republic* 76 (8 November 1933): 349–350; "All Power to the Trade Associations?" *New Republic* 76 (15 November 1933): 4–5; "What to Do with the N.R.A.," *New Republic* 74 (30 March 1933): 144–146.

12. James T. Patterson, *Congressional Conservatism and the New Deal* (Lexington: University of Kentucky Press, 1967), 340–350; Ronald A. Mulder, *The Insurgent Progressives in the United States Senate and the New Deal, 1933–1939* (New York: Garland, 1979), 309–313.

13. John A. Rohr, *To Run a Constitution: The Legitimacy of the Administrative State* (Lawrence: University Press of Kansas, 1986), 117; Wolfe, *Modern Judicial Review,* 242–250.

14. William G. Ross, *A Muted Fury* (Princeton: Princeton University Press, 1994); William E. Leuchtenburg, *The Supreme Court Reborn* (New York: Oxford University Press, 1995), 84–85; Thurman Arnold, "The New Deal Is Constitutional," *New Republic* (15 November 1933): 8–10.

15. "One Insurance Plan—Or Forty–Eight?" *New Republic* 81 (2 January 1935): 206–207; Schlesinger, *Politics of Upheaval,* 253–254.

16. "The Week," *New Republic* 81 (16 January 1935): 259.

17. *Schechter Poultry Corp. v. United States*, 293 U.S. 495 (1935), *Humphrey's Executor v. United States*, 295 U.S. 602 (1935), *Local 167 v. United States*, 291 U.S. 293 (1935).

18. "Social Control vs. the Constitution," *New Republic* 82 (12 June 1935): 116–118; Schlesinger, *Politics of Upheaval,* 490–496; Leuchtenburg, *Supreme Court Reborn*, 96–131.

19. Feinman, *Twilight of Progressivism,* chaps. 7 and 8.

20. Sidney M. Milkis, *The President and the Parties* (New York: Oxford University Press, 1993), chap. 5.

21. Patterson, *Congressional Conservatism,* chap. 3; Leuchtenburg, *Supreme Court Reborn*, chap. 5.

22. "Remaking the Judiciary," *New York Times,* 6 February 1937, 16; "Tampering with the Court," *New York Times,* 7 February 1937, sec. 4, p. 8; "Time for Deliberation," *New York Times*, 19 February 1937, 18.

23. *New York Times,* 20 March 1937, 8.

24. For labor union endorsements and activities, see *New York Times*, 7 February 1937, 33; 9 February 1937, 1; 18 February 1937, 2; 19 February 1937, 1, 3; 24 February 1937, 1; 5 March 1937, 15; 6 March 1937, 2; 9 March 1937, 1, 15; 17 March 1937, 11; 2 April 1937, 1; 20 April 1937, 16, 17; 15 May 1937, 1. For the NFU, see *New York Times,* 20 February 1937, 4, and 9 March 1937, 1, 15. The Harlem Lawyers Association endorsement is in the *New York Times,* 14 March 1937, 3.

25. "Purging the Supreme Court," *Nation* 144 (13 February 1937): 173–174; "Curbing the Supreme Court," *New Republic* 89 (17 February 1937): 31–32.

26. C. Herman Pritchett, *The Roosevelt Court* (Chicago: Quadrangle Books, 1948), chap. 1; Patterson, chap. 3; Leuchtenburg, *Supreme Court Reborn*, 154–162.

27. Milkis, *President and the Parties,* 114–115.

28. "New Tools for Uncle Sam," *New Republic* 89 (27 January 1937): 371–372; "Adventure in Blueprints," *Nation* (30 January 1937): 116–117; "Democratic Government," *New York Times*, 13 January 1937, 22. Subsequent supportive editorials in the *Times* include "The Administration Loses," 9 April 1938, 16.

29. On interest triangles, see Marver H. Bernstein, *Regulating Business by Independent Commission* (Princeton: Princeton University Press, 1955); and Arthur Maass, *Muddy Waters* (Cambridge: Harvard University Press, 1951). Rohr, *To Run a Constitution,* 157–160, and the *New York Times,* 27 November 1940, 1, 24; and 19 December 1940, 1, 18, discuss the Walter–Logan bill controversy.

30. "Congress Adjourns," *New Republic* 94 (28 June 1938): 200; "The President Reports," *New Republic* 95 (6 July 1938): 237–238; "The Shape of Things," *Nation* 147 (13 September 1938): 213; Milkis, *President and the Parties,* chap. 4.

31. Richard H. Pells, *The Liberal Mind in a Conservative Age* (New York: Harper & Row, 1985), 8–26.

32. Pritchett, *Roosevelt Court,* chap. 10; Alpheus Thomas Mason, *The Supreme Court from Taft to Warren* (Baton Rouge: Louisiana State University Press, 1958), chaps. 5 and 6.

33. For a good discussion of Black, see Fred Rodell, "The Case for Judicial

Activism," reprinted in *Basic Issues of American Democracy* , ed. Samuel Hendel, 8th
ed. (Englewood Cliffs, NJ: Prentice-Hall, 1976), 117–122.

34. "Social Control vs. the Constitution," *New Republic* 94 (12 June 1935):
116–118. Maverick was the lone Southern Democrat to support the federal antilynching bill in 1937. Pepper and Kefauver supported federal abolition of the poll
tax, which kept many Southern blacks (as well as poor whites) from voting. On
the sit-down strikes and federalism, see *New York Times,* 3 April 1937, 3.

35. The Holmes position is discussed by Pritchett, *Roosevelt Court,* 266; and
Leuchtenburg, *Supreme Court Reborn,* 4.

# 5

# The Conservative Theory of Governance

The theory of governance advanced by most of the anti–New Deal conservative coalition of 1933–45 was in large part the mirror image of that put forward in the name of liberalism. Yet on some components, substantial overlapping existed; and on some points, the prescriptions were simply different, rather than arrayed at opposite ends of a continuum.

Where the liberals tended to perceive a living, flexible Constitution and often described constitutional law as little more than a reflection of preferences or moral philosophy, conservatives of the New Deal period conceptualized it in rather rigid terms, emphasizing the need for strict construction of constitutional language and adherence to the original intent of the framers when the language did not provide the obvious answer. Justice George Sutherland doubtless spoke for most conservatives: "The whole aim of the construction, as applied to a provision of the Constitution, is to discover the meaning, to ascertain and give effect to the intent, of its framers and the people who adopted it." However, even some conservative scholars have since noted that judicial conservatives of the period often went beyond the Constitution to "natural justice," or "natural law," particularly with regard to the doctrine of economic substantive due process, which conservative justices often employed to strike down various liberal-backed policies as unconstitutional. When conservatives invoked "natural justice" or "natural law" in support of laissez-faire economic positions, they of course opened themselves to liberal charges of hypocrisy. Yet most conservatives continued to insist, often with apparent sincerity, that theirs was a position of obedience to a rigidly defined Constitution.[1]

Prior to 1933, the conservative record on federalism had been a mixture of centralism and decentralism, with little to distinguish it from the ambiguous pattern among progressives on the subject. Republican conservatives, in particular, had tended toward the centralist views that Hamiltonian Federalists had put forward in the early days of the Republic and that the Republican party had promulgated during and after the Civil War. In the Democratic party, on the other hand, states' rights had long been a cherished tenet that some conservative Republicans had come to embrace, at least on certain socioeconomic issues, in the twentieth century. Despite this background of diversity, the second major component in the anti–New Deal conservatives' theory of governance soon came to be an embrace of states' rights that cut across party lines. Though some conservatives demurred on some specific policy matters and a few favored cooperative federalism or even centralist approaches, most took positions markedly more decentralist than their liberal contemporaries and usually voiced these in terms of states' rights, rather than other possible decentralized modes.

The third major element in the conservatives' theory of governance was a preference for a nightwatchman state (albeit one with some administrative support for business development and protection) over a regulatory and welfare-oriented administrative state of the sort envisioned by liberals. Whether the state bureaucracy was patronage based or professionalized, it was an object of great distrust for most conservatives. Not all would go as far as Albert Jay Nock in denouncing "Our Enemy, the State," but most—with some big-business dissent—agreed that liberal versions of the administrative state were a clear threat to negative freedom.[2]

A fourth ingredient in the conservative theory of governance came to be a congressionally centered check-and-balance system. Though the Congresses of the First and Second New Deals inspired far less conservative confidence than later Congresses did, and though conservatives until 1937 usually saw the Supreme Court as the key checking institution vis-à-vis the presidency, the administrative state, and centralization, conservatives generally—after some initial waffling—preferred a national legislative-executive relationship closer to the congressional than to the presidential end of the continuum. However, judicial conservatives, and internationalist conservatives after 1939, tended to accept and even welcome the presidential roles of chief diplomat and commander-in-chief more than they did the other liberal presidential roles.

Finally, there was the matter of the judiciary. In the early 1930s, when the Supreme Court and the federal judiciary were generally sympathetic to conservative values and programmatic aims, most conservatives favored active judicial negation of executive and legislative liberal policies, particularly when these threatened private property rights. However, they did not explicitly endorse a judicial activism position at the opposite end of the restraint-activism scale from their liberal opponents. Most conservatives portrayed judicial invalidation of executive actions and legislation not as activism but simply as adherence to strict construction of the Constitution and the original intent of its framers, though such invalidation was certainly activist in the sense that it entailed active judicial overturning of lawmaking majorities. As liberals tightened their grip on the Supreme Court and the federal judiciary generally in the years after 1937, the conservative coalition tended to shift its focus to other prescriptions in its theory of governance.

## Conservative Institutional Prescriptions, 1933–1936

Initial conservative responses to the Roosevelt administration's Hundred Days proposals were for the most part cautiously favorable and included support for measures that dramatically increased both presidential powers vis-à-vis Congress and national government powers in relation to those of the states. Even such a strict-constructionist advocate of states' rights and congressional prerogatives as Representative James M. Beck of Pennsylvania, solicitor general in the Harding administration and author of a 1926 book, *The Vanishing Powers of the States*, that had articulated much of what would become the conservative theory of governance, favored the broad grants of authority in the economy bill, passed by the House of Representatives in the first week of the New Deal. In both houses of Congress, in fact, most conservatives voted for the economy bill and the emergency banking bill. In fact, in each instance higher proportions of conservatives than liberals supported the bills, despite their centralizing and presidential-power-enhancing characteristics.[3]

Even as late as May 1933, the Roosevelt-backed National Industrial Recovery Act, encompassing broad grants of power to the executive as well as centralization of authority that had previously resided in state governments and private businesses, gained the support of majorities of conservatives voting in the House and the Senate, albeit now by slender margins and over the vehement denunciations of Beck, who led the opposition to the bill in the House of Representatives. Attacking the efficiency arguments made by proponents of the bill on behalf of national action and delegation to the executive and raising the specter of Caesarism that would become a staple of conservative warnings, Beck thundered: "A Caesar may be far more efficient than a senate, but the Roman Republic came to an end when the policies of Rome were determined by Caesar and not by the senate."[4]

By May, despite the NIRA vote, most conservatives were increasingly concerned about the institutional changes and programmatic effects of the early First New Deal. Conservative columnists Frank R. Kent and Mark Sullivan had voiced their opposition in April and would magnify that opposition in the months and years to come. Even Hamilton Fish, a leading conservative House Republican leader who in May still expressed general support for what he termed Roosevelt's "American dictatorship," stressed the "temporary" and "emergency" nature of the power shifts and noted other proposed enhancements of presidential authority that he would oppose. Charles D. Hilles, the New York Republican national committeeman widely regarded as a spokesman for New York big-business interests, was closer to Beck than to his fellow New Yorker, Fish, in a 25 May address warning of centralization and stressing states' rights, although avoiding Beck's frontal attack on the emergent liberal theory of governance. Soon the positions taken by Beck, Kent, Sullivan, and Hilles would rally most opponents of the New Deal around a distinctive conservative governance approach.[5]

During the summer of 1933, the American Bar Association and some state bar associations became key focal points for developing consensus on conservative institutional prescriptions. Charles E. Martin, president of the ABA, roused his organization's convention in late August with a ringing appeal to states' rights, tracing what he viewed as a dangerous trend toward centralization back to Progressive Era grants-in-aid and calling for a return to the "basic and fundamental doctrine of dual powers" between narrowly defined spheres of national govenmental action on the one hand and "reserved" spheres of state action on the other. "So rapidly are the rights of the states waning," proclaimed Martin, "that legal writers are beginning to assert that soon they will be reduced to administrative districts."[6]

Conservative Democratic Senator Patrick McCarran of Nevada broadened the attack at the American Bar Association convention two days later, denouncing the National Industrial Recovery Act and the banking and agricultural legislation of the New Deal for their institutional effects: "They constitute an avalanche that sweeps away the structures fought for and reared by Jefferson and his adherents."[7]

Addressing the Maryland Bar Association convention shortly thereafter, Beck returned to the fray, weaving together most of the conservative institutional prescriptions into the theme that the Constitution was being "demolished" by the Roosevelt administration. Through 1933, however, the conservative opposition remained disorganized; and many conservatives gave less than full endorsement to the theory of governance put forward by Beck, the American Bar Association leadership, and others.[8]

The *Chicago Tribune*, long a bastion of the Republicanism of the American heartland, was a good barometer of developing conservative ideas. In 1932 the *Tribune* had endorsed Herbert Hoover, as expected, for reelection; but it had noted that Roosevelt's victory would not be "a calamity" and had said of FDR: "He himself is a man of conservative breed and upbringing." During Roosevelt's first month in office, the *Tribune* editorialists waxed enthusiastic over many broad grants of authority to the president and expressed scorn for the capabilities of Congress as an institution. Its comments on the Economy Act were typical: "The reasons for granting the President the power he demanded to slash government expenditures are so concrete and so pressing that he had to act as he did in demanding immediate authority to carry out a program of economy. . . . More congressional promises and pledges of economy would be merely more promises and pledges."[9]

By the end of the Hundred Days, the *Tribune* was more cautious but still not hostile to the new presidential powers and the centralization of authority that were evident. "That the administration's program is susceptible of grave abuse no one who knows our political or economic conditions can doubt. The proof of the pudding is in the eating of it. Legislation has granted new and extensive powers to administration. The real test will come with their application." Reflective of their continuing preference for presidential power over congressional power at this point was the fact that two of the *Tribune* editors' six "platform planks," printed prominently on the editorial page, attacked Congress and targeted it for major reforms, while the editors praised the president's "extraordinary gift of public leadership."[10]

Nor was the *Tribune* yet prepared during the early months of the Roosevelt administration to lift the banner of states' rights. The first indication that its editors were leaning in that direction came in early September 1933, when they praised the states' rights address of conservative Democrat Patrick McCarran to the ABA convention. By February 1934, however, the *Tribune* editors—noting their break with the conservative Republican and Federalist heritage as they viewed it—were ready with a rationale for warmly embracing the doctrine of states' rights: "The roles of the parties are now reversed. . . . The need for a strengthening of the federal authority which justified, at least to Federalists and Republicans, the policies of their parties has been replaced by the need for restraints upon the swift and inordinate growth of centralization, burocracy, and the extension of political regulation over the conduct and activities of the people."[11]

The *Chicago Tribune*'s opposition to the New Deal and its entire approach to governance solidified in the next few months, with regular attacks on "burocracy," "the planned society," "the federal Christmas tree," and "tyranny." By 13 May 1934, the *Tribune* was ready to declare all-out war on the New Deal liberal governance prescriptions. Denouncing a "Hitlerite tendency" in the Roosevelt whom they had praised the previous year, the editors now made their first "platform" priority "Repeal of the Tyranny Laws," a number of which they had endorsed during the Hundred Days.[12]

As the *Chicago Tribune* moved to increasingly vehement denunciations of the liberal institutional prescriptions during 1934, a sizable group of major business leaders and prominent politicians—including James Beck; two former Democratic presidential candidates, Alfred E. Smith and John W. Davis; J. Howard Pew, of the Sun Oil Company; Sewell Avery, of Montgomery Ward; the du Ponts; and Alfred P. Sloan and William S. Knudsen, of General Motors, among others—formed the American Liberty League. Unlike some organizations fighting the New Deal, the Liberty League made the governance recommendations its central theme. "For the Liberty League," George Wolfskill has written, "protection of the Constitution was its *raison d'etre*, its moral issue. . . . The pose of the Liberty League as the handmaiden of the Constitution may well have been sincere; but it was also conscious, deliberate, and calculated."[13]

Although the Liberty League occupied the central role in the conservative propaganda campaign to mobilize popular support for its theory of governance over the next three years, the bar associations, newspapers such as the *Chicago Tribune*, prominent conservatives of both parties in Congress, former President Hoover and his ex–treasury secretary Ogden Mills, much of the Republican party apparatus, and judicial conservatives also operated somewhat independently on behalf of conservative governance ideas during that time.

Some of the most notable movement toward the conservative theory of governance between 1933 and 1936 occurred in the Republican party organization, where the change was most evident on the states' rights component. Both the *New York Times* and the *Chicago Tribune* took note of the Republicans' departure from centralist traditions. William Allen White, noted journalist and himself a life-long Republican, described the transformation as a "party revolution" by 1936, with the Republicans moving from Hamiltonian to Jeffersonian positions on the issue. The *Chicago Tribune*, of course, had endorsed and encouraged the Republican shift for more than two years.[14]

Then, too, there was Albert Jay Nock, widely recognized in later years as the most notable conservative intellectual of the 1930s, whose book *Our*

*Enemy, the State,* published in 1935, advanced many of the propositions of what was becoming the conservative theory of governance but particularly attacked the evils of the liberal administrative state.

Still, as late as the spring of 1935, many conservatives in Congress, despite loud grumbling, were willing to acquiesce in authorizing the president to spend $4.8 billion in emergency relief, with few strings attached. The House of Representatives passed the bill by a vote of 329 to 18. In the Senate, Warren Austin led a band of conservatives in opposition; but after a few concessions by the administration and extensive debate, the Senate followed suit.[15]

It was the judicial conservatives of the Supreme Court who delivered the most effective blows against the New Deal institutional reforms, felling the National Industrial Recovery Act, the Agricultural Adjustment Act, and other major pieces of New Deal legislation, as well as overturning Roosevelt's removal of William Humphrey as a Federal Trade Commissioner on grounds that this action exceeded presidential powers. The Supreme Court's majority opinions in a series of 1935 and 1936 cases read like a summary of the conservative institutional prescriptions: strict construction and original intent, states' rights and dual federalism, and congressional lawmaking powers that could not be delegated to administrative agencies or the president. Of course, the decisions themselves exemplified the judicial roles that conservatives cherished (though in fact often moving well beyond the obvious meaning of the Constitution, despite claims to the contrary).[16]

Hailing the three Supreme Court decisions of the liberals' Black Monday, 27 May 1935, the *Chicago Tribune* exulted: "These are tremendous decisions because, dealing with the policies of the present government, they check its . . . intent of centralizing power by congressional delegation to a semi-legislative, semi-judicial burocracy controled [sic] by the President, of subjecting the states to a loss of sovereignty and control, and of depriving the individual of free will, free action, and free decisions under law conforming to constitutional principles."[17]

## The Conservative Counterattack on the Third New Deal

When the Roosevelt administration launched its postelection attack on the Supreme Court and the federal judiciary early in 1937, the conservative coalition mobilized quickly in opposition. Branding FDR's proposals "revolutionary," the *Chicago Tribune* likened the president to Stalin, Hitler, and Mussolini. In contrast to earlier clashes between theories of governance, this time the conservatives proved far more united than the liberals on their mode of action and considerably more capable of gaining the support of key moderates. By July 1937, a unanimous Senate conservative bloc had won a spectacular victory over the divided and demoralized liberals by recommitting Roosevelt's Court-packing bill to the Judiciary Committee. However, the triumph proved largely illusory, as shifts by Justices Hughes and Roberts combined with the replacement of Willis Van Devanter with Hugo Black to end the conservatives' dominance on the Supreme Court. By 1939, most conservatives appeared to agree with Frank Hogan, the conservative president of the American Bar Association, that "reliance against the exercise of arbitrary power must be placed by the people henceforth in the legislative rather than the judicial department of the National Government. . . . There rest now America's hopes." The *Chicago Tribune* concurred. Noting in 1940 that "there is now a New Deal court," it called upon Congress to take the central place in our check-and-balance system and "write into the law provisions which permitted no other interpretation than the one intended." Gone were the days of 1933 when Congress had been the chief target of the *Tribune*'s institutional critiques.[18]

In Congress, the Court fight had brought the conservative coalition new recruits, some of whom became long-term adherents, abandoning moderation or "progressivism" to take conservative stands on other governance issues and on quite a few programmatic policy matters as well. Democratic Senator Burton K. Wheeler of Montana was a case in point. The Progressive party's 1924 vice-presidential nominee, Wheeler possessed impressive "progressive" credentials and had appeared between 1933 and 1937 to be a solid member of the "new" liberal coalition. He had even spoken out against conservative Supreme Court rulings and had urged a constitutional amendment to curb the Court's power. However, Wheeler disliked centralized power, whether in big business or in government, and had become resentful of Roosevelt personally. When conservatives asked him to take public leadership of the fight against FDR's Court-packing plan, he readily agreed. Soon, Wheeler was aligned with the conservative cause not only on the Court issue but also on opposition to Roosevelt's executive reorganization ideas, his attempted party purge, and his quest for additional powers in foreign policy and national security. Though never a full-fledged conservative, in the wake of the battle over the judiciary Wheeler moved much closer than before to the conservative theory of governance and even conservative programmatic goals.[19]

Nor was Wheeler an isolated example. After careful analysis, James Patterson concluded that "for many it was a turning point. . . . The court plan undermined Roosevelt's powerful senatorial coalition; it alienated many western progressives and moderate Democrats; it helped to unite Republicans and to transform their strategy; and it led conservatives of both parties to begin to work together in bipartisan fashion."[20]

The other major legislative dimension of the Roosevelt administration's Third New Deal drive for institutional reform, executive reorganization, at first produced limited conservative opposition. While Senator Harry F. Byrd of Virginia and conservative columnist Frank R. Kent almost immediately denounced the measure for allegedly building a bureaucratic behemoth and fostering presidential dictatorship, conservative opposition to it was relatively slow to develop, in part because of preoccupation with the battle over the judiciary, in part because of widespread initial big-business support for what appeared to many to be a streamlining of the government bureaucracy to reflect a generally corporate model. Despite denunciations of the administrative state idea by such conservatives as Nock, many in the conservative coalition favored neither a state wholly confined to a nightwatchman role (which Nock favored) nor a fragmented, machine-style administration. What most of them did share, at least by the late 1930s, was a preference for a congressionally centered system of checks and balances and a fear of presidential dominance. It was these themes that increasingly drew most conservatives into opposition to the Roosevelt-backed proposals for reorganization. Frank Gannett's National Committee to Uphold Constitutional Government shifted easily from the Court battle to attacks on executive reorganization and sought to mobilize public opinion over the next several years.[21]

Despite the efforts of Gannett and others, conservatives could not achieve the unanimity in Congress that they had attained on the Court-packing issue. This matter was one with many complex nuances, "efficiency" seemed to be on the side of the liberals, and the administration proved willing to win support with key compromises. On the most critical Senate vote, 81 percent of the conservatives joined in opposition but could not win enough moderate or liberal allies to prevail. They did nonetheless force Roosevelt to retreat from some of his more radical proposals (such as merging independent commissions into departments) and to accept partial victories on a number of other points.[22]

Not surprisingly, Roosevelt's efforts to "purge" Democratic party conservatives and replace them with liberals in the 1938 primaries aroused almost universal conservative outrage. Linking the purge to attempts at Court-packing and executive reorganization, conservatives portrayed all three moves as steps toward dictatorship. Hiram Johnson, once a progressive but now a staunch conservative, was typical in declaring that the president's "ruthlessness . . . seems to me compelling proof that he has reached such a despotic and unreasonable state of mind that he will tolerate no man who disagrees with him at all."[23]

FDR's bid for an unprecedented third term in 1940 and liberal claims of popular presidential "mandates" only added to conservative fears. The 1938 purge failed almost completely, with Roosevelt clearly successful only in securing the defeat of the conservative chair of the House Rules Committee. Conservatives emerged from the 1938 elections with added strength in Congress and the state governments and encouraged to continue to fight for their theory of governance, despite their inability to retain control over the federal judiciary or to block an executive reorganization that enhanced both the liberal administrative state and presidential power.

As an aftermath of the Third New Deal, demonstrating both continued conservative suspicions of an administrative state and hopes for the federal judiciary, came the conservative drive for the Walter-Logan bill in 1940. Though the chief sponsors of the bill were moderate Democrats, most support came from the conservative alliance. This measure would have empowered the federal courts to review any rule of an administrative agency to determine its constitutionality and its compliance with congressional statutes. With the aid of a majority of moderates, but with virtually no liberal support, conservatives pushed the bill through both congressional chambers in the face of Roosevelt's denunciations of it. On key votes, 98 percent of House conservatives and 77 percent of Senate conservatives supported the Walter-Logan measure. Vetoed by FDR in December 1940, the bill lacked sufficient support for a successful override. Another conservative effort to hamper the administrative state had fallen short.[24]

### World War II and the Conservative Governance Theory

Prior to the outbreak of World War II, judicial conservatives had, in the *United States v. Curtiss-Wright Export Corporation* case of 1936, held that congressional delegations of powers to the president in foreign affairs could more easily pass the test of constitutionality than those concerning domestic matters. Conservative Justice Sutherland had, in *obiter dicta,* gone beyond that point to endorse "the exclusive power of the President as the sole organ of the federal government in the field of international relations—a power which does not require as a basis for its exercise an act of Congress." The following year, in *United States v. Belmont,* the High Court had shown in addition a high tolerance for executive agreements made without the two-thirds Senate vote of approval requisite for treaties. Taken together, these two decisions offered strong endorsement of presidential government in foreign affairs.[25]

Furthermore, "internationalist" conservatives, particularly prominent in Eastern financial, industrial, and publishing circles, by the late 1930s demonstrated considerable willingness to support presidential leadership as commander-in-chief and chief diplomat far beyond what they would tolerate concerning presidential initiation of social reforms, mobilization of popular majorities, or direction of a domestic administrative state.[26]

Despite the judicial conservatives' precedents and the inclinations of the internationalist conservatives, many, probably most, members of the conservative coalition viewed expanded presidential powers in the foreign and national security areas in the same light that they viewed them in the other realms—as steps toward dictatorship. When Roosevelt moved to make his destroyer deal with Britain and to seek congressional modification of the Neutrality Laws and congressional endorsement of lend-lease to Britain and other countries fighting the Axis powers, these conservatives were determined to resist vigorously. The *Chicago Tribune* announced its strong opposition to the lend-lease measure in familiar terms: "This is a bill for the destruction of the American Republic. It is a brief for an unlimited dictatorship with power over the possessions and lives of the American people, with the power to make war and alliances forever."[27]

In the U.S. House of Representatives, most conservatives opposed grants of presidential authority in foreign affairs. On the key lend-lease bill roll call of 6 February 1941, for instance, 70 percent were in opposition. In the Senate, the picture was rather different. There, a larger proportion of conservatives than in the House hailed from the South or from urban Eastern states where internationalism was strong. Moreover, Roosevelt had agreed to some compromise language on appropriations procedures prior to the Senate vote. In the end, only 40 percent of Senate conservatives cast their ballots in the negative on lend-lease. Thus, a deep split in the conservative movement, especially notable in the Senate, facilitated the expansion of presidential government in the international sphere as the United States drew closer to entering the war. Once again, the liberal governance model had triumphed.[28]

Following the Pearl Harbor attack on 7 December 1941, most conservatives acknowledged the necessity of presidential leadership in World War II and offered little resistance as Roosevelt and his advisers set grand strategy and shuffled agencies related to the war itself, with little specific guidance from Congress. They continued to attack domestic aspects of the strong presidency and other components of the liberal theory of governance. On the genuine government abuses of the liberties of the Japanese-Americans, most conservatives, like most liberals, supported big government in practice.

As the 1933–45 period drew to a close, with the death of Roosevelt and the end of World War II, conservatives could derive some satisfaction from the fact that they had slowed the momentum for liberal institutional reform and had blocked some liberal initiatives and forced compromises on others. Nevertheless, their inability to win the presidency, or even a major-party nomination for the presidency, for one of their own and the paucity of conservative intellectuals to articulate their theory of governance were handicaps in their struggles against liberalism and its institutional prescriptions. And the internal unity so evident in the fight over Court-packing in 1937 was lacking on many other matters, particularly on those pertaining to the president's international roles.

## Conservative Consensus and Discord

As was true of liberal opinion, conservative recommendations concerning government institutions usually spread across a range on continuums pertinent to each component of their theory of governance. Certainly, over a period spanning twelve years, such a pattern was to be expected. Then, too, there were conservatives whose views overlapped with those of liberals, particularly those of moderate liberals, and particularly on the issues of the administrative state and presidential foreign roles. However, few, if any, acknowledged conservatives took positions at the extreme liberal end of any of the scales.

### Constitutional Immutability

Near the extreme conservative end of the flexibility-rigidity continuum concerning the nature of the Constitution lay Justice Sutherland's opinion that government "powers are rigidly limited to the enumerations of the Constitution." Justice Roberts's discussion of "mechanical jurisprudence" was in a similar vein: "When an act of Congress is appropriately challenged in the courts as not conforming to the constitutional mandate, the judicial branch of the Government has only one duty—to lay the article of the Constitution which is invoked beside the statute which is challenged and to decide whether the latter squares with the former." Whether the matter was one of interpretation of the Constitution by a judge or by someone else, this position conceived of the Constitution as rigid and unchanging in its meaning. However, Roberts at times found the Constitution considerably more flexible than his comments indicated, and Sutherland and most conservative jurists often drew upon such extraconstitutional concepts as natural justice to apply economic substantive due process restrictions that appeared neither in the text of the Constitution nor in the expressed intentions of most framers. Moreover, as previously indicated, in Congress and elsewhere many conservatives were willing to support the idea—especially in the economic-emergency conditions of 1933—that the Constitution was sufficiently malleable to permit the accretions of presidential power and centralization of federal powers embodied in much of the Hundred Days legislation that they endorsed at that time. Therefore, while displaying pronounced tendencies, especially in their rhetoric, toward a position of constitutional immutability, conservatives were sometimes willing to support considerable flexibility of interpretation in practice. None, however, went so far as to embrace the "legal realist" views at the extreme liberal end of the scale.[29]

*States' Rights*

On the matter of centralization or decentralization of the federal system, most conservatives of 1933–45 came to embrace the idea of states' rights. However, what they meant by that term and how extensively they wished to apply it varied considerably. Southern Democratic conservatives, such as Josiah Bailey, Carter Glass, and Harry Byrd, invoked the concept regularly and linked it to their Jeffersonian Democratic heritage. Some conservative Republicans, such as James Beck, emulated them and, like them, possessed records of decentralization advocacy that predated the New Deal period and cut across many policy issues. However, many conservative Republicans had taken Hamiltonian centralist positions in the past, and quite a number of them continued to do so on some issues— antilynching and anti–poll tax legislation, for example—that divided them sharply from their Southern Democratic colleagues in the conservative camp. Even some conservative Southern Democrats abandoned their states' rights advocacy and called for new national-government intrusions on selected issues, such as suppressing sit-down strikes in Michigan, when state policy outcomes were particularly unsatisfactory to them. Much of conservative big business was even less inclined than the rest of the coaliton to support states' rights in practice, particularly when it came to business regulation; for the prospect of national uniformity in regulations often seemed preferable to an array of forty-eight distinctive, and possibly contradictory, sets of state regulations. Therefore, the nearly universal conservative lip service to states' rights from the mid-1930s onward concealed considerable discord as to application.[30]

### Nightwatchman State Providing Limited Aid to Business

On this dimension, too, conservative opinion spread over a considerable range. While almost all conservatives of the period regularly denounced bureaucratization in government (the *Chicago Tribune*'s notorious "burocracy"), only a minority were probably as strongly and consistently opposed to the administrative state as Nock or other libertarian intellectuals, such as Ludwig von Mises and Friedrich A. Hayek, whose ideas gained wide currency during World War II. Many conservatives, such as Harry Byrd and Herbert Hoover, had in fact instituted administrative-state moves of their own, based on businesslike concerns for economy and efficiency, within their own bailiwicks. Byrd, for example, as governor of Virginia, had drawn upon Luther Gulick's talents to develop an executive reorganization plan in his own state. Business corporate leaders initially gave considerable support to the Roosevelt proposals of 1937, though most retreated into opposition or silence once the conservative battle against them went into high gear. Moreover, most conservatives of the period favored state-imposed protective tariffs, corporate-assistance agencies such as the Reconstruction Finance Corporation (instituted under Hoover), and even, in its early stages, the National Recovery Administration. Although virtually none of them favored a fully developed, hierarchical, and professionalized administrative-state apparatus in the national government, neither did most conservatives during this period cluster at the other extreme, favoring a purely nightwatchman state.[31]

### Congressionally Centered Checks and Balances

Although conservatives initially accepted dramatic expansions of presidential powers during the First New Deal, their hostility to presidential government grew as their confidence in Roosevelt and his hoped-for conservatism diminished. Congressional conservatives, judicial conservatives, and an array of conservative pundits usually opposed broad congressional delegations of powers domestically after 1937. As the Supreme Court became increasingly liberal and Congress became increasingly conservative, Congress occupied the center stage in most conservatives' domestic prescriptions for the national government. The advent of World War II, however, highlighted what already appeared to be a developing conservative split over presidential and congressional roles in the international sphere. A few conservatives, such as Nicholas Murray Butler, president of Columbia University, offered another variation in occasional calls for a cabinet-parliamentary system, but these were rare. Despite important differences among conservatives, almost all rejected liberal "plebiscitary" presidential roles and the liberal conception of the president as agenda-setter for social reform; and most preferred congressional management of whatever administrative state was to exist on domestic matters.[32]

*Active Judicial Protection of Property Rights*

The clearest common denominator in the conservative theory of governance concerning the judiciary was the recommendation that the courts should actively prevent popularly elected branches of the government from trampling constitutionally guaranteed property rights. As noted previously, many liberals of the 1933–37 period portrayed their conservative opponents as judicial activists while asserting the need for judicial restraint; yet most conservatives did not perceive themselves as advocates of activism. Even when the Supreme Court departed from precedent (as in the *Humphrey's Executor* case involving Roosevelt's removal of a member of the Federal Trade Commission) or chose some precedents over others and appealed to natural justice (as in a number of cases), most conservatives denied that the justices were being activist in any sense except doing their constitutional duty to overrule an erring Congress or president. As the Supreme Court and the federal judiciary in general became increasingly liberal after 1937, conservatives continued to advocate what they viewed as traditional jurisprudence by the courts. But they displayed little willingness to challenge FDR's liberal judicial appointments and generally shifted their focus after 1937 to other components of their theory of governance. In 1940, however, they did mount an effort on behalf of courts versus administrative tribunals, in the instance of the Walter-Logan bill.

## Conclusions

The conservatives' institutional prescriptions, as they commonly defined them, usually meshed without sharp contradictions. Strict construction and original intent were generally supportive of a fairly state-oriented federalism, a congressionally centered check-and-balance system, and a rather limited state that provided some support for private business. However, conservative judicial activism to protect property rights seemed to most liberal and neutral eyes to stretch beyond recognition the supposedly rigid constitutional boundaries of original intent or strict construction. Conservatives dealt with this apparent contradiction by simply denying it—and by appearing quite sincere in their denials.

Clearly, most conservatives also believed that their theory of governance and its components fostered their core values. They could at least make a strong case that this was so with regard to negative freedom (especially the liberty to use one's private property free from government restraint), traditional republicanism, and economic growth. However, whether a congressionally centered, check-and-balance national structure, lacking a significant administrative state apparatus and severely constrained by states' rights and judicial intervention, could actually have provided a high level of order or national security or anything approaching legal equality in the circumstances of the Great Depression and World War II is certainly subject to doubt. One suspects that the conservative waffling on presidential power, the administrative state, and centralization in the emergencies of both 1933 and 1941–45 reflected the concerns of many conservatives themselves on these matters.

## Notes

1. *Home Building and Loan v. Blaisdell,* 290 U.S. 398 (1934); Christopher Wolfe, *The Rise of Modern Judicial Review* (Lanham, MD: Rowman & Littlefield, 1994), 145–160.

2. Albert Jay Nock, *Our Enemy, the State* (New York: William Morrow, 1935).

3. *Cong. Rec.,* 73rd Cong., 1st sess. (11 March 1933), 218. On Beck's book, see Arthur M. Schlesinger Jr., *The Crisis of the Old Order* (Boston: Houghton Mifflin, 1957), 72. For key votes, see table 4.1 in this book.

4. The quotation is from Beck's remarks in the House of Representatives, 25 May 1933, reprinted in *Congressional Digest* (December 1933).

5. On Kent and Sullivan, see Gary Dean Best, *The Critical Press and the New Deal* (Westport, CT: Praeger, 1993), 39–40; on Fish, see *New York Times,* 13 May 1933, 4; on Hilles, see *New York Times,* 26 May 1933, 1.

6. *New York Times*, 31 August 1933, 11.

7. *New York Times*, 1 September 1933, 9.

8. *New York Times*, 3 September 1933, 15.

9. "The National Election," *Chicago Sunday Tribune,* 6 November 1932, sec. 1, p. 10; "The Paramount Issue," *Chicago Daily Tribune,* 11 March 1933, 10.

10. "The President's Appeal," *Chicago Daily Tribune,* 19 June 1933, 12; "Elect Better Men to Congress," *Chicago Daily Tribune,* 18 June 1933, 14.

11. "A Jeffersonian Speaks Out," *Chicago Daily Tribune*, 4 September 1933, 12; "Opposition," *Chicago Suncay Tribune*, 18 February 1934, sec. 1, p. 14.

12. "The Tenons and Mortises of the New Deal," *Chicago Sunday Tribune*, 13 May 1934, sec. 1, p. 16.

13. George Wolfskill, *The Revolt of the Conservatives* (Boston: Houghton Mifflin, 1962), 110–111.

14. *New York Times*, 14 February 1934, 18; *Chicago Sunday Tribune*, 18 February 1934, sec. 1, p. 14; *New York Times*, 18 June 1936, 2.

15. Wilfred E. Binkley, *Powers of the President* (Garden City, NY: Doubleday, Doran & Co., 1937), 282–284; Arthur M. Schlesinger Jr., *The Politics of Upheaval* (Boston: Houghton Mifflin, 1960), 268–270.

16. Schlesinger, *Politics of Upheaval,* 447–496.

17. "The Constitution Rules the United States," *Chicago Daily Tribune*, 29 May 1935, 12.

18. "The Future of the Supreme Court," *Chicago Sunday Tribune*, 7 February 1937, sec. 1, p. 16; Frank J. Hogan, "Important Shifts in Constitutional Doctrines," *American Bar Association Journal* 25 (July 1939): 638; "The Luxury of Liberty," *Chicago Daily Tribune*, 20 December 1940, 16.

19. Ronald A. Mulder, *The Insurgent Progressive in the United States Senate and the New Deal* (New York: Garland, 1979), 178–213, 254–256, 272–274, 313; Ronald L. Feinman, *Twilight of Progressivism* (Baltimore: Johns Hopkins University Press, 1981), 125–134, 195–197.

20. James T. Patterson, *Congressional Conservatism and the New Deal* (Lexington: University of Kentucky Press, 1967), 126. William E. Leuchtenburg, *The Supreme Court Reborn* (New York: Oxford University Press, 1995), 156–161, largely concurs.

21. Richard J. Polenberg, *Reorganizing Roosevelt's Government* (Cambridge: Harvard University Press, 1966), chap. 3; Best, *Critical Press,* 116, discusses Kent's opposition.

22. Polenberg, *Reorganizing Roosevelt's Government*; John A. Rohr, *To Run a Constitution* (Lawrence: University Press of Kansas, 1986), pt. 2; Sidney M. Milkis, *The President and the Parties* (New York: Oxford University Press, 1993), chap. 6.

23. Feinman, *Twilight of Progressivism,* 144.

24. Rohr, *To Run a Constitution*, 157–160; Milkis, *President and the Parties,* 144; *New York Times*, 27 November 1940, 1, 24; December 19, 1940, 1, 18.

25. *United States v. Curtiss-Wright Export Corporation*, 299 U.S. 304 (1936); *United States v. Belmont*, 301 U.S. 324 (1937); Arthur M. Schlesinger Jr., *The Imperial Presidency* (New York: Popular Library, 1974), 108–111.

26. James MacGregor Burns, *Roosevelt: Soldier of Freedom* (New York: Harcourt Brace Jovanovich, 1970), 37–40; Jordan A. Schwarz, *The New Dealers* (New York: Alfred A. Knopf, 1993), 324–342.

27. Cited by Burns, *Roosevelt: Soldier of Freedom,* 45.

28. See table 4.1. Discussion of the lend–lease controversy is found in Schlesinger, *Imperial Presidency* , 115–120, and Burns, *Roosevelt: Soldier of Freedom,* 43–49.

29. Sutherland's opinion is from *Home Building and Loan v. Blaisdell,* 290 U.S. 398 (1934); Roberts's is from *United States v. Butler,* 297 U.S. 1 (1936).

30.  Patterson, *Congressional Conservatism,* discusses Bailey, Glass, and Byrd. For Beck, see Schlesinger, *Crisis of the Old Order* (Boston: Houghton Mifflin, 1957), 72, 178. The regionalism on antilynching and anti–poll tax legislation is evident in the voting study of the *New Republic,* 18 May 1942, 699–705. On the sit-down strikes, see *New York Times,* 3 April 1937, 3. On big business, see Michael W. Miles, *The Odyssey of the American Right* (New York: Oxford University Press, 1980), 42–43; Kim McQuaid, *Big Business and Presidential Power* (New York: William Morrow, 1982), chap. 1.

31.  Ludwig von Mises, *Omnipotent Government* (New Haven, CT: Yale University Press, 1944); Ludwig von Mises, *Bureaucracy* (New Haven, CT: Yale University Press, 1944); Friedrich A. Hayek, *The Road to Serfdom* (Chicago: University of Chicago Press, 1944). The Byrd–Gulick relationship is discussed by Polenberg, *Reorganizing Roosevelt's Government,* 31–35. On administrative support for business, see McQuaid, *Big Business,* chap. 1; and *New York Times,* 20 January 1937, 10.

32.  On Butler, see *New York Times,* 4 September 1933, 1.

# 6

# Theories of Governance: Instrumentalism and Impact

Despite some discord within each ideological coalition over institutional prescriptions, and especially over preferred modes for effecting these, both the conservative and liberal camps of the 1933–45 period developed distinctive theories of governance. A flexible constitutional framework, fairly centralized federalism, an administrative state, presidential government, and judicial restraint on socioeconomic questions usually won liberal endorsement. Most conservatives tended to support constitutional immutability, states' rights federalism, a modified nightwatchman state, congressionally centered checks and balances, and judicial activism vis-à-vis lawmaking majorities on issues of private property. Each coalition, as has been indicated, drew upon its own sense of traditions, extending back at least to the Progressive Era, in crafting its theory of governance but made significant amendments that reflected its current assumptions and core values and programmatic policy preferences, as well as the power realities of the period.

The first part of this chapter addresses the question of how instrumentalist the liberal and conservative institutional prescriptions were during the 1933–45 period and what priority liberals and conservatives assigned to them in comparison with other tenets of their ideologies. In the process, it examines the extent and nature of the continuity of each theory of governance, the types of justifications that proponents offered in support of their institutional prescriptions, and the willingness of adherents to persist in institutional prescriptions even when they contradicted power or policy goals. To the extent that there existed continuity, justifications in terms of high principles, and support for institutional recommendations even when they conflicted with other movement goals—especially the last of these—there is evidence that the prescriptions were more than mere means toward short-term power and policy ends. The converse is likewise the case.

The second section of this chapter focuses on the impact of the theories of governance and their components, regardless of the motives of their advocates. What effects did they actually have on the ways government institutions operated? What were their programmatic policy consequences? Did they promote the superior ends desired by their proponents? What was their impact on political parties and interest groups? How did they shape the overall content of the ideologies themselves in the future?

### Instrumental Links to Power and Programmatic Policy Ends

Most social scientists have portrayed ideologically based theories of governance as little more than means toward short-term power and programmatic policy ends. William G. Andrews's comment "The constitutional theory follows the party flag" has been widely echoed by such major analysts as Arthur M. Schlesinger Jr., Samuel H. Beer, David Kairys, and James MacGregor Burns.[1]

However, "new institutionalists," who emphasize that institutions are often intervening and independent variables, as well as many ideological proponents of theories of governance, have seen these theories as more than mere means. Some of the proponents have even portrayed their own institutional prescriptions as "the end which would legitimate and fortify all the other ends" (C. P. Ives) or have denounced instrumental treatment of institutions as "the totalitarian philosophy that the end justifies the means" (Barry Goldwater).[2]

For the 1933–45 period, as demonstrated in chapters 4 and 5, considerable continuity and consistency existed in liberal and conservative theories of governance, extending over more than a decade. Nevertheless, it is important to note that this longevity was in part a reflection of medium-term patterns in the power positions occupied by each coalition. Therefore, particularly close attention should be paid to the extent to which recommendations shifted in those instances where power positions changed. In addition, both liberals and conservatives thought certain traits to be inherent in particular government institutions and saw connections between these traits and their own policy agendas.

With regard to ideological power positions, chapter 3 has shown that liberals enjoyed the advantage in the national executive branch, particularly among the New Dealers who staffed much of the new Executive Office of the President and many departments and independent agencies. Conservatives held the upper hand before 1937 on the Supreme Court and throughout the federal judiciary but lost it thereafter; however, they gained dominance in Congress following the 1938 elections and held it through 1945. There can be little doubt that liberal endorsement of presidential government and the administrative state and conservative attacks on Caesarism and bureaucracy throughout most of the period related in part to each side's perceptions of control of the executive branch. Liberals' efforts to centralize federalism and conservatives' growing enthusiasm for states' rights may be seen in a similar light.

The timing of prescription changes also suggested a strong dose of instrumentalism linked to perceptions of power realities. After the ideological inclinations of the courts and Congress underwent major changes in 1937–38, liberals became less inclined than previously to advocate judicial restraint as a general principle. Their considerable discord over preferred freedoms and deference to lawmaking majorities after 1937 illustrated the liberal coalition's adjustment difficulties during a period of transition in the judiciary. Similarly, the conservative *Chicago Tribune* shifted from expressing scorn for Congress and making it the prime target of calls for institutional reform during 1933 and 1934 to proposing by 1940 that it be the center of the national government. Frank Hogan, conservative president of the American Bar Association, urged conservatives in 1939 to switch their emphasis from judicial checks on presidential and bureaucratic authority to congressional checks. Frank Gannett of the National Committee to Uphold Constitutional Government wrote in 1938: "Since the President now controls the Supreme Court, our only hope lies in influencing the members of Congress."[3]

Predominant liberal and conservative perceptions of Roosevelt's ideological inclinations underwent major changes during 1933, with consequent effects for prescriptions concerning presidential government. As noted in chapter 4, a significant number of those who would soon be leading lights of the liberal coalition were hesitant about granting broad, undefined powers to the president during the Hundred Days. However, warnings, such as those of Paul Anderson in June 1933, that presidential powers could be employed by future conservative presidents to bring dire results virtually disappeared in liberal commentaries as Roosevelt established his liberal credentials and proceeded to win reelection three times.[4]

Meanwhile, growing recognition among conservatives that Roosevelt would not join their camp led to a sharp reduction of initial conservative support for broad grants of authority to the presidency. The president, whom Newton D. Baker still saw in May 1933 as a "devoted public servant" deserving of major power grant, had by 1934 become an executive whose "unconstitutional" designs must be sharply checked. Hamilton Fish, the *Chicago Tribune* editorialists, and many other conservatives altered their assessments and their recommendations concerning presidential government.[5]

Beyond the issue of the strength of each ideological coalition within the institutions of government lay other instrumental considerations—those linked to liberal and conservative perceptions of the *inherent* characteristics of government institutions that possessed implications for programmatic policies as well as for basic values. Congress, for example, was widely seen in each camp to be more fragmented and slower to act than the relatively cohesive and quick-acting presidency. If one favored major social-reform initiatives, as the liberals did, only the presidency could likely provide the leadership to attain positive freedom, equality of opportunity, and social security. A strong presidency was necessary but not sufficient to gain these; the president must also be a liberal. But the election returns of the 1930s and 1940s increasingly led liberals (and many conservatives) to associate the presidency *as an institution,* beyond FDR's occupation of the presidential office, with leadership in developing social welfare and business regulatory policies linked to liberal values. Wilfred E. Binkley's historical analysis of president and Congress, first published in 1937 and widely read and praised by liberals, portrayed a recurring pattern of battles between strong presidents who were popular tribunes (Jackson, Lincoln, Wilson, the two Roosevelts) and vested business interests. When the president violated civil liberties, as in the Japanese-American internment of World War II, some liberals expressed concerns. But most liberals of the period emphasized socioeconomic goals far more than they did civil liberties and were quite content to hail presidential government most of the time.[6]

Similarly, both liberal and conservative political leaders and activists who thought United States intervention in the international sphere desirable usually saw the potential for decisiveness, speed, and secrecy in presidential government to be far preferable to the compromising, slowness, and proclivity to leak information that they felt were characteristic of Congress. Therefore, as World War II created increased support for internationalist public policies, endorsement among internationalists for presidential power grew accordingly.

In contrast to the national presidency, the states were thought by most observers to be inherently conservative in their public policy and values biases—again, beyond their current incumbents' own ideological proclivities. State governments were sharply restricted in their ability to run deficits (unlike the national government), they competed against one another to attract business investment in a time of economic disaster, and they were generally too narrow in their scope and too limited in their power resources to regulate multistate and multinational business corporations effectively. Therefore, in the eyes of many liberals and conservatives, a states' rights emphasis effectively foreclosed most egalitarian redistribution of wealth, social welfare programs, or regulation of the national economy in accord with liberal values. Even when liberals occupied governorships or other state government positions, the above factors were generally perceived to be effective constraints on "little New Deals."[7]

Prior to the late 1930s, and even beyond to some extent, the judiciary, too, was widely presumed by many liberals and conservatives to be inherently conservative. This was probably one reason that conservative preferences for courts over administrative tribunals and liberal preferences in the reverse lingered beyond 1937, as was evident in the battle over the Walter-Logan bill in 1940. It also helped explain why many liberals continued to favor judicial restraint even after they gained dominance on the Supreme Court. One common version of the allegedly inherent conservatism of the Supreme Court was articulated by Robert Jackson just before his own elevation to the Court: "The alternations of our national moods are such that a cycle of liberal government seldom exceeds eight years, and by living through them the Court could go on without decisive liberal infusions. So well has this strategy worked that never in its entire history can the Supreme Court be said to have for a single hour been representative of anything except the relatively conservative forces of its day."[8]

Others stressed the entire federal judiciary's inherent insulation from popular pressures due to lifetime appointments, lack of current information, and preoccupation with precedents and legalisms, and its lack of accessibility to average individuals due to high litigation costs. Roosevelt's veto message regarding the Walter-Logan bill drew upon these arguments, as did Charles Groves Haines's presidential address to the American Political Science Association in 1939 and numerous articles in liberal publications.[9]

Before concluding that even medium-term liberal and conservative institutional recommendations were shaped extensively by power and policy considerations, it is useful to review the justifications offered at the time by liberal and conservative proponents of their theories of governance and the extent to which medium-term commitments to institutional prescriptions were jettisoned in favor of immediate power or programmatic policy ends.

Most justifications fell into two broad categories: (1) those stressing values directly linked to the ideology in question, and (2) those emphasizing values of a more universal, nonideological nature. Some arguments were, of course, frankly and overtly instrumentalist, as were a number of the 1933–34 justifications for flip-flops on presidential powers and centralization noted previously among both conservatives and liberals. However, most were not. Among conservatives, advancement of liberty was by far the most widely cited argument in favor of all components of the conservative theory of governance. The American Liberty League and Herbert Hoover's book, *The Challenge to Liberty,* set the tone early that was carried on by most conservatives throughout the period, pointing to the primacy of the libertarian strand, at least among conservatives focusing on governance questions. Preservation of republican traditions, or simply "tradition," also was prominently featured as a justification in the conservative camp. Among liberals, there was greater diversity, with democracy being cited very frequently in support of judicial restraint and often for presidential government (particularly its tribune role). However, liberals advanced nonideological efficiency most often as an argument for their administrative state and frequently for centralization and presidential power also, as well as for the specific Roosevelt Court-packing endeavor. Ideologically linked values of equality of opportunity, positive freedom, and social security sometimes made an appearance in liberal institutional arguments; but none equaled the frequency of citation that liberty enjoyed on the conservative side. Both conservatives and liberals often portrayed their institutional recommendations as more likely than their opponents' to foster economic growth—liberals, through the mixed economy's use of Keynesian and other economic management tools; conservatives, through much greater reliance on free markets. If one were to assess motivations solely on the basis of the publicly offered justifications (an approach not recommended by the author), ideologically linked values appeared to be the most obvious stimulators of institutional prescriptions.[10]

However, the relative frequency with which both conservatives and liberals abandoned major institutional tenets when these contradicted immediate power or policy goals suggests that institutional prescriptions were often treated as means toward even short-term ends. In the realm of general constitutional prescriptions, liberal notions of flexibility, particularly in legal realist form, offered a virtual carte blanche to pursue any power or policy goal that liberals might favor at any point in time. However, such liberals as Hugo Black found the Constitution quite rigid on certain matters, particularly those dealing with the First Amendment. Conservative prescriptions for strict construction and original intent appeared to impose more genuine constraints on their adherents. In practice, however, as previously noted, judicial and other conservatives frequently went beyond their stated precepts in their efforts to find grounds to rule against congressional power delegations to executives or against the uses of national government powers. Sometimes, they even appeared to override their own precedents to do so, as in *Humphrey's Executor v. United States* in 1935. In this case, the justices ruled that the president lacked the power to remove a conservative Republican commissioner from a regulatory commission because the commission was not a purely "executive" agency, despite the fact that nine years previously the conservative-dominated Court had granted the president sweeping removal powers. While some conservatives appeared oblivious to their own constitutional flexibility in such matters, the general patterns of contravening their theory of governance when it suited their policy and power interests to do so aroused considerable skepticism about their motivations.[11]

On the matter of centralized versus decentralized federalism, each side could claim, with some justification, that any departures from the general prescriptions of the ideology reflected merely a recognition of particular needs in particular cases and did not challenge the general validity of centralized federalism (for the liberals) or states' rights (for the conservatives). Nonetheless, the number and timing of the exceptions that proponents of each theory made were sufficient at least to raise questions about short-term and issue-specific instrumentalism. The rejection by most Southern liberals, such as Senator Lister Hill of Alabama or even Senator Claude Pepper of Florida, of centralized or cooperative federalism on race relations but acceptance of it on virtually all other major matters was striking. Even more noteworthy were the demands of Southern conservatives Josiah Bailey, James Byrnes, and Walter George for national action against a 1937 wave of sit-down strikes in Michigan despite their long-term advocacy of states' rights on just such socioeconomic issues and their loud denunciation of a federal antilynching bill on states' rights grounds just two weeks later. Similarly, liberal Senators Sherman Minton and Prentice Brown objected to proposed federal intervention in the sit-down strikes on states' rights grounds that they had rarely, if ever, cited previously.[12]

Presidential government and administrative-state issues offered some similar examples. A substantial number of liberals voiced more opposition to the power delegations in the Economy Act and the Emergency Banking Act in 1933 than their theory suggested and than they themselves ever expressed again during the New Deal era, because they disliked the goals of cutting government employees' salaries or veterans' benefits or simply lacked confidence that Roosevelt would use his new powers to pursue liberal ends. Conservatives, as previously indicated, voiced much less opposition to these early New Deal measures than they did later, at least in part because they still perceived the strong possibility of public policy outcomes that they favored. Conservatives, including much of big business, over half of the congressional contingent, and former President Hoover, initially supported both the presidential and administrative powers in the National Industrial Recovery Act, as well as its centralization of authority, when they thought that the NRA would further their policy goals, only to reject them all decisively as unconstitutional after a relatively short time span. While he was governor of Virginia, Senator Harry Byrd had employed Luther Gulick's advice on designing an administrative state, only to denounce Gulick's similar plan for the national government in 1937, when it appeared linked to Rooseveltian purposes of which Byrd by then thoroughly disapproved. Pro-British Eastern conservatives who had just recently denounced presidential "dictatorship" in the battles over executive reorganization and the Walter-Logan bill between 1937 and 1940 usually endorsed the broad grants of authority to the president in the Lend-Lease Act of 1941. Meanwhile, antiwar liberals centered in the Midwest and West—adherents of presidential government in most respects—demurred on grants of power to the president to aid Britain in 1940 and 1941.[13]

In the judicial sphere, both liberal and conservative theories of governance showed the obvious effects of policy preferences, with conservative judicial activists overruling lawmaking majorities much more readily on matters of property rights than on civil liberties or civil rights, while liberal judicial activists reversed the pattern to a considerable degree. As for particular modes of operation, the outraged opposition of the conservative American Bar Association to FDR's proposed enlargement of the Supreme Court in 1937 stood in stark contrast to its previous advocacy of additional Supreme Court justices in 1921, during the conservative Harding administration.[14]

Of course, there were counterexamples of individuals, such as Senator William E. Borah, who took a states' rights stance on a wide array of issues, including some, such as his refusal to join most Republicans in support of a federal antilynching law, which hurt his own campaign for the Republican presidential nomination in 1936. On lynching, sit-down strikes, and a number of other issues, Borah advocated decentralization and states' rights even when doing so went against his programmatic policy preferences and even when it hampered his drives for power. But Borah was a highly unusual figure, never really a part of either ideological coalition. There was also, of course, Felix Frankfurter, a charter member of the New Deal liberal coalition. Frankfurter usually continued to adhere to a position of judicial restraint (as did some other liberal justices, but less consistently than he), even when he strongly disagreed with the legislative actions at issue in the cases before him. Yet another example was Representative Maury Maverick, who stood out as a rare Southern liberal willing to endorse centralized federalism on racial as well as on other matters—though he did not survive long as an elected Texas member of the U.S. House of Representatives.[15]

The prevailing pattern was one of a moderately high level of medium-term continuity and consistency in both the conservative and the liberal theories of governance. Justifications for the theories were phrased in terms of a mixture of ideological and nonideological values. There were only occasional overt references to power or policy instrumentalism, but only scattered clear examples in either camp of adherence to institutional prescriptions when they clearly collided with major power or policy goals. Usually, such collisions were not in evidence; but when they were, faithfulness to institutional prescriptions was a relatively rare commodity. The evident continuity over time was probably due more to the medium-term power patterns and perceptions of inherent institutional characteristics linked to programmatic policy preferences than to either coalition's pursuit of theories of governance as ends in themselves. Nevertheless, the liberal and conservative theories of governance did take on a life of their own over time. And they did have an impact (though not always the intended one) on various features of American politics.

## Impact of the Theories of Governance

The liberal theory of governance had a greater immediate impact on government institutions, programmatic public policies, and political parties and interest groups than its conservative counterpart did, though conservatives were frequently strong enough to modify the effects of liberal ideas. Each theory of governance, becoming an important set of symbols, would also have some effects on future ideas emanating from its coalition.

Without doubt, federalism became more centralized (or, at least, cooperative) and the national government became more focused around an administrative state and more subject to presidential leadership than had been the case before the New Deal. More people than ever before regarded the Constitution as flexible. However, in each respect, the changes fell short of what even some moderate liberals favored, largely but not wholly because of strong conservative resistance.

In the federal system, only a few New Deal reforms—the Wagner Act, title 2 of the Social Security Act, and the Fair Labor Standards Act, among them—really created coherent, centrally directed national policies. The numerous grant-in-aid programs left considerable discretion in the hands of state and local officials—to an extent that dismayed both contemporary and subsequent liberal analysts, while failing to please most conservatives.[16]

The administrative state that emerged from the struggles over the Brownlow-Gulick-Merriam proposals and the Walter-Logan counterattack left independent regulatory commissions outside the departments and permitted subgovernments or interest triangles to flourish even as it created a more hierarchical and professionalized apparatus than had previously existed. Presidential powers were enhanced by the New Deal legislative grants, executive reorganization, court rulings and *dicta* in the foreign realm, the effects of World War II, and the overwhelming Rooseveltian personality—but not, especially in domestic affairs, to the extent that many liberals favored or most conservatives feared. The federal courts did come to be self-restrained on most socioeconomic matters, to a degree almost unimaginable before 1937, though sharp liberal disputes and weak definition of what judicial liberalism really entailed limited the liberal ideas' impact on the judiciary. Finally, the Constitution itself came to be seen as more flexible than before, by some conservatives as well as by the liberals who had first promoted the idea, though flexibility gave no clear directions.[17]

The partial liberal success in revamping American government institutions did have some of the public-policy consequences that liberals desired. Keynesian fiscal policy became possible to an extent that it could not have without considerable federal centralization, movement toward an administrative state, and enhancement of presidential power, though it would often (even usually) take on coloration more favorable to private business corporate development in the postwar period than most of its New Deal liberal proponents advocated. A variety of regulatory and social welfare policies also emerged more fully than before, facilitated by the liberal presidency and administrative state, centralizing of authority, and judicial embrace of constitutional flexibility on socio-economic questions. However, at the same time, these were constricted by the compromises which left interest triangles and state and local governments as major institutional actors. National economic planning never really resulted in the forms that some New Dealers foresaw, but many liberals had not favored it in any event.[18]

As for the political parties and interest groups, the effects of the partial triumph of the liberal theory of governance were only to some extent those intended by its progenitors. Sidney Milkis has demonstrated that the subsequent erosion of the American party system had at least some of its roots in the liberal presidential government and administrative state of the New Deal period. By providing the means for policy innovation and administration from the presidency and a professionalized career civil service in the national government, the liberal reforms weakened the decentralized machines that previously had been critical units in both the Democratic and Republican parties, freed the presidents of the future considerably from ties to their party organizations, and set the stage for eventual dealignment of the party system.[19]

Furthermore, the expansion of the liberal administrative state—but without the clear presidential direction favored by most liberals of the period—fostered enhanced activity by interest groups, aimed at influencing the portions of the bureaucracy pertinent to each. Interest-group liberalism began to emerge within the liberal ideological coalition itself, as the labor unions, farm groups, and ethnic and racial groups within the alliance pursued their own particular goals. Big business, regularly denounced by many liberals of the period, suffered fewer negative effects of the institutional changes than the *New Republic,* the *Nation,* or most left-liberals of the 1930s had hoped for. Throughout the period, business corporate leaders proved quite capable of adapting to the government changes that transpired. Moreover, its importance to the war effort and the upsurge of economic growth in the 1940s enabled big business to regain most of the popular prestige that had been lost during the Great Depression.[20]

Finally, there was the impact of the theories of governance on the future ideas of the conservative and liberal coalitions themselves. Though adopted and pursued in the 1933–45 period largely but not entirely as means toward the ends of power, policy, and promotion of ideological values, the institutional prescriptions, once entrenched in adherents' minds, could in turn shape future ideological policy choices, uses of power, and even values. From the perspective of the 1950s, Samuel Lubell, one of the most insightful analysts of the period, would remark on the great extent to which "the Presidency has become the symbol of the political revolution wrought by Roosevelt, while Congress has become the symbol of the counterrevolution which has been seeking to reverse the New Deal." The same could have been said of centralized federalism and states' rights.[21]

Scholars including Richard H. Pells, Alonzo L. Hamby, and Arthur M. Schlesinger Jr. have noted the tendency of post-Roosevelt liberals to continue to look almost automatically to the presidency for leadership in defining their public policies. While Pells may exaggerate a bit in portraying a liberal "cult of leadership" centered on the presidency, the notion of presidential government unquestionably influenced subsequent liberal behavior. Moreover, its growing linkage to the national security bureaucracy, combined with its guiding function for the liberal coalition, probably facilitated the building of liberal support for Cold War policies and, according to such diverse scholars as Richard Barnet, Henry Steele Commager, and Jordan Schwarz, even shaped the nature of those policies.[22]

Another aspect of later liberal ideology influenced by the liberal governance theory of the 1930s was "interest-group liberalism," referred to previously. Theodore J. Lowi, author of the term, emphasized its roots in the liberal institutional prescriptions of the 1930s, at least in the form that they took in practice because of compromises and later developments. The trend to interest-group liberalism, its seeds sown in the New Deal era, would after the early 1960s increasingly undermine much of what coherence had been attained by the "new" liberal ideology.[23]

In the conservative coalition, too, the subsequent effects of institutional prescriptions adopted in the 1930s for generally instrumentalist reasons could be seen. One was the widespread expectation, even demand, that any administration seeking to demonstrate conservative credentials should advance some sort of new federalism, as the administrations of Eisenhower, Nixon, and Reagan did in the decades to follow. Doctrines of states' rights, while not always strictly adhered to by conservatives, nonetheless had become important symbols influencing behavior in the conservative coalition.[24]

The following sections of this book, which deal with later time periods, will further analyze issues pertaining to the impact of the New Deal–era theories of governance on future ideological choices; but the preceding points have indicated the importance of the subject and some of its dimensions.

### Conclusions

Developed in part from past progressive and conservative conceptions, shaped rather pragmatically as political leaders and activists created the New Deal programs and responded to them, the liberal and conservative theories of governance would have an impact on American politics for years, sometimes decades, to come. At times, this impact would be in expected directions; at other times, it would be quite far removed from the origins of the ideas. The instrumentalist concerns with the ends of power, programmatic policy, and ideological values—rather evident in the emergence of the liberal and conservative institutional prescriptions during the 1930s—would reshape them over time, as they did even during the 1933–45 period. Yet many of the components of the theories of governance would become symbols important in their own right, capable of exerting influence on the behavior of political actors.

The death of Franklin D. Roosevelt, long the central figure in the liberal-conservative struggle in the United States, and the end of World War II, both occurring in 1945, marked the end of a distinctive period in the development of American conservatism and liberalism, particularly since there was no return to the socioeconomic conditions of the Great Depression during the postwar years. In the new era, there would be new leaders—though none so capable of dominating the political scene as FDR had been—and changing issues, power balances, and perceptions. There would be alterations in the ideologies, too, including their theories of governance. However, most of the components of each major governance theory were to endure with but few modifications through the years 1945–66. Only in the turbulent 1960s would they undergo significant transformation.

## Notes

1. William G. Andrews, "The Presidency, Congress, and Constitutional Theory," in *Perspectives on the Presidency,* ed. Aaron Wildavsky (Boston: Little, Brown, 1975), 38; Arthur M. Schlesinger Jr., in Schlesinger and Alfred de Grazia, *Congress and the Presidency* (Washington: American Enterprise Institute, 1967), 8–9; Samuel H. Beer, "Introduction," in *New Federalism,* by Timothy J. Conlan (Washington: Brookings Institution, 1988); David Kairys, ed., introduction to *The Politics of Law* (New York: Pantheon Press, 1990), 5; James MacGregor Burns, *Presidential Government* (Boston: Houghton Mifflin, 1965).

2. C. P. Ives, "The Well–Intending Judges," *Modern Age* 13 (Summer 1969): 242; Barry M. Goldwater, "My Case for the Republican Party," *Saturday Review* 47 (17 October 1964): 23.

3. C. Herman Pritchett, *The Roosevelt Court* (Chicago: Quadrangle Books, 1948), chaps. 9, 10, on liberals and the judiciary; Frank J. Hogan, "Important Shifts in Constitutional Doctrines," *ABA Journal* 25 (July 1939): 629–638; "The Luxury of Liberty," *Chicago Daily Tribune,* 20 December 1940, 16; Gannett is cited in William E. Leuchtenburg, *The Supreme Court Reborn* (New York: Oxford University Press, 1995), 155.

4. Paul Y. Anderson, "In Defense of Congress," *Nation* 136 (28 June 1933): 722.

5.  On Baker, see *New York Times*, 20 May 1933, 5; and Arthur M. Schlesinger Jr., *The Coming of the New Deal* (Boston: Houghton Mifflin, 1959), 476, 483. Fish and the *Tribune* are discussed in chap. 5 of this book.

6.  Wilfred E. Binkley, *The Powers of the President* (Garden City, NY: Doubleday, Doran, 1937), 301–309. Liberal concern for the Japanese-Americans' civil liberties but continued praise for presidential government is evident, for example, in "Liberty and War," *New Republic*, 15 June 1942, 815–816, and "Civil Liberties and War," *New Republic*, 22 June 1942, 848–849.

7.  James T. Patterson, *The New Deal and the States* (Westport, CT: Greenwood Press, 1969), 202–205.

8.  Robert H. Jackson, *The Struggle for Judicial Supremacy* (New York: Alfred A. Knopf, 1941), 187.

9.  Sidney M. Milkis, *The President and the Parties* (New York: Oxford University Press, 1993), 144; Charles Groves Haines's address, cited by John A. Rohr, *To Run a Constitution* (Lawrence: University Press of Kansas, 1986), 160; and the articles in *Nation,* 10 July 1935, 39–43.

10.  George Wolfskill, *The Revolt of the Conservatives* (Boston: Houghton Mifflin, 1962); Herbert Hoover, *The Challenge to Liberty* (New York: Charles Scribner's Sons, 1934). The continued emphasis on liberty and republican traditions is evident in such later pieces as E. F. Albertsworth, "The New Constitutionalism," *American Bar Association Journal* 26 (November 1940), 865–869; and "The Luxury of Liberty," *Chicago Daily Tribune*, 29 December 1940, 16.

11.  *Humphrey's Executor v. United States* , 295 U.S. 602; Arthur M. Schlesinger Jr., *The Politics of Upheaval* (Boston: Houghton Mifflin, 1960), 279–280.

12.  *New York Times*, 3 April 1937, 1, 3; 15 April 1937, 1; 16 April 1937, 1; 27 July 1937, 1, 2.

13.  Chap. 4 discusses the noted liberal switches; chap. 5, the conservative ones.

14.  For the ABA switch, see *New York Times*, 12 March 1937, 8.

15.  On Borah, see *New York Times,* 29 January 1936, 13; 30 January 1936, 18. On Frankfurter, see William G. Ross, *A Muted Fury* (Princeton: Princeton University Press, 1994), 322, who describes Frankfurter as uniquely principled in this regard and contrasts him with most other liberals. See also C. Herman Pritchett, *The Roosevelt Court* (Chicago: Quadrangle Books, 1948), 280–284. On Maverick, see Jonathan Mitchell, "Front Fighters in Congress," *New Republic* 19 June 1935, 156–157; and *New York Times*, 16 April 1937, 1.

16.  David B. Robertson and Dennis R. Judd, *The Development of American Public Policy* (Glenview, IL: Scott, Foresman, 1989), chap. 4; Patterson, *New Deal and the States*, chap. 8.

17.  On the administrative state, see Sidney M. Milkis, *The President and the Parties* (New York: Oxford University Press, 1993), 125–134; Richard J. Polenberg, *Reorganizing Roosevelt's Government* (Cambridge: Harvard University Press, 1966); Rohr, *To Run a Constitution*, pt. 3. On presidential powers, see Arthur M. Schlesinger, *The Imperial Presidency* (New York: Popular Library, 1974), 107–130. On the federal judiciary, Pritchett, *Roosevelt Court,* chap. 10, is particularly insightful. On constitutional interpretation, Christopher Wolfe, *The Rise of Modern Judicial Review* (Lanham, MD: Rowman & Littlefield, 1994), 3–10, 242.

18. Robertson and Judd, *American Public Policy,* chap. 6.

19. Milkis, *President and the Parties,* chaps. 5 and 6.

20. Kim McQuaid, *Big Business and Presidential Power* (New York: William Morrow, 1982), chaps. 2 and 3; G. William Domhoff, *The Higher Circles: The Governing Class in America* (New York: Vintage Books, 1970), esp. chap. 6.

21. Samuel Lubell, *The Future of American Politics* , 2d ed. (Garden City, NY: Doubleday Anchor Books, 1956), 26.

22. Richard H. Pells, *The Liberal Mind in a Conservative Age* (New York: Harper & Row, 1985), 8–26, 57–60; Alonzo L. Hamby, *Beyond the New Deal* (New York: Columbia University Press, 1973), 63; Schlesinger, *Imperial Presidency,* 129–130, 169. Richard J. Barnet, *Intervention and Revolution* (New York: New American Library, 1972); Henry Steele Commager, *The Defeat of America* (New York: Simon & Schuster, 1974); Jordan A. Schwarz, *The New Dealers* (New York: Alfred A. Knopf, 1993), 337–350.

23. Theodore J. Lowi, *The End of Liberalism: The Second Republic of the United States,* 2d ed. (New York: W. W. Norton, 1979), esp. 273–274.

24. A. James Reichley, *Conservatives in an Age of Change* (Washington: Brookings Institution, 1981), 18–19, 36; Conlan, *New Federalism.*

# 1945–1966

# 7

# Liberal and Conservative Values and Programmatic Policies

Forged in the crucible of depression-era crisis, shaped by the Roosevelt-ian New Deal initiatives and responses to them, and modified by the external threat of the Axis powers, American liberal and conservative ideologies confronted a changing world after 1945. Franklin Delano Roosevelt died in April 1945, and neither Harry Truman nor any of the other political leaders of the next period would be the focal point—positively or negatively—for the ideological coalitions to the extent that FDR had been. Despite widespread initial concerns among conservatives and liberals, the postwar economic picture was one of unparalleled growth, not depression, creating a politics of affluence quite different from the grim socioeconomic struggles of the 1930s. With the surrender of Japan in August 1945, the Axis threat was ended. But the Cold War soon replaced it with a fear of the Soviet Union, and of Communism generally, that came to pervade both conservatism and liberalism, altering some of their values and policy recommendations.

Moreover, African Americans, mobilized by the war effort and accelerating their mass migration from the rural South to urban centers where they could voice their political demands, were to be increasingly insistent in forcing issues of racial justice onto the ideological agenda to a degree far exceeding that of the 1933–45 period. All of these significant contextual changes would effect shifts in the values and programmatic policies of liberalism and conservatism. Yet continuity probably outweighed change. The 1945–66 period was in many respects a time of consolidation in each ideological coalition, despite the need to face new issues under new leadership.

## Liberal Assumptions and Values

Assumptions in the liberal coalition continued to include considerable faith in basic human equality and a proclivity to rationalism, but these were now more tempered than before by frequent liberal perceptions of a need for leadership by enlightened elites and fears of popular irrationality. Mary Sperling McAuliffe has noted the shift in mood, but probably overstated it when she wrote that the postwar liberals "abandoned many traditional liberal tenets—the belief in progress, in man's goodness, in popular democracy, and in world peace—replacing them with a chastened and, in their view, 'realistic' philosophy which stressed man's sinfulness, the seeming inevitability of conflict among nations, and the dangers of democratic rule."[1]

What McAuliffe discerned was more true of the mainstream liberals' view of international politics than of their domestic vision; for domestically the liberals' embrace of the reformist goals of the Fair Deal, the New Frontier, and the Great Society bore a strong resemblance to the optimistic hopes for societal improvement through a mix of government effort, social scientific knowledge, and private enterprise that had characterized the New Deal. Gary Gerstle has argued convincingly that a constant "was the liberal commitment to rationality. . . . Many liberals believed that their contributions to New Deal policy-making and to war mobilization proved their capacity for social engineering on the grandest scale. No problem was too great for them to handle."[2]

Even in the foreign sphere, the postwar liberal "realism" was not a dramatic break from the mixture of "Four Freedoms" idealism and pragmatic pursuit of "national interests" that the Roosevelt administration, backed by most of the liberal movement, had undertaken during World War II. The leading account of FDR's war leadership, for example, has concluded that Roosevelt was "a deeply divided man—divided between the man of principle, of ideals, of faith, crusading for a distant vision on the one hand; and, on the other, the man of *Realpolitik* . . . intent always on protecting his power and authority in a world of shifting moods and capricious fortune." If liberal assumptions did shift away from egalitarianism and rationalism, the change was neither as uniform nor as dramatic after 1945 as McAuliffe and many left critics have suggested.[3]

Other liberal assumptions also underwent some alterations in the postwar years. The materialism of the 1930s did not dissipate altogether, as evidenced by the continuing stress on FDR's economic bill of rights and on increasing the gross national product. However, the affluence of the postwar era led to some diminishment of liberal emphasis on material gains. Meanwhile, the rise of civil rights activism and increasing liberal embrace of the black civil rights movement as a moral crusade lent a moralistic tone of social uplift and promotion of moral virtue that had been atypical of New Deal liberalism and tended to displace a materialistic "social class" emphasis with a concern for the evils of racial segregation.[4]

Finally, the previously-noted liberal combination of collectivist faith in social engineering and individualistic assumptions about the benefits of the free marketplace of ideas continued after 1945. Despite the jibes from both libertarians and critics of market models that the underlying premises of the two approaches did not mesh well, liberals generally continued to adhere to them simultaneously.[5]

In the realm of expressed value preferences, liberal continuity with the New Deal era was also more evident than change. Equality of opportunity continued to be invoked regularly by liberals but was now extended to blacks as well as whites, unlike the predominant pattern in the New Deal era. But if this move represented a leftward shift, it was counterbalanced by the declining number of liberals desiring to push beyond equality of opportunity to a social democratic equality of results. Whereas in the 1933–45 period such "left-liberals" constituted a substantial minority, strong in the CIO unions and among the *New Republic* and *Nation* intellectuals, their numbers and influence were diminished by the intense anti-Communism and the growing affluence of the postwar era. More liberals now saw themselves as "the vital center" than as "the left." Only a few, mostly intellectuals, continued to call publicly for a Swedish-style social democracy, as Irwin Ross did in his 1949 book, *Strategy for Liberals*.[6]

As in the New Deal era, "positive freedoms" were a frequent emphasis of postwar liberalism. Eugene McCarthy, writing *A Liberal Answer to the Conservative Challenge* in 1964, more than two decades after Roosevelt's Four Freedoms speech and his positive freedom program drawn from the National Resources Planning Board, quoted extensively from both to justify the liberal programs of the 1960s as mandated by the "economic bill of rights." Americans for Democratic Action, the leading group of liberal intellectuals throughout the postwar period, agreed, repeatedly citing positive freedoms in its policy statements.[7]

The social security theme also remained central to liberalism, with liberals seeking to extend the concept further and to more of the population than had been feasible in the economically distressed 1930s. By the 1950s the heart of the program going by the name Social Security, the Old Age and Survivors' Insurance Program, had attained such popularity that even most conservatives viewed it as irreversible. Other social security ideas, such as national health insurance, enjoyed wide liberal support but were unacceptable to conservatives and many moderates of the period.

Diminishing liberal materialism, rooted largely in the postwar economic boom, might have been expected to deflect liberals from their previous pursuit of economic growth as a high priority; and it did lead some of them—particularly intellectuals from the mid-1950s onward—to shift their focus to "quality of life" issues. Arthur Schlesinger Jr., for example, in various articles in the mid-1950s, called for de-emphasizing economic growth in favor of a "qualitative liberalism dedicated to bettering the quality of people's lives and opportunities." Liberals should focus more attention than before, he argued, on "the more subtle and complicated problems of individual dignity, identity, and fulfillment in a mass society." Liberals should take steps to "improve our schools, our hospitals, our cities, our natural resources, our public domain." Quite a few liberals echoed Schlesinger. Yet economic growth continued to be a major liberal concern. Even some intellectuals, such as Leon Keyserling, reasserted its importance, and labor union leaders and liberal politicians still gave it very high priority. As the years advanced, a sort of balance came to characterize liberal values, with liberals weighing the benefits of growth against such other values as a clean environment, and seeking compromises between them.[8]

Probably the greatest liberal value shifts occurred in the area of majoritarian procedural democracy. During the late 1940s and 1950s, many liberals were frightened by the mass anti-Communist hysteria triggered by Senator Joseph McCarthy and by social scientific studies indicating "working-class authoritarianism" and widespread aversion to the protection of civil liberties. These developments pushed many, especially liberal intellectuals like Seymour Martin Lipset, Daniel Bell, Talcott Parsons, and Leslie Fiedler, in the direction of pluralism, or what some termed "democratic elitism." Other liberals, such as A. A. Berle, embraced these concepts less from fear of the masses than from a faith in technocracy. In contrast, there emerged in the 1960s an opposing "new politics" liberalism, influenced by the participatory democratic demands of Students for a Democratic Society and other New Leftists, which found the old procedural democracy—and certainly the democratic elitism of Lipset and others—insufficiently populistic. Differences in values concerning democracy were an important source of conflict within the liberal coalition by the 1960s, far more than they had been in the 1933–45 years.[9]

One other value, increasingly evident in liberalism after 1939 and becoming long-term and pervasive during the Cold War, was national security. Its effects during World War II had led many liberals to downgrade civil liberties, particularly in the cases concerning the internment of the Japanese-Americans. Though most postwar liberals did not embrace the order-national security values with as much warmth as did order-conscious and Communist-hating conservatives, they did modify their values to fit a national-security model more than in the New Deal era, particularly in the late 1940s and early 1950s.

Overall, despite challenges for primacy, particularly from national security values, equal opportunity, positive freedom, social security, and economic growth remained of central importance to liberalism. Growth was now balanced, however, against newer quality-of-life concerns. Negative freedom in the area of civil liberties continued to be of importance to most liberals. Despite subordination to national security in the 1947–54 period, civil liberties again became a major liberal value after the decline of anti-Communist hysteria. Liberalism had changed, but it had also continued to be recognizable as a child of the New Deal.

### Liberal Programmatic Public Policies

Against a backdrop of assumptions and values still linked to the New Deal era, the liberal movement not surprisingly maintained many of the programmatic commitments of the past. However, here the changes were sometimes quite significant—especially with regard to foreign policy and black civil rights. Both of these issues often occupied center stage in the 1945–66 period and took forms quite different from those of the past. Even in the socioeconomic and civil liberties spheres, where policy recommendations shifted less dramatically than in the other domains, there were some notable departures.

Liberal social welfare policies probably displayed the greatest continuity with the New Deal. Drawing upon Roosevelt's 1944 and 1945 pledges and building upon the base established in the 1930s, the Truman administration proposed a Fair Deal program, including national health insurance, general federal aid to education, an expanded public housing program, and extended social security benefits and coverage. However, proposing and gaining enactment were two different matters. The Truman-liberal health care and education proposals never gained congressional passage because of intense conservative opposition and conflicts concerning Roman Catholic Church demands for parochial school aid. The public housing program barely squeaked through Congress in modified form, and it was poorly administered, distorted by many local governments, and underfunded. Only in areas like social security that built incrementally on what already existed and granted benefits to the broad middle class did Truman and the liberals enjoy much success. The major outcomes of Truman's Fair Deal socioeconomic efforts were mainly consolidation and moderate extension of the Rooseveltian partial welfare state.[10]

The unfinished liberal social welfare agenda—notably national health insurance and general federal aid to education—remained on the back burner during the Eisenhower administration (though Eisenhower unsuccessfully called for federal aid for public school construction). This agenda also lacked the necessary congressional backing under Kennedy, even with national health insurance trimmed back to medicare for just the elderly. Finally, in 1965, fortified by liberal strength in Congress following the 1964 elections, Lyndon Johnson pushed through medicare for the elderly, medicaid for the poor, general federal aid to elementary and secondary education, and an array of new Great Society social welfare programs.[11]

From Truman through Johnson, the liberals' advocacy of their social welfare reforms nearly always stressed the values of equal opportunity, positive freedom, and social security. Though critics on both their left and right often questioned whether the programs actually promoted these values, few liberals had doubts on the matter, at least until the late 1960s. The only major liberal social welfare policy not yet accomplished in 1966 was national health insurance. But with a conservative trend soon to develop, this goal would remain unachieved.

In the domain of government management of the economy, liberals became somewhat more unified than they had been in the 1930s, mainly around a Keynesian strategy of indirect management to steer the economy toward growth and enhanced employment, without either deep recessions or steep inflation. Deliberate budget deficits in economic downturns followed by balanced budgets in upswings, it was thought, would keep the economy moving forward on an even keel. Overt government planning, government ownership of major financial or industrial corporations, or other direct challenges to private business corporate prerogatives were now seen as less desirable or necessary than in the past. Considerable success in both the Truman and Kennedy-Johnson administrations in attaining balanced growth using variations of the basic Keynesian approach encouraged liberals to persist in this basic strategy, though signs of economic dislocation were becoming evident by 1966. Even in this realm, some notable liberal differences existed—for example, the sharp dispute between the Galbraith-led liberals who favored increased government spending to stimulate the economy in the early 1960s and the Kennedy administration, which opted for major stimulative tax cuts. Moreover, liberal efforts requiring congressional action often fell short of the liberals' intentions, as was the case with the Employment Act of 1946, which was watered down extensively from the liberals' original goal of establishing a firm and enforceable government commitment to "full employment."[12]

Other liberal economic management proposals of the period included periodic and largely unsuccessful efforts to revamp the conservative-backed Taft-Hartley Act of 1947, which most of the liberal coalition, and especially union leaders, viewed as overly hostile to the interests of organized labor. There was also the Truman administration's abortive effort to gain passage of the so-called Brannan Plan, which would have sought to maintain farm income through direct payments to farmers rather than through crop restrictions and would have placed a cap on the government subsidy to each farm. This plan, like the efforts to reverse the Taft-Hartley labor legislation, came to naught because of strong conservative opposition.[13]

In the domain of civil rights, liberals of the period moved far beyond their record in the New Deal era, prodded by the developing civil rights movement and by judicial liberals, whose *Brown v. Board of Education* decision in 1954 was a spur to action. Well before *Brown,* the Truman administration had taken effective steps to desegregate the armed forces and had made an unsuccessful effort to persuade Congress to establish a permanent Fair Employment Practices Commission, pass an antilynching law, and abolish the poll tax, which had disfranchised many blacks and poor whites throughout most of the South. During the Eisenhower administration, congressional liberals joined with many moderates and Northern conservatives to pass two weak civil rights measures, the first of any kind to be enacted by Congress since 1875. But it was in the 1960s that liberals in all government institutions and throughout the country made a strong commitment to racial desegregation. Though the Kennedy administration approached the subject gingerly at first, it eventually endorsed a strong civil rights bill that became the main basis for the landmark Civil Rights Act of 1964, signed into law by Lyndon Johnson. This act included a guarantee of equal access to public accommodations, provisions aimed at ending discrimination in employment practices, powers for the attorney general to initiate school desegregation suits, and provisions to terminate federal funding for programs in which there was found to be racial discrimination. Again with the support of a broad coalition extending well beyond the boundaries of liberalism, the Johnson administration gained congressional passage of the Voting Rights Act of 1965. It then proceeded to enforce it with particular effectiveness, enabling over seven hundred thousand African Americans in the South to register and vote for the first time in their lives. By the 1960s, liberalism was coming to be clearly identified—by its adherents, as well as by the general public—with attempts to extend not just formal, legal equality, but also equal opportunity and positive freedoms to black Americans. Whether there should be moves beyond these to equality of outcomes between the races, as implied by some affirmative action programs, would soon badly divide liberals and alienate a considerable portion of the liberal base of popular support among whites. Even before affirmative action became a byword of American politics, however, a white backlash against liberalism was emerging. Soon the civil rights controversies would play a major role in the unraveling of the liberal coalition.[14]

Civil liberties questions still often divided liberals, as they had in the 1933-1945 period. Issues centering on the free expression rights (if any) of Communists and other "security risks" came to the forefront, particularly during the late 1940s and early 1950s. While some liberals, especially those in the American Civil Liberties Union, took "preferred freedom" or even "absolute freedom" positions regularly, others saw a "clear and present danger" or even a "dangerous tendency" as sufficient cause to restrict civil liberties. However, Supreme Court liberals and the liberal movement in general increasingly favored relaxation of government restrictions on civil liberties as McCarthyism and fears of internal Communist subversion subsided. The *Yates v. United States* case in 1957, in which the High Bench held that the mere advocacy of overthrow of the government provided insufficient grounds for conviction of Communists, aroused a storm of conservative protest but won general liberal support. Often, in fact, liberals came to define liberties more broadly than before, finding individual rights to privacy, for example in the "penumbra" of the Bill of Rights. The increased linkage after the late 1950s of liberalism to civil libertarianism, like the parallel growing association of liberalism with black civil rights, would play a part in eroding liberal support among the voting public.[15]

The new foreign policy issues that centered around the containment of the Soviet Union and Communism at first badly divided the liberal coalition as the Cold War began. On one side, favoring the containment doctrine and advocating military and economic aid to Greece and Turkey, the Marshall Plan of massive economic assistance to non-Communist European governments, and eventually (in 1949) the United States' entry into the North Atlantic Treaty Organization, stood President Truman and most of his administration, backed by the majority of congressional liberals, and such liberal groups as the new Americans for Democratic Action. On the other side, favoring a policy of cooperation with the Soviet Union and acceptance of a Soviet "defensive" sphere of influence in Eastern Europe, stood Henry A. Wallace, former vice president and soon to be ex-secretary of commerce, backed at the outset by a few congressional liberals such as

Glen Taylor and Claude Pepper and by the Progressive Citizens of America. Following his ouster from the Truman cabinet, Wallace broke sharply with the "Cold War liberals" and mounted a campaign for the presidency against Truman, running on the Progressive party ticket. However, most liberals rallied behind Truman in the face of Communist influence on Wallace's Progressive party and widespread perceptions of a Soviet/Communist international threat.

From 1948 through 1965, most of the liberal coalition united behind an international policy based on the containment of Communism. When Communist North Korea invaded South Korea in June 1950, even Wallace announced his support for the Truman administration's commitment of troops through the United Nations. The stalemated war in Korea, which essentially reinstated the preinvasion dividing line between North and South, would be accompanied by a growing United States role in containing Communism globally. And American involvement in Vietnam grew steadily and then at an increasingly rapid pace as the years advanced.

The liberals' anti-Communist foreign policies overlapped with the policies favored by much of the conservative coalition during the period. Both entailed a huge defense apparatus and massive military spending, covert activities in other countries, and frequent reliance on the dispatch of troops overseas. However, the liberals' policies differed from those of conservative anti-Communist interventionists in several important respects. Few liberals joined in conservative demands to roll back Communism rather than contain it. Most liberals placed more reliance on foreign economic aid, were more tolerant of Third World neutralism, and were more inclined to seek allied cooperation than most conservatives. And whether it was Harry Truman's Point Four program, John Kennedy's Peace Corps, Eugene McCarthy's plea to "conspire together" with other nations to promote global economic justice, or Lyndon Johnson's vision of a Tennessee Valley Authority for the Mekong River Valley in Southeast Asia, liberal foreign policy themes contained more than a dash of New Dealish social reform that was notably absent from most conservative foreign policy prescriptions. Nonetheless, Cold War liberal and conservative foreign policy distinctions in practice were often blurred.[16]

## Conservative Assumptions and Values

If the conservative coalition of the 1930s had sometimes been troubled by the tensions between classical liberal and traditional conservative assumptions and values in its ranks, the growing numbers of conservative intellectuals after 1945 heightened conflict between the two but also produced major efforts to synthesize them into a coherent whole. George Nash has chronicled effectively the growth of the conservative intellectual movement after World War II. Prominent among those espousing the libertarian conservative outlook were economists, from Friedrich A. Hayek and Ludwig von Mises in the 1940s through Milton Friedman, whose *Capitalism and Freedom,* published in 1962, proved very influential in the 1960s and the following decades. Other intellectuals, too, such as Albert Jay Nock and Felix Morley, contributed libertarian conservative ideas. Certainly, the assumptions and values of "Manchester" classical liberalism, dominant in the conservative movement in the preceding period, were now articulated more clearly than before and constituted the major strand in conservative thinking. However, Russell Kirk and Richard Weaver, more than any other intellectuals, articulated a traditional, Burkean conservative value system that also won considerable conservative support. Loosely associated with this view was another version of traditional conservatism put forward by the followers of political philosopher Leo Strauss and grounded in the ideas of Plato and other thinkers of Greek antiquity. An influx of intense anti-Communists—activists committed to strong government to combat Communism—into the conservative movement tended to supplement the ranks of the traditionalists, though anti-Commuinists entered both camps. Sensing the danger of an outright split between the two main wings of American conservatism, intellectuals such as Frank Meyer and, to a great extent, William F. Buckley, sought to fuse them. Meyer, admittedly more of a libertarian conservative than a traditional one, stressed that the libertarians' negative freedom was the ultimate *political* end but that the traditionalists' virtue was the ultimate end of man as man. Though Meyer's formulation did not satisfy all conservatives, especially the traditionalists, Buckley's new weekly magazine, *National Review,* became a major forum for interchanges among conservative intellectuals of both schools and various hues after its founding in 1955.[17]

Skepticism about liberal social engineering continued to unite most conservatives at a fundamental level. In its inaugural issue, *National Review* portrayed an irreconcilable conflict between "Social Engineers" and "conservative" disciples of Truth, who defend the organic moral order. However, "liberationist" conservatives who embraced international interventionism often perceived a government capacity to reshape the globe in an American image even while rejecting the possibilities for domestic social reform. James Burnham, for instance, declared, "The reality is that the only alternative to the communist World Empire is an Amer-

ican Empire which will be, if not literally world-wide in formal boundaries, capable of exercising decisive world control." Certainly, the goal of
dominating the world went far beyond what conservatism had usually
seen as possible or desirable in the New Deal era. It also conflicted with
the underlying assumptions about the limits of government that animated leaders such as Robert Taft and Felix Morley.[18]

In the sphere of values, the predominant conservative position, as previously, was that equality entails no more than formal equality before the
law. A few prominent conservatives, notably Harry Jaffa, pushed a bit
beyond this in positing "the principle of the natural equality of political
rights of all men," appealing to the ideas of Abraham Lincoln and Thomas
Jefferson for support. But Jaffa drew quick rebukes from many fellow conservatives; and most traditionalists, such as Russell Kirk, Richard Weaver,
and James J. Kilpatrick, as well as fusionist Frank Meyer, rejected the
value of equality altogether.[19]

"Liberty" remained the foremost value for the libertarians and the
fusionist conservatives. But while some traditionalist conservatives, such
as Brent Bozell, conceded the value of private property, they firmly denied
that freedom in and of itself was an important value. Foreshadowing
intraconservative disputes between the Christian right and libertarian
conservatives in later eras, Bozell argued for the need "to build a Christian civilization" and to employ government action to "ease the way to
virtue." Therefore, in light of the emergent virtue-oriented strand of traditionalist conservatism, private property, rather than liberty itself, was
the value around which conservatives could unite. Private property, the
most important basis for liberty to libertarian and fusionist conservatives,
was instead primarily a building block of a well-ordered society to most
traditionalists. Nevertheless, the rhetoric of liberty continued to echo
widely through the conservative movement.[20]

Order and national security came to occupy higher positions in the conservative hierarchy of values than previously, particularly as the movement rallied around the themes of anti-Communism at home and abroad.
Even most libertarian conservatives were willing to support Joseph
McCarthy's efforts to root out alleged domestic subversives in the name of
national security, though some conservatives eventually turned against
him. When the Senate in December 1954 voted to censure McCarthy, two-
thirds of the conservatives remained loyal to the Wisconsin senator, while
one-third voted against him. After the mid-1950s, most conservatives of all
stripes also accepted a huge military-industrial complex as essential to
security against the perceived Communist threat internationally. Nash has
concluded that conservative internal harmony "was immensely assisted

by the cement of anti-Communism" during this period. E. J. Dionne, and Linda Medcalf and Kenneth Dolbeare, have concurred.[21]

As in the liberal camp, economic growth remained important to the conservative coalition, particularly for libertarians and the sizable numbers of conservatives who were engaged in business. Like the conservatives of the previous period, however, their analysis differed from liberals' in holding that free-market capitalism was the key to maximizing growth. Milton Friedman typified this group. In *Capitalism and Freedom* and in a subsequent monetary history, he sought to bolster this argument by demonstrating that the Great Depression had been caused not by flaws in the capitalist system but by government mismanagement. Friedman also attacked the Keynesian theories favored by liberals and pioneered a monetarist approach that relied on prudent control of the money supply. Among traditionalist conservatives, however, economic growth rarely stimulated much discussion. Viewing the movement as a whole, it can be concluded that economic growth was probably less central to conservative thought than in the Depression era.[22]

Finally, the conservatives' belief that the United States should be viewed as a constitutional republic and not a democracy was reiterated in most quarters of the conservative movement. Clarence Manion, longtime dean of the Notre Dame College of Law and a prominent figure in the conservative movement, was typical. Noting "that our Founding Fathers managed to write both the Declaration of Independence and the Constitution without using the term 'democracy' even once," Manion stressed that a republic protected the "God-given attributes of the individual human being, majorities to the contrary notwithstanding." Barry Goldwater concurred. Calling for a return to the intent of the constitutional framers, he then asked, "Was it then a *Democracy* the framers created? Hardly. The system of restraints, on the face of it, was directed not only against individual tyrants, but also against a tyranny of the masses." Even Willmoore Kendall, who was more majoritarian than the norm, took a dim view of "plebiscitary," or direct democracy. Not until the late 1960s would a substantial number of conservatives embrace majoritarian democracy as a value.[23]

Support for national security and domestic order (especially against Communism), for private property (either as a key to liberty or as a basis for order), and for a constitutional republican form of government lay at the heart of conservative consensus as the movement developed between 1945 and 1966. Equality of opportunity and especially equality of outcomes held little attraction for conservatives, but equality before the law enjoyed considerable conservative support. Values of liberty and virtue were sources of internal conflict, especially among conservative intellectuals, though commitment to economic marketplace liberty remained widespread and often intense. Economic growth was generally perceived to be desirable but was less a focus of concern that it had been in the 1930s.

### Conservative Programmatic Public Policies

The core values emphasizing national security, protection of private property, and a constitutional republic eventually provided a foundation for considerable agreement among conservative politicians, intellectuals, and other activists concerning major public policies. Consensus was most evident on socioeconomic policies, but it developed after the mid-1950s even in some domains, such as foreign policy, where there was considerable discord between 1945 and 1954.

As during the 1930s, conservatives advocated tax cuts, particularly geared to business and upper-income groups; reductions in government spending, at least in domestic affairs; a balanced budget rather than Keynesian fiscal policies (though some, especially in big business, came to accept Keynesian principles); and reliance upon private property exchanges through free markets to an extent that liberals found unacceptable. They were also united in support of tightened regulation of labor unions, with congressional conservatives voting unanimously for the Taft-Hartley Act in 1947 and vehemently opposing its repeal. To be sure, there were areas of internal disagreement. While many conservatives followed Barry Goldwater, the 1964 Republican presidential candidate and the first conservative "movement" choice to win a major-party nomination since the New Deal, in calling for an end to the graduated income tax and a massive rollback of the New Deal regulatory state, others were content to cut taxes and retain most regulations but have them administered by sympathetic, probusiness conservatives—a strategy broadly pursued by the moderate-to-conservative Eisenhower administration. Overall, government economic management policy issues in Congress divided conservatives from liberals more sharply than did any other kinds of issues during the period.[24]

In the social welfare policy domain, conservatives united in opposing major new programs, such as national health insurance or even medicare under the social security program. Most sympathized with Goldwater's warning that "Socialism through Welfarism poses a far greater danger than Socialism through Nationalization. . . . The effect of welfarism on freedom will be felt later on—after its beneficiaries have become its victims; after dependence on government has turned into bondage and it is too late to unlock the jail." But many wished only to rein in the growth of the welfare state rather than to reduce it by 10 percent per year until it was gone, as Goldwater proposed. Even as noted a conservative as Robert Taft was prepared to accept modest welfare state additions such as those embodied in the Housing Act of 1949.[25]

If the range of conservative views was relatively narrow on government management and even on social welfare policy matters, it was somewhat broader on issues pertaining to the civil rights of black Americans—and conservatism fractured along new lines as the years advanced, especially after 1954, when the pace of change accelerated. Before 1954, the conservative split was largely along regional lines, with most Northern conservatives (mostly Republicans after World War II) willing to support modest federal intervention to protect voting rights and equal protection of the law in some spheres and virtually all Southern conservatives (mostly Democrats) citing both white supremacy and states' rights arguments in opposition to such intervention. Following the *Brown* decision on school desegregation, the Northern conservatives increasingly split among themselves. Barry Goldwater and William F. Buckley's *National Review* both joined the Southern conservatives in denouncing the ruling and opposing federal desegregation efforts generally. Other Northern conservatives, such as the editors of the *Chicago Tribune*, called for support of national intervention on behalf of black civil rights. The *National Review*'s position was quite close to that of most white Southerners, even opposing black voting rights in the South. "The central question," it declared editorially in 1957, "is whether the White community in the South is entitled to take such measures as are necessary to prevail, politically and culturally, in areas where it does not predominate numerically? The sobering answer is Yes—the white community is so entitled because, for the time being, it is the advanced race." In contrast, Goldwater cited only strict constructionist and states' rights arguments, not white supremacist ones, to support his stance. Most Northern congressional conservatives still voted for moderate civil rights bills. Though Goldwater strongly opposed the far-reaching Civil Rights Act of 1964, a substantial number of conservatives voted for it, with Senate Republican Leader Everett McKinley Dirksen leading the way.[26]

In the civil liberties domain, conservatives were less deeply divided than they were on black civil rights. On issues pertaining to domestic Communists and their alleged sympathizers, most conservatives were even more inclined than liberals in the late 1940s and early 1950s to crack down. Conservatives, including leaders with civil libertarian records, such as Taft, supported the House of Representatives Committee on Un-American Activities and Senator Joseph McCarthy in their often-authoritarian methods of rooting out alleged subversion. The McCarran Act of 1950, a sweeping and broadly defined antisubversion measure that was vetoed by Truman but passed over his veto by Congress, won a unanimous conservative vote. Not until McCarthy tangled with the United States Army and the Eisenhower administration did many conservatives resist his tactics, and even then, the majority of Senate conservatives rallied around him in a losing cause as the Senate voted for censure. Most of the vehement attacks against the post-1956 Supreme Court civil liberties decisions also emanated from conservatives, though a conservative minority accepted them, and moderate conservative Justice John M. Harlan even delivered the Court's opinion in the *Yates* case of 1957 that loosened previous restrictions on Communists.[27]

Foreign policy questions found the conservative movement badly divided in the first part of the period but increasingly unified after the mid-1950s. As the Cold War developed in the late 1940s and conservatives reacted to the containment-of-Communism policies of the Truman administration, they split into several ill-defined but often contentious factions. Some conservatives, led by moderate-to-conservative Republican Senator Arthur Vandenberg and such Southern conservative Democrats as Senator Walter George, joined moderates and Cold War liberals in endorsing most of the containment approach, usually differentiating themselves from the liberals by adopting a greater emphasis on Asia and by rejecting the New Dealish focus on global socioeconomic justice and advancement (termed "globaloney" by Clare Booth Luce). Others, often styled "liberationist" conservatives and typified by General Douglas MacArthur, Senators Barry Goldwater and William Knowland, and a host of staunchly anti-Communist intellectuals such as Burnham and Buckley, called for strong, usually unilateral, United States action to roll back Communism, not just contain it. John Foster Dulles, Eisenhower's secretary of state, often employed the rhetoric of this faction, usually without acting upon it. Still others, led by Taft but including some libertarian conservative intellectuals such as Felix Morley and John T. Flynn, stressed the dangers of a militarized central government and favored limited and defensive foreign policy goals. This third faction particularly resisted such policies as joining the NATO alliance and making large military commitments in Europe. Following the death of Taft in 1953, this faction lacked a strong leader and gradually disintegrated. The Eisenhower administration sought to bridge the first two factions in its rhetoric but nearly always carried on the same containment policies pursued by the preceding Truman administration and the succeeding Kennedy and Johnson administrations. Most of the conservative movement, now largely shedding Taftite qualms, urged strengthened actions against international Communism. Intense anti-Communism and national security values led even most libertarian conservatives to agree by the early 1960s, usually arguing, as Friedman did, that Communism posed such a great threat to negative freedom that "big government" in the military sphere was essential to the defense of liberty, even though it had the potential to restrict it domestically.[28]

## Liberal and Conservative Internal Conflicts

The liberal coalition saw its social democratic tendency shrink and almost disappear in the late 1940s, undermined by the backlash against any ideas even remotely associated with Communism and by the booming prosperity of the regulated capitalist system. By the early 1960s, however, left-liberalism was reviving, though in a "new politics" form different from that of the 1930s and 1940s. The new politics liberalism did constitute a threat to the "vital center," Cold War liberalism that had prevailed until then. The full force of its challenge would be felt in the next political epoch and would alter the liberal coalition substantially. Southern liberalism, an important factor in the coalition during the New Deal era, virtually disappeared in the 1940s as most Southern politicians avoided association with a liberalism that now incorporated a strong challenge to white supremacy and seemed otherwise linked to urban and labor interests of the North. The Western progressives had already disintegrated as a political force before the end of the Roosevelt administration. Except for the period of the mid-1960s, the net result of these changes was a somewhat diminished liberal alliance, but a liberalism less internally divided than before by old cleavages over basic assumptions and values. After the consolidation of the postwar years, however, new fissures, already becoming apparent by the early 1960s, would emerge to fracture liberal unity. Just when liberalism seemed once again triumphant following the 1964 landslide victory over Goldwater and his conservatives, upheaval loomed on the horizon.

In the conservative movement, the emergence for the first time of a sizable intellectual contingent helped to create a good deal more questioning of basic assumptions and values than the pragmatic anti-New Deal conservatives had usually engaged in during the 1930s and early 1940s. At the deepest level, these intellectual conflicts pitted libertarian conservatives against traditional or organic conservatives. But complicating matters further were serious public policy differences among conservatives, especially over foreign policy in the first part of the period and over civil rights policy after the *Brown* decision and the civil rights movement forced the issue to the center of the national agenda. Still, there were unifying elements in the conservative movement: national security/anti-Communist values, strong support for private property, and endorsement of a constitutional republic. Moreover, the establishment of the *National Review* provided a focal point and Goldwater's capture of the 1964 Republican party presidential nomination (despite his landslide defeat in the general election) provided a hope for future success.

### Beyond and between Liberalism and Conservatism

From late in 1948 to the early 1960s, ideological movements clearly to the left of liberalism declined into insignificance. However, with the emergence of a New Left, centered around the ideas of C. Wright Mills and Herbert Marcuse and Students for a Democratic Society, that situation was changing as the period drew to a close. As previously noted, the "new politics" movement within the liberal coalition showed influences from the New Left. A counterculture largely separate from the New Left, and certainly from the old liberalism, was generally nonpolitical; yet it was gaining the potential for political impact in the 1960s and came to be linked by many to the civil libertarian strand in liberalism. Although the civil rights movement also existed somewhat separately from the liberal mainstream, its connections to liberalism were so strong that Martin Luther King Jr., Roy Wilkins of the National Association for the Advancement of Colored People, Whitney Young of the Urban League, and most of its other spokespersons really represented a wing of liberalism. Of course, the emergent black power movement of the 1960s did not.[29]

On the far right of the spectrum were racist authoritarians and the so-called radical right, the latter centered around such organizations as the John Birch Society. The radical right generally possessed sufficiently strong ties to the conservative movement to classify as extreme conservatism. Figures such as Clarence Manion and M. Stanton Evans bridged the gap between the radical right and mainstream conservatism. On the other hand, the various Ku Klux Klans and the American Nazis were distinctly different phenomena but they enjoyed little real influence in national politics.[30]

Probably even more important than in the 1930s were the moderate and nonideological actors whose ideas and policy stances placed them between or straddling liberalism and conservatism. Party organization politicians and pragmatic material and solidary interest groups were often resolutely nonideological and continued to be significant factors in American politics. However, of key importance during the middle stages of this period was the moderate or moderate conservative president, Dwight D. Eisenhower. Eisenhower characterized himself as "liberal on human issues, conservative on economics." Assessments of him have varied, from those of many academic scholars, who have emphasized his essential (albeit moderate) conservatism on all but foreign-policy matters, to those of most contemporary political actors—either critics or supporters—who often saw him as an independent moderate figure standing between or bridging the two ideological coalitions. Certainly most in the conservative movement attacked him and his administration for excessive moderation, even liberalism; his supporters, such as Arthur Larson, usually praised his approach as embodying a new "modern Republicanism" distinct from conservatism. Though Presidents Truman, Kennedy, and Johnson were, like Eisenhower, often criticized by the movement closest to them for insufficient loyalty to ideological principles, these leaders' attachments to the liberal coalition were markedly more evident than Eisenhower's to the conservative alliance. Eisenhower was almost certainly closer to conservative than to liberal ideology in his personal outlook. Nonetheless, he had a nonideological background and his presidential candidacy had been put forward by Eastern big-business moderates, not by the conservative movement. His detachment from the conservative coalition and the perceptions of most of its active members before and during his administration, combined with his conservative instincts, merit treating him as a moderate conservative but one distinctly outside the movement.[31]

## Conclusions

For liberalism, the 1945–66 period was one of adjusting previous assumptions and values but retaining most of their core, consolidating New Deal reforms and extending them when possible (mainly in the last two years of the period, following Johnson's landslide victory over Goldwater), responding to the demands of the civil rights movement, and coping with the perceived threats of the Soviet Union and of Communism. Although the liberal coalition appeared on the surface less divided than before in its basic assumptions and values, it was about to face severe new internal fissures just as it appeared to triumph in 1964 over its conservative opposition. Soon the liberal consensus on containment of Communism and the meaning of black civil rights would crumble, and underlying liberal disagreements over the meaning of democracy would burst forth in sharp disputes over reforming the political process. The interest group components of the liberal coalition would also assert their distinctive agendas even more insistently than before, often obscuring common yearnings and a sense of purpose.

For conservatism, the years between 1945 and 1966 brought to the surface underlying differences between two rather divergent schools of thought, as well as sharp conflicts over some specific public policy issues. But they also brought a much more self-conscious, highly organized, and articulate conservative movement than had previously existed. The foundations had been laid for conservative victories in the years ahead, as liberals stumbled.

### Notes

1. Mary Sperling McAuliffe, *Crises on the Left* (Amherst, MA: University of Massachusetts Press, 1978), 63.

2. Gary Gerstle, "The Protean Character of American Liberalism," *American Historical Review* 99 (October 1994): 1071.

3. James MacGregor Burns, *Roosevelt: Soldier of Freedom* (New York: Harcourt Brace Jovanovich, 1970), vii. Also see Alonzo L. Hamby, *Liberalism and Its Challengers*, 2d ed. (New York: Oxford University Press, 1992), 36–49.

4. Gerstle, "The Protean Character," 1070–1071; Allen J. Matusow, *The Unraveling of America* (New York: Harper & Row, 1984), 6, 60–62; Hamby, *Liberalism and Its Challengers*, esp. chap. 4.

5. For a libertarian critique, see Murray N. Rothbard, "The Great Society: A Libertarian Critique," in *The Great Society Reader: The Failure of Liberalism*, ed. Marvin E. Gittleman and David Mermelstein (New York: Random House, 1967), 502–511. Garry Wills, *Nixon Agonistes* (New York: New American Library, 1970), 490–506, provides a criticism from a nonmarket perspective.

6. Richard H. Pells, *The Liberal Mind in a Conservative Age* (New York: Harper & Row, 1985), 117–121; Alonzo L. Hamby, *Beyond the New Deal* (New York: Columbia University Press, 1973), esp. chap. 12; Arthur M. Schlesinger, *The Vital Center* (Boston: Houghton Mifflin, 1949); Irwin Ross, *Strategy for Liberals* (New York: Harper & Brothers, 1949).

7. Eugene J. McCarthy, *A Liberal Answer to the Conservative Challenge* (New York: MacFadden, 1964), 37–41, 77–86. For a typical ADA statement of principles propounding positive freedoms, see *ADA World*, 3 March 1948, 3–6, esp. the sections on rights to education and civil rights.

8. The Schlesinger quotations and discussion of the perspective they represented, are taken from Steven M. Gillon, *Politics and Vision* (New York: Oxford University Press, 1987), 124–125, and Matusow, *Unraveling,* 8.

9. Pells, *Liberal Mind,* esp. 334–340; Peter Bachrach, *The Theory of Democratic Elitism* (Boston: Little, Brown, 1967). For the "new politics" liberal drive for more participatory democracy, see Arnold S. Kaufman, *The Radical Liberal* (New York: Atherton Press, 1968), 56–75; and E. J. Dionne Jr., *Why Americans Hate Politics* (New York: Simon & Schuster, 1991), 45–54.

10. Hamby, *Liberalism and its Challengers,* 63–66.

11. James L. Sundquist, *Politics and Policy* (Washington: Brookings Institution, 1968), esp. chaps. 4, 5, 7, 11.

12. Stephen K. Bailey, *Congress Makes a Law* (New York: Columbia University Press, 1950) is the most thorough work on the Employment Act struggle. On Keynesianism and liberalism and the Kennedy–era disputes, see Arthur Schlesinger, *A Thousand Days: John F. Kennedy in the White House* (Greenwich, CT: Fawcett Crest, 1965), chap. 23; Bruce Miroff, *Pragmatic Illusions* (New York: David McKay, 1976), chap. 5; and Matusow, *Unraveling,* chap. 2.

13. On Taft–Hartley, see R. Alton Lee, *Truman and Taft-Hartley* (Lexington: University of Kentucky Press, 1966). Hamby, *Beyond the New Deal,* 303–310, provides a good account of the Brannan plan controversy.

14. Robert A. Garson, *The Democratic Party and the Politics of Sectionalism, 1941–1948* (Baton Rouge: Louisiana State University Press, 1974), chaps. 5–9; William C. Berman, *The Politics of Civil Rights in the Truman Administration* (Columbus: Ohio State University Press, 1970); John Frederick Martin, *Civil Rights and the Crisis of Liberalism* (Boulder, CO: Westview Press, 1979), chaps. 5–9.

15. Pells, *Liberal Mind,* chap. 5; William L. O'Neill, *A Better World* (New York: Simon and Schuster, 1982), esp. chaps. 8, 10, 11; *Yates v. United States,* 354 U.S. 298 (1957); *Griswold v. Connecticut,* 381 U.S. 479 (1965); G. Theodore Mitau, *Decade of Decision* (New York: Charles Scribner's Sons, 1967). John G. Broesamle, *Reform and Reaction in Twentieth Century American Politics* (New York: Greenwood Press, 1990), 167, stresses the negative effects of judicial activism on public support for liberalism.

16. Richard J. Walton, *Henry Wallace, Harry Truman, and the Cold War* (New York: Viking Press, 1976) and Hamby, *Beyond the New Deal,* esp. chaps. 4, 7, 8, 16–19, offer differing perspectives on liberal foreign policy in the early period. Richard J. Walton, *Cold War and Counterrevolution* (Baltimore: Penguin Books, 1973) and Schlesinger, *A Thousand Days,* do so for the Kennedy years. McCarthy, *A Liberal Answer,* 123–128.

17. "The Magazine's Credenda," *National Review* 1 (19 November 1955): 6; the Burnham quotation is from George H. Nash, *The Conservative Intellectual Movement in America since 1945* (New York: Basic Books, 1976).

18. Burnham quoted in Nash, *Conservative Intellectual Movement,* 93. For discussions of Taft, Morley, and other dissenters, see Hamby, *Liberalism and Its Challengers,* 106–110, 114–116, and Nash, *Conservative Intellectual Movement,* 123–130.

19. Nash, *Conservative Intellectual Movement,* 223–225.

20. Nash, *Conservative Intellectual Movement*, 175–178; Kenneth M. Dolbeare and Patricia Dolbeare, *American Ideologies*, 2d ed. (Chicago: Markham, 1973), chap. 5.

21. Nash, *Conservative Intellectual Movement*, 179; Dionne, *Why Americans Hate Politics*, 161; Linda J. Medcalf and Kenneth M. Dolbeare, *Neopolitics* (New York: Random House, 1985), 131.

22. Nash, *Conservative Intellectual Movement*, 284–289; Milton Friedman, *Capitalism and Freedom* (Chicago: University of Chicago Press, 1962); Milton Friedman and Anna Schwartz, *A Monetary History of the United States, 1867–1960* (Princeton: Princeton University Press, 1963), chap. 7.

23. Clarence Manion, "The United States Should Be a Republic," in James A. Gould and Willis H. Truitt, *Political Ideologies* (New York: Macmillan, 1973), 174; Nash, *Conservative Intellectual Movement*, 248–252; Barry M. Goldwater, *Conscience of a Conservative* (Shepherdsville, KY: Victor, 1960), 18–19; Willmoore Kendall, *The Conservative Affirmation* (Chicago: Henry Regnery, 1963), esp. 16, chap. 2.

24. Barry M. Goldwater, *Conscience of a Conservative* (Shepherdsville, KY: Victor Publishing, 1960); Herbert S. Parmet, *Eisenhower and the American Crusades* (New York: Macmillan, 1972), esp. chap. 24. On congressional voting patterns of the period, see Aage R. Clausen, *How Congressmen Decide* (New York: St. Martin's Press, 1973).

25. The Goldwater quote is from *Conscience*, 72; the reductions, Goldwater, *Conscience*, 68–69. Taft's position is discussed by Michael W. Miles, *The Odyssey of the American Right* (New York: Oxford University Press, 1980), 182.

26. Goldwater, *Conscience*, chap. 4; "Why the South Must Prevail," *National Review* (24 August 1957): 149; "Segregation Outlawed," *Chicago Daily Tribune*, 18 May 1954, sec. 1, p. 14; "Transitional Help for Southern Schools," *Chicago Daily Tribune*, 19 May 1954, sec. 1, p. 16; Sundquist, *Politics and Policy*, 259–271.

27. Miles, *Odyssey*, 123–147, 208–238, 245–249; Hamby, *Beyond the New Deal*, 408–415; Stephen M. Ambrose, *Eisenhower: The President* (New York: Simon & Schuster, 1984), 162–168, 219–221; Parmet, *American Crusades*, 372–375; Mitau, *Decade of Decision*, chap. 1; *Yates v. United States*, 354 U.S. 298 (1957).

28. Miles, *Odyssey*, esp. chaps. 4–7, 9, 15; Nash, *Conservative Intellectual Movement*, esp. chap. 4; Friedman, *Capitalism and Freedom*, 201–202.

29. Matusow, *Unraveling*, esp. chaps. 10–12; Dionne, *Why American Hate Politics*, 31–54, 81–90. Hamby, *Liberalism and Its Challengers*, chap. 4, places King and the bulk of the civil rights movement within the liberal alliance, as this author does.

30. Miles, *Odyssey*, 246–251; Daniel Bell, ed., *The Radical Right* (Garden City, NY: Doubleday Anchor Books, 1964). Gilbert Abcarian and Sherman M. Stanage, "Alienation and the Radical Right," *Journal of Politics* 27 (November 1965): 776–796, note major values close to those of mainstream conservatism but suggest stylistic differences.

31. Stressing Eisenhower's essential conservatism on all but international affairs are Gary Reichard, *The Reaffirmation of Republicanism* (Knoxville: University of Tennessee Press, 1975), esp. 227–237; Ambrose, *Eisenhower: The President*, 115–116; and Hamby, *Liberalism and Its Challengers*, 115–128. Parmet, *American Crusades*, 340–341, 574–576; and James MacGregor Burns, *Deadlock of Democracy*

(Englewood Cliffs, NJ: Prentice–Hall, 1963), 193–195, portray him as a moderate outside the conservative movement and, in Parmet's case, "containing" it. Nash, *Conservative Intellectual Movement*, 253–256, demonstrates the almost universal alienation of the conservative movement's intellectuals from the Eisenhower administration. Arthur Larson, *A Republican Looks at His Party* (N.Y: Harper & Brothers, 1956) makes the case for Eisenhower-style "new" Republicanism.

# 8

# Liberal and Conservative Power Centers

---

The relative powers of each ideological coalition in the various institutions of the government continued, for the most part, to reflect the basic patterns of the late New Deal era. Liberalism was usually strongest in the executive branch (despite the partial exception of the Eisenhower administration) and on the Supreme Court (though conservative shifts by ostensibly liberal justices in the 1949–52 years called this pattern into question), while conservatism was usually strongest in Congress, where it not only enjoyed substantial numerical advantages most of the time but also possessed the ability to use congressional rules for ideological advantage, much to the frustration of liberals. The state government picture, as before, was mixed in terms of personnel but structurally biased toward conservative goals. In the realm of political parties and interest groups as well, continuity with the past was evident. However, the emergence of significant new wordsmiths introduced some power shifts worthy of note.

## Government Institutions

The presidency of Franklin D. Roosevelt had firmly attached an institutionalized presidency to the liberal movement and had locked thousands of New Dealers into the executive branch of government for the long term by extending the merit system rules to cover their positions. The Truman administration continued the pattern. Despite the hopes of the conservative coalition, Truman succeeded in asserting control over the staffs of the new National Security Council and the Council of Economic Advisers. Furthermore, through his Reorganization Plan 8, he attained additional power over the independent regulatory commissions.[1]

Thus, even Eisenhower, the lone Republican president of the postwar period, found himself presiding over an executive bureaucracy that, below the top level, was almost certainly more liberal than conservative in orientation. Eisenhower's lack of interest in fundamentally reshaping the bureaucracy in a conservative mold was one of the great disappointments of the conservative movement in his administration.[2]

The three Democratic presidents of the period—Harry S. Truman, John F. Kennedy, and Lyndon B. Johnson—all possessed solid ties to the liberal coalition, though their relations with liberals, especially in the case of Johnson, were often strained. Truman and Kennedy had both earned liberal plaudits for their congressional voting records before entering the White House. Truman's *New Republic*/Union for Democratic Action score for the 78th Congress (1943–44) was 93 percent (with 100 percent the most liberal possible). Kennedy consistently voted the liberal line between 1947 and 1960, earning an Americans for Democratic Action rating of 100 percent in 1960 and averaging a 91 percent rating from the *New Republic* over the entire period from his first year in Congress through 1958. Nevertheless, neither Truman nor Kennedy had been the initial first choices for the presidency of many liberals. Truman's background in Kansas City's Pendergast machine and Kennedy's failure to condemn Joseph McCarthy were blots on their records that liberal intellectuals, in particular, found difficult to forget or forgive. Moreover, once each man was in the White House, the liberal coalition often criticized each for inadquate commitment to the cause.[3]

In the case of Johnson, liberal distrust extended beyond the complaints about Truman and Kennedy. Nonetheless, Johnson had compiled a voting record as a solid New Deal liberal after his first election to Congress in a special 1937 election in which he had pledged full support to FDR, including his court-packing plan. As late as the seventy-eighth Congress, LBJ was voting 78 percent of the time in accordance with the *New Republic*/ UDA preferences. However, his liberal ratings sagged to a 62 percent *New Republic* average score during his Senate years. In 1960, his ADA rating was 67 percent, and his conservative rating from the Americans for Constitutional Action for 1955–59 was a puny 10 percent (compared with Kennedy's 11 percent). Overall, his record was a far cry from a conservative one, though it did not satisfy many liberals. When JFK picked Johnson as his running mate, much of the liberal movement protested; and Johnson's elevation to the presidency in November 1963, aroused much liberal apprehension. Nevertheless, LBJ carried on the programs that Kennedy and the liberals had endorsed and, indeed, added to them. He also enjoyed considerably more success in gaining their passage through Congress than Kennedy had.[4]

If the presidencies of Truman, Kennedy, and Johnson were linked to the liberal coalition, that of Eisenhower possessed but very tenuous ties to the conservative movement. As noted previously, Eisenhower was a man whose personal domestic policy orientations tended toward moderate conservatism. However, Eisenhower, unlike the three Democratic chief executives, had never worked with either coalition prior to seeking the presidency and had been bitterly opposed in 1952 for the Republican presidential nomination by the bulk of the conservative movement. It is true that the Eisenhower administration did include a few prominent conservative coalition figures, such as Secretary of Agriculture Ezra Taft Benson, and that its "cabinet of millionaires" certainly possessed very close ties to the business elements at the heart of that coalition. Moreover, many of its domestic policy proposals (and evasions, as on black civil rights) had a distinctly conservative coloration. Its institutional prescriptions, however, rarely pleased the conservative movement. Active conservatives were generally quite critical of the Eisenhower administration for what they saw as its excessive moderation or even liberalism; and, except for the 1959–61 period, the Eisenhower administration was probably less conservative than Congress as a whole.[5]

Congress was usually dominated numerically by conservatives during the period; and even when conservatives lacked majorities or near-majorities, they occupied key power positions in Congress and showed remarkable ability to use congressional rules to gain an advantage. As table 8.1 illustrates, the *New Republic*'s scoring system showed that conservatives (scores 0–33 percent) held the edge over liberals (scores 67–100 percent) in every Senate and in every House of Representatives but one during the fourteen-year period following 1945, often by a decisive margin. The *Congressional Quarterly*'s "conservative coalition" scoring began in 1959, just as the *New Republic*'s ended; and it showed that, even in the wake of the Democratic party's gains in Congress after the 1958 elections, the conservative coalition of most Republicans and Southern Democrats won on more roll-call votes than it lost in every Congress until the Eighty-ninth (1965–66). Nor do these figures tell the full story. The seniority system gave such leading conservatives as Howard Smith of Virginia (chair of the House Rules Committee, which controlled the flow of all major legislation to the floor of the chamber), Harry Byrd of Virginia (chair of the Senate Finance Committee, which was responsible for tax legislation, including social program proposals requiring tax changes), and James Eastland of Mississippi (chair of the Senate Judiciary Committee, in charge of civil rights legislation and judicial nominations) enormous power even when conservatives lacked a clear voting majority in

Table 8.1
Ideological Divisions in Congress, 1945–1959

| Congress | Liberals | | Moderates | | Conservatives | |
|---|---|---|---|---|---|---|
| | N | % | N | % | N | % |
| House of Representatives | | | | | | |
| 79 | 129 | 30.4% | 78 | 18.5% | 215 | 51.5% |
| 80 | 66 | 15.6 | 96 | 22.6 | 262 | 61.8 |
| 81 | 159 | 37.9 | 76 | 18.1 | 184 | 43.9 |
| 82 | 141 | 33.3 | 79 | 18.7 | 203 | 48.0 |
| 83 | 138 | 32.9 | 112 | 26.7 | 170 | 40.5 |
| 84 | 154 | 36.3 | 124 | 29.2 | 146 | 34.4 |
| 85 | 153 | 36.4 | 92 | 21.9 | 175 | 41.7 |
| Senate | | | | | | |
| 79 | 29 | 30.9 | 15 | 16.0 | 50 | 53.2 |
| 80 | 27 | 28.4 | 21 | 22.1 | 47 | 49.5 |
| 81 | 27 | 28.4 | 26 | 27.4 | 42 | 44.2 |
| 82 | 29 | 30.5 | 26 | 27.4 | 40 | 42.1 |
| 83 | 29 | 30.5 | 21 | 22.1 | 45 | 47.1 |
| 84 | 33 | 35.1 | 21 | 22.3 | 40 | 42.6 |
| 85 | 37 | 38.5 | 19 | 19.8 | 40 | 41.7 |

Congress. Moreover, traditions such as the Senate filibuster, which could then be terminated only by a two-thirds majority of those present and voting to impose closure of debate, enabled conservatives to prevent votes on issues when they knew that they would lose. Until 1965, when liberal strength in Congress swelled in the wake of the 1964 Democratic landslide over Goldwater and the Republicans, "the obstacle course on Capitol Hill," as Robert Bendiner put it, was a daunting reality for any advocate of liberal legislation.[6]

Overall, then, congressional-presidential relations usually reflected a conservative-liberal struggle, as had been the case regularly since the late 1930s. Truman, Kennedy, and Johnson took liberal policy initiatives in most cases, often seeking to bypass Congress if majorities could not be found there. Truman did this, for instance, in establishing the President's Committee on Civil Rights and by desegregating the armed forces by executive orders. In addition, liberals filled many (but far from all) key slots in the executive branch of government during their administrations.

Conservatives sought to kill, delay, or water down liberal executive initiatives in Congress and to mount investigations and other attacks on liberal administrators from their power bases within the congressional committee system. Sometimes, when they held majorities or near-majorities in Congress, the conservatives were themselves able to seize the legislative initiative, as they did on issues such as tidelands oil, Taft-Hartley labor legislation, and the Bricker Amendment. The Eisenhower years offered a partial respite from this pattern of warfare, but conflicts between a conservative Congress and a moderate executive occurred to some extent even during those years over executive agreements, demands for executive branch information for congressional committee investigations, federalism, and Supreme Court jurisdictional issues.

The liberalism of the Supreme Court waxed and waned and waxed again over the two decades of this period, shaped not only by the new justices who took their seats on the High Bench but also by the general political moods in the country. The most thorough statistical analysis of Supreme Court voting patterns found two positively correlated but distinct scales of liberalism and conservatism—one centered on civil liberties, the other on socioeconomic issues. The least liberal part of the era was between 1949 and 1952, when Truman's appointees proved surprisingly inclined toward general judicial restraint and scored relatively low on civil liberties liberalism, just at the time that McCarthyism was at its peak in the country. By the end of the period, however, judicial liberal activism had regained dominance on the Court and was becoming especially evident in expanding the previous concepts of civil liberties and civil rights. While such liberal justices as Hugo Black and William O. Douglas were feted by the liberal movement, and Douglas was even widely viewed as a potential liberal Democratic presidential candidate in both 1948 and 1952, none of the less liberal justices had similar connections to the conservative coalition.[7]

Beyond the national government institutions lay the state governments. There, basic patterns had changed little since the New Deal era. State legislatures throughout the period heavily overrepresented conservative rural and small-town areas (though that was in the process of change by 1966, because of a series of controversial Supreme Court rulings between 1962 and 1964 that mandated "one person, one vote" reapportionment). Other factors continuing to have conservative effects in the states included constitutional financial restrictions on state governments, competition among states to attract business by creating a "favorable business climate," and limited state capacities for reform. However, the proportions of moderate governors appeared to increase, especially in the

Republican party, where such governors often contended with congressional conservatives over Republican presidential nominations (favoring Eisenhower over Taft in 1952 and Scranton over Goldwater in 1964) and over public policies (increasingly favoring cooperative federalism that allowed states and localities considerable leeway while providing federal funds).[8]

The overall pattern in government institutions was clear to most in both the liberal and conservative movements. In 1964, Barry Goldwater aptly summed it up in terms that few in either coalition would dispute: "[T]he state governments and the Congress by and large stand on one side of the battle line. They face, across that battle line, the Executive Branch and, usually, the Judicial Branch, the Supreme Court."[9]

## Political Parties

Both major political parties saw a gradual displacement of machine-style politics and a growth of citizen activism, often but not always stimulated by ideology, during the period. In the Democratic party the Stevenson presidential campaigns of 1952 and 1956 galvanized thousands of "amateur Democrats" to become politically active; and many of these remained committed to political action, providing through groups such as the California Democratic Clubs, the Independent Voters of Illinois, and the reform clubs of New York a base for an emergent "new politics" liberalism in the 1960s. In the Republican party, the Goldwater campaign of 1964 brought a massive influx of conservative activists who put an end to the tradition of moderate presidential Republicanism that had nominated Wendell Willkie in 1940, Thomas Dewey in 1944 and 1948, and Dwight Eisenhower in 1952 and 1956.[10]

In the "four-party" context described by James MacGregor Burns, the Democratic presidential party remained the chief center for liberal strength. Truman, Stevenson, and Kennedy all relied heavily on the liberal coalition for their election campaigns. Johnson also drew upon it but sought in 1964 to reach beyond it into the business community for support as well, succeeding to an extent unparalleled by any Democratic presidential candidate since 1932. In the late 1950s, Democratic National Chair Paul Butler established the Democratic Advisory Council to develop liberal Democratic program proposals, with little cooperation from congressional Democratic leaders. The Democratic congressional party remained deeply divided between conservatives (now usually composed almost entirely of Southerners), who controlled most of the key standing committee chairmanships, and Northern liberals possessing strong ties to the presidential Democratic party but unable to dominate the Democratic caucuses in Congress. In the House, frustrated liberals formed their own caucus within the party caucus, called the Democratic Study Group, while in the Senate a less formalized liberal "activist bloc" took shape. Seeking to hold the Southern conservatives and the liberals together in precarious unity were two Texas Democrats, Sam Rayburn, speaker of the House during almost all of the era, and Lyndon Johnson, Democratic Senate leader through most of the 1950s.[11]

The Republican congressional party remained as conservative as before, particularly in the House of Representatives. Among Senate Republicans, the old progressives of the West were no longer a significant factor, but a cluster of moderates, centered primarily in the urban states of the Northeast and Midwest, emerged to complicate conservative unity efforts in the upper chamber. However, it was in the presidential Republican party that the most dramatic power shift occurred. There, as noted before, a huge influx of conservative activists in 1964, backed by financial contributions from Southern and Western businessmen in particular, dislodged the combination of Eastern big business and moderate governors that had long held sway. Though the Goldwater campaign ended in short-term disaster for the Republican party, undiscouraged conservative activists and their financial backers maintained a significant presence in the party. Henceforth, conservative ideology would more fully unite presidential and congressional Republicans than had previously been the case.[12]

### Interest Groups

Between 1945 and 1966, the liberal and conservative coalitions made some new interest group recruits, while some of the older group participants merged with one another, loosened their coalitional ties, or disappeared. But the overall continuity with the late New Deal patterns was striking.

In the ranks of the liberal coalition, the Union for Democratic Action, now supplemented by additional activists, became the basis for the new Americans for Democratic Action in 1947. This group was to endure for the long term and become the premier interest group of prominent liberal intellectuals. Usually led by a renowned intellectual, such as Reinhold Niebuhr or John Kenneth Galbraith, or by a liberal member of Congress, such as Don Edwards, the ADA published a monthly magazine, *ADA World*, rated members of Congress on their voting records, developed policy statements, and sought to mobilize public and government support for its positions. An ongoing debate within the organization concerned its close links to the Democratic party and whether they should be loosened or tightened. While the ADA promoted Cold War liberalism during this period, another purposive group of liberal intellectuals, the Progressive Citizens of America (PCA), became a vehicle between 1946 and 1948 for those who favored close relations with the Soviet Union. After the unsuccessful Henry Wallace presidential campaign of 1948, into which it merged, PCA never reappeared.[13]

In the late 1940s and early 1950s, the mainly middle-class liberals of the Americans for Democratic Action included a number of labor union leaders, placed many labor issues on their agenda, and received over one quarter of their financial support from unions. By the late 1950s and 1960s, however, a gap developed between labor and the intellectuals of the liberal coalition. Union contributions constituted only 10 percent of ADA financial support by 1959, and only a few labor union leaders remained active in the organization.[14]

The labor union movement, while still maintaining many links to the liberal coalition, was undergoing changes. The clear differences between the liberal Congress of Industrial Organizations and the much less liberal American Federation of Labor had blurred by the 1950s, as had other distinctions between them; and in 1955, the two federations merged into the AFL-CIO. Although Walter Reuther, head of the United Auto Workers and chief of the CIO, became vice president of the new organization and sought to carry on the militancy of the old CIO, George Meany, a "bread-and-butter" unionist of the AFL, became president of the AFL-CIO. Through its political action committee, the Committee on Political Education (COPE), the AFL-CIO was a major source of organizational and financial support for liberal candidates for Congress, the White House, and state and local offices. The merged union federation was also usually a major part of liberal lobbying alliances on the big issues, extending far beyond those that pertained to the immediate material interests of the unions.[15]

Also linked to each of the above liberal interest groups was the National Farmers Union. The NFU occasionally broke with the liberal coalition, especially on international issues in the 1946–48 years; but it was a very strong supporter of the Truman administration's Brannan Plan for agriculture, worked closely with the Kennedy administration, and was a generally dependable member of the liberal alliance. James Patton, its leader throughout the period, was widely viewed as a spokesman for an important, but declining, segment of American liberalism.[16]

As the National Farmers Union lost some of its clout, civil rights interest groups proliferated and became of increasing importance to the liberal coalition. Most of them did not engage overtly in partisan electoral politics and kept their focus primarily on civil rights issues; but in their congressional lobbying and public educational efforts, their general thrust was clearly liberal. Many new organizations joined the National Association for the Advancement of Colored People and the National Urban League in the emerging civil rights movement during and after World War II. The Congress of Racial Equality, founded in 1942, and Martin Luther King Jr.'s Southern Christian Leadership Conference were among the most significant ones. The Leadership Conference on Civil Rights, founded in 1950 with 30 groups as its original sponsors, swelled eventually to include over 150, and loosely coordinated the efforts of the member organizations and linked them with the rest of the liberal coalition.[17]

Another component of the liberal coalition of the period was the American Civil Liberties Union (ACLU). Although it assigned higher priority to civil liberties than the liberal movement in general did, even the ACLU made some compromises between liberty and security in the 1947–54 years. Since the 1930s, the ACLU had close ties with the National Association for the Advancement of Colored People, and it broadened these and played a significant supportive role in the development of the civil rights movement during the 1950s and 1960s. Its overall agenda and outlook, while focused on civil liberties, blended autonomistic civil libertarianism with collectivist liberalism on socioeconomic issues in the same general way that most liberals did. Surveying its philosophy and policy positions, a leading scholarly study of the organization concluded: "As with collectivistic liberals the Union looks favorably on using government to further social reforms; when it comes to social justice and egalitarian ends, the ACLU has no problem in supporting big government."[18]

Increasingly linked to the liberal alliance and to the Democratic party during the period was the National Education Association, largest of the teachers' groups in the United States. Since 1919 the NEA had pushed for federal aid to education, and the Truman administration's embrace of most of the NEA's goals (and conservative opposition to them) brought the organization closer to liberals and Democrats than previously. By the 1950s, a major policy analyst reported, the Democratic party's "inner councils" were maintaining "continuous consultation" with the NEA, as they did with the AFL-CIO and other key liberal interest groups.[19]

Not until the middle-to-late 1960s did the "advocacy explosion" generate dozens of new "public interest" groups that would affiliate with the liberal coalition. However, the growing prominence of Ralph Nader in the mid-1960s, the formation of the National Organization for Women in 1966, and the growing cooperation between environmental interest groups and the mainstream of the liberal alliance on matters such as clean air and clean water legislation and highway beautification, hinted at developments that would add new elements to the liberal movement in the next era, even as the influence of the AFL-CIO and the NFU in the alliance would wane.[20]

Though business groups of the postwar period continued to affiliate mainly with the conservative coalition, a new organization, first established in 1942, the Committee for Economic Development (CED), provided an additional bridge between big businessmen of the Business Council and the liberals in government. William Benton, later to become a liberal Democratic senator from Connecticut, and Ralph Flanders, later to take office as a moderate-to-conservative Republican senator from Vermont, were among those active in the CED's founding and in its early years. Never a part of the liberal coalition, and generally dedicated to research rather than to overtly partisan activities or even lobbying, the committee was a check on the efforts of left-liberal interest groups to pull the liberal coalition in directions deemed undesirable by the big-business community. As such a check, it enjoyed considerable success during this period.[21]

Finally, outside the realm of interest groups but often providing a base of support for liberalism, and certainly seen by the conservative opposition as part of the "liberal establishment," were think tanks such as the Brookings Institution, which conducted research on important institutional and public policy issues, published books, and helped to set the political agenda, and such foundations as the Ford Foundation, which often funded liberal projects and research. In the New Deal era, the Brookings Institution had possessed a strong conservative coloration and had played a major role in seeking to block Roosevelt's efforts to reorganize the national government. In the postwar period, however, it shifted in the direction of moderate liberalism.[22]

Like their ideological counterparts, conservative purposive groups in the postwar era in some instances had direct connections to those of the New Deal era. For example, Frank Gannett's National Committee to Uphold Constitutional Government, organized to fight Court-packing and executive branch reorganization in 1937, was renamed the Committee for Constitutional Government. Still largely funded by Gannett's publishing fortune, the committee launched drives such as the one in support of the Bricker Amendment. New conservative purposive groups also appeared. Americans for Constitutional Action emulated the ADA by developoing a conservative score card for congressional roll call votes.

Other new conservative interest groups that took stands on a broad array of issues included the Young Americans for Freedom, founded in 1960 in William F. Buckley's living room and swelling to a membership of more than 50,000, and the American Conservative Union, established after Goldwater's defeat in 1964.[23]

The business and professional interest groups previously associated with one another and with the conservative cause continued to be active on behalf of most conservative endeavors. The National Association of Manufacturers and the United States Chamber of Commerce formed the core of these groups, but they were nearly always joined by the American Bar Association, as in the 1930s. The American Medical Association, previously less active than these groups in support of general conservative causes, now moved increasingly to align with them. Frightened by Roosevelt's hints that he would support national health insurance and horrified by Truman's actual commitment to a program on the subject, the AMA became increasingly politicized in a conservative direction. In 1944, the organization had set up a permanent Washington office for the first time in its history. In 1951, it joined with the American Bar Association, the National Association of Manufacturers, the U.S. Chamber of Commerce, an array of business trade associations, and the American Farm Bureau Federation to launch the first of a long series of Greenbrier Conference sessions. These provided a means for coordinating the efforts of much of the conservative coalition of interest groups. Albert Melone's systematic analysis of the congressional testimony of interest groups during the period found that the American Bar Association, for example, agreed with other Greenbrier Conference members 82.1 percent of the time.[24]

Among the agricultural interest groups, the Farm Bureau became even more actively involved than before in the conservative coalition, while the National Grange's politicization decreased. Not only was the American Farm Bureau Federation a charter member of the Greenbrier Conference, but it also associated with the ABA, NAM, and the U.S. Chamber of Commerce in the Conference of National Organizations. On agricultural issues, it became the leading spokesman for the conservative coalition, embracing "free market" imagery (in contrast to its positions of the 1930s) and supporting Ezra Taft Benson's efforts as Eisenhower's secretary of agriculture to move from fixed to variable price supports, while denouncing both the Truman and Kennedy farm program proposals.[25]

Just as the liberals could increasingly count on support from the Brookings Institution think tank in the postwar era, the American Enterprise Institute became the premier think tank for conservatives. Founded in 1943 as the American Enterprise Association, the renamed institute gained prestige and enhanced funding under the leadership of William Baroody, who became a key adviser to Barry Goldwater's presidential election campaign. Also a center for support of conservative policy research and books was the Hoover Institution, honoring the former Republican president, which gained influence under the auspices of a new director, W. Glenn Campbell, appointed in 1959. Conservative foundations such as that established by John M. Olin further helped to counter the influence of liberal-oriented foundations.[26]

In general, the 1945–66 period was one in which both the liberal and conservative coalitions solidified old bases of support, incorporated new interest groups, and gained additional backing from think tanks and foundations. Though many interest groups remained outside the two ideological coalitions, few could doubt that the liberal and conservative networks of groups were important factors shaping the contours of American politics.

### Wordsmiths

The intellectual power bases of the two movements, especially the conservative one, probably underwent more significant changes from the New Deal era than any other aspects of power centers. While a number of new liberal publications appeared, and the prestigious *Washington Post* shifted to the liberal camp from its previous association with conservatism, the major new developments concerned the conservative coalition.

The sheer number of conservative intellectuals multiplied many times from what had been a very small base. New publications such as *Human Events*, founded in 1944 by Felix Morley, William Henry Chamberlin, and Frank Hanighen, gave voice to conservative ideas throughout the period; but the most significant development was the new "fusionist conservative" weekly publication, *National Review*, established in 1955, which reflected William F. Buckley's directing role and was open to conservatives of all persuasions. It more than any other journal or magazine came to fulfill the sort of role that the *New Republic* and the *Nation* had long performed for liberalism. Another influential new conservative center for wordsmiths was *Modern Age,* founded by Russell Kirk in 1957. More traditionalist conservative and higher in intellectual content than the *National Review* or *Human Events,* it also became an important center of conservative ideas.[27]

Despite a few prominent defections to the liberal camp, most daily newspapers continued to favor conservatism on their editorial pages, though it was often the moderate conservatism typified by the *New York Herald Tribune.* The death in 1955 of the *Chicago Tribune*'s long-time conservative publisher and dominant figure, Colonel R. R. McCormick, did little to deflect that newspaper from its firm conservatism. However, the *Tribune* did soften its conservative stridency a bit by the late 1950s and 1960s and increasingly kept its political views confined to the editorial page, in contrast to the past. The ranks of older conservative columnists, such as David Lawrence, Westbrook Pegler, and George Sokolsky, were joined by newcomers, such as Buckley, who also used television effectively. Nevertheless, widespread editorial criticism of the Goldwater campaign in 1964, together with evidence that most working journalists and broadcasters were inclined away from conservatism, led to increasingly shrill conservative attacks on the "liberal press."[28]

On the liberal side, the *Nation* and the *New Republic* remained of central importance, but their efforts were now supplemented by such new publications as the *Reporter,* founded by Max Ascoli in 1949. The *Reporter* was more strongly supportive of military containment than the *Nation* or the *New Republic* and more inclined to focus on particular themes, especially in international affairs. The *Progressive,* founded by the LaFollettes, was reorganized and brought out as an independent liberal monthly beginning in 1947 and continuing throughout the period. Somewhat more peripheral to the liberal mainstream but often including pieces by major liberal intellectuals were the *New Leader* and *Commentary,* the latter a new publication launched in 1945 as a monthly under the sponsorship of the American Jewish Committee. Meanwhile, the *New York Times* left the liberal camp altogether during most of the late 1940s and 1950s, only to move into it more solidly than before in the 1960s; and the *Washington Post* came to be seen, as noted previously, as a citadel of liberalism in the 1960s.[29]

## Conclusions

The major power center differences between the postwar era and that of the New Deal were the vastly increased activity among conservative intellectuals and the concomitant development of conservative magazines and journals that published their work; the increased importance of black civil rights groups and, toward the end of the period, environmental and other "public interest" groups within the liberal coalition; and the slight weakening of labor unions' commitment and contributions to the liberal coalition. These trends and the rise of citizen activism in the presidential

Democratic and Republican parties on behalf of liberalism and conservatism, respectively, gave each movement a more middle-class character than before, though business groups continued to provide much of the muscle and financial support for the conservative coalition and labor unions did the same for liberals.

In general, the period was one in which the patterns of power remained remarkably similar to those of the late New Deal era, even with regard to wordsmiths and interest groups and certainly in reference to the party system and government institutions. The Republican party did become more clearly conservative at the presidential level than previously, but this new pattern was not really in evidence until the early 1960s. With regard to government institutions, the long-term pattern was (with the partial exception of the Eisenhower years) that the liberal coalition enjoyed a strong base of support in the executive and judicial branches of the national government while the conservative movement found its greatest strength in Congress and the state governments. This institutional/ideological lineup would, not surprisingly, be reflected in the ideological theories of governance.

### Notes

1. Sidney M. Milkis, *The President and the Parties* (New York: Oxford University Press, 1993), 132–133, 159–161.

2. Milkis, *President and the Partiest*, 167. The study of career executive officials in the Nixon administration by Joel D. Aberbach and Bert A. Rockman, "Clashing Beliefs within the Executive Branch: The Nixon Administration Bureaucracy," *American Political Science Review* 70 (June 1976): 456–468, shows a liberal predominance early in the Nixon administration that likely characterized the postwar era generally.

3. The author has tabulated the *New Republic*/UDA and *New Republic* scores from the original sources. The 1960 ADA score is from *Congressional Quarterly Weekly Reports*, 7 October 1960, 1659. On liberals' relations with Truman, see Alonzo L. Hamby, *Beyond the New Deal* (New York: Columbia University Press, 1973). On their relations with Kennedy, see Arthur M. Schlesinger Jr., *A Thousand Days* (New York: Fawcett Books, 1965), esp. 17–26, 68–69; David Burner and Thomas L. West, *The Torch Is Passed* (New York: Harper & Row, 1984), chap. 1; Allen J. Matusow, *The Unraveling of America* (New York: Harper & Row, 1984), chap. 1; and Steven M. Gillon, *Politics and Vision* (New York: Oxford University Press, 1987), chap. 6.

4. Author's tabulation of liberalism scores. *Congressional Quarterly Weekly Reports*, 6 October 1960, 1659, for the 1960 ADA score. Matusow, *Unraveling*, 16–17, 151–152; Schlesinger, *A Thousand Days*, 55–60, 68–69; Gillon, *Politic and Vision*, chap. 7.

5. George H. Nash, *The Conservative Intellectual Movement since 1945* (New

York: Basic Books, 1976) 253–256, discusses the conservative movement's generally negative relationship with Eisenhower. See also chap. 7, n. 31 of this book for full citations on this subject.

6. Robert Bendiner, *Obstacle Course on Capitol Hill* (New York: McGraw-Hill, 1964); Hamby, *Beyond the New Deal,* chap. 14; James L. Sundquist, *The Decline and Resurgence of Congress* (Washington: Brookings Institution, 1981), 179–187. In table 8.1, as in other tables, conservatives are those with scores in the 0–33 range, moderates in the 34–66 range, and liberals in the 67–100 range. The author tabulated each score from the original records in the *New Republic.*

7. Glendon Schubert, *The Judicial Mind* (Evanston, IL: Northwestern University Press, 1965), 99–157. On Douglas's presidential prospects, see Hamby, *Beyond the New Deal* , 55, 226, 229, 242, 485.

8. See David B. Robertson and Dennis R. Judd, *The Development of American Public Policy* (Glenview, IL: Scott, Foresman, 1989), chap. 5 on grants-in-aid cooperative federalism policy compromises of the period and chap. 11 on structural conservatism of the states. Nicol C. Rae, *The Decline and Fall of the Liberal Republicans from 1952 to the Present* (New York: Oxford University Press, 1989) stresses the gubernatorial moderate–congressional conservative conflicts of the period.

9. Barry M. Goldwater, *Where I Stand* (New York: McGraw-Hill, 1964), 91.

10. James Q. Wilson, *The Amateur Democrat* (Chicago: University of Chicago Press, 1962); Nelson W. Polsby and Aaron Wildavsky, *Presidential Elections,* 4th ed. (New York: Charles Scribner's Sons, 1976), 29–40.

11. James MacGregor Burns, *Deadlock of Democracy* (Englewood Cliffs, NJ: Prentice-Hall, 1963), 194–203; James L. Sundquist, *Politics and Policy* (Washington: Brookings Institution, 1968), 405–415.

12. Rae, *Decline and Fall*; Thomas Byrne Edsall and Mary D. Edsall, *Chain Reaction* (New York: W. W. Norton, 1991), esp. chaps. 2 and 3.

13. Gillon, *Politics and Vision,* chaps. 1–7; Hamby, *Beyond the New Deal*, 159–168, 215, and 271–272.

14. Gillon, *Politics and Vision,* 123.

15. J. David Greenstone, *Labor in American Politics* (New York: Alfred A. Knopf, 1969), 54–58; Philip Taft, "Political Activity of Organized Labor: 1948–55," in *Labor and American Politics,* ed. Charles M. Rehmus and Doris B. McLaughlin (Ann Arbor: University of Michigan Press, 1967), 191–196; V. O. Key Jr. *Politics, Parties, and Pressure Groups* (New York: Thomas Y. Crowell, 1964), 57–68; Harmon Zeigler, *Interest Groups in American Society* (Englewood Cliffs, NJ: Prentice–Hall, 1964), 152–161.

16. John O. Crampton, *The National Farmers Union* (Lincoln: University of Nebraska Press, 1965); Hamby, *Beyond the New Deal* , 223–224, 358, 365, 497; Key, 37–38; Zeigler, *Interest Groups,* 196–197.

17. Jeffrey M. Berry, *The Interest Group Society*, 2d ed. (Glenview, IL: Scott, Foresman, 1989), 167, discusses the Leadership Conference and its political roles; John Hope Franklin, *From Slavery to Freedom*, 3d ed. (New York: Alfred A. Knopf, 1967), chaps. 30 and 31, provides a good overview.

18. The quotation is from William A. Donohue, *The Politics of the American Civil Liberties Union* (New Brunswick, NJ: Transaction Books, 1985), 13. Donohue notes

the compromises on civil liberties (162–191). Charles Lam Markmann, *The Noblest Cry* (New York: St. Martin's Press, 1965), 257–275, discusses the links to civil rights groups.

19. Sundquist, *Politics and Policy*, 393, is the source of the quotes; see also 177–188, 392, and "The Question of Federal Funds for Public Schools," *Congressional Digest* 25 (February 1946), 35–36.

20. Berry, *Interest Group Society*, chap. 2; H. R. Mahood, *Interest Group Politics in America* (Englewood Cliffs, NJ: Prentice–Hall, 1990), chap. 2. Liberal–environmental group cooperation in the early 1960s is discussed in Sundquist, *Politics and Policy* , chap. 8.

21. Kim McQuaid, *Big Business and Presidential Power* (New York: William Morrow, 1982), 109–121, 233–235.

22. Sidney Blumenthal, *The Rise of the Counter-Establishment* (New York: Harper & Row, 1986), 4–5, 38; Richard J. Polenberg, *Reorganizing Roosevelt's Government* (Cambridge: Harvard University Press, 1966), 35–41.

23. See Duane Tananbaum, *The Bricker Amendment Controversy* (Ithaca, NY: Cornell University Press, 1988), ll6; and Stuart Long, "Thunder on the Right," *Reporter* 2 (6 June 1950): 11–13, for the CCG; Berry, *Interest Group Society*, 108–109, on the ACA; and Nash, *Conservative Intellectual Movement*, 334–335, 337, on the YAF and ACU.

24. For in-depth discussion of the ABA of the period, see Albert P. Melone, *Lawyers, Public Policy, and Interest Group Politics* (Washington: University Press of America, 1977), esp. 111–116 and chap. 5. James G. Burrow, *AMA: Voice of American Medicine* (Baltimore: Johns Hopkins Press, 1963), covers the AMA.

25. Samuel R. Berger, *Dollar Harvest: The Story of the Farm Bureau* (Lexington, MA: D. C. Heath, 1971), esp. 103–109; Key, *Politics, Parties, Pressure Groups*, 33–37.

26. Blumenthal, *Rise of the Counter-Establishment*, 32–35, 38–39; Nash, *Conservative Intellectual Movement*, 335, 345.

27. Nash, 14, 144–145, 148–153.

28. Lloyd Wendt, *The Chicago Tribune* (Chicago: Rand McNally, 1979), 690–705, 724, 733, 744–745; Stephen M. Shadegg, *What Happened to Goldwater* (New York: Holt, Rinehart, and Winston, 1965), chap. 25; and M. Stanton Evans, *The Liberal Establishment* (New York: Devin-Adair, 1965), develop the "liberal press" theme.

29. Hamby, *Beyond the New Deal* , 107–108, 283. On the *Washington Post* 's editorial shift toward liberalism during the late 1950s and early 1960s under Philip and then Katharine Graham, see Chalmers M. Roberts, *In the Shadow of Power* (Washington: Seven Locks Press, 1989), 280–285, 301, 303, 309, 327–330, 337. On the *New York Times,* see Joseph C. Goulden, *Fit to Print: A. M. Rosenthal and His Times* (Secaucus, NJ: Lyle Stuart, 1988), 200–205.

# 9

# The Liberal Theory of Governance

The theory of governance that most liberals had come to embrace during the late New Deal era persisted in most respects during the post-World War II period. Liberals' perceptions of the need for both domestic reform and an internationalist foreign policy inclined them to continue their support for the idea of a Constitution flexible enough to permit civil rights actions by the national government above and beyond those that they had previously advocated, new initiatives for national health insurance and general federal aid to education, presidential dispatch of troops overseas, and the mounting of executive branch-developed covert actions in other countries. Therefore, if anything, the "living" Constitution was stretched to accommodate even more changes than in the 1930s. However, as previously, certain liberals found the Constitution to be uncharacteristically rigid in its requirements in some areas, mainly with regard to the First Amendment and some other parts of the Bill of Rights.

Liberals in the postwar years came closer to unanimity than before in rejecting the "states' rights" imagery, in large part because of the defection of most white Southern liberals (who had been the liberals most prone to employ it) to the conservative coalition or at least to the ranks of the moderates. The growing association of that imagery with white supremacist notions also made it unattractive to liberals. However, at the same time, liberals shifted, at least in practice, toward cooperative federalism and away from centralization on most non–civil rights issues, although a few continued to call for movement to a highly centralized unitary structure. Judging from the generally negative liberal assessments of the state governments' orientations and capacities during the period, and their obvious preference for national solutions on matters ranging from offshore oil and operation of employment services to civil rights and health insurance, it is probable that the growing reliance on the use of cooperative federalist grant-in-aid strategies owed more to their need for political compromises with moderates and conservatives to enact any new federal programs than to dramatic shifts in liberal preferences from the New Deal era. Even in the 1930s, of course, cooperative federalism had generally prevailed over centralization in practice.

The liberal administrative state erected during the Third New Deal continued to enjoy the support of most of the liberal coalition. Though conservative opposition to it softened a bit at times, liberals still had to fight against efforts in Congress by conservatives and various interest-group spokesmen to fragment and micromanage it and to penetrate it with demands for executive-branch information.

Presidential government, like the administrative state to which liberals linked it, continued to be central to most liberal thought of the postwar era. Although a few liberals balked at such extreme actions as Truman's seizure of the steel industry during the Korean "police action," they generally applauded presidential exercises of power, including many that broke new ground. Moreover, the liberal rhetoric consistently exalted the ideas of presidential government, hailing strong presidential roles as commander-in-chief and chief diplomat more enthusiastically than ever and continuing to portray the president as properly the chief administrator of the domestic bureaucracy, the initiator of social reform, and the tribune of a national popular majority (though many modified this last role with claims that he should also be chief defender of minority civil rights and civil liberties). Even the Republican president of the period was urged by liberals to be "strong"; and liberals, far more than conservatives, supported the Eisenhower administration on institutional issues pertaining to executive agreements, treaty powers, and executive privilege.

As far as the Supreme Court was concerned, liberal views solidified during the period, particularly as the "Warren Court" after 1954 moved in directions that they endorsed. The liberal commitment to judicial activism on behalf of preferred freedoms grew. Increasingly, however, this concept broadened to include black civil rights in various new realms as well as rights of alleged Communists, atheists, and religious minorities, and criminal suspects, rights of all to "privacy," and rights to equal representation on the basis of "one person, one vote." By the 1960s, this type of expanded judicial activism had come to be far more associated with liberalism and the liberal coalition than in the days of FDR or Truman, despite some liberal objections to it.

## The Truman Administration and the Liberal Theory of Governance

The linkage between the Truman administration's approaches to institutional questions and the liberal governance theory became evident early. Agreement between the Truman administration and the liberal coalition on major programmatic policy ends and insitutional means to achieve them characterized most of the debates of 1945 and 1946. Constitutional flexibility, centralized or cooperative federalism, an enlarged administrative state, and strong presidential leadership enjoyed Truman administration and liberal coalition support with regard to the Fair Deal domestic reform agenda: national commitment to full employment, national health insurance, federal aid to education, and federal protection of black civil rights.

Even on matters peripheral to the liberals' main policy concerns, the Truman administration generally selected approaches drawn from the prevailing liberal theory of governance and won liberal backing for such approaches. A good example was the tidelands oil issue, which bubbled to the surface shortly after Truman's accession to the presidency.  The questions here primarily involved just three states and seemed rather narrowly legal and technical: would the federal government or the states control the oil resources in submerged coastal lands within a three-mile zone? With Secretary of the Interior Harold Ickes leading the way, however, most liberals in and out of the administration soon perceived the issue in terms of their theory of governance. The matter was one of centralized federalism versus states' rights and defense of the Supreme Court versus attacks on its jurisdiction. When Congress voted in favor of the states' claims, almost all congressional liberals (89 percent in the House, 85 percent in the Senate) resisted; and Truman promptly vetoed the measure, expressing a desire to await a High Court ruling. The *New Republic*'s comments summed up most liberal sentiments: "Rarely has Congress subordinated the public interest to special interests so clearly and so openly as in its approval of legislation giving away the federal government's claim to ownership of the rich submerged oil lands off the coast of California." Moreover, reflecting the new liberal solicitude for the Supreme Court, the congressional move was "congressional usurpation of the Supreme Court's jurisdiction."[1]

Once the Supreme Court majority ruled, as the liberals had wished, that the national government possessed "paramount rights" over the submerged lands at issue, the liberals and the Truman administration engaged in a prolonged battle with congressional and other conservatives to keep control in national government hands. Truman again successfully used his veto in behalf of the liberal effort. As with so many institutional struggles of the period, the tidelands oil controversy pitted the presidency and the Supreme Court on the liberal side, fighting for centralized federalism, against Congress and most state governments on the conservative side, fighting for states' rights. When Eisenhower won the presidency on a platform promising state control over the tidelands oil, however, the liberals met defeat. But the main point was that an issue fairly remote from the central policy concerns of the liberal coalition had nonetheless been viewed in terms of the general theory of governance and had mobilized most leading members of the coalition for a period extending over more than seven years.[2]

Though liberals usually rallied in support of the Truman administration's stances that accorded with the liberal theory of governance, there was one notable exception during the first two years under Truman. Angered by what he perceived to be the recalcitrance of railway union leaders in a period when strikes had been unusually troublesome, the president in 1946 asked that Congress authorize him to draft strikers into the armed forces in emergencies. Liberal denunciations of this particular "power grab" were loud and clear. Liberal columnist Max Lerner compared Truman to Hitler; Helen Fuller saw a parallel with Mussolini. Liberal Senator Claude Pepper joined with conservative leader Robert Taft to mobilize Senate support to delete the Truman proposal from the measure in which it had been included, as most Senate liberals united against the request for new presidential power. However, Truman soon repaired his relations with the liberal coalition by vetoing antiunion legislation passed by congressional conservatives; and most liberals forgot quite soon how easily presidential power in the hands of the "wrong" president might be used for illiberal ends.[3]

The tidelands oil pattern was far more typical than the pattern on the Truman proposal for drafting strikers. Certainly, on employment matters, national health insurance, and black civil rights, the unifying point was a desire for centralized federal approaches. A 1945–46 effort by conservatives to return employment services to the state level as quickly as possible incurred strong Truman administration and liberal opposition before Truman reluctantly acquiesced to Congress on the subject. Health insurance also presented an area where Truman and the liberal movement agreed on a centralized federal approach, but Congress blocked their efforts. In the black civil rights domain, the Truman administration, backed strongly and emotionally by the liberal coalition, proposed national abolition of the poll taxes applied mainly in Southern states, a federal antilynching law, and a national government Fair Employment Practices Commission with genuine enforcement powers. Southern conservative filibusters blocked these measures in the Senate, with covert assistance from many other conservatives.[4]

On the question of federal aid to education, the Truman administration and most liberals advocated cooperative federalism, with considerable state and local autonomy, rather than centralized federalism. However, this approach involved a larger national government role than in the past and also stirred much states' rights opposition in Congress and elsewhere. Liberals divided among themselves not over a national government role but over the question of parochial school assistance; and this internal conflict helped to defeat the Truman education proposals.[5]

If federalism issues were of major concern to the liberal coalition during the Truman administration, so, too, were an array of matters pertaining to presidential-congressional relations. Some of these focused directly on the presidency, as in the case of the Twenty-Second Amendment to the Constitution, which limited the president to two elected terms of office. Designed to weaken the presidency as an institution, this Amendment gained the requisite two-thirds majority in Congress in 1947 over the opposition of 90 percent of the Senate liberals and 87 percent of those in the House of Representatives. Most liberal opponents echoed liberal historian Henry Steele Commager in denouncing the amendment as a "vote of no confidence in democracy" and fought against its ratification by the state legislatures, to no avail. The amendment became a part of the Constitution in 1951 and has served to lessen presidential influence during the second term when all political actors know that the incumbent cannot serve another term. A few liberals, notably Richard Neuberger, abandoning their "anti-democratic" arguments, next called for term limits for congressmen and state legislators. But, perhaps because it contradicted their recently expressed views about the people's right to a democratic choice on retaining officeholders, most of the liberal coalition did not take up this cause.[6]

Other liberal prescriptions focused directly on Congress. Throughout the Truman administration, but with particular zeal after their disappointments with the Democratic-controlled eighty-first Congress, for which they had held high hopes, liberals advocated an array of reforms aimed at making the congressional process more subject to majority rule and speedier than it customarily was. Chief among these were proposals to permit termination of a Senate filibuster, an extended debate intended to prevent a vote on an issue, by a simple majority vote rather than a two-thirds majority. Other proposals included bypassing the House Rules Committee by a procedure called the "21-day rule" after the committee had failed to act for a three-week period, and abolishing the seniority system, whereby the longest-serving majority party members of each standing committee automatically became chairs (giving conservative Democrats who faced few, if any, challenges to their reelections in the one-party South a disproportionate advantage). Liberals also mounted an attack in the courts on apportionment schemes for the U.S. House of Representatives and state legislative bodies that overrepresented rural areas. Of all of these efforts, none was crowned with success during the Truman years except for the adoption by the House in 1950 of the 21-day rule; and even it proved short-lived when a more conservative House repealed it at the beginning of the eighty-second Congress.[7]

The Truman administration's initiatives, usually backed by most liberals, primarily had the effect of strengthening presidential powers as commander-in-chief, chief diplomat, chief domestic administrator, and instigator of social reform. In the social reform sphere, Truman established the President's Committee on Civil Rights and then desegregated the military by executive orders, effectively bypassing Congress. Liberal endorsement of these actions was virtually unanimous. Though liberals were disappointed that Truman often failed to drive reform legislation through Congress and questioned his leadership abilities as a result, they placed most of the blame on Congress and pushed for the above-noted reforms of that institution.[8]

As chief domestic administrator, Truman was able to enhance presidential powers, at least marginally, by gaining control over two new staff agencies, the Council of Economic Advisors and the National Security Council, that Congress created in 1946 and 1947, respectively. He also obtained, under his Reorganization Plan 8 (1950), the power for himself and future presidents to appoint the chairs of "independent" regulatory commissions and have them serve at his pleasure, thus partially undermining the autonomy that these commissions had gained from the *Humphrey's Executor* decision during the Roosevelt administration. The Hoover Commission on the organization of the executive branch, headed by former President Hoover, also proved helpful to Truman in gaining added legitimacy for his role as chief administrator. On the other hand, Truman engaged congressional conservatives in battle over their demands for access to executive branch information. In response to Truman's claims of executive privilege, House conservatives, over almost unanimous liberal opposition, pushed through a resolution calling for executive disclosure of all information needed to help Congress perform its duties. Once again, liberals stood in defense of the administrative state and presidential powers over it.[9]

Even more significant presidential power enhancements under Truman came in foreign affairs. Though Truman worked closely with Congress in designing his early containment doctrine policies in Europe, he dispatched troops to join the Korean conflict in June 1950 without a congressional declaration of war or substantial consultation; sent additional troops to Europe to support the North Atlantic Treaty Organization (NATO) there; continued Roosevelt's practice of negotiating numerous executive agreements that took effect without being sent, as treaties were, to the Senate for ratification by a two-thirds majority; fired General Douglas MacArthur as head of the forces in Korea when he judged the general's behavior to be insubordinate; and seized the steel industry to avert a strike that he believed would endanger the American police action in Korea. In all of these actions save the last, Truman enjoyed nearly unanimous liberal support. The *New Republic,* the *Nation,* the *Progressive,* Americans for Democratic Action, the National Farmers Union, and virtually all other components of the liberal coalition hailed Truman's initial actions in Korea without Congress as necessary and appropriate. The "Great Debate" that erupted in the Senate in 1951 over presidential powers to send additional troops to Europe culminated in Senate votes in which over 90 percent of the liberals supported broad presidential powers. Liberal Senator Wayne Morse of Oregon, later to shift his views dramatically, typified liberals by citing the *Curtiss-Wright* precedent to support "a discretionary power which I believe is inherent in the President of the United States in the field of foreign policy." Such other prominent liberals as Herbert Lehman, Henry Steele Commager, and Arthur Schlesinger Jr. concurred. As for the executive agreements, few liberals perceived a problem. When conservative Senator John Bricker sought support to restrict their use, he encountered nearly solid liberal opposition. In the case of Truman's removal of MacArthur from his Korean command, liberals were effusive in their praise for what Max Lerner termed the president's "resolution and courage."[10]

For some members of the liberal coalition, the limits of proper presidential powers were exceeded by Truman's seizure of the steel industry to avert a steel strike in April 1952. Truman himself asserted in this instance that the president possesses "very great inherent powers to meet great national emergencies." When asked if he could also seize newspapers and broadcasting stations as part of his "inherent" powers, Truman impulsively responded, "Under similar circumstances the President of the United States has to act for whatever is for the best of the country." Many in the liberal movement backed Truman's actions to the fullest extent. The *New Republic,* for instance, hailed it as a "logical act" and declared,

"President Truman would have been delinquent in his duty had he failed to seize the steel mills." But the coalition split badly. Remembering Truman's previous threat to draft strikers, the *Nation's* editors saw a potential "threat against labor." Moreover, they argued, "Nothing in the Constitution, directly or by implication, authorizes the President to take the step he did" and deemed Truman's action "dictatorial." A divided Supreme Court ruled against Truman, with the prime liberal leaders on it, Black and Douglas, voting in the majority to overturn his action as invalid. Though most of the liberal opponents, like the Supreme Court justices, drew no clear line of demarcation, it was evident that their support for presidential government had its limits, even in the Truman era and even regarding war powers.[11]

Despite occasional liberal discord over institutional prescriptions and modes for implementing them during the 1945–53 years, consistency and coherence were the predominant liberal patterns. Disagreements were mainly centered on a few instances of presidential power deployment and on the degree and extent of centralized federalism. As between 1937 and 1945, the boundaries of judicial activism were also a source of some liberal tensions; but during the Truman years, that conflict was largely confined to the judiciary and the relatively few liberal activists and intellectuals who followed the courts closely. Whether intended by him or not, Truman's appointees shifted the Supreme Court in the direction of judicial restraint, leaving the liberal activists usually in the minority—until new members and a changing political atmosphere led to a dramatic shift in the Eisenhower years.[12]

### The Liberal Governance Theory in the Eisenhower Years

When Eisenhower supported the conservative coalition on the federalism governance issue and finally defeated in 1953 the liberal coalition's efforts to maintain national control over tidelands oil, liberals feared the beginning of a period where the power of the presidency might regularly be brought to bear against their ideas. The actual pattern was not to be as simple or as negative for their purposes as that. The so-called Bricker Amendment controversy had been simmering through the last year of the Truman administration, and liberals continued to be intent on blocking this measure on grounds that it would undermine presidential diplomatic powers (by placing new restrictions on both treaties and executive agreements), curb administrative state discretion (in the same ways), and weaken the central government vis-à-vis the states (by limiting the effects of national government treaties and other agreements on state laws). The American Federation of Labor, Congress of Industrial Organizations, American Civil Liberties Union, and Americans for Democratic Action were early and vociferous in their denunciations of the conservative effort. The AFL summed up most of their views, decrying the proposed amendment as an attempt to "curb the treaty-making power of the government, cripple United States participation in the United Nations, and put a brake on U.S. action in Jim Crow laws." (The last point apparently referred to liberal hopes that international conventions would prod the United States to action against segregation.) Both they and the conservatives breathlessly awaited the verdict of Eisenhower and his administration. The fate of the Bricker Amendment hung in the balance.[13]

When a series of negotiations between the Eisenhower administration and the conservative coalition backing the Bricker resolution broke down without agreement being reached, liberal hopes soared; and the Eisenhower presidency soon became an ally of the liberals in battling the pro-congressional, pro-states' rights, anti–administrative state Bricker endeavor. The battle raged through all of 1953 and into early 1954 before liberal victory was achieved. Even a watered-down substitute for the original Bricker Amendment failed to win the necessary two-thirds vote in the Senate. Most liberals cheered.[14]

Nor was this to be the only major institutional issue on which the liberal movement found itself on the same side as the Eisenhower administration. As previously noted, liberals had generally supported the Truman administration in its refusal to provide confidential information to congressional investigators. In part, this position had reflected liberal distaste for the character and purposes of the conservative anti-Communists in Congress who were making most of the demands, in part it reflected loyalty to the Truman administration, and in part it signified general liberal support for presidential government and an executive administrative state protected from congressional infringements on its prerogatives. Though feeling little loyalty to the Eisenhower administration, liberals had no sympathy for demands for executive information from the likes of conservatives Joseph McCarthy, Karl Mundt, and John McClellan, three frequent investigators; and liberals' general ideas about an executive-led administrative state continued to operate. Therefore, when the Eisenhower administration greatly expanded claims of executive privilege to cover all exchanges within the executive branch, ushering in what Arthur Schlesinger Jr. later termed "the greatest orgy of executive denial in American history," most liberals applauded. Wilfred Binkley, writing in the *New Republic,* hailed it as "a turning point in a current trend of the Presidency" and likened congressional opponents of executive privilege to Henry Clay during Andrew Jackson's presidency. "Let Clay's sad experience be a lesson to those who have not yet learned, in our day, what the Presidency has become—both as an office and as an institution cherished by the American people." TRB added his endorsement. Telford Taylor, a liberal Americans for Democratic Action activist and New York attorney who had previously urged the Eisenhower administration to resist forcefully any congressional encroachments of executive control of the administrative state, was one of the few who saw its extremely broad assertion of executive privilege as excessive.[15]

Other areas in which the liberal proclivity to support presidential government and to protect executive administrative powers meshed with the Eisenhower administration's instincts for self-protection included reciprocal trade agreements, the use of troops overseas, and discretionary foreign aid. Particularly regarding trade and foreign aid, liberals were often more supportive of executive discretion than conservatives were. On presidential leeway concerning troop commitments, the congressional votes favoring the Formosa and Middle East resolutions of 1955 and 1957, respectively, showed strong support from liberals, moderates, and conservatives.[16]

On judicial roles, too, the liberal coalition found some common ground with the Eisenhower administration in that both strongly resisted the efforts of most of the conservative coalition to get Congress to restrict the Supreme Court's appellate jurisdiction following a series of "activist" Warren Court decisions. In the general judicial sphere, however, there were marked differences between the institutional prescriptions of liberals and those of Eisenhower. Despite appointing liberal activists Earl Warren and William Brennan to the Supreme Court, Eisenhower himself was not in sympathy with their activism on the bench. It was often said later that he regretted the Warren appointment in particular, and he privately opposed even the *Brown v. Board of Education* school desegregation decision. Most of the liberal coalition, in contrast, came to applaud the judicial activism of the Warren-Brennan-Black-Douglas variety during the Eisenhower years. Thus, the coalition's defense of the High Bench against conservative assaults was enthusiastic and entailed strong support for liberal judicial activism, not mere defense of the Supreme Court as an institution, as was the case for Eisenhower.[17]

A bill sponsored by Senator William Jenner, an Indiana Republican, imposing curbs on the appellate jurisdiction of the Supreme Court, represented the most direct and forceful attack on the judiciary as an institution during the Eisenhower years. Liberals again worked closely with the

Eisenhower administration and they jointly blocked Jenner's effort in the Senate, with 89 percent of the liberals voting to kill the Court-curbing bill and succeeding by an eight-vote margin.[18]

Another significant theory of governance matter that linked the liberals and the Eisenhower administration against the conservative coalition was one that related to both the judiciary and federalism: the issue of federal preemption. In *Pennsylvania v. Nelson* (1956), the Supreme Court reiterated a previously developed doctrine of federal preemption, holding in this case that federal law against subversion had preempted the field, thus negating a Pennsylvania state law under which Nelson had been convicted. Anticipating this Supreme Court decision, the conservative coalition put forward a bill, sponsored by Representative Howard Smith of Virginia, which provided that "no Act of Congress shall be construed as indicating an intent on the part of Congress to occupy the field in which such Act operates, to the exclusion of all State laws on the same subject matter, unless such Act contains an express provision to that effect." Liberals viewed this measure not only as a move toward states' rights but, as the *New Republic* described it, part of "the drive to put the Supreme Court in its place." In the House, 85 percent of liberals opposed it; in the Senate, 84 percent did so. With the help of moderates and a scattering of conservatives, they defeated the Smith bill in the Senate by one vote.[19]

Throughout the Eisenhower years, the liberal movement continued to be generally supportive of its previous governance theory, but it strengthened its commitment to judicial activism and defense of the Supreme Court as an institution (in contrast to 1933–37). Strong conservative assaults on the Court doubtless spurred liberals in this direction. On many of the major institutional controversies, including several concerning presidential powers, liberals were able to come to substantial agreement with the Eisenhower administration, despite some major domestic programmatic policy differences. Nonetheless, there were significant institutional conflicts between the liberals and Eisenhower, most notably in the realm of federalism. The tidelands oil dispute has been discussed previously. In addition, federalism arguments separated them on such matters as civil rights and environmental protection. In 1960, in vetoing a liberal environmental bill to expand federal aid to localities for sewage treatment works, Eisenhower highlighted the differences. "Water pollution is a uniquely local blight," declared the Republican president. "Primary responsibility for solving the problem lies not with the Federal Government but rather must be assumed and exercised, as it has been, by State and local governments." Despite frequent cooperative federalist compromises, a clear gap persisted between most liberals' desire for a more centralized federalism and the states' rights proclivities of the Eisenhower administration. Nonetheless, areas of agreement between Eisenhower and the liberals were sufficiently broad on institutional matters to arouse considerable conservative indignation.[20]

## The Liberal Governance Theory
## in the Kennedy-Johnson Years to 1966

The return of relative liberalism to the White House in January 1961 only heightened the liberal enthusiasm for presidential government and an administrative state that had persisted for the most part even through the Eisenhower interlude. Now liberals not only defended executive power in administrative, commander-in-chief, and diplomatic roles, as they had between 1953 and 1961, but also called upon the president to seize the initiative on social reform and to mobilize a popular majority for liberal principles. Historian John Morton Blum, writing in the *New Republic* just before Kennedy's inauguration, stressed that such difficult times "demand the tough, hard work on large planning and detail that only the executive establishment can undertake, the work so long neglected." TRB, regular *New Republic* columnist, hoping that Kennedy would rouse a popular majority, wrote approvingly in March 1961: "He is appealing over the head of Congress to the public using every publicity means available." Disappointed by congressional resistance to Kennedy's initiatives, but encouraged by a 1961 success in enlarging the House Rules Committee, liberals renewed their Truman-era demands for major congressional reforms and urged Kennedy to push hard against the filibuster, the seniority system, and other bastions of congressional conservative power (though he rarely did so). Quite a few liberal intellectuals called, as they had for years, for "responsible party" reforms but mainly to bring party discipline to Congress to enable liberal Democratic presidents now and in the future to gain congressional Democratic approval of their initiatives.[21]

Occasionally, Kennedy initiated liberal reforms through executive orders, bypassing Congress as Truman had done on such matters as desegregation of the military. But this was not his usual approach, and liberals were often impatient over what they viewed as inadequate presidential leadership. Their complaints were particularly loud in the area of black civil rights during the first two years of the Kennedy administration. While most recognized the difficulties of gaining meaningful civil rights legislation from Congress, they expected dramatic executive actions by the president. During the 1960 campaign, for example, Kennedy had assured liberals that he would forbid discrimination in federal housing programs "with the stroke of a pen." As the months passed and no executive order was forthcoming from Kennedy, angry civil rights liberals started mailing pens to the White House in a sarcastic effort to ease the president's apparently difficult task. Finally, after nearly two years in office, Kennedy did issue the promised executive order, but it was less sweeping than most liberals had hoped it would be.[22]

The liberal drive for full-scale presidential government continued into the Johnson administration, despite initial liberal misgivings about LBJ's liberal credentials. Liberal political scientist Louis Koenig, writing in 1964, called for "more power to the President (not less)" and urged "very considerable tightening of party discipline" and a presidential item veto. "Peoples must be aroused, Congress moved, the bureaucracy stirred, and alliances redirected," proclaimed Koenig. "Only the President can do it." James MacGregor Burns in 1965 saw Goldwater's defeat as "the triumph of Presidential government" and exclaimed: "The Presidency today is at the peak of its prestige." Burns now even saw it as the "main governmental bastion for the protection of individual liberty and the expansion of civil rights." Liberal disillusionment with presidential power would soon take root, however, as Lyndon Johnson plunged more deeply into a war in Southeast Asia, the purposes and methods of which were stirring deep liberal doubts by 1965.[23]

Meanwhile, liberal drives for centralized or cooperative federalism continued, though there were a few modifications. Most liberal preferences had long been for centralized federalism, especially where black civil rights were concerned. However, freedom riders and the activities of other civil rights activists in the South were now provoking such violence that new questions of police powers arose. Kennedy-Johnson administration officials, such as Burke Marshall, head of the Justice Department's Civil Rights Division, tended to hold that constitutional constraints limited federal powers sharply, particularly regarding police powers to cope with the violence. Many other liberals, particularly in the civil rights movement, demanded strong national action. Apart from civil rights, cooperative federalist grant-in-aid approaches that in practice permitted considerable state and local autonomy proliferated, often representing liberals' compromises to gain congressional endorsement. Rarely was there enactment of any major liberal-backed socioeconomic legislation that was as centralizing in its effects as title 2 of the Social Security Act, the (Wagner) National Labor Relations Act, or the Fair Labor Standards Act had been in the 1930s. Moreover, by the 1960s, bypassing of established state and municipal governments in favor of federal grants to communi-

ty groups (most controversially in the community action programs) illustrated some liberal shifting away from previous centralist proclivities in
response to New Left and "new politics" liberal critiques calling for
decentralization.[24]

Finally, liberal judicial activism continued to stir controversies during
the Kennedy-Johnson years over both the nature of the Constitution and
the appropriate roles of the Supreme Court. Virtually all liberals accepted
the Supreme Court's flexible interpretation of the Fourteenth Amendment
in the *Brown* decision and subsequent civil rights cases. They believed
that, although the intent of the framers in 1868 might well have been to
permit school segregation, times had changed, sociological and psycho-
logical evidence of the ill effects of segregation were now available, and
desegregation should be national policy. If this entailed judicial legislation, as many conservatives charged, the liberal response was that such
"lawmaking" by the Court had existed since the days of John Marshall
and was inevitable. Judicial activism to protect the rights of alleged subversives, of criminal suspects, and of non-Christians generally won liberal support, or at least acquiescence, during these years. That which mandated redistricting of the United States House of Representatives and
many state legislatures on a "one person, one vote" egalitarian basis generated active liberal endorsement and a major (and ultimately successful)
drive to block both new Court-curbing moves by conservatives and Senator Everett Dirksen's effort to overturn the decisions in question by a
constitutional amendment.[25]

The liberals' association with a judicial activism that by 1966 went far
beyond that of the 1940s, and often well beyond what public opinion
favored in its substantive policy results, brought estrangement of liberal
elites from some of the constituencies at the base of the liberal coalition, particularly blue-collar whites. Combined with liberal defense of an administrative state that also aroused considerable popular distrust and outright
opposition, support for judicial activism made liberals increasingly vulnerable to charges of elitism—most importantly, from an emergent "populistic" wing of conservatism that was taking shape in the late 1960s.

## Liberal Consensus and Discord

Table 9.1 provides a cross-section of liberal and conservative voting patterns in Congress on key governance issues during the 1945–66 period.
Although it omits some issues that were heavily imbued with programmatic policy considerations and some votes that were simply repetitive of

Table 9.1
Congressional Ideological Divisions on Key Governance Roll Calls

| Bill | Date/House | | Governance Issues | % for "Liberal" Position. | | Lib.-Cons. Gap |
|---|---|---|---|---|---|---|
| | | | | Lib. | Cons. | |
| Employment service | 9/19/45 | S | Fed. | 74 | 5 | 69 |
| Employment service | 1/29/46 | H | Fed. | 91 | 0 | 91 |
| Tidelands oil | 7/22/46 | S | Fed. | 85 | 14 | 71 |
| Tidelands oil | 8/2/46 | H | Fed. | 89 | 7 | 82 |
| Pres. term limits | 2/6/47 | H | Pres. | 87 | 0 | 87 |
| Pres. term limits | 3/12/47 | S | Pres. | 90 | 0 | 90 |
| Executive privilege | 4/22/48 | H | Pres.-Cong. | 98 | 10 | 88 |
| 21-day rule | 1/20/50 | H | Cong. | 99 | 22 | 77 |
| 21-day rule | 1/3/51 | H | Cong. | 96 | 5 | 91 |
| Pres. troop discretion | 4/2/51 | S | Pres.-Cong. | 97 | 24 | 73 |
| Pres. troop discretion | 4/3/51 | S | Pres.-Cong. | 92 | 10 | 82 |
| Bricker amendment | 2/25/54 | S | Pres.-Cong./Fed | 93 | 33 | 60 |
| George substitute | 2/26/54 | S | Pres.-Cong. | 66 | 22 | 44 |
| Federal preemption | 7/17/58 | H | Fed./Jud. | 85 | 3 | 82 |
| Federal preemption | 8/21/58 | S | Fed./Jud. | 84 | 11 | 73 |
| Supreme Court jurisdiction | 8/20/58 | S | Jud. | 89 | 11 | 78 |
| House Rules enlargement | 1/31/61 | H | Cong. | 100 | 5 | 95 |
| Fed. court jurisdiction | 8/19/64 | H | Jud. | 94 | 5 | 89 |
| Fed. court jurisdiction | 9/15/64 | S | Jud. | 100 | 40 | 60 |
| Dirksen amend./reapp. | 8/4/65 | S | Fed./Jud. | 86 | 0 | 86 |

others, and does not cover the considerable number of institutional issues that were never subjects of congressional roll calls, it does provide a good measure of the overall picture. Clearly, the liberal coalition continued to take governance positions that were consistent with each other and in accord with the recent past. Clearly, too, liberals and conservatives differed in regular and predictable ways. Liberals usually favored constitutional flexibility, a more centralized federalism than most conservatives preferred, an administrative state structure that was executive in nature, presidential government, and liberal judicial activism on civil liberties and civil rights—with rights conceptualized in terms that gave them broader definition than in the past.

Nevertheless, some discord over institutional prescriptions did disturb liberal harmony on governance theory. Most of the disagreements concerned particular modes of implementing general prescriptions, but there were also several fundamental liberal disputes concerning basic conceptions.

### Flexible Constitution

As in the New Deal era, almost all liberals employed the language of a "living" Constitution. They ranged in their outlooks from those in what Arthur Schlesinger Jr. termed the "Yale school," (associated with Fred Rodell and Walton H. Hamilton, in particular), who took legal realist approaches; through those such as Henry Steele Commager, who perceived the need for grounding constitutional law in historical precedents, however selective they might be; to those such as Burke Marshall and (by the mid-1960s, sometimes) even Justice Hugo Black, who focused on constitutional language and framers' intentions to a degree approximating the views of moderate conservatives. The Yale school, popular among many in the liberal coalition, including Justices Douglas and Black in the late 1940s and 1950s, held that judicial legislation was "inevitable." In its view, as described by Schlesinger, "Conservative majorities in past Courts have always legislated in the interests of the business community; why should a liberal majority tie its hands by a policy of self-denial that conservatism will never follow when it is in power?" Law itself, including consitutional law, was "a means to an end—the achievement of social justice, especially for the otherwise unprotected—instead of an end in itself." Commager's approach, used in numerous institutional battles during the period and typical of many other liberals, argued that "Our Constitution is not only the original document; it is also a century and a half of interpretation, a century and a half of tradition, practice, and custom." In addressing presidential-congressional war powers, Commager proceeded, for example, to cite an array of presidential actions from the earliest days to the present, as well as Supreme Court opinions and *dicta.* Still less flexible than this approach was that taken by Burke Marshall concerning civil rights enforcement or by Hugo Black in 1965, when he denounced the Supreme Court majority's "discovery" of individual rights of privacy in the "penumbras of the Bill of Rights" in *Griswold v. Connecticut.* Black, nonetheless, did not take such a position consistently over time.[26]

## Centralized or Cooperative Federalism

On the continuum ranging from centralized national power to states' rights decentralization, most liberals continued to be inclined in the centralist direction. Christopher Jencks, writing in the *New Republic* in 1964, summed up a widespread liberal view: "Even a casual survey of 20th century American politics suggests that the major pillars of the *status quo* have been the 50 states. Conversely the major force for innovation and progress has been the federal government." Liberal thought inclined more than previously toward centralization on black civil rights (and other "rights") issues. Political scientist William Riker, analyzing federalism in 1964, spoke for many in concluding: "The main beneficiaries [of federalism] throughout American history have been the southern whites, who have been given the freedom to oppress Negroes. . . . The judgment to be passed on federalism in the United States is therefore a judgment on the values of segregation and racial oppression." Even on civil rights, however, as noted before, liberals such as Burke Marshall were hesitant to push too far in a centralist direction. Along with fairly marked civil rights centralizing trends, however, went increased liberal willingness to adopt cooperative federalist compromises on many other matters. Grants-in-aid permitting considerable autonomy proliferated in the 1950s and 1960s with liberal endorsement. Partially in response to participatory democratic, decentralist ideas bubbling up from "new politics" liberals as well as New Leftists, the liberal mainstream showed some receptivity in the 1960s to federal grants to decentralized units other than state or municipal governments. These grants, however, sometimes split the liberal coalition, opening a widening gap by 1966 between many state and local officials previously linked to the liberal movement and "radical decentralist" liberals who wanted to decentralize outside of the traditional government framework. Meanwhile, New Deal liberal centralizers continued to endorse a more centralist approach than either most liberal state and local officials or radical decentralizers thought appropriate. The limits of liberal consensus on the federal aspect of their theory of governance were becoming strained to the breaking point after years of relative internal harmony.[27]

## Administrative State

In this domain, too, liberal consensus overshadowed discord until very late in the period. Enlarging the national administrative state's scope and functions, minimizing congressional intrusions into its workings through "micromanagement" efforts or investigative "witch hunts," and expanding civil service merit coverage—these were ideas that won wide liberal endorsement from the 1940s to the 1960s. As Theodore Lowi has illustrated, the era was also one in which clear directives to administrative agencies became increasingly rare, in part by design, in part because of compromises on vague statutory language. In any event, as statutory guidelines weakened, administrative discretion increased. Often the result was not power for professional administrators drawing upon their vast expertise but rather what Lowi termed "interest-group liberalism." When participatory democratic denunciations of "bureaucracy" began to emanate from within the liberal ranks in the 1960s, mainly from the young, cracks became evident in what had been remarkable harmony in the liberal coalition in support of the administrative state. The subsequent attacks by Lowi, Grant McConnell, and others would further undermine that consensus in the years ahead.[28]

## Presidential Government

This component remained a centerpiece of the liberal theory of governance throughtout the period, until the erosion of support for it began during 1965. Even during the Eisenhower administration, liberals' commitment to presidential government remained largely intact. A few liberal voices, such as Herman Finer in 1960, issued general warnings about the dangers of excessive presidential powers, but these were rarities in the liberal coalition. Much more commonplace were the paeans of praise to presidential power from Burns, Binkley, Koenig, and others. The major internal liberal disagreements were primarily over specific uses of presidential power, with many liberals objecting to its proposed employment to draft striking workers, quite a few to the steel seizure, and a small cluster to the broad power delegations in the Formosa, Middle East, and Gulf of Tonkin resolutions. The expansive presidential roles as commander-in-chief, chief diplomat, chief administrator, leader of social reform, and tribune of a national popular majority continued to enjoy solid liberal support, despite some diminishment of liberal enthusiasm for majoritarianism. Liberal faith, almost blind faith, in presidential leadership was illustrated well in the *New York Times'* editorial endorsement of the broad congressional grant of authority to Lyndon Johnson at the time of the Tonkin Gulf incident off the coast of Vietnam in August 1964: "The President has rightly asked that the resolution express a determination that 'all necessary measures' be taken," leaving it to the chief executive to define these. "The nation's united confidence in the Chief Executive is vital. No one else can play the hand." The editors of the *Times* would themselves soon find reason to question this judgment.[29]

### Judicial Activism in Behalf of Civil Liberties and Rights

During the postwar period, especially from 1954 onward, the liberals' prescriptions for the judiciary were transmuted from an emphasis on restraint on socioeconomic questions to an increasingly warm endorsement of "liberal" judicial activism. Fears that a conservative Supreme Court might again, as in the past, employ judicial activism in support of business interests and against liberal government executives and legislators waned as the 1890–1937 era became a distant memory. Liberals did continue to favor judicial self-restraint vis-à-vis "lawmaking majorities" on most socioeconomic questions but discussed and debated the matter much less openly and often than in the 1930s and early 1940s. Now the chief focus of the liberals' institutional prescriptions was for activist overturning of mainly state and local laws and practices in support of "rights" or "liberties," especially those of persons or groups deemed "disadvantaged." Frankfurter, no longer viewed by most as a liberal, often continued to object on grounds of judicial restraint, as did, with some regularity. Truman's Supreme Court appointees. However, the prevailing winds of liberalism blew in the direction of liberal judicial activism during the years of the Warren Court.[30]

### Conclusions

By 1966, several long-term components of the liberal theory of governance were beginning to come under challenge from within the liberal movement. Foremost among these was presidential government, but centralized federalism and the administrative state as previously conceived were also being questioned, especially by young, new politics liberals.

From 1945 to 1965, however, there had been remarkable continuity with the early 1940s, consistency over time, and harmony across the liberal coalition on most basic governance issues. If judicial activism, especially in support of disadvantaged minorities' liberties and rights, potentially clashed with liberal majoritarianism, that majoritarianism was more tepidly endorsed by liberals than previously; and many simply insisted that there was no conflict. If presidential power occasionally served illiberal ends, those situations appeared to be exceptions to the general rule. Nevertheless, the liberals' growing emphasis on qualitative, not quantitative, goals; their rising questions about the Vietnam War and general Cold War containment doctrine assumptions; and the near-completion of the New Deal/Fair Deal/New Frontier/Great Society legislative program of socioeconomic reform all possessed implications for the liberal theory of governance in the future. So, too, would the loss of the presidency in the 1968 elections and the emergence of new liberal power bases in a partially "reformed" Congress.

## Notes

1. "The Smell of Oil," *New Republic* 115 (5 August 1946): 12; Ernest R. Bartley, *The Tidelands Oil Controversy* (Austin: University of Texas Press, 1953), esp. chaps. 8–9.

2. Bartley, *Tidelands Oil*, chaps. 10–15. More detailed discussion of this case appears in chap. 11 of this book.

3. Alonzo L. Hamby, *Beyond the New Deal* (New York: Columbia University Press, 1973), 76–78; James T. Patterson, *Mr. Republican* (Boston: Houghton Mifflin, 1972), 306–307.

4. "The Question of Federal or State Control of the Employment Services," *Congressional Digest* 25 (April 1946): 99–128; Sidney M. Milkis, *The President and the Parties* (New York: Oxford University Press, 1993), 151–159; "The Controversy in Congress over Federal 'Civil Rights' Proposals," *Congressional Digest* 29 (February 1950) 37–64; "The Proposal for a Federal Compulsory Insurance System for Citizens' Medical Care," *Congressional Digest* 25 (August–September 1946): 193–224; Hamby, *Beyond the New Deal*, chaps. 13 and 14.

5. "Should the State Public School Systems Be Subsidized by Federal Funds?" *Congressional Digest* 25 (February 1946), 35–64.

6. See table 9.1 for this and other congressional votes referred to in the text. Henry Steele Commager, "Only Two Terms for a President?" *New York Times Magazine,* 27 April 1947, 48; Richard Neuberger, "Let's Limit All Terms of Office!" *New Republic* 23 June 1952, 10.

7. James L. Sundquist, *The Decline and Resurgence of Congress* (Washington: Brookings Institution, 1981), 179–182; *ADA World* (September 1950), Congressional Supplement; *Colegrove v. Green,* 328 U.S. 549 (1946). See the congressional voting patterns in table 9.1.

8. Milkis, *President and the Parties*, 158; Hamby, *Beyond the New Deal* , 62–64.

9. Milkis, *President and the Parties*, 160; Arthur M. Schlesinger Jr., *The Imperial presidency* (New York: Popular Library, 1973), 154–155.

10. On the liberal endorsement of the initial Korean commitment, see Hamby, *Beyond the New Deal*, 403–405; on troops to Europe, see Schlesinger, *Imperial Presidency*, 139–142; on executive agreements, Duane Tananbaum, *The Bricker Amendment Controversy* (Ithaca, NY: Cornell University Press, 1988), chap. 4; on the MacArthur firing, Hamby, *Beyond the New Deal, 425*. Key congressional votes are in table 9.1.

11. "Steel—What Next, Mr. President?" *New Republic* 128 (21 April 1952): 5; "Steel and Stabilization," *Nation* 174 (19 April 1952): 360; "Seizure—Threat against Labor," *Nation* 174 (10 May 1952): 443–444; Hamby, *Beyond the New Deal*, 454–458; Schlesinger, *Imperial Presidency, 144–152*.

12. Glendon Schubert, *The Judicial Mind* (Evanston, IL: Northwestern University Press, 1965), 99–157; Arthur M. Schlesinger Jr., "The Supreme Court: 1947," *Fortune* 35 (January 1947): 73–79, 201–202, 204, 206, 211–212.

13. Tananbaum, *Bricker Amendment*, chaps. 1–3.

14. Tananbaum, *Bricker Amendment,* chaps. 4–11. However, many liberals felt the Eisenhower administration conceded too much on international human rights in order to "win" on the Bricker amendment.

15. Wilfred E. Binkley, "Andrew Jackson's Defiance," *New Republic* 130 (14 June 1954): 16–17; TRB, "Washington Wire," *New Republic* 130 (24 May 1954): 2; Telford Taylor, "Congress vs. the President," *ADA World*, March 1954, 2; Taylor, *Grand Inquest* (New York: Simon & Schuster, 1955), 133; Schlesinger, *Imperial Presidency, 159*.

16. Major roll-call votes where liberals were more supportive of Eisenhower administration presidential/executive powers than conservatives include the Kerr Senate amendment on reciprocal trade (22 July 1958), the Reed motion in the House on reciprocal trade (11 June 1958), and the Knowland Senate foreign aid amendment (5 June 1958). All are discussed by the *New Republic,* 22 September 1958.

17. Eisenhower's views on Warren and the *Brown* decision are discussed by Herbert S. Parmet, *Eisenhower and the American Crusades* (New York: Macmillan, 1972), 438–439. For Eisenhower's hesitancy about civil liberties activism, see Walter F. Murphy, *Congress and the Court* (Chicago: University of Chicago Press, 1962), 117. For the general liberal shift to support judicial activism, see Murphy, *Congress and the Court*, 76, and Christopher Wolfe, *The Rise of Modern Judicial Review* (Lanham, MD: Rowman & Littlefield, 1994), chap. 12.

18. G. Theodore Mitau, *Decade of Decision* (New York: Charles Scribner's Sons, 1967), 32–34; Murphy, *Congress and the Court*, 154–169.

19. Murphy, *Congress and the Court, 182–217*; C. Herman Pritchett, *Congress versus the Supreme Court, 1957–1960* (New York: DeCapo Press, 1973), chap. 6; table 9.1.

20. The Eisenhower veto message is quoted in James L. Sundquist, *Politics and Policy* (Washington: Brookings Institution, 1968), 323.

21. John Morton Blum, "Congress and the President," *New Republic* 144 (9

January 1961): 9–10; "TRB from Washington," *New Republic* 144 (6 March 1961): 2; Alan Rosenthal, "Could Kennedy Budge the Congress?" *New Republic* 148 (4 May 1963): 13–15; James MacGregor Burns, *The Deadlock of Democracy* (Englewood Cliffs, NJ: Prentice-Hall, 1963), chaps. 13–14.

22.  Arthur M. Schlesinger Jr., *A Thousand Days* (New York: Fawcett Crest, 1965), 857–858; Richard Reeves, *President Kennedy* (New York: Simon & Schuster, 1993), 432; Bruce Miroff, *Pragmatic Illusions* (N.Y: David McKay, 1976), 244.

23.  Louis Koenig, "More Power to the President (Not Less)," *New York Times Magazine*, 3 January 1965, 7, 42–43, 45–46; Gerald Johnson, "The President and His Power," *New Republic*, 28 November 1964, 19–20; James MacGregor Burns, *Presidential Government* (Boston: Houghton Mifflin, 1965), 312–313, 329.

24.  On the civil rights federalist disputes, see Allen J. Matusow, *The Unraveling of America* (New York: Harper & Row, 1984), 66–67, 71–74; Schlesinger, *A Thousand Days*, 870–873; and Burke Marshall, *Federalism and Civil Rights* (New York: Columbia University Press, 1964). On the comparison with the 1930s, cooperative federalism, and bypassing, see David B. Robertson and Dennis R. Judd, *The Development of American Public Policy* (Glenview, IL: Scott, Foresman, 1989), 114–116, 134–149; and Matusow, *Unraveling*, chap. 9.

25.  Mitau, *Decade of Decision*, covers all of these topics thoroughly.

26.  Schlesinger, "The Supreme Court: 1947," 73–79; Henry Steele Commager, "Presidential Power: The Issue Analyzed," *New York Times Magazine*, 14 January 1951, 11, 23; Henry Steele Commager, "The Perilous Folly of Senator Bricker," *Reporter* 146 (13 October 1953): 12–17; Marshall, *Federalism and Civil Rights;* Wolfe, *Judicial Activism*, 291; Philip B. Kurland, *The Constitution and the Warren Court* (Chicago: University of Chicago Press, 1970), 43.

27.  Christopher Jencks, "Why Bail Out the States?" *New Republic* 151 (12 December 1964): 8; William H. Riker, *Federalism: Origin, Operation, Significance* (Boston: Little, Brown, 1964), 152–153; Robertson and Judd, *American Public Policy*, 134–149; Matusow, *Unraveling*, chap. 9.

28.  Theodore J. Lowi, *The End of Liberalism*, 2d ed. (New York: W. W. Norton, 1979), esp. 276; Grant McConnell, *Private Power and American Democracy* (New York: Vintage, 1966), esp. chap. 10.

29.  Herman Finer, *The Presidency: Crisis and Regeneration* (Chicago: University of Chicago Press, 1960), esp. chap. 6; "Wider War," *New York Times*, 6 August 1964, 28.

30.  Schubert, *Judicial Mind*, 99–159; Wolfe, *Judicial Activism*, chap. 12.

# 10

# The Conservative Theory of Governance

---

If the liberals maintained their theory of governance largely intact for two decades after World War II, so, too, did the conservatives. The harmony on institutional prescriptions within the conservative coalition occurred despite the rising consciousness after 1945 of conservative intellectual bifurcation along libertarian-traditionalist lines and the marked policy cleavages over foreign policy and civil rights.

The New Deal–era conservative theory of governance had taken shape when conservatives were primarily libertarian, opposed global interventionism, and ignored any black civil rights claims that went beyond restrictions on lynching and mild support of voting rights. Such intellectual and public policy inclinations generally had meshed well with a governance theory emphasizing original intent and strict construction of the Consititution, states' rights, checks and balances, a modified nightwatchman state, and judicial invalidation of executive or legislative departures from "traditional" constitutionalism. The conservatives of the 1930s who were more traditionalist than libertarian had also found the governance theory generally compatible with their beliefs, though it was at least questionable whether national security and domestic order could be sustained while implementing the theory strictly.

Postwar libertarian-traditionalist lines were drawn somewhat more sharply than before. Placing even more potential strain on conservative harmony on governance issues were the 1945–55 conflict over foreign policy and the 1954–66 division over civil rights policy. Regarding the former, such defenders of neoisolationism as Robert Taft, Felix Morley, and Murray Rothbard continued to be wary of American overseas involvement. Though they detested Communism as the greatest threat to liberty, they also feared big government in the United States. A desire to avoid presidential government, enlargement of the administrative state, and centralization of authority restrained them from embracing a global anti-Communist crusade. On the other hand, the liberationist foreign policies of leaders such as James Burnham, William F. Buckley, and Barry Goldwater seemed to necessitate strong presidential leadership (energy, unity, speed, and secrecy being essential to mount a successful effort to roll back Communism globally), a large defense establishment, and a good deal of centralization of authority. Nonetheless, the liberationist conservatives of 1945–66 maintained strong rhetorical support for congressionally centered checks and balances, a limited administrative state, and states' rights. Similarly, on civil rights, the potential for policy-driven sharp splits in conservative governance approaches generally did not spread beyond specific measures. Those conservatives, such as Goldwater, Buckley, and James Kilpatrick, who favored little or no national government action on the subject, of course found the conservative governance theory congenial to their policy inclinations. However, even those conservatives, such as Everett Dirksen and the *Chicago Tribune* editorialists, who came to embrace a broadened national commitment on black civil rights, usually maintained strong verbal support for states' rights generally and other aspects of the long-term governance theory.[1]

A likely reason for the continuing rhetorical unity among conservatives on their theory of governance lay in the power structures discussed in chapter 8. Despite differences over intellectual foundations and programmatic policies, almost all conservatives in all camps perceived that the presidency, the national executive bureaucracy, and increasingly the federal courts had become *institutionally* linked to the liberal coalition and its values. Seeing no short-term possibility for reversing that linkage, and maintaining continuity with the past and their conservative colleagues by sustaining most of the governance theory intact, they continued their institutional advocacy of the past, making some small adjustments on specific policy matters in particular situations and on the Supreme Court generally as these seemed appropriate to them.

Therefore, just as the liberal coalition made only a few verbal alterations in its theory of governance, primarily in the judicial realm, the same was true of the conservative movement between 1945 and 1966. There, too, the most obvious change lay in the area of attitudes toward the Supreme Court. The rising hostility of conservatives to the Court and their efforts to curb its liberal judicial activism offered a sufficiently dramatic contrast to past conservative deference to the judiciary that many felt called upon to seek to justify the apparent change. On the other hand, a growing conservative willingness, especially as the liberationist conservatives gained predominance in the movement, to add to the defense establishment and even accept strong presidential powers in the international realm rarely had much impact on conservatives' verbal support for antibureaucratic tirades or congressionally centered checks and balances until after 1966.

## The Conservative Governance Theory in the Truman Years

Political leaders such as Robert Taft and intellectuals like Felix Morley had set the course for the conservatives' institutional prescriptions in the 1930s and continued to pursue it with marked consistency after 1945. Most other conservatives joined them. The American Bar Association's leadership was typical. Surveying the political scene in February 1945, the new president of the association, David Simmons, saw the need to return America to the "republican form of government, with checks and balances" that had been established by the framers. Redistribution of national government power "back to the several states and to the people at home" seemed highly desirable to Simmons but "at the moment hardly feasible." However, Congress should, in his view, "reestablish the checks and balances in our government and thus prevent the misuse of that power." By January 1947, the *American Bar Association Journal* had decided that the time was ripe to mount a major political effort on behalf of states' rights, as well as for strict construction, a strengthened Congress, and a congressionally checked administrative state reduced in size. Uncertain what to do about the Supreme Court, the *Journal* essentially urged repentance and improved behavior. "The Supreme Court, which has by judicial legislation caused or cleared the way for much of the centralization, can undo much that it has done and start America on the long road back to government according to the constitutional pattern."[2]

Specific modes for effecting conservative institutional prescriptions were becoming clear in 1945 and 1946. Besides fighting against the Truman administration's proposals for national health insurance, a national Fair Employment Practices Commission with enforcement powers, and other measures that would enhance national government powers over the states and/or executive powers over the legislature, conservatives initiated efforts to weaken federal price controls and to return the employment services to the state governments, from which they had been transferred to the national level in December 1941, at the request of President Roosevelt. Enjoying success in these endeavors, they hoped to use their power in Congress to prevent the federal government from gaining control of tidelands oil from the states. On this matter, however, they encountered difficulties from the Supreme Court and were unable to override President Truman's veto of their measure. Thus, the stage was set for a prolonged states' rights battle pitting conservatives against liberals from 1945 into 1953.[3]

Truman's proposed general federal aid to public education raised for most conservatives yet another states' rights issue. Although a few prominent conservatives, notably Senate leader Robert Taft, endorsed a moderate course entailing some limited federal aid, most conservatives took a strong stance against Truman's proposals, arguing that education was an area reserved for state control by the Tenth Amendment to the Constitution. Inside the House of Representatives' Rules Committee, a bastion of strength for the conservative coalition, conservatives combined with some Catholic opponents of Truman's bill (who disliked its noninclusion of aid to parochial schools) to kill the measure.[4]

In the realm of the administrative state, conservatives continued to engage in loud denunciations of bureaucracy (or "burocracy," as Colonel McCormick of the *Chicago Tribune* insisted on spelling it), although the American Bar Association, and perhaps others, were reassured that congressional-presidential concurrence on the Administrative Procedures Act of 1946 had at least made a "good beginning" at reining in bureaucratic tyranny. Most conservatives vehemently opposed the Truman administration's refusal to yield executive-branch information to congressional investigative committees. Young Representative Richard Nixon was, in fact, among those opposing Truman's claim of what came to be termed "executive privilege," insisting that "it cannot stand from a constitutional standpoint." Conservatives in the House of Representatives voted by a 90 percent–10 percent margin in favor of the Hoffman resolution demanding full executive disclosure and won House passage of the measure in May 1948, but they failed to carry the day in the Senate. Despite continuing conservative hostility to the administrative state apparatus, when the Hoover Commission, chaired by former president (and conservative) Herbert Hoover, made a 1949 report broadly accepting the administrative state and presidential direction of it, few conservatives attacked the report. The presence of Hoover gave the report some legitimacy in conservative eyes, as did its emphasis on achieving "economy and efficiency" in administration. Though some analysts see the conservative acceptance of the Hoover Commission Report of 1949 as a turning point, that is probably an exaggeration in light of subsequent conservative attacks on the administrative-state concept that endured through the 1950s and 1960s.[5]

An early postwar governance initiative by the conservative movement aimed against presidential government was the successful drive to restrict the president to two elective terms. Backed unanimously in 1947 by both Senate and House conservatives, who remembered Roosevelt's four terms with resentment and bitterness, this resolution in 1951 became the Twenty-second Amendment to the Constitution. Foreign military policy also became a matter of sharp conservative criticism. Although most conservatives initially acquiesced in Truman's dispatch of troops to Korean combat in 1950 without congressional consultation or a request for a declaration of war, many soon joined Taft in accusing the president of acting in Korea "without authority of law." In 1951, when Truman sent additional troops to Europe on his own authority, most conservatives exploded with rage. The ensuing "Great Debate" in the Senate captured national attention. Taft opened the debate with a ringing attack on "secret executive agreements" that had brought the United States "to danger and disaster." In the end, the most the conservatives could enact, however, was a "sense of the Senate" resolution that approved the sending of the troops to Europe but insisted that no additional troops could be dispatched by the president "without further congressional approval."[6]

Two other Truman exercises of presidential powers excited especially vehement conservative condemnations: his firing of General MacArthur and his seizure of the steel industry. While Taft and some others conceded that Truman as commander-in-chief did possess the constitutional power to remove the general, most of the conservative movement went to extremes in opposing the action, with the *Chicago Tribune,* Senator Joseph McCarthy, and Senator William Jenner calling for Truman's immediate impeachment and removal from office. The steel seizure provoked even more nearly unanimous conservative opposition, this time on much more solid constitutional grounds than in the case of the MacArthur firing. Columnist David Lawrence perceived "a Constitutional crisis of great magnitude." Senator John Bricker, Taft's conservative Ohio colleague, characterized Truman's justifications for his actions to be "totalitarian philosophy." Senator Richard Russell, a leading Southern conservative who had defended Truman on the removal of MacArthur, denounced the steel seizure as establishing "a pattern that a potential dictator later on could follow and use as a precedent." Taft concurred, in almost identical language. When the Supreme Court overruled Truman's actions, conservatives breathed a collective sigh of relief.[7]

At the time of the steel-seizure controversy in 1952, congressional hearings were just getting under way on a proposed constitutional amendment, authored by Senator Bricker, who was cooperating with much of the leadership of the American Bar Association in the endeavor. This proposal tied together conservative concerns about preservation of the "traditional"

Constitution, states' rights, congressionally centered checks and balances, and distrust of both the administrative state and the Supreme Court. For good measure, it also appealed to American nationalistic feelings and conservative fears of the United Nations and potential world government as threats to the Constitution and the laws made under it. By tapping all dimensions of the conservative theory of governance and other conservative sentiments, too, the proposed amendment would be at the center of conservative-liberal controversy for the next two years. At its heart were provisions to restrict presidential use of executive agreements as substitutes for treaties, prevent either treaties or executive agreements from abridging any constitutionally guaranteed freedoms, and protect state laws against treaties or executive agreements. As far as the states were concerned, conservative fears were that a 1920 Supreme Court precedent for using a treaty to overrule state law might be employed by the current High Bench to apply such documents as the United Nations charter or other international agreements to the same effect. Thus, anti–United Nations sentiments merged with the United States governance issues for most of the conservative coalition. Because of the complexity of the proposed amendment and several possible variations of it, no congressional action was taken in 1952. Therefore, the Bricker amendment was near the top of the agenda as the new Eisenhower administration took office on 20 January 1953.[8]

### The Eisenhower Administration
### and the Conservative Governance Theory

Although most Republican conservatives had preferred Taft for the party's presidential nomination in 1952, and although both they and the conservative Southern Democrats distrusted Eisenhower's links to such Eastern moderates as Henry Cabot Lodge, Herbert Brownell, and Thomas E. Dewey, the new president's rhetoric on governance matters and the language of the 1952 Republican platform on which he ran seemed to offer hope to the conservative coalition. Eisenhower had personally pledged to grant the states control over tidelands oil and often used decentralist rhetoric in his campaign. The platform had made several states' rights pledges, the broadest being: "We believe that it is the primary responsibility of each State to order and control its own domestic institutions, and that this power, reserved to the states, is essential to the maintenance of our Federal Republic." With specific reference to education, it had stated: "The responsibility for sustaining this system of popular education has always rested upon the local communities and the states. We subscribe fully to this principle." Other states' rights pledges had been scattered through the platform, reassuring conservatives. Moreover, Eisenhower himself frequently called for "restoring the balance" between president and Congress and ending "executive usurpations of power" and had spoken of the need to "restore Congress to its rightful place in the government." He even declined to present Congress with a legislative program at the outset of his presidency, arguing that Congress should take the legislative lead (though this stance did not last long).[9]

As president, Eisenhower usually took positions on federalism issues well to the right of the liberal coalition, as in his stance on tidelands oil, his total rejection of national health insurance, his veto on states' rights grounds of such measures as area redevelopment and expanded federal aid for sewage treatment plants, and his expressed hopes (largely unfulfilled) to decentralize functions and resources to the states—a matter on which he appointed the Kestnbaum Commission and later a joint federal-state action committee. Even so, he did not see the merit of the Bricker amendment's effort to protect state laws from the effects of treaties or executive agreements. Privately, he expressed fears that the amendment would seriously disrupt American international trade because it would render the federal government incapable of protecting foreigners' property against state expropriation or eminent domain proceedings. Secretary of State John Foster Dulles voiced the concern that the Bricker amendment "cuts the treaty power back to what it was under the Articles of Confederation."[10]

If the Eisenhower administration rejected the states' rights aspects of the Bricker amendment, it even more vehemently opposed the provisions aimed at curtailing executive powers vis-à-vis Congress. Although Eisenhower was more deferential to Congress than Truman or Roosevelt or than his successors, he believed that the Bricker amendment would "cripple executive power to the point that we become helpless in world affairs." Therefore, on both federalist and executive-power grounds, Eisenhower and his administration moved into opposition to what was at the outset a virtually united conservative movement.[11]

At the time that the Eisenhower administration announced its determination to block the Bricker amendment, Senate Joint Resolution l, as it was known, already enjoyed the sponsorship of sixty-four senators, mostly conservatives. If these all voted for it—a reasonable assumption—then it would be assured of the two-thirds majority required for Senate approval. It never achieved that endorsement, however. The Eisenhower administration, and Eisenhower himself (employing his renowned "hidden-hand" techniques), pried off enough of the original sponsors (including one-third of the conservatives) to defeat the measure, even in a watered-down form, in February 1954, with the active assistance of most of the liberal coalition. In the final votes, 67 percent of the Senate conservatives voted for Bricker's resolution; and 78 percent of them endorsed a milder version of it offered by Senator Walter George. But their effort was to no avail. The George substitute failed by one vote to obtain the requisite two-thirds majority. Although Bricker and his backers made further efforts over the next several years to revive the Bricker amendment, it was dead—killed through the efforts of a Republican administration, which now appeared insufficiently conservative, even liberal, to much of the conservative coalition.[12]

The Bricker amendment controversy was not the only governance question to divide the conservative movement from the Eisenhower administration. When a conservative-dominated Senate investigative committee in 1954 demanded executive branch information, the Eisenhower administration responded with what a leading historian has termed "the most absolute assertion of presidential right to withhold information from Congress ever uttered to that day in American history." Nor was this an isolated incident. Articulating a doctrine that Attorney General William Rogers termed "executive privilege," the Eisenhower administration refused information to Congress on that basis at least forty-four times.[13]

Most of the conservative movement reacted in outrage to the sweeping claims of executive privilege. The *Chicago Tribune* saw it as an issue of both presidential government and the administrative state: "If, on the claim of executive privilege, the administration can suppress anything unfavorable to it, while disseminating thru [sic] thousands of press agents what redounds to its credit, the public is cheated." Referring to the administrative state apparatus, the *Tribune* deplored the fact that "the executive department has proliferated until it now numbers more than 2 million civilian employees. Its control by Congress is tenuous at best." In subsequent executive privilege disputes, the new *National Review* termed the Eisenhower administration's actions an "arresting demonstration of a bureaucracy in almost complete control, of a massive and arrogant contempt, by the Executive, for the legislature." Fusionist conservative philosopher Frank Meyer saw it as part of a "revolt against Congress" and called the Eisenhower administration's use of executive privilege "outrageous."[14]

Increasing conservative disenchantment with the Supreme Court, including Eisenhower's appointees Chief Justice Earl Warren and Associate Justice William Brennan, also eventually brought much of the conservative movement into another governance clash with the administration. The unanimous *Brown v. Board of Education* school desegregation decision handed down by Warren in May 1954 badly divided the conservative movement, in contrast to the liberals, who united behind it. However, later civil liberties and rights decisions were to unite most conservatives—in strong opposition to the Court.

Registering vehement objections to the *Brown* decision were Republican senator and future presidential candidate Barry Goldwater, William F. Buckley, the *National Review* and most of its staff and writers, and, of course, an array of white Southerners, mainly Democrats but mainly part of the conservative coalition. All of these agreed that the decision was improper because of its disregard for original intent (evidenced by the approval of segregated schools in the District of Columbia by the same Congress that in 1868 had drafted the Fourteenth Amendment) and its injection of the national government into an area (public education) that the Tenth Amendment reserved, in their view, for the states alone. Eisenhower himself harbored a private distaste for the *Brown* decision, insisting that it would "set back progress in the South," but he did not make these views public. Some conservatives pushed states' rights ideas in reaction to *Brown* much further than others. Much of the Southern contingent rejuvenated the nineteenth-century John C. Calhoun doctrine of interposition, whereby it was asserted that state governments could interpose their authority between their citizens and the federal govenment when they disagreed with national actions on constitutional grounds. The *National Review* and long-time conservative federalism theorist Felix Morley also warmly endorsed interposition. Furthermore, many went beyond even these arguments to assert white supremacy—a position that Goldwater, among many others, refused to endorse.[15]

At the same time, many other conservatives, largely Northern Republicans, endorsed the *Brown* decision and the theory of governance that it embodied, at least on the issue of school desegration and the federal government. Typical was the *Chicago Tribune,* which declared that "the state governments, north and south, must regard all men as created equal so far as the opportunities at the disposal of the state are concerned. That idea may appear dangerously novel to some, but the Supreme Court didn't invent it. Indeed, they can be said to have borrowed it from a distinguished Virginian named Thomas Jefferson." The *Tribune,* long a foe of federal aid to education on states' rights grounds, even suggested that it might be able to endorse ("very tentatively") some federal grants or loans to state and local school systems "to ease the transition." The majority of the Northern Republicans in Congress, probably reflecting public opinion polls in the North, generally fell in line with the *Tribune*'s position.[16]

When Eisenhower in 1957 felt compelled to enforce a federal court order to desegregate Central High School in Little Rock, Arkansas, by federalizing the Arkansas National Guard and dispatching regular military forces as well, his actions predictably split the conservative coalition again. Raising the specter of presidential dictatorship, the *National Review* editorialized that Eisenhower's behavior showed "that we are a nation in which one man, and that man, the prisoner of the nation's most dangerous and extreme Liberal ideologues, is powerful enough, and power-hungry enough, to trample under foot the nation's oldest legal tradition, namely: that of the division of power between the federal government and the states." In contrast, Senator William Knowland of California, the Senate Republican leader, probably spoke for most non-Southern congressional conservatives in declaring that Eisenhower "should have the support of the entire nation." As Knowland phrased it, "When mob violence or nullification undermines our American system anywhere, it endangers the whole structure everywhere."[17]

If the institutional recommendations of conservatives concerning federalism and presidential powers varied in regard to black civil rights issues, they came to be increasingly unified on the matter of the Supreme Court itself. During the 1940s and early 1950s, there was considerable conservative discontent with the Supreme Court, evident in American Bar Association criticisms of it for "judicial legislation," references to it as the "New Deal Court," and criticisms of its judgment by most backers of the Bricker amendment and the state claims to tidelands oil. Conservative columnist David Lawrence had even launched an unsuccessful 1947 campaign to amend the Constitution to replace life tenure for justices with ten-year terms. After the *Brown* decision, conservative criticisms escalated sharply. But it was a series of High Court civil liberties decisions between 1955 and 1957, including the *Watkins v. United States* (1957) restrictions on congressional investigatory powers, that galvanized the conservative coalition into major actions against the Supreme Court.[18]

The most direct and potentially far-reaching conservative assault on the High Bench was the effort, led by Republican Senator William Jenner of Indiana in 1957 and 1958, to restrict its appellate jurisdiction. Since this Court-curbing measure bore some resemblance to Franklin Roosevelt's Court-packing effort of the 1930s, many conservatives took pains to draw a distinction, fearful of being seen as opportunists since their movement had defended the High Court so strenuously in 1937. Brent Bozell, brother-in-law of William F. Buckley and himself a leading conservative intellectual, insisted that there was no inconsistency: "Conservatives opposed efforts [in 1937] to force the Court to deviate from the Constitution. Today, the Supreme Court is *violating* the Constitution in case after case. Senator Jenner's bill seeks to enforce judicial observance of the Constitution. The common denominator in the two situations is allegiance to the Constitution."[19]

Unconvinced of the merits of the Jenner endeavor, the Eisenhower administration announced its opposition, once again moving into alliance with the liberal coalition on a major institutional issue. Several pillars of the conservative establishment, including the *Chicago Tribune* and the American Bar Association, also declined to support Jenner. In the Senate, however, 89 percent of the conservatives present and voting cast their votes in favor of a modified version that would still have restricted Supreme Court jurisdiction, though less extensively than in Jenner's original measure. Liberals and moderates killed the proposed legislation in a close 49-41 vote.[20]

Gathering wider support than the Jenner bill, but also facing the combined opposition of the Eisenhower administration and the liberal coalition, was another governance measure, the Smith bill, House Resolution 3. Sponsored by conservative Democratic Representative Howard W. Smith of Virginia, it focused on restoring states' rights allegedly trampled by Court decisions, rather than on altering the Supreme Court's appellate jurisdiction. By instructing the Supreme Court to refrain from using the federal preemption doctrine to negate state laws without the expressed wish of Congress to preempt, it represented a slap at the High Bench but was centered primarily on states' rights and congressional prerogatives. The American Bar Association applauded it, as did the National Association of Manufacturers, the United States Chamber of Commerce, the American Farm Bureau Federation, and an array of other conservative interest groups. In the House of Representatives, the Smith Bill won an overwhelming 97 percent of the conservatives' voting support in July 1958 and gained passage (with a repeat performance and similar pattern in 1959). In the Senate, despite the positive votes of 89 percent of the conservatives present and voting, the measure lost by a one-vote margin. Once again, a major conservative institutional "reform" had been defeated by the Eisenhower administration–liberal coalition combination, though Walter Murphy has concluded that the Warren Court made a "tactical withdrawal" for the next few years in the face of strong conservative opposition.[21]

As the Eisenhower administration drew to a close, conservatives could look back with some satisfaction on the administration's frequent inclinations toward conservative governance theory on federalism and presidential government. Perhaps, too, they derived some pleasure from the partial (but temporary) retreat by the Warren Court. However, on the major controversies concerning governance issues, conservatives had been bitterly disappointed, losing often on close votes, owing to hostility from the Eisenhower administration. And on the civil rights controversies, they had divided sharply among themselves concerning the proper interpretation of the Constitution and the proper extent of states' rights and presidential powers.

### The Conservative Governance Theory in the Kennedy-Johnson Years to 1966

The conservatives' support for states' rights continued to appear often during the Kennedy-Johnson years. Sometimes the conservatives were able to block liberals' efforts to move in a centralizing direction, as on the Kennedy administration's measure to provide federal aid to elementary and secondary public schools, where the events of the Truman-era struggle were largely replayed. At other times, the conservative coalition was able to compel a compromise, as on a 1964 amendment to permit state governors to veto most antipoverty projects within their own states. In both of these instances, however, Lyndon Johnson and the larger than usual congressional liberal contingent in 1965 were able to enact cooperative federalist measures that were more centralized than most conservatives could accept.[22]

Another major states' rights issue that united most conservatives in this period was reapportionment. Back in 1946, the Supreme Court had declined to rule on whether the Fourteenth Amendment required legislative apportionment on the basis of one person, one vote, declaring this to be a political question to be worked out among state politicians. By 1962, however, the Court majority saw the matter differently and, in *Baker v. Carr* and several subsequent decisions, made state election districts subject to close federal court scrutiny and to national standards of equality. The result was to be massive redistricting for many state legislatures, as well as for the U.S. House of Representatives, in order to comply with the new national requirements. The conservative coalition swung quickly into action, at first throwing its support in 1964 behind a bill authored by conservative Democratic Representative William Tuck of Virginia. Like the Jenner bill of 1958, the Tuck bill sought to restrict the jurisdiction of the Supreme Court; but it also aimed to extend this restriction on state apportionment matters to the entire federal court system. In the House of Representatives, 94 percent of the conservatives present and voting backed the measure; and it passed the House in August 1964. However, as in 1958, the conservative coalition split on the matter of altering judicial jurisdiction. Once again, the American Bar Association came out in strong opposition to the idea. In the Senate, where there was already talk of supporting a constitutional amendment instead of the Tuck bill, 40 percent of the conservatives defected on the crucial vote on the measure, and the Tuck bill went down to defeat.[23]

Next, Republican Senator Everett Dirksen of Illinois, who had opposed the Tuck bill, stepped forward with another approach to protect states' rights (and reapportionment methods that had long sustained conservative power): a constitutional amendment to allow the states to consider factors other than population in the apportionment of one legislative chamber. Almost the whole array of conservative interest groups now endorsed this proposal, as did the Republican party platform of 1964, and it won unanimous support from Senate Republicans. Nonetheless, the measure fell seven votes short of the requisite two-thirds majority. Reapportionment of the state legislatures and of the U.S. House of Representatives proceeded. However, because of conservative strength in the fast-growing suburbs, the new districting did less damage to conservative power bases than many in the movement had feared.[24]

During these years, probably the most positive development for advocates of the conservative theory of governance, now modified to include a strong judicial restraint plank, was the Goldwater presidential campaign of 1964. Far more than any other presidential candidate of the modern era, Goldwater emphasized his theory of governance, and his rhetoric matched the conservative institutional prescriptions point for point.

Goldwater was a strong proponent of original intent as a guide in matters of constitutional interpretation. "The Constitution is what its authors intended it to be and said it was," he declared, "not what the Supreme Court says it is. If we condone the practice of substituting our own intentions for those of the Constitution's framers, we reject, in effect, the principle of Constitutional government: we endorse a rule of men, not of laws." He was equally vehement about decentralization to the state governments. "States' rights is no mere slogan," he proclaimed. "It is the backbone of our Constitutional system." And he very specifically applied that doctrine in rejecting federal aid to education, the *Brown* decision, the Civil Rights Act of 1964 (particularly its equal-employment and public-accommodation guarantees), and a variety of other programs. Nor was cooperative federalism a satisfactory compromise in Goldwater's eyes. He condemned federal grants-in-aid, widely used since the 1930s, as no more than "a mixture of blackmail and bribery." He deplored "the steady accumulation of massive power in the hands of national bureaucrats" and called for drastic reductions in both the functions and size of the administrative state apparatus. As for the presidential office that he was seeking, "Some of the current worship of powerful executives may come from those who admire strength and accomplishment of any sort. Others hail the display of Presidential strength . . . simply because they approve of the result reached by the use of power. This is nothing less than the totalitarian philosophy that the end justifies the means." Goldwater was having none of it. He regretted that "the power of Congress to initiate legislation has slowly passed to the Executive" and pledged to reverse the trend toward presidential government. Goldwater had enthusiastically supported the Jenner bill aimed at curbing the Supreme Court's jurisdiction. The High Court's "decisions have clearly shown that it has no disposition whatever to support the states or the Congress against the Executive or to prevent the Congress from abdicating more and more of its powers—despite the allocation of those powers by the Constitution itself," he declared. Goldwater's assessment was: "Inside the federal government, both the executive and judicial branches have roamed far outside their constitutional boundary lines." He pledged to make things right again.[25]

Though Goldwater suffered a crushing defeat in the 1964 general election, taking many Republican congressional candidates down with him, his campaign gave the conservatives a strong foothold in the presidential Republican party that they had previously lacked, articulated their theory of governance and the rest of their ideology consistently, and brought Ronald Reagan on the national political stage as a conservative leader for the future.

Despite his consistent reference to the conservative theory of governance in his rhetoric, however, Goldwater—like Burnham, Buckley, Reagan, and most others who dominated conservatism in the 1960s and later—favored a highly interventionist American national security/foreign policy aimed at vanquishing Communism around the world, which seemed virtually to require presidential leadership of defense and foreign policy, a national security administrative state bureaucracy of enormous magnitude, and considerable centralization in practice. Already by the mid-1950s, conservatives had endorsed broad grants of Cold War authority to the president and had supported what some observers termed the military-industrial complex, including a large defense bureaucracy, by their congressional votes and their often silent acquiescence. These patterns continued in the Kennedy-Johnson years. Not a single conservative member of Congress raised a voice or cast a vote against the August 1964 Gulf of Tonkin resolution granting the president a blank check to take "all necessary measures" in Vietnam. Outside Congress, the *Chicago Tribune*, heir to an older, more libertarian, more isolationist conservative tradition, sounded a rare conservative alarm, based on the conservative theory of governance, in opposition to the resolution:

> Congress and the American people have developed a considerable tolerance for military blank checks. They have also developed a remarkable apathy toward the constitutional mandate that only Congress shall have the power to declare war. . . . innovations in the exercise of the war power deal with as momentous a subject as the Constitution treats, and innovations there can lead to innovations elsewhere, with a restricting and stifling effect upon liberty.[26]

By the early 1970s, Goldwater himself, long-time advocate of congressionally centered checks and balances and vigorous denouncer of those who treated institutions as means toward ends, would be defending Richard Nixon's imperial presidency and attacking most congressional efforts to curb it. His rhetoric would be reflective of his policy goals. Like Goldwater, many conservatives would soon be shifting their governance stances, too.

## Conservative Consensus and Discord

As the array of institutional liberal-conservative struggles between 1945 and 1966 and Goldwater's 1964 positions indicated, most of the conservative coalition of the postwar period supported a theory of governance that stressed strict constitutional construction and respect for original intent, decentralized federalism with a focus on states' rights, a limited administrative state that was more oriented toward Congress than liberals thought appropriate, congressionally centered checks and balances, and a Supreme Court wedded to strict construction and original intent and operating on principles of judicial restraint, at least in most spheres where it had been active since 1937.

Yet lip service to these institutional ideals by almost all conservatives did not always translate into agreement on particular courses of action. Slogans often obscured the fact that different conservatives took positions at various points on what were really continuums with regard to each major institutional issue.

## Constitutional Immutability

"Strict construction" and "original intent" were the terms most widely used by conservatives of the period to describe what they viewed as proper constitutional jurisprudence. No member of the Supreme Court in the 1950s or 1960s articulated a position as far toward the inflexibility end of the continuum as Justice Sutherland, and sometimes Justice Roberts, had done in the 1930s, but that might well reflect the fact that there were no real movement conservatives on the Supreme Court in the postwar period. The impression gained from reading conservative treatises on the subject, ranging from those of 1945–46 American Bar Association President David Simmons to those of 1964 presidential candidate Barry Goldwater, is of some slight movement away from the extreme pole, when compared with the preceding era. These two conservative leaders, however, were quite close to Sutherland. Simmons, for example, insisted that "Constitutional law means what the people wrote and intended. . . . I vigorously dissent from any theory that the law means whatever the judges say it means." Some conservatives—especially Northern congressional Republicans on civil rights matters—unquestionably favored less rigidity of interpretation than others. The editors of the *Chicago Tribune* even seemed willing, for instance, to use Jefferson's Declaration of Independence to supplement the Constitution as a basis for school desegregation—a thought doubtless horrifying to some of their fellow conservatives.[27]

## States' Rights

As in the preceding era, states' rights was a slogan to which virtually all conservatives paid obeisance. Traditionalist conservative intellectual Harry Jaffa was one of the rare exceptions. Yet some carried the principle to much greater extremes on a much wider variety of issues than others did. Almost all conservatives favored approaches that were more oriented toward the state governments than liberals did. Few were receptive to the "new-politics" liberal inclination toward decentralizing to institutions other than state or local governments. Such decentralization was neither called for by the Constitution nor associated with the traditional republican values stressed by most conservatives. Nor did it usually place power in the hands of conservatives. Almost no conservatives favored national health insurance proposals or, indeed, centralized federalism on any but black civil rights issues, the latter point being one on which conservatives were bitterly divided between Goldwater, Buckley,

Morley, and Southern Democratic conservatives on the one hand and the *Chicago Tribune* and Republican congressional leaders such as Dirksen and Charles Halleck on the other. Moreover, cooperative federalist compromises became acceptable to some conservatives, especially big businessmen and many congressional politicians, while they remained repellent to others, such as Goldwater, with his "blackmail and bribery" characterization.[28]

## A Limited Administrative State

On this dimension, conservative positions moved a little in the aggregate toward the center. Mollified by the Administrative Procedures Act of 1946, which afforded some protection against arbitrary bureaucratic edicts, reassured by Herbert Hoover's blessings on an "economic and efficient" administrative state, and cognizant of the need for a large bureaucratic apparatus to implement the conservatives' own increasingly predominant preferences in the world struggle against Communism, conservatives edged away from the nightwatchman state in practice. Nonetheless, antibureaucratic verbiage remained almost universal in the conservative camp. Moreover, many congressional conservatives, in particular, were quite intent on obtaining broad investigatory powers and in micromanaging the administration as much as possible. Conservatives such as Goldwater, Joseph McCarthy, Karl Mundt, and John McClellan were certainly less accepting of an administrative state than Herbert Hoover or many big businessmen who had experience in supervising huge bureaucracies themselves.[29]

## Congressionally Centered Checks and Balances

Only a few self-styled conservatives departed verbally from the stated goal of a check-and-balance national structure centered on Congress. The scattering who advocated presidential government, mainly Clinton Rossiter and Walter Lippmann, were scorned as nonconservatives by most in the movement. Those few who called for a legislatively oriented parliamentary or responsible-party system, such as David Lawrence and Henry Hazlitt, remained in good standing as conservatives. Even the most militant conservative proponents of a foreign policy aimed at liberating the entire Communist world and reshaping it in an American image, such as Burnham and Goldwater, were staunch proponents of a congressionally centered system. Burnham, for example, wrote an entire book on the subject in 1959, and Goldwater's views have already been discussed.

Most of the internal conservative-coalition differences on this continuum appeared on concrete measures, mainly in the foreign policy realm, as in the great debate on presidential troop commitments in 1951 or the Bricker amendment controversy. But, as previously noted, the most striking overall pattern was the growing gap from about 1955 onward between the conservatives' rhetoric and their willingness in practice to grant the president extensive powers as commander-in-chief and chief diplomat as long as the cause was clearly anti-Communist. Almost all conservatives, however, agreed that liberals' notions of the president as a tribune of a popular majority were completely inappropriate. Even those, like Willmoore Kendall, who conceded that there was a presidential majority as well as a congressional one saw congressional, "Madisonian" representation of structured communities as clearly preferable.[30]

*Judicial Restraint*

The conservatives' judicial prescriptions, while still linked to their past recommendations by their emphasis upon Court applications of the framers' intent, placed an increased stress on judicial restraint, despite the fact that no justice (not even Frankfurter, according to Harold Spaeth's empirical analysis) consistently applied it. Probably this shift reflected the conservatives' growing assessment that the Supreme Court was, by the mid-1950s, very unlikely in the foreseeable future to be conservative-activist, as the High Bench of 1890–1937 had been, in defense of property rights. As the Court's liberal activism intensified and became increasingly obnoxious to conservatives, they sought to curb it by limiting the Court's appellate jurisdiction, overturning decisions with constitutional amendments, and/or persuading the justices to engage in self-restraint by mounting attacks on their activism. David Lawrence suggested a constitutional amendment prescribing ten-year terms but won only limited support. The *Chicago Tribune* and the American Bar Association demurred on proposals to curb the Court's jurisdiction. But virtually all conservatives were united in a call for greater judicial restraint in the areas where the Court had become most active.[31]

## Conclusions

At the level of rhetorical commitment, the most marked adjustments in conservative governance theory in the postwar period were those in the judicial realm, where lingering deference to the Supreme Court gave way to a grim determination to restrain its activism. Still, old respect for the judiciary as an institution put limits on how far many conservatives would go to impose that restraint. In regard to the administrative state, there was at least marginal movement by conservatives toward the center of the spectrum, but in the aggregate, it was no more than marginal. Somewhat enhanced tolerance of cooperative federalist approaches was evident on the states' rights–centralist federalism dimension, particularly among congressional conservatives. However, almost certainly the greatest conservative behavioral changes during the postwar period were the growing acceptance of expansive presidential national security and foreign policy roles in the quest to combat international Communism. Nevertheless, these effected little or no change in conservatives' verbal denunciations of presidential government and calls for congressionally centered checks and balances.

Even though most conservatives echoed Goldwater in asserting that they, unlike the liberals, refused to treat institutions as mere means to power or programmatic policy ends, there can be little doubt that both the continuity and the change that occurred had definite connections to the conservatives' preferred programs and their perceptions of where their power centers and those of the opposition lay. The extent and nature of both liberal and conservative instrumentalism and the impact of their theories of governance form the subject matter of the next chapter.

## Notes

1. For clear and full endorsement of the conservative theory of governance, see esp. James Burnham, *Congress and the American Tradition* (Chicago: Henry Regnery, 1959); Barry M. Goldwater, *Conscience of a Conservative* (Shepherdsville, KY: Victor, 1960); and Barry M. Goldwater, *Where I Stand* (New York: McGraw–Hill, 1964), 88–93.

2. David A. Simmons, "Reorganization of the Federal Government," *American Bar Association Journal* 31 (February 1945): 63–66; "For a Republican Form of Government," *American Bar Association Journal* 33 (January 1947): 4–5.

3. "The Question of Federal or State Control of the Employment Services," *Congressional Digest* 25 (April 1946); Alonzo L. Hamby, *Beyond the New Deal* (New York: Columbia University Press, 1973), 79–80; Ernest R. Bartley, *The Tidelands Oil Controversy* (Austin: University of Texas Press, 1953), chaps. 9–11.

4. James T. Patterson, *Mr. Republican* (Boston: Houghton Mifflin, 1972), 320–326; "Should the State Public School Systems Be Subsidized by Federal Funds?" *Congressional Digest* 25 (February 1946).

5. "The Federal 'Administrative Procedure Act' Becomes Law," *American Bar Association Journal* 32 (July 1946): 377–386; Arthur M. Schlesinger Jr., *The Imperial*

*Presidency* (New York: Popular Library. 1973), 155; Sidney M. Milkis, *The President and the Parties* (New York: Oxford University Press, 1993), 160–161; 94 *Cong. Rec.* (13 May 1948), 5818–5822.

6. Schlesinger, *Imperial Presidency,* 138–143; James L. Sundquist, *The Decline and Resurgence of Congress* (Washington: Brookings Institution, 1981), 111.

7. On the reactions to the MacArthur firing, see David McCullough, *Truman* (New York: Simon & Schuster, 1992), 843–856; and Patterson, *Mr. Republican,* 487–488. On the steel seizure, Duane Tananbaum, *The Bricker Amendment Controversy* (Ithaca, NY: Cornell University Press, 1988), 50, quotes Bricker and Russell. Lawrence's views appear in 98 *Cong. Rec.* (1952), A 2544; Taft's views are in 98 *Cong. Rec.* (16 April 1952), 4014.

8. Tananbaum, *Bricker Amendment,* chaps. 1–4.

9. Bartley, *Tidelands Oil,* 229–230, on the tidelands oil pledge; Kirk H. Porter and Donald Bruce Johnson, eds., *National Party Platforms, 1840–1968* (Urbana: University of Illinois Press, 1970), 496–505; Sidney M. Milkis, *President and the Parties* (New York: Oxford University Press, 1993), 161–162, 168; Schlesinger, *Imperial Presidency,* 154; Marcus Cunliffe, *American Presidents and the Presidency* (London: Eyre & Spotteswoode, 1969), 113.

10. James L. Sundquist, *Politics and Policy* (Washington: Brookings Institution, 1968), 69, 323; Samuel H. Beer, introduction to *New Federalism,* by Timothy J. Conlan (Washington: Brookings Institution, 1988), xiv–xv; Tananbaum, *Bricker Amendment,* 100–102.

11. Tananbaum, *Bricker Amendment,* 72.

12. Tananbaum, *Bricker Amendment,* esp. 68–71 on the early support and 157–190 on the final debates and votes. The percentages were tabulated by the author, based as elsewhere on the *New Republic* scoring system. "Conservatives" had *New Republic* scores of 0–33.

13. Schlesinger, *Imperial Presidency,* 157, 159.

14. "Executive Secrecy and the Fifth Amendment," *Chicago Daily Tribune,* 18 May 1954, sec. 1, p. 14; "Congress Keep Out," *National Review* 1 (7 March 1956): 6; "The McClellan Investigation," *National Review* 1 (14 March 1956): 6; "Contempt for Congress," *National Review* 1 (30 May 1956): 6; Frank S. Meyer, "The Revolt against Congress," *National Review* 1 (7 March 1956): 6.

15. On Eisenhower, see Emmet John Hughes, *The Ordeal of Power* (New York: Atheneum, 1963), 201–202. "The South Girds Its Loins," *National Review* 1 (29 February 1956): 5; Felix Morley, *Federalism and Freedom* (Chicago: Henry Regnery, 1959); "Why the South Must Prevail," *National Review* 3 (24 August 1957): 149.

16. "Segregation Outlawed," *Chicago Daily Tribune,* 18 May 1954, sec. 1, p. 14; "Transitional Help for Southern Schools," *Chicago Daily Tribune,* 19 May 1954, sec. 1, p. 16. Comments in the *Congressional Record* and votes on the Powell amendments and other civil rights matters indicate substantial Northern Republican support.

17. "The Lie to Mr. Eisenhower," *National Review* 3 (5 October 1957): 297–298; the Knowland quotation is from the *New York Times,* 27 September 1957, 12.

18. "For a Republican Form of Government," *American Bar Association Journal* 33 (January 1947): 4–5; David Lawrence, "The 'New Deal' Lives On," *U. S. News and*

*World Report* 22 (10 January 1947): 26–27; Tananbaum, *Bricker Amendment*, 51–52; G. Theodore Mitau, *Decade of Decision* (New York: Charles Scribner's Sons, 1967), 23–32.

19.  L. Brent Bozell, "A Bill to Curb the Court," *National Review* (1 March 1958): 200–201.

20.  Walter F. Murphy, *Congress and the Court* (Chicago: University of Chicago Press, 1962), 161–162, discusses the Eisenhower administration's position. For a conservative attack on the *Chicago Tribune* and the ABA for opposing the Jenner bill, see "Assault from Strange Quarters," *National Review* 5 (8 March 1958): 220–221. For further discussion of the vote, see Mitau, *Decade of Decision,* 32–34.

21.  Murphy, *Congress and the Court*, 91–94, 182–183, 214–217, 246.

22.  Sundquist, *Politics and Policy,* 147–150, 187–195, 211–214.

23.  Mitau, *Decade of Decision,* chap. 3. On ABA opposition, see Albert Melone, *Lawyers, Public Policy, and Interest Group Politics* (Washington: University Press of America, 1977), 127.

24.  Mitau, *Decade of Decision,* chap. 3.

25.  The original intent quotation is from Goldwater, *Conscience of a Conservative,* 37; the states' rights and bureaucracy quotations are from Goldwater, *Where I Stand,* 38; the presidential quotation is from Barry M. Goldwater, "My Case for the Republican Party," *Saturday Review* 47 (17 October 1964): 23; the congressional-executive quotation is from Goldwater, *Where I Stand,* 90; and the Supreme Court quote is from the same book, 91; the final executive–judicial quotation is from Goldwater, *Conscience of a Conservative,* 19–20.

26.  "Age of Nondeclared Wars," *Chicago Tribune,* 9 August 1964, sec. 1, p. 24.

27.  David A. Simmons, "The Supremacy of Law," *American Bar Association Journal* 32 (January 1946): 17–21; "Segregation Outlawed."

28.  Jaffa's atypical position is set forth in "The Case for a Stronger National Government," in *A Nation of State,* ed. Robert A. Goldwin (Chicago: Rand McNally, 1963), 106–125. It stressed primarily concerns related to national security. Robertson and Judd, *American Public Policy,* 145–149, stresses accommodation on cooperative federalism but also notes continuing liberal–big business differences over how centralized Johnson's "creative federalism" should be in practice.

29.  Milkis, *President and the Parties,* 160–161, has stressed conservative accommodation to the administrative state during this period; but the rhetoric and behavior cited throughtout this chapter show considerable continuing conservative resistance.

30.  For conservative attacks on Lippmann and Rossiter, see Willmoore Kendall, *The Conservative Affirmation* (Chicago: Henry Regnery, 1963), chap. 1; "The Liberal Line," *National Review* 1 (4 January 1956): 8; "Moon–Struck Madness," *National Review* 2 (13 June 1956): 16; "Lippmann on the Rack," *National Review* 2 (18 July 1956): 16–17; Burnham, *Congress and Tradition,* 256–257. For the two-majorities idea, with preference for the congressional majority, see Kendall, *Conservative Affirmation,* 16, chap. 2.

31.  On Frankfurter's inconsistent application of restraint, see Herbert J. Spaeth, *Supreme Court Policy Making* (San Francisco: W. H. Freeman, 1979), 75–80. L. Brent Bozell especially emphasized the need "to chasten the Court, to make it behave,"

in "A Bill to Curb the Court," *National Review*, 1 March 1958, 200–201; Lawrence, "The New Deal Lives On," 26–27; "A Dangerous Bill," *Chicago Daily Tribune*, 24 February 1958, sec. 1, p. 12; "Assault from Strange Quarters," *National Review* 5 (8 March 1958): 220–221.

# 11

# Theories of Governance: Past Influences, Instrumentalism, and Impact

A s we have seen, both liberal and conservative theories of governance underwent some changes during the 1945–66 period. Liberals put increasing emphasis on judicial activism in additional spheres, while conservatives moved toward advocacy of overt curbs on the Supreme Court to impose judicial restraint on it. Conservative behavior, if not rhetoric, increasingly supported aspects of presidential government, especially in its international dimensions, but also, to a more limited extent, in its general chief administrative roles. Moreover, each coalition's behavior shifted somewhat toward cooperative federalism, though a sizable gap between the two sides remained. Nonetheless, the general patterns were ones in which continuity outweighed change.

Why? In an attempt to find answers, this chapter focuses on the continuing impact of previous ideologically based institutional prescriptions on the theories of governance that liberals and conservatives advocated in the postwar era and the degree and nature of instrumentalism in the governance positions taken by major liberals and conservatives of the period. It also examines the long-term impact of the choices about governance that each ideological coalition made between 1945 and 1966.

## The Influence of Past Prescriptions

Political leaders, activists, and intellectuals prefer to appear to be consistent with their previously announced positions whenever possible, for inconsistency opens one to charges of insincerity and opportunism from political opponents. Therefore, the persistence of old patterns of expression and behavior in the postwar era should be unsurprising. Yet the ways in which the past exerted influence deserve some attention. One important way in which previous commitments shaped behavior on new issues and caused that behavior to resemble preexisting patterns was evident in the tidelands oil controversy that emerged after the end of World War II and then raged for over seven years.

On the surface, there was little to suggest that the tidelands oil issue would become a major subject of liberal-conservative debate centering on states' rights versus centralized federalism. The matter of legal title to, and effective control over, a narrow three-mile strip of submerged lands that primarily affected only three states hardly seemed a prime candidate for sharp ideological conflict. Although Roosevelt's liberal interior secretary, Harold Ickes, had come by the late 1930s to see the issue in ideological terms as one necessitating national government control of precious oil reserves to conserve them from weak state governments that he saw as subject to contol by greedy oil interests, that perspective was not widely shared as the postwar era began. In fact, Robert Kenny, the California Attorney General who took the lead in 1945 in representing California's state claim and enlisting the support of other state attorneys general to urge a federal quitclaim (ceding control to the states), was himself a renowned liberal, active in the National Citizens Political Action Committee.[1]

Despite the technical, legal aspects of the matter and the fact that the oil companies were at least somewhat divided in their preferences between federal and state control, the liberal coalition came during 1945 and 1946 to perceive the issue as one of federal control in the public interest versus weak or corrupt state control that would pass natural resources into the hands of rapacious oil company bosses. The *New Republic* explained the issue for its readers in these terms and also proclaimed the need to defend the Supreme Court, which had not yet heard even the first tidelands oil case. Meanwhile, on the conservative side, the states' rights banners were beginning to fly. Though the tidelands oil issue might be expected to be of little interest to those in inland states and others having little or no oil off their shores, conservatives came to believe that there was a matter of principle potentially affecting everyone. As a brief prepared for the state attorneys general proclaimed, "There is no middle ground. If Mr. Ickes can seize one square foot of tide or submerged land in any State and maintain his seizure, it will be the official duty of Federal officers everywhere to complete the conquest of all like areas in all the States."[2]

By the time the submerged lands quitclaim measure came to a vote in Congress in July and August 1946, the ideological lines had been sharply drawn. In the House, 89 percent of liberals voted against the quitclaim, as did 85 percent of liberals in the Senate. Among conservatives, 93 percent in the House and 86 percent in the Senate voted the opposite way. Even in

California, the state whose claim was directly at issue and whose liberal attorney general was leading the drive for the quitclaim, prominent liberals Helen Gahagan Douglas and Jerry Voorhis broke with their state to vote with the liberal coalition. Declared Voorhis, in clear liberal governance theory rhetoric: "I do not believe that by and large the States have successfully protected the public interests of the American people in those oil resources which lie in these submerged lands."[3]

Truman's 1946 and 1952 vetoes of congressionally passed legislation and the liberal Supreme Court's pro-federal rulings in the California, Texas, and Louisiana cases only intensified the liberal-conservative cleavage on the issue. By 1952, it had become a major ideological issue in the presidential election campaign, with Eisenhower staking out a clear states' rights position and Stevenson asserting the national government's responsibilities.[4]

No single case study can fully illustrate a general pattern. However, the tidelands oil case suggests how new issues, perceived by prominent members of each coalition through the lenses of past governance theories, could be fitted into old patterns by both the liberal and conservative coalitions in the postwar years. The states' rights cues in this instance, absent any other major counterpressures, drew elected officials and activists toward support for, or opposition to, a position consistent with the past. Much the same pattern appeared in 1945–46 concerning the return of the employment services to the states.

In areas where the coalitions were shifting their institutional prescriptions or behavior, there is evidence that previous governance positions imposed some constraints on such movement in the postwar period. When conservatives moved from deference to the judiciary to efforts to curb judicial activism, most of them were clearly reluctant to be seen as attacking the courts or abandoning past conservative positions. Walter Murphy, in a thorough scholarly study of the subject, commented on this reticence. Almost certainly, considerations of past stances and continuity with them kept the conservative American Bar Association from endorsing either the Jenner or Tuck efforts to limit court jurisdiction. After careful analysis of the ABA, Albert Melone found deep bar association dislike of many Warren Court decisions but an unwillingness to attack the Supreme Court *as an institution.* Even the most militant proponents of curbing the federal courts, such as Brent Bozell, perceived the need to justify extensively their recommendations and actions in ways that attempted to establish linkages to conservative positions during the court battles of the 1930s.[5]

In the sphere of presidential government, as previously noted, conservative behavior, especially after the mid-1950s, increasingly accepted expansive roles for the chief executive in national security policy. In this area, however, allegiance to past principles probably played a part (along with genuine distrust of particular occupants of the White House and a perception of Congress's relative conservatism) in keeping their rhetoric virtually unchanged. The theories of governance thus tended to perpetuate themselves, barring strong pressures (as in the judicial sphere during the Warren Court era) to alter them.

### Instrumental Links to Power and Programmatic Policy Ends

Much of the continuity and consistency in the ideological theories of governance between 1945 and 1966, and with the previous era, reflected perceptions of where liberal and conservative strength lay, rather than representing mere application of past precepts. How much should be explained in these terms, it is difficult to assess; but there are helpful clues.

Barry Goldwater was far from alone in saying that the liberal power base rested in the presidency, the executive bureaucracy, and the Supreme Court and the conservatives' strength resided in Congress and the state governments. Similar formulations were offered by conservatives as different from one another as liberationist James Burnham, libertarian republican Alfred de Grazia, and the distinctive Straussian traditionalist Willmoore Kendall, as well as by a variety of liberal analysts, including Wilfred Binkley, R. Alton Lee, and James MacGregor Burns. Given such widespread agreement on where the ideological movements' power bases within government institutions lay, the high level of cohesion in each camp on institutional prescriptions that comported well with these perceptions is unsurprising.[6]

More frequently than in the New Deal era, conservative and liberal leaders admitted openly that instrumental calculations lay behind their theories of governance. Even as he pushed strenuously for a congressionally centered check-and-balance system, conservative James Burnham conceded, "It cannot be held that an American conservative always and necessarily favors the legislature; and an American liberal, the executive. Today this is so, but it has not always been and may not forever be." Burnham went on to state: "Primary allegiance shifts from executive to legislature to Court as this or that branch seems the most likely to foster the other elements of the political syndrome."[7]

Brent Bozell's instrumentalism was a little more veiled than Burnham's but not markedly so. Defending the Jenner bill to alter the jurisdiction of the Supreme Court, he addressed those conservatives who worried that "it smacks of the Liberals' method of dealing with institutions that do not do their bidding." While such fears represented "a commendable concern for consistency—a consideration one seldom finds Liberals worrying about," Bozell argued that conservatives of both the 1930s and the 1950s were showing "allegiance to the Constitution." However, he then proceeded to stress the need "to chasten the Court, to make it behave," suggesting his embrace of rather heavy-handed methods indeed to deal with a recalcitrant institution.[8]

In the liberal camp, similar openly instrumentalist justifications appeared also. Averell Harriman frankly saw the institutional issues as a matter "of whose ox is getting gored: who is in or out of power, and what actions either side may want." Arthur Schlesinger Jr. described the "Yale school" liberals in terms that almost mirrored Bozell's views: "Why should a liberal majority [on the Supreme Court] tie its hands by a policy of self-denial that conservatism will never follow when it is in power?" In each instance, one side sought to justify its own instrumentalism by alleging that the other camp regularly employed government institutions as mere means to power or policy ends.[9]

Another area of rather transparent institutional instrumentalism for both conservatives and liberals in this period concerned reforming the electoral college for presidential elections. Although most liberals in the 1930s had favored direct popular vote for president—an obvious choice given their majoritarianism and portrayal of the president as the tribune of a national majority—while most conservatives had defended the electoral college with traditionalist and states' rights arguments, the 1945–66 period found many on both sides altering their positions, often with clear power and policy ends in mind.[10]

Conservatives generally threw their support behind a proposed constitutional amendment, sponsored by conservatives Senator Karl Mundt and Representative Frederick Coudert, that would give each House of Representatives district one electoral vote, with each state additionally receiving two electoral votes to cast for the statewide winner. The *National Review*, immediately perceiving the power and policy implications of terminating the winner-take-all electoral vote system, offered its enthusiastic endorsement, stressing that the measure "would reduce the excessive weight of the two or three most heavily populated states; and would help frustrate the balance-of-power maneuvers of small but tightly organized political groupings" (i.e., liberal blacks and Jews). Another proposal engendering somewhat less conservative enthusiasm, but winning the backing of some moderates unwilling to embrace the Mundt-Coudert plan, which would have given the presidency the same rural and small-town bias as Congress, was the Lodge-Gossett plan to divide each state's electoral votes in proportion to the popular vote in the state. This, too, would reduce the influence of the largest states but would not have the strong rural orientation of the Mundt-Coudert proposal.[11]

Most liberals reacted in horror to the district plan and came eventually to oppose the proportional plan also. Many now found great merit in an electoral-college system that liberals had seen as unsatisfactory in 1934, when liberal Senator George Norris had mounted his attack on it. As James MacGregor Burns explained, "The spread of urbanization and the electoral college 'gerrymander' have made New York and the other big urban states 'preponderate' in most recent presidential elections." A result, he noted, was that "whatever his political party, the modern President must be sensitive to the needs of the cities." However shaky the facts underlying this proposition, many liberals (and conservatives) believed them to be true. Therefore, while Charles M. LaFollette, national director of the Americans for Democratic Action, conceded that the "Electoral College is an anti-democratic anachronism," he asserted that "liberals can ill afford drastic change in the system of electing a President until either of two developments occur": federal enforcement of voting rights throughout the country or "improvement in the political climate of the traditionally conservative, one-party South."[12]

However, instances of instrumentalism as blatant as these examples were still relatively uncommon. In fact, some advocates, such as Goldwater, were vehement in denouncing the treatment of institutions in instrumental terms. Scorning what he viewed as liberals' instrumental advocacy of presidential government, Goldwater denounced those who "hail the display of Presidential strength simply because they approve of the result reached by the use of power. This is nothing less than the totalitarian philosophy that the end justifies the means. . . . If ever there was a philosophy of government totally at war with that of the Founding Fathers, it is this one." However, as noted previously, Goldwater himself would soon dramatically alter his expressed views on the presidency and Congress. Most conservative and liberal proponents of institutional prescriptions, as in the New Deal era, employed the language of high principles drawn from their ideology and other, less ideological, values to justify their institutional prescriptions.[13]

These principles and values resembled those of the past, with a few exceptions. While the *Chicago Tribune*, Robert Taft, Felix Morley, Alfred de Grazia, and even Barry Goldwater and the *National Review*, regularly justified their governance prescriptions in terms stressing liberty or negative freedom, grounded usually in property rights, traditionalists, such as

Russell Kirk, rarely, if ever, did so. In this period, the greatest consensus in the conservatives' governance justifications appeared to be Madisonian tradition and avoidance of plebiscitary democracy and Caesarism. These were points on which the various conservative schools of thought could at least agree on language. Thus, traditionalist-organic conservative Russell Kirk denounced "'plebiscitary democracy' in which the executive of a unitary state, . . . elected nominally by the masses but actually brought to office and kept there by the publicist and the manipulator, is compelled to make all the decisions for everyone—and must, in the circumstances, make most decisions imprudently." Pursuing this line, Kirk heaped praise on James Madison for his conservative wisdom. Like Madison, he believed, "the American conservative is truly a federalist, a balancer of authority, a restrainer of power." Libertarian conservative Alfred de Grazia wholeheartedly concurred. Attacking presidential majoritarian-mandate ideas and proposals for responsible-party government as well, he declared, "Congress is the spearhead of the Republican Force" but saw it linked in this respect to "federalism, free enterprise, and an independent and precedent-based judiciary." He noted, however, "There exists a continuous abuse of republican government in America so long as the Supreme Court engages unrestrainedly in legislation." For both traditionalists and libertarians, then, there were some common justifications for strict construction of the Constitution, states' rights, congressionally centered checks and balances, and a "non-legislating" judiciary.[14]

Among liberals, probably the greatest shift in justifications was in the direction of civil liberties and minority rights arguments. Majoritarian rationales declined in frequency from the New Deal era, but many liberals still advanced them—now often combining them with civil libertarian and minority rights arguments. James MacGregor Burns, for example, saw the president as "majority leader" but perceived no attendant danger of majority tyranny over minorities' civil liberties or rights, because the president's majority "embraces a great variety of interests and attitudes." Later, Burns elaborated further: "By the 1930's and 1940's the Presidency had become sensitive to the political power of groups that had been socially and economically disadvantaged, and to liberal intellectuals who took a militant stand on civil liberties." Grant McConnell generally concurred. Writing of the presidency in 1966, he concluded: "The constituency of this majestic office is all the people. The prestige of its occupant is so great that when his power is husbanded and skillfully used he can make innovations of policy in the interest of those who are outside the pluralist scheme of rule." Thus, to many liberals, the president was at the same time both a tribune of a popular majority and a defender of minority civil liberties and rights, conveniently reconciling these two somewhat divergent elements of the liberals' value system.[15]

The extent to which short-term power or programmatic policy ends affected conservatives' and liberals' adherence to their theories of governance can be tested by considering the effects, if any, of the Supreme Court's shift toward moderate conservatism from 1949 to 1952 and toward liberal activism after 1954 and the presidency's shift toward moderate conservatism during the Eisenhower administration, 1953–61. Did these shifts measurably affect the prescriptions of the two coalitions or their behavior patterns concerning the Supreme Court and the presidency?

During the 1949–52 period, liberals voiced numerous complaints about Truman's judicial appointees and the overall record of the Supreme Court. TRB in the *New Republic* sniffed that "Truman does not have an intellectual grasp of the difference between conservatism and liberalism in the judicial sense." Harold Ickes observed acidly on the Supreme Court's decisions, "Leave all hope behind, ye who enter here to seek the civil rights that once were yours." But this was a time when the liberal movement's commitment to liberal judicial activism was still not solidified, and no major shifts in liberal institutional prescriptions for the Court were forthcoming.[16]

Among conservatives, the years 1949–52 had slightly greater effects. Delighted with the Supreme Court's overturning of Truman's steel-industry seizure and generally pleased by its relative conservatism on civil liberties issues, the American Bar Association decided that the time was ripe for a constitutional amendment that would forever fix the High Court's membership at nine (negating any possibility of future FDR-type Court-packing efforts) while imposing a mandatory retirement age of seventy-five on federal judges. Conservative Republican Senator John Butler of Maryland served as the chief sponsor of the proposed amendment, and most of its support came from the conservative coalition. Before the necessary backing could be enlisted, however, the Supreme Court began outraging conservative opinion with its shift to liberal judicial activism. By 1957, as has been discussed in chapter 10, the same Senator Butler was working with Senator Jenner to alter the Supreme Court's appellate jurisdiction, and the conservative coalition was arrayed in favor of curbing the Court that they had quite recently viewed with considerable favor.[17]

As for the Eisenhower administration and its effects on the presidential-congressional prescriptions of the two coalitions, the observed shifts were in predictable directions but were relatively slight. One area where conservative movement toward a propresidential pattern was evident concerned the Bricker amendment. Even though all Senate conservatives had supported the proposed amendment during the Truman administration, when all but two were official sponsors, one-third voted against it on 25 February 1954; and 22 percent opposed even a weakened version of it on the following day. There can be little doubt that the change of presidencies was the key factor here; but it is also noteworthy that most conservatives openly opposed the Eisenhower administration on a critical measure, while most liberals supported it. In fact, the pattern of conservative opposition to, and liberal support for, presidential power was repeated on issues of executive privilege, foreign-aid discretionary powers, and reciprocal trade powers, among others, though some conservative support on congressional roll calls did shift toward the presidency on the last two matters because of Eisenhower's presence in the White House.[18]

Several factors explain the continued strong liberal loyalty to presidential government and the relatively small and halting conservative moves toward embracing it (and almost no shifts in their rhetoric in this direction) during the Eisenhower years. Habitual patterns and loyalty to them were a part of the story, but probably not the major part, for it was clear how rapidly conservatives grew hostile to the Supreme Court during and after 1954, and it would be evident how quickly and extensively liberals would abandon presidential government in the late 1960s. Rather, the major explanations appear to be that both conservatives and liberals perceived the presidency and the executive branch to be more liberal than Congress over the medium-to-long term; that neither perceived the Eisenhower administration to be distinctly more conservative than Congress (and many, especially conservatives, saw it as more liberal than Congress); and that each side perceived its medium- to long-term programmatic policy goals to be linked institutionally to the presidency for liberals and to Congress for the conservatives.

Regarding the medium- to long-term liberal or conservative occupancy of power seats in the executive branch and Congress, general outlooks focused on the electoral college gerrymander that seemed to give the advantage to large, urban states and the rural biases in the apportionment of both the House of Representatives and the Senate, as well as on the seniority system that regularly awarded prime chairmanships of congressional committees to Southern conservatives and the merit system that had entrenched liberals in the executive bureaucracy since the New Deal. Time and again, each side made reference to these, indicating their importance.[19]

Furthermore, particularly in the conservative movement, few saw the Eisenhower administration as occupying an ideological position to the right of Congress. The most credit that Willmoore Kendall could give to Eisenhower was that "Dwight Eisenhower, though recognizably a Liberal, is not the Liberal propaganda machine's favorite kind of Liberal." According to Kendall, "undermining the power and prestige of Congress" was a top priority for the liberal machine. It was the official editorial position of the *National Review* that the Eisenhower administration constituted a "pedestrian blend of pragmatism, mid-century liberalism, and undifferentiated goodnaturedness."[20]

Finally, the liberals widely perceived that the speed, efficiency, decisiveness, and uniformity that they associated with the presidency and the executive branch suited their policy goals of social reform at home and containment abroad better than the slowness, inefficiency, compromises, and fragmentation that appeared endemic to the legislative processes. Libertarian conservatives, such as Morley, usually agreed readily and took the procongressional perspective. Making this point, Morley titled one of his pieces "Deliberate Pace in Congress Safeguards Your Freedom." However, some interventionist-liberationist conservatives, such as Burnham, seeing the potential peril in conceding at least the speed and efficiency arguments, simply denied that speed and efficiency were, in fact, more characteristic of the presidency than of Congress.[21]

Some issue-specific instrumentalism, where coalition members blatantly abandoned their general prescriptions to achieve particular policy ends, was in evidence. Southern conservatives, whose embrace of states' rights had the longest heritage and whose application of it on civil rights issues went to the point of interposition, often eagerly sought federal grants-in-aid for a variety of other projects. In fact, they often played the roles of moderates in securing cooperative federalist compromises during this period. Ralph McGill, editor of the *Atlanta Constitution*, commented on the apparent hypocrisy of many of his region's spokespersons: "The South has got to make up its mind. It cannot have its cake and eat it, too. It cannot ask for government aid in one field and deny government aid, or 'interference' in another." But much of the white South, especially in Congress, continued to do just that.[22]

Nor was such a pattern confined to Southern conservatives. Liberals, enthusiastic about presidential powers on almost every issue during the period, recoiled in horror from the prospect that the president might obtain power to draft labor unionists who went on strike during emergencies, and they joined with conservatives to kill the measure that would have granted such broad powers. Yet such instances were not common.[23]

In general, the 1945–66 period was one of marked continuity and consistency in liberal and conservative theories of governance and the arguments that each side marshaled in behalf of its institutional prescriptions. While the 1949–52 and 1953–61 interludes on the Supreme Court and in the presidency, respectively, yielded some deviations in liberal and conservative prescriptions and behavior, these were relatively slight. Issue-specific abandonment of the theories of governance was also fairly rare. However, genuine and strong dedication to the governance theories, while certainly present and operative on questions, such as tidelands oil, when other cues were weak or mixed, probably was not the sole, or even the major, reason for the consistency over time. Openly instrumentalist arguments appeared on each side with considerable frequency. And even when such arguments were not apparent, they were almost certainly part of most political actors' calculations. A view toward medium- to long-term power and policy ends appeared to guide both coalitions toward fairly consistent prescriptions and behavior between 1945 and 1966.

### The Impact of the Theories of Governance

Even more than in the 1933–45 years, the postwar era was one in which results were often compromises between the two coalitions, reflecting the fairly even balance of power between them. In areas of compromise, including many aspects of federalism and the administrative state, the result was something that fell short of what either side favored. On most key questions of constitutional interpretation, presidential government, and judicial roles, the liberal coalition usually prevailed after 1945—but sometimes by a precariously narrow margin of victory. What emerged from the clashes over institutional prescriptions, then, was a continuation of flexible constitutional interpretation and presidential government, heightened judicial activism from 1954 onward, and a highly fragmented and often confusing pattern of intergovernment relations and administration.

The biggest institutional changes to emerge in the postwar era were the Warren Court's expanded judicial activism, the accretions of presidential power (especially in national security and foreign policy), and the increasingly intricate network of fragmented national administrative and cooperative federalist structures. Each of these would have significant impacts, though these effects were often unforeseen and unintended.

The Warren Court's judicial activism in the sphere of black civil rights infuriated most of the white South. Because the liberal coalition endorsed the Court's civil rights activism, Southern white voters became increasingly alienated from liberal candidates and from the Democratic party, especially at the presidential level. As the Court's activism extended to protecting the rights of alleged Communists, criminal suspects, atheists,

religious minorities, and others from state laws and state and local traditional practices, the new liberal version of judicial activism eroded general popular support for liberalism, the Democratic party, the Supreme
Court itself, and (some have argued) government institutions generally.
By November 1966, the Harris Poll indicated that 70 percent of the general public opposed the High Court's rulings on prayer in schools; 65 percent the decision disallowing confessions without first informing suspects
of *Miranda* legal rights; and 51 percent the ruling allowing Communists to
obtain passports. In the same survey, 52 percent of the public gave the
Supreme Court an overall negative assessment. What was perhaps the liberal coalition's greatest institutional victory over the conservatives during
the postwar period thus had among its consequences some distinctly negative repercussions for its proponents.[24]

The other major liberal institutional victory of the postwar era, the continued growth of presidential power, also had an impact that was largely
unforeseen by liberal advocates. Even as late as 1965, James MacGregor
Burns was exulting that "presidential government, far from being a threat
to American democracy, has become the major single institution sustaining it—a bulwark of individual liberty, an agency of popular representation, and a magnet for political talent and leadership." Events such as Truman's threat to use presidential powers against striking labor unionists
made little long-term impression on liberals. Very soon, however, liberals
themselves would be denouncing "the imperial presidency" and fighting
to strengthen Congress at the expense of presidential power. But even
with the liberals' post-1965 shift away from presidential government,
many segments of the general public would blame liberals for what they
viewed as its excesses, not only in Vietnam but in social engineering at
home as well. The impact of presidential government, partially resem-
bling that of liberal judicial activism, was ultimately to weaken public
support for liberalism, the Democratic party, the presidency itself, and
(more clearly in this instance) government institutions generally. However, as Sidney Milkis has stressed, presidential government also continued
to erode the political party system in general, contributing to a sustained
period of party dealignment that was already becoming evident during
the 1950s.[25]

Finally, there was the combination of cooperative federalism and an
administrative state apparatus that mainly represented compromises
among liberals, conservatives, and assorted other political actors, including many pragmatic interest groups. Theodore Lowi has portrayed the
results of this combination as a "second republic," fully emergent in the
1960s but with roots in the New Deal, based on what he termed "interest-

group liberalism." Unclear statutory standards combined with a fragmented administrative apparatus, complex cooperative federalist structures, and a developing advocacy explosion (fed in part by these other structures and practices) to produce a melange of logrolling policy outcomes. David Robertson and Dennis Judd, from a somewhat different angle, have described the results as "incoherent policy activism" by the federal government and have argued convincingly that the impact was to make the national government appear "inept." To the extent that this was so, the mixture of cooperative federalism and a fragmented administrative state would have some of the same consequences as liberal judicial activism and presidential government, including a waning of popular support for liberalism and the government institutions most associated with it.[26]

## Conclusions

By the late 1960s, liberalism was fragmenting and increasingly on the defensive, in part because of the impact of the outcomes of the governance struggles of 1945–66 and their consequences, in part for other reasons, including public policy issues, leaders' personalities and characters, and changes in the interest-group system.

The liberals and conservatives of the postwar era had maintained their late New Deal theories of governance largely intact, usually but not always because they perceived them to fit their power and programmatic policy designs well. When they did not perceive a good fit, liberals and conservatives generally altered their institutional prescriptions, or at least their behavior regarding them. But few major adjustments had seemed necessary until 1966.

What was developing by 1966 was an upheaval in which the power bases of the two ideological coalitons would change fairly dramatically. Goldwater's capture of the Republican presidential nomination in 1964 and developing liberal unease with the Johnson administration's use of presidential power overseas in 1965 and 1966 were early indicators of a coming change. As the movements' power bases shifted, so, too, did some of their values and programmatic policy commitments and priorities. The results were rising questions of fit between the old theories of governance and the emergent power bases and goals of each coalition after 1966. By the early 1980s, most conservatives were advocating presidential government, though in a partially new form, and most liberals were heralding the advantages of congressionally centered checks and balances. How that new pattern grew out of a period of considerable upheaval is the subject to which we next turn.

## Notes

1.  Ernest R. Bartley, *The Tidelands Oil Controversy* (Austin: University of Texas Press, 1953), chap. 8 discusses Ickes's role; chap. 9, Kenny's. Alonzo L. Hamby, *Beyond the New Deal* (New York: Columbia University Press, 1973), 34–35, documents Kenny's liberal credentials.

2.  On divisions among oil companies, see Bartley, *Tidelands Oil*, 119–120, 147, 221; The *New Republic*'s views are in "The Smell of Oil," 5 August 1946, 12. Bartley, *Tidelands Oil*, 150, cites the states' rights quotation.

3.  Conservatives and liberals are defined as elsewhere, using *New Republic* scores. Voorhis' quotation is from Bartley, *Tidelands Oil*, 155.

4.  See Bartley, *Tidelands Oil*, 156–157, 227–228 on the Truman vetoes; chaps. 10 and 12 on the Court cases; and 229–230 on the 1952 campaign.

5.  Walter F. Murphy, *Congress and the Court* (Chicago: University of Chicago Press, 1962), 260; Albert P. Melone, *Lawyers, Public Policy, and Interest Group Politics* (Washington: University Press of America, 1977), 116–133; L. Brent Bozell, "A Bill to Curb the Court," *National Review* 5 (1 March 1958): 200–201.

6.  Barry M. Goldwater, *Where I Stand* (New York: McGraw–Hill, 1964), 91–92; James Burnham, *Congress and the American Tradition* (Chicago: Henry Regnery, 1959), esp. 119–120, 166; Alfred de Grazia, *Republic in Crisis* (New York: Federal Legal Publications, 1965), esp. 28 & 79; Willmoore Kendall, *The Conservative Affirmation* (Chicago: Henry Regnery, 1963), esp. chap. 2; Wilfred E. Binkley, "The Decline of the Executive," *New Republic* 128 (18 May 1953): 13–16; R. Alton Lee, *Truman and Taft–Hartley* (Lexington: University of Kentucky Press, 1966), 3–6; James MacGregor Burns, *Deadlock of Democracy* (Englewood Cliffs, NJ: Prentice–Hall, 1963), esp. chap. 10.

7.  Burnham, *Congress and Tradition*, 119–120.

8.  Bozell, "A Bill to Curb the Court," 200–201.

9.  Harriman quoted in Arthur M. Schlesinger Jr., *The Imperial Presidency* (New York: Popular Library, 1973), 386; on the Yale school, see Schlesinger, "The Supreme Court: 1947," *Fortune* 78 (January 1947): 202.

10.  For the electoral college disputes of the 1930s, see 78 *Cong. Rec.* 2d sess. (22 May 1934), 9243–9245.

11.  "Electing a President," *National Review* 1 (28 March 1956): 6; Lawrence D. Longley and Alan G. Braun, *The Politics of Electoral College Reform* (New Haven: Yale University Press, 1972); "The Revived Controversy over the Electoral College System," *Congressional Digest* 27 (April 1948), 101–128.

12.  James MacGregor Burns, *Presidential Government* (Boston: Houghton Mifflin, 1965), 317–318; Charles M. La Follette, "A Dangerous Method of Electoral Reform?" *ADA World*, 18 February 1950, 5; Longley and Braun, *Electoral College Reform*, 100–103, challenge the full accuracy of the liberals' and conservatives' perceptions of the effects of the electoral college.

13. Goldwater's quotation is cited by Marcus Cunliffe, *American Presidents and the Presidency* (London: Eyre & Spotteswoode, 1969), 111.

14. For examples of emphases on liberty in governance justifications, see "Age of Undeclared Wars," *Chicago Tribune*, 9 August 1964, sec. 1, p. 24; Taft's comments in 98 *Cong. Rec.* (16 April 1952), 4014, and his philosophy discussed by James T. Patterson, *Mr. Republican* (Boston: Houghton Mifflin, 1972), esp. 332–333; Felix Morley, *Federalism and Freedom* (Chicago: Henry Regnery, 1959); de Grazia, *Republic in Crisis*, foreword and 24–26; Goldwater, *Where I Stand*, 92–93; and "The Magazine's Credenda," *National Review* 1 (19 November 1955): 6. The Madisonian, antiplebiscitary emphasis is found, for example, in Russell Kirk, *A Program for Conservatives*, rev. ed. (Chicago: Henry Regnery, 1962), 257–259, 263; Kendall, *Conservative Affirmation*, 16 and chap. 2; Burnham, *Congress and Tradition*, 262–267; and de Grazia, *Republic in Crisis*, 21 and chap. 3. Typical conservative attacks on Caesarism appear in "Caesarism," *National Review* 1 (26 November 1955): 3–4; Burnham, *Congress and Tradition*, 297–298; and Amaury de Riencourt, *The Coming Caesars* (New York: Coward–McCann, 1957).

15. James MacGregor Burns, *Congress on Trial* (New York: Harper & Brothers, 1949), 188; Burns, *Presidential Government*, 287; Grant McConnell, *Private Power and American Democracy* (New York: Vintage, 1966), 351.

16. Alonzo L. Hamby, *Beyond the New Deal* (New York: Columbia University Press, 1973), 337–338; Walter F. Murphy, *Congress and the Court* (Chicago: University of Chicago Press, 1962), 76.

17. Murphy, *Congress and the Court*, 77–78, 79–99.

18. Duane Tananbaum, *The Bricker Amendment Controversy* (Ithaca, NY: Cornell University Press, 1988), 69, chap. 10. Aage R. Clausen, *How Congressmen Decide* (New York: St. Martin's Press, 1973), chap. 8.

19. See the sources in notes 11 and 12. Also see Burnham, *Congress and Tradition*, esp. 119–120; de Grazia, *Republic in Crisis*, esp. chap. 3, 110; Wilfred E. Binkley, "Decline of the Executive," 13–16; Burns, *Congress on Trial*, 49, 188.

20. The Kendall quotations are from *National Review* 1 (21 March 1956): 8, and (1 February 1956): 8, respectively. "Mr. Eisenhower's Third Party," *National Review* 2 (18 July 1956): 5–6. George H. Nash, *The Conservative Intellectual Movement since 1945* (New York: Basic Books, 1976), 253–256, makes it clear that these views were widespread.

21. Felix Morley, "Deliberate Pace in Congress Safeguards Your Freedom," *Nation's Business* 51 (March 1963): 27–28; Burnham, *Congress and Tradition*, 262–263.

22. Ralph McGill, "The South Must Decide," *Forum* 105 (January 1946): 526–527.

23. Hamby, *Beyond the New Deal*, 76–78; Patterson, *Mr. Republican*, 306–307.

24. The Harris Poll results appear in G. Theodore Mitau, *Decade of Decision* (New York: Charles Scribner's Sons, 1967), 5–7. John G. Broesamle, *Reform and Reaction in Twentieth Century American Politics* (New York: Greenwood Press, 1990), 167, makes the case that liberal judicial activism undermined popular faith in government.

25. James MacGregor Burns, *Presidential Government*, 346; Sidney M. Milkis, *The President and the Parties* (New York: Oxford University Press, 1993).

26.  Theodore J. Lowi, *The End of Liberalism* (New York: W.W. Norton, 1979), esp. 62–63, 274–277; David B. Robertson and Dennis R. Judd, *The Development of American Public Policy* (Glenview, IL: Scott, Foresman, 1989), esp. 153–163, 376.

# 1966–1981

# 12

# Liberal and Conservative Values and Programmatic Policies

The late 1960s were a time of unusual turbulence in American politics. Not only was domestic peace ripped asunder by massive urban riots, antiwar protests, and assassinations of major leaders; but the global scene was marked by diminished American capacities to assert dominance over the non-Communist world as well as by an increasingly open rift between the Communist giants, China and the Soviet Union. An end to the long postwar pattern of economic growth, which became increasingly evident in the early 1970s and was characterized by a frustrating combination of inflation and unemployment, added to the atmosphere of change.

All of these developments, together with the cumulative effects of other trends already in progress, substantially reshaped the liberal and conservative movements after 1966. A new and relatively stable pattern was to emerge eventually with the advent of Ronald Reagan's presidency in January 1981. In the meantime, however, flux was almost as characteristic of the two coalitions as consolidation had been from 1945 to 1966. The spectacular fall of Richard Nixon following the revelation of his attempted cover-up of the Watergate affair probably delayed the ascendancy of a new conservatism and made that conservatism less moderate than it would have been, and the election of the relatively nonideological Jimmy Carter as president considerably blurred ideological conflict lines for a time. In the end, however, the decline of liberalism under way by 1966 gave way to the ascendancy in 1981 of a conservative movement that encompassed a variety of sometimes conflicting factions and tendencies but that nonetheless united around the leadership of Reagan and a core of common assumptions, values, and programmatic policies.

## Liberal Assumptions and Values

The liberal coalition began to shift to a revised "new-politics," reformist, "postcontainment" belief system after 1966, spurred in that direction by pressures from new sociopolitical movements, growing disenchantment with the Vietnam War and to some extent the Great Society programs, and perceptions of new global realities. Although quite a few elements of this reform liberalism were continuous with the liberalism that had emerged from the New Deal, World War II, and the early Cold War—particularly broad assumptions about human equality and rationality and commitments to social security, positive freedom, and civil liberties—there were substantial alterations also. Even some basic assumptions became subject to reassessment, though none was fully rejected. Perhaps most subject to growing doubt among the underlying assumptions was the efficacy of large-scale social engineering. Governor Edmund G. (Jerry) Brown, for example, represented a significant new liberal strand in this regard. "Our technology can take us only so far. Our government can give us only so much," declared Brown. "Human nature is constant. It is weak. It needs a type of government that recognizes that mankind is really brought down by its own instincts." In a similar vein, Simon Lazarus, a leading intellectual proponent of the new reformism, attacked the "liberal statism fostered by the New Deal." Michael McCann, analyzing a wide array of what he termed "public-interest" liberals, concluded: "Reflecting the pervasive disillusionment with the shattering of New Deal ideals by the Johnson and Nixon administrations, the new reformers have adamantly resisted the common temptation to invest any leadership at all with high hopes." The new-politics liberal changes provoked a strong reaction from defenders of "old-politics," consolidationist, Cold War liberalism, who fought to preserve the commitments of the liberal movement and the Democratic party to the old beliefs. As the new-politics liberalism gained the upper hand by the early 1970s, many old-politics liberals declared themselves (or were declared to be) neoconservatives. Others, such as long-time liberal leader Hubert Humphrey, struggled to bridge the widening gap.[1]

New-politics liberalism drew support from most of the new liberal sociopolitical movements of the 1960s—the civil rights, antiwar, feminist, environmental, consumer-rights, and procedural-reform movements in particular. It also gained the endorsement of the Americans for Democratic Action (ADA) as the result of a power struggle that reoriented that organization between 1965 and 1968. Such elected officials as Robert and Edward Kennedy, Eugene McCarthy, George McGovern, Frank Church, and Don Edwards provided political leadership, as did some nonelected activists, such as Ralph Nader and his associates; and such intellectuals as Arnold Kaufman, Christopher Jencks, John Kenneth Galbraith, Simon Lazarus, and John Rawls offered the core ideas of the revised version of liberalism.[2]

The assumptions of new-politics liberalism differed from previous liberalisms since 1933 not only in questioning the prospects for large-scale social engineering but also in conceptualizing politics as, in Alonzo Hamby's phrasing, "an exercise in the higher morality rather than in the enhancement of personal interests." Trends in this direction in the postwar era now accelerated, according to Hamby, Kenneth and Patricia Dolbeare, Michael McCann, and other analysts. Gus Tyler, a trade unionist long active in liberal circles, including the Americans for Democratic Action, protested what he viewed as the liberal movement's shifting "away from economics, to ethics and aesthetics, to morality and culture." But the new-politics alterations that brought the strongest negative reactions within the liberal coalition were those concerning the values of national security, equality of opportunity, procedural democracy, and economic growth.[3]

As far as national security was concerned, new-politics liberals downplayed nationalistic values and stressed global security, linking it to such long-term liberal values as social security, positive freedom, and civil liberties. The Americans for Democratic Action, for example, revamped its foreign-policy prescriptions in 1969 to call for "a fundamental restructuring of U.S. foreign policy" to address "the needs and demands of the poorest countries." It also urged "development of a regime of enforceable world law to insure peaceful settlement of international disputes, immediate elimination of international armed conflict, and the international recognition of human rights." After extensive interviews with congressional liberals between 1970 and 1976, Jerrold Schneider concluded that their chief aim abroad was "to end wide-scale human suffering and save the planet from both nuclear war developing out of nuclear proliferation, and from destruction of the environment and the world's natural resources, through international cooperation and redistribution." The contrast with the national security emphasis of the liberalism of even the early 1960s was sharp.[4]

New-politics liberalism still frequently employed the language of equality of opportunity. Increasingly, however, its leading advocates favored "more equality," as Herbert Gans put the issue in a 1973 book. Christopher Jencks, another new-politics liberal intellectual, concluded somewhat reluctantly that programs aimed at promoting equality of opportunity through education had failed to achieve their goals and called for efforts to redistribute incomes in the direction of equality. In 1969, the Americans for Democratic Action urged a "massive redistribution of wealth and power in America." John Rawls, almost certainly the most renowned liberal philosopher of the 1970s, accepted a presumption that equality is desirable and placed the burden of justification on those who supported any inequality. Still, Rawls concluded that "social and economic inequalities are permissible, provided they are (i) attached to the greatest expected benefit of the least advantaged, and (ii) attached to positions and offices open to all under conditions of fair equality of opportunity." While moving somewhat beyond most previous liberal conceptions of equality of opportunity in an egalitarian direction, most new-politics liberals, like Rawls, Jencks, Gans, and the ADA activists, did not embrace full equality of results, despite what many of their critics claimed.[5]

Some new-politics liberals advocated a rather different value concerning equality: "equality of group results," primarily in reference to affirmative action programs. This approach stressed not equality of outcomes overall but simply the same distribution of inequalities within each designated racial, gender, or ethnic group. As some critics have emphasized, this value entailed less change from the status quo than genuine equality of opportunity would; but it was often perceived as a move to the left by both supporters and opponents in the late 1960s.[6]

With regard to democratic values, most new-politics liberals placed considerably more emphasis on popular participation than their predecessors had or than the old-politics liberals thought advisable. Arnold Kaufman was typical, advocating "a new politics of radical pressure that synthesizes in mutually reinforcing ways welfare politics, coalition politics, and participatory democracy"; for, in his view, "morally and politically, the development of a more deliberative process of coalition politics, the growth of participatory institutions, and the completion of the welfare state are concomitant enterprises." The Americans for Democratic Action added its call for "effective democratic control over the economic organization of the country." Reflecting these values of participatory democracy, many new-politics liberals pushed for expanded presidential primaries and a democratization of the party conventions to dislodge the power of party bosses, such as Chicago's Mayor Daley; others stressed "opening up" the processes of the administrative state through creative new strategies of legal challenges.[7]

Finally, in relation to economic growth as a value, most new-politics liberals, especially in the public-interest groups, lowered its priority markedly below the place assigned to it even by liberal intellectuals such as Arthur Schlesinger Jr. in the previous period. Influenced by the counterculture and by ecologists like Barry Commoner and Paul Ehrlich and distrustful of the giant corporations' roles in steering and managing economic expansion efforts, new-politics liberals came increasingly "to question the logic of commitments to maximizing economic growth that were so important to earlier generations of American liberals."[8]

For most of the 1966–76 decade, the liberal coalition was torn by battles between the new politics, reformist, postcontainment liberals and the old-politics, consolidationist, Cold War liberals. The latter, some of whom organized the Coalition for a Democratic Majority to fight for control of the Democratic party, included in the 1966–76 years many members of the Johnson administration; most of the leadership of the American Federation of Labor-Congress of Industrial Organizations (AFL-CIO); such elected public officials as Henry Jackson, Gale McGee, and Thomas Dodd; and an array of intellectuals including Nathan Glazer, Jeane Kirkpatrick, Samuel Huntington, Norman Podhoretz, and Daniel Bell. Most of them stressed national security values in conventional Cold War terms and strongly opposed postcontainment notions. On equal-opportunities values, Nathan Glazer's comments were typical of the group: "The demand for economic equality is now not the demand for equal opportunities for the equally qualified: it is now the demand for equality of economic results." Samuel Huntington, writing in 1975, deplored the "excess of democracy" in the United States and called for "a greater degree of moderation in democracy," rather than the enhanced participation demanded by new-politics liberalism. Gus Tyler of the AFL-CIO wanted the focus kept on economic growth. Despite mounting a major battle to "save" the liberal coalition from undesirable reformism, members of the old-politics faction either eventually made their accommodations to change or left the movement to become "neoconservatives"—sometimes even defecting to the Republican party in the 1970s.[9]

The old politics–new politics split was not the only fracture in the liberal coalition after 1966. Civil libertarian values, as in the past, also stimulated some disputes, largely independently of the major cleavage. Probably the sharpest of these concerned the insistence of a majority of liberals that abortion rights centered around a woman's rights of privacy, while others challenged this rationale, and still others (mainly liberal Roman Catholics) conceptualized the matter as a right to life for the unborn child. Still other lines of conflict pitted the material self-interests of various interest groups in the coalition against one another and against the principled moralism of the increasingly new politics–oriented liberal mainstream.

## Liberal Programmatic Public Policies

In light of the shifting assumptions and values of liberalism, it is unsurprising that the liberal movement's foreign policy and civil rights policy prescriptions also changed, the former quite markedly. To a lesser degree, its civil liberties policies underwent adjustment also, mainly by coming to give a great deal of emphasis to privacy rights on the abortion issue. The liberals' social welfare and government management prescriptions probably changed the least dramatically in practice, despite all the rhetoric about questioning social engineering and promoting "more equality."

The Great Society of the Johnson administration had seen the enactment of most liberal social welfare proposals into law, the major exception being national health insurance, which continued to be a plank in the liberal platform after 1966, though it lacked sufficient political support to win congressional passage. A source of great controversy in social welfare in the 1960s and 1970s were ideas about replacing Aid to Families with Dependent Children with a negative income tax or a guaranteed annual income. These notions appealed to a number of liberals, who viewed them as a vehicle for movement toward greater equality, as well as a means for moving away from the bureaucracy of the "liberal statism" decried by Lazarus and many new-politics liberals. George McGovern, in his 1972 presidential campaign, proposed a "demogrant" to pay everyone in the United States $1,000 per year, to be taxed as regular income. When the Nixon administration incorporated some aspects of a guaranteed annual income into its proposed Family Assistance Plan, liberals divided over the measure, which provided low levels of support and included work requirements for recipients. Internal liberal disagreements over the guaranteed-income approach and specific means for implementing it, liberals' inability to win substantial moderate or conservative support for their national health insurance proposals (and their general unwillingness to accept what Nixon was willing to offer), and liberal preoccupation with foreign policy, civil rights, civil liberties, and regulatory issues tended to diminish the emphasis of the liberal movement on its social welfare agenda after 1966.[10]

In the realm of government economic management, liberal commitment to a Keynesian indirect macroeconomic management policy wavered a bit under the pressures of stagflation and was supplemented by frequent endorsement of wage-price controls during periods of soaring inflation, common in the 1970s. However, the centerpiece of liberal concerns was a strong emphasis on expanded environmental, occupational safety and health, and consumer protection regulations and creative legal means for enforcing them—most of which aroused passionate business opposition. In the late 1960s and early 1970s, liberals enjoyed a number of successes in these endeavors. However, the business community became increasingly adept at resisting effective regulation of its behavior; and liberal efforts to establish an Agency for Consumer Advocacy went down to defeat in 1978, heralding a new era in which conservative hostility to business regulation would be ascendant. The stagflation of the 1970s not only sapped liberal self-confidence but also undermined popular support for Keynesianism as a grand strategy, preparing the way for a shift toward conservative monetarism and supply-side economics.[11]

In the civil liberties domain, the judicial liberals' Warren Court decisions had set most of the standards for liberalism that continued into the 1970s. However, the *Roe v. Wade* decision handed down in 1973 by Nixon appointee Harry Blackmun (but concurred in by liberals Thurgood Marshall, William O. Douglas, and William Brennan) invoked the right of privacy in behalf of a woman's right to choose an abortion and won wide liberal endorsement. Other liberals, while agreeing on the right to choose abortion, preferred to justify such a right in terms of women's rights to equal protection of the law or through equal-opportunities rationales. A minority of liberals, including *Commonweal* magazine's editors, who supported new-politics liberalism in virtually all other respects, dissented forcefully, asserting that the *Roe* decision "diminished the whole concept of what it means to be a person."[12]

The chief liberal shifts regarding civil rights policies were twofold: (1) their increasing extension of the civil rights concept to apply not only to blacks but also to other disadvantaged groups, including women, gays, the elderly, and the handicapped; and (2) their increasing embrace of court-ordered school busing to achieve black-white target percentages in the public schools and of affirmative action programs in higher education and employment to achieve similar targets. Although Lyndon Johnson himself moved at least tentatively in the general new-politics liberal direction on these issues, most of the rest of the old-politics liberal camp were strongly resistant, especially to the second dimension, which treated people as members of groups and emphasized equality of group outcomes—both unacceptable in their view.[13]

The most dramatic change in liberals' policy prescriptions occurred in the foreign and defense policy sphere. While liberals had previously mingled their Four Freedoms imagery with support for military containment of Communism and had endorsed American armed intervention in Korea, Vietnam, and the Dominican Republic, the dominant new-politics liberals centered their major proposals around promoting international law and human rights, while they called for sharp reductions in arms spending and withdrawal of American troops from Vietnam. Their down-playing of nationalistic values gave rise to a preference for policies that were multilateral, rather than unilateral, in nature. Though they were often accused by their critics of favoring a "new isolationism" and did often stress the need to shift financial resources from the military to domestic social programs, their main policy thrust was usually quite internationalist, while it attacked militarism and nationalistic unilateral-ism in American foreign policy.[14]

Finally, contributing to a widespread impression that the liberal coali-tion was splintering more severely than the facts probably justified were the differing emphases of various groups within the coalition during the period 1966–81. Liberal feminist groups, such as the National Organiza-tion for Women, stressed the proposed Equal Rights Amendment to the Constitution and abortion rights; black civil rights groups such as the National Association for the Advancement of Colored People focused heavily on affirmative action and school busing for desegregation; envi-ronmental groups stressed the enactment and enforcement, often through court battles, of new environmental statutes; Public Citizen pushed hard-est for the Agency for Consumer Advocacy; and on and on. Although new-politics liberal assumptions and values were present in all of these groups, and although even the old-politics liberal belief system of most AFL-CIO leaders still provided some strong links to the rest of the liberal coalition, the absence of recognized liberal leadership at the center, capa-ble of articulating liberal values, policies, and theory of governance and mobilizing mass popular support for them, proved a critical problem for the coalition, particularly once Ronald Reagan emerged to provide such leadership for the rival conservative movement.[15]

## Conservative Assumptions and Values

In some respects, the conservative movement of 1966–81 was more fun-damentally split than was the liberal coalition of the 3period. To the old libertarian-versus-traditionalist cleavage, partly papered over by fusion-ism, were added two major new streams of thought: neoconservatism, the belief system of those old-politics, consolidationist, Cold War liberal intel-lectuals who shifted into the conservative movement as the period pro-gressed; and the New Right, distinguished from the old right mainly by its greater proclivity to embrace majoritarian democracy and populistic methods, but also including a subgroup, the new religious right, which blended the populism of the New Right generally with the emphasis on morality and order long associated with traditional-organic conservatism. Moreover, a broad big-business conservatism, possessing closest ties to the libertarian conservatism of the old right but some links to all versions of conservatism, gathered new recruits and added militancy during the 1970s. Unlike liberalism, however, conservatism by the late 1970s was clearly a movement rising in power; and in Ronald Reagan it found a leader who could transcend its internal divisions and rally all components for a common effort. Shared hostility to liberal ideas about "more equality" and past liberal social engineering and a common commitment to private property rights and anti-Communism provided the foundations for Reagan's leadership to succeed in unifying conservatives.

At least at the outset, the neoconservatives differed from the bulk of the conservative movement primarily in their emphasis on social security, positive freedom, and equality of opportunity. Most of the old-politics liberals who made the switch to neoconservatism—in contrast to the AFL-CIO leadership and the Democratic party officeholders, such as Senator Jackson, who remained at least on the fringes of liberalism—were Jewish intellectuals of a rather elitist bent who had long harbored doubts about majoritarianism, especially in its participatory forms, and assigned high priority to order and national security within an anti-Communist framework. Therefore, bridges to mainstream conservative values were already present. The neoconservatives' perception that liberalism was now extending positive freedom too far in seeking to guarantee new rights to additional groups and was shifting to equality of outcomes or equality of group results instead of equal opportunity also impelled them toward alliance with the conservative movement, particularly since growing numbers of conservatives, such as Jack Kemp and Newt Gingrich, were employing at least the slogan "equality of opportunity." As the decade of the 1970s proceeded, the neoconservatives increasingly merged with the conservative mainstream, though they retained some distinctiveness on social security, positive freedom, and equal-opportunity values and in the nature of their elitism.[16]

The New Right stream of thought was quite different from neoconservatism in its origins and its greatest sources of support; but it was also able to blend at least temporarily with the conservative mainstream by the end of the 1970s. Most analysts have agreed with Richard Viguerie, one of the founders of the New Right, in marking 1974 as the year it crystallized and in seeing president Gerald Ford's nomination of Nelson Rockefeller (perceived by its adherents to be a major symbol of Establishment liberalism) to be his vice president as the single event that most triggered its formation. However, mass sources of support for a populistic conservatism had been rising since the 1950s; and reactions against judicial liberalism and supposed liberal permissiveness regarding the 1960s counterculture enlarged its potential base. Where analysts have seriously disagreed with one another has been in assessing the New Right's distinctiveness. Some, such as Alan Crawford, Linda Medcalf and Kenneth Dolbeare, and Kevin Phillips, have seen it as sharply differentiated from the old right (and the neoconservatives) by populistic, majoritarian values and a lower-middle-class social base. "To be radical, majoritarian, lower-middle class, and conservative at the same time," wrote Medcalf and Dolbeare, "is completely unprecedented in American politics." On the other hand, Jerome L. Himmelstein and James C. Roberts, among others, have found few clear-cut distinctions beyond chronology, personalities, and style separating the New Right from the old. "Differences between the New Right and the Old Right were usually superficial," concluded Himmelstein, after a lengthy analysis. Himmelstein's assessment is fairly close to the mark, though it underestimates the significance of New Right populistic imagery and of the religious right segment of the New Right, the latter of which did bring important new combinations of themes and new voting strength to the conservative coalition.[17]

Some of the problems of assessment lay in the way analysts defined the boundaries of the New Right; for some scholars associated it primarily with a subgrouping often termed the new religious right. Led by such figures as Jerry Falwell, Howard Phillips, and Ed McAteer in the 1970s, this group not only employed extensive populistic rhetoric but also gave special emphasis to "traditional" moral values. Angered by cultural changes that they attributed to liberal permissiveness and especially to judicial liberal activism on the Supreme Court, they established links to the old traditionalist conservatism in their stress on virtue and order; but their social base and populistic style made them distinctive from it.[18]

During the 1970s, another stream of conservative activism came from the business community, especially from big business. Previously, some important sectors of large corporate business had accommodated themselves to the liberals' domestic and foreign policies and even certain aspects of their value system and its assumptions. A few continued to do so; but by the early 1970s, the chief executive officers of most major American business corporations had, in the words of Sidney Blumenthal, become "profoundly disillusioned with the post–World War II consensus." In large part, their swing to the political right was a response to an economic slowdown and increased foreign competition throughout the First World, and it certainly had its parallels in Britain and much of Western

Europe in the 1970s. However, there were also particular aspects of new-politics liberalism that especially galvanized big business into alliance with the conservative movement, persuading it to organize politically and bankroll a wide variety of conservative foundations, publications, and political campaigns. Chief among these were the reform liberals' successes in turning public opinion against big business and in promoting passage and enforcement of new-style regulatory policies that cut across business as a whole (i.e., environmental, safety and health, equal employment opportunities regulations). Big-business conservatism emphasized private property rights and economic growth above all other values but also was interested in domestic order and security against Communist and other third-world revolutionary threats. While its intellectual links were probably strongest to old-right libertarian conservatism, it proved willing to support the conservative movement generally and thus by 1980 became an important force for conservative political success.[19]

Tying together the old right libertarians, traditionalists, and fusionists, the New Right and its rather distinctive religious right tendency, the neo-conservative recruits from liberalism,and most of big business were some basic likes and dislikes, if not a coherent set of assumptions. At the level of basic assumptions and values lay some critical differences. However, shared aversion to past liberal social engineering and current liberal calls for more equality, common commitments to private property rights, and an intense anti-Communism united almost all conservatives. A common desire to reactivate economic growth and a belief that market-oriented approaches were most likely to achieve this goal also animated most conservatives, particularly by the end of the 1970s. Considerable conservative consensus on public policies by 1980, despite noteworthy differences, was a result.

### Conservative Programmatic Public Policies

In each major public policy domain, the Nixon administration's public policy stances between 1969 and 1974 produced considerable conservative confusion and pulled some conservatives toward centrist positions, though in a number of key instances the Nixon administration itself proved quite conservative. Unlike Eisenhower, Nixon possessed deep roots in the conservative coalition, and he took pains even as president to maintain strong emotional links to the conservative mainstream. Thus, when his administration departed from what had been conservative policy proposals, conservative reactions tended to be mixed; and the effect on the movement was frequently moderating. However, the Watergate affair and Nixon's personal complicity in the cover-up that followed it destroyed the Nixon administration's legitimacy for almost all political actors. President Ford, though himself quite conservative, pursued a policy course that also often moved pragmatically toward centrism, but after 1974 most conservative policy positions veered to the right.[20]

With regard to social welfare policies, the Nixon administration mingled a conservative attack on the Office of Economic Opportunity and vetoes of congressional measures to expand day-care facilities with endorsement of a centrist Family Assistance Plan (FAP) that entailed a $1,600 guaranteed annual income for a family of four coupled with work requirements. The FAP split conservatives and blurred long-term liberal-conservative cleavages on social welfare issues. With its defeat and the demise of the Nixon administration, conservatives generally renewed their previous broad attacks on the welfare state, favoring reduced spending on welfare programs for the poor and work requirements without most aspects of a guaranteed income, though conservative elected officials usually took care (unlike Goldwater in 1964) to protest their devotion to social security for the elderly as something quite separate from welfare. Many neoconservatives and some traditionalists, such as George Will, favored more extensive government provision of social welfare than most libertarian conservatives did; but virtually all of the conservative movement favored less than most liberals thought appropriate.[21]

Similarly, in the sphere of government economic management policies, Nixon's proclamation that he was a Keynesian and, even more so, his administration's adoption of of program of wage and price controls broke with past conservative policy prescriptions and created considerable disarray among conservatives. Later in the decade, however, most of the conservative movement rallied around either Milton Friedman's monetarist policy approach, shunning Keynesian fiscal policy efforts to manipulate demand, or supply-side economics, put forward by Arthur Laffer and popularized by Jude Wanniski and others, calling for massive tax cuts and business deregulation that would supposedly provide incentives for business to bring forth an enhanced supply of goods and services. Despite some major contradictions between these two approaches, both were oriented toward markets and the private sector. Quite a few conservatives joined Ronald Reagan in endorsing both as the period drew to a close. Of the two, however, supply-side economics, embodied in the Kemp-Roth plan of Representative Jack Kemp and Senator William Roth, came to enjoy the wider popular constituency among conservatives (though not among professional economists).[22]

In the civil rights domain, too, the mixed record of the Nixon administration exerted at least a partial moderating influence on the conservative coalition, though this was much less notably the case than on social welfare and economic management issues. In the centrist-to-liberal direction lay the Nixonian policies of supporting a Labor Department-sponsored "Philadelphia plan" for affirmative action and of providing financial incentives for Southern school desegregation. However, the Nixon administration also denounced court-ordered busing for desegregation in terms that roused conservative audiences, filed briefs in support of a Mississippi effort to delay school desegregation there, sought to appoint white Southerners with segregationist backgrounds to the Supreme Court, and engaged openly in a "Southern strategy" to woo Southern white voters. Overall, then, the Nixon administration's efforts probably reinforced, more than moderated, conservative trends in this sphere of public policy. Later in the decade, particularly after the Supreme Court limited mass busing for desegregation in most of the North and sent mixed signals on affirmative action in its *Bakke* decision, conservatives shifted their major focus from the antibusing crusade to attacks on affirmative action. By the time of the Reagan presidential campaign of 1980, these had become central to conservative ideology, despite the record of the Nixon administration on the subject.[23]

In what the liberals conceptualized as the civil liberties policy domain, conservatives increasingly perceived a sphere of social or sociocultural public policy—one in which the New Right joined traditionalist old-right conservatives in demanding government preservation of traditional values: prohibition of abortions, promotion of prayer and Bible-reading in public schools, curbs on pornography, restrictions on homosexual behavior, and loosening of court-ordered restraints on law enforcement officers so that they could allegedly restore order. However, most libertarian conservatives, some neoconservatives, and some fusionists, such as Barry Goldwater, rejected important parts of this agenda, splitting the conservative movement badly on many of these issues. The Nixon administration moved cautiously, appealing to law and order and the vague cultural conservatism of the "silent majority" without taking concrete steps that would offend too many libertarian or other conservative sensibilities. This policy domain, more than any other, became one in which the conservative movement could not reach consensus, though it shifted in the late 1970s, at least in its rhetoric, in the direction advocated by the New Right–traditionalist conservative alliance. As it did so, some libertarians abandoned the conservative coalition altogether, adding to the small group who had done so previously, largely over defense and foreign policy matters. Most, however, remained in the conservative camp and supported Ronald Reagan in 1980 on other grounds.[24]

Finally, there was the foreign and defense policy sphere, an area of considerable conservative consensus around anti-Communist, interventionist themes since the mid-1950s. Here, the Nixon administration mixed policies of détente with the Soviet Union, an opening to the People's Republic of China, and gradual troop withdrawal from Vietnam with expansion of the Indochinese conflict into Cambodia, massive bombing of North Vietnamese cities, and heavy pressures to bring down the Socialist-Communist coalition headed by Salvador Allende that had won power constitutionally and democratically in Chile. Once again, many conservatives were uncertain in their reactions to the moderate strand in the Nixonian policy mix. As in other areas, the demise of the Nixon administration brought a sharp conservative move toward the right of the policy spectrum, as conservatives called for a major military buildup, an end to détente, and an array of covert (and not-so-covert) efforts to roll back Communism in various parts of the globe. Though some conservatives were considerably more optimistic and ambitious than others about the possibilities of remolding the world in an American image and some important internal differences existed over policies toward China and over human rights, virtually all conservatives favored an array of anti-Communist policies, including major new armaments. Anti-Communism linked to national security concerns still provided important glue to maintain conservative unity.[25]

### Liberal and Conservative Internal Conflicts

Although each major ideological coalition maintained a distinctive identity during the period of flux from 1966 to 1981, to an extent understated by many analyses that focus on factions or tendencies within each movement, each was also riven by fairly sharp conflicts, as has already been noted. For liberalism, the most serious of these was certainly that between the new-politics, reformist, postcontainment liberals and the old-politics, consolidationist, Cold War liberals, for it provoked a substantial exodus by the neoconservatives to the main opposition movement. Within the conservative coalition, the overall adjustments stemming from the influx of the New Right (and especially its new religious right subgrouping) and the neoconservatives drove some libertarian conservatives, but not most of them, out of the coalition—but into independence rather than allegiance to the liberal coalition. The increased activism and commitment of big-business conservatives probably fostered conservative political success and unity by funneling additional money and other organizational resources into a variety of conservative causes. Therefore, despite considerable flux and some sharp internal conflicts within each ideological coalition, a broad liberal-versus-conservative division still shaped American politics in 1980, as it had done since the New Deal years.

## Beyond and between Liberalism and Conservatism

The New Left, a significant factor outside the two main coalitions at the beginning of this period, splintered and went into a sharp decline in the late 1960s; and the counterculture never became explicitly political. Both of these, however, had important influences on new-politics liberalism and produced sharp reactions among many already conservative activists and others who were soon to be conservatives. A few libertarians detached themselves from the conservative coalition in the late 1960s, and others did so later, making radical libertarianism a force outside both major alliances and a base for a small Libertarian party. To some extent, a vague populism also existed, at least in popular attitudes, outside the liberal and conservative coalitions of the era.[26]

Of the three presidencies of the period, that of Jimmy Carter was the least attached to either ideological coalition. Carter himself had virtually no previous links to the liberal coalition from his prepolitical career or his years in Georgia state politics. He was viewed with distrust by most major leaders of the liberal movement in Congress and in the sphere of intellectuals and interest groups. When Edward Kennedy challenged Carter's bid for reelection in 1980, Kennedy was able to draw upon substantial support from the liberal coalition. Carter's most insightful political biographer has characterized his basic personal views on politics as "centrist" and has concluded: "He lacks, it seems, a well-thought-out conceptual framework to guide his concrete political choices." James Fallows, one of his leading speechwriters, expressed the view that "Carter believes fifty things, but no one thing." The Carter administration did unquestionably include more liberals than conservatives, a point stressed by Alonzo Hamby in placing Carter within the liberal tradition. Yet Hamby himself notes Carter's appointment of monetarist Paul Volcker to head the powerful Federal Reserve Board. Hamby notably neglected to point out such other Carter appointees to key posts as James Schlesinger, Bert Lance, Griffin Bell, and Zbigniew Brzezinski. Carter himself should probably be classified as a moderate, generally seeking to find a centrist course between the two coalitions. His administration, despite his nonliberal appointments to key posts, was moderate-liberal in orientation.[27]

Nixon and Ford, in contrast to Carter, personally possessed strong ideological movement ties—to the conservative movement. James Reichley, in particular, has made a strong case for classifying them and their administrations as conservative, albeit of moderate-conservative coloration. Nixon personally appears to have been "aprincipled" in his behavior as president, however, a point made by Joan Hoff in particular but shared by other observers. Ford, despite displaying more genuine conservatism than Nixon, almost lost his renomination bid in 1976 to Ronald Reagan, who drew strong support from the conservative movement. Though both Nixon and Ford and their administrations sometimes strayed from the path desired by the bulk of the conservative coalition, they maintained fairly solid conservative links.[28]

So, too, did the "peak" interest groups of the business community. However, despite a shift toward conservatism, many large business corporations and trade associations continued to operate largely outside the boundaries of ideological coalition politics in pursuit of specific material interests. Through the business political action committees that proliferated after the campaign finance law changes of 1974 and their new or upgraded Washington lobbying efforts, they channeled campaign contributions and made contacts that often cut across ideological lines, especially when dealing with powerful congressional incumbents, to an extent that upset some conservatives.[29]

Many, probably most, nonbusiness interest groups also pursued strategies that led them to operate frequently outside either ideological coalition in order to seek support wherever they could find it—from liberals, moderates, and conservatives. As one leading scholar of interest groups later noted, "the norm among interest groups in Washington is that *no one is too evil to work with.*"[30]

The continuing decline of old-style machine politics meant that elected politicians were more likely to have clear ties to one ideological coalition or the other than had been true even in the 1940s or 1950s. Schneider found considerable evidence to this effect in his congressional interviews. However, Reichley was probably correct (despite some problems of operationalizing his definitions) to distinguish Republican "stalwarts" and Democratic "regulars" who were less strongly committed to the ideologies of the conservative and liberal coalitions, respectively, than their "fundamentalist" and "liberal" colleagues, despite usually voting with them.[31]

## Conclusions

The years between 1966 and 1981 were a time of considerable turbulence and upheaval in American politics. They also represented a period of transition between the New Deal and post–World War II years, during which the political initiative had usually rested with the liberal coalition, and the Reagan period, when the conservative alliance gained the upper hand in setting the American political agenda.

Each coalition underwent considerable flux and was ruptured by new cleavages. Liberalism shifted generally in the direction of new-politics, reformist, postcontainment liberalism; suffered the defection of the small but politically significant faction that came to be dubbed neoconservatives; and became increasingly segmented into separate movements and interest groups with different priorities but fairly broadly shared assumptions and values. Conservatives lost some libertarian support but made net gains from the addition of neoconservatives and new religious rightists and from additional big-business organizational and financial backing. After considerable confusion during the Nixon administration, conservatives attained considerable consensus on public policies stressing tax cuts and deregulation of business, staunchly anti-Communist foreign and defense efforts, and opposition to affirmative action and attained somewhat less marked agreement on social-policy matters.

Next, this study turns its attention to the changes in the power bases of conservatism and liberalism that accompanied these alterations of principles and public policy preferences. These were particularly noteworthy with regard to Congress and the presidency, the two most central shapers of American public policy, but shifts occurred in other areas also.

### Notes

1. Brown quoted in "Big Turnabout among U.S. Liberals," *U.S. News & World Report,* 80 (15 March 1976): 18. Simon Lazarus, *The Genteel Populists* (New York: Holt, Rinehart, & Winston, 1974), 230. Alonzo L. Hamby, *Liberalism and Its Challengers,* 2d ed. (New York: Oxford University Press, 1992), 279; Michael W. McCann, *Taking Reform Seriously* (Ithaca, NY: Cornell University Press, 1986), esp. 72–79.

2. Linda Medcalf and Kenneth Dolbeare, *Neopolitics* (New York: Random House, 1985), chap. 5, discusses the liberal programmatic movements and links them to reform liberalism. Also see McCann, chap. 2; and Kenneth M. Dolbeare and Patricia Dolbeare, *American Ideologies,* 2d ed. (Chicago: Markham, 1973), chaps. 3 and 4. Steven M. Gillon, *Politics and Vision* (New York: Oxford University

Press, 1987), chaps. 8–10, discusses the transformation of the ADA.

3.  Hamby, *Liberalism and Its Challengers,* 279; Tyler's quotation is cited in Gillon, *Politics and Vision,* 193. Also see K. Dolbeare and P. Dolbeare, *American Ideologies,* chaps. 3 and 4, and McGann, *Taking Reform Seriously,* esp. chap. 2.

4.  Gillon, *Politics and Vision,* 228–229; Jerrold L. Schneider, *Ideological Coalitions in Congress* (Westport, CT: Greenwood Press, 1979), 80.

5.  Herbert J. Gans, *More Equality* (New York: Pantheon Books, 1973); Christopher Jencks, *Inequality* (New York: Basic Books, 1972); Gillon, *Politics and Vision,* 229; the Rawls quotation, from *Political Liberalism* (New York: Columbia University Press, 1993), 271, is cited by Vernon Van Dyke, *Ideology and Political Choice* (Chatham, NJ: Chatham House, 1995), 83.

6.  Richard Kahlenberg, "Class, Not Race: An Affirmative Action That Works," *New Republic* 212 (3 April 1995): 21–27.

7.  Arnold S. Kaufman, *The Radical Liberal* (New York: Simon & Schuster, 1968), 72. The ADA quotation is from Gillon, *Politics and Vision,* 229. Also see McCann, *Taking Reform Seriously,* esp. 24, 90–105.

8.  McCann, *Taking Reform Seriously,* 24.

9.  Peter Steinfels, *The Neoconservatives* (New York: Simon & Schuster, 1979), quotes Glazer on 217, Huntington on 262. Gillon, *Politics and Vision,* 193, discusses Tyler's views.

10.  A. James Reichley, *Conservatives in an Age of Change* (Washington: Brookings Institution, 1981), chap. 7; Daniel Patrick Moynihan, *The Politics of a Guaranteed Income* (New York: Random House, 1973).

11.  Kim McQuaid, *Big Business and Presidential Power* (New York: William Morrow, 1982), chap. 9; David Vogel, *Fluctuating Fortunes* (New York: Basic Books, 1989), chaps. 3–8; William Greider, *Who Will Tell the People? The Betrayal of American Democracy* (New York: Simon & Schuster, 1992), esp. 123–130, on regulatory implementation difficulties; E. J. Dionne Jr., *Why Americans Hate Politics* (New York: Simon & Schuster, 1991), esp. 242–249, on the decline of liberal Keynesianism.

12.  "The Abortion Decision," *Commonweal* 97 (16 February 1973): 435–436; Van Dyke, *Ideology and Political Choice,* 69–70.

13.  Thomas Byrne Edsall and Mary D. Edsall, *Chain Reaction,* (New York: W. W. Norton, 1991), esp. 87–90, 116–129.

14.  Schneider, *Ideological Coalitions,* chap. 3; K. Dolbeare and P. Dolbeare, *American Ideologies,* 92–93, 95.

15.  Medcalf and K. Dolbeare, *Neopolitics,* chap. 5.

16.  The literature on the neoconservatives from which this paragraph was drawn is vast. See, for example, in addition to the Steinfels work cited previously, Gary Dorrien, *The Neoconservative Mind* (Philadelphia: Temple University Press, 1993); Irving Kristol, *Reflections of a Neoconservative* (New York: Basic Books, 1983); Paul Gottfried and Thomas Fleming, *The Conservative Movement* (Boston: Twayne, 1988), chap. 4; Sidney Blumenthal, *The Rise of the Counter-Establishment* (New York: Harper & Row, 1986), chap. 6; Medcalf and K. Dolbeare, *American Ideologies,* chap. 8; and Van Dyke, *Ideology and Political Choice,* chap. 13.

17.  The quotations are from Medcalf and K. Dolbeare, *American Ideologies,* 166,

and Jerome L. Himmelstein, *To the Right* (Berkeley and Los Angeles: University of California Press, 1990), 85. See also Alan Crawford, *Thunder on the Right* (New York: Pantheon Books, 1980); Kevin P. Phillips, *Post–Conservative America* (New York: Random House, 1982); and James C. Roberts, *The Conservative Decade— Emerging Leaders of the 1980s* (Westport, CT: Arlington House, 1980).

18. Gottfried and Fleming, *Conservative Movement,* esp. 82–84; Dionne, *Why Americans Hate Politics,* chap. 8; Van Dyke, *Ideology and Political Choice,* chap. 11.

19. Blumenthal, *The Rise of the Counter-Establishment,* 55, contains the quotation; chaps. 3 and 4 cover the topic of rising big-business conservatism well, as do Himmelstein, *To the Right,* chap. 5; Vogel, *Fluctuating Fortunes,* chaps. 6–8; and Thomas Byrne Edsall, *The New Politics of Inequality* (New York: W. W. Norton, 1984), esp. chap. 3. Useful comparative perspectives are found in Joel Krieger, *Reagan, Thatcher, and the Politics of Decline* (New York: Oxford University Press, 1986), esp. the introduction and chap. 1; and Mark Kesselman, et. al., *European Politics in Transition* (Boston: D.C. Heath, 1987), esp. 17–22.

20. Hamby, *Liberalism and its Challengers,* chap. 7, treats the Nixon administration in these general terms, although he misleadingly labels it "neoconservative." Dionne, *Why Americans Hate Politics,* 189–208, labels the Nixon–Ford policies a continuation of Eisenhower-style modern Republicanism—which is probably closer to the mark than Hamby's label but still does not capture the complexity of the reality. Reichley, *Age of Change,* places the Nixon-Ford administration more firmly within the conservative camp than the others do.

21. On FAP, see Reichley, *Age of Change,* chap. 7; and Moynihan, *Guaranteed Annual Income.* On the OEO battle, see Joan Hoff, *Nixon Reconsidered* (New York: Basic Books, 1994), 60–65; and Arthur M. Schlesinger Jr., *The Imperial Presidency* (New York: Popular Library, 1973), 235–236. On day care, see Gary Orfield, *Congressional Power* (New York: Harcourt Brace Jovanovich, 1975), 302–306. For neoconservative social welfare views, see Steinfels, *Neoconservatives,* esp. 219–224; and Van Dyke, *Ideology and Political Choice,* 228–229. On Will, see Van Dyke, *Ideology and Political Choice,* 206–207.

22. On the Nixon administration's economic management policies, see Leonard Silk, *Nixonomics* (New York: Praeger, 1972), and Reichley, *Conservatives,* chap. 10. Blumenthal, *Rise of the Counter-Establishment,* chap. 5, provides a good discussion of monetarism and its relation to conservative politics, while chap. 7 does the same for supply–side economics.

23. T. Edsall and M. Edsall, *Chain Reaction,* esp. chap. 4, 123–128, 186–187; Hamby, *Liberalism and Its Challengers,* 320–321.

24. Dionne, *Why Americans Hate Politics,* 219–241, chap. 10; Gottfried and Fleming, *Conservative Movement,* esp. 84–86.

25. On the Nixon and Ford administrations' foreign policies and their relationships to conservatism, see Reichley, *Age of Change,* chaps. 6 and 16. Schneider, *Ideological Coalitons,* chap. 3, provides useful insights into the foreign and defense policy view of congressional conservatives. Medcalf and K. Dolbeare, *Neopolitics,* 156–157, captures the essence of 1980 conservative foreign and defense policy.

26. Christopher Lasch, "The Disintegration of the New Left," in *Political Ideologies,* ed. James A. Gould and Willis H. Truitt (New York: Macmillan, 1973),

336–348; K. Dolbeare and P. Dolbeare, *American Ideologies,* chap. 8; Dionne, *Why Americans Hate Politics,* 259–270; William S. Maddox and Stuart A. Lilie, *Beyond Liberal and Conservative* (Washington: Cato Institute, 1984); Jerome Tuccille, *Radical Libertarianism* (Indianapolis, IN: Bobbs–Merrill, 1970); Donald I. Warren, *The Radical Center* (South Bend, IN: Notre Dame University Press, 1976).

27.  Betty Glad, *Jimmy Carter* (New York: W. W. Norton, 1980), 476; James Fallows, "The Passionless Presidency," *Atlantic Monthly* 243 (May 1979): 42; Hamby, *Liberalism and Its Challenges,* 353–354; Dionne, *Why Americans Hate Politics,* chap. 5.

28.  Reichley, *Age of Change.*

29.  T. Edsall, *New Politics of Inequality,* esp. 128–136; Vogel, *Fluctuating Fortunes,* 206–213.

30.  Jeffrey M. Berry, *The Interest Group Society,* 2d ed. (Glenview, IL: Scott, Foresman, 1989), 169.

31.  Schneider, *Ideological Coalitions,* esp. 47–90; Reichley, *Age of Change,* 22–28, 80–85.

# 13

# Government Institutions:
# Liberal and Conservative Power Centers

The long-term linkage of the presidency and the centralized bureaucracy to the liberal coalition virtually disintegrated during the 1966–81 period, though a strong new connection between them and the conservative movement did not emerge clearly. Lyndon Johnson's already ambivalent ties to liberalism gave way to increased rancor between the president and much of the liberal coalition after 1966, and no other president of the period possessed even the liberal links that Johnson had. Jimmy Carter, the sole Democratic chief executive for more than two decades after 1969, was a moderate who, prior to his run for the presidency, had rarely even interacted with the liberal coalition. Though, as discussed in the previous chapter, his administration drew upon a significant number of liberals to fill important slots, even the administration should be classified only as moderate-liberal, given its inclusion in key positions outright conservatives, such as James Schlesinger, and prominent nonliberals including Paul Volcker, Bert Lance, Griffin Bell, and Zbigniew Brzezinski.[1]

Nixon and Ford and their administrations were more clearly conservative than Carter and his administration were liberal, but most of the conservative movement expressed some dissatisfaction with the depth and extent of their conservatism. Nixon, particularly, often appeared to display an aversion to consistent ideological principles. Ford, while personally more inclined than Nixon to adopt the current norms of conservative philosophy as his own, in 1976 faced a sharp conservative challenge, unlike Nixon in 1972, to his bid for the Republican presidential nomination. Both administrations included a number of staunch conservatives with movement linkages, such as Patrick Buchanan, Earl Butz, and Alan Greenspan, and Nixon's "administrative presidency" efforts, intended to make the career bureaucracy much more conservative than it had been, achieved some marked successes in that regard for a time, as Richard Cole and David Caputo have documented. However, moderate conservatives and nonideologues generally predominated at the top levels in each administration, much to the dismay of conservatives such as Buchanan, who strongly urged Nixon to recast his administration along sharply conservative lines.[2]

Meanwhile, inside Congress, changes were occurring that shifted power in a generally liberal direction, even as the overall membership shifted only slightly to the left. One of the biggest alterations in Congress that added to liberal strength took place in the standing committee system. From the 1930s to the 1960s, committee chairs had disproportionately been Southern Democratic conservatives, who piled up seniority without significant challenges to their bids for reelection in the one-party South and then automatically gained key committee positions and great legislative power. As recently as the Eighty-seventh Congress (1961–62), there had been only two liberal chairs of sixteen in the Senate, and most of the important standing committees in each chamber were run by conservatives. (Liberals were those voting with the conservative coalition, as measured by *Congressional Quarterly,* on one third or fewer of the pertinent roll calls; liberalism scores were calculated on the basis of the percentage of the time that a member opposed the conservative coalition.) By the Ninety-fourth Congress (1975–76), party competition in the South combined with deaths and retirements to give liberals seven standing committee chairmanships in the Senate and eight in the House of Representatives. Among these were Ray Madden, who was at the helm of the key House Rules Committee, which controlled the flow of legislation to the floor, and Brock Adams and Edmund Muskie, who were chairs of the two new Budget Committees, slated to play a major role under the budgetary reform rules adopted in 1974. Moreover, the liberalism scores of committee chairs had risen dramatically in the Senate and somewhat in the House, as table 13.1 illustrates. Perhaps even more significantly, the House Democratic Caucus ousted three conservative chairs in 1975, sending a message to all chairs that resistance to the liberalism predominant in the caucus might be dangerous to one's hold on power. Meanwhile, power was increasingly flowing into the hands of subcommittee chairs, many of them fairly junior liberal Democrats. The 1974 House Democrats' adoption of "the subcommittee bill of rights" accelerated this trend.[3]

Also nudging Congress in a liberal direction during the late 1960s and early 1970s was the rising pressure generated by the new-politics liberal movements and interest groups. Especially those that stressed the public interest won wide popular backing for a time, and Congress paid them

Table 13.1
Standing-Committee Chairs, 87th and 94th Congresses

|  | House | Senate |
|---|---|---|
| 87th Congress (1961–1962) | | |
| Liberal chairs/total chairs | 7/20 | 2/16 |
| Average liberalism scores of chairs | 51.7 | 32.6 |
| 94th Congress (1975–1976) | | |
| Liberal chairs/total chairs | 8/20 | 7/16 |
| Average liberalism scores of chairs | 55.4 | 59 |

heed in enacting new regulatory legislation in a number of spheres. Although this "advocacy explosion," as Jeffrey Berry termed it, on the political left would soon be counteracted by a combination of New Right and big-business activism, it had a temporary liberalizing effect on Congress, as did the institutional struggles with the Nixon administration during that same period.[4]

Still, the conservative coalition in Congress continued to win more often than it lost on roll-call votes, as tabulated by the *Congressional Quarterly*. Although Congress hardly became a citadel of liberalism between 1966 and 1981, change in the relative ideological positions of the national legislative and executive branches became evident. The growing liberal power in the House Democratic Caucus and within the committee and subcommittee systems in each chamber combined with the liberals' inability to win the presidency and the partial success of Nixon's conservatizing administrative-state changes to create a new pattern in which it could no longer be assumed that the presidency and the upper reaches of the executive branch would necessarily, or even ordinarily, be more liberal than Congress. Whether the reverse would come to be true for the long term remained uncertain as the decade of the 1970s drew to a close, but there were some indicators that it might.[5]

On the Supreme Court and in the federal court system generally, old patterns were also giving way to new ones. Nixon's four appointees to the Supreme Court and Ford's single appointee unquestionably shifted the High Bench somewhat in a conservative policy direction on both economics and civil liberties but less dramatically and consistently than most of the conservative coalition had hoped and expected. Conservative legal scholar Christopher Wolfe delineated "a few definite conservative shifts" but concluded that the picture was "complex and mixed, and very difficult to characterize simply." From the liberal perspective, law professor Bernard Schwartz saw the High Court increasingly engaged in a "rootless activism." Most justices now "dealt with cases on an essentially *ad hoc* basis, inspired less by moral vision than by pragmatic considerations." The liberal Court majority of the Warren era dwindled steadily. With the retirement of William O. Douglas, the last of the Roosevelt-appointed justices was gone; and the liberal bloc was reduced to just two: Thurgood Marshall and William Brennan. However, of the Nixon and Ford appointees, only William Rehnquist and Chief Justice Warren Burger were dependable supporters of conservatism on most matters, and Burger was far from a consistent proponent of conservative governance theory. In "the middle," tending toward a pragmatic and partial conservatism but engaging in widespread judicial activism, were Harry Blackmun, Lewis Powell, John Paul Stevens, and holdovers Potter Stewart and Byron White. No longer liberal, the Supreme Court in the 1970s was not fully conservative.[6]

In the lower federal courts, the picture was even more mixed and shifting. There, in contrast to the Supreme Court, to which Carter was able to make no appointments whatsoever, he enjoyed considerable impact. In fact, during his four years in office, he appointed 40 percent of the entire federal bench, a figure greater than for any previous president in a single term; and his appointees' decisional patterns resembled those of other Democratic presidents' appointees, according to Jon Gottschall's studies. Of at least equal significance, the federal district and appellate courts became major arenas for an array of liberal public-interest litigation during the 1970s, primarily with regard to interpretations of statutes, particularly in the regulatory field. This rash of litigation—at least before the major counterattacks by business and business-funded conservative public-interest groups—sometimes elicited pro-liberal decisions even from nonliberal judges, a point stressed heavily by such new-politics liberals as Simon Lazarus in arguing for this strategy. Thus the judicial scene overall appeared more supportive of liberalism during this period than a focus on Supreme Court justices alone would suggest. In fact, quite a few liberals and conservatives now perceived the judiciary to be institutionally oriented toward liberalism, in almost a perfect reversal of perceptions during the struggles of 1890–1937, and even those of the early 1940s, that it was inherently conservative.[7]

Out among the state and local governments, court-mandated legislative reapportionment ended rural overrepresentation, but population shifts from the cities to frequently conservative suburbs prevented the effects from boosting liberalism as much as many liberals had hoped. State government reform capacities improved but still usually lagged behind those of the national administrative state. Although governors such as Edmund G. (Jerry) Brown of California, Milton Shapp of Pennsylania, Patrick Lucey of Wisconsin, and Michael Dukakis of Massachusetts represented various tendencies within the liberal coalition, and often outnumbered clear-cut conservative governors such as Ronald Reagan of California, Meldrim Thomson of New Hampshire, or William Clements of Texas, many state structural features, including competition to attract and hold business investment, constitutionally imposed fragmentation and limits, narrowness of scope, and artificiality of boundaries, continued to hamper liberal social reform below the national level.[8]

The overall pattern in government institutions was probably less clear to the leaders of the liberal and conservative coalitions by the mid-1970s than at any time since the beginning of the New Deal era. The presidency seemed to be more conservative than any major analysts had foreseen as recently as 1965, but the independent Carter won in 1976 and the series of three consecutive conservative presidential election victories was still in the future. Moreover, the liberals retained considerable support in the upper reaches of the civil service even under conservative presidencies. Congressional liberals had made noticeable power gains, but the conservative coalition still won more roll-call votes than it lost in most congressional sessions. While more conservative than in the period 1954–66, the Supreme Court was usually dominated by a moderately conservative center that lacked strong connections to the conservative movement; and the lower federal courts were even less clearly conservative than the Supreme Court. Finally, the reapportioned and partially reformed state and local governments were a somewhat less inhospitable environment for liberalism than previously.

### Political Parties

The four-party model of James MacGregor Burns (liberal presidential Democrats, moderate-conservative congressional Democrats, moderate presidential Republicans, conservative congressional Republicans)—already in flux before 1966—underwent further transformation. Although the presidential Democratic party remained generally liberal, the new-politics/old-politics split complicated matters; and Carter's winning of the Democratic presidential nomination in 1976 and renomination in 1980 indicated the limits of that liberalism. In fact, the congressional Democrats, led by Northern liberals Tip O'Neill and Mike Mansfield, were more inclined toward liberalism on quite a few issues, including natural gas and gasoline price regulation, social security, national health insurance, and urban aid legislation, than the Carter administration was. Meanwhile, the ideological pattern of moderate presidential Republicans versus conservative congressional Republicans never reappeared after 1964. Instead, the Senate Republican party, especially when led between 1969 and 1977 by moderate Hugh Scott of Pennsylvania, was usually the least conservative sector of the Republican party, while the House Republicans remained the bastion of conservatism that they had been without interruption since the New Deal.[9]

## Interest Groups

The most significant new developments reshaping the interest-group and mass-movement bases of the liberal and conservative coalitions were the waves of new-politics liberal movements and groups that were the center of the advocacy explosion of the late 1960s, the counterwaves of religious right and other New Right groups that emerged shortly thereafter, and the new business groups and enhanced political involvement of business corporations and older business groups that were in large part a reaction during the 1970s to the new-politics liberal activism in the domestic socioeconomic sphere.

Just as the civil rights movement had added new components to the liberal coalition and altered its orientations in the 1950s and early 1960s, so, too, on an even larger scale, did the antiwar, feminist, environmentalist, consumer protection, workplace health and safety, and procedural reform movements of the late 1960s and 1970s. Each of these spawned new interest groups, many of which endured and became long-term centers of new-politics liberalism. Although most of the anti–Vietnam War interest groups did not long survive the end of that conflict, their legacy to liberalism was a continuing skepticism about overseas interventions and a disinclination to see the containment doctrine as a sound basis for public policy. The National Organization for Women, Environmental Action, the Health Research Group, Public Citizen, and Common Cause were just a few of the most prominent new organizations that proved durable bases for new-politics liberalism. Largely composed of middle-class liberals, they increasingly edged aside such old liberal interest groups based among working-class and lower-income groups as the

National Farmers Union and the AFL-CIO, though some of them did seek out and maintain alliances with organized labor. Older middle-class liberal groups, such as the Americans for Democratic Action and the American Civil Liberties Union, remained important and linked themselves to the new groups ideologically and strategically, but they were less central to defining liberalism than previously.[10]

The chief organizational power base after 1966 for the old-politics, consolidationist, Cold War liberalism was unquestionably the AFL-CIO, headed by an aging oligarchy of mostly white males of working-class backgrounds, typified by its top leader of the period, George Meany of the Plumbers' Union. After a decade of often intense struggle for control of the liberal movement and the Democratic party, the old-politics and new-politics forces eventually came to terms—but the terms reflected the declining potency of labor. Organizing 31.4 percent of the workforce in 1960, unions enrolled only 23.6 percent by 1978. Moreover, driven in part by a fear of increased international competition, organized business was demonstrating heightened determination to combat trade unionism rather than to compromise with it. These factors, together with the end of the Vietnam War, which had divided most AFL-CIO leaders from most new-politics liberals, made possible a rapprochement of sorts within the liberal coalition in the late 1970s. However, organized labor no longer played what Thomas Byrne Edsall termed "the central role in the lobbying process" for the entire liberal agenda that it often had from the 1930s to the 1960s. Moreover, by 1978, liberals faced a conservative movement rapidly gaining strength and intent on seizing control of the national political agenda.[11]

Two major streams of new interest-group/mass-movement activity flowed into the conservative coalition during the 1970s. The first sprang from a long-term, conventional source of conservative support: the business community. Fearful of the new-politics liberals and angered by their successes in the regulatory and judicial arenas and concerned about rising worldwide economic pressures, big business became more politically active and more clearly attached to the conservative coalition. One indication of the shift in the big-business approach was the creation in 1972 of the Business Roundtable, an organization composed of about two hundred of the chief executive officers of the nation's largest business corporations. Involving the CEOs themselves in lobbying and drawing extensively on the resources of giant corporations, the Roundtable very quickly became an important factor in politics. "Although other business peak associations have long existed, including the Chamber of Commerce and the National Association of Manufacturers," concluded a leading scholar of interest groups, "none has so effectively utilized the resources of its members as the Roundtable."[12]

But the Business Roundtable was only one indicator of the new business conservative activism. New conservative foundations, such as the Heritage Foundation and the Institute for Educational Affairs, and old foundations that became newly linked to the conservative cause, such as the John M. Olin Foundation, received millions of dollars from America's corporate elite in the 1970s and funneled it into new conservative journals, books, issues research, and other efforts aimed at establishing a business-oriented conservative agenda for the nation and "educating" the public to support it. Wordsmiths from all factions and tendencies within the conservative movement, including the ostensibly populistic New Right, gained considerable big-business financial backing. Moreover, the changes in the federal campaign finance laws in 1974, ironically endorsed by organized labor and most new-politics liberals, enabled corporations to form hundreds (and eventually over two thousand) new political action committees to give campaign contributions to political candidates. Many corporations also set up new Washington lobbying offices or signed on with Washington law firms to gain increased representation of their interests during the 1970s.[13]

While big business was mobilizing and deploying its resources with increasing effectiveness after 1972, often in behalf of conservatism generally, the New Right, and especially its religious right segment, was drawing hundreds of thousands of activists into the conservative movement, many of them from the lower middle class. Some groups associated with the New Right, such as Phyllis Schlafly's Stop-ERA, were already on the scene before the term "New Right" came into currency. The so-called (by its opponents) radical right of the 1950s and 1960s also provided a base of support. But 1974 appears to have been the most critical formative year. The Supreme Court's abortion decision in *Roe v. Wade* (1973) and President Ford's designation of Nelson Rockefeller as his vice presidential choice (1974) were key events. The newest elements of the New Right were the groups constituting the religious right movement. Unlike such New Right leaders as Richard Viguerie, Howard Phillips, Paul Weyrich, Patrick Buchanan, and Phyllis Schlafly, who had long been active in conservative politics, most of the religious right movement consisted of political newcomers, many of whom had been resolutely nonpolitical in the past. Jerry Falwell, for example, during the 1960s had preached to his Baptist congregation, like most white Protestant evangelicals of the time, against political involvement of religious figures. However, growing concern about the counterculture and liberal "permissiveness," accentuated by the abortion decision, galvanized the religious right into action. By the end of the decade, Falwell's Moral Majority would become a household name, and the religious right would have channeled an army of new participants into the conservative coalition.[14]

Some of the mainstays of the conservative movement, such as the American Bar Association, ceased in the late 1960s and 1970s to be closely associated with it. The ABA even occasionally endorsed liberal proposals, such as the Equal Rights Amendment, and incurred some conservative wrath over its roles in the judicial selection process. Others, such as the American Farm Bureau Federation and the American Medical Association, became less centrally involved than before but retained close ties. Still others, such as the National Association of Manufacturers and the United States Chamber of Commerce, remained at least as active as previously but shared the conservative podium with new spokespersons reflective of new business groups and the New Right and the religious right.

Although some interest groups left one coalition or the other or dissolved and many other interest groups never associated extensively with either ideological movement, the period from 1966 to 1981 was marked by a proliferation of interest-group activity linked to the two coalitions. At first, from 1966 to 1972, the influx was most obviously to the liberal coalition, enabling it to score some victories on socioeconomic regulatory issues despite the loss of the presidency. Subsequently, however, heightened business involvement combined with the somewhat independent surge of the New Right and the religious right (and the intellectual contributions of the neoconservatives and other wordsmiths) to give the conservative movement the edge.

## Wordsmiths

If liberal and conservative interest groups and movements proliferated between 1966 and 1981, the surge of new wordsmiths was also impressive. In this sphere, however, actual realignments of allegiance were more noteworthy than among interest groups.

New journals and magazines were among the most evident developments in the conservative movement. Although *National Review* remained the most important, it lost some of its centrality to the conservative movement and came to be seen increasingly as an outlet primarily for the old right. *Modern Age* continued to be identified with traditionalist intellectual conservatism. Beginning operation in 1968, *Reason* articulated libertarian views. The New Right had its own publication, *Conservative Digest;* and *Policy Review,* published by the new and influential Heritage Foundation, included both New Right and old right authors. The most prolific writers of all were the neoconservatives, who transformed *Commentary* from a liberal to a neoconservative journal and who also dominated the new journal *The Public Interest* and came to be increasingly influential in another new publication, *American Spectator.* Among major newspapers, the *Wall Street Journal* editorial page became much more a center of conservative political interchange and ideas than previously, bringing together many strands of conservatism with a large business readership. While it remained generally conservative, the *Chicago Tribune* did not play a role equivalent to that of the *Journal.*[15]

On the liberal side, the *New York Times* and the *Washington Post* editorials remained the bellwethers of mainstream liberal thought that they had become by the early 1960s. The *Times* moderated its new-politics liberalism somewhat after its publisher forced John Oakes out as its editorial page editor in 1977, allegedly for being too antibusiness and as a result of a dispute over a senatorial-primary endorsement; but both newspapers remained broadly committed to the liberal movement as the period drew to a close. The *New Republic* flirted with new-politics liberalism in the late 1960s and early 1970s but included contributions from all branches of liberalism, and sometimes neoconservatism also, as the decade advanced. As in the case of the *New York Times*, its publisher's inclinations had some constraining effects on liberalism. The *Nation* and the *Progressive,* on the other hand, tended toward the left wing of new-politics liberalism, as did the *New York Review of Books. Commonweal* represented a blending of mainly new-politics liberalism with distinctively Roman Catholic thought.

Even a brief review of the changes in the liberal-conservative wordsmith lineups indicates the power shift here, too, in a generally conservative direction as the decade of the 1970s moved toward a conclusion.[16]

## Conclusions

The changes in liberal and conservative power bases between 1966 and 1981 contrasted sharply with the continuity that had usually prevailed from 1945 to 1966. Organized labor lost much of its clout in the liberal coalition and found itself at odds with the new-politics tendency in that coalition during most of the period. Middle-class, citizen-based movements and interest groups grew markedly in importance in each coalition, but big business made strong gains also from 1972 onward. An array of new publications appeared, mainly on the political right, and usually funded by wealthy contributors based in big business. Even liberal publications, such as the *New York Times* and the *New Republic,* sometimes found limits placed on their liberalism by the pressures exerted by the power of money. Clearly, the societal power balance was shifting toward conservatism by the late 1970s.

As for government institutions, liberal and conservative power balances there shifted to such an extent that each coalition found it necessary to reassess Barry Goldwater's 1964 conclusions that "the state governments and the Congress by and large stand on one side of the battle line. They face across that battle line, the Executive Branch and, usually, the Judicial Branch, the Supreme Court." Liberals' inability to win the presidency, growing liberal power in Congress, a mixed ideological picture inside the executive branch, centrism on the Supreme Court and a confused judicial pattern overall, and state reforms mingled with continuing conservative structural biases—this combination might be expected to provoke some changes in the theories of governance long prevalent within each ideological movement, if instrumental pursuit of power and policy goals was indeed as important in shaping those theories as this book has suggested.[17]

## Notes

1. Betty Glad, *Jimmy Carter* (New York: W. W. Norton, 1980); E.J. Dionne Jr., *Why Americans Hate Politics* (New York: Simon & Schuster, 1991), chap. 5; Sidney M. Milkis and Michael Nelson, *The American Presidency,* 2d ed. (Washington: Congressional Quarterly Press, 1994), 353–355; and Iwan W. Morgan, *Beyond the Liberal Consensus* (New York: St. Martin's Press, 1994), 161–162, support these conclusions, Alonzo L. Hamby, *Liberalism and Its Challengers,* 2d ed. (New York: Oxford University Press, 1992), 353–354, sees Carter as more liberal than this account does. Technically, Volcker may not be seen as part of the administration, but he was appointed by Carter to chair the Federal Reserve Board and was widely identified with the administration.

2. A. James Reichley, *Conservatives in an Age of Change* (Washington: Brookings Institution, 1981), esp. chap. 19; Hamby, *Liberalism and Its Challengers,* chap. 7 and 352–353; Dionne, *Why Americans Hate Politics,* 193–200; Joan Hoff, *Nixon Reconsidered* (New York: Basic Books, 1994), 3, 300; and Morgan, *Beyond the Liberal Consensus,* 96, all support these conclusions. On the bureaucracy, see Joel D. Aberbach and Bert A. Rockman, "Clashing Beliefs within the Executive Branch: The Nixon Administration Bureaucracy," *American Political Science Review* 70 (June 1976): 456–468, and Richard L. Cole and David A. Caputo, "Presidential Control of the Senior Civil Service: Addressing the Strategies of the Nixon Years," *American Political Science Review* 73 (June 1979): 399–413. Stephen Ambrose, *Nixon: The Triumph*

*of a Politician, 1962-1972* (New York: Simon & Schuster, 1989), 405, 407, discusses Buchanan's complaints and efforts to "conservatize" the administration.

3. Gary Orfield, *Congressional Power* (New York: Harcourt Brace Jovanovich, 1975), esp. 7–12; Hedrick Smith, *The Power Game* (New York: Ballantine Books, 1988), 24–25.

4. Jeffrey M. Berry, *The Interest Group Society,* 2d ed. (Glenview, IL: Scott, Foresman, 1989), chap. 2; Michael W. McCann, *Taking Reform Seriously* (Ithaca, NY: Cornell University Press, 1986); David Vogel, *Fluctuating Fortunes* (New York: Basic Books, 1989), chaps. 3–5.

5. *Congressional Quarterly Almanac,* 1980, 35–C, indicates conservative coalition victories, by year.

6. Christopher Wolfe, *The Rise of Modern Judicial Review,* rev. ed. (Lanham, MD: Rowman & LIttlefield, 1994), 292–293; Bernard Schwartz, *The Ascent of Pragmatism* (Reading, MA: Addison–Wesley, 1990), 410, 412; Sheldon Goldman, *Constitutional Law and Supreme Court Decision-Making* (New York: Harper & Row, 1982), esp. 539–543.

7. On Carter's judicial appointments, see Thomas G. Walker and Deborah J. Barrow, "The Diversification of the Federal Bench: Policy and Process Ramifications," *Journal of Politics* 47 (May 1985): 596–619; Jon Gottschall, "Carter's Judicial Appointments: The Influence of Affirmative Action and Merit Selection on Voting on the U.S. Court of Appeals," *Judicature* 67 (October 1983): 165–173; Jon Gottschall, "Reagan's Appointments to the U.S. Courts of Appeals: The Continuation of a Judicial Revolution," *Judicature* 70 (June/July 1986): 48–54. Simon Lazarus, *The Genteel Populists* (New York: Holt, Rinehart, & Winston, 1974), chap. 10. The contrast between Lazarus and the New Deal liberals is sharp.

8. For a contemporary fair assessment of federalism in terms pertinent to liberalism and conservatism, see Duane Lockard, *The Perverted Priorities of American Politics,* 2d ed. (New York: Macmillan, 1976), chap. 4.

9. On congressional Democratic liberalism relative to that of the Carter Administration, see Betty Glad, *Jimmy Carter,* 422, 426–427. On Senate Republican moderation versus House Republican conservatism, see Orfield, *Congressional Power,* 8–9.

10. McCann, *Taking Reform Seriously,* esp. 17–18, 151; Berry, *Interest Group Society,* 27–31; Andrew McFarland, *Common Cause: Lobbying in the Public Interest* (Chatham, NJ: Chatham House, 1984), esp. 25–29; Vogel, *Fluctuating Fortunes,* esp. chaps. 3, 5.

11. Thomas Byrne Edsall, *The New Politics of Inequality* (New York: W. W. Norton, 1984), chap. 4; the quotation is from p. 162.

12. The quote is from Berry, *Interest Group Society,* 38. Also see T. Edsall, *New Politics of Inequality,* chap. 3; Sidney Blumenthal, *The Rise of the Counter-Establishment* (New York: Harper & Row, 1988), esp. 69–80; Vogel, *Fluctuating Fortunes,* chaps. 7 and 8; and Jerome L. Himmelstein, *To the Right* (Berkeley and Los Angeles: University of California Press, 1990), 139–140.

13. Blumenthal, *Rise of the Counter-Establishment,* chaps. 2–4; Himmelstein, *To the Right,* chap. 5; T. Edsall, *New Politics of Inequality,* chap. 3.

14. Paul Gottfried and Thomas Fleming, *The Conservative Movement* (Boston:

Twayne, 1988), chap. 5; Dionne, *Why Americans Hate Politics,* chap. 8; Linda J. Medcalf and Kenneth M. Dolbeare, *Neopolitics* (New York: Random House, 1985), chap. 10; Berry, *Interest Group Society,* 31–34; Himmelstein, *To the Right,* chap. 4.

   15.   Most of these assessments are based upon Gottfried and Fleming, *Conservative Movement,* esp. 63, 72, 93–94; Blumenthal, *Rise of the Counter-Establishment,* 5, 8, 179–182; Lloyd Wendt, *Chicago Tribune* (Chicago: Rand McNally, 1979), 756, 777–779, 789; and judgments by the author from his own reading of these publications.

   16.   Joseph C. Goulden, *Fit to Print* (Secaucus, NJ: Lyle Stuart, 1988), 206–208, 211–216; Chalmers Roberts, *In the Shadow of Power* (Washington: Seven Locks Press, 1989); author's assessments.

   17.   Barry M. Goldwater, *Where I Stand* (New York: McGraw–Hill, 1964), 91.

# 14

# The Liberal Theory of Governance in Flux

The emergence of new-politics, reform liberalism as the predominant strain in liberal ideology, combined with the shifting power bases discussed in chapter 13, had a profound impact on liberals' institutional prescriptions between 1966 and 1981. In early 1965, most liberals were still enthusiastic, even rhapsodic, in their praise of presidential government, and most perceived Congress to be the "sapless branch," as liberal Joseph Clark of Pennsylvania, himself a member of the Senate, described it that year. Lyndon Johnson's creative federalism was still fairly centralized, at least by conservatives' standards. Although a few liberals, such as Walter Heller, were advocating decentralization to state and local governments through a sharing of federal revenues with few strings attached and liberal acceptance of cooperative federalist compromises in congressional legislation had become commonplace, most of the liberal movement remained scornful of states' rights and cool to ideas that might weaken central government authority. Complaints about bureaucracy occasionally emanated from the ranks of liberal politicians and intellectuals, but the professionalized administrative state remained of central importance in most liberal governance prescriptions. Then, too, judicial activism was now almost universally embraced by liberals, and in a more expansive form than in the 1940s. Undergirding all of these institutional prescriptions lay a perception of constitutional flexibility that had been shaped extensively by legal pragmatism and realism. But, of course, the liberals' "living" Constitution could be reshaped to permit different institutional arrangements should a changing situation demand them. After 1966, it increasingly seemed to liberals to require just that.[1]

Despite major liberal shifts in their institutional prescriptions between 1966 and 1981, a new liberal theory of governance, capable of generating a liberal consensus, such as that which usually prevailed from the late

1930s to the mid-1960s, never fully crystallized. Instead, new-politics liberals mounted attacks on presidential government during the later part of the Johnson administration, accelerated and expanded those attacks in the Nixon-Ford administrations, and then moderated them without returning to the old embrace of a strong presidency during the Carter administration. Old-politics liberals generally remained supportive of a strong presidency, though quite a few of them shifted, too, during the Republican administrations. Accompanying the shifts concerning presidential power were growing liberal endorsements of a congressionally centered system of checks and balances. However, the liberal enthusiasm for Congress was often tempered, especially by new-politics liberals like Mark Green, with caveats about the need for further reforms of that institution. Liberal support for revenue sharing grew after 1966, as did liberal decentralist rhetoric, though liberal decentralizing proposals rarely emphasized the states, were often unclear as to precise means of implementation, and failed to generate full consensus across the liberal coalition. As for the administrative state, new-politics liberals increasingly critiqued its underlying premises and attacked its modes of operation after 1966. Often, in a real reversal from the 1930s and 1940s, they sought to check the power of supposedly expert administrators and to open up administrative processes. Not surprisingly, many liberal administrators and old-politics practitioners were less than enthusiastic about the new approaches in this realm. Meanwhile, the prospect of growing judicial conservatism during parts of the period raised questions about the long-term likelihood that judicial activism or a jurisprudence based on constitutional flexibility would help to achieve liberal power and policy goals. Liberal prescriptions concerning the judiciary and the Constitution itself changed less dramatically than those conerning the presidency, Congress, the administrative state, and federalism. But even here, the combination of new-politics redefinition and expansion of judicial activism, new efforts to link constitutional interpretation to moral rights or procedures more than to the constitutional text or the framers' intents, and widespread uncertainty about the future composition and orientation of the federal judiciary created considerable flux in prescriptions.

### The Shifts Begin: The End of the Johnson Administration

The most important initial stimulus for the earliest major liberal shifts in institutional prescriptions was the rising opposition of many liberals to the Johnson administration's policies in Vietnam. This opposition spread fairly quickly to other aspects of defense and foreign policy, increasingly calling into question past liberal commitments to an expansive presidential role as commander in chief and leader of American foreign policy. Once these came under increased challenge from new-politics liberals, it required no great leap to broaden the attack to presidential government generally. Though the most prominent erstwhile presidential government advocates in the new-politics liberal camp, such as Henry Steele Commager, Arthur M. Schlesinger Jr. and James MacGregor Burns, sought to focus the calls for limiting presidential powers on the war-making role, they were only partially successful. And by the middle of the Nixon administration, even many of them were broadening the attack on presidential powers. Meanwhile, other aspects of the old liberal theory of governance began to be questioned by liberals, too, particularly the administrative state idea, with its emphasis on expertise and hierarchy.

Johnson's dramatic escalation of the Vietnam War in 1965 and his dispatch of troops to the Dominican Republic the same year stirred considerable liberal opposition. Although Senator J. William Fulbright, chair of the Senate Foreign Relations Committee, was hardly a charter member of the liberal coalition, he was widely repected among liberals. When he began to render pointed attacks on presidential diplomatic and war powers, introducing a sense of the Senate resolution in July 1967 aimed at curbing executive branch commitments to other nations without congressional approval, such prominent liberals as George McGovern, Mike Mansfield, Gaylord Nelson, and Jacob Javits rallied to the cause. By the early Nixon administration, there was sufficient Senate support to win passage of a modified version of Fulbright's proposals.[2]

Liberal historian Henry Steele Commager, staunch defender of an expansive presidential role as leader of foreign policy during the great debate of 1951 and the Bricker amendment controversy, now found "ambiguity" in the Constitution, "not clarified by miscellaneous Supreme Court decisions" on the matter of presidential-congressional war powers. By April 1968 he was lamenting "presidential abuse of power in foreign affairs" in the *New Republic* and speculating about how Congress might effectively restrict presidential powers.[3]

Saul K. Padover, writing in *Commonweal* in August 1968, was among many liberals advancing proposals to check presidential war and diplomatic powers. Padover endorsed legislation to require presidential consultation with Congress before any commitment of troops abroad, place limits on the size of such forces in the absence of a congressional war declaration, and restrict the time that troops could remain abroad without explicit congressional extensions. In addition, he called for enlarged congressional staff support and enhanced congressional oversight of the Central Intelligence Agency.[4]

Dwight Macdonald went even further, attacking the whole edifice of presidential government. While conceding that the strong presidency had brought advantages in the New Deal era, Macdonald now saw a dangerous concentration of presidential powers. The tribune role was particularly undesirable: "Because he is elected by everybody, the president has too much prestige and too much freedom of action." The presidency should be abolished altogether, thought Macdonald, to be replaced by a "Chairman," selected by the majority party in Congress and serving for one six-year term or until his party lost a congressional vote on a major issue. [5]

Eugene McCarthy, in his campaign for the presidency in 1968, was somewhat less extreme than Macdonald but, like him, criticized presidential powers generally and suggested that perhaps the president should be limited to a single term in office. Arthur Schlesinger Jr., disapprovingly, saw McCarthy as "the first liberal candidate in the century to run against the Presidency; doing this moreover, in times of turbulence that seemed to call for a strong Presidency to hold the country together." Even Robert Kennedy, long identified with presidential government, during his 1968 campaign expressed the need for widened sharing of chief - executive powers. Thus, by late in the Johnson administration, the old liberal consensus on presidential government was unraveling rather generally in new-politics liberal quarters.[6]

The old-politics liberals, however, were fiercely resistant. Lyndon Johnson challenged Congress to rescind the Gulf of Tonkin resolution of 1964, claiming that the president needed no authorization from Congress for his actions in Vietnam. Objecting to Fulbright's national commitments resolution, Senator Henry Jackson declared that "it trespasses on the President's authority in the national security field" and "fails to recognize the constitutional powers of the President as Commander-in-Chief." Senator Gale McGee agreed. Such a resolution would "hobble the president in the execution of his legitimate duties." Making the explicit link between presidential government and containment of Communism, Senator Thomas Dodd, another old-politics liberal, termed Fulbright's effort "an invitation to Communist aggression in both Europe and Asia." Thus, liberal consensus on presidential government gave way to sharp internal conflict.[7]

Shifts concerning other components of the liberal theory of governance were less dramatic than these but also noteworthy in the years from 1966 to 1969. Commitment to the old New Deal liberal ideal of centralized federalism, in particular, eroded considerably. As early as 1964, liberal intellectuals such as David Hackett had pushed for a new type of decentralization, a community-action approach, within the War on Poverty. The new Community Action Program, endorsed by Robert Kennedy and accepted by Johnson (though scholars still debate the extent of his comprehension of its implications), invited local communities to establish new organizations or designate existing ones as community action agencies to coordinate federal antipoverty programs, provide new services to the poor, and promote institutional change in the interests of the poor. Also given a mandate that they employ "maximum feasible participation" of the target populations themselves, these agencies were often far from what conservative states' rights advocates had favored; and they soon proved quite controversial. Many of the emerging new-politics liberal activists, intellectuals, and political leaders, however, wanted to extend this decentralization theme further.[8]

Richard Goodwin, new-politics liberal intellectual and political speechwriter for Johnson, McCarthy, and Robert Kennedy (no mean achievement!), in 1967 declared: "The idea of decentralization is making its first tentative appearance in political rhetoric. . . . the first party to carry this banner (if buttressed by a solid political program) will find itself on the right side of the decisive issues of the 1970s." But Goodwin took pains to separate new-politics liberal decentralism from that advanced by conservatives: "Many conservatives have welcomed the idea of decentralization, hearing in it comforting echoes of old battle cries about states' rights. They are mistaken, for decentralization, if it is to work, will require even larger public programs and even more money for public ends." A major problem for new-politics liberals, however, was just how to make their decentralism work effectively to the satisfaction of the general public, how to buttress it with a "solid political program." It was a problem they never really would resolve.[9]

Among the liberal presidential candidates of 1968, Robert Kennedy went furthest to embrace the decentralizing themes that were emerging in the liberal camp. Kennedy had been closely associated with Hackett and the formative stages of the Community Action Program; and he embraced both its decentralizing and its participatory themes. Conservative commentator M. Stanton Evans, writing in the *National Review Bulletin*, noted with some surprise that Kennedy repeatedly "called for a return of decision-making powers to states and local communities" in his 1968 primary campaigns for the Democratic presidential nomination. However, the precise nature of Kennedy's decentralization approach remained unclear; and his assassination in June 1968 removed his possible opportunity to put his rhetoric into action.[10]

Still another area of changing liberal institutional prescriptions was the administrative state. The new liberal interest in participatory democracy, seen in the Community Action Program but also in calls for citizen participation in running schools and other agencies and, less directly, in the "genteel populism" of the burgeoning liberal public-interest groups of the late 1960s, came increasingly into conflict with the long-term liberal emphasis on a hierarchical administrative state run by professional experts. Reflecting some of the values of the counterculture and the New Left, many new-politics liberals evinced, as Michael McCann has emphasized, "inherent distrust of the professional ranks of bureaucratic elites in whom earlier generations placed their greatest hopes for social improvement." Already evident by 1968, this pattern would develop further in the early 1970s.[11]

In the realm of the judiciary, the last year of the Johnson administration witnessed what many viewed as another major extension of liberal judicial activism, moving beyond overturning legislative and executive actions to ordering judicial remedies that were often quite detailed in their mandates. The most controversial Supreme Court decision illustrative of this type of liberal judicial activism during the Johnson years was *Green v. School Board of New Kent County*. In this 1968 decision, the High Bench invalidated the "freedom of choice" approach to school desegregation, which had been adopted in New Kent County, Virginia, as in much of the South, as grossly insufficient to achieve desegregation. The decision set the federal courts on a course that would entail prescribing school busing to achieve target percentages for racial groups attending the public schools. While most liberals agreed with Bernard Schwartz and the Supreme Court justices that such decisions were based on "the traditional enforcement powers of courts of equity, which rested on the principle that the chancellor may order whatever may be deemed necessary to correct the wrong done in the given case," most conservatives perceived yet another dangerous extension of judicial "lawmaking" and responded with howls of outrage.[12]

Therefore, as the Johnson administration gave way to that of Nixon, liberals were fighting liberals over presidential government, especially its foreign policy and war powers roles; and many elements in the liberal coalition were seriously questioning both centralized federalism and the administrative state forms that liberals had long endorsed. Meanwhile, liberals were expanding their judicial activism prescriptions. The accession to the presidency of Richard Nixon, faced by a Democratic Congress that was in a number of respects more liberal than he, would promote further change in liberal prescriptions, particularly concerning Congress and the presidency .

## The Liberal Institutional Prescriptions in the Nixon-Ford Years

In light of the sharp internal conflicts over presidential government and the growing liberal disarray concerning federalism and the administrative state, a coherent liberal theory of governance no longer really existed by 1969. Still, there came to be a number of institutional prescriptions around which most liberals could unite, especially in relation to presidential authority. As President Nixon displayed an increasing tendency to expand power, bypass Congress altogether, and adopt confrontational stances toward his critics, he helped to create substantial liberal unity on a new model of congressionally centered checks and balances. Eventually, most old-politics liberals joined new-politics liberals in efforts to check presidential powers and assert those of Congress. Often, they were assisted by many moderates and conservatives. In the Nixon years, the chief areas of combat were diplomatic and war powers, the budgetary process, executive privilege versus congressional demands for information, and reorganization powers.

In the sphere of diplomatic and war powers, most liberals—including many who had refrained from actively opposing Johnson—joined in June 1969 to endorse a version of Fulbright's National Commitments Resolution to the effect that a "national commitment by the United States results only from affirmative action taken by the executive and legislative branches. . . ." On the key vote to reject a weaker substitute, 95 percent of the liberals took the position favoring additional restrictions on presidential powers; 97 percent of the liberals voted for the resolution in its final form. Though this measure was a mild one and only expressed the sense of the Senate, it would subsequently be followed by liberal efforts to impose some genuine constraints on presidents.[13]

Probably the most significant of these, at least symbolically, for the long term was the War Powers Resolution of 1973, which mustered the support of 95 percent of Senate liberals and 93 percent of House liberals on final passage and similar percentages to override Nixon's veto—a veto that was overcome by the requisite two-thirds majorities in each chamber, thanks to substantial moderate and conservative backing. A few liberals who opposed the resolution on final passage, such as Senator Thomas Eagleton and Representative Bella Abzug, were new-politics liberals who felt that its restraints on presidential war powers were insufficient; a few others were old-politics devotees of presidential prerogatives. The resolution laid out requirements for presidential consultation with Congress "in every possible instance" prior to introducing American military forces into hostilities, called for a presidential report to Congress within forty-eight hours of such an introduction of troops, and provided mechanisms for Congress to terminate military action (including a controversial legislative-veto procedure). Under the terms of the resolution, congressional approval would also be required to sustain military deployment beyond ninety days. Although the resolution's effects have been mixed, most liberals agreed at the time with its chief Senate sponsor, liberal Republican Jacob Javits of New York, that at last Congress had taken action "about codifying the most awesome power in the possession of every sovereignty."[14]

Beyond the War Powers Resolution, congressional liberals took the lead in employing the power of the purse to force Nixon to agree to halt military operations in and over Vietnam, Cambodia, and Laos after 15 August 1973 and then to restrict Ford from resuming military actions. They also moved in other foreign and national security areas to curb presidential powers and assert congressional roles: requiring that executive agreements be submitted to Congress, establishing congressional surveillance over the covert activities of the Central Intelligence Agency, and applying the legislative veto to arms sales and international atomic energy agreements, for example.[15]

Assertive use of congressional budgetary powers had effects on diplomatic and war powers, as noted above; but the greatest controversies over the power of the purse concerned Nixon's expanded use of impoundment, or presidential withholding of money appropriated by Congress. Though previous presidents had employed impoundment from time to time, most frequently to defer spending temporarily or following consultation with Congress, Nixon's use of it went far beyond of his predecessors' in both volume and intent. Not only did Nixon impound on an unprecedented scale, but he did so to kill programs that he disliked and to pressure Congress to give him what he wanted. Congressional liberals united, again with substantial backing from moderates and conservatives, and passed the Budget and Impoundment Control Act of 1974, which revamped the congressional budgetary process in an effort to enhance its effectiveness and counter presidential charges that it lacked coherence. The act also placed tight restrictions on the president's ability to withhold funds appropriated by Congress. In the face of overwhelming congressional support for this measure, Nixon reluctantly signed it, just four weeks before being forced from office.[16]

In the area of executive privilege, where liberals had rallied behind Truman and had generally supported even Eisenhower's vast claims, they now almost unanimously denounced the Nixon administration's invocation of the Eisenhower formula. And in the realm of reorganizing the executive branch, they withdrew their support for the approach, used since 1932, whereby the president could initiate most executive branch reorganizations, subject to a legislative veto by Congress. Clearly, by 1973 and 1974, liberals appeared united in most congressional votes and actions, on an approach that now emphasized congressionally centered checks and balances on a variety of major matters.[17]

There were, however, a few exceptions that indicated less than complete commitment to reducing presidential powers. The most notable of these was the Senate liberals' vote in May 1971 to grant the president broad authority to impose wage and price controls. It was likely that most expected Nixon would refuse to use such authority, proclaiming his devotion to free enterprise; and liberals could then attack him for failing to deal adequately with inflation despite their giving him weapons to do so. Nixon believed this to be their rationale. If true, the maneuver backfired on the liberals when Nixon imposed controls of his own choosing. Since most liberals had called for such presidential action, they were hardly well positioned to complain about excessive presidential power. Although this was an exception to the general pattern of liberal efforts to cut presidential powers during the Nixon years, it indicated some liberal ambivalence about a strong presidency. Moreover, in 1974, congressional liberals were to show themselves far more willing than their conservative colleagues to grant the president standby authority in the energy sphere also.[18]

Like most of the liberal action in Congress, most of the published works of liberal intellectuals, activists, and politicians after 1969 indicated a shift of basic perspectives away from presidential government and toward a more benign assessment of Congress as an institution than in the preceding thirty-five years, when liberals had regularly described the national legislature as "a broken mirror" or a "House out of order" and had deplored the "obstacle course on Capitol Hill."[19]

In an editorial in early 1971, the *New Republic* addressed the need for liberals to shift their basic allegiance from the presidency to Congress. Using the language of new-politics liberalism, it hailed Congress as "an institution of participatory democracy." Unlike the presidency, according to the *New Republic*'s editors, "Congress is the institution where we do not merely hold our government to account, but can take some part in it." The "unchecked dominion" of presidential powers, insisted the editorial, must be tackled in domestic as well as in foreign policy spheres. *Commonweal* in 1973 demanded that Congress "get tough with the President" and called for "reestablishment of the Constitutional checks and balances." However, like much of the new-politics liberal movement, it also emphasized the need for Congress to "work on the internal reforms that will reenergize it and regain it its lost respect." The *New York Times* added

its editorial voice. Denouncing presidential use of war powers, impoundment, and executive privilege, the *Times* proclaimed: "Congress cannot
escape responding to these direct challenges to its authority."[20]

In March 1973, John Herbers of the *New York Times* concluded after
interviewing numerous liberal intellectuals and activists that "liberals who
have long viewed the presidency as the best means of achieving a humane
foreign policy and helping the needy at home are crying for restraints on
the President." Certainly that was true of a broad cross-section, particularly of new-politics liberals. But there were still quite a few prominent liberals who urged the liberal movement not to reject all of the tenets of presidential government.[21]

Arthur M. Schlesinger Jr. was one. Although Schlesinger admitted his
past "errors" in praising broad presidential war powers, he insisted, "It
would be a mistake to cripple the presidency at home because of presidential excesses abroad." History shows, he argued, "the Presidency to be
the most effective instrumentality of government for justice and
progress." Joseph Califano even proposed adding new presidential powers to impose wage and price controls, alter tax rates subject to a legislative veto, assert further control over the Federal Reserve Board of Governors, and shift funds. Rexford Tugwell remained negative in his
assessments of Congress: "The most casual examination of experience
will cause anyone to shudder at the suggestion of the actual sharing of
presidential power with any members of the Congress or with any of its
committees." Even Gary Orfield, who generally favored a shift away from
presidential government, cautioned: "It would be tragic if we replaced the
idealization of the Presidency . . . with the idealization of Congress."
Thus, despite numerous lopsided votes by congressional liberals to curb
presidential powers in particular respects and much liberal endorsement
of a major shift of institutional commitments, there remained considerable reluctance in the liberal movement, even in the Nixon-Ford era, to
embrace fully a recommendation for congressionally centered checks and
balances. A new liberal consensus was beginning to take shape but was
far from complete; and the Carter years would nudge some liberals back
into a pro-presidential direction.[22]

Meanwhile, liberals lacked as much consensus as in the past with
regard to both federalism and the administrative state. Even on judicial
activism and constitutional flexibility, internal splits often appeared.

Already divided over proposals for revenue sharing from Walter
Heller (and eventually Joseph Pechman, after initial doubts), and uncer-
tain about decentralization ideas broached by Richard Goodwin, Robert
Kennedy, and others, the liberal coalition was unable to develop a unified

response when Nixon unveiled his "New Federalism" proposals. Central to these was a version of general revenue sharing, under which the federal government would provide about five billion dollars per year, with almost no strings attached, to the state and local governments. In addition, the Nixon administration proposed to switch many specific categorical grants-in-aid to broad block grants to permit state and local governments greater flexibility.[23]

Much of the early liberal reaction was negative. "What's New?" asked the *New Republic* editorially in February 1971. "As a philosophy of government the New Federalism is as new as the States' Rights doctrine. It presumes that the federal government is a less beneficent and responsive servant of the people than the state, city, or county governments. The idea finds little support in experience." Max Frankel of the *New York Times* denounced the proposals as based upon faulty assumptions about local and state popular control. "The nearer our elections get to the local level, the less adequate the public discussion, the smaller the participation." State and county governments, in his rather traditional liberal view, were "mostly weak, outmoded, or corrupt." Frankel concluded: "If we followed his [Nixon's] advice, what is deceptively called revenue sharing would become a constant flow of money out of the Federal treasury that would not bring anything for the national interest. The new revolution is in fact a counterrevolution." Echoing the *New Republic,* Henry Steele Commager complained: "It's not new and it's not Federalism."[24]

However, a number of liberals embraced major portions of Nixon's proposals, particularly general revenue sharing. State and local officials of most political persuasions became lobbyists for revenue sharing. Carl Stokes, the mayor of Cleveland, for example, persuaded his brother, liberal Representative Louis Stokes, to endorse it. Liberals who had already embraced decentralist themes, especially younger, new-politics liberals, were often sympathetic, too. By the time general revenue sharing came up for a final vote, majorities of liberals in both chambers endorsed it. Even the *New Republic* had decided by the fall of 1972, to support general revenue sharing. Although its editors still expressed fears that state and local governments were "often corrupt, racially biased, or beholden to all kinds of business or other pressures," they had concluded that some state and local autonomy in spending federal funds was in order. "The merit of revenue sharing is precisely that the man who wears the shoe knows best when it pinches, and that in this vast and varied country, the shoe pinches quite differently in New York and in Montana."[25]

The block grants aspects of Nixon's New Federalism, however, evoked fairly solid liberal opposition, particularly when the grants were to be block grants to states, rather than to cities. In instances where mayoral lobbying was not a major factor, Conlan's analysis of the voting patterns has concluded, the partisan and ideological proclivities of Northern Democrats inclined them strongly against this type of decentralization.26

Many liberals' prescriptions concerning the administrative state related in part to their increasing disenchantment with a strong presidency, and with the presidency of Richard Nixon in particular. Liberal attacks on the expansion of the Executive Office of the President, refusal to countenance renewal of presidential authority to reorganize subject to a legislative veto, and denunciation of the Nixon administration's "responsiveness program" designed to link the administrative state to the Nixonian agenda by exerting pressure on career civil servants all blended with their rejection of most aspects of presidential government during the Nixon years. But liberal prescriptions went beyond opposition to tightened chief executive control over the administrative state. Continuing trends under way during the Johnson years, new-politics liberals in particular questioned the value of bureaucratic expertise. In a typical expression of this view, Friends of the Earth noted skeptically that the effects of the traditional New Deal liberal administrative state were too often "to reserve for the judgment of experts decisions where their expertise is of very little relevance." Moreover, as McCann has emphasized, new-politics liberal values came to embrace a "code of conflict" quite unlike the "cooperation, conformity, and consensus in which modern elite bureaucratic politics thrives."[27]

One result was an effort by many new-politics liberals in the early 1970s to "judicialize" the administrative state and its processes. Unlike most conservative critics of the past, who had sought to destroy the administrative state or at least sharply reduce its scope, the new-politics liberals wished to extend its regulatory sway over the private corporate sector. However, their distaste for the strong presidency, distrust of expertise, and proclivity toward a conflict model impelled most of the liberal public interest groups to make creative use of the Administrative Procedure Act of 1946, such new legislation as the Magnuson-Moss Act of 1975, and various other techniques to open up administration and turn it into an open adversary process much like that in the courts. The operations of some agencies, such as the Federal Trade Commission, were literally transformed by these liberal efforts. Richard Stewart, analyzing these developments in 1975, described a "reformation of American administrative law."[28]

An additional aspect of the new-politics liberals' novel approach to the administrative state was an expansion of liberal judicial activism into the economic regulatory spheres from which New Deal liberalism and its successors had usually barred it. The contrast with liberal attitudes toward the roles of the judiciary and the administrative state in the past was striking. Back in 1940, when Roosevelt had vetoed the Walter-Logan Act to ringing applause from the liberal movement, the liberal consensus had been that relative autonomy of the administrative state from judicial intervention would further the public interest. Now Simon Lazarus spoke for much of the new-politics liberal movement in rejecting judicial restraint and deference to administrators in the economic regulatory field. According to Lazarus, "the federal courts have to assume a more decisive role in regulatory affairs than they have traditionally played." Judges "have to begin to assume a greater share of responsibility for interpreting and enforcing the substance of regulatory statutes."[29]

This style of judicial activism did not generally entail overruling Congress or other bodies on constitutional grounds but rather centered on prodding judges to assign "populist interpretations to ambiguous statutes and then enforcing them vigorously," as Lazarus put it. Yet broad liberal support for this approach grew out of the previous expansion of liberal judicial activism. With the loss of the presidency and growing uncertainties about the characteristics of the administrative state, it seemed to many liberals a natural progression. To criticisms that it vested economic management lawmaking powers in courts far removed from public opinion, Joseph Sax, an environmental movement leader and staunch proponent of the new approach, responded that "the role of the courts is not to make public policy, but to help assure that public policy is made by the appropriate entity, rationally, and in accord with the aspirations of the democratic process." Nonetheless, even many liberals found the linkage between the judiciary and democracy to be a tenuous one, in light of federal judges' insulation from popular accountability and input. And comments such as Sax's did suggest an expansive judicial policy role.[30]

Furthermore, there were indications that the federal judiciary was becoming increasingly conservative, at least in some realms, and thus an undependable ally of the liberal cause. Nixon had pledged in his 1968 presidential election campaign to appoint judges who were strict constructionists and who would promote a conservative version of law and order" (though these two promises might not be fully compatible). In practice, neither pledge was completely redeemed—partly, but not primarily, because of strong liberal opposition to some of Nixon's judicial appointees. The most notable of the liberal-conservative battles over appointments occurred at the level of the Supreme Court, where almost the entire liberal coalition, with the AFL-CIO joining forces with the Leadership Conference on Civil Rights at the core of the effort, mobilized to block Senate confirmation first of Clement Haynsworth and then of G. Harrold Carswell to the High Bench. Still, new-politics liberals and other liberals had cause to worry. Not only were the Nixon and Ford administrations increasing the conservative coloration of the federal courts through their appointments, but big business in particular and the conservative movement generally were working strenuously to counter the new-politics liberals' public-interest litigation strategies.[31]

While many new-politics liberals sought to push judicial activism into the economic regulatory sphere and much of the liberal mainstream worried about the conservatizing effects of Nixon and Ford judicial appointments, some liberal legal scholars called for increased judicial self-restraint and found the Constitution less flexible than their colleagues or the Supreme Court majority, especially in cases such as *Roe v. Wade*. Yale law professsor Alexander Bickel, a frequent contributor to *New Republic* who possessed long-term ties to liberalism, had grown increasingly disenchanted with liberal judicial activism in the 1960s. His 1970 book *The Supreme Court and the Idea of Progress* criticized the Warren Court for frequently abandoning "reason" and for a "web of subjectivity." He also questioned the capacity of the courts, given their institutional characteristics, to direct major sociopolitical change in positive directions, let alone achieve "the heavenly city." Concluded Bickel: "The only abiding thing, as Brandeis liked to say, is change, and in those broad realms of social policy where that is so, judicial supremacy, we must conclude, is not possible." Though Bickel's criticisms of liberal judicial activism brought angry retorts from many in the liberal movement, a few liberals went even further than he, criticizing both what they viewed as excessive judicial activism in overturning laws and overly loose judicial construction (or nonconstruction) of the Constitution. After the 1973 *Roe v. Wade* decision, for example, Louis Lusky, in *By What Right?*, accused the Supreme Court majority of being "ready to engage in freehand constitution-making in order to combat what they viewed as a basic injustice, in any field where they thought that the Court's intervention would be helpful and effective."[32]

Despite new-politics liberal efforts to expand judicial activism and calls by some other liberals for limits to such activism and stricter construction of the Constitution, liberals' prescriptions on the judiciary and constitutionalism during the Nixon-Ford years were fairly continuous with their past theory of governance. Yet much of that theory, even in these realms, was obviously in flux in the new political environment of the 1970s.

## The Liberal Institutional Prescriptions
## and the Carter Administration

The liberal coalition did not generally view President Carter as its leader, and its members often distanced themselves from the Carter administration despite its inclusion of a number of prominent liberals, such as Joseph Califano, Patricia Roberts Harris, Brock Adams, Cyrus Vance, Andrew Young, Michael Pertschuk, and Patricia Derian. Still, the hostility that most of the liberal movement had directed at presidential government in the Nixon years had moderated marginally under Ford and moderated somewhat further during the Carter administration, at least when that administration was taking actions favored by most liberals.

In the sensitive diplomatic powers realm, for example, when Carter unilaterally terminated the United States's treaty ties with Taiwan in order to establish full diplomatic relations with the People's Republic of China, Senate liberals unanimously voted against a 1979 sense-of-the-Senate resolution by Harry Byrd Jr. that "approval of the United States Senate is required to terminate any Mutual Defense Treaty between the United States and another nation." However, Senator Frank Church spoke for many liberals in stating that he hoped that presidents would seek Senate concurrence on treaty terminations in the future.[33]

Furthermore, 89 percent of the liberals present and voting voted to restore to the president in 1977 the power to reorganize the executive branch, subject to a legislative veto—an authority that had been denied to Nixon and Ford. Since Carter had made reorganization a central campaign theme in 1976, this was an important victory for him. Though he and much of Congress were generally at odds over the matter of legislative vetoes, he willingly accepted the long-employed combination of such a veto with reorganization authority in this instance.[34]

Cutting across both presidential power and administrative state concerns was the general issue of the legislative veto, which became a classic case in this period of both liberals' and conservatives' use of a particular institutional device as a means toward different power and policy ends. Back in 1976, liberals had divided badly (44 percent to 56 percent) over a proposed measure, falling just two votes short of the needed two-thirds majority in the House of Representatives, to require that all new regulations proposed by federal agencies be submitted to Congress for sixty days, where they could be blocked by a legislative veto. However, liberals had almost unanimously endorsed the use of the same device to curb presidential-executive war powers, overseas military sales, executive branch reorganization, and other actions. During the Carter administration, Elliott Levitas of Georgia, a moderate-to-conservative Southern Democrat, made repeated efforts to gain passage of a bill similar to that barely blocked in 1976. Falling short in that endeavor, he and his supporters targeted particular regulatory agencies disliked by the business community, especially the Federal Trade Commission, which new-politics liberals had succeeded in "reforming." Mark Green, director of Ralph Nader's Congress Watch and himself a leading force in opening up the administrative process, did not like the new business enthusiasm for the legislative veto in the regulatory context. Deploring "anti-bureaucracy hysteria," he now proclaimed, "The Legislative Veto Is Bad Law." "It makes little sense to replace an Imperial Presidency with an Imperial Congress," argued Green and his coauthor Frances Zwenig in the *Nation,* denying "the inherent right of the legislature to paralyze the executive power" and objecting to the legislative veto on constitutional, separation-of-powers grounds. The *New York Times* and the *Washington Post* added their editorial voices to the widespread liberal opposition to the legislative veto. Senator Edward Kennedy spoke out as a leading opponent, as he had in the 1976 battle. However, liberals' record in the recent past and congressional liberals' continuing insertion of such vetoes into legislation when it suited them suggested an ad hoc approach to the subject during the Carter years, rather than a consistent liberal position.[35]

Also bridging both presidential government and administrative state subject areas during the Carter administration was the Civil Service Reform Act of 1978, one of Carter's highest priorities, though a matter of little interest to most of the liberal coalition. By creating a new Senior Executive Service composed of high-level civil servants to be subject to presidential control through demotion, transfer, or removal and replacing the bipartisan Civil Service Commission with an Office of Personnel Management, to be headed by political appointees, the act reinforced a hierarchical administrative state and potentially enhanced presidential powers. As Sidney Milkis and others have stressed, this measure was very much in the "Third New Deal" mode of presidential government and an administrative state under presidential authority. Although Carter never really used the new mechanisms to tighten his control over the bureaucracy, the Reagan administration would prove both willing and able to do so. That liberals would accept this approach without major objections is somewhat surprising in light of their recently growing commitment to congressional power enhancement and a fragmented and open administrative state model.[36]

This other, "judicialized" model lay at the heart of the liberal drive to enact consumer protection legislation establishing an Agency for Consumer Advocacy (ACA). Put forward by Ralph Nader's movement in particular, but supported by a wide array of new-politics liberals and some others, the proposed ACA would have had the authority to initiate lawsuits for judicial review of administrative agency policies affecting consumers and would have had a mandate to expand consumer participation in making administrative rules and regulations. In short, it was a clear expression of the new-politics liberal version of the administrative state. Despite endorsement by the Carter administration and the support of 93 percent of the congressional liberals, the bill to set up the ACA went down in February 1978 to a 189-227 defeat in the House of Representatives, at the hands of the Business Roundtable, a wide array of other business and conservative groups, and a highly united congressional conservative coalition.[37]

In the judicial realm, liberals during the Carter years continued their consistent practice since the 1950s of ardently defending the Supreme Court and the federal courts generally against periodic conservative efforts to restrict the courts' jurisdiction over certain types of cases. In the late 1960s, liberals had presented a unified front, supplemented by a number of moderates and a few conservatives, to delete provisions from the crime bill of 1968 that would have curbed federal courts' jurisdiction in several criminal justice domains. Now, in 1976, they succeeded in defeating a measure by conservative Senator William Scott of Virginia to remove all cases involving public schools from federal court jurisdiction and a measure by conservative Senator William Roth of Delaware to remove cases involving school busing for desegregation. Again in 1979, they mobilized their forces to defend the courts, this time against a drive by conservative Senator Jesse Helms of North Carolina to restrict federal court jurisdiction on matters concerning prayers in public schools. Overall, then, despite some growth of judicial conservatism in the 1970s, the liberals were the chief protectors of the federal courts against continuing periodic conservative efforts to limit their jurisdiction.[38]

The issues of constitutional interpretation also were the subject of continuing debate in the late 1970s. When Raoul Berger, a Harvard legal scholar independent of either ideological coalition, published *Government by Judiciary: The Transformation of the Fourteenth Amendment* in 1977, adding his voice and prestige to what had become the conservative original-intent cause, he provoked a wave of liberal scholarly and political rebuttals. Arthur S. Miller, noted liberal law professor at George Washington University, described Berger's originalism (or interpretavism, as most legal scholars now termed it) as "simplistic at best, puerile at worst."

Echoing sentiments widespread in the liberal movement, Miller wrote:

> The Constitution, as Woodrow Wilson said in 1906, is not a mere lawyer's document; it is much more; it is the vehicle of the nation's life. To interpret it in the same way as, say, a contract or even a statute is to forget that it is the fundamental law. The intention of those who wrote the Constitution is not the sole criterion of judgment. . . . We have married legislation with adjudication and look for statesmanship in our courts.[39]

Stanford law professor Paul Brest concurred in the *New York Times*, citing wide agreement "that whatever the Framers' expectations may have been, broad constitutional guarantees require the Court to discern, articulate, and apply values that are widely and deeply held by our society. . . . these values, though rooted in our historical traditions and beliefs, may evolve over time." Robert Cover in the *New Republic* and E. Richard Larson in the *Nation* also weighed in with quick attacks on Berger's jurisprudence, though Larson (unlike most liberals) challenged what he found to be Berger's faulty originalism rather than original-intent jurisprudence itself.[40]

Nor did liberal legal scholars merely seek to rebut Berger and other advocates of extreme originalism (interpretavism). As in previous periods, liberal outlooks on constitutional interpretation were ranged along a continuum. Taking a moderate position, Stanford law professor Thomas Grey stressed the constitutional background of "'higher law,' protecting 'natural rights,' and taking precedence over ordinary positive law" and argued, in terms broadly similar to those that conservative scholar Robert Bork had employed, that "the Ninth Amendment is the textual expression of this idea in the federal Constitution." However, Grey's interpretation of natural rights was distinctly liberal, compared with Bork's version. Another major liberal legal academic scholar, John Hart Ely of Harvard Law School, deplored the "false dichotomy" that he saw dominating contemporary constitutional debates. Seeking to articulate and defend what he himself conceived as a "moderate interpretavism," as opposed to Berger's "clause-bound interpretavism," Ely, in his influential *Democracy and Distrust: A Theory of Judicial Review,* published in 1980, called for a jurisprudence of procedure, based largely upon a return to an emphasis on the famous footnote of Harlan Stone in the 1938 *Carolene Products* case—the footnote that had underlain much of the early liberal jurisprudence of the post–New Deal era. Ely's process-centered constitutional interpretations focused on protecting the "process rights" of minorities that are included in, or implied by, "the Constitution's open-ended provisions."[41]

Ronald Dworkin, author of the 1977 book *Taking Rights Seriously,* staked out a liberal position closer to the high-flexibility pole than Ely's or Grey's but one that was still linked to constitutional text. Calling for a "fusion of constitutional law and moral theory," Dworkin emphasized the latter and the need for "fresh moral insight," drawing upon John Rawls's theoretical foundations, so important in new reform liberal thinking, to shape his prescriptions. "Our constitutional system rests on a particular moral theory, namely that men have moral rights against the state," declared Dworkin. "The difficult clauses of the Bill of Rights . . . must be understood as appealing to moral concepts rather than laying down particular conceptions."[42]

Conservative reactions to the revised liberal formulations of Grey, Ely, and Dworkin were generally negative. Walter Berns, for example, commented acidly on Dworkin: "Unfortunately, this way of taking rights 'seriously' treats the Constitution frivolously, and ultimately will undermine its structure." Similarly, Gary McDowell claimed that Grey's understanding of natural rights was seriously flawed and attacked Ely's procedural approach as nonconstitutional.[43]

### Liberal Consensus and Discord

In marked contrast to the New Deal and postwar eras, liberal governance ideas and actions fragmented and fluctuated throughout the 1966–81 period. The previous liberal theory of governance eroded, but no new one capable of generating strong intellectual support or consistently mobilizing action appeared to replace it. Although congressional roll-call voting patterns provide only a partial picture, table 14.1 illustrates some major differences from the past and considerable fragmentation and even inconsistency. On the presidential-congressional relations continuum, liberals shifted strongly in the procongressional direction during the Nixon-Ford years but even then took pro-presidential power positions on selected matters, particularly those pertaining to economic management (e.g., wage and price control authority and energy regulatory authority). Use of the legislative veto won strong liberal support on some matters (such as the War Powers Resolution) but split congressional liberals badly when posed as a general proposition (9/21/76). During the Carter administration, congressional liberals proved willing to support presidential powers on executive reorganization, civil service reform, and treaty termination that they would almost certainly have opposed had a conservative Republican been in the White House. Federalism questions sometimes split the liberals fairly sharply, too, most notably on the key vote for a

Table 14.1
Congressional Ideological Divisions on Key Governance Roll Calls

### Presidential-Congressional Issues

| Bill | Date/House | | % Favoring Presidential Power | | Lib.-Cons. Gap |
|------|------------|---|------|------|------|
| | | | Lib. | Cons. | |
| National commitments | 6/25/69 | S | 5% | 61% | 56% |
| National commitments | 6/25/69 | S | 3 | 34 | 31 |
| OMB/Domestic Council reorg. | 5/13/70 | H | 20 | 76 | 56 |
| Wage-price control | 5/3/71 | S | 93 | 31 | -62 |
| Impoundment | 3/7/72 | S | 7 | 73 | 66 |
| War powers | 7/20/73 | S | 0 | 63 | 63 |
| War powers | 11/7/73 | H | 7 | 65 | 58 |
| Energy reg. powers | 3/6/74 | S | 92 | 24 | -68 |
| Energy reg. powers | 5/21/74 | H | 96 | 15 | -81 |
| Destabilization of foreign govt. | 9/24/74 | S | 32 | 98 | 66 |
| Foreign military sales | 2/18/76 | S | 8 | 57 | 49 |
| Foreign military sales | 3/3/76 | H | 10 | 73 | 63 |
| Exec. branch reorg. | 3/29/77 | H | 89 | 66 | -23 |
| Energy reg. powers | 6/5/79 | S | 87 | 32 | -55 |
| Treaty termination | 6/6/79 | S | 100 | 2 | -98 |

### Federalism Issues

| Bill | Date/House | | % for Revenue Sharing | | Lib.-Cons. Gap |
|------|------------|---|------|------|------|
| | | | Lib. | Cons. | |
| Block grant (Esch amendment) | 6/2/71 | H | 5% | 8% | -77% |
| Revenue sharing (closed rule) | 6/21/72 | H | 64 | 46 | 18 |
| Revenue sharing | 6/22/72 | H | 87 | 56 | 31 |
| Revenue sharing | 9/12/72 | S | 74 | 74 | 0 |

### Administrative-State Issues

| Bill | Date/House | | % Favoring New Checks | | Lib.-Cons. Gap |
|------|------------|---|------|------|------|
| | | | Lib. | Cons. | |
| Access to information | 11/20/74 | H | 100% | 84% | 16% |
| Access to information | 11/21/74 | S | 100 | 31 | 69 |

*Continued on next page*

Table 14.1—*Continued*

| Administrative-State Issues—*continued* | | | | |
|---|---|---|---|---|
| | | % Favoring New Checks | | |
| Bill | Date/House | Lib. | Cons. | Lib.-Cons. Gap |
| Legislative veto | 9/21/76  H | 44 | 84 | -40 |
| Agency for Consumer Advocacy | 2/8/78  H | 93 | 2 | 91 |

| Judicial Issues | | | | |
|---|---|---|---|---|
| | | % Opposing Court-Curbing | | |
| Bill | Date/House | Lib. | Cons. | Lib.-Cons. Gap |
| Criminal justice | 5/21/68  S | 97% | 28% | 69% |
| Criminal justice | 5/21/68  S | 97 | 33 | 64 |
| Public schools | 4/1/76  S | 97 | 38 | 59 |
| School busing | 4/1/76  S | 95 | 18 | 77 |
| School prayer | 4/9/79  S | 96 | 3 | 93 |

closed rule allowing an up-or-down vote on general revenue sharing, though Conlan has interpreted their 95 percent opposition to the Esch block grant amendment as indicative of a continuing preference for centralized federalism in the absence of pressure from liberal Democratic mayors to vote otherwise. Only on defemse of the federal judiciary from efforts to limit its jurisdiction did congressional liberals demonstrate consistency and unity during the 1966–81 period. Yet when judicial questions extended beyond mere defense, as they did not in congressional roll-call votes, considerable liberal dissension on judicial activism and even constitutional interpretation was evident. In sum, then, the era was one of flux in liberal prescriptions.

## A Flexible Constitution

Most liberals still agreed that the Constitution was flexible. Modest moves toward centrist positions on the rigidity-flexibility scale by such liberals as Bickel, Grey, and Ely generated some liberal support, but most liberals were closer to the positions taken by Dworkin and Miller. Historian Henry Steele Commager, who had previously employed constitutional text, Supreme Court precedents, and historical examples to bolster the case for presidential domination of war making and diplomacy, now employed the same types of evidence, again selectively, to justify curbing these presidential powers. None of the remaining Supreme Court liberals gave as much emphasis to strict construction or the framers' intent as Hugo Black sometimes did in the preceding period. Although liberal views and actions occupied a fairly wide range of positions, they still tended to fall markedly toward the flexibility end of the continuum, mostly rejecting clause-related original-intent jurisprudence and strict construction as impossibilities. Overall, this was the area of most marked continuity with the past.

## Federalism

On this continuum, liberals spread out over a much broader range than at any time since the early 1930s (and new-politics decentralization constituted a somewhat different continuum altogether from that of the past). Although several distinct clusters of liberal thought could be delineated, none constituted *the* liberal prescription. Many new-politics liberals (but not all) favored decentralization to agencies outside direct state government controls, hoping to link them to their participatory democratic goals. Richard Goodwin, Robert Kennedy, and David Hackett typified this school of thought. Others were willing to decentralize to the state and local governments in the name of participatory democracy. "There is a chance to have genuine participatory democracy if government can be meaningful at the state level and at the local level," wrote liberal legal scholar Bernard Schwartz in 1978, for example. Quite a few liberals were eager to embrace general revenue sharing as a boon to energize state and local governments. Often state or local officials themselves or linked closely to them, these liberals were motivated, at least in part, by a self-interested desire for additional funds, as Conlan and others have demonstrated. On the other hand, many liberals remained wedded to the ideals of centralized federalism, illustrated by the large liberal vote against block grants, Max Frankel's negative assessments of state and local governments and denunciations of revenue sharing as counterrevolutionary, and the significant liberal minority who voted against general revenue sharing. Even as the *New Republic* shifted editorially to a position more sympathetic to the states than in the past, it still tended to see state governments as often retrograde on racial issues and beholden to big business—views long held by most in the liberal movement. Schwartz, too, conceded that "the states have not been responsible, workable centers of government as compared with government from Washington." A conservative would have been extremely unlikely to make such an assessment.[44]

*An Administrative State*

Liberals still largely agreed on the need for an administrative state in the sense that virtually all of them favored a public sector larger than that endorsed by conservatives and perceived the need for a sizable civil service to administer it. However, most of the new-politics liberals, especially within the public-interest groups, came to endorse what McCann has termed a "judicialized" model of the administrative state, rather than the hierarchically organized, expertise-based administrative state embraced by most liberals since the New Deal and still supported by many old-politics liberals and, for the most part, by Jimmy Carter. The new-politics liberals were suspicious of bureaucratic expertise claims and of hierarchy and were wedded to citizen participation, or at least participation by public-interest groups claiming to represent the citizens' interests. They saw adversarial relationships centered around public-interest litigation as the best means to achieve their goals and favored not only a transformation of administrative law but also (in a striking departure from the liberal past) increased judicial intervention in the administrative sphere. Nevertheless, the growing effectiveness of the conservative and business counterattack against liberal public-interest activism raised liberal doubts about the desirability of the new administrative state model. Though a "judicialized" administrative state won fairly wide new-politics liberal support, especially in the early 1970s, it did not achieve the level of liberal consensus that the New Deal administrative state had once been able to mobilize.

*Presidential-Congressional Relations*

The presidential government model, with its emphasis on chief executive discretion as commander in chief and leader of foreign policy, as well as presidential roles as chief administrator, tribune of a popular majority, and chief instigator of social reform, lost its allure for a broad array of liberals from 1966 onward. Some of their rejection stemmed from the same proparticipatory, antihierarchical attitudes common among new-politics liberals that have already been noted in discussion of the administrative state. Yet much of it related to distaste for particular presidents and their policies and to more generalized new-politics liberal shifts away from an embrace of policies such as containment of Communism or even major new social welfare reforms that almost required presidential leadership. It is noteworthy that many old-politics liberals and most neoconservatives maintained their previous support for a strong presidency in most, if not all, of its dimensions.

Beginning in the Johnson administration and accelerating during the Nixon-Ford years, there was a particularly sharp liberal turn against expansive conceptions of the president's diplomatic and war powers. Although many liberals claimed (with some justification) that their positions had not shifted but rather that Johnson and especially Nixon were pushing far beyond previous presidents in their use of these powers, wide liberal endorsement of congressional curbs on war powers, military sales, executive agreements, covert CIA actions, and trade indicated a general shift from their recent past. Arthur Schlesinger Jr., Hans Morgenthau, Henry Steele Commager, Tom Wicker, Wayne Morse, and many other liberals admitted to some change in their basic perspectives. Morgenthau was fairly typical in this respect. Writing in 1969, he ruefully confessed: "I remember how I used to implore a succession of Presidents to assert their constitutional powers against Congress as long as I disagreed with the foreign policies to which Congress appeared to be committed."[45]

Quite a few liberals remained attached to other aspects of the past liberal presidential government model, even as they now favored congressionally centered checks and balances in the defense and foreign policy realm. Schlesinger was particularly concerned with preserving the presidential role as chief instigator of social reform, through both executive orders and legislative leadership. Califano even wanted to expand the president's economic regulatory powers; and many congressional liberals, with their votes for presidential wage-price control and energy controls, appeared to agree. But the old liberal embrace of the president as the tribune of the majority disappeared almost as completely as the liberal endorsement of broad presidential war and diplomatic powers. Although he claimed that he wished only to curb "Presidential excesses abroad," Schlesinger also became vehement in his denunciation of the "plebiscitary Presidency" and the "mystique of the mandate," employing precisely the same terminology against the tribune role that such conservative intellectuals as Burnham and de Grazia had employed in previous decades. Alexander Bickel and a number of other prominent liberals concurred with Schlesinger. As noted previously, *New Republic* now found Congress more "participatory democratic" than the presidency was.[46]

In general, new-politics liberals shifted most dramatically on the presidential-congressional continuum, and their change of positions was most evident regarding the foreign policy and tribune roles, least evident on the social reform leadership role. Nonetheless, liberals were much more internally divided and less consistent over time on presidential-congressional relations during this period than at any point since 1933. Some, such as Theodore Sorensen and Louis Koenig, continued to defend most or all of the presidential government model; others, such as Bernard Schwartz, Anthony Lewis, and Theodore Lowi, became strong proponents of a congressionally centered checks-and-balances model; quite a few wanted a strong presidency or a strong Congress only when it served their immediate power and/or policy ends. The old cohesiveness in support of presidential government was gone, but a new liberal model had not emerged to replace it.

*Expanded Judicial Activism*

The liberals' institutional prescriptions concerning the Supreme Court and the federal judiciary generally changed less dramatically than in any other area except basic constitutional conceptions. Despite strong general support for judicial activism, however, particularly when it came under conservative court-curbing attacks, liberal splits existed on this dimension, too. Alexander Bickel questioned the competency of judicial activists to direct social change in desirable directions, in addition to raising the old liberal judicial self-restrainers' concerns about overturning "lawmaking majorities." Moving in a contrary direction were the large number of new-politics liberals, typified by Simon Lazarus, who argued that the federal courts were no less democratic than the executive and legislative branches and called upon judges to insert themselves actively into the economic regulatory processes where liberals had long discouraged their intrusion.

## Conclusions

The liberal theory of governance that had guided most of the liberal coalition most of the time from the 1930s to the mid-1960s disintegrated with surprising rapidity after 1966. Although clusters of liberals continued to adhere to significant portions of the previous liberal theory, new-politics liberalism strongly challenged presidential diplomatic and war powers and the president's roles as tribune of a popular majority and as chief administrator. The questioning of the last of these mingled with emergence of a new, judicialized conception of how the administrative state itself ought to operate. New-politics liberalism's embrace of increased decentralization (though usually without enthusiasm for the state governments) and its support for regulatory judicial activism also differentiated liberal prescriptions of this period from those of the past.

However, not all of the observed flux was due to the ideological innovations of new-politics liberalism. Changes in the institutional power centers of both liberalism and conservatism led to marked shifts toward liberal endorsement of congressional powers and away from the presidency—much more clearly during the Nixon and Ford administrations than in those of Johnson and Carter. Overt and openly admitted treatment of institutional prescriptions as means toward short-to-medium term power and policy ends became more widespread than at any time since the New Deal.

The next chapter discusses the extent to which, and ways in which, new ideological strands and changes in the institutional power centers affected the conservative coalition and its institutional prescriptions from 1966 to 1981.

## Notes

1. Joseph S. Clark, *Congress: The Sapless Branch* (New York: Harper & Row, 1965). On Heller's early advocacy of revenue sharing and liberal coolness to it, see A. James Reichley, *Conservatives in an Age of Change* (Washington: Brookings Institution, 1981), 155.

2. *New York Times,* 17 August 1967, 1; *New York Times,* 17 November 1967, 1; "Congress and U.S. Military Commitments, *Congressional Digest* 48 (August–September 1969): 193–224.

3. Henry Steele Commager, "Can We Limit Presidential Power?" *New Republic,* 6 April 1968, 15–18.

4. Saul K. Padover, "The Power of the President," *Commonweal,* 9 August 1968, 521–525.

5. Dwight Macdonald, "The Constitution of the United States Needs to Be Fixed," *Esquire,* October 1968.

6. Tom Wicker, "The Presidency under Scrutiny," *Harper's,* October 1969, 92–94; Arthur M. Schlesinger Jr., *Robert Kennedy and His Times* (New York: Ballantine Books, 1978), 960.

7. *New York Times,* 19 August 1967, 1; the Jackson, McGee, and Dodd quotations are from "Congress and U.S. Military Commitments," *Congressional Digest* 48 (August-September 1969): 193–224.

8. Schlesinger, *Robert Kennedy and His Times,* 688–690; Allen J. Matusow, *The Unraveling of America* (New York: Harper & Row, 1984), 243–245.

9. The first quote is cited by M. Stanton Evans, "At Home," *National Review Bulletin,* 11 June 1968, B94. The second is cited by Garry Wills, *Nixon Agonistes* (New York: New American Library, 1969), 459. Wills also points out a number of difficulties with Goodwin's conception.

10. On RFK's role in the formation of the Community Action Program, see Schlesinger, *Robert Kennedy and His Times,* 688–690. Evans, "At Home," B94.

11. The quotation is from Michael W. McCann, *Taking Reform Seriously* (Ithaca, NY: Cornell University Press, 1986), 99. Also see Sidney M. Milkis, *The President and the Parties* (New York: Oxford University Press, 1993), 211.

12. *Green v. New Kent County* 391 U.S. 430 (1968). Bernard Schwartz, *The New Right and the Constitution* (Boston: Northeastern University Press, 1990), 161. For a typical conservative denunciation, see Lino Graglia, *Disaster by Decree* (Ithaca, NY: Cornell University Press, 1976), chap. 5.

13. "Congress and U.S. Military Commitments," *Congressional Digest* 48 (August–September 1969): 193–224; see also table 14.1 in this chapter.

14. Louis Fisher, *Constitutional Conflict between Congress and the President* (Princeton, NJ: Princeton University Press, 1985), 307–318; James L. Sundquist, *The Decline and Resurgence of Congress* (Washington: Brookings Institution, 1981), 257–260. The Javits quotation is cited in Sundquist, 260.

15. Sundquist, *Decline and Resurgence,* 275–279.

16. Louis Fisher, *Presidential Spending Power* (Princeton, NJ: Princeton University Press, 1975), esp. chap. 8; Sundquist, *Decline and Resurgence,* 199–215.

17. Norman Dorsen and John H. F. Shattuck, "Executive Privilege: The President Won't Tell," in *Resolved: That the Powers of the Presidency Should Be Curtailed,* by the Congressional Research Service, Library of Congress (Washington: U.S. Government Printing Office, 1974), 172–187; Fisher, *Constitutional Conflicts,* 164–166.

18. Richard M. Nixon, *RN: The Memoirs of Richard Nixon,* (New York: Warner Books, 1978), 1:638–647; Leonard Silk, *Nixonomics* (New York: Praeger, 1972), chaps. 7–8.

19. The "broken mirror" quote is from Wilfred E. Binkley, "The Decline of the Executive," *New Republic,* 18 May 1953, 15–16; Richard Bolling, *House Out of Order* (New York: Dutton, 1966); Robert Bendiner, *Obstacle Course on Capitol Hill* (New York: McGraw–Hill, 1964). A good collection of liberal reappraisals is Rexford G. Tugwell and Thomas R. Cronin, eds., *The Presidency Reappraised* (New York: Praeger, 1974).

20. "Swing of the Pendulum," *New Republic,* 27 March 1971, 6–7; "The Challenge to Congress," *Commonweal,* 26 January 1973, 363–364; "No Exit for Congress . . .," *New York Times,* 3 January 1973, 38.

21. John Herbers, "Nixon's Presidency: Expansion of Power," *New York Times,* 4 March 1973, 1, 47.

22. James A. Schlesinger Jr., *The Imperial Presidency,* (New York: Popular Library, 1973), 384; Joseph A. Califano Jr., *A Presidential Nation* (New York: W. W. Norton, 1975), esp. 312–318; Rexford G. Tugwell, "The Historians and the Presidency," *Political Science Quarterly* 86 (June 1971): 202; Gary Orfield, *Congressional Power* (New York: Harcourt Brace Jovanovich, 1975), 11.

23. Reichley, *Age of Change,* chap. 8; William Safire, *Before the Fall* (Garden City, NY: Doubleday, 1975), 218–231; Timothy J. Conlan, *New Federalism* (Washington: Brookings Institution, 1988), pt. l.

24. "What's New?" *New Republic,* 6 February 1971, 13; Max Frankel, "Revenue Sharing Is a Counterrevolution," *New York Times Magazine,* 25 April 25, 1971, 28–29, 91; Commager's comments are cited by Safire, *Before the Fall,* 229.

25. Reichley, *Age of Change,* chap. 8; "Divvying Up the Dollars," *New Republic* 167 (14 October 1972): 7–8.

26. Conlan, *New Federalism,* 70–75.

27. The Friends of the Earth quotation is cited by McCann, *Taking Reform Seriously,* 100; his "code of conflict" comments are on 101.

28. McCann, *Taking Reform Seriously,* 196–121; Milkis, *President and the Parties,* 245–255; Stewart's quotation is cited by McCann, 111.

29. Lazarus, *The Genteel Populists,* (New York: Holt, Rinehart & Winston, 1974), 230.

30. Sax is cited by McCann, *Taking Reform Seriously,* 111.

31. Lazarus, *Genteel Populists,* noted these liberal concerns and sought to respond to them. On the liberals' battles against judicial appointments, see *Congressional Quarterly Weekly Report,* 28 November 1969, 2420; 3 April 1970, 903–908; 10 April 1970, 943–946; 15 May 1970, 1311–1314; on business-conservative counteraction, see McCann, *Taking Reform Seriously,* 232–237.

32. Alexander Bickel, *The Supreme Court and the Idea of Progress* (New York: Harper & Row, 1970), chap. 2, develops the "heavenly city" theme; chap. 4 focuses on "the web of subjectivity." The quotation is from p. 175. Lusky is cited by Gary McDowell, *Curbing the Courts* (Baton Rouge: Louisiana State University Press, 1988), 35.

33. Fisher, *Constitutional Conflicts,* 269–272.

34. Fisher, *Constitutional Conflicts,* 167–168.

35. *Congressional Quarterly Weekly Report,* 25 September 1976, 2637, 2662–2663; Michael Pertschuk, *Revolt against Regulation* (Berkeley and Los Angeles: University of California Press, 1982), chap. 3; Mark Green and Frances Zwenig, "The Legislative Veto Is Bad Law," *Nation,* 28 October 1978, 434–436; *Congressional Quarterly Weekly Report,* 24 May 1980, 1407–1409.

36. Milkis, *President and the Parties,* 257–258, 277–278; *Congressional Quarterly Weekly Report,* 15 July 1978, 1777–1784.

37. McCann, *Taking Reform Seriously,* 113; Kim McQuaid, *Big Business and Presidential Power* (New York: William Morrow, 1982), 300–301; *Congressional Quarterly Weekly Report,* 11 February 1978, 323–325.

38. *Congressional Quarterly Almanac,* 1976, 396–398; *Congressional Quarterly Almanac,* 1979, 426–427.

39. Arthur S. Miller, "Do the Founding Fathers Know Best?" *Washington Post,* 13 November 1977, sec. E, pp. 5, 8.

40. Paul Brest, "Berger v. Brown et al.," *New York Times Book Review,* 11 December 1977, 44; Robert M. Cover, "Books Considered," *New Republic* 198 (13 January 1978): 26–28; E. Richard Larson, "Misreading the Fourteenth Amendment," *Nation* 225 (10 December 1977): 628, 630; "An Exchange of Views," *Nation* 226 (25 February 1978): 26–28.

41. Thomas Grey, "Origins of the Unwritten Constitution: Fundamental Law in American Revolutionary Thought," *Stanford Law Review* 30 (1978): 843. Also see Robert H. Bork, "Supreme Court Needs a New Philosophy," *Fortune,* December 1968, 138–141. John Hart Ely, *Democracy and Distrust* (Cambridge: Harvard University Press, 1980), vii, 172, 181.

42. Ronald Dworkin, *Taking Rights Seriously* (Cambridge: Harvard University Press, 1977), vii, 137, 147.

43. Walter Berns, cited by McDowell, *Curbing the Courts,* 22; McDowell's

assessment of Grey, "Unwritten Constitution," is on pp. 49–50; for his assessment of Ely, *Democracy and Distrust,* see pp. 30–32.

44. Bernard Schwartz, "Imperial Presidential Power," *Center Magazine* 11 (January 1978): 20–21.

45. Hans Morgenthau, "Congress and Foreign Policy," *New Republic* 160 (14 June 1969): 17.

46. Schlesinger, *Imperial Presidency,* 287; Alexander Bickel, ed., *Watergate, Politics, and the Legal Process* (Washington: American Enterprise Institute, 1974), 41–42; Alexander Bickel, "Swing of the Pendulum," *New Republic* 164 (27 March 1971): 6–7.

# 15

# The Conservative Theory of Government in Flux

The years from 1966 to 1981 constituted a period of considerable flux for the conservative theory of governance. As in the case of liberalism, the entry of new ideological strains and the shifts in institutional power centers operated concurrently to erode some conservative institutional prescriptions that had endured for more than a generation. Neoconservative entrants into the conservative coalition usually brought presidential government and often administrative state ideas with them. New Rightists employed populistic majoritarian rhetoric that they frequently linked to a tribune role for the president, and their attacks on liberal judicial "elites" often took on a populistic tone unusual in the conservative movement. Much of the old right, which had often acquiesced in practice in presidential war powers and a large defense establishment as means of at least containing Communism (and someday rolling it back), now openly embraced expanded presidential powers and a Cold War administrative state. Others, however, especially those representing the libertarian tendency within the old right, continued to advocate congressionally centered checks and balances.

Changing perceptions of where the power centers of conservatism lay also played a part in altering conservative prescriptions. The partially reformed, reconstituted (and more liberal) Congress became a major target for conservative wrath during this period, for the first time since the early New Deal. Yet past habits, misgivings that Nixon might be aggrandizing presidential powers on too grand a scale, and doubts about the depth of the conservatism of the Nixon and Ford administrations, restrained conservative moves toward full-scale presidential government. Deep-seated preferences for private rather than public socio-economic management among both old and new rightists also operated to limit enthusiasm for an administrative state and certain types of presidential powers (such as wage-price or energy regulatory authority).

In the areas of constitutional immutability and states' rights, conservatives' basic prescriptions remained in close alignment with those of the past. Their "original intent" jurisprudence won important support from outside the movement with the publication of Raoul Berger's *Government by Judiciary*; and the wide debate that it generated gave conservatives renewed faith in their cause. Richard Nixon's rhetorical support for "strict construction" also won wide conservative acclaim, though the depth of his adherence to strict constructionism and its meaning for his court appointees came into question. Some conservatives even embraced openly the idea of constitutional flexibility, though most did not. Meanwhile, Nixon's revenue-sharing proposals, presented as a means to revitalize the states, won some conservative support for a new approach to decentralization but failed to generate much real conservative enthusiasm. Somewhat stronger and more enduring conservative support was forthcoming for his block-grants approach. By 1980, conservatives were again rallying around the states' rights flag of Ronald Reagan's presidential campaign in a fashion clearly reminiscent of the old days of the Goldwater campaign.

In the sphere of judicial roles, the oft-stated conservative preference for judicial restraint, imposed if necessary on specific issues by curtailment of federal court jurisdiction, continued to echo through the conservative coalition. The actual behavior of supposedly conservative justices, however, indicated that the Burger Court was no different from the Warren Court in its readiness to overturn "lawmaking majorities" and judicial precedents—two key manifestations of judicial activism that conservatives had come to denounce so loudly in the previous era. Outraged by new-politics liberal efforts to promote liberal judicial regulatory activism, most conservatives reiterated their opposition to judicial "lawmaking"; but others focused mainly on enlisting the judiciary in their own deregulatory efforts.

As the period came to an end, most conservatives—unlike most liberals—looked forward to a Reagan era in which they felt confident that their ideas would be translated into public policy. Whether they could agree on a common theory of governance for the long term remained in doubt.

## Conservative Institutional Prescriptions and the Nixon-Ford Administration

In contrast to the liberal coalition's moves toward new institutional prescriptions during the Johnson administration, major shifts in the conservative movement's governance theory became overt primarily after Richard Nixon was in the White House. These alterations were most evident with regard to the presidential-congressional powers continuum but could also be detected in reference to the administrative state and federalism. Of course, there had been factors encouraging change in the preceding era, particularly the general conservative ideological move toward overseas interventionism in the Cold War against Communism, with its implications for the governance theory of the past. However, the Nixon administration itself was a major catalyst for change until it became embroiled in the Watergate coverup and lost its legitimacy. At that point, conservatism was set adrift and failed to coalesce around a coherent new governance theory until the dawn of the Reagan era. Short-term instrumentalism aimed at specific power and policy ends became increasingly evident in conservative behavior in the meantime.

Many leading figures of old-right conservatism shifted overtly toward presidential government during the Nixon administration, most dramatically with regard to presidential war and diplomatic powers but also on impoundment of funds and an array of other issues pertaining to the general direction of the administrative state. Some even shifted toward support for the presidential tribune and instigator of social reform roles, though these roles were much less widely advocated than the others. Support for them was more likely to emanate from the New Right or the neoconservative movement than from the old right. Another presidential role emphasized by Nixon that most conservatives of all camps welcomed was that of remolder of the federal judiciary. Nixon had campaigned in 1968 on pledges that he would not only appoint strict constructionists to the federal courts but also that he would effect judicial promotion of strengthened law enforcement—two points that were not fully compatible with one another but that were both cheered by most conservatives.[1]

Barry Goldwater typified the shifts of much of the old right during the first term of the Nixon administration. "I would put more faith in the judgment of the Office of the president at this time than I would of Congress," he declared in 1971. Goldwater vehemently and vocally opposed the War Powers Resolution and even the mild National Commitments Resolution of 1969, which merely asked for congressional concurrence in national commitments to foreign nations. Furthermore, Goldwater was quite willing to cede broad impoundment powers to the president. The principled opponent of presidential government was now apparently altering his principles.[2]

Jeffrey Hart, a prominent old-right *National Review* intellectual, writing in 1974, shortly after the downfall of Nixon and at a time of considerable conservative disarray, urged conservatives to unite around a presidential government model. "Historically, I submit," wrote Hart, "the Nixon administration, whatever else may be said about it, will be seen to have been the first to understand the revolution that has taken place." Noting what he interpreted as the "revolutionary" rise of a conservative popular majority and liberal control over the mass media and much of the bureaucracy and Congress, Hart even endorsed the tribune aspects of the presidential government model. In Hart's view, what was needed, as Nixon had recognized, was "a powerful President who is willing virtually to go to war within his own executive branch in order to carry out his mandate. . . . Armed with his 49-state landslide, President Nixon was making modest moves to try to get the giant brontosaurus of the federal bureaucracy under some sort of executive control. Almost immediately, however, these efforts were frustrated by Watergate."[3]

Old-right critiques of Congress as an institution were also becoming increasingly common. James J. Kilpatrick complained of the "macaroni Congresses" that lacked any fiscal discipline or willingness "to bite anything tougher than macaroni." William F. Buckley deplored "legislative tyranny" and what he perceived to be an attitude that "every congressman is entitled to know all the nation's secrets but, in fact, to use his own judgment on whether to share them with the Associated Press." Now conservatives in Congress began to author books denouncing their own institution in a manner previously fashionable only among liberals, as in conservative Republican Representative Marjorie Holt's edited book of nineteen articles by congressional conservatives, titled *The Case against the Reckless Congress.* [4]

The strongest support for presidential majoritarianism came from those who would soon emerge as leaders of the New Right. Patrick J. Buchanan was typical. Hailing the "new American majority" that had rejected Hubert Humphrey in 1968 and reelected Nixon in a landslide in 1972, Buchanan perceived "a collision between Congress and President, between the nation's regnant ideology on the one hand and the nation's political majority on the other." In Buchanan's view, "While the Nixon landslide was a victory of the man over McGovern, it was also a victory of 'the new American majority' over the 'New Politics,' a victory of traditional American values and beliefs over the claims of the 'counter-culture,' a victory of 'Middle America' over the celebrants of Woodstock Nation." However, much of the old right (despite Hart) continued to find such plebiscitarianism inappropriate. Henry Regnery denounced "democratist ideology" as opposed to "constitutional principle," the *National Review* editorially warned against the "Caesarist mass democra-

tization" implicit in the tribune role of Nixon, and Alfred de Grazia asserted that "Presidents often represent fractions and other politicians are
more representative of the whole."[5]

Neoconservatives, not surprisingly in light of their backgrounds as
longtime liberals, tended to be dependable conservative backers of presidential government in a general sense. Typically, Samuel P. Huntington in
1975 warned against the shifting of power from the chief executive to
Congress: "When the president is unable to exercise authority, when he is
unable to command the cooperation of key decision-makers elsewhere in
society and government, no one else has been able to supply comparable
purpose and initiative." Continuing in this line of thought, Huntington
stressed: "In recent years, the increase in the power of Congress has out-
stripped an increase in its ability to govern." The likely consequences,
Huntington and many other neoconservatives foresaw, were "financial
insolvency" for the country and "a relative downturn in American power
and influence in world affairs." But even in neoconservative ranks, some
discord existed on the subject, with Michael Novak, Aaron Wildavsky,
and Nelson Polsby voicing some reservations about the new conservative
version of presidential government.[6]

If a few neoconservatives expressed concerns about presidential government, a sizable bloc of old right conservatives remained strong adherents of a congressionally centered system of checks and balances. Conservative Southern Democrats, such as Senator Sam Ervin of North Carolina,
were prominent in this bloc. Ervin not only headed the Senate Watergate
Committee that contributed greatly to the termination of the Nixonian
imperial presidency, but he was also the leading architect of restrictions
on presidential impoundment of funds. He authored bills (never enacted)
giving Congress absolute authority to veto all executive agreements within sixty days, requiring all executive branch officials to appear in person
when summoned by congressional committees even if they were intending to claim executive privilege, and restricting presidential use of the
pocket veto; and articulated a broad scheme for subordinating the presidency to Congress across the board. Not all conservative Southern
Democrats were as consistent as Ervin, but the majority remained opponents of presidential government.[7]

Another major element in this procongressional, checks-and-balances
conservative bloc were many intellectual conservatives of a libertarian
bent. Writing in 1975, Alfred de Grazia declared that "Congress . . . should
logically develop new institutions and devices to justify the commanding
position it holds under the Constitution." He denounced Nixon's "unnec-
essary, sharp intrusions on the constitutional prerogatives of Congress"

and the "abrupt and callous forays that he ordered in Cambodia," argued that instead of the president's really controlling the bureaucracy it "uses him to expand its own powers," and scornfully rejected the tribune role. Felix Morley, M. Stanton Evans, and Jeffrey St. John were other prominent libertarian conservatives who expressed broadly similar views of congressional-presidential relations.[8]

Thus, the Nixon-Ford era witnessed a general conservative trend toward presidential government but with conservatives divided even over presidential diplomatic and war powers (where the trend was most evident) and very fractured on other aspects of the model. Though neoconservatives and New Rightists tended to be most inclined to support a new conservative model of presidential government and conservative Southern Democrats and libertarian conservative intellectuals were the least favorable to it, even the conservative subgroups were often internally divided.

No other governance issues created as much turmoil and flux among conservatives as presidential-congressional powers issues did between 1969 and 1977; but there also were notable alterations concerning some of the other conservative governance dimensions. As far as the administrative state was concerned, Nixon, of course, sought to enhance presidential control over it—in part to decentralize some of its domestic functions to state and local governments and in part to increase his own power and punish those whom he perceived to be his enemies. Although 76 percent of conservatives in the House of Representatives supported Nixon's Office of Management and Budget and Domestic Council reorganizations of 1970 and most congressional conservatives went along with his early justifications for impoundments, their patience eventually wore thin. Most conservatives strongly opposed giving the executive branch authority over prices and wages, and most remained skeptical of the administrative state. The strongest conservative supporters of a hierarchical, expert national administrative state under presidential control were usually neoconservatives; administration operatives such as Richard Nathan, who wrote extensively on the subject; and big-business conservatives, long accustomed to both business corporate and government bureaucracies. When Nixon sought to tighten his controls over the administrative state in 1973 and 1974, just as the Watergate affair was undermining his credibility, most conservative backing for his endeavors evaporated. Continuing conservative suspicions of career civil servants surfaced in the struggle, mainly during the Ford administration, over revision of the Hatch Act to permit federal employees to engage in a widened range of political activities. Backed by a blue-ribbon commission report, the labor unions that organized executive branch employees, and almost all congressional liberals, the measure met stiff conservative opposition—from 80 percent of congressional conservatives in both chambers on key roll-call votes and from President Ford, who vetoed the bill.[9]

Nixon's efforts to alter the contours of the conservative consensus on states' rights also fell short of full accomplishment, despite some results favorable to his New Federalism perspective. Since general revenue sharing—granting upwards of five billion dollars in federal funding per year for state and local governments to spend largely as they wished—was the most novel departure from traditional conservative states' rights ideas in his package, Nixon made a major effort to convince the conservative movement that his move was a logical extension of their long-held ideas. He was only partially successful. *National Review* ran articles both supporting and attacking revenue sharing, William F. Buckley saw it as insufficiently different from the past to accomplish much of value, Goldwater opposed it, and congressional conservatives split badly, opposing giving it a closed rule by a 54 to 46 percent margin on what Timothy Conlan saw as the critical vote in the House of Representatives but supporting the measure on final passage in both the House (56 to 44 percent) and the Senate (74 to 26 percent). Nixon's effort to enhance state and local government powers by shifting from specifically drawn categorical grants-in-aid to broadly defined block grants also won generally mixed conservative support. Although the concept gained wide conservative backing, specific efforts to apply it resulted in a "fragmented politics," according to Conlan's scholarly analysis of the patterns, in which instrumental calculations of specific power and policy gains and losses predominated.[10]

As for the judiciary and constitutional interpretation, most conservatives continued their previous rhetoric about judicial restraint, strict construction, and original intent. Solid majorities (72 percent on one item, 67 percent on another) of congressional conservatives had made additional unsuccessful stabs at federal court-curbing as part of the crime bill of 1968, and most appeared supportive of Gerald Ford's unsuccessful drive in the early years of the Nixon administration to impeach liberal Justice William O. Douglas on several grounds, including his writings about revolutionary change and his alleged breaches of ethics. Despite losses on key Senate confirmation votes concerning Nixon's appointments of Clement Haynsworth and G. Harrold Carswell, conservatives were generally pleased initially by the new Nixon-named justices: Chief Justice Warren Burger, William Rehnquist, Harry Blackmun, and Lewis Powell. By July 1972, the *National Review*'s editors were feeling quite optimistic about the direction of the High Bench:

it is fair to say that the requirements of order and stability received a far more favorable hearing from the Nixon Court than from its predecessor. With Kennedy appointee Byron White often providing the swing vote, and the four Nixon appointees usually voting as a bloc, the Court strengthened law enforcement by expanding the authority of the police to 'stop and frisk' and by curbing the right to counsel. In its 6 to 3 ruling that racially restrict- ed private clubs could hold a state liquor license, the Court indicated its willingness to call a halt to government intrusion upon the private life.[11]

It was noteworthy that *National Review* made no comment on the adherence of the "Nixon Court" to judicial restraint in this editorial, since studies would soon show that the High Bench was overruling judicial precedents and lawmaking majorities just as frequently as the Warren Court had done. According to David O'Brien's analysis, the Burger Court overruled acts of Congress an average of 2.0 times per year (1.6 times per year for the Warren Court), state laws an average of 11.3 times per year (9.4 times per year for the Warren Court), and previous Supreme Court decisions an average of 2.9 times per year (the same as the Warren Court figure). Bernard Schwartz came up with slightly different figures but showed the same pattern. Moreover, much of the early conservative enthusiasm for the policies emerging from the new Supreme Court would wane fairly soon. The 1973 *Roe v. Wade* decision, rendered by a 7-2 major- ity, in an opinion written by Nixon appointee Blackmun (and joined by Burger and Powell) came as a rude shock. Not only did it go against the antiabortion policy position of a majority of conservatives, but it also overturned the statutes in many states beyond the Texas law at issue and cited a "right to privacy" not present in the language of the Constitution. To most conservatives, it appeared to entail judicial lawmaking and departure from the text of the Constitution at their worst extremes. Jerry Falwell was to assert that this Supreme Court decision was what drove him into politics. Well beyond the confines of the new religious right, however, conservatives expressed genuine horror at the new directions of what they had just begun to think was "their" Supreme Court.[12]

Meanwhile, the liberal public-interest group drive for expansion of lib- eral judicial review into the economic regulatory sphere, coupled with a judicialized administrative state, was provoking a conservative reaction. The intellectual challenge came initially and most forcefully from the neo- conservative camp, particularly from Donald Horowitz, Nathan Glazer, David Kirp, and Franklin Hunt. The first argument that they usually put forward alleged that this form of judicial activism was undemocratic, since judges were too insulated from the give-and-take of the democratic process and from democratic accountability through elections to make economic management policy. Since the late 1930s, judicial activism had only occasionally entered the field of detailed regulation. Franklin Hunt typified many neoconservatives in seeing the new-politics liberal efforts as a "lawyers' war against democracy," in sharp contrast to the assertions of Lazarus and other new-politics liberals that it was, on the contrary, opening up the administrative processes and enhancing participatory democracy. Two very different conceptions of democracy were obviously at war here. But neither conception was the old right's model of "a republic, not a democracy," even though the neoconservatives' vision was much closer to it than was Lazarus's. The other major argument of the neoconservative intellectuals was one of judicial competence and capacity. This fit old-right conservative conceptions quite well and was soon widely adopted throughout the conservative movement. According to Horowitz, who stressed this argument, a key question "relates not to legitimacy but to capacity, not to whether the courts *should* perform certain tasks but to whether they *can* perform them competently." While conceding that the judicial process "reduces the number of participants and makes it possible to cut through to an apparent solution," Horowitz believed the appearance to be illusory. A "complex pattern of interests" would still "reappear and make their influence felt at the implementation stages." Judges and courts, in Horowitz's view and that of many other neoconservatives, were ill-suited to the task at hand. Judicial restraint was in order.[13]

Big businessmen were unwilling to wait and hope for judicial restraint. They moved quickly into action with their own legal teams; with new corporate-funded conservative "public-interest" law organizations, such as the Pacific Legal Foundation and the Rocky Mountain Legal Foundation; with massive campaign contributions and lobbying to reshape congressional attitudes; and with advertising and other "educational" campaigns to shift public opinion toward free-enterprise points of view. Much of this activity, both by business groups and by conservative intellectuals and political activists, really began to have major effects during the Carter administration; but the acceleration of such efforts began in the early 1970s, partly in response to liberal initiatives.[14]

As the Nixon-Ford years ended with the election of the centrist Jimmy Carter to the presidency, conservative internal consensus appeared moderately high on constitutional interpretation and the need to restrain liberal judicial activism, rather divided on particular means of decentralization such as modes of revenue sharing but high on the concept of states' rights, and quite fractured over the administrative state and especially presidential-congressional relations. The Carter years would do little to clarify this last point for conservatives, but they did set the stage for the election of Ronald Reagan to the presidency and thus some eventual conservative moves toward unity on a new presidential government model to suit their perceived needs.

### Conservative Institutional Prescriptions in the Carter Years

Conservatives spent much of the Carter period battling liberal judicial activism through additional, unsuccessful efforts to curb federal court jurisdiction on school busing and school prayer issues, and on public school matters generally; drives for constitutional amendments on the abortion matter to overturn *Roe v. Wade* and subsequent abortion rulings; and attempts to either restrain or influence the views of the judges in regulatory cases where the judiciary had gained a significant role in the early 1970s.

As far as presidential-congressional relations were concerned, conservatives swung back generally in the direction of congressionally centered checks and balances, but in a hesitant fashion suggestive of short-term instrumentalism rather than a return to where most of the conservative movement had stood a decade before. The most noteworthy apparent break with the recent past was the 98 percent solid conservative vote to insist that the Senate play a mandatory role in the termination of treaties, a subject on which constitutional language was of little help. Goldwater, who had become a strong proponent of presidential powers, especially in the diplomatic and war powers arena, now became the most vocal and active opponent of the Carter administration's unilateral termination, without Senate approval, of the United States' treaty with Taiwan in order to open formal diplomatic relations with the People's Republic of China. Not only did Goldwater fight the issue in the Senate, but he also filed suit in federal court, challenging the constitutionality of Carter's action, though he failed in both arenas.[15]

Despite nearly unanimous conservative opposition to presidential power on the treaty termination issue, conservatives were less intolerant of modest exercises of power by Carter in some other spheres. Most voted for his Civil Service Reform Act of 1978 (which possessed considerable potential, mostly unused by Carter, for enhanced presidential control over the administrative state) and even agreed to permit the president to once again reorganize the executive branch, subject to a legislative veto.[16]

Where conservatives challenged presidential power and the administrative state most directly in the domestic sphere under Carter was on the matter of legislative vetoes, especially in the regulatory domain. Late in the Ford administration, a united conservative coalition had nearly succeeded in gaining House passage of a bill to require that all new federal regulations be subject to a legislative veto by Congress. Failing in that endeavor, they targeted the regulatory agencies which were most disliked by business for legislative vetoes during the Carter years. A particularly acrimonious battle over the Federal Trade Commission finally ended in 1980 with a "compromise" that gave the conservatives more than their opponents.[17]

Perhaps the clearest triumph for the conservatives on an institutional issue during the Carter administration was their blocking of the new-politics liberals' keystone for the judicialized administrative state that they had hoped to build, the Agency for Consumer Advocacy. Lobbied heavily by an array of corporations and business-backed interest groups, led by the Business Roundtable, which threw the efforts of top corporate chief executive officers directly into the battle, the House of Representatives rejected the liberals' measure in February 1978. House conservatives voted 98 percent to 2 percent against the bill and picked up an array of moderates and a scattering of liberals. This vote was a harbinger of future patterns.[18]

Despite occasional outright triumphs and some partial victories, as in the legislative veto-Federal Trade Commission battle, the conservative movement was far from satisfied with the institutional or policy outcomes of the 1970s. The Nixonian judicial "revolution" for which many of them had held high hopes had fizzled, states' rights appeared almost as much in jeopardy as ever despite a revenue sharing process initiated by a Republican president, and the Constitution continued to be stretched almost beyond recognition (most shockingly, many conservatives thought, by the abortion "right to privacy" decisions). Though conservatives had inflicted some key defeats on the new-politics liberals in the administrative state sphere, the bureaucracy remained large, mostly unsympathetic, and threatening in most conservatives' eyes. Worst of all, perhaps, conservatives remained deeply divided among themselves over what they wished to prescribe concerning presidential-congressional relations.

## Conservative Consensus and Discord

As noted, conservative discord was most serious on the issue of presidential-congressional relations as the 1966–81 period drew to a close. This had also been true throughout most of these years. Ideological and power

changes had helped to shatter the old rhetorical consensus on a congressionally centered system of checks and balances. For a time, during the
Nixon years and before the Watergate revelations, a new conservative
consensus favoring presidential government (and perhaps even an
administrative state linked to it) had appeared to be forming. However,
that had dissipated during the upheavals of 1973 and 1974. Other aspects
of the old conservative institutional doctrines remained largely in place,
though each had generated some degree of debate; and some had been
turned in slightly different directions.

### Constitutional Immutability

"Strict construction" and "original intent" remained the key phrases
for most conservatives, though there was considerable shift from emphasis on the former in the first part of the period (when Nixon stressed it
repeatedly) to stress on the latter in the second half of the period (when
Raoul Berger's *Government by Judiciary* widened its popular appeal). The
two phrases had similar meanings to most conservatives but were not
synonymous. "Strict construction" referred to serious attempts to adhere
as closely as possible to the textual language of the Constitution; "original
intent" suggested a preoccupation with adherence to the intentions of
those who had penned that language (and those involved in the ratification process). Most liberals questioned whether either was really even
practicable, let alone desirable. In actuality, most conservatives with judicial or legal experience recognized that there were unavoidable ambigui-
ties of both constitutional language and framers' intentions, as Justice
William Rehnquist of the Supreme Court, usually its most conservative
member, noted in a widely cited 1976 article on the "living Constitution."
But Rehnquist, like most conservatives, still found objectionable the "sub-
stitution of some other set of values for those which may be derived from
the language and intent of the framers." Some conservatives, however,
notably Robert Bork, while emphasizing constitutional language and the
framers' intentions, also drew upon a philosophy of natural rights. Bork,
in particular, linked it to the Constitution through the Ninth Amendment.
A few conservatives of the period openly described the Constitution as
flexible. Perhaps the most blatantly instrumentalist statement in this connection was expressed by Donald E. Santorelli, associate deputy attorney
general in the Nixon administration: "The Constitution is flexible. Period.
Your point of view depends on whether you're winning. . . . The Constitution isn't the real issue in this; it's how you want to run the country."

The decisions of many of the new judicial conservatives raised questions as to how many of them may have privately shared Santorelli's outlook.[19]

## States' Rights

Conservatives appeared, at least on the surface, to be more unified on federalism issues than did the liberals of the period. Most agreed that they disliked both the centralized federalism of the past liberal model and the new-politics liberal proclivity to bypass the states in a new quest for a participatory decentralist formulation. However, conservatives' deep divisions over revenue sharing and conflicts over block grants in practice raised questions of whether their unity really extended far beyond the slogan of states' rights. As the 1970s ended and conservatives of all factions and tendencies ralled around Reagan's states' rights new federalism appeals, their dislocations of the early 1970s appeared to be behind them. When the editors of *Publius: The Journal of Federalism* tabulated the "federalist stance" scores of congressmen for 1979 and 1980, they found, not surprisingly, that conservatives generally took more pro-decentralist positions in their roll-call voting than liberals did. Still, it should be recalled that even conservative state and local officials had generally accommodated themselves to the routines of cooperative federalism and resisted any changes that appeared threatening, even if they bore a "states' rights" label.[20]

## A Limited Administrative State

Conservatives still loved to rail against government bureaucracy and generally favored a reduction of the public regulatory and social services sector. However, all except a few diehard libertarian conservatives recognized that the administrative state was here to stay. The widespread conservative as well as liberal support for the Civil Service Reform Act of 1978 illustrated that a broad area of consensus existed across the political spectrum. What now mobilized conservatives most effectively in unified opposition was the new-politics version of the administrative state. With its liberal public-interest group litigation, judicialized administrative processes, link to liberal judicial activism, and perceived threat to big business and propertied interests generally, it made an excellent target for conservatives. Conservative unity on the vote to kill the Agency for Consumer Advocacy was noteworthy: 98 percent voted against the agency.

*Presidential-Congressional Relations*

On this continuum, or cluster of dimensions, conservative disparities stood in sharpest contrast to the past. Since this set of institutional issues dealt with the two major institutional power centers most capable of altering the nation's agenda, conservatives' inability to achieve even a semblance of medium-term unity posed a significant problem for the coalition.

Most neoconservatives, echoing James Neuchterlein in a 1979 *Commentary* article, continued to believe that "our constitutional arrangements are such that national leadership must come from the President. The Congress is simply not constructed to provide coherent direction to the nation in either foreign or domestic spheres." A number of other conservative intellectuals, notably including many traditional conservatives of the Straussian school of thought (followers of the late political philosopher Leo Strauss), such as Harvey Mansfield, James Ceaser, and Carnes Lord, were beginning to articulate a strong presidency model shorn of its tribune and social reform leadership roles but capable of strong and fairly autonomous leadership, especially in national security and foreign policy matters. But in 1980, both of these forces together constituted a minority in the conservative camp. They faced another organized minority, centered among libertarian conservatives, which favored congressionally centered checks and balances. Still another organized minority cluster, centered in the New Right, favored a full-scalle presidential government model, highlighting the president's role as a popular tribune—a role shunned by many other conservatives. Apart from all of these lay many conservatives who had become rather overtly short-term instrumentalist in their approach to the question and had shifted in several different directions during the 1970s. Whether the new Reagan administration that would take office in January 1981 could reunify the conservatives, this time around a reconceptualized presidential government model, remained to be seen.[21]

*Judicial Restraint*

Throughout this period, almost all conservatives from Richard Nixon to Ronald Reagan, including all of the supposed conservatives on the Supreme Court, gave verbal endorsement to judicial restraint. Conservatives usually asserted the need for judges to restrain themselves from overturning both lawmaking majorities and precedents (unless the framers' intent or constitutional language really demanded that they do so). Yet the intent or the language apparently did make such demands often, at least in the minds of the sitting justices of the Supreme Court. The Burger Court proved just as activist in both senses as the Warren Court had been. Sometimes, as in *National League of Cities v. Usery* (1976), in which the High Bench overturned congressional extension of the Fair Labor Standards Act to state and local employees, conservatives generally applauded "activism." In this particular case, the states' rights prescription apparently took precedence for most of them over judicial restraint. More commonly they were outraged, as in *Roe v. Wade,* which seemed to them to combine judicial activism with extremely loose construction of the Constitution (even "Constitution-making") by the Court. Conservatives now also urged restraint with regard to judicial "legislation" in the regulatory field, mainly in response to the new-politics liberals' extension of liberal judicial activism into that sphere. Major arguments for judicial restraint now came to be both democratic ones (stressing the need for deference to lawmaking majorities, borrowed largely from Felix Frankfurter's longtime strictures on the subject) and competency ones (stressing judges' and courts' unsuitability for handling complex social policy matters, drawn extensively from Alexander Bickel's ideas). Despite widespread conservative rhetorical support for judicial restraint, backed by strong (but unsuccessful) conservative efforts to curb judicial activism via restrictions on federal court jurisdiction, the behavior of conservative justices and the willingness of the conservative movement to elevate other institutional and policy choices above judicial restraint called the commitment of the coalition to judicial restraint into question during this period.[22]

## Conclusions

Conservatives had adjusted their judicial restraint prescription somewhat to cope with new situations (mainly liberal initiatives), but they also needed to address the failure of supposed judicial conservatives to restrain themselves. But aside from seeking to curb federal court jurisdiction in specific subject areas in which they disagreed with the judicial decisions, or sponsoring specific constitutional amendments, conservatives did not really do so. In the administrative state sphere, conservatives also made some adjustments, becoming more willing to accept its existence than in the past, but also uniting in very strong opposition to the judicialized administrative state advanced by many new-politics liberals and typified by the proposed Agency for Consumer Advocacy. States' rights continued to be a dominant conservative theme in the late 1960s and 1970s, but conservatives were compelled to respond to Nixon's New Federalism initiatives as well as new liberal versions of decentralization. Constitutional immutability also won at least rhetorical support from most conservatives, though a few openly admitted to treating the Constitution as a highly flexible document; and many conservatives disagreed over just how immutable the Constitution was. In these four fields, then, conservative continuity generally outweighed change and conservative consensus generally outweighed discord. However, in the very important sphere of presidential-congressional relations, the conservative coalition was so marked by flux and so rent by disagreements that its commitment to an overarching theory of governance was about as much in doubt as that of the liberal coalition.

Overt instrumentalism for short-to-medium-term power and policy ends by conservatives as well as liberals became more widespread than in previous periods, perhaps because the changes in the institutional power centers of the two broad ideological movements seemed to many to mandate altered behavior patterns that could hardly be explained in any but crude mean-ends terms. In less obvious ways than the power shifts, however, changing ideological goals also effected alterations in the institutional prescriptions made by each coalition. The next chapter analyzes the impact of the past, the extent and nature of contemporary instrumentalism in the 1966–81 period, and the future effects of the institutional prescriptions of these years.

## Notes

1. Patrick J. Buchanan, *The New Majority* (n.p.: Girard Bank, 1973), 28–29, notes Nixon's two pledges and priorities.

2. Arthur M. Schlesinger Jr., *The Imperial Presidency* (New York: Popular Library, 1974), 286; also see James L. Sundquist, *The Decline and Resurgence of Congress* (Washington: Brookings Institution, 1981), 292, for Goldwater's pro–presidential power views during the Ford administration.

3. Jeffrey Hart, "The Presidency: Shifting Conservative Perspectives," *National Review* 26 (22 November 1974): 1351–1355.

4. James J. Kilpatrick, "The Macaroni Congresses," *Nation's Business* 62 (December 1974): 13–14; William F. Buckley, "And Now Legislative Supremacy," *National Review* 39 (6 June 1975): 630–631; Marjorie Holt, ed., *The Case against the Reckless Congress* (Ottawa, IL: Green Hill Publishers, 1976).

5. Buchanan, *The New Majority*, 67, 63–64; Henry Regnery, "Emerging Conservatism: Kilpatrick, Morley, and Burnham," *Modern Age* 22 (Summer 1978): 242; *National Review* editorial of 17 May 1974, quoted by Hart, "The Presidency," 1352; Alfred de Grazia, *Eight Bads—Eight Goods* (New York: Doubleday Anchor, 1975), 32.

6. Samuel P. Huntington, "The United States," in *The Crisis of Democracy,* by Michel Crozier, Samuel P. Huntington, and Joji Watanuki, (New York: New York University Press, 1975), 92, 102, 106; Michael Novak, *Choosing Our King* (New York: Macmillan, 1974), esp. ch.ap 32; Aaron Wildavsky's discussion in Alexander Bickel, ed., *Watergate, Politics, and the Legal Process* (Washington: American Enterprise Institute, 1974), 39; Nelson W. Polsby, "Against Presidential Greatness," *Commentary* 63 (January 1977): 61–64.

7. Schlesinger, *Imperial Presidency,* 373–383; "Controversy over the Presidential Impoundment of Appropriated Funds," *Congressional Digest* 52 (April 1973): 99–128; author's analysis of congressional voting patterns.

8. De Grazia, *Eight,* 171, 26, 32; Felix Morley, *For the Record* (South Bend, IN: Regnery/Gateway, 1979), esp. 437–438, 44l, 462; M. Stanton Evans, *Clear and Present Dangers* (New York: Harcourt Brace Jovanovich, 1975); Jeffrey St. John, "A Document for Dictatorship," *New York Times,* 3 October 1970, 31.

9. Richard P. Nathan, *The Plot That Failed* (New York: Wiley, 1975); Sidney M. Milkis, *The President and the Parties* (New York: Oxford University Press, 1993), 228–238; Kim McQuaid, *Big Business and* Presidential *Power* (New York: William Morrow, 1982), chap. 8. On Hatch Act reform, see *Congressional Quarterly Almanac,* 1976, 490.

10. A. James Reichley, *Conservatives in an Age of Change* (Washington: Brookings Institution, 1981), chap. 8; Timothy J. Conlan, *New Federalism* (Washington: Brookings Institution, 1988), chaps. 2–5; chap. 3 discusses fragmented politics; Milkis, *President and the Parties,* 225–228; William F. Buckley Jr., "Revenue Sharing," *National Review* 33 (6 April 1971): 390–391; J. A. Maxwell, "Yes, to Revenue Sharing," *National Review* 35 (31 March 1972): 341–343; W. G. Fredericks, "No, to Revenue Sharing," *National Review* 34 (13 July 1971): 754–757.

11. "The First Nixon Court," *National Review,* 21 July 1972, 785.

12. David M. O'Brien, *Storm Center,* 2d ed. (New York: W. W. Norton, 1990), 60–61; Bernard Schwartz, *The Ascent of Pragmatism* (Reading, MA: Addison–Wesley, 1990), 408. On Falwell, see Paul Gottfried and Thomas Fleming, *The Conservative Movement* (Boston: Twayne, 1988), 82, and Jerome L. Himmelstein, *To the Right* (Berkeley and Los Angeles: University of California Press, 1990), 118.

13. Franklin Hunt, "The Lawyers' War against Democracy," *Commentary* 68 (October 1979): 45–51; Donald L. Horowitz, "Are the Courts Going Too Far?" *Commentary* 63 (January 1977): 42, 44.

14. Michael W. McCann, *Taking Reform Seriously* (Ithaca, NY: Cornell University Press, 1986), esp. 232–237.

15. Sundquist, *Decline and Resurgence,* 295–296; Louis M. Fisher, *Constitutional Conflicts between Congress and the President* (Princeton, NJ: Princeton University Press, 1983), 269–272.

16. Fisher, *Constitutional Conflicts,* 167–168; Milkis, *President and the Parties,* 257–258, 277–278; *Congressional Quarterly Weekly Report,* 15 July 1978, 1777–1784.

17. Sundquist, *Decline and Resurgence,* 350–366.

18. McCann, *Taking Reform Seriously,* 113; McQuaid, *Big Business,* 300–301; *Congressional Quarterly Weekly Report,* 11 February 1978, 323–325.

19. Raoul Berger, *Government by Judiciary* (Cambridge: Harvard University

Press, 1977); for an early popular-press example of Bork's efforts, see Robert Bork, "Supreme Court Needs a New Philosophy," *Fortune* 78 (December 1968): 138–141; William H. Rehnquist, "The Notion of a Living Constitution," *Texas Law Review* 54 (May 1976): 695; Santorelli is quoted by Novak, *Choosing Our King,* 248.

20.  "Federalism in the 96th Congress," *Publius* 11 (Summer 1981): 155–192.

21.  James A. Nuechterlein, "Watergate: Toward a Revisionist View," *Commentary* 68 (August 1979): 39; Robert Devigne, *Recasting Conservatism* (New Haven: Yale University Press, 1994), esp. 69–74, 176–189, discusses the Straussians' ideas and what he sees as their links to neoconservatism.

22.  On the *Usery* case and alleged conservative inconsistencies concerning judicial restraint, see Herman Schwartz, *Packing the Courts* (New York: Charles Scribner's Sons, 1988), 39–40.

# 16

# Theories of Governance: Past Influences, Instrumentalism, and Impact

───────────

The preceding two chapters have illustrated that the 1966–81 period was one of much more flux in both the liberal and conservative theories of governance than had been true during the 1945–66 years. On the really critical issues of presidential-congressional relations, there was not simply major change in the prescriptions of many liberals and conservatives by the mid-1970s but so much diversity within each coalition that it became difficult to describe a predominant theory of governance for either one. Thus, in chapters 14 and 15, references have been made to institutional prescriptions rather than to theories of governance.

Nevertheless, it would be a mistake to suggest that all institutional prescriptions were in flux or to convey the impression that conservative or liberal consensus on governance theory completely disappeared in the late 1960s and 1970s. Even on presidential-congressional relations, there were some patterns in the general chaos. Furthermore, in the sphere of constitutional interpretation, marked continuity persisted, at least in the rhetoric employed by most liberals and conservatives. On issues of federalism, the administrative state, and judicial review, significant adjustments occurred; but these were less extensive and fundamental than on executive-legislative relations.

Following the same general format as chapters 6 and 11, this chapter will focus on three major themes concerning the institutional prescriptions of the ideological coalitions: the influences of past commitments on present recommendations, the nature and extent of instrumentalism underlying current choices (particularly, in this period, the noteworthy alterations of choices), and the long-term impact of the outcomes of the liberal-conservative institutional struggles of the late 1960s and the 1970s.

## The Influence of Past Prescriptions

As previously discussed, sheer force of habit and a desire to avoid opposition charges of insincerity and opportunism have usually persuaded political actors to apply past institutional prescriptions to new situations unless there are clear power and/or policy-values reasons to do otherwise. The shifting power bases of the two major ideological coalitions, of course, provided some important stimuli for altered institutional prescriptions after 1966. So, too, did the differing values and policy preferences injected into each coalition—especially by the rise of new-politics liberalism in the liberal movement and by the concomitant rise of the New Right and the acquisition of the neoconservative faction in the conservative alliance. However, past prescriptions continued to exert influence in each ideological camp, particularly on those politicians, intellectuals, and activists who had already gone on record with a particular institutional recommendation or set of recommendations.

In the area of greatest change in the 1966-81 period, that pertaining to presidential-congressional relations, the liberals who had helped to design the presidential government model and/or who had participated actively in making it a reality were generally more reluctant than others to reject it altogether. Among these were two major subsets: old-politics liberals who had gone on record for presidential government and who retained the old values and goals, and new-politics liberals who had similarly gone on record but whose values and goals now embraced most of new-politics liberalism. In the first category were such figures as Henry Jackson, Gale McGee, and Thomas Dodd. Not surprisingly, they continued to be generally sympathetic to presidential power. The second category included a large number of liberal leaders. Theodore Sorensen (a proponent and participant in presidential government in the Kennedy administration) and Joseph Califano (playing similar roles in the Johnson administration) sympathized with much of new-politics liberalism but remained among the strongest defenders of the old institutional model. Louis Koenig continued to support most aspects of presidential government, though in a more restrained fashion than in his 1965 article calling for major new presidential powers. Arthur Schlesinger Jr. made major admitted shifts on the diplomatic-war powers aspect (and also rejected plebiscitarianism) but remained quite intent on preserving presidential preeminence in social reform leadership and administration. In fact, he took great pains in *The Imperial Presidency* to separate his own position from that of those who sought a congressionally centered system of checks and balances, lest he be misunderstood. James MacGregor Burns moved away from his extremely pro-presidential positions of 1965 but only back toward his responsible party government prescriptions of the previous two decades, though he gave these a little less pro-presidential twist than he had done previously. A few past advocates of presidential government who became new-politics liberal proponents did shift almost completely away from presidential government, as Eugene McCarthy and (eventually) Henry Steele Commager did, but most were reluctant to shift quickly and drastically. The past did exert an influence in restraining change. However, the combination of an altered power structure and postcontainment and participatory values pulled many old liberals who had new-politics liberal sympathies a good distance away from their previous moorings.[1]

Among conservatives, too, many of those who had gone on record most vehemently in favor of congressionally centered checks and balances remained faithful to the cause or at least were reluctant to contradict their previous positions directly. Prime examples of those who continued to advocate consistently the old conservative model included Alfred de Grazia, Felix Morley, Henry Regnery, Sam Ervin, Ernest Griffith, Henry Hazlitt, and (despite some wavering) M. Stanton Evans. William F. Buckley did not retract his previous recommendations but became markedly less enthusiastic about Congress than before. On the other hand, Jeffrey Hart, James J. Kilpatrick, David Lawrence, and James McClellan did shift markedly in a pro-presidential direction. Barry Goldwater moved toward endorsement of presidential power during the first Nixon administration and then back toward his previous model, especially during the Carter years, as did many congressional conservatives. A few of the most vociferous old-right intellectual defenders of a congressionally centered check and balance model, such as James Burnham, barely addressed the subject any longer, though Hart saw Burnham's influence in *National Review*'s editorial resistance to the pro-presidential government advocacy that Hart favored.[2]

Even some of the ideologically based innovations of 1966–81 looked to the past institutional recommendations for guidance in their new endeavors. Consider, for example, the case of the "new" liberal judicial activism. When new-politics liberals were considering how to open up the administrative state to greater participation in accord with their new ideological vision, they selected expanded judicial activism as one significant mechanism for doing so. Such a choice was far from obvious. The Nixon administration, in office at the time that this strategy was being designed and pursued most aggressively, had pledged to make the judiciary an institution oriented toward conservative social policy and judicial restraint. The courts themselves, insulated from electoral pressures and indeed from most direct contact with the general public, and using procedures that generally confined the scope of conflict, hardly seemed the ideal vehicles for populism, even of a "genteel" variety. Of course, as many conservatives charged, the new-politics liberals may have been insincere in their participatory commitments and may have selected the judicial activism approach because they thought it suited their power interests as members of the "new class" of discontented middle-class professionals who were envious of businessmen's power and wealth. However, the fact that the courts appeared to be growing increasingly conservative at the time, and the wide variety of new-politics liberal arguments and actions in behalf of participatory democracy, make this conservative critique less than fully persuasive. Rather, the new-politics liberals' decision to seek extension of judicial activism into new regulatory areas appears to have been primarily a case of reaching into the old liberal armory for weapons in a new battle. It was a choice that seemed highly risky in light of the ability of the business-conservative coalition to counter their efforts, as well as Nixonian aims of conservatizing the judiciary.[3]

On administrative state issues, the effects of past prescriptions were also evident. As in the past, liberals, even the new-politics liberals who wished to remold the administrative state, still wanted to expand its scope—this time, to encompass consumer protection, workers' safety and health, and additional environmental spheres. The hold of past prescriptions was also evident in their willingness to acquiesce in Carter's reorganizations (subject to legislative veto, as in the past) and most of his Civil Service reform package of 1978, even though the latter had strong ties to presidential government. Among conservatives, the old hostility to the administrative state, though muted a bit more in some quarters than previously, still burst forth in frequent tirades against bureaucracy, typified by Barry Goldwater's 1976 book, *The Coming Breakthrough,* which devoted considerable space to excoriating the "army of government bureaucrats" that really "runs the government" and regularly thwarts the will of elected officials and the people.[4]

Similarly, when the Nixon administration was seeking innovation in national-state-local relations, it looked both to past conservative block-grant ideas advocated in the 1960s by Representative Albert Quie and other states' rights proponents and to the general revenue sharing notions of former conservative Representative Melvin Laird, then secretary of defense. It was Nixon's hope to link his restructuring to traditional conservative notions of states' rights and thus win strong conservative backing. Despite the Nixon administration's efforts, however, conservative enthusiasm for the New Federalism proved less widespread and deep than administration leaders had hoped. By the end of the decade, conservatives had mostly reverted to the traditional states' rights rhetoric of the past; and in the Reagan era, they would support the new administration's proposal to jettison general revenue sharing. Thus, the influence of the past was often evident, even in spheres where some notable changes in institutional prescriptions were occurring.[5]

## Instrumental Links to Power and Public Policy Ends

Since changes in institutional prescriptions were far more evident in this period than in the preceding one, these years offer a unique opportunity to analyze the nature and extent of the instrumental calculations that contributed to major changes. Of course, it should be remembered that continuity was also often based on medium-to-long-term perceptions regarding power and/or policy ends, as has been previously discussed.

Three major sources of innovations in ideologically based institutional prescriptions can be identified in the 1966–81 period, though they were to some extent intertwined, hampering separate analysis. One source related to the new values and programmatic policy ends introduced on a major scale into each ideological coalition. Another derived from the realignment of the major institutional power centers and societal bases of the two alliances. Still another stemmed from the institutional innovations advanced by the leadership of the Nixon administration, which reflected both efforts to develop a new synthesis of ideas in the new political environment of these years and pragmatic desires to build a solid power base capable of securing control over state and society, much as Roosevelt had done in the 1930s.

The values and policy goals of the new-politics liberalism which became the predominant tendency in the liberal coalition during this period were widely perceived to mesh rather poorly with some aspects of the old New Deal/Cold War liberal theory of governance, particularly its presidential government, hierarchical and professionalized administrative state, and general proclivity toward centralization of government authority. The justifications offered in the liberal camp for major new institutional prescriptions—congressionally centered checks and balances, decentralization with community control, a judicialized administrative state, and regulatory judicial activism—nearly always cited the distinctive new values of new-politics liberalism, participatory democracy and more equality in particular, as the ultimate ends of institutional reforms. With regard to presidential-congressional relations, the policy goals of terminating American military involvement in Indochina and avoiding "another Vietnam" in the future and the general postcontainment values also drove liberals away from presidential power prescriptions. As noted previously, old-politics liberals and neoconservatives generally remained allegiant to presidential government, while new-politics liberals (especially those who had not actively helped build it in the past) moved strongly against it.[6]

However, some problems were evident in the new formulations of the new-politics liberals. For one thing, liberals employed the term "participatory democracy" quite differently to justify varied institutional prescriptions. In the context of calling for the enhancement of congressional power and checks on the president, the *New Republic* justified its new editorial position in 1971 by declaring that "while the Presidency is unquestionably a democratic institution, it is not, as compared with Congress, an institution of participatory democracy." But Congress, with its logrolling among elected politicians (often entrenched long-term occupants of their power positions) and hired lobbyists, was hardly the kind of participatory democracy that Arnold Kaufman or David Hackett had in mind when justifying "radical decentralization" or "community control" in participatory democratic terms. And the type of participatory democracy that Simon Lazarus, Ralph Nader, and other public interest–group liberals employed as a value to justify judicialized public administration and judicial activist intrusion into its processes was something else again.[7]

"More equality," another major value associated with the new-politics brand of liberalism, also permeated liberal justifications of their institutional prescriptions of the period. Though the use and meanings of equality were less varied than the participatory democratic justifications, there were certainly questions as to whether either it or participatory democracy was in fact likely to be maximized by the institutional prescriptions of the new-politics liberals. Congress continued to be notoriously vulnerable to high-pressure, well-financed combinations of lobbying and campaign contributions, as Nader associate Mark Green himself stressed in *Who Runs Congress?*; and business elites proved quite adept at mounting such campaigns after some initial losses to new-politics liberals. The new-politics liberals' ignominious congressional defeat on the Agency for Consumer Advocacy legislation in 1978 was symptomatic of the problem. A fragmented, judicialized administrative state, checked by frequent judicial interventions, might also prove quite susceptible to conservative-business counterstrategies and pressures. And the judiciary itself seemed unconvincing to many in a long-term role as an effective advocate of participatory democracy or more equality, given its composition, procedures, and traditions. In the end, the clearest policy/value linkage to the new liberal institutional prescriptions was between postcontainment values globally and congressionally centered checks and balances on diplomatic and war powers. Here perhaps was a basis for growing liberal consensus, especially as old-politics liberalism waned.[8]

Although many new-politics liberals appeared quite sincere in offering their justifications, their arguments were not fully convincing within the liberal camp itself. One of the reasons that liberals were divided and often inconsistent in their institutional prescriptions of this period was that the justifications were often less than fully convincing in terms of the links to values or policy outcomes. Moreover, there was the inherent problem of reconciling participatory democracy with civil libertarian and minority rights values that most liberals still stressed. If the old liberal theory of governance seemed poorly suited to the values and policy goals of the new reform liberalism, the proposed new one appeared to offer little improvement.

In addition, there was the matter of power centers. Liberals began to despair in the 1970s that they would be able to win the presidency with any frequency, if at all, in the foreseeable future. Gone were the days when the electoral college "gerrymander" favoring the largest states would insure a presidency sympathetic to liberal concerns. Nixon was anathema to most liberals, Ford was barely tolerable to them, and few viewed Carter as any great improvement. On the other hand, liberals' gains in Congress, particularly with the decentralization of congressional power to subcommittees where liberals often enjoyed positions of strength, offered some hope. But Congress was far from a liberal-dominated institution, and new-politics liberalism was weaker there than was the movement as a whole. Liberal congressional gains in the early to mid-1970s began to erode in the face of the increased effectiveness of business and other conservative forces in influencing Congress. The judiciary was also less clearly liberal than in the past, and even the upper levels of the civil service were partially conservatized by the efforts of Nixon to build his "administrative presidency." Out in society, of course, the liberal coalition still enjoyed considerable bases of power. Yet there, too, the rising power of the conservative movement relative to that of the liberal coalition was evident by the late 1970s. Problems of linking the proposed new theory of governance to realistic medium-to-long-term power bases also complicated the task of developing liberal cohesion and consistency on institutional prescriptions in the 1966–81 period.

The third major factor, the assertive Nixon administration, united the liberal movement in 1973–74 around most elements of the proposed new theory of governance. The reaction against its excesses also gave liberals enough moderate and conservative assistance to enjoy some notable successes—on war powers legislation, budgetary process reform and curtailment of impoundment powers, restrictions on the Central Intelligence Agency, freedom of information, and various other matters. However, detestation of Nixon and a grim determination to block his power aggrandizement proved unreliable bases for development of unity on a long-term theory of governance. With the demise of the Nixon presidency and the developing problems in linking institutional prescriptions as convincingly to power and values/policy ends as in the past, liberal fragmentation and short-term instrumentalism became common.

In the conservative coalition, this new era of change also posed difficulties for developing and maintaining consensus on a theory of governance. No faction or tendency oriented toward change in the institutional prescriptions of the past gained the preeminence in the conservative movement that new-politics liberalism did in its liberal counterpart. However, the New Right, with its emphasis on democracy, and the neoconservative faction, carrying much of the old liberal theory of governance with it, both introduced some new justifications for prescriptions not previously put forward by most conservatives. Both the New Right and the neoconservatives frequently employed "democratic" arguments to attack liberal judicial activism and call for restraint. Typically, New Rightist Patrick J. Buchanan called for reforms to be "the work of elected legislators, answerable at the polls, not of appointed judges with tenure for life, answerable only to themselves." New Right legal scholar Lino Graglia found fault with the *Brown v. Board of Education* decision, primarily on the grounds that "so important a social change should not have been made by unelected, lifetime appointees." In a similar vein, neoconservative Franklin Hunt perceived a "war against democracy" in liberal judicial activism.[9]

Adherents of both of these segments also generally pushed for a strong presidency. Although New Rightists were more prone than neoconservatives to stress a presidential role as popular tribune and justify it with majoritarian democratic rhetoric, Irving Kristol, perhaps the most prominent of the neoconservatives, would eventually endorse the New Right's brand of populism. However, Jeane Kirkpatrick was probably more typical of neoconservatives in finding this populism naïve and critically flawed. Above all, she thought the New Right exaggerated the extent to which the public was likely to endorse any coherent ideology, conservative or otherwise, in an election. The main shared justification between the New Right and the neoconservatives concerning the presidency was their common view of national security, which they believed required presidential preeminence in the sphere of defense and foreign policy.[10]

Some old rightists, such as Jeffrey Hart, James McClellan, and (sometimes) Barry Goldwater, came to agree with them on this point. However, quite a few libertarian and fusionist conservatives, who remained important elements of the conservative movement, cited negative freedom as the prime justification for all of their institutional prescriptions, including a congressionally centered system of checks and balances. Alfred de Grazia, writing of the presidency in 1975, summed up the arguments of most of this group: "It is all in all a dangerous institution for a free culture . . . [the presidency] attracts great powers into the central government; serves to keep them there; and helps to enlarge the great bureaucracy." Thus, conflicting emphases of values among conservatives spawned justifications for contrary prescriptions on what was probably the most important of the institutional issues.[11]

In the conservative coalition, changing calculations of medium- to long-term power distributions of ideological strength were also reshaping governance ideas. Jeffrey Hart, in a major *National Review* article in 1974, cited previously, made the case for a conservative model of presidential government almost entirely in terms of the ends of power. Paul Weaver, writing in *Commentary* the following year, mixed power and policy ends as explicit justifications for a preeminent presidency, noting what he perceived to be the liberals' reasons for shifting in the opposite direction. However, many of the factors that produced liberal uncertainty had the same effects among conservatives. It remained unclear through the 1970s what the medium-to-long-term institutional power centers of each coalition would be. Carter's presidency, certainly not viewed by most conservatives as expressive of their values or policy goals, elicited little conservative enthusiasm for presidential power, as was evident in both the congressional roll-call votes and various commentaries during his years in office. However, even then, a number of conservative intellectuals and activists were calling for a strong presidency, hopeful that a staunch "movement" conservative would be elected soon. The Reagan candidacy of 1980 seemed likely to fulfill their fondest hopes.[12]

The Nixon presidency, of course, had raised those hopes only to dash them. During Nixon's first term in office, he was able not only to pull many conservatives toward support of his presidential government model (including roles as foreign policy leader, chief administrator, tribune of the "silent majority," and remolder of the federal judiciary) but also, to some extent, toward his New Federalism model and his administrative state prescriptions, both of which required substantial breaks with the past, despite Nixon's efforts to promote them in terms of their links to previous conservative ideas. However, Nixon's values and programmatic policies were suspect in the eyes of a number of conservatives, and the Watergate fiasco destroyed his legitimacy in his second term and ultimately brought his downfall.

Although, unlike liberals, conservatives sensed a promising future, particularly in the wake of the 1980 election results, they were unable to achieve full consensus on a revised theory of governance as the period drew to a close. That task awaited conservatives in the new Reagan-Bush era.

The general breakdown of consensus on governance theory in each ideological coalition after 1966 unquestionably related to changes in values and programmatic policy preferences within each alliance, the shifting institutional and other power bases of the two coalitions, and the rather unique effects of the Nixon presidency. It is impossible to assign precise weights to each of these factors, but the first two were probably of about equal importance and had greater long-term significance than did the Nixon administration's legacy.

Short-term power and policy calculations appeared to grow in importance as motivators for institutional prescriptions during this period—or at least more political actors confessed openly to them. Donald Santorelli, I.F. Stone, Bryce Harlow, Averell Harriman, and Hans Morgenthau were just a few of those who admitted to treating government institutions as means toward short-term, immediate ends. Moreover, congressional voting patterns of both coalitions showed a fluidity in response to short-term power and policy considerations that extended well beyond what had been evident in the preceding several decades. Timothy Conlan's vivid description of the highly fragmented politics of block grants was just one of many possible illustrations. The proliferation of legislative vetoes by both liberal and conservative coalitions for their own immediate goals was another. Liberals promoted legislative vetoes on war powers and other foreign policy actions, while conservatives used them to hit such regulatory agencies as the Federal Trade Commission. The flip-flops concerning presidential powers by Goldwater, who in 1964 had so vehemently denounced the very idea of treating institutions as means toward ends, was symptomatic of the new age in which key aspects of the old theories of governance were eroding.[13]

### The Impact of the Institutional Prescriptions

One result of the fragmented and fluid conflictual patterns of the 1966–81 period was a presidency weakened by its occupants' own miscalculations as well as by new restrictions placed upon it by an aroused and resurgent Congress, mainly (but not entirely) at the behest of the liberal coalition that had so recently been an ardent defender of presidential government. However, the extent and effectiveness of the new or restored checks and balances could easily be exaggerated. Some of the restrictions, such as those in the War Powers Resolution, were already beginning to appear less effective by the end of the decade than the authors had hoped. Moreover, the Reagan presidency would soon demonstrate some of the significant power capacities remaining in the White House. Thus, the dire 1975 predictions by Samuel Huntington of a loss of overall governing authority, an "excess of democracy," a "downturn in American power and influence," and other allegedly unfortunate results of a crippled presidency appear to have been overdrawn.[14]

Huntington was not completely wrong, however. The new budgetary procedures adopted in 1974 combined with the explosion of interest-group activity to contribute to the "financial insolvency" that he predicted, though president Reagan in particular would share the responsiblity. And congressional micromanagement, particularly through legislative vetoes instigated by both liberals and conservatives, did sometimes paralyze future implementation of public policy.[15]

In the federalism sphere, the decentralizations inspired by new-politics liberalism rarely lasted long enough to have much long-term impact, though community-control struggles in some locales did exacerbate racial tensions that then lasted for years. Among the Nixonian New Federalism reforms, only general revenue sharing and a few block grants were enacted. Some of the projected revitalization of state and local governments did ensue, but much less was due to the New Federalism than had been envisioned by proponents. As federal government deficits ballooned in the Reagan era, the general revenue sharing program was terminated. Reagan himself, like many other conservatives, had never cared much for the concept. However, block grants, especially those directed to state governments, increasingly became an important element in conservative platforms, both under Reagan and in the 1990s.[16]

The judicialized administrative state extended into numerous new regulatory areas, especially in the early part of the period, but generally failed to spur participatory democracy or enhanced equality over the long term to the extent that its proponents had hoped. Part of the problem was that business interests proved frequently to be more than a match for the liberal public-interest groups, as Michael McCann, William Greider, and others have illustrated. However, McCann has also argued that "disaggregated" public authority and "obsession with legal rules" worked to "undercut effective policy making in many cases," even apart from the issue of business influences.[17]

Judicial activism remained the norm in the federal judiciary. The Supreme Court under Burger overturned legislation and judicial precedents as frequently on an annual basis as the Warren Court had done. However, the policy effects were now haphazard and confusing much of the time. What Bernard Schwartz accurately termed a "rootless activism" had come to replace liberal activism oriented in an egalitarian direction. As Schwartz noted: "[T]he center Justices did not have anything like a defined juristic weltanschauung. And that was true of the Burger Court as an institution." The liberal coalition clearly could no longer be blamed—or blamed alone—for the results of judicial activism. But the impact, especially of such controversial decisions as *Roe v. Wade*, continued to be widespread political agitation that would rage for years and continued public unease about judicial "lawmaking."[18]

Finally, there was the matter of constitutional interpretation and its impact. Despite continuing conservative prescriptions for strict construction and a jurisprudence of original intent, probably heightened by Nixon's and Reagan's campaigning on these issues, as well as by proselytizing by conservatives and the independent scholar Raoul Berger, little of either was in evidence, even among ostensibly conservative Supreme Court justices. Constitutional flexiblity remained the norm governing behavior. Even some conservatives, such as Donald Santorelli, proclaimed the Constitution's flexibility and indicated their eagerness to use it for their own purposes. At the same time, several liberal legal scholars made renewed efforts to establish clearer moral and procedural guidelines for constitutional interpretation than in the recent past.[19]

### Conclusions

After a brief resurgence in the form of new-politics liberal successes in the regulatory sphere, the forced departure from office of Richard Nixon, and some congressional gains, liberalism was again on the defensive at the end of the 1970s, as it had been in the late 1960s. This time, though, it was more for reasons of Carter's inadequacies (for which liberalism was often unfairly blamed) and economic (stagflation) and foreign-policy (Iran, Panama Canal, Soviet intervention in Afghanistan) problems that much of the public associated with liberalism than for reasons of liberal governance theory and its effects.

As for conservatism, it had risen phoenix-like from the ashes after the debacle of the Nixon administration and conservatives' crushing defeat in the mid-term elections of 1974. Fueled by large-scale business support, the continuing shift into its ranks by neoconservatives, and the development of the new religious right beginning in 1974, the conservative coalition made solid gains, culminating in the election of Ronald Reagan as president and the victories of many new congressional conservatives in the 1980 elections.

However, neither ideological coalition was able to attain internal consensus on a full-scale governance theory that would relate to its values and policy ends and its real bases of power and integrate its various components into a coherent whole—partly because the power bases had not been very clear for more than a decade, partly because the values and policy ends were more complex than previously in each camp.

The fragmented and fluid patterns of the late 1960s and 1970s had left an uncertain legacy. Although some new trends were evident, they might either crystallize or dissipate. What the new Reagan-Bush era would bring remained to be seen.

## Notes

1.  For Jackson, McGee, and Dodd, see "Congress and U.S. Military Commitments," *Congressional Digest* 48 (August–September, 1969): 193–224; Theodore Sorensen, "Political Perspective: Who Speaks for the National Interest?" in *The Tethered Presidency,* ed. Thomas M. Franck (New York: New York University Press, 1981), 12–15; Joseph A. Califano Jr., *A Presidential Nation* (New York: W. W. Norton, 1975), esp. 312–318; Louis Koenig, "Historical Perspective: The Swings and Roundabouts of Presidential Power," in Franck, *Tethered Presidency,* 40–61; Arthur M. Schlesinger Jr., *The Imperial Presidency* (New York: Popular Library, 1973), esp. 247–248 and chap. 11; James MacGregor Burns, *Uncommon Sense* (New York: Harper & Row, 1972), 124; James MacGregor Burns, "King of the Rock," *Commonweal* 97 (9 February 1973): 415–418; On Eugene McCarthy, see Schlesinger, *Imperial Presidency,* 363–364, and Tom Wicker, "The Presidency under Scrutiny," *Harper's* 239 (October 1969): 92–94; Henry Steele Commager, "Can We Limit Presidential Power?" *New Republic* 156 (6 April 1968): 15–18; Henry Steele Commager, *The Defeat of America* (New York: Simon & Schuster, 1974).

2.  Alfred de Grazia, *Eight Bads—Eight Goods* (New York: Doubleday Anchor, 1975), 16–26, 30–32, 163, 171; Felix Morley, *State and Society* (Menlo Park, CA: Insitute for Human Studies, 1976), 6; Felix Morley, *For the Record* (South Bend, IN: Regnery Gateway, 1979), 437, 462; Henry Regnery, "Emerging Conservatism: Kilpatrick, Morley, and Burnham," *Modern Age* 22 (Summer 1978): 237–245; Sam J. Ervin, *The Whole Truth* (New York: Random House, 1980); Schlesinger, *Imperial Presidency,* 373–385, also analyzes Ervin's views extensively; Ernest S. Griffith and Francis R. Valeo, *Congress: Its Contemporary Role,* 5th ed. (New York: New York

University Press, 1975); Henry Hazlitt, foreword to *A New Constitution*, rev. ed. (New York: McGraw–Hill, 1976); M. Stanton Evans, *Clear and Present Dangers* (New York: Harcourt Brace Jovanovich, 1975), esp. 51–87; William F. Buckley Jr., "Mr. Reid's Bill," *National Review* (16 March 1973): 331; William F. Buckley Jr., "And Now Legislative Supremacy," *National Review* (6 June 1975): 630–631; Jeffrey Hart, "The Presidency: Shifting Conservative Perspectives?" *National Review* 26 (22 November 1974): 1351–1355; James J. Kilpatrick, "The Macaroni Congresses," *Nation's Business* 62 (December 1974): 13–14 and 1976 analysis cited by R. Gordon Hoxie, *Command Decision and the Presidency* (New York: Reader's Digest Press, 1977), 383; David Lawrence, "Read Your History," in *The Editorials of David Lawrence* (Washington: U.S. News, 1970), 4: 429; David Lawrence, "Why an 'Undeclared' War Is Constitutional," in *Editorials*, 4:444; James McClellan, "The State of the American Congress," *Modern Age* 21 (Summer 1977): 227–239. See Goldwater's voting record, his suit in *Goldwater v. Carter* (1979), and his retrospective analysis in "The War Powers Act Controversy," *Congressional Digest* 62 (November 1983): 257–288.

3.  Michael W. McCann, *Taking Reform Seriously* (Ithaca, NY: Cornell University Press, 1986). Conservative charges are found, for example, in Franklin Hunt, "The Lawyers' War Against Democracy," *Commentary* 68 (October 1979): 45–51.

4.  Barry M. Goldwater, *The Coming Breakthrough* (New York: Macmillan, 1976), esp. chap. 4.

5.  Quie's block-grant ideas in the 1960s are discussed by David B. Robertson and Dennis R. Judd, *The Development of American Public Policy* (Glenview, IL: Scott, Foresman, 1989), 262–263; other points are covered by Timothy J. Conlan, *New Federalism* (Washington: Brookings Institution, 1988), chaps. 2–5, and A. James Reichley, *Conservatives in an Age of Change* (Washington: Brookings, 1981), chap. 8.

6.  Paul Weaver, "Liberals and the Presidency," *Commentary* 60 (October 1975): 48–53, suggests some of these themes.

7.  "Swing of the Pendulum," *New Republic* 164 (27 March 1971): 6–7; Arnold Kaufman, *The Radical Liberal* (New York: Simon & Schuster, 1968), chap. 5; Simon Lazarus, *The Genteel Populists* (New York: Holt, Rinehart, & Winston, 1974), chap. 10.

8.  Mark Green, James Fallows, and David Zwick, *Who Runs Congress?* (New York: Bantam/Grossman, 1972); McCann, *Taking Reform Seriously*, chap. 5; Weaver, "Liberals and the Presidency," 48–53.

9.  Patrick J. Buchanan, *The New Majority* (n.p.: Girard Bank, 1973), 29; Lino Graglia, *Disaster by Decree* (Ithaca, NY: Cornell University Press, 1976), 32; Hunt, "Lawyers' War," 45–51.

10. Irving Kristol, "The New Populism: Not to Worry," *Wall Street Journal*, 25 July 1985, 20; Jeane Kirkpatrick, "Why the New Right Lost," *Commentary* 63 (February 1979): 34–39.

11. De Grazia, *Eight*, 33.

12. Hart, "Presidency," 1351–1355; Weaver, "Liberals and the Presidency," 48–53.

13. On Santorelli and Stone, see Michael Novak, *Choosing Our King* (New York: Macmillan, 1974), 248–249; on Harlow and Harriman, see Emmet J. Hughes, *The*

*Living Presidency* (New York: Coward, McCann & Geohegan, 1973), 345, 349; Morgenthau's statement is in Hans Morgenthau, "Congress and Foreign Policy," *New Republic* 160 (14 June 1969): 17. Conlan, *New Federalism,* chap. 3; James L. Sundquist, *The Decline and Resurgence of Congress* (Washington: Brookings Institution, 1981), 350–365.

14.  Sundquist, *Decline and Resurgence,* 261–272, writing in 1981, found the impact of the War Powers Resolution to be considerably greater than did Louis Fisher, *Constitutional Conflicts between Congress and the President* (Princeton: Princeton University Press, 1985), 313–318. Fisher's assessment appears the more persuasive of the two with the passage of time. Samuel P. Huntington, "The United States," in *The Crisis of Democracy,* by Michel Crozier, Samuel P. Huntington, and Joji Watanuki (New York: New York University Press, 1975), 106.

15.  Huntington, "The United States," 106. James A. Thurber, "The Impact of Budget Reform on Presidential and Congressional Governancee," in *Divided Democracy,* ed. James A. Thurber (Washington: Congressional Quarterly Press, 1991), 145–167.

16.  Allen J. Matusow, *The Unraveling of America* (New York: Harper & Row, 1984), chap. 9; Conlan, *New Federalism,* 160–162.

17.  McCann, *Taking Reform Seriously,* chap. 5; William Greider, *Who Will Tell the People?* (New York: Simon & Schuster, 1992), esp. chap. 5. The McCann quotes are from *Taking Reform Seriously,* 225, 231.

18.  Bernard Schwartz, *The Ascent of Pragmatism* (Reading, MA: Addison–Wesley, 1990), 401.

19.  Novak, *Choosing Our King,* 248; Ronald Dworkin, *Taking Rights Seriously* (Cambridge: Harvard University Press, 1977); John Hart Ely, *Democracy and Distrust* (Cambridge: Harvard University Press, 1980).

# 1981–1993

# 17

# Conservative and Liberal Values and Programmatic Policies

The outcomes of the 1980 elections appeared to many to signify the ascendancy of conservative ideology and the conservative movement. Although analyses of public opinion showed a highly mixed set of patterns at that level, among elites there was a distinct shift to the right. Indeed, during the next decade, it was usually the conservatives more than the demoralized liberals (many of whom even shunned the liberal label they had worn proudly since the New Deal era) who set the agenda for American politics: reductions of taxes, deregulation of business, and rolling back Communism.

However, the conservative coalition remained a loose alliance of rather diverse elements. For a time, the leadership of Ronald Reagan, the intensity of conservatives' devotion to national security values linked to anti-Communism, and a shared dedication to private property rights and market-oriented economic growth sustained substantial conservative unity. However, Reagan's luster dimmed with the passage of time, and Bush was never able to fulfill his leadership role for the conservative movement. In an interesting paradox, the long-hoped-for collapse of Communism and the demise of the Cold War in the late 1980s and early 1990s removed another source of conservative unity. Furthermore, the unequal effects of economic growth and then the stagnation of the early 1990s weakened the popular appeal of conservative socioeconomic ideology and produced some internal disunity. That left defense of private property rights as one of the few common foundations for conservatives in 1992, and conservatives did not agree among themselves as to why these rights were of primary importance.

As the Bush administration floundered in 1991 and 1992, the challenge to Bush's renomination from Patrick Buchanan opened new conservative fissures; and predictions of a "conservative crackup," heard since 1987, became increasingly widespread, even within the movement itself. Libertarian, traditionalist, old right fusionist, New Right and religious right, neoconservative and big business factions or tendencies retained somewhat separate identities that continued to hamper unity. Some observers even discerned the emergence of a new "progressive conservative" tendency to complicate matters further.[1]

Meanwhile, although liberals recuperated partially from the shocks of 1980 and 1981 as the conservatives' disarray became increasingly evident, their movement was no more clearly defined or cohesive than it had been since the disintegration of the late Johnson administration. During the 1980s, it witnessed the emergence of several strands of "neoliberalism," splitting off from new-politics liberalism in the direction of the broad center of the political spectrum. At the same time, there were several efforts, none very successful, to update and integrate the movements of new-politics liberalism along left-liberal lines, as a "rainbow coalition" (in Jesse Jackson's terms) or around themes of "economic democracy" (Tom Hayden and the Americans for Democratic Action) or "social democracy" (Robert Kuttner). Perhaps the most significant was a major effort by so-called New Democrats to win back white Southerners and other "Reagan Democrats" with an attempted synthesis of liberal, moderate, and conservative ideas that threatened to displace liberalism from the central seats of power in the political party which it had dominated since the New Deal. When Bill Clinton gained the presidency in 1993, bringing the Reagan-Bush era to a close, he did so as a "New Democrat" and with only 43 percent of the popular vote in a race that had threatened for a time to give the White House to H. Ross Perot, a man more clearly outside the boundaries of both major ideological coalitions than even Jimmy Carter had been.

At least for the conservative coalition, the 1980s were more stable years than the previous decade and a half had been. However, by the early 1990s, fluidity and flux were returning. Whether the conservative-liberal division would even continue to be central to American political debate, as it had been since the 1930s, became a serious question. Liberalism had suffered from exhaustion since the mid-1960s; now the conservative coalition appeared to be on the verge of disintegration.

## Conservative Assumptions and Values

In the early 1980s, the Reagan presidency provided a focal point around which most conservatives wished to rally, much as Franklin Roosevelt's presidency had offered leadership for liberals in the 1930s. Also like the

Roosevelt presidency, it appointed to numerous posts in the executive and judicial branches movement activists and intellectuals who aspired to public service. Even apart from Reagan's leadership, there was some movement toward synthesis. For example, William Kristol, son of neoconservative Irving Kristol, studied at Harvard under neo-Straussian traditionalist conservative Harvey Mansfield Jr., and went to work for old-right conservative Vice President Daniel Quayle in the Bush administration. Such interchanges were not uncommon. Moreover, some of the new conservative intellectuals—George Gilder and Michael Novak in particular—made explicit efforts to create a fusion of the new array of conservatisms. However, significant factionalism remained. And especially as the Cold War ended and the Bush administration lost its bearings, the movement fractured badly.[2]

Lack of a broad and solid foundation of common assumptions and values, obscured for a time by support for Reagan and his major policies, increasingly became a problem for conservatives, particularly as the foundation narrowed further following the collapse of Communism, the common enemy. Distaste for liberal social engineering and egalitarianism was continuous with the past and widespread in the current period within the conservative coalition, but libertarian conservatives extended free-market assumptions and an emphasis on negative freedom in the use of one's property considerably further than most other conservatives were willing to do. Dissenting from market capitalist assumptions, Clyde Wilson, for example, declared: "Free enterprise is not an absolute. It is a means, not an end. New Rightists. . . do not intend to establish a religion of the dollar bill." Neoconservative leader Irving Kristol was willing to offer only "two cheers," not three, for capitalism. Such varying assumptions often led to sharp intraconservative conflicts on issues of immigration, regulation of "adult" activities, drug use, and abortion, most frequently pitting libertarian conservatives and some old-right fusionists on one side against the religious right and traditionalist conservatives of various hues on the other, with the neoconservatives and big business conservatives falling somewhere in the middle.[3]

Traditionalist conservatism continued to flourish among conservative intellectuals. In fact, the followers of the late political philosopher Leo Strauss, including Harvey Mansfield Jr., Walter Berns, James Ceaser, Gary McDowell, Charles Kesler, Allan Bloom, and many others, gained new prominence and became particularly important in the realm of conservative governance theory. Shifting their focus from the classical political thought of antiquity (Strauss's emphasis) to the American constitutional system and (notably in Bloom's case) to current American political and social problems, the neo-Straussians gained wide publicity and exerted some influence in the Reagan and Bush administrations. Meanwhile, Russell Kirk, dean of the Burkean traditionalists, continued to play a significant role; and some younger conservative intellectuals, such as columnist and television commentator George Will, carried on many of the tenets of Burkean conservatism, adding their own unique twists. Among traditionalists of both schools, "virtue" and "order" continued to be primary values.[4]

Libertarian conservatism also remained a vital force, despite some continuing defections from the conservative movement by libertarian thinkers. Libertarian conservatism gained important new recruits in the 1980s from young philosophers inspired by Robert Nozick's *Anarchy, State, and Utopia;* Charles Murray, author of *Losing Ground,* and his followers, who focused largely on attacking the liberal welfare state; Richard Posner and others of the "law and economics" school of constitutional jurisprudence; and an array of "public choice" theorists in the social sciences, building on the model of James Buchanan and Gordon Tullock. The Cato Institute, linked more to independent libertarianism than to the conservative movement, also enjoyed new influence in the 1980s. Tying a variety of new libertarian conservative ideas to those of longtime libertarian conservative figures such as Milton Friedman and Friedrich Hayek, who continued to contribute to the movement, was a preoccupation with negative freedom (especially in the use of private property) as the supreme value.[5]

Neoconservatism retained some of its previous attachments to the values and assumptions of old-politics liberalism. These usually placed them on the "centrist" side of the conservative movement on an array of domestic issues, though in the national security/foreign sphere, that certainly was not the case. Neoconservatives themselves were not always certain as to what separated them from the rest of the conservative movement. Dan Himmelfarb, the assistant managing editor of the neoconservative journal, *The Public Interest,* reviewed four differences (timing of entry, attitudes toward the social sciences, religious differences, and locations on the political spectrum) and concluded that "each of these explanations is only partially correct. There is another, better way of explaining the tensions between the two conservatisms [neo- and "paleo-" in his terms]—namely as a tension between two distinct philosophical traditions." Elaborating, Himmelfarb argued that "neoconservatives belong to the tradition of liberal-democratic modernity . . . paleoconservatives are heirs to the Christian and aristocratic Middle Ages." However, there were more than two conservatisms, and Himmelfarb's explanation did not go far enough to encompass even the Straussian version of traditionalism, let alone the variety of conservative tendencies.[6]

The New Right as a broad movement continued to be most distinguished by its emphasis on populistic democracy as a value. Perhaps this was more a matter of style and an effort to win popular support than of deep-seated philosophy. Nonetheless, it often produced conflicts with other segments of the conservative movement, especially traditionalists, but often neoconservatives as well. Even more productive of conflicts than this matter, however, was the stress given to "virtue" as an ultimate value by the new religious right. Both Patrick Buchanan in 1992 and 1996 and Pat Robertson in 1988 employed new religious right themes of populistic democracy and virtue in their quests for the Republican presidential nomination; and such new leaders as Ralph Reed also emerged to articulate these themes, even as the influence of some early New Rightists, such as Jerry Falwell, waned.[7]

At least the hint of a new conservative grouping clustered around the initiatives of Jack Kemp, New York Republican representative and then secretary of housing and urban development in the Bush administration, appeared during this period. Kemp declared himself to be a "radical, bleeding-heart progressive conservative." Themes of including the poor in a market-oriented economy through economic "empowerment" were of central importance to Kemp, Representative Vin Weber of Minnesota, and a number of Heritage Foundation scholars who formed the core of the nascent progressive conservative tendency. Whether this group will ever be large enough and distinctive enough to constitute an important segment of the conservative coalition remains doubtful, though Kemp's renewed prominence in 1996 makes that development at least a greater possibility than it seemed to be a short time ago.[8]

Finally, the heads of the giant business corporations continued to be an important source of funding for most components of the conservative coalition, though their zeal for the cause showed signs of diminishing by the late 1980s. This was most apparent in the patterns of corporate political action committee campaign contributions. In contrast to the late 1970s and early 1980s, when business made major investments in young conservative challengers to liberal incumbents, its contributions shifted by 1986 back toward incumbents of both major parties. Although still clearly hostile to most aspects of liberalism, big business became less attached to the conservative coalition than in the 1970s and more pragmatic in its political strategies. Still, it remained the major source of support for the conservative policy-discussion and policy-formulating organizations so important to the continuing success of the varied parts of the conservative movement.[9]

The greatest changes having implications for conservative assumptions and values during the 1981–93 period were the dominance and then the retirement of Ronald Reagan, the uneven effects of economic growth and then the stagnation of the economy in the early 1990s, and the end of the Cold War and the consequent fragmentation of conservative conceptions of national security. Each of these issues played an important part in fracturing the conservative coalition in the early 1990s.

Reagan was able to transcend internal conservative internal divisions and make symbolic appeals to all conservative schools of thought in a way that no other political leader could duplicate. Though his own views and the policies of his administration most closely approximated the assumptions and values of the fusionist old right and the business corporate leadership, Reagan incorporated numerous traditional conservative, New Right/religious right, and neoconservative values into his speeches and substantive policies. While the religious right and the progressive conservatives gained less of substance from the Reagan presidency than the others did, Reagan's verbal support for "traditional moral values" and his appointment of a number of New Right judges were reassuring to the religious right, and his perennial optimism appealed to progressive conservatives. Bush, however, lacked strong appeal to any but the business conservatives. *Human Events* even endorsed the Buchanan insurgent candidacy against him in 1992, as did the American Conservative Union; and *National Review* gave Buchanan what it termed a "tactical endorsement." In contrast, the *Wall Street Journal* was probably Bush's strongest proponent. While most conservatives (with the exception of a few prominent neoconservatives) did support Bush in the 1992 general election campaign, their endorsements were often lukewarm.[10]

The unequal impact of the economic growth of the 1980s, which significantly widened the gap between rich and poor in the United States, and to an even greater extent the combination of massive budget deficits, trade deficits, and economic stagnation of the early 1990s, served to undermine the appeal of conservatism to the mass electorate. However, these developments also encouraged the religious right and traditionalist conservatives, whose commitment to market-oriented economic growth had never been very deep, to push their separate agendas with renewed vigor by 1992.[11]

Probably most significant of all for the long term, the demise of the Cold War brought new diversity in conservatives' interpretations of the meaning of national security values. Since the mid-1950s, the conservative conception of national security had rested firmly on shared and intense anti-Communism. According to leading neoconservative Norman Podhoretz, conservative disintegration "no doubt became inevitable once the end of the cold war had eliminated the great purpose that more than any other factor had brought so many disparate groups together into a working coalition." Now that Communism had been vanquished, conservative responses diverged. Some, such as neoconservative Charles Krauthammer, proposed development of a "confederated West" to be at the center of a "unipolar world." His fellow neoconservative Irving Kristol, however, took a position close to that of William Bennett and an important cross-section of traditionalist conservatives. They recommended "realistic" pursuit of the "national interest," based upon "selective engagement" overseas on a case-by-case basis. Still other conservatives, particularly neoconservatives, including Paul Johnson, Joshua Muravchik, Michael Ledeen, Ben Wattenberg, and Francis Fukuyama, envisioned a policy of spreading democracy globally. However, libertarian conservatives, such as Burton Yale Pines, editor of a 1992 *Blueprint* for the Heritage Foundation, warned against "an ambitious foreign policy," seeing it as almost certain to entail big government that endangered liberty at home. According to Pines, the conservative "bargain" to permit a warfare state had been solely to combat Communism and was now terminated. Traditionalist conservative Russell Kirk lashed out at neoconservative global democratizers as "cultural and economic imperialists" bent on "pursuing a fanciful Democratic globalism rather than the national interest of the United States." Patrick Buchanan also rejected global democratization as a value linked to national security, but he combined political unilateralism with economic protectionism. Calling for an emphasis on "America first, second, and third," he portrayed national security in terms of "tough" political and economic nationalism. Numerous conservative critics of Buchanan described his approach as neoisolationist and denied that it would produce national security. However, others, such as old-right editor Samuel Francis, offered formulations similar to Buchanan's. Clearly, national security values no longer served as a basis for conservative cohesion. Even factions were now often rent by disagreements over how to pursue national security in the new global environment. Though "realism" probably enjoyed the widest conservative support, it was doubtful whether it could be the basis for the kind of unity enjoyed in the past.[12]

## Conservative Programmatic Public Policies

Reagan, far more than Eisenhower, Nixon, or Ford, was accepted as the leader of the conservative movement. For the most part, the major public policies of his administration won broad conservative endorsement, despite neoconservative dissatisfaction with his arms control negotiations, religious right questioning of his administration's priorities, and various other policy disputes. In contrast, the Bush administration received numerous criticisms from conservatives, particularly when it sought compromises with liberals on tax, affirmative action, and Nicaraguan aid issues.

The Reagan administration's greatest domestic policy successes came in the spheres of government economic management and social welfare policies and occurred during the first year. With virtually unanimous conservative backing in Congress, the Reagan administration pushed through an array of domestic social welfare spending cuts and tax reductions in 1981. Simultaneously, it took a number of administrative steps to deregulate business, from requiring Office of Management and Budget clearance of all new regulations to starving regulatory agencies for funds and/or appointing probusiness regulators such as Anne Burford at the Environmental Protection Agency and James Watt to head the Interior Department. Later, in response to liberal resurgence and liberal interest-group pressures, some of these steps were partially reversed, and Burford and Watt were forced from office. Nevertheless, a major legacy of the Reagan era—in part because of the huge government deficits that resulted—was a halt to government expansion at the national level and a new climate of opinion which stressed the limits of government in domestic affairs. Most conservatives applauded these developments while regretting the deficits and the lack of further cuts in social welfare programs. The Bush administration's economic management and welfare record proved less satisfactory to them. Though they endorsed Bush's veto of a liberal-backed family leave policy for business employees, some of the deregulatory efforts run under the auspices of Vice President Quayle, and Bush's repeated (but unavailing) calls for cuts in the capital gains tax, most were unforgiving of his failure to keep his 1988 campaign pledge of "no new taxes" and disturbed by his overall management of the economy.[13]

In the civil rights policy domain, the Reagan administration proved the least sympathetic to federal civil rights guarantees for African Americans of any modern administration, at least since Eisenhower's. Although Reagan himself had opposed the Civil Rights Act of 1964, he made no direct attack on it. However, his administration did seek to grant tax-exempt status to private schools with discriminatory practices and acted at first to block full extension of the Voting Rights Act in 1982. In each case, the administration was forced to retreat in the face of strong liberal opposition and a divided conservative movement. Congress also overrode a

1988 Reagan veto of legislation overturning a Supreme Court ruling and restored the power of the federal government to end financial aid to institutions with records of discrimination. In steps widely popular among conservatives, Assistant Attorney General for Civil Rights William Bradford Reynolds made repeated verbal and policy-implementing attacks on quotas, goals, and timetables linked to affirmative action. The Reagan administration also significantly reduced funding for the Equal Employment Opportunity Commission and the Office of Federal Contract Compliance Programs, necessitating major staffing reductions in the two major agencies charged with curbing discrimination in the private sector. The Bush administration continued attacks on "quotas" in affirmative action programs but compromised with liberals and moderates on the Civil Rights Act of 1991 and generally took a more centrist stance on civil rights issues than the Reagan administration had done or than most of the conservative movement preferred.[14]

In the sociocultural policy sphere, both the Reagan and Bush administrations repeatedly stressed their opposition to abortion and their endorsement of "family values" and patriotism. In the Reagan administration, Attorney General Edwin Meese mounted well-publicized attacks on pornography; William Bennett as education secretary stressed "back to basics" in public schools and "back to the classics" in higher education; and the president himself made clear his support for prayer and the teaching of so-called "creationism" in the public schools. The administration also made a concerted effort to appoint social conservatives to the federal courts. Though these combined efforts still fell short of achieving the religious right's agenda, anything beyond them would likely have jeopardized the support of libertarian conservatives, some of whom defected in any event. The Bush administration was less socially conservative than Reagan's. However, Bush's 1988 campaign prominently featured his "patriotic" opposition to Michael Dukakis's defense of a teacher's right not to pledge allegiance to the flag; and the Bush administration called loudly for a constitutional amendment to ban flag-burning and remained adamantly opposed to abortion.[15]

In the foreign and defense policy domain, conservatives of the 1980s enjoyed their greatest triumph, not only greatly expanding the defense budget in the early part of the period and advancing such projects as the Strategic Defense Initiative, but above all seeing the collapse of their great nemesis, the Soviet Union, and the Communist movement generally. Of course the irony, as noted previously, was that this foreign policy victory contributed to eventual conservative disunity and defeat in the 1992 elections. Although almost all conservatives had warmly endorsed

the military buildup under Reagan in the early 1980s, the Bush administration could sustain nothing more than an extremely vague vision of a
"new world order" to try to maintain conservative unity on foreign policy after the Cold War. The effort fell flat. Most leading conservatives
(notably excepting Patrick Buchanan) did support the Persian Gulf War
effort and Bush's efforts leading up to it. However, the aftermath was
unsatisfying to many; and conservative prescriptions for American foreign policy fragmented badly in the 1990s.[16]

Overall, the rather remarkable conservative unity on public policies in
the early 1980s gave way to considerable quarreling by the 1990s. Probably the most serious conflicts concerned sociocultural policies, particularly abortion, where even Reagan failed to paper over libertarian conservative versus religious right and traditionalist conservative differences. But
now foreign policy was also a major source of disputes. Even socioeconomic and civil rights policy domains were scenes of some conservative
disunity as the period drew to a close. Underlying disagreements over
basic assumptions and values now related to policy conflicts in ways that
made harmony difficult for the conservative coalition to achieve.

### Liberal Assumptions and Values

The liberal coalition began the decade of the 1980s without the focal point
enjoyed by the conservatives and in a state of demoralization and disarray. Despite some political gains over the next twelve years and the election of a Democratic president in 1992, liberals remained unable to find
significant cohesion around central assumptions and values. Perhaps
even more than in the case of the conservative movement, the future of
liberalism was in doubt by the mid-1990s.

Liberalism remained more egalitarian and rationalistic in its basic
assumptions than conservatism (with the possible and partial exception
of progressive conservatism). As before, it generally struggled to balance
its individualism in the sociocultural sphere with its fairly communitarian emphasis (but mainly using the language of positive freedom) in the
socioeconomic domain. However, a quasi-libertarian attraction to entrepreneurialism and markets infected the ranks of liberalism—both neoliberal and "New Democrat" varieties, in particular—more than at any time
since the New Deal. Simultaneously, some liberals (especially those influenced by the New Democrats) edged toward an increased emphasis on
the collective whole in the sociocultural realm, at least in their rhetoric
about patriotic values, cracking down on illegal drug use and crime gen-

erally, and fostering "family values." The long-term division between sociocultural individualism and socioeconomic collectivism in the liberal camp thus blurred a bit but did not disappear.

New-politics liberalism, though fading and fragmenting somewhat, remained central to the liberal coalition. However, the 1980s spawned several efforts to redefine it and move it further to the left, stressing values of more equality, more meaningful participatory democracy, more "rights" to positive freedom, and more global cooperation to promote global democracy and human rights. Of these endeavors, Jesse Jackson's move to forge a rainbow coalition around his own candidacy for the Democratic presidential nomination in 1984 and 1988 gained the most public attention, though Jackson experienced great difficulty in expanding his base beyond African American voters; and some analysts viewed Jackson's ideology as little different from New Deal–Great Society liberalism. "Economic democracy" themes, long associated with the New Left, continued to be articulated by Tom Hayden and his Campaign for Economic Democracy, as well as by the Americans for Democratic Action. New proponents, such as Martin Carnoy and Derek Shearer, gave these themes added intellectual respectability, but economic democracy never gained a solid base of support in the entrepreneurial, market-oriented climate of the period. Still others among the left-liberals, such as Robert Kuttner, favored a social democratic ideology, an idea almost always present in the liberal movement since the 1930s. But the socioeconomic collectivism that it implied won even less support than the ideas of economic democracy did in the era of Reagan and Bush. Efforts to move new-politics liberalism to the left thus enjoyed little success in the 1981–93 years.[17]

The 1984 presidential campaign witnessed an effort by Senator Walter Mondale, long a protege of Hubert Humphrey, to win the presidency largely by shifting new-politics, reformist, postcontainment liberalism back a bit in the direction of New Deal liberalism. While Mondale's global outlook was closely attuned to new-politics liberalism, the rest of his ideological appeal, and his strong base of support in organized labor, were reminiscent of an earlier period. This combination gained Mondale the Democratic presidential nomination, but the inadequacy of this appeal was evident in his landslide defeat by Reagan in November.[18]

Neoliberalism became one of the major new forces reshaping liberalism in the 1980s and 1990s. Like the left-liberal efforts, it was an offshoot of new-politics liberalism; but unlike them, it sought to position the movement near the "vital center" of a new era. Charles Peters, editor of the *Washington Monthly,* and an array of journalists associated with him played important roles in launching the movement. In "A Neoliberal's

Manifesto," published in 1983, Peters declared community, democracy, and prosperity to be the primary goals of the neoliberals. However, he gave less attention to the first two than to the third. "Economic growth is most important now," Peters emphasized. "It is essential to almost everything else we want to achieve. Our hero is the risk-taking entrepreneur who creates new and better products." There followed calls for business-government partnerships and government deregulation aimed at encouraging competition. More market-oriented and less concerned with social security values than either new-politics liberalism or New Deal liberalism, neoliberalism still favored a larger stimulating and supportive role for government in the economy than most conservatives found palatable. Two neoliberal Democratic presidential candidates, Senator Gary Hart of Colorado in 1984 and Senator Paul Tsongas of Massachusetts in 1992, made strong bids for the presidential nomination; but both fell short, in large part because of limited appeal to traditional Democratic constituencies among low-income voters. Although neoliberals did usually emphasize equality of opportunity and (to a lesser extent) positive freedom and social security, their preoccupation with entrepreneurial roles in promoting economic growth failed to strike a responsive chord with the low-income segments of the population that had responded most warmly to New Deal liberalism.[19]

The New Democrat movement, centered around the Democratic Leadership Council, established in 1985, and its Public Policy Institute, originated largely outside the boundaries of liberalism. Most of its founders were moderate or even moderate-conservative Democrats disturbed by left-liberalism, the new-politics liberal mainstream, and the Mondale campaign approach. Over time, however, the New Democrats incorporated a number of neoliberal ideas and served as a potential bridge between the liberal coalition and disaffected Democrats and independents who had flirted with Reagan-Bush conservatism. Generally more socially conservative and communitarian on sociocultural matters than the neoliberals, they shared with them a fascination with entrepreneurialism, business-government partnerships, and a market orientation.[20]

Arkansas Governor Bill Clinton, for a time the chair of the New Democrats' Democratic Leadership Council, won the Democratic presidential nomination and then the presidency in 1992. However, in doing so, Clinton positioned himself closer to the new-politics liberal mainstream than did most New Democrats. On the one hand, he heavily stressed the New Democrat/neoliberal theme of reinventing government to make it less bureaucratic and more entrepreneurial and responsive than in the past. He also borrowed from New Democrat/conservative values emphasizing the community obligations of welfare recipients (to "end welfare as we know it") and law and order regarding crime control (including endorsement of the death penalty). Yet at the same time, Clinton's past record also linked him to the McGovern campaign of 1972 and to new-politics liberalism. Clinton drew upon new-politics liberal values of global cooperation and human rights, positive freedom, more equality, and social security in proposing to reorient American foreign policy, develop a national health insurance program, and restore progressivity to the United States income tax. Clearly, Clinton hoped to redefine liberalism (while shunning the label for himself as much as possible) in a way that would appeal to enough moderates and even conservatives to insure winning electoral margins, at least for his own reelection bid. Whether liberalism itself would survive in a recognizable form remained in some doubt, though its past resilience suggested that it probably would.[21]

### Liberal Programmatic Public Policies

Often during the 1981–93 period, the liberals defined their public policy choices more by what they defended and opposed than by what they proposed. As their prospects for resurgence improved, however, some liberal proactive consensus emerged, mainly around socioeconomic policies stressing strategies for creating economic growth and for bringing the poor into the growth process and distributing the benefits more evenly than in the Reagan-Bush era.

Reaganite shifts in government taxing and spending in ways that effected an upward redistribution of wealth evoked loud denunciations from most liberal commentators and political leaders as promoting "Robin Hood in reverse" economics. However, a number of liberals had engaged in a bidding war with the Reagan administration over tax cuts in 1981 and thus bore at least some of the responsibility for the results. Much of the Reagan-Bush deregulation policy also came in for sharp liberal attacks, a number of which brought about partial reversals, especially in the realm of environmental policy. Defensive efforts by liberals were often successful during this period. When Reagan proposed to dismantle the Department of Education, liberals were critical to maintaining it; and strong liberal defense of social security for the elderly, supplemented by the activism of the American Association of Retired Persons and other interest groups of senior citizens, dissuaded the Reagan administration from attempting major revisions. After initial defeats in 1981, the liberals were generally able to temper the conservative initiatives of the Reagan and Bush administrations in the socioeconomic policy sphere. However, the huge government deficits and the antitax sentiments continually fanned by conservatives proved to be effective deterrents to any new liberal initiatives that bore significant costs. As Walter Mondale noted ruefully:

> Reagan has practiced the politics of subtraction. He knows the public wants to spend money on the old folks, protecting the environment, and aiding education. And he's figured out the only way to stop it is to deny the revenues. No matter how powerful the argument the Democrats make for the use of government to serve some purpose, the answer must be no.[22]

In the civil rights domain, liberals found themselves in an even more defensive posture than on socioeconomic matters. Backed by many moderates and even some conservatives, they triumphed in forcing the Reagan administration to retreat on tax exemptions for segregated private schools and on extension of the Voting Rights Act. However, on the important affirmative action/quotas issues, liberals themselves were divided and had great difficulty in clarifying for the public the distinctions that they often sought to delineate between quotas and affirmative action. Nonetheless, the liberal coalition did manage to compel the Bush administration to accept a compromise on the Civil Rights Act of 1991, largely defusing the issue for the 1992 campaign. Meanwhile, liberals continued for the most part to favor extension of government protections to other minorities, perhaps most controversially, to homosexuals.[23]

In the sociocultural policy sphere, most liberals continued to stress civil liberties, defending individual choice regarding abortion, the exclusionary rule as a protection against unreasonable search and seizure, the prohibition on public prayer in public schools, and other civil libertarian positions that placed them at odds with most of the Reagan-Bush conservative social agenda. However, New Democrats and even some neoliberals also increasingly stressed such nonlibertarian, community-focused sociocultural policies as the "war on drugs," the expanded use of the death penalty and increased reliance on incarceration in efforts to reduce crime, and the fostering of "family values" by government policies.[24]

Finally, in the foreign and defense policy sphere, the end of the Cold War at least temporarily eased intraliberal movement tensions rather than undermining consensus, as it did in the conservative coalition. New-politics liberalism had embraced since the late 1960s a policy stressing global cooperation, human rights, and defense spending cuts that had never won full support in the liberal coalition, being challenged both by pro-containment liberals and by assorted "realists" who felt that it short-changed careful assessment of national interests and was often naive. Such policy proposals as those of the nuclear-freeze movement of the early 1980s had split the liberal coalition rather sharply. Although the collapse of Communism did not end realist-idealist and other disagreements among liberals, it did remove a major source of contention. In the short run, it also permitted liberals to downgrade the importance of foreign policy and get by with lip service to the ideals of new-politics liberalism that concealed some real policy differences.[25]

## Conservative and Liberal Internal Conflicts

Despite continuing distinctions among libertarian, traditionalist, New Right/religious right, neoconservative, and business corporate factions and the partial emergence of progressive conservatism, conservative unity that was centered around the leadership of Ronald Reagan, support for national security values and policies linked to anti-Communism, and protection of private property rights overshadowed the internal divisions of the movement until the late 1980s. After that time, however, centrifugal forces badly fragmented the conservative coalition, causing even some of its own leaders to question its future viability. Nonetheless, there were indications of renewed efforts to forge conservative cohesion even on a somewhat reduced intellectual foundation in the mid-1990s. The economic interests of a well-organized constituency drawn primarily from the upper- and upper-middle classes, together with an emphasis linking private property rights to economic growth, might be sufficient to sustain the coalition indefinitely.

The liberal coalition floundered badly during the 1980s. Its predominant new-politics, reformist, postcontainment ideological tendency split between neoliberalism on the one hand and several strands of left-liberalism on the other. Meanwhile, its distinctive feminist, African American rights, gay-rights, environmentalist, consumer-protection, procedural-reform, and other components often disagreed over priorities and strategies. Organized labor remained another, rather separate, force, no longer really liberal in the eyes of many and losing in its major bid for renewed influence in 1984 in the Mondale campaign. Finally, the New Democrat movement, originating outside the liberal coalition, threatened by 1992 and 1993 to take over the presidential Democratic party, much of the congressional Democratic party, and (especially in the eyes of many left-liberals) to dilute the content of liberalism itself. Nevertheless, the Clinton presidency held the potential to revitalize liberalism even while redefining it. Whether that potential can be achieved remains to be seen.

### Beyond and between Conservatism and Liberalism

Much of the political action in American politics in the 1980s and 1990s lay between the two major ideological coalitions. Very little of major impact existed either to the left or the right of them. The era began with the John Anderson independent candidacy for the presidency and ended with that of H. Ross Perot. Despite major differences in their appeals, both men sought to build on a center base positioned between conservatism and liberalism. Among intellectuals and commentators, there were increasing calls for a new synthesis of liberal and conservative ideas to address the problems of the future. Former elected officials Paul Tsongas and Warren Rudman used their Concord Coalition to make such an appeal. Books by E. J. Dionne, David Osborne and Ted Gaebler, Thomas Byrne Edsall and Mary D. Edsall, Alice M. Rivlin, and James Davison Hunter won widespread attention with their similar pleas. New Democrats and progressive conservatives in particular sought to move their respective coalitions in the direction of such a synthesis. The Clinton administration frequently aimed to move toward it, particularly after the 1994 elections.[26]

### Conclusions

As the United States faced a changing and uncertain world in the mid-1990s, some observers foresaw an end to the conservative-liberal ideological battle that had raged, albeit in changing forms, since the early New Deal. Conservatives talked of a "conservative crackup," while many long-time liberals shunned the liberal label, seeking others that would carry less baggage from the past. Widespread calls for a centrist synthesis echoed throughout the land.

However, strong centrist forces also had existed in the 1970s and indeed in most previous periods. The New Democrats of the 1990s had parallels in the Modern Republicans of the Eisenhower era of the 1950s. Yet for sixty years ideological conflict along conservative-liberal lines has persisted. Given the dualism of the well-entrenched two-party system and the wide gap between rich and poor in the United States, there certainly remained in place in the 1990s foundations for continuing ideological conflict along the broad lines seen since 1933 (and to some extent since the 1890s). The industrial age that spawned the conservative-liberal cleavage has given way to a postindustrial age in which global ties are more important than ever. However, predictions that the 1981–93 period will be the last one to pit a conservative movement against a liberal one are probably premature.

## Notes

1. Norman Podhoretz, "Buchanan and the Conservative Crackup," *Commentary* 93 (April 1992): 30–34; R. Emmett Tyrell, "The Coming Conservative Crack–Up," *American Spectator* 20 (September 1987): 17–19, 51.

2. On William Kristol, see Gordon S. Wood, "The Fundamentalists and the Constitution," *New York Review of Books,* 18 February 1988, 34; and E. J. Dionne Jr., *Why Americans Hate Politics* (New York: Simon & Schuster, 1991), 73. Dionne, 253–255, discusses Gilder's fusionist efforts. Also see Michael Novak, *The Spirit of Democratic Capitalism* (New York: Simon & Schuster, 1982).

3. Wilson's quote is cited by Linda J. Medcalf and Kenneth M. Dolbeare, *Neopolitics* (New York: Random House, 1985), 175; Irving Kristol, *Two Cheers for Capitalism* (New York: Basic Books, 1978).

4. Wood, "The Fundamentalists," 33–40; Robert Devigne, *Recasting Conservatism* (New Haven: Yale University Press, 1994); Medcalf and K. Dolbeare, *Neopolitics,* chap. 9; Vernon Van Dyke, *Political Ideology and Political Choice* (Chatham, NJ: Chatham House, 1995), chap. 9.

5. Van Dyke, *Ideology and Political Choice,* chaps. 7, 8, 10; Bernard Schwartz, *The New Right and the Constitution* (Boston: Northeastern University Press, 1990), chaps. 3 and 4; Medcalf and K. Dolbeare, *Neopolitics,* chap. 9; Dionne, *Why Americans Hate Politics,* chaps. 9 and 10.

6. Dan Himmelfarb, "Conservative Splits," *Commentary* 85 (May 1988): 56. Also see Gary Dorrien, *The Neoconservative Mind* (Philadelphia: Temple University Press, 1993); Van Dyke, *Ideology and Political Change,* chap. 13; and Medcalf and K. Dolbeare, *Neopolitics,* chap. 8.

7. Dionne, *Why Americans Hate Politics,* chap. 8; Medcalf and K. Dolbeare, *Neopolitics,* chap. 10. Ralph Reed, "Casting a Wider Net," *Policy Review* 65 (Summer 1993): 31–35. Matthew Moen, "The Evolving Politics of the Christian Right," *PS: Political Science & Politics* 29 (September 1996): 461–464.

8. Van Dyke, *Ideology and Political Choice,* chap. 12, discusses this tendency but probably exaggerates its significance.

9. Jerome L. Himmelstein, *To the Right* (Berkeley and Los Angeles: University of California Press, 1990), 204–206.

10. Podhoretz, "Buchanan," 30–34.

11. Kevin Phillips, *The Politics of Rich and Poor* (New York: Random House, 1990); Thomas Byrne Edsall and Mary B. Edsall, *Chain Reaction,* (New York: W. W. Norton, 1991), esp. 219–220.

12.  Podhoretz, "Buchanan," 33; Charles Krauthammer, "Universal Dominion: Toward a Unipolar World," in *America's Purpose,* ed. Owen Harries (San Francisco: ICS Press, 1991), 5–15; Irving Kristol, "Defining Our National Interest," Harries, 69–70, 72; William Bennett, "Rebirth of a Nation," *National Review* 72 (18 March 1991): 44; Paul Johnson, "Wanted: A New Imperialism," *National Review* 75 (14 December 1992): 28–34; Joshua Muravchik, *Exporting Democracy: Fulfilling America's Destiny* (Washington: American Enterprise Institute Press, 1991); Michael Ledeen, "Common Sense 1992," *American Spectator* 25 (June 1992): 23–26; Ben J. Wattenberg, *The First Universal Nation* (New York: Free Press, 1991); Francis Fukuyama, "The End of History?" *National Interest* 16 (Summer 1989): 3–18; Burton Yale Pines, "A Primer for Conservatives," *National Interest* 23 (Spring 1991): 68; Kirk is quoted by Krauthammer, "Universal Dominion." 7; Patrick Buchanan and Samuel Francis are both cited by Van Dyke, *Ideology and Political Choice,* 256–257.

13.  Paul E. Peterson and Mark Rom, "Lower Taxes, More Spending, and Budget Deficits," in *The Reagan Legacy: Promise and Performance,* ed. Charles O. Jones (Chatham, NJ: Chatham House, 1988), 213–240; Christopher H. Foreman Jr., "Legislators, Regulators, and the OMB: The Congressional Challenge to Presidential Regulatory Relief," in *Divided Democracy,* ed. James A. Thurber (Washington: Congressional Quarterly Press, 1991), 123–144; Paul J. Quirk, "Domestic Policy: Divided Government and Creative Presidential Leadership," in *The Bush Presidency: First Appraisals,* ed. Colin Campbell and Bert A. Rockman (Chatham, NJ: Chatham House, 1991), 69–91; Sidney M. Milkis, *The President and the Parties* (New York: Oxford University Press, 1993), chaps. 10, 11; Sidney M. Milkis and Michael Nelson, *The American Presidency,* 2d ed. (Washington: Congressional Quarterly Press, 1994), 362–387.

14.  T. Edsall and M. Edsall, *Chain Reaction,* 172–197 and 230; Laurence I. Barrett, *Gambling with History* (New York: Penguin Books, 1984), chap. 24; Milkis, *President and the Parties,* 297–298; Michael Foley, "The President and Congress," in ed. *The Bush Presidency: Triumphs and Adversities,* ed. Dilys M. Hill and Phil Williams (New York: St. Martin's Press, 1994), esp. 55–56.

15.  Dionne, *Why Americans Hate Politics,* 236–239; Marjorie Randon Hershey, "The Campaign and the Media," in *The Election of 1988,* ed. Gerald M. Pomper (Chatham, NJ: Chatham House, 1989), 81–82, 85–86; Wilson Carey McWilliams, "The Meaning of the Election," in *Election of 1988,* ed. Pomper, 190; Tinsley E. Yarbrough, "Bush and the Courts," in *Bush: Triumphs and Adversities,* 84–108.

16.  I. M. Destler, "Reagan and the World: An 'Awesome Stubbornness,'" in *Reagan,* 241–262; Dionne, *Why Americans Hate Politics,* 317–318, 348–352; Larry Berman and Bruce W. Jentleson, "Bush and the Post–Cold War World: New Challenges for American Leadership," in *Bush: First Appraisals,* 93–128; Milkis, *President and the Parties,* 294–296; Milkis and Nelson, *American Presidency,* 378–382.

17.  On Jesse Jackson, see Dionne, *Why Americans Hate Politics,* 306–308; and T. Edsall and M. Edsall, *Chain Reaction,* esp. 206–207. Treatment of Jackson's ideology as in the New Deal–Great Society liberal tradition is found in Paul R. Abramson, John H. Aldrich, and David W. Rohde, *Change and Continuity in the 1988 Elections,* rev. ed. (Washington: Congressional Quarterly Press, 1991), esp. 34–36. Tom Hayden, *The American Future* (Boston: South End Press, 1980); Stephen M. Gillon,

*The Politics of Vision* (N.Y: Oxford University Press, 1987), 239–243; Martin Carnoy and Derek Shearer, *Economic Democracy* (White Plains, NY: M. E. Sharpe, 1980); Robert Kuttner, *The Life of the Party* (New York: Viking Press, 1987). The Social Democrats U.S.A. used the social democratic label for a centrist agenda.

18. Harry Plotkin, "Issues in the Campaign," in *The Election of 1984*, ed. Gerald M. Pomper (Chatham, NJ: Chatham House, 1985), 35–59; Wilson Carey McWilliams, "The Meaning of the Election," in *Election of 1984*, 157–184.

19. Charles Peters, "A Neoliberal's Manifesto," *Washington Monthly* 15 (May 1983): 10; Paul Tsongas, *The Road from Here* (New York: Alfred A. Knopf, 1981); Gary Hart, *A New Democracy* (New York: Quill, 1983); Randall Rothenberg, *The Neoliberals* (New York: Simon & Schuster, 1984); Medcalf and K. Dolbeare, *Neopolitics,* chap. 4; Van Dyke, *Ideology and Political Choice*, chap. 15.

20. Van Dyke, *Ideology and Political Choice*, 276–279; David Osborne, *Laboratories of Democracy* (Boston: Harvard Business School Press, 1990), esp. the foreword by Bill Clinton, and l–17, 83–110.

21. Van Dyke, *Ideology and Political Choice,* 276–283; Gerald M. Pomper, "The Meaning of the Election," in *The Election of 1992*, ed. Gerald M. Pomper (Chatham, NJ: Chatham House, 1993), 132–156; and Wilson Carey McWilliams, "The Meaning of the Election," in *Election of 1992*, 190–218.

22. Mondale cited by Milkis and Nelson, *American Presidency*, 370. Also see Peterson and Rom, "Lower Taxes," 213–240; Quirk, "Domestic Policy," 69–92.

23. Barrett, *Gambling with History,* chap. 24; T. Edsall and M. Edsall, *Chain Reaction,* 110, 172–197, 230; Milkis, *President and the Political Parties,* 297–298.

24. Van Dyke, *Ideology and Political Choice*, 274–283; McWilliams, "The Meaning of the Election," in *Election of 1992,* 190–218; Patrick M. Garry, *Liberalism and American Identity* (Kent, OH: Kent State University Press, 1992), esp. chap. 8 and 148–160.

25. Van Dyke, *Ideology and Politcal Choice,* chap. 14; Garry, *Liberalism and American Identity,* 142–148; Alonzo L. Hamby, *Liberalism and Its Challengers,* 2d ed. (New York: Oxford University Press, 1992), 379, 394.

26. Dionne, *Why Americans Hate Politics*; Osborne, *Laboratories of Democracy;* David Osborne and Ted Gaebler, *Reinventing Government* (Reading, MA: Addison–Wesley, 1992); T. Edsall and M. Edsall, *Chain Reaction;* Alice M. Rivlin, *Reviving the American Dream* (Washington: Brookings Institution, 1992); James Davison Hunter, *Culture Wars* (New York: Basic Books, 1991).

# 18

# Conservative and Liberal Power Centers

---

The fluidity of the post-1960s power centers of the conservative and liberal ideological movements gave way to considerably more stable patterns between 1981 and 1993. A fairly clear distribution was most evident
concerning the presidency and Congress, but it held true for the federal
judiciary as well. Even among the state governments, a long-term post-
1960s trend toward centrist reformism based on enhanced government
capacities and redistricting of legislatures became more clearly defined than
in the 1970s. Of course the outcomes of the 1992 and 1994 elections were to
bring pronounced movements in new directions—a more-liberal executive
branch and a Congress shifted notably to the right, with the conservative
coalition gaining firm control over both chambers in 1995. The 1996 elections reinforced this pattern. More than anything else, these election results
were an indicator that the Reagan-Bush era was giving way to another.

Societal power bases for each ideological movement during the
1981–93 period were also relatively stable between 1981 and 1993, though
there was more flux on the liberal side than among conservatives. Both
the roles of the large business corporations (especially dollars and organizational clout) and those of the new religious right (new votes from
beyond the conventional conservative constituencies in the upper-middle
and upper classes) remained important to the conservative coalition, but
business corporate leaders became more pragmatic and less conservative
ideologically as the period advanced. In the liberal coalition, the new-politics interest groups and movements remained important, organized labor
attempted a comeback but continued its steady decline, and liberal politicians sought desperately to attract new constituencies or to woo back old
ones in presidential elections. There were no major new movements to
reshape the coalitions, as there had been during the preceding period. The
liberal dominance of the Democratic party, in question during the Carter

years, continued to be in some doubt, while conservatives maintained firm control over the Republican party.

## Government Institutions

"Ronald Reagan was the most ideological president, and the leader of the most ideological administration in modern American history." So concluded political scientist Walter Dean Burnham in a review of the Reagan heritage. Most analysts concurred. It went without saying that the ideology to which Reagan adhered was conservatism, though he gave it some of his own unique twists. "Reaganism," noted one early student of his administration, "entered the argot before Ronald Reagan entered the White House. . . . it became a valid point of reference for a simple reason: Reagan had been clear enough, sincere enough, consistent enough long enough for the term to take on meaning." Moreover, Reagan pledged to remold both the executive branch and the federal judiciary in his own conservative image, and the leadership of his administration made a concerted effort to fulfill that pledge in ways that extended far beyond its predecessors' moves. Joel Aberbach's comparative analysis of the outlooks of political appointees and civil servants in 1970 (early in the Nixon administration) and 1986–87 (late in the Reagan administration) showed that the percentages of officeholders taking the conservative position of opposing an active role for government in the economy rose from 19 percent to 72 percent among political appointees and from 13 percent to 47 percent among top civil servants from the first period to the second. The percentages of Republican administrative officeholders also soared. Therefore, there is solid empirical evidence that the Reagan administration produced an executive branch markedly more conservative than it had been under Nixon.[1]

The orientations of George Bush and the Bush administration were also generally conservative, but less clearly so than in the case of Reagan and his administration. Though judged by many to be an "instinctive moderate," Bush had compiled a solidly conservative voting record during his brief tenure in the House of Representatives (83 percent support for the conservative coalition versus 10 percent opposition to it during the Ninetieth Congress) and had loyally served Republican administrations in various capacities, including the vice presidency for eight years under Reagan. Despite Bush's solid conservative credentials, his conservatism was closely tied to business corporate outlooks and to the old right and did not inspire and mobilize the conservative coalition as a whole in the way that Reaganism did. The Bush administration was widely perceived to be less conservative than its immediate predecessor. While noting the absence of systematic studies, Aberbach, for example, concluded that Bush "cabinet members were primarily establishment types with reputations as pragmatists, and subcabinet members were, for the most part, chosen by cabinet appointees."[2]

The sharp rightward shift of the presidency and the upper levels of the executive branch after 1981 were at first accompanied by growing conservatism on a less dramatic scale in Congress, especially in the Senate, which was captured by the Republicans in the 1980 elections for the first time since the Eisenhower landslide of 1952. However, the still-sizable bloc of Republican Senate moderates and the liberal congressional gains in 1982 and 1986 placed Congress normally well to the left of the Reagan and Bush administrations, though certainly not under the full control of new-politics liberals. In another major development, Southern Democrats increasingly detached themselves from the conservative coalition. A clear indicator of the change was the declining percentage of roll calls in which a majority of Southern Democrats aligned with a majority of Republicans. In contrast to the 1966–81 period, when majorities of Southern Democrats joined Republican majorities on 24 percent of the roll calls, they did so on only 13 percent of the roll calls between 1981 and 1993. Moreover, on almost all major public policy issues during the period from 1983 onward, liberals in Congress were strong enough to force the conservatives to compromise and sometimes to reverse themselves. Using their overall strength and their power in certain subcommittees in particular, congressional liberals blocked most social welfare cuts after the first year, forced the ouster of a few of the most extreme conservative administrators, such as James Watt and Anne Burford, modified some of the conservatives' deregulatory policies, blocked several Reagan administration and Supreme Court civil rights rollback efforts, helped to craft the tax reforms of 1986, compelled the Bush administration to compromise on taxes and affirmative action, and imposed restraints on conservative foreign policies from Nicaragua to South Africa. A few observers, notably Samuel Francis and David Brock, questioned the extent to which Congress was likely to be more liberal than the executive branch over the long term and cited a few examples of recent congressional conservatism relative to the executive branch, but their views were in a distinct minority.[3]

The Supreme Court and the federal judiciary in general shifted in an increasingly conservative direction after 1981, although many conservatives perceived the continuation of institutional factors that effectively constrained the conservatism of the judiciary during the period. Christopher Wolfe spoke for much of the conservative movement in describing the judicial changes as the "revolution that didn't quite happen."[4]

On the matter of court appointments, Reagan and Bush between them were able to name three-quarters of the federal judges sitting at the end of 1992 and five of the nine Supreme Court justices. The Reagan administration made a special point of carefully screening all potential judicial appointees, subjecting them to daylong interviews that included questions about their views on sensitive issues. It also minimized the previous roles of the American Bar Association (no longer a bulwark of the conservative coalition as it once had been) and of home-state senators in the selection process. Occasionally, Senate liberals mobilized successfully to reject conservative nominees, as they did in the controversial cases of Reagan's nomination of Robert H. Bork to the Supreme Court and Jefferson B. Sessions III to the federal district court in Alabama. Several other nominations were withdrawn, including Lino Graglia's, in the face of strong liberal and/or American Bar Association disapproval. However, such administration defeats were infrequent. Although the Bush administration was less overt than the Reagan administration in its efforts to "conservatize" the federal judiciary, Reagan's attorney general and close associate, Edwin Meese, proclaimed: "The results are the same as in the Reagan Administration." George Kassouf, director of the Judicial Selection Project for the liberal Alliance for Justice, agreed, noting that Bush's judicial nominees "don't bring out the same kind of controversies as the Reagan nominees, but they are the same good soldiers in the conservative movement." Most independent observers concurred.[5]

On the Supreme Court itself, the only two remaining clear-cut liberals both retired, William Brennan in 1990 and Thurgood Marshall in 1991. By the end of the period, moderate justices John Paul Stevens and Harry Blackmun (appointed by Ford and Nixon, respectively) usually took the most liberal positions on the High Bench. Sometimes they aligned with some or all of the moderate conservatives to form a majority. The moderate conservatives occupying the center of the Court spectrum were Byron White, Sandra Day O'Connor, David Souter, and Anthony Kennedy. On the clearly conservative end of the continuum sat Antonin Scalia, Clarence Thomas, and William Rehnquist, the last of whom was elevated to be chief justice by Reagan in 1986, when Warren Burger retired. Although the High Bench now handed down a number of decisions, especially concerning civil rights, that outraged liberals and provoked congressional liberal efforts to clarify civil rights legislation to negate the results of Court rulings, many conservatives were unhappy both with the Court majority's jurisprudence and the policy results.[6]

Some conservatives, such as Gary McDowell, found the basic continuing problem with the courts in general to lie in judicial procedures. According to this analysis, "a move from concrete standards to more abstract standards governing the conduct of judicial business," including loosened requirements for standing, broadened use of consent decrees, and a widened understanding of equitable relief, had all developed over several decades and continued to orient the judiciary toward an activism that often had liberal policy effects.[7]

New Right law professor Lino Graglia spoke for even more conservatives than McDowell when he blamed the law schools and the mass media for what he viewed as the institutional liberalism of the courts. His explanation, not fully convincing, was that "Academia is not only the molder of judges but also, along with the media, their source of approval and protection." According to this view, even judges appointed after careful screening could not be depended upon to make the "right" rulings. One problem, however, was that conservatives increasingly disagreed among themselves (as the next chapter will detail) over what the criteria for proper judicial behavior were.[8]

Meanwhile, the state governments continued to evolve away from the rural-based conservatism that had typified them in the past. While structural obstacles to liberal redistributive reforms remained significant at this level, broad reform capacities of state governments continued to increase, with the growth of professionalized bureaucracies, upgraded legislative bodies and staffs, and improved revenue bases in many states. A number of states became what David Osborne and others termed "laboratories of democracy," pointing the way to "creating economic growth" and even "bringing the poor into the growth process." Osborne's view of the states stressed the creative centrist ideas both of Democratic and of Republican governors, including Bill Clinton of Arkansas, Bruce Babbitt of Arizona, and Michael Dukakis of Massachusetts among Democrats and Richard Thornburgh of Pennsylvania, Thomas Kean of New Jersey, and Robert Orr of Indiana among Republicans. Although somewhat overstated, Osborne's analysis captured the essence of major patterns at the state level during this period, which continued trends that had begun to develop in the 1970s. These, too, would have some bearing on conservative and (especially) liberal theories of governance.

## Political Parties

Conservatives tightened their control over the Republican party, both in presidential and congressional sectors. No moderate of the period could hope to score even as well as Nelson Rockefeller had in 1968 in a Republican presidential nominating contest. Republican nominating convention delegates were overwhelmingly conservative, well to the right of the electorate on most issues. Among congressional Republicans, it was no longer possible for a leader as moderate as Hugh Scott to head the Senate Republican party, despite its less-intense conservatism compared to the House Republican Conference. Nevertheless, so-called "gypsy moth" moderates (named for the moth characteristic of the Northeastern region where such moderates were most common) continued to be a force, especially in the Senate.[10]

In the Democratic party, the neoliberal split with the dominant new-politics liberalism and the rising influence of the New Democrats, especially after three successive presidential election defeats, led to continuing reassessments of the party's link to liberalism. Southern Democrats remained more conservative than the rest of the party, though North-South differences were more muted than they had been in the 1960s. Carter's triumph in 1976 had already advertised the weakening hold of liberalism on the presidential Democratic party apparatus; and the long-term strength of conservative Southern Democrats in Congress was legendary. Therefore, the novelty of liberals' struggling for the soul of the Democratic party should not be exaggerated. In fact, despite his New Democrat credentials, Bill Clinton possessed far more ties to the liberal mainstream of 1992 than Carter had to the liberalism of 1976 or 1980. Not only had Clinton headed the McGovern campaign effort in his native Arkansas in 1972, but he had sustained links to most of the liberal power centers in the national Democratic party throughout his political career, in contrast to Carter's pre-presidential record. Although Clinton rejected the liberal label, both liberals and conservatives most commonly viewed him as a part of the liberal coalition.[11]

### Interest Groups

No major new streams of interest group/mass movement activity flowed into either major ideological coalition on a scale to match the late 1960s or the 1970s. Some of the new groups of the previous period changed names and/or declined in influence. The Moral Majority, for example, did both, merging into the new Liberty Federation and losing clout. Neoliberalism and the New Democrat movement caused some flux in the liberal coalition but were not mass movements and had less impact on interest-group activity than had the new-politics movements of the previous period.[12]

Later in this period, the Business Roundtable, a number of business trade associations, and quite a few individual business corporations shifted back toward a pragmatic strategy less closely tied to the conservative movement than in the 1970s and early 1980s. However, the National Association of Manufacturers and the United States Chamber of Commerce continued to be the conservative bastions that they had been since the 1930s. In fact, most of the organized business community remained pro-conservative in orientation. Among the large array of business-backed conservative think tanks, which continued to proliferate, the Heritage Foundation became the largest and most powerful of the period, churning out books and position papers, publishing a journal of conservative analysis, and suggesting personnel for the staffing of the Reagan and Bush administrations (particularly the former). The New Right/religious right interest groups underwent considerable reshuffling, as the Christian Coalition and the Family Research Council displaced the Moral Majority. Increasingly, the religious right groups came to be accepted as an integral part of the Republican party coalition. Some observers, such as Matthew Moen, even went so far as to describe a "transformation" from social protest movement to electoral coalition partner.[13]

Neoliberals and New Democrats wooed business support with some success, but the main base of the liberal movement remained the new-politics liberal movements and the interest groups that they had spawned; the older liberal groups such as the American Civil Liberties Union, the Americans for Democratic Action, the National Farmers Union, and the National Committee for an Effective Congress; and the still-weakening AFL-CIO. Throughout most of the period, the AFL-CIO was more outraged by the blatant antiunionism of the Reaganites than it was attracted to the ideals of liberalism. Overall union membership as a percentage of the workforce continued its long-term decline, falling to less than 15 percent during this period. By the mid-1990s, however, the labor movement was displaying signs of renewed energy—and liberalism. Among the think tanks, the prominent Brookings Institution, once seen as clearly liberal, continued its centrist approach and even veered at times to the center-right of the spectrum.[14]

While liberals frequently portrayed the conservative movement as little more than a front for big business interests and/or as a vehicle for the religious right, conservatives heatedly attacked liberalism as a mere cover for selfish interest groups of labor union bosses, "new class" professionals jealous of business success, and racial, ethnic, and sexual minorities demanding special privileges. Each accusation rang true enough to give it considerable credibility, although each was only a partial truth.

## Wordsmiths

The alignments among major wordsmiths also remained quite continuous with the late 1970s and fairly stable over time between 1981 and 1993. On the conservative side, the *Wall Street Journal* editorial page linked, even more than previously, various conservatisms (but now especially the neoconservatism of editor Robert Bartley and frequent columnist L. Gordon Crovitz) with the business corporate world. Less influential and successful was the new *Washington Times,* which sought to provide a strong conservative presence in the journalism of the nation's capital in competition with the liberal *Post. National Review* spoke still for the old right but featured a variety of conservative viewpoints. Less influential but also possessing deep old-right roots was *Human Events. The National Interest,* founded in 1985, joined *The Public Interest* and *Commentary* as a major mouthpiece for neoconservatism. *Modern Age* continued as a voice for mainly traditionalist conservatism and was joined by *Chronicles of Culture,* published by the Rockford Institute. *Reason,* as well as Cato Institute publications, sustained libertarian perspectives. The Heritage Foundation's *Policy Review* and R. Emmett Tyrell's *American Spectator* rounded out the list of influential conservative periodicals of the period. Major conservative syndicated columnists included George Will, William F. Buckley, James J. Kilpatrick, Joseph Sobran, Charles Krauthammer, William Safire, and Robert Novak and Rowland Evans.[15]

Among liberals, the *New York Times* and *Washington Post* editorials continued to be near the center of the liberal mainstream. However, neoconservatism came to be featured on the *Times*'s op-ed page and in the *New York Times Magazine* more frequently than in the past. The *New Republic* veered toward neoliberalism but also encompassed writers further to the left and from the neoconservative movement. More clearly neoliberal than the *New Republic* was the *Washington Monthly* of Charles Peters, which spawned a variety of talented journalists who became influential in other mass media outlets, including James Fallows, Gregg Easterbrook, Nicholas Lemann, Joseph Nocera, Mickey Kaus, and others. *Commonweal* continued its blend of liberalism and Roman Catholicism. The *Progressive* and to an even greater extent the *Nation* occupied the left wing of the liberal movement and primarily addressed it. Two left-liberal policy quarterlies, *Working Papers for a New Society* and *Democracy,* ceased publication after enjoying some influence in the early part of the period. Major liberal syndicated columnists of these years included Anthony Lewis, Tom Wicker, Joseph Kraft, Mary McGrory, Molly Ivins, Edwin Yoder, and Jack Germond and Jules Witcover.[16]

## Conclusions

Viewed in retrospect, the 1981–93 period was one in which the societal power centers of both the conservative and liberal coalitions changed but little from the patterns crystallizing in the late 1970s. Wordsmiths, political parties, and interest groups assumed postures that were generally quite predictable, though there were notable fluctuations pulling the liberal coalition toward the center of the political spectrum.

Inside government, the presidency and the upper reaches of the executive branch became more conservative than at any time since 1933. This development gave the conservative coalition a distinct edge in setting the national political agenda. On the other hand, after some brief successes in Congress, the conservatives found themselves usually frustrated there by resurgent liberal strength and self-confidence and frequent use of power bases within congressional subcommittees to block Reagan-Bush initiatives and hold executive branch officials at least partially accountable to them and their liberal agendas. The federal judiciary became increasingly conservative, mainly due to the appointment process of the Reagan and Bush administrations. However, conservatives divided over their judicial goals, and many of them continued to believe that the courts were institutionally liberal or at least nonconservative by their criteria. Finally, more than at any time since 1933, the state governments appeared to offer no clear advantage to either the conservative or the liberal coalition (after years of relative conservatism), though inequalities among them, competitive pressures, and other factors still made them unlikely laboratories for a successful left-liberal brand of democracy.

Whether twelve years of relative stability in the institutional power centers of the two major ideological coalitions also stabilized conservative and liberal prescriptions for government institutions and crystallized new theories of governance is the issue addressed by the next three chapters.

## Notes

1.  Walter Dean Burnham, "The Reagan Heritage," in *The Election of 1988,* ed. Gerald M. Pomper, (Chatham, NJ: Chatham House, 1989), l. The Reaganism quotation is from Laurence I. Barrett, *Gambling with History* (New York: Penguin Books, 1984), 46. Joel Aberbach, "The President and the Executive Branch," in *The Bush Presidency: First Appraisals,* ed. Colin Campbell and Bert A. Rockman (Chatham, NJ: Chatham House, 1991), 229–235. For similar assessments, see also John L. Palmer and Isabel V. Sawhill, "Overview," in *The Reagan Record,* ed. Palmer and Sawhill (Cambridge, MA: Ballinger, 1984), 2; Alonzo L. Hamby, *Liberalism and*

*Its Challengers,* 2d ed. (New York: Oxford University Press, 1992), 363; Iwan W. Morgan, *Beyond the Liberal Consensus* (New York: St. Martin's Press, 1994), 173; and Sidney M. Milkis and Michael Nelson, *The American Presidency,* 2d ed. (Washington: Congressional Quarterly Press, 1994), 362.

2. Hamby, *Liberalism and Its Challengers,* 389, terms Bush an "instinctive moderate." For Bush's House voting record, see *Congressional Quarterly Almanac,* 1968, 825; and Aberbach, "The President and the Executive Branch," 239.

3. The author calculated the figures on Southern Democratic–Republican majority agreements from data in *Congressional Quarterly Almanac.* Samuel Francis, "Imperial Conservatives?" *National Review* 68 (4 August 1989): 37–38; David Brock, "Mr. Symms Goes to Jamba: A Kind Word for Congress in Foreign Policy," *Policy Review* 59 (Winter 1992): 32–39.

4. Christopher Wolfe, *The Rise of Modern Judicial Review,* rev. ed. (Lanham, MD: Rowman & Littlefield, 1994), 365–369.

5. David M. O'Brien, "The Reagan Judges: His Most Enduring Legacy?" in *The Reagan Legacy,* ed. Charles O. Jones (Chatham, NJ: Chatham House, 1988); Lincoln Caplan, "The Reagan Challenge to the Rule of Law," in *The Reagan Legacy,* ed. Sidney Blumenthal and Thomas Byrne Edsall (New York: Pantheon, 1988), 213–249; the Meese quotation and a review of independent assessments of the Bush judicial appointees are in Joan Biskupic, "Bush Boosts Bench Strength of Conservative Judges," *Congressional Quarterly Weekly Report,* 19 January 1991, 171–174. Kassouf's quote is from Tinsley E. Yarbrough, "Bush and the Courts," in *The Bush Presidency: Triumphs and Adversities,* ed. Dilys M. Hill and Phil Williams (New York: St. Martin's Press, 1994), 92–93.

6. Wolfe, *Modern Judicial Review,* 360–361; Linda Greenhouse, "Changed Path for Court?" *New York Times,* 26 June 1992, sec. A, pp. 1, 10; Thomas Byrne Edsall and Mary D. Edsall, *Chain Reaction* (New York: W. W. Norton, 1991), 186–192, discusses such decisions as *Grove City v. Bell* and *Ward's Cove Packing Co., Inc. v. Atonio* and the successful congressional liberal efforts to negate or modify their effects.

7. Gary L. McDowell, *Curbing the Courts* (Baton Rouge: Louisiana State University Press, 1988), chap. 6; the quotation is from p. 170.

8. Lino Graglia, "Judicial Activism: Even on the Right, It's Wrong," *Public Interest* 95 (Spring 1989): 74.

9. David Osborne, *Laboratories of Democracy* (Boston: Harvard Business School Press, 1990), esp. 1–17. For an assessment noting the persistence of inherent conservatism in state-centered federalism, see David B. Robertson and Dennis R, Judd, *The Development of American Public Policy* (Glenview, IL: Scott, Foresman, 1989), esp. chap. 11.

10. Nicol C. Rae, *The Decline and Fall of the Liberal Republicans from 1952 to the Present* (New York: Oxford University Press, 1989); Gerald M. Pomper, "The Presidential Nominations," in *The Election of 1988,* ed. Gerald M. Pomper (Chatham, NJ: Chatham House, 1989), esp. 53–65.

11. Nicol C. Rae, *Southern Democrats* (New York: Oxford University Press, 1994); a useful review of conservative and liberal assessments of Clinton's ideolo-

gy appears in Vernon Van Dyke, *Ideology and Political Choice* (Chatham, NJ: Chatham House, 1995), 283.

12.  On the Moral Majority, see Jeffrey M. Berry, *The Interest Group Society,* 2d ed. (Glenview, IL: Scott, Foresman, 1989), 34.

13.  Jerome L. Himmelstein, *To the Right* (Berkeley and Los Angeles: University of California Press, 1990), 200–208; John B. Judis, "Conservatism and the Price of Success," in *The Reagan Legacy,* ed. Blumenthal and T. Edsall, 135–171; Sara Diamond, *Roads to Dominion* (NY: Guilford, 1995), esp. chap. 10. Matthew Moen, *The Transformation of the Christian Right* (Tuscaloosa: University of Alabama Press, 1992); and Matthew Moen, "The Evolving Politics of the Christian Right," *PS* 29 (September 1996): 461–464.

14.  Michael W. McCann, *Taking Reform Seriously* (Ithaca, NY: Cornell University Press, 1986), chap. 5; Steven M. Gillon, *Politics and Vision* (New York: Oxford University Press, 1987), 238–243; Berry, *Interest Group Society,* 23–24; "AFL–CIO's Brash Boss Jump–Starts Labor," *St. Petersburg Times,* 2 September 1996, sec. A, pp. 5, 6.

15.  The best overviews of conservative wordsmiths of the period are in Paul Gottfried and Thomas Fleming, *The Conservative Movement* (Boston: Twayne, 1988), 63, 72, 93–94; and Diamond, *Roads to Dominion,* esp. chap. 12.

16.  A good summary appears in Robert Kuttner, *The Life of the Party* (New York: Viking Press, 1987), 20, 170–175; also see Fred Barnes, "Media Realignment," *New Republic* 192 (6 May 1985): 12–16.

# 19

# Conservative Institutional Prescriptions

---

With conservatives in firm control of the presidency, the upper reaches of the executive branch, and increasingly the federal judiciary, the conservative movement enjoyed more opportunities to effectuate its institutional recommendations (when it could reach consensus on them) than at any time since 1933. However, liberal obstacles in Congress, never absent, grew from 1983 onward, and the states frequently became arenas for centrist reform. Moreover, conservatives' actions were sometimes at odds with their rhetorical prescriptions, particularly concerning decentralized federalism, judicial restraint, and constitutional immutability. In the last two realms, the conservative split became wider than it had ever been, engendering philosophical debates over the principles themselves.

Not surprisingly in light of the power bases of the coalitions of the period, conservative coalescence around a presidential government model became more evident than at any previous time. However, there remained a sizable minority bloc of dissenters. A few new conservative proponents of congressionally centered checks and balances even entered the fray. On the related issue of the administrative state, the predominant conservative approach stressed presidential administrative leadership, privatization and decentralization in many domestic spheres, and (as long as the Cold War endured) a large national security administrative state under presidential direction. Deeply held suspicions of civil service bureaucrats and their perceived proclivities toward trade unionism and liberalism caused many conservatives to continue to resist efforts to grant civil servants additional political rights.

Overall, the period was one of considerable conservative stability on the important subject of presidential-congressional relations, though the end of the conservatives' foreign policy/national security values and policy consensus, the election of Clinton to the presidency in 1992 and 1996 and of a conservative Congress in 1994 and 1996, and the poor fit between presidential government and prescriptions for a constitutional jurisprudence of original intention and perhaps for liberty, all raised questions as to whether the new conservative pattern in support of presidential government would endure much longer. Stability also characterized most conservative rhetoric during these twelve years about the administrative state and federalism, despite the fact that conservative actions sometimes failed to reflect such stability. In matters of judicial review and constitutional interpretation, intraconservative conflict became more notable than at any previous time, though conservative majorities remained wedded to past prescriptions. More stable overall than the 1966–81 years were for conservative institutional ideas, the 1981–93 period still did not generate full conservative unity on a theory of governance.

### The Reagan Administration and Conservative Institutional Prescriptions

As the chief focal point for the conservative movement, the Reagan administration took initiatives that often reflected a conservative consensus that had already been achieved, but they sometimes helped to shape a new consensus. Certainly the administration's loud and frequent rhetoric about states' rights, judicial restraint, and constitutional immutability fell into the former category. On the other hand, its presidential government and administrative state initiatives—broadly similar to those undertaken by the Nixon administration despite some obvious differences in modes of implementation—pushed the conservative movement closer to an embrace of presidential government and establishment of a conservative state than Nixon had ever been able to do.

On the subject of federalism, Reagan's inaugural address expressed the extreme states' rights "compact theory" that "the Federal Government did not create the states; the states created the Federal Government" (rather than conceptualizing "the people" as the creators of the federal government). Reagan at the same time endorsed the "dual federalism" idea, prevalent before 1937, by proclaiming: "It is my intention to curb the size and influence of the Federal establishment and to demand recognition of the distinction between the powers granted to the Federal Government and those reserved to the states or the people." This suggested a replacement of the existing "marble-cake federalism" of shared federal and state responsibilities with sharply delineated policy domains for each level of government. If put into action, the ideas of the Reagan inaugural address would certainly have meant revolutionary change in the federal system in a states'-rights direction.[1]

However, the actual picture was a mixed one. In a few areas, the Reagan administration sought and achieved changes of a decentralist nature, with solid conservative backing by the conservative coalition. The most significant measure of this type came in the first year when the Omnibus Budget Reconciliation Act consolidated fifty-seven existing categorical grant-in-aid programs into seven broad block grants that gave the states extensive leeway in their spending priorities and administration. One hundred percent of the conservatives present and voting in the Senate endorsed this measure (compared with 25 percent of the liberals); on the most critical vote on it in the House of Representatives (the Gramm-Latta amendment), 80 percent of the conservatives and only 1 percent of the liberals voted in the affirmative, creating an exceedingly thin majority. "We're talking about a very revolutionary change," claimed White House adviser Robert B. Carleson, with some exaggeration. The block grants "move in the direction of Reagan federalism . . . [and] show a significant start in reversing the direction of government." Unlike Nixon, who had advocated block grants as a managerial device, Reagan saw them as a means "to help the federal government disengage itself from what were considered to be traditional state and local responsibilities," according to the leading analyst of the subject. Also unlike Nixon, Reagan had no sympathy for general revenue sharing; and that program expired in 1986, partially because of ballooning federal deficits which necessitated budget-cutting and partially because of Reagan's hostile view of it.[2]

After its first year, the Reagan administration enjoyed only a few new successes, most notably the replacement of categorical grants with block grants in 1987. More typically, it was able to achieve funding reductions for categorical grant programs that left the states with less federal money than previously. (The Reagan efforts to shift to block grants had also usually entailed spending reductions.) Even in the administration's first year, liberals in Congress picked up enough moderate and conservative votes to negate a Reagan administration effort to fold the legal services for the poor program into a block grant, which might well have killed the program in most states (the real Reagan goal, according to many liberals). When the Reagan administration in 1982 proposed a "big swap" in which the states would assume responsibilities for more than forty federal aid programs while the national government would take full financial responsibility for medicaid, it encountered strong resistance in both Congress and the states, to such an extent that the administration never even presented a formal legislative request on the subject.[3]

However, far from all of the failures to decentralize stemmed from external opposition. In many respects, the Reagan administration and Reagan himself were "Janus-faced" on the subject of federalism. As Joseph Zimmerman has noted of Reagan: "His 'public' face emphasized initiatives promoting a return of political power to the states and local governments. His 'silent' face encouraged additional centralization of political power in several functional areas." Reaching similar conclusions, Timothy Conlan found "strong temptations for policy advocates to seek a single national solution, a temptation that afflicts conservatives and liberals alike." Among the areas in which the Reagan administration actually favored centralization of power at the expense of states' rights were its support for national product liability legislation (to replace traditional state regulations in this sphere), national regulation of trucking and drinking-age standards (successfully employing threats of federal funding cuts to force state compliance here), limitations on state abilities to veto nuclear waste dump sites, and reduction of state roles in the granting of offshore oil and gas drilling leases. Moreover, a study of proposed federal preemptions found that the Reagan administration "supported moves to take regulatory powers from the states" in 75 percent of the cases studied.[4]

Conservatives in general displayed a similar ambivalence on federalism issues. Studies of congressional voting patterns in the 97th Congress (1981–82) found a small cluster of conservatives in each chamber who voted consistently for states' rights; but only 15 of 58 (26 percent) in the Senate and 16 of 225 (7 percent) in the House of Representatives did so on three-fourths or more of the roll calls analyzed by the researchers for *Publius: The Journal of Federalism*. In fact, a slightly larger number of conservative representatives (17, or 8 percent) took consistently procentralist positions than took consistently decentralist ones, though no conservative senators did so. Overall, the nature of the substantive policy issues involved and the positions taken by the Reagan administration went much further toward explaining congressional conservatives' behavior than the philosophy of states' rights did. Although conservatives inside and out of government regularly employed the rhetoric of decentralized federalism during this period, the actions of conservative officeholders suggested a picture that was far from clear on the subject.[5]

Much more consistency between rhetoric and behavior existed for both the Reagan administration and the conservative movement in the realm of presidential government. However, there were some significant differences over what the conservative model of presidential government should entail. And there remained pockets of conservative resistance to the model itself from advocates of congressionally centered checks and balances.

The greatest degree of internal conservative disagreement about presidential powers centered around whether the president should play a role as tribune of a popular majority, claiming policy mandates from his electoral victories and using his office as a "bully pulpit" to reach out to the mass public over the heads of Congress members, media interpreters, and other intermediaries to sustain and expand majority support. The strongest advocacy of this component of presidential government, not surprisingly, came from Richard Viguerie, Patrick Buchanan, and other leaders of the New Right. Viguerie, expressing his position in terms that evoked religious right sentiment, phrased his position thus: "Teddy Roosevelt said he believed in using the Presidency as a bully pulpit. I agree that the Presidency affords a tremendous opportunity for a good person to lead the people in a righteous direction." Viguerie also stressed the need for a conservative president to reach out to "the people" over the heads of "media elites." Nor were such views confined entirely to the New Right. Senator John Tower, a pillar of the old right, proclaimed: "The President, along with the Vice President, is the only officer of government who is elected by and responsible to the nation as a whole. As such only he possesses a national mandate." Neoconservatives Irving Kristol and Michael Horowitz also embraced the tribune role warmly. Eroding partisan ties among the public and a "democratized" presidential nomination process increased the likelihood that presidents of any ideological bent would cast themselves as popular tribunes and habitually "go public" to assist them in governing, as Theodore Lowi, Samuel Kernell, and other political scientists have noted.[6]

The extent to which Reagan himself embraced the tribune role and utilized it is subject to some dispute. While James Ceaser has portrayed him as uncomfortable with the role, and Irving Kristol complained that he did not carry it as far as he should have, others, including an otherwise sympathetic Harvey Mansfield Jr., have noted a streak of Reagan populism; and Lowi has treated him as a prime example of a "plebiscitarian" president.[7]

Much of the conservative movement, especially traditionalist conservatives, denounced the tribune role as incompatible with the original intent of the framers of the Constitution and as damaging to republicanism in general. George Carey spoke for many, protesting that "Ours is not a plebiscitary republic . . . [T}he *deliberate* sense of the *community* ought to prevail." Alan Crawford reiterated the old conservative warnings against "Caesarism." Neo-Straussian traditionalist conservative scholars, including James Ceaser, Jeffrey Tulis, and Harvey Mansfield Jr., blamed the emergence of the tribune conception of the presidency on Woodrow Wilson and likewise rejected it. But the conservative movement, and perhaps Reagan himself, remained divided on the matter.[8]

On the other hand, conservative rhetorical and behavioral consensus generally prevailed during the Reagan years on presidential roles as leader of foreign and defense policies, chief administrator, and remolder of the federal judiciary and legal system. Certainly, Reagan and his administration displayed zeal in all three realms. Though each of these roles provoked some conservative dissent, and a few conservatives rejected all of them, fairly wide conservative agreement was in evidence, both in books and articles and in congressional voting patterns, on the modes of implementation.

Expansive presidential roles as commander-in-chief and chief diplomat were Reagan administration goals endorsed by almost all conservatives, with the exception of a libertarian conservative contingent (who stressed the likely negative impact on liberty and/or republicanism and/or made objections on constitutional grounds) and a few others whose prime argument was that Congress was more conservative over the long run than the presidency. Conservative intellectuals from varied camps stressed inherent presidential characteristics of energy, unity, speed, and secrecy; called upon Alexander Hamilton as a constitutional framer sympathetic to a powerful presidency in foreign affairs; and frequently emphasized John Locke's conception of an "executive prerogative" to cope with emergencies. In Congress, some roll-call votes, notably those concerning presidential discretion in Angola and Nicaragua, found a unanimous or nearly unanimous conservative coalition in opposition to an almost equally united liberal movement. Although other foreign and national security presidential powers did not rally quite this much conservative support, the presidential-congressional roll calls consistently showed conservatives favoring presidential power markedly more than their liberal rivals did.[9]

The Reagan administration also took steps—widely endorsed by the conservative movement, despite some criticisms from a few conservative legal scholars, such as Philip Kurland—to use the presidency very consciously and overtly to remold the federal judicial and legal system. Not only did this entail the careful screening of judicial appointees, as detailed in chapter 18, but it also involved assertion of tightened presidential control of the solicitor general's office (representing the government's legal interests), active litigation of the presidential agenda by the full staff of the Justice Department, rejection or attempts at substantial modification of the previously enacted provisions for independent prosecutors in cases of alleged executive branch legal infractions, and repeated calls for depoliticization of the Senate judicial confirmation process. On the last point, energetic and successful Senate liberal blocking of Reagan's appointment of Robert Bork to the Supreme Court, in the midst of what became a virtual political campaign, drew particularly intense administration and conservative ire. Taken as a whole, these modes represented a substantial effort to expand presidential powers. Without exaggeration, government professor David O'Brien concluded: "Reagan's administration had a more coherent and ambitious agenda for legal reform and judicial selection than any previous administration."[10]

Finally, with regard to presidential powers, there were the conservative-endorsed efforts by the Reagan administration to increase presidential direction of the executive branch. In addition to the conscious and generally successful effort to appoint conservatives to political executive posts, the Reagan administration used the new Civil Service Reform Act of 1978 to the fullest to move conservative-oriented civil servants into key positions and tightened the political control and coordination of both policy formulation and implementation through such devices as the use of a cabinet council system and the expansion of the regulatory clearance functions of the Office of Information and Regulatory Affairs in the Office of Management and Budget. When the Reagan administration sought to build its administrative control still further by persuading Congress to cede the president an item veto and/or various excision or rescission powers, most congressional conservatives gave their support but were unable to overcome strong liberal and moderate opposition. Quite a few conservatives went even beyond the Reagan administration's agenda by calling for elimination of all independent agencies and commissions and placing them under presidential control in a single, hierarchical chain of command. Certainly such ideas were a far cry from what conservatives had advocated from the 1930s through the 1960s.[11]

While conservatives of the period mostly united around the goal of enhancing presidential control over the administrative state, they remained generally hostile to government bureaucracy, at least in the domestic sphere. Their attacks on it, usually supported by the Reagan administration, included loud and widespread demands for "privatization," emanating especially from libertarian conservative scholars and activists in the Heritage Foundation and the Cato Institute. Specific Reagan administration privatization endeavors included creation of a Commission on Privatization, sale of Conrail and some federal loans to the private sector, and increased reliance on contracting out to private firms to deliver goods or services previously delivered by government employees. With less success, the administration urged expanded use of vouchers to give citizens a wider set of choices in education, medical care, and other fields. Also reflecting a general lack of enthusiasm for the career civil service, the

Reagan administration opposed efforts to grant additional political rights to federal civil servants, whose ability to engage in political activities had long been sharply restricted by the Hatch Act. Although some saw the conservative embrace of presidential control of the administrative state as tantamount to acceptance of that state itself, such a reading underestimated the continuing conservative hostility to government bureaucracy. That hostility, and the privatization movement in particular, sometimes operated at cross-purposes with the drive for presidential-hierarchical control, since privatization, as Peter Benda and Charles Levine have demonstrated, often created networks "so tangled that clear lines of accountability disappeared." These authors noted pointedly that both the Iran-Contra and *Challenger* disasters illustrated the difficulties of monitoring privatized administration. Most conservatives, however, perceived no conflict between tightened presidential controls and privatization of administration and endorsed both of these goals.[12]

Finally, the Reagan administration and much of the conservative movement mingled prescriptions for judicial restraint with calls for constitutional interpretation based upon original intent. They also expressed wishes for judicial outcomes consonant with conservatives' preferred public policies, even though these might sometimes be incompatible with the other stated objectives. The 1980 Republican party platform described model judges as those

> who respect and reflect the values of the American people, and whose judicial philosophy is characterized by the highest regard for protecting the rights of law-abiding citizens . . . [and] is consistent with the belief in the decentralization of the federal government and efforts to return decision-making power to state and local elected officials . . . who respect traditional family values and the sanctity of innocent human life . . . [and] who share our commitment to judicial restraint.[13]

To these the Reagan administration in general, and Edwin Meese, attorney general from 1985 to 1988, in particular, added a heavy emphasis on what Meese termed "a jurisprudence of original intention." This he defined as follows:

> Where the language of the Constitution is specific, it must be obeyed. Where there is a demonstrable consensus among the framers and ratifiers as to a principle stated or implied by the Constitution, it should be followed as well. Where there is ambiguity, as to the precise meaning or reach of a con-

stitutional provision, it should be interpreted and applied in a manner so as to at least not contradict the text of the Constitution itself.[14]

In taking this position and linking it to judicial restraint, Meese and the Reagan administration aligned themselves with an array of conservatives, including legal scholars Lino Graglia (discussed previously) and Robert Bork and political scientists Walter Berns and Gary McDowell (both neo-Straussian traditionalists). In making their arguments for judicial restraint, Bork, Graglia, and Meese included deference to lawmaking majorities and majority rule generally, in common with most of the populistic New Right. In contrast, neo-Straussian traditionalists saw the restraint on judges imposed solely by the Constitution and its framers' intentions, shying away from majoritarianism in their treatment of the judiciary, as in other matters.[15]

As noted previously, a number of conservative judges appointed by Reagan (like many appointed by Nixon and Ford) proved to be activists in practice, not only in the sense of overturning statutes adopted by lawmaking majorities and precedents established by predecessors but also in emphasizing "natural law" not found in the Constitution but reflective of conservative versions of moral theory. Back in the 1890-1937 period, when similar conservative judicial activism in behalf of negative freedom and property rights had been commonplace, no prominent conservatives had defended such judicial behavior as "activism" or in terms of a flexible Constitution. In the 1980s, although most still did not do so, there emerged for the first time on a major scale a group of conservative intellectuals who argued explicitly for supplementing constitutional text and original intent with natural law and sometimes even public-choice theory. Prime among these were legal scholars Bernard Siegan, Richard Epstein, and Stephen Macedo—all of a libertarian conservative bent—and the *Wall Street Journal* editorial staff under Robert Bartley—mostly neo-conservative but with strong ties to big business.

Bernard Siegan's major work, *Economic Liberties and the Constitution,* was published in 1980, shortly before the Reagan administration took office, but remained a center of heated controversy throughout the Reagan years and played an important part in derailing Siegan's own appointment to a federal appellate judgeship by Reagan. Its chief theme was "the great need under our government system for judicial oversight of economic legislation." While proclaiming his support for libertarian approaches to both economic and noneconomic matters on the basis of a "substantive" interpretation of the due process clauses of the Fifth and Fourteenth Amendments, Siegan put his main emphasis on reviving the doctrines set forth back in the 1905 *Lochner v. New York* case and a generally activist judicial approach to protecting property rights, overturning economic legislation when necessary to accomplish his libertarian conservative goals. Behind Siegan's praise for *Lochner* lay a Social Darwinist conception of natural rights similar to that which Oliver Wendell Holmes had protested against back in 1905, not the original intent proclaimed by the Reaganite conservatives and others.[16]

University of Chicago law professor Richard Epstein arrived at similar economic libertarian recommendations but by a somewhat different route. Instead of focusing on the due process clauses as Siegan did, Epstein in his 1985 book *Takings: Private Property and the Power of Eminent Domain* used as his basis the "takings" clause of the Fifth Amendment, which provided: "[N]or shall private property be taken for public use, without just compensation." Epstein proposed activist judicial attacks on most liberal socioeconomic regulation from the New Deal onward, since in his view any regulation that imposed limits on property owners or diminished the value of their property constituted a taking for which the government must pay compensation. The Supreme Court should, in this analysis, also prohibit progressive taxation on such grounds. Delighted by Epstein's approach, the *Wall Street Journal* took up the cause eagerly on its editorial page. Some conservative judges, such as Richard Posner, praised Epstein's work, and Chief Justice William Rehnquist and Associate Justices Antonin Scalia and Sandra Day O'Connor appeared to be influenced by it. In the meantime, Posner developed his own "law and economics" approach that emphasized a pursuit of economic "efficiency" as the foundation of jurisprudence.[17]

Both Siegan and Epstein provoked sharp attacks from fellow conservatives who advocated a jurisprudence of original intention and judicial restraint. Bork's conclusions were fairly typical. In reference to both Siegan and Epstein, he noted: "Though I am more in sympathy with their political ends than I am with the objectives of the ultraliberals, I do not think that they establish that these ends may be reached through the Court." On Epstein's work specifically, Bork concluded that it was "a powerful work of political theory" but that Epstein "has not convincingly located that political theory in the Constititution." Graglia concurred: "Epstein's theory is indistinguishable from the theory of Ronald Dworkin, his liberal counterpart. . . . [T]hey differ only in that Dworkin would have the Supreme Court enact John Rawls's egalitarian program because it is required by natural law and therefore the Constitution, whereas Epstein would have the Court enact Robert Nozick's libertarian program on a similar basis."[18]

At the same time, libertarian conservative advocates of judicial activism lashed back with direct attacks on the conservative proponents of original intent and judicial restraint. Probably the harshest and most thorough of these was Stephen Macedo's *The New Right v. the Constitution*, published by the Cato Institute in 1987 with an introduction by Epstein. In this work, Macedo criticized New Rightists Bork, Graglia, and Meese by name and repeatedly. His four-point indictment argued that the jurisprudence of original intent was naive and "patently at odds with the spirit of the Constitution"; that the "democratic" justification for judicial restraint distorted the fact that the Constitution established "a scheme of limited government," not a democracy; that the New Right's disdain for abstract philosophical principles reflected in fact a "moral skepticism that is deeply at odds with the Constitution"; and that liberty and community can be mutually supportive in ways that the New Rightists fail to comprehend. Offering his own prescriptions, Macedo called for "a principled activism in service of individual rights both personal and economic" that would "fuse" constitutional interpretation and libertarian conservative moral philosophy.[19]

Unpersuaded, conservative proponents of judicial restraint continued to seek curbs on judicial activism of any variety. Deploring the congressional conservatives' issue-by-issue (and consistently unsuccessful) efforts to restrict federal court jurisdiction on such matters as school busing and school prayer and noting the inherent difficulties of achieving the supermajorities needed for constitutional amendments to overturn particularly egregious examples of judicial activism, Gary McDowell proposed that conservative advocates of judicial restraint target federal court procedures instead. Writing in 1988, near the end of the Reagan administration, McDowell called upon Congress to erect "procedural fences" that would restrict standing, class action suits, intervention or joinder, declaratory relief, consent decrees, and equitable relief. He believed that through this self-styled "modest remedy" lay the most effective route to restricting judicial activism. Although a number of conservatives voiced agreement, congressional conservatives, generally more interested in overturning or blocking particular "liberal" substantive outcomes of judicial decisions than in the abstract principle of judicial activism, continued to emphasize an issue-by-issue approach, as they did on abortion, school prayer, and (during the Bush years) flag-burning.[20]

As the Reagan administration drew to a close, the conservative movement echoed as never before with the cries of the contending sides in the internal debates over constitutional jurisprudence and judicial activism. The new conservative judges themselves split, with quite a few taking positions more situational than any of the schools of thought proposed. Judicial restraint and a jurisprudence based upon original intent still retained the support of a majority in the conservative coalition, at least at the rhetorical level. Yet these principles were now facing strong conservative challenges for the first time.

### Judicial Conservative Rulings on Governance Issues

The Supreme Court, dominated by moderate-to-conservative justices throughout the 1981–93 period, was another potential source of influence, in addition to the Reagan administration, on conservative institutional prescriptions. However, it was much more detached from the conservative movement at large than the administration was, and its decisions often moved in unclear or even contradictory directions.

On the subject of federalism, the High Bench's record was decidedly mixed. But, of course, so was that of the Reagan administration and the conservative movement in general when it came to actual behavior. In *Garcia v. San Antonio Metropolitan Transit Authority* (1985), the Court overturned its states' rights decision handed down nine years previously in *National League of Cities v. Usery,* this time upholding the extension of the coverage of the national Fair Labor Standards Act to fourteen million state and local employees. In *Missouri v. Jenkins* (1990), it also took a procentralist position, holding that a federal judge could order a local legislative body to raise taxes to support a racially integrated magnet school. On the other hand, the Supreme Court appeared to shift in a states' rights direction (with the notable exception of the *Jenkins* case) after 1989, largely due to the influence of the Reagan appointees, although Associate Justice Scalia paid less deference to the states than the other Reagan-named justices did.[21]

On the matter of presidential powers, the Supreme Court in *Immigration and Naturalization Service v. Chadha* (1983) overturned the use of the legislative veto in an apparent victory for presidential power. However, the effects were far from clear-cut, liberals joined conservatives on the Court in the majority, and the legislative veto had been employed (and continued to be used) by both conservatives and liberals in Congress in attempts to achieve their power and policy ends. Again, in *Bowsher v. Synar* (1986), the High Bench took a pro-presidential position, agreeing with the solicitor general's argument that the Gramm-Rudman-Hollings Act unconstitutionally gave executive functions to agents of Congress. In both of these cases, the Supreme Court majority made separation-of-powers arguments that became quite common in conservative defenses of presidential powers during the period. However, the two liberal justices voted with the majority in each.Nonetheless, in *Morrison v. Olson* (1988), with only Scalia in dissent, the Supreme Court surprised and disappointed most pro-presidential government conservatives by upholding the independent counsel legislation which the Reagan administration had vigorously opposed.[22]

Overall, although the Supreme Court—and especially its most conservative members—tended toward pro-states' rights and pro-presidential power rulings during this period, the tendency was not a pronounced one. Moreover, the decisions on governance issues often found a blurring of liberal-conservative lines on the High Bench and rarely made the kinds of direct links to conservative ideology that the Reagan administration (or the Siegan-Epstein-Posner school) nearly always did.

### The Bush Administration
### and Conservative Institutional Prescriptions

The Bush administration broke no new ground on governance issues. In most respects, it sought to continue on the path charted by its predecessor, although it displayed somewhat less hostility to the administrative state and placed somewhat less stress than the Reagan administration on rhetoric extolling states' rights and original intent. In the conservative movement generally, however, there appeared to be heightened emphasis on decentralization to the states. And battles over presidential government, the administrative state, original intent, and judicial restraint continued.

According to Joel Aberbach, writing before the end of the Bush administration, "Bush has been careful to treat the role and mission of career civil servants with respect, he has appointed cabinet officials who are not hostile to the statutory goals of their agencies, and he has allowed these officials much greater leeway than his predecessor did in selecting their subordinates." Despite a better relationship with civil servants than Reagan had, Bush continued the privatization drive and was just as determined as his mentor to block revision of the Hatch Act to allow executive branch employees below the top levels to engage in previously proscribed political activities. When he vetoed the measure passed by Congress, however, Bush argued that he was seeking to protect civil servants against possible pressures from political supervisors. Most executive employees appeared to view the matter differently. Congressional conservatives provided enough support for Bush to sustain his veto, but much less than they had for President Ford in similar circumstances back in 1976. Then 80 percent of the conservatives in both chambers had opposed Hatch Act revision to permit employee political participation; this time only 40 percent of conservative representatives and 63 percent of conservative senators did so, probably reflecting a shift in conservatives' assessments of the career civil service.[23]

As for federalism, the Bush administration "left office without having articulated clearly the priority of federalism's principles in informing its proposals," according to Michael Pagano and Ann Bowman. There was no dramatic pledge of a New Federalism, such as Reagan had offered; but there were further efforts to reduce funding for categorical grants and a general, if vague, commitment to decentralization. On the subject of constitutional jurisprudence, no administration official assumed the proselytizing role that Meese had played. Overall, the tone of the Bush administration was generally more subdued and moderately conservative than that of the Reagan administration.[24]

Nonetheless, congressional conservatives showed a more marked proclivity than in the early Reagan years toward decentralist positions concerning federal relationships, at least in their roll-call voting patterns. Such positions were most evident, according to a thorough study by Michael Malaby and David Webber, on issues of allocative federalism concerning funding issues, and fairly evident on questions of federal authority. However, Malaby and Webber's findings also emphasized, as previous ones had, that federalism voting patterns in Congress were not unidimensional. In fact, factor analysis yielded four different dimensions on national-state matters in the 101st Congress, only two of which placed conservatives clearly at the decentralist end of the continuum.[25]

On presidential government, the intraconservative debates heated up as the end of the Cold War and the departure of the charismatic Reagan diminished the forces that had supported it most strongly in the conservative camp. Proponents of a strengthened presidency, especially among New Rightists and neoconservatives, became even more active than before in support of their own versions, with Terry Eastland presenting a New Right case in his *Energy in the Executive* in 1992 and L. Gordon Crovitz and Jeremy Rabkin bringing together a wide array of conservatives, heavily populated with neoconservatives but also including New Rightist Robert Bork and several neo-Straussian traditionalist conservatives, in their book *The Fettered Presidency,* in 1989. Meanwhile, the *Wall Street Journal*'s editorialists and numerous writers on the newspaper's editorial page escalated their already vocal campaign for a strengthened presidency. The Heritage Foundation meanwhile started a major fundraising drive to finance a campaign against what it termed "the imperial Congress." Heritage Foundation President Edwin Feulner, Heritage Foundation Research Director Burton Yale Pines, and New Rightist Paul Weyrich all prodded the Bush administration to take steps to enhance presidential powers. Although Bush himself challenged Congress periodically over the pocket veto, his refusal to be bound by language in committee reports or to execute portions of laws that he deemed unconstitutional, covert actions overseas, and several other matters, his actions were insufficiently bold to satisfy many of the conservative proponents of presidential government.[26]

At the same time, the conservative minority calling for a return to the old conservative doctrine of congressionally centered checks and balances voiced its dissent with increasing force, as Representative Mickey Edwards, former head of the American Conservative Union, assumed a leading advocacy role, supplemented by Forrest McDonald, Christopher Layne, Ted Galen Carpenter, Samuel Francis, David Brock, and Philip Kurland, among others. Columnist George Will weighed in with ambivalent recommendations that called for congressional term limits (likely to decrease congressional expertise and power vis-à-vis the executive) but at the same time enhanced roles for Congress as "deliberative" body in a revived "classical republicanism" of checks and balances. The *Wall Street Journal*, in particular, lashed back at conservative critics of presidential government, even questioning their motives. Despite the changeover in the presidency from Reagan to Bush and the demise of the Communist threat that had long buttressed the conservative presidential government model, most congressional conservatives, and probably most in the movement at large, remained allegiant to a strong presidency as the Reagan-Bush period drew to a close. Early indicators were that it was coming under increased challenge but still surviving during the Clinton administration.[27]

In the meantime, the struggles over original intent and judicial restraint continued. Christopher Wolfe emerged as another major defender of the originalist/interpretativist and judicial restraint positions, especially with his historical study of *The Rise of Modern Judicial Activism* and his multiple efforts to rebut his numerous critics in and out of the conservative movement. Despite strong challenge, the positions that Wolfe defended remained the dominant ones among conservatives, at least at the rhetorical level.[28]

## Conservative Consensus and Discord

A conservative governance theory enjoying fairly wide conservative movement support did emerge as dominant during the Reagan-Bush era. However, it was always subject to enough internal conservative challenges that it never quite became the conservative governance theory to the extent that such a theory had prevailed between the 1930s and the 1960s. The conservative coalition was now probably too complex and diverse for that past record to be duplicated. Moreover, several components of the dominant theory of the 1980s and 1990s failed to mesh well with one another and with some other aspects of conservative ideology. And two key underpinnings for conservative advocacy of presidential government—a presidency more conservative than Congress and a common conservative commitment to use presidential government to win the Cold War—had disappeared by 1993.

The most widely shared conservative institutional prescriptions of 1981–93 emphasized constitutional immutability, states' rights, a limited administrative state under presidential supervision, a three-pronged presidential government model, and judicial restraint. The most problematic component, and the one most likely to be altered significantly in the near future, was presidential government. However, constitutional immutability and judicial restraint were under challenge as never before, and conservative officeholders' behavior deviated frequently from the path of states' rights as well as from these two precepts.

Table 19.1 illustrates congressional voting patterns on some key aspects of institutional prescriptions, although quite a few components and modes of implementing them were never the subjects of roll-call votes and thus do not appear. The highest levels of conservative cohesion (over 90 percent) generally appeared on roll calls supportive of presidential diplomatic and war powers that also tapped anti-Communist sentiments, in particular the Boland amendment restricting executive assistance to the Nicaraguan contras fighting against what conservatives viewed as a "Communist" regime, and the Clark and Solarz amendments similarly restricting executive assistance to anti-Communist forces in Angola. Other presidential powers in different contexts also often drew strong conservative support, though it rarely reached these levels and occasionally fell below the 50 percent mark, as on the independent counsel legislation of 1987. As previously noted, federalism and judicial roll calls saw significant shifts in conservatives' institutional positions, depending on the nature of the policies at issue. Finally, on the administrative state roll calls concerning civil servants' political activities, conservative unity was

Table 19.1
Congressional Ideological Divisions on Key Governance Roll Calls, 1981–1993

| | Presidential-Congressional Issues | | | | |
|---|---|---|---|---|---|
| | | % Favoring Presidential Power | | | |
| Bill | Date/House | | Cons. | Lib. | Cons.-Lib. Gap |
| Military sales (Saudi Arabia) | 10/14/81 | H | 45% | 0% | 45% |
| Military sales (Saudi Arabia) | 10/28/81 | S | 77 | 10 | 67 |
| Boland amendment (Nicaragua) | 7/28/83 | H | 94 | 4 | 90 |
| Troop commitment (Lebanon) | 9/28/83 | H | 79 | 37 | 42 |
| Troop commitment (Lebanona) | 9/29/83 | S | 83 | 5 | 78 |
| Export authority | 10/27/83 | H | 77 | 10 | 67 |
| Export authority | 10/27/83 | H | 61 | 2 | 59 |
| Impoundment powers | 11/16/83 | S | 76 | 0 | 76 |
| Clark amendment (Angola) | 6/11/85 | S | 100 | 5 | 95 |
| Clark amendment (Angola) | 7/10/85 | H | 98 | 3 | 95 |
| Item veto (2-yr. trial) | 7/24/85 | S | 87 | 18 | 69 |
| Independent counsel | 10/21/87 | H | 42 | 0 | 42 |
| Independent counsel | 11/3/87 | S | 21 | 0 | 21 |
| Waive Budget Act/ Rescission | 11/9/89 | S | 76 | 4 | 72 |
| Solarz amendment (Angola) | 10/17/90 | H | 91 | 2 | 89 |
| Troop commitment (Persian Gulf) | 1/12/91 | S | 81 | 0 | 81 |
| Trade negotiation authority (Mexico) | 5/23/91 | H | 74 | 28 | 46 |

| | Federalism Issues | | | | |
|---|---|---|---|---|---|
| | | % for Decentralization | | | |
| Bill | Date/House | | Cons. | Lib. | Cons.-Lib. Gap |
| Legal Services block grant | 6/18/81 | H | 76 | 0 | 76 |
| Legal Services block grant | 6/25/81 | S | 60 | 0 | 60 |

Continued on next page

Table 19.1—*Continued*

## Federalism Issues—*Continued*

| Bill | Date/House | | % for Decentralization | | Cons.-Lib. Gap |
|------|------------|---|------|------|------|
| | | | Cons. | Lib. | |
| Budget reconciliation (incl. block grants) | 6/26/81 | H | 80 | 1 | 79 |
| Budget reconciliations (incl. block grants) | 6/28/81 | S | 100 | 25 | 75 |
| State vetoes of dump sites | 4/29/82 | S | 33 | 71 | -38 |
| State vetoes of dump sites | 11/29/82 | H | 24 | 94 | -70 |
| Truck width (state requirements) | 12/2/82 | S | 24 | 63 | -39 |

## Judicial Issues

| Bill | Date/House | | % Favoring Override/Curb of Supreme Court | | Cons.-Lib. Gap |
|------|------------|---|------|------|------|
| | | | Cons. | Lib. | |
| Antiabortion constitutional amendment | 6/28/83 | S | 76 | 5 | 71 |
| School prayer constitutional amendment | 3/20/84 | S | 83 | 12 | 71 |
| Curb federal court jurisdiction (school prayer) | 9/10/85 | S | 61 | 0 | 61 |
| Civil Rights Restoration Act | 3/22/88 | H | 39 | 100 | -61 |
| Civil Rights Restoration Act | 3/22/88 | S | 53 | 100 | -47 |
| Flag-burning constitutional amendment | 6/21/90 | H | 92 | 6 | 86 |
| Flag-burning constitutional amendment | 6/26/90 | S | 86 | 12 | 74 |
| Civil rights bill of 1990 | 10/17/90 | H | 27 | 98 | -71 |
| Civil rights bill of 1990 | 10/24/90 | S | 35 | 100 | -65 |

*Continued on next page*

Table 19.1—*Continued*

| | | Administrative-State Issues | | |
| | | % Favoring Restrictions on Political Activity | | |
| Bill | Date/House | Cons. | Lib. | Cons.-Lib. Gap |
| --- | --- | --- | --- | --- |
| Revise Hatch Act | 6/20/90  H | 40 | 2 | 38 |
| Revise Hatch Act | 6/21/90  S | 63 | 4 | 59 |

far less marked than on similar matters in the past and much less evident than contemporary liberal cohesiveness.

## Constitutional Immutability

The conservative emphasis on a jurisprudence of original intent continued to predominate during the 1981–93 period, at least in conservatives' verbal expressions on the subject. Attorney General Meese and a wide array of conservative intellectuals articulated this position repeatedly. However, it came under challenge from a significant conservative minority, mainly libertarian conservatives, including Bernard Siegan, Richard Epstein, and Stephen Macedo, who supplemented the Constitution with "natural law" and, in various ways, libertarian conservative moral philosophy. Even Robert Bork, who portrayed himself and was widely viewed as a defender of originalism in this period, had flirted with natural law as a basis for constitutional jurisprudence in the past and still displayed a proclivity to treat the Constitution more flexibly than the conservative mainstream. New Supreme Court Associate Justice Clarence Thomas, as well as several other Reagan-Bush appointees, showed signs of the influence of conservative natural law thinking toward the end of the period. Richard Posner's "law and economics" emphasis on economic efficiency as a basis for jurisprudence also gathered a significant cluster of conservative supporters.[29]

## States' Rights

No prominent conservatives verbally challenged the long-dominant conservative doctrine of decentralized federalism during the period, and Ronald Reagan rhetorically championed it to a greater extent than any president since 1933. Nevertheless, conservative officeholders' behavior, including that of members of Congress, Supreme Court justices, and

Reagan himself, displayed a mixed pattern that fell far short of the verbal commitments to states' rights. When decentralized federalism conflicted with other conservative values, conservative executives, legislators, and judges frequently sacrificed states' rights. Some conservatives in the judiciary departed from decentralized federal precepts even when other major conservative values were not clearly at issue, as in the *Garcia* and *Jenkins* decisions by the Supreme Court. Associate Justice Scalia of the Supreme Court, a firm conservative in most respects, displayed little interest in this point of the dominant conservative governance theory.

### A Limited Administrative State under Presidential Supervision

The new conservative elements grafted onto the long-term conservative prescription for a limited administrative state were a wider commitment than before by most conservatives (following the Reagan administration's lead) to presidential control and to a variety of specific "privatization" schemes concerning public administration. The conservative preference for cutting back on federal categorical grants in favor of reduced spending on broad block grants to the states and localities also became more closely tied to the ideas of attacking the administrative state than had previously been the case, again due in part to Reagan administration efforts. However, the Bush administration was less hostile to the career civil service bureaucracy than Reagan's was, and quite a few conservatives demurred on individual privatization and devolutionist proposals. Bush's efforts to continue restrictions on civil servants' political activities were successful, thanks to congressional conservative backing; but that support was far less widespread than in the past, indicating some possible softening of conservatives' hostile views of government "bureaucrats."

### Presidential Government

The conservative movement came to embrace presidential government more fully during the 1980s than it had ever done previously. However, the tribune role enjoyed significantly less conservative support than did roles as leader of defense and foreign policy, chief administrator, and remolder of the judicial/legal system. A few conservatives, mainly in the libertarian conservative camp, strongly resisted the general conservative shift toward presidential government that had begun under Nixon. With the retirement of Reagan and the dissipation of the Communist threat, the proportion of dissenters appeared to grow; and the election results of 1992, 1994, and 1996 seemed likely to spur further conservative questioning of their movement's commitment to presidential government. Since presidential government, especially its tribune role but also some major aspects of its expansive war powers, fitted poorly with constitutional interpretations based on original intent (despite various conservative efforts to make the latter mesh), there were also other reasons to question the durability of the conservative commitment to presidential government.

*Judicial Restraint*

Although this prescription continued to be offered regularly in the conservative camp, and a few conservative analyses of judicial behavior claimed to find evidence of increased adherence to it among conservative judges, most of its proponents continued to be disappointed by conservative judicial behavior. Most of them remained eager to find means of curbing judicial activism but continued to rely on unsuccessful issue-by-issue approaches involving constitutional amendments (very difficult in light of the required two-thirds majorities in both chambers of Congress and concurrence of three-fourths of the state legislatures) or limiting federal court jurisdiction (deemed too drastic by enough conservatives to block even a simple majority in Congress). Gary McDowell's advocacy of a new approach, tightening judicial procedural rules, won some conservative endorsement as a general curb on judicial activism; but few saw it as sufficient.[30]

In a significant new development, however, an important minority bloc of conservatives—mainly the same scholars and jurists who rejected constitutional interpretations based solely or primarily on original intent and strict construction of the Constitution—openly embraced judicial activism in a manner not previously seen. The pragmatic and aimless activism previously seen on the Burger Court continued to characterize some conservative judges, but now there was also a conservative "principled activism," as Stephen Macedo aptly termed it.[31]

## Conclusions

An overview of conservative institutional prescriptions from 1981 to 1993 shows the emergence of a dominant conservative governance theory with several significant new elements. However, conservative dissents to some of its components were vocal and influential. The presidential govenment model adopted by most conservatives provoked strong opposition from a mainly libertarian conservative minority, while the conservative movement was split almost evenly over the merits of a tribune role for the president. Developments in the 1990s appeared likely to lead to further internal dissension on presidential-congressional prescriptions. In the meantime, overt conflicts over judicial restraint and constitutional immutability and frequent behavioral deviance on these and on states' rights called these elements of the dominant conservative governance theory into question. That left a limited state with an increasingly privatized administration as probably the greatest point of conservative agreement. Yet even in administrative state matters, differing degrees of distrust of government bureaucracy and differences about the advisability and extent of presidential direction of the administrative state were sources of dissension. In sum, then, although the period was one in which some stability and consensus developed around a conservative theory of governance, that theory failed to evoke strong and universal conservative endorsement. Additional flux, much of it shaped by instrumental calculations concerning power and policy ends, appeared likely in the late 1990s.

## Notes

1.  Ronald Reagan, "Inaugural Address," reprinted in Gerald Pomper, ed, *The Election of 1980* (Chatham, NJ: Chatham House, 1981), 191.

2.  Carleson is quoted in *Congressional Quarterly Almanac*, 1981, 463. Timothy J. Conlan, *New Federalism* (Washington: Brookings Institution, 1988), 151, is the source of the quotation contrasting Reagan's goals with Nixon's; on the death of general revenue sharing, see Conlan, *New Federalism*, 161–162.

3.  The success/failure rate is discussed by Conlan, *New Federalism*, chap. 8. The 1987 successes are discussed by Joseph F. Zimmerman, "Federal Preemptions under Reagan's New Federalism," *Publius* 21 (Winter 1991): 10–11. On legal services, see *Congressional Quarterly Almanac*, 1981, 37–H, 38–H; and Larry Hunter, "U.S. Senate Votes in the 97th Congress on Federalist Issues," *Publius* 13 (Spring 1983): 123–128. On the "big swap," see Richard S. Williamson, "The 1982 Federalism Negotiations," *Publius* 13 (Spring 1983): 11–32; and Conlan, *New Federalism*, chap. 9.

4.  Zimmerman, "Federal Preemptions," 7; Timothy J. Conlan, "Federalism and Competing Values in the Reagan Administration," *Publius* 16 (Winter 1986): 42; Felicity Barringer, "U.S. Preemption: Muscling in on the States," *Washington Post*, 25 October 1982, sec. A, p. 11.

5.  John E. Haynes, "U.S. House Votes in the 97th Congress on Issues with Implications for Federalism," *Publius* 16 (Spring 1983): 107–121; Hunter, "Federalist Issues," 123–128. The numbers and percentages were calculated by the author,

defining conservatives as those having conservative coalition scores of 67 percent and above.

6.  Richard Viguerie, *The Establishment vs. the People* (Chicago: Regnery Gateway, 1983), 242; John Tower, "Congress versus the President: The Formulation and Implementation of American Foreign Policy," *Foreign Affairs* 60 (Winter 1981/82): 232; Irving Kristol and Michael Horowitz, "Commentary and Exchanges," in *The Fettered Presidency*, ed. L. Gordon Crovitz and Jeremy A. Rabkin (Washington: American Enterprise Institute, 1989), 316–317, 320, respectively; Theodore J. Lowi, *The Personal President* (Ithaca, NY: Cornell University Press, 1985); Samuel Kernell, *Going Public* (Washington: Congressional Quarterly, 1986).

7.  James Ceaser, "The Theory of Governance of the Reagan Administration," in *The Reagan Presidency and the Governing of America*, ed. Lester Salamon and Michael S. Lund (Washington: Urban Institute Press, 1985), 65. Harvey C. Mansfield Jr., "The American Election: Toward Constitutional Democracy," *Government and Opposition* 16 (1981): 3–18. Lowi, *Personal President*, 160.

8.  George W. Carey, "Thunder on the Right, Lightning from the Left," *Modern Age* 25 (Spring 1981): 132; Alan Crawford, *Thunder on the Right* (New York: Pantheon Books, 1980), 326–327; Robert Devigne, *Recasting Conservatism* (New Haven: Yale University Press, 1994), 56–58, 73–74.

9.  Libertarian conservative dissents may be seen in Crawford, *Thunder on the Right*; Mickey Edwards, "Of Conservatives and Kings," *Policy Review* 48 (Spring 1989): 24–31; Mickey Edwards, "A Conservative Defense of Congress," *Public Interest* 100 (Summer 1990): 81–88; Robert Higgs and Charlotte Twight, "National Emergency and the Erosion of Private Property Rights," *Cato Journal* 6 (Winter 1987): 747–773. For conservative defenses of Congress emphasizing its allegedly greater long–term conservatism, see Samuel Francis, "Imperial Conservatives?" *National Review* 68 (4 August 1989): 37–38; and David Brock, "Mr. Symms Goes to Jamba," *Policy Review* 59 (Winter 1992): 32–39. Conservative defenses of presidential primacy in national security and foreign affairs are very numerous. Good samplings are in L. Gordon Crovitz and Jeremy A. Rabkin, eds., *The Fettered Presidency* (Washington: American Enterprise Institute, 1989); and Gordon S. Jones and John A. Marini, eds., *The Imperial Congress* (New York: Pharos Books, 1988).

10.  Kurland's objections are noted by David M. O'Brien, "The Reagan Judges," in *The Reagan Legacy*, ed. Charles O. Jones (Chatham, NJ: Chatham House, 1988), 67; the final quotation is from O'Brien, "The Reagan Judges," 62; this full piece, 60–101, covers most other points well. See also Terry Eastland, *Energy in the Executive* (New York: Free Press, 1992), pt. 3, for a sympathetic conservative assessment of the Reagan administration's judicial/legal efforts.

11.  Sidney M. Milkis, *The President and the Parties* (New York: Oxford University Press, 1993), chap. 10; Peter M. Benda and Charles H. Levine, "Reagan and the Bureaucracy: The Bequest, the Promise, and the Legacy," in *The Reagan Legacy*, ed. Charles O. Jones (Chatham, NJ: Chatham House, 1988), 102–142; Christopher H. Foreman Jr., "Legislators, Regulations, and the OMB," in *Divided Democracy*, ed. James A. Thurber (Washington: Congressional Quarterly Press, 1991), 123–144; Nolan Clark, "The Headless Fourth Branch," in *Imperial Congress*, ed. Jones and Marini.

12. Stuart M. Butler, "Overview," in *Mandate for Leadership II,* by Butler, et al. (Washington: Heritage Foundation, 1985), 6–7, stresses privatized administration; *Congressional Quarterly Almanac,* 1990, 408–411, discusses efforts at Hatch Act revision; the quotation is from Benda and Levine, "Reagan and the Bureaucracy," 138.

13. Cited by Herman Schwartz, *Packing the Courts* (New York: Charles Scribner's Sons, 1988), 5.

14. Edwin Meese III, "Interpreting the Constitution," in *Interpreting the Constitution,* ed. Jack N. Rakove (Boston: Northeastern University Press, 1990), 17.

15. Lino Graglia, "Judicial Activism: Even on the Right, It's Wrong," *Public Interest* 95 (Spring 1989): 57–94; Robert H. Bork, *The Tempting of America* (New York: Free Press, 1990); Walter Berns, *Taking the Constitution Seriously* (New York: Simon & Schuster, 1987); Gary L. McDowell, *Curbing the Courts* (Baton Rouge: Louisiana State University Press, 1988); see also William A. Stanmeyer, "Judicial Supremacy," in *The New Right Papers,* ed. Robert W. Whitaker (New York: St. Martin's Press, 1982), 142–168.

16. Bernard H. Siegan, *Economic Liberties and the Constitution* (Chicago: University of Chicago Press, 1980); the quotation is from p. 7. For Siegan's rejection by the Senate Judiciary Committee, see the *New York Times,* 15 July 1988, sec. A, p. 12.

17. Richard A. Epstein, *Takings* (Cambridge: Harvard University Press, 1985). For the *Wall Street Journal's* endorsement of this approach, see "Economic Civil Rights," *Wall Street Journal,* 5 July 1985, 6; and Herman Schwartz, *Packing the Courts* (New York: Charles Scribner's Sons, 1988), 40; the impact on Posner, Rehnquist, Scalia, and O'Connor is assessed by Bernard Schwartz, *The New Right and the Constitution* (Boston: Northeastern University Press, 1990), 131–135. Also see Richard A. Posner, *Economic Analysis of the Law,* 3d ed. (Boston: Little, Brown, 1986).

18. Bork, *The Tempting of America* (New York: Free Press, 1990), 223, 230; Graglia, "Judicial Activism," 67.

19. Stephen Macedo, *The New Right v. the Constitution* (Washington: Cato Institute, 1987), 23, 3, 4, 5.

20. McDowell, *Curbing the Courts,* esp. 1–12, 168–205. See table 19.1 for major congressional court-curbing roll-call votes of the period.

21. David B. Walker, "American Federalism from Johnson to Bush," *Publius* 21 (Winter 1991): esp. 115–117; *Garcia v. San Antonio Metropolitan Transit Authority,* 105 S. Ct. 1105 (1985); *Missouri v. Jenkins* 109 S. Ct. 1150 (1990).

22. *INS v. Chadha* 103 S. Ct. 2764 (1983); *Bowsher v. Synar* 106 S.Ct. 3181 (1986); *Morrison v. Olson* 487 U.S. 654 (1988). See the discussions in Louis Fisher, *Constitutional Conflicts between Congress and the President* (Princeton, NJ: Princeton University Press, 1985), 178–183; and Eastland, *Energy,* 75, 80, 87, 93, 177, 270.

23. Joel D. Aberbach, "The President and the Executive Branch," in *The Bush Presidency: First Appraisals,* ed. Colin Campbell and Bert A. Rockman (Chatham, NJ: Chatham House, 1991), 223; Walker, "American Federalism," 114; *Congressional Quarterly Almanac,* 1990, 408–411.

24. Michael A. Pagano and Ann O'M. Bowman, "The State of American Federalism, 1992–1993," *Publius* 23 (Summer 1993): 1.

25. Michael R. Malaby and David J. Webber, "Federalism in the 101st Congress," *Publius* 21 (Summer 1991): 77–92.

26. Eastland, *Energy*; Crovitz and Rabkin, *The Fettered Presidency*; examples of *Wall Street Journal* editorials include "Real Reform for Congress," 5 June 1989, sec. A, p. 14; "Taking Stock of the Presidency," 8 August 1989, sec. A, p. 10; "Budget Therapy," 20 October 1989, sec. A, p. 14; "Terms of Limitation," 11 December 1989, sec. A, p. 14. On Bush administration efforts, see Gerald F. Seib, "Is the President's Authority Being Nibbled Away?" *Wall Street Journal,* 11 September 1989, sec. A, pp. 1, 12; Gerald F. Seib, "Bush Vows to Protect Authority, Yet Brings Congress into Decisions," *Wall Street Journal,* 12 September 1989, sec. A, pp. 1, 12; *Congressional Quarterly Weekly Report*, 3 February 1990, 291–295.

27. Mickey Edwards, "A Conservative Defense of Congress," *Public Interest* 100 (Summer 1990): 81–88; Mickey Edwards, "Of Conservatives and Kings," *Policy Review* 48 (Spring 1989): 24–31; Forrest McDonald, foreword to *The Constitution and the American Presidency,* ed. Martin L. Fausold and Alan Shank (Albany: State University of New York Press, 1991), ix–xi; "Gulf 'Victory' Could Lead to Entanglement, Study Says," *Cato Policy Report* 13 (January/February 1991): 10–11; Samuel Francis, "Imperial Conservatives?" *National Review* (4 August 1989): 37–38; Brock, "Mr. Symms Goes to Jamba," 32–39; Philip B. Kurland, "More Power for the President?" *New York Times Book Review,* 6 September 1992, 25; George F. Will, *Restoration* (New York: Free Press, 1992); "Mickey's Enchanted Kingdom," *Wall Street Journal,* 21 November 1989, sec. A, p. 18.

28. Christopher Wolfe, *The Rise of Modern Judicial Review,* rev. ed. (Lanham, MD: Rowman & Littlefield, 1994), and Christopher Wolfe, *Judicial Activism* (Pacific Grove, CA: Brooks-Cole, 1991).

29. See the discussion of Thomas in Sotirios A. Barber, *The Constitution of Judicial Power* (Baltimore: Johns Hopkins University Press, 1993), 239. Mark Kelman, "A Critique of Conservative Legal Thought," in *The Politics of Law,* ed. David Kairys, rev. ed. (New York: Pantheon Books, 1990), 436–452, especially emphasizes Posner's contributions.

30. Craig Stern, "Judging the Judges: The First Two Years of the Reagan Bench," *Benchmark* 1 (July–October 1984), cited by Eastland, *Energy,* 274, claimed that Reagan's appointees adhered fairly regularly to judicial restraint, but the study covered a short period, and its measures of restraint are subject to debate.

31. Macedo, *New Right,* 5.

# 20

# Liberal Institutional Prescriptions

Lacking the focal point that Ronald Reagan and his administration provided for conservatism in the 1980s, the liberal coalition—fragmented along various lines and tugged toward the center of the political spectrum by successive presidential election defeats and by the neoliberal and New Democrat movements—drifted uncertainly between 1981 and 1993 toward prescribing congressionally centered checks and balances while tending toward centrist positions on the other major institutional prescriptions. Even on the cluster of presidential-congressional dimensions, the continuing pockets of liberal advocacy for presidential power or responsible party government throughout the period and the accession of Bill Clinton to the White House in January 1993 and of the Republicans to congressional control in January 1995 suggested the likely impermanence of liberal attachments to procongressional recommendations. On the other hand, the liberal search for credible middle-of-the-road positions on the administrative state, federalism, judicial review, and the interpretation of the Constitution showed signs of some durability, though each aroused liberal opposition in certain quarters. No really clear liberal theory of governance emerged to replace that which had badly eroded since the 1960s.

## Reactions to the Conservative Administrations and the Supreme Court

The fairly decisive liberal shifts toward advocacy of congressionally centered checks and balances and rejection of the "imperial presidency" had begun in the mid-1960s but had stalled and were partially reversed in the late 1970s. The initiatives of the Reagan administration, and to some extent the Bush administration, reactivated the liberal trend of the Nixon-

Ford years. As table 19.1 indicated, large liberal majorities in Congress (usually over 90 percent) favored congressional restrictions on presidential discretion over foreign military sales, covert activities as in Angola and Nicaragua, troop commitments overseas, and export regulations. Moreover, they favored continuing tight restrictions on presidential impoundment of funds and rescission authority and maintenance of the independent counsel provisions of the 1970s to curb executive-branch abuses. Even on issues of joint troop commitments with allies in Lebanon, free-trade negotiations with Mexico, and a trial item veto for the president, on which substantial minorities of congressional liberals took pro-presidential positions, liberals were far more inclined than conservatives to insist upon checking presidential discretion. Beyond roll-call voting, congressional liberals also used their bases of power in congressional committees and subcommittees to hold hearings, launch investigations, add restrictive riders to legislation, and in various other ways impose curbs on presidential power. Even after the *Immigration and Naturalization Service v. Chadha* (1983) decision overruled legislative vetoes, congressional liberals still employed them, and sometimes the presidents acquiesced, as Bush did, for example, in accepting an "informal" legislative veto on the Nicaraguan aid matter in 1989. One analyst counted over one hundred uses of the legislative veto following the Supreme Court decision that had supposedly terminated its employment.[1]

Outside of Congress, many liberal intellectuals wrote in support of a model of congressionally centered checks and balances. Liberal columnist Anthony Lewis and independent scholars of generally liberal bent Theodore Lowi and Louis Fisher were among those making the case most fully and consistently—Lewis, in his regular syndicated columns on a variety of subjects; Lowi, particularly in his 1985 book, *The Personal President*, and in his calls for "radical constitutionalism"; Fisher, in several books and articles during the period that mainly continued themes that he had developed in the 1970s. Many of the arguments, especially those of Lowi, were strikingly reminiscent of the justifications employed by conservatives in a previous era on behalf of congressionally centered checks and balances, including the need for deliberation, not a "plebiscitary" presidency, and even appeals on occasion to original intent. Lowi, for example, insisted that "consideration of original intent reveals a theory of government in which the place of the presidency is profoundly at odds with that of today." Unlike the conservatives of the past, however, these authors accepted an expansive government/executive regulatory social welfare state—what Lowi termed "the irreversible reality of big government and a big president."[2]

Some liberals made a particular effort to advance a theoretical model in support of enhanced congressional influence over the administrative state as an antidote to the Reagan "administrative presidency" embraced by most conservatives. Of these, the piece by scholars William F. West and Joseph Cooper was among the most convincingly presented. West and Cooper, writing in 1989, called for increased congressional oversight of administration, stressing the representational diversity that the legislative body introduced and challenging the type of "ad hoc political coordination" that had emanated from the Office of Management and Budget of the Reagan administration. While conceding that presidential administrative leadership was more likely than active congressional oversight to promote executive efficiency, West and Cooper stressed that the "goal of efficiency is necessarily subordinate to constitutional democratic goals." Certainly, congressional liberal efforts to oppose an item veto or expanded rescission powers for the president, together with liberals' reliance on legislative veto provisions and riders attached to omnibus appropriations measures and periodic investigations, indicated a fairly wide liberal eagerness to orient the administrative bureaucracy toward increased accountability to Congress (or at least to certain portions of Congress).[3]

Many liberal intellectuals and politicians centered most of their presidency-curbing efforts on the expansive roles of commander-in-chief and chief diplomat rather than on domestic dimensions of presidential power. Lowi, in fact, chided liberal advocates of what he termed the "Domestic Necessity Model" of presidential power, including Arthur Schlesinger Jr., James MacGregor Burns, and Richard Neustadt. These liberals favored imposing additional congressional checks on external presidential powers, especially war powers, but warned against crippling the presidency's domestic leadership capacities. Schlesinger's 1987 *New Republic* article on "The Imperial Temptation" typified this perspective. Reviewing the Reagan administration's efforts, Schlesinger declared: "The imperial presidency in the United States has staged a comeback some 13 years after the fall of Richard Nixon. The congressional reclamation of power after Watergate turned out to be largely make-believe. The War Powers Resolution had no effect in restraining presidents from sending troops into combat, whether in Lebanon or Grenada or Libya. Reagan re-established the executive secrecy system. He brought the CIA back. . . ." According to Schlesinger, "The imperial temptation is the consequence of a global and messianic foreign policy," which he and most 1980s liberals opposed. However, at the same time Schlesinger saw the need for presidential "energy" (quoting Alexander Hamilton) and proclaimed: "The executive branch must take the initiative if the system is to move."[4]

Reflecting a similar bifurcated view, Senator Edward Kennedy favored curbs on presidential war-making and other foreign initiatives but saw the presidency as more capable than Congress of providing needed domestic leadership. Kennedy also stressed that "Congress has too much power over the purse and the President has too little." He therefore endorsed Reagan's request for a line-item veto for the president, breaking with most liberals on this issue. Lining up in solid opposition to giving the president (at least Reagan or Bush) the line-item veto were most of the major liberal interest groups, including the AFL-CIO, the National Education Association, the National Farmers Union, the Americans for Democratic Action, the National Association for the Advancement of Colored People, Common Cause, and the Consumer Union of America, as well as most congressional liberals.[5]

In contrast to the congressionally centered model of Lowi and the dualistic model of Schlesinger, a few liberals continued to support a fairly general presidential dominance model similar to that of the New Deal and post-New Deal years. Representative Les Aspin of Wisconsin, chair of the House Armed Services Committee, stated that "Congress as an institution is conservative, cautious, and reluctant to initiate change. . . . When it opposes the executive, it is usually to protect some interest group or some aspect of the status quo." Stuart Eizenstat, who had been Jimmy Carter's chief domestic policy adviser, argued in 1989 that "institutionally, the office of the president must be strengthened." Another former Carter administration official, Lloyd Cutler, called for movement toward a parliamentary system but primarily as a means of strengthening presidential leadership. Although the majority of the liberals of the 1981–83 period moved in the direction of advocacy of congressionally centered checks and balances, a large minority clustered around a bifurcated domestic necessity model; and even the old full-scale presidential government of the liberal past had its advocates. Moreover, the depth of the liberals' intellectual commitment to a congressionally oriented model was questionable.[6]

The growing conservatism of the Supreme Court and the federal judiciary during the 1981–93 years also aroused considerable liberal reaction. Writing about the High Bench in 1988, analyst William Lasser noted that "vociferous critics of the Court can now be found on both sides of the political spectrum. Frequently, the Court finds itself under fire from liberals and conservatives simultaneously, often on the same issue." However, liberal coalition opposition to the judiciary did not take the court-curbing forms that conservative attacks often did. Partly due to the fact that the Supreme Court decisions which most upset liberals were in the civil rights domain and involved statutory interpretations, the liberal coalition focused most of its efforts on obtaining "corrective" legislation from Congress, as on both the *Grove City College* and affirmative action decisions, where unanimous or nearly unanimous liberal coalitions in Congress picked up sufficient moderate and conservative support to reverse (at least partially) the effects of conservative Supreme Court rulings.[7]

On the matter of constitutional interpretation, the prominent advocacy by Attorney General Meese and others of a "jurisprudence of original intention" evoked negative liberal reactions that were sharply worded and virtually unanimous. A rebuttal from liberal Associate Justice William Brennan gained particularly wide publicity and liberal applause. Without responding to Meese by name, Brennan dismissed his jurisprudence as both impractical and inadequate. According to Brennan,

> The Constitution embodies the aspiration to social justice, brotherhood and dignity that brought this nation into being. The Declaration of Independence, the Constitution and the Bill of Rights solemnly committed the United States to be a country where the dignity and rights of all persons were equal before all authority. . . . Our amended Constitution is the lodestar for our aspirations. Like every text worth reading, it is not crystalline.[8]

As for the position advocating strict adherence to original intention, Brennan declared critically:

> It is a view that feigns self-effacing deference to the specific judgments of those who forged an original social compact. But in truth it is little more than arrogance cloaked as humility. It is arrogant to pretend that from our vantage we can gauge accurately the intent of the Framers on application of principle to specific, contemporary questions. . . . [O]ur distance of two centuries cannot but work as a prism refracting all we perceive.[9]

Brennan also proudly made the case for liberal judicial activism against conservative critics of it. He attacked the majoritarianism that underlay most of the conservative advocacy of judicial restraint:

> It is the very purpose of a Constitution—and particularly of the Bill of Rights—to declare certain values transcendant, beyond the reach of temporary political majorities. The majoritarian process cannot be expected to rectify claims of minority right that arise as a response to the outcomes of that very majoritarian process.[10]

In offering a spirited defense of liberal conceptions of both constitutional flexibility grounded in a broadly egalitarian moral philosophy and liberal judicial activism devoted to protection of minority rights within that same context, Brennan's views probably came close to expressing the essence of the dominant liberal consensus in these two realms of institutional prescription. His words echoed those of the *Carolene Products* footnote of 1938 that had for years buttressed liberal judicial activism. Certainly, too, the ideas developed by legal scholars Ronald Dworkin, John Hart Ely, Arthur Miller, Laurence Tribe, and Michael Perry, and the views expressed by such prominent liberal intellectuals as columnist Anthony Lewis and historians Arthur Schlesinger Jr. and Gordon Wood, meshed well with Brennan's.[11]

To the left of the liberal mainstream, but largely outside the liberal movement and identified with neo-Marxist ideas, grew up the critical legal studies movement. Identified with Mark Kelman, Duncan Kennedy, Mark Tushnet, and others, this movement scorned the widespread liberal quest for "principled" legal decisionmaking. Within the liberal mainstream, however, a few legal scholars, notably political scientist Sotirios Barber, staked out positions more centrist than Brennan's on matters of constitutional jurisprudence and exercised some moderating influence. Barber attacked the legal realism that underlay much of the modern liberal conceptualizing on the subject for going "too far" in downplaying the possibility of "an independent constitutional meaning." Calling for a return to what he viewed as the "classical theory" of constitutional interpretation embodied in *The Federalist* and John Marshall's Supreme Court opinions from the late eighteenth and early nineteenth centuries, Barber nonetheless took positions far from the originalism of Meese and most conservatives. In his view, "by the intentions of the framers, we are entitled to mean not their mere immediate wants and aversions but the general purposes that we believe made up what they believed would be a good and just society." As for judicial activism, moreover, Barber came down firmly in support of it and against those cautioning self-restraint by judges, concluding: "No real constitutional defense seems available for judicial self-restraint."[12]

At the same time, some liberals, especially in the neoliberal camp, broke with the liberal mainstream on judicial activism rather than on constitutional flexibility. Robert Kaus, for example, deplored an overly large role for "unelected judges" and accused liberal proponents of judicial activism of "having contempt for the democratic process." This line of thinking, of course, had strong roots in the previous views expressed by such figures as Felix Frankfurter in the New Deal and post-New Deal periods, though it now appeared most typical of the neoliberals.[13]

## Neoliberal and New Democrat Contributions

Many of the revisions in liberal institutional prescriptions of the 1981–93 period stemmed primarily or in part from the neoliberal and New Democrat movements, both of which stressed generally "centrist" recommendations. The impact of these was most evident concerning judicial activism, the administrative state, and federalism.

Neoliberalism, spawned by intellectuals associated with the *Washington Monthly* and taken up by a number of political leaders (including presidential candidates Gary Hart and Paul Tsongas), was most distinctive in its institutional prescriptions from the rest of the liberal coalition in its critiques of new-politics liberal reliance on the courts and judicialized administration. While it shared new-politics liberal suspicions of large bureaucracies, both government and business corporate, its adherents were more inclined to support privatization and decentralization as desirable alternatives than were most other liberals. Emphasizing a preference for "democratic" responsiveness, Robert Kaus, for example, complained that "liberals, on the questions of broad social policy, have become addicted to using the courts to accomplish their ends." Declared Kaus: "I think that the basic divide between the liberal and neoliberal positions is over whether you think litigation is a good way of resolving disputes, a good way of settling broad questions of social policy." Among neoliberals, the general consensus was that it was not.[14]

Moreover, most neoliberals were critical of long-term civil servants, perceiving the need for "risk-taking" in administration that such officials allegedly avoided. Charles Peters, widely recognized as the founding father of the movement, even called for half of the executive bureaucracy to be appointed for a term of office of not more than five years. Although much of the rest of the liberal movement now also questioned the traditional New Deal liberal support for hierarchical public administration, it was not generally on the entrepreneurial, risk-taking grounds stressed by Peters and other neoliberals.[15]

Later in the period, New Democrats (or neoprogressives, in David Osborne's preferred term) were to make "reinventing government" with an "entrepreneurial" emphasis central to their program. David Osborne and Ted Gaebler, authors of *Reinventing Government* in 1992, were among the most influential spokespersons for the reinvention approach to public administration. A few government services, such as social security, they believed, could be delivered effectively by a traditional, hierarchical administrative state apparatus. "But most government institutions perform increasingly complex tasks, in competitive, rapidly changing environments, with customers who want quality and choice." Under these conditions, the proper approach to public administration was, in their view, one of entrepreneurial government, promoting competition, empowering citizens by "pushing control into the community," focusing on outcomes, redefining clients as customers and offering them choices, and being driven by missions (not bureaucratic rules and regulations). "Participatory management" should replace the hierarchies of the past. The old liberal-conservative debate over more versus less government should be discarded in favor of a focus on "better governance." "We do not need another New Deal nor a Reagan Revolution. We need an American *perestroika*," proclaimed Osborne and Gaebler. Bill Clinton, governor of Arkansas, soon picked up this theme in his ultimately victorious presidential election campaign and as president assigned the responsibility for overseeing the reinvention to Vice President Gore.[16]

The common meeting ground for most neoliberals and the New Democrats, who increasingly merged with them and displaced them as the years progressed, lay not only in their "entrepreneurial-competitive" administrative preferences but also in a proclivity to embrace a fairly decentralized federalism. Governor Bruce Babbitt of Arizona, identified with both the neoliberal and the New Democrat movements, highlighted this approach as early as 1981, in a *New Republic* article seeking to win liberal support for the cause of states' rights. A number of neoliberals added their voices, and New Democrats later made the revitalization of the states an important part of their governance approach. Again, Osborne was in the forefront, publishing *Laboratories of Democracy* in 1990 about creative state governments and then expanding on the decentralist theme in *Reinventing Government* two years later.[17]

Alice Rivlin, long the head of the Congressional Budget Office and later to direct the Office of Management and Budget in the Clinton administration and serve on the Federal Reserve Board of Governors, added major contributions with her *Reviving the American Dream* in 1992. Joining many conservatives in seeking to resuscitate the "dual federalism" of the past, in which the powers of the federal government and those of the state governments were treated as separate and distinct, she advocated placing the states in charge of what she termed "the productivity agenda" while eliminating most national government programs in education, housing, highways, social services, economic development, and job training. In her prescription, the national and state governments would share common taxes according to a formula, and the national government would provide national health insurance and finance it for all. While Osborne and Gaebler's approaches differed somewhat from hers, there were broad similarities. Rejecting states' rights rhetoric and emphasizing the need for major national government domestic policy roles in setting broad standards, raising revenues, and providing certain services, the New Democrats hoped to transcend old liberal-conservative divisions pitting centralized federalism against states' rights. Only time would tell how successful they would be.[18]

Some mainstream and left-liberals also moved to embrace a more decentralized federalism than most liberals had previously favored. In a number of states, including New York, California, and Hawaii, judicial activist liberals took the lead in handing down interpretations of state constitutions that expanded "rights" well beyond what increasingly conservative federal judges found in the U.S. Constitution. Francis Flaherty, writing in the *Progressive* in 1982, noted this growing pattern and proclaimed that "states' rights are our rights, too." In New York, for example, state courts held that article 17 of the state constitution mandated extensive social services to the poor in light of language to the effect that the "aid, care and support of the needy are public concerns and shall be provided by the state." Furthermore, new-politics liberals and their heirs sometimes succeeded in pushing state liberal initiatives further than was possible in the national political arena, most often in the environmental protection realm but sometimes in domains like health care as well.[19]

However, there remained considerable liberal attachment to the prescriptions for centralized federalism or just plain centralism. Michael Kinsley of the *New Republic* even called for abolition of federalism in favor of a unitary approach, following a long line of liberal thinkers extending back at least to the *New Republic* editors of the New Deal period. Characterizing the state governments as "independent duchies, free to join with or join battle with all the other special interests," Kinsley urged extensive centralization in the pursuit of uniformity, fairness, and efficiency and to "assure that society as a whole makes rational, democratic decisions about issues that affect society as a whole." Most liberals did not go so far as Kinsley. Yet the majority of those who addressed the matter explicitly still inclined more toward centralized federalism than toward states' rights. Sar Levitan probably spoke for most: "We live in one nation. In an era when so many of our economic and social problems take on global proportions, a return to an outmoded concept of states' rights may not be in our collective best interests." Henry Steele Commager added his assessment of the historical record and concluded: "From the beginning, it has not been the states that have been the chief instruments of democracy but the central government in Washington." Whether the issue was one of positive freedom for the ex-slaves, for women, or for laborers, or one of promotion of equal educational opportunity or protection of the environment, Commager found the national government's record far superior to that of the states. Former Americans for Democratic Action head Samuel Beer, Vernon Jordan of the Urban League, and the editors of the *Nation* were among other liberal voices that concurred.[20]

## Liberal Consensus and Discord

Led particularly by neoliberals and New Democrats but joined by a number of others, the liberal coalition moved hesitantly toward centrist positions on the administrative state, federalism, and (to a lesser degree) judicial review continuums. Somewhat independently, and without clear backing from any organized groups, there were also liberal efforts from scholars such as Sotirios Barber and John Hart Ely, in particular, to find a centrist position on constitutional interpretation. Liberals tended more than previously to take strong antipresidential power positions, especially concerning war powers, in contrast to their views on other continuums, where centrism proved attractive.

Much of the inconsistency seen in the previous period on federalism issues in Congress appeared again among liberals (and conservatives) on roll calls in the 1981–93 years (see table 19.1). Without question, the substantive policy issues at stake shaped the observed behavior more than did the principles concerning federalism. On the principles themselves, however, a major gap opened between neoliberal and New Democratic advocates of enhanced state powers and many liberals' continuing belief in centralized federalism. Regarding the judiciary, liberals proved themselves eager to reverse major Supreme Court decisions with which they disagreed, though they refrained from the jurisdiction-tampering efforts undertaken repeatedly by conservatives—perhaps out of principle, perhaps because they did not need to employ them or did not wish to appear hypocritical in light of their past harsh criticisms of such conservative endeavors. For the most part, liberals' votes were to uphold Supreme Court decisions against conservative attacks and to defend the federal courts' jurisdiction from court-curbing attempts. On presidential power questions, whether the matter was one of war powers, diplomacy, budgetary processes, or control of the executive branch, most liberals voted on a regular basis for restrictive positions. In relation to public administration, the congressional liberals almost unanimously favored Hatch Act revision to permit civil servants to engage more extensively than in the past in political activities, despite the declared opposition of Common Cause to the measure on grounds that it might lead to political abuses.[21]

Although no clear liberal theory of governance came to predominate, a consensus pattern prevailed among liberals on four of the five continuums or sets of continuums. Yet the range of liberal positions on most dimensions was wider than previously, and the integration of the positions fell short of establishing a theory enjoying strong and enthusiastic support. To summarize, the patterns were as follows:

## A Flexible Constitution

Although liberals remained more inclined to conceptualize the Constitution as "living" and adaptable than conservatives did, increased overlap developed between the two major ideological movements on this continuum, mainly because of conservative shifts toward supplementing original intent and strict construction with moral philosophy, but partly as the result of liberal moves away from legal realism. In the latter respect, Sotirios Barber made the most direct challenge to the realist tradition, but an array of liberal legal scholars had been laboring for a generation to ground constitutional jurisprudence in moral philosophy and/or procedural considerations rather than judges' personal values. The philosophical and/or procedural conceptions of the liberals, however, were generally quite incongruent with those of conservatives, making a genuine synthesis unlikely in the center of this continuum. While centrist conservatives drew upon market-oriented, private-property-emphasizing philosophies, centrist liberals stressed preferred freedoms and/or built on broadly egalitarian foundations.

## Federalism

In this sphere, many liberals, led by an overlapping group of New Democrats and neoliberals, became considerably more enthusiastic about the states and even the old conservative doctrine of "dual federalism" than had been the case at any time since the New Deal. However, such serious fragmentation characterized the liberal coalition on this set of issues that it constituted the one continuum on which a consensus liberal position was impossible to discern. Most congressional liberals shifted back and forth with abandon, depending on the particular policy issues at hand. Liberal intellectuals staked out philosophical positions ranging from the extreme centralism of Michael Kinsley to the highly decentralized prescriptions of Alice Rivlin, David Osborne, and Ted Gaebler. To a greater extent than on constitutional jurisprudence, liberal and conservative recommendations really overlapped, making synthesis a realistic possibility.

## An Administrative State

Neoliberals and New Democrats challenged both the "judicialized" administrative state of the new-politics liberals (which many of the latter continued to seek to implement) and the hierarchical New Deal liberal administrative state (which continued to enjoy some liberal support). In addition, an increasing number of liberals from all camps found more merit than in the past in congressional efforts to make bureaus accountable to Congress or congressional committees or subcommittees, but some remained oriented toward an administrative state under presidential control. Despite marked liberal fragmentation on these important matters, liberals—even New Democrats and neoliberals—usually viewed themselves and were seen by others as more sympathetic to civil servants and the idea of an administrative state than were most conservatives. Nevertheless, here, too, as on federalism, a centrist synthesis of neoliberal/New Democrat and conservative prescriptions appeared to be a distinct possibility in the future, for the liberal-conservative gap had narrowed appreciably.

## Presidential-Congressional Relations

On this continuum, three distinct liberal clusters were in evidence. The largest one, but one lacking great intellectual depth and links to other aspects of liberal ideology that would stabilize its support over time, called for a general model based on congressionally centered checks and balances. A second one, smaller than the first but including many liberal intellectuals, prescribed new or at least continued checks on presidential foreign policy and war powers but favored enhanced presidential leadership capacities domestically. Finally, a few liberals favored presidential government, either through outright presidential dominance (as Eizenstat did and Aspin appeared to do) or through the vehicle of parliamentary or responsible-party government (as Cutler proposed). Congressional liberals voted quite consistently to restrict presidential powers and enhance those of Congress, giving an extra edge to the first of these three sets of liberal prescriptions on presidential-congressional relations.

*Judicial Activism*

Although some liberals, such as Arthur Miller, called for still further judicial activism, most liberals of the period did not. The emergence of neoliberalism, with its usual coolness toward litigation in general and the increased involvement of judges in economic regulatory processes in particular, had the effect of weakening the overall liberal push for enhanced judicial roles. Some neoliberals, such as Robert Kaus, were critical of judicial activism even in its pre-new-politics liberal form, stressing "democratic" arguments that federal judges were "unelected." Growing conservatism in the federal judiciary and rising support among conservatives for their own forms of judicial activism may also have operated to cool liberal ardor for judicial activism. On this continuum, as on that concerning constitutional jurisprudence, the overlap between liberals and conservatives increased. However, the purposes guiding their respective activisms were so different that the likelihood of a synthesis was remote.

## Conclusions

On federalism and administrative state issues, the prescriptions of liberals, especially those of a neoliberal or New Democratic bent, increasingly meshed with those of many conservatives, although quite a few prominent liberals remained philosophically wedded to centralized federalism. A movement toward centrist positions was also evident among liberals on matters of constitutional interpretation and judicial behavior. On these latter two continuums, however, the common ground with conservatives was shaky at best. Though there was overlap between liberal and conservative judicial activists and room for agreement in overruling lawmaking majorities on the basis of some shared libertarian understandings of freedom of expression, the general policy thrusts of the two judicial activisms were dramatically different. Furthermore, the preferred moral philosophies of the liberal fusers of constitutional text, original intention, and moral philosophy were quite distinct in most instances from those of conservatives pursuing fusion of text, original intention, and philosophy. A wide gap yawned between the liberal natural law of Dworkin and Rawls and the conservative natural law of Epstein and Nozick—a gap not easily bridged. Meanwhile, on presidential-congressional relations, the differences between the liberal and conservative positions became wider than they had been in the 1970s.

As in earlier periods, the new institutional recommendations that emerged from both the liberal and conservative camps reflected ideological innovations concerning values and policy preferences as well as changes in the institutional power centers where each coalition had its major bases. The following chapter will take up the influences of the past and the instrumental calculations made by conservatives and liberals in the 1981–93 years before briefly raising questions concerning the potential impact of their institutional prescriptions on the future of the American political system.

## Notes

1.  Louis Fisher, "Micromanagement by Congress: Reality and Mythology," in *The Fettered Presidency,* ed. L. Gordon Crovitz and Jeremy A. Rabkin (Washington: American Enterprise Institute, 1989), 139–157; James P. Pfiffner, "Divided Government and the Problem of Governance," in *Divided Democracy,* ed. James A. Thurber (Washington: Congressional Quarterly Press, 1991), 56, 60, discusses the "informal" legislative veto of 1989.

2.  For samples of Lewis's prescriptions, see "Constitutional Issues Central to Iran-Contra Affair," *St. Petersburg Times,* 14 March 1990, sec. A, p. 16; "War in the Gulf?" *New York Times,* 22 October 1990, sec. A, p. 15; "The President's Power in War Has Become Too Great," *St. Petersburg Times,* 14 January 1992; "George Milhouse Bush," *New York Times*, 28 December 1992, A11; "Two Cents Plain," *New York Times*, 11 January 1993, sec. A, p. 15. Theodore J. Lowi, *The Personal President* (Ithaca, NY: Cornell University Press, 1985); and Theodore J. Lowi, "Presidential Power and the Ideological Struggle over Its Interpretation," in *The Constitution and the American Presidency,* ed. Martin L. Fausold and Alan Shank (Albany: State University of New York Press, 1991), 227–244. Louis Fisher, *Constitutional Conflicts between Congress and the President* (Princeton: Princeton University Press, 1985); and Fisher, "Micromanagement by Congress." The quotations are from Lowi, *The Personal President,* 34, and Lowi, "Presidential Power," 240.

3.  William F. West and Joseph Cooper, "Legislative Influence v. Presidential Dominance: Competing Models of Bureaucratic Control," *Political Science Quarterly* 104 (Winter 1989/90): 581–606. The quotation is from p. 600.

4.  Lowi, "Presidential Power," 233–234; Arthur Schlesinger Jr., "The Imperial Temptation," *New Republic* 196 (16 March 1987): 17–18.

5.  Edward M. Kennedy, "Line–Item Veto: Out of the Shambles," *Los Angeles Times*, 23 July 1985, sec. 2, p. 5; the list of groups is from the *Wall Street Journal,* 22 July 1985, 18.

6.  Les Aspin, "Congress versus the Defense Department," in *The Tethered Presidency,* ed. Thomas M. Franck (New York: New York University Press, 1981), 262; Eizenstat quoted by Gerald Seib, "Is the President's Authority Being Nibbled Away?" *Wall Street Journal,* 11 September 1989, sec. A, pp. 1, 12; Lloyd N. Cutler, "To Form a Government—On the Defects of Separation of Powers," *Foreign Affairs* 39 (Fall 1980): 126–143.

7.  William Lasser, *The Limits of Judicial Power: The Supreme Court in American Politics* (Chapel Hill: University of North Carolina Press, 1988), 243.

8.  William J. Brennan, "The Constitution of the United States: Contemporary Ratification," reprinted in *Interpreting the Constitution,* ed. Jack N. Rakove (Boston: Northeastern University Press, 1990), 23.

9.  Brennan, "The Constitution," 25.

10.  Brennan, "The Constitution," 26.

11.  Dworkin, Ely, and Miller were discussed in chap 14. For Laurence Tribe's views, see Laurence H. Tribe and Michael C. Dorf, *On Reading the Constitution* (Cambridge: Harvard University Press, 1991), esp. the specific endorsement of Brennan's views on p. 106; Michael J. Perry, *The Constitution, the Courts, and Human Rights* (New Haven: Yale University Press, 1982); Lewis and Schlesinger are discussed by Jack N. Rakove, introduction to *Interpreting the Constitution,* ed. Rakove, 4; Gordon S. Wood, "The Fundamentalists and the Constitution," *New York Review of Books,* 18 February 1988, 33–40.

12.  On critical legal studies, see David Kairys, ed., *The Politics of Law: A Progressive Critique,* rev. ed. (New York: Pantheon Books, 1990). Sotirios A. Barber, *On What the Constitution Means* (Baltimore: Johns Hopkins University Press, 1993), 14, 36, 219; see also Barber, *The Constitution of Judicial Power* (Baltimore: Johns Hopkins University Press, 1993).

13.  Kaus's comments are in Charles Peters and Phillip Keisling, eds., *A New Road for America* (Lanham, MD: Madison Books, 1985), 44, 145.

14.  Kaus, in *A New Road,* ed. Peters and Keisling, 44, 43.

15.  Peters, in *A New Road,* ed. Peters and Keisling, 148.

16.  David Osborne and Ted Gaebler, *Reinventing Government* (Reading, MA: Addison–Wesley, 1992), 15–16, 19–20, 23–24.

17.  Bruce Babbitt, "States Rights for Liberals," *New Republic* 184 (24 January 1981): 21–23; David Osborne, *Laboratories of Democracy* (Boston: Harvard Business School Press, 1990).

18.  Alice M. Rivlin, *Reviving the American Dream* (Washington: Brookings Institution, 1992), esp. the summaries in chaps. 1 and 10.

19.  Francis J. Flaherty, "States' Rights Are Our Rights, Too," *Progressive* 46 (February 1982): 40–43; John J. Marchi, "New York's Welfare Meltdown," *New York Times,* 12 August 1996, sec. A. p. 15.

20.  Michael Kinsley, "The Withering Away of the States," *New Republic* 184 (28 March 1981): 17–21; Sar A. Levitan, "Budgeting States Rights," *Society* 19 (July/August 1982): 75–78; Henry Steele Commager, "Tocqueville's Mistake: A Defense of Strong Central Government," *Harper's* 269 (August 1984): 70–74; Samuel H. Beer, "The Idea of the Nation," *New Republic* 187 (July 19–26, 1982): 23–29; Vernon E. Jordan Jr., "Surrender of Federal Programs to the States," *Vital Speeches* 47 (1 May 1981): 421–423; and "State of Disunion," *Nation* 234 (6 February 1982): 129.

21.  *Congressional Quarterly Almanac,* 1990, 408–411.

# 21

# Institutional Prescriptions: Past Influences, Instrumentalism, and Impact

As the preceding two chapters have shown, there was less dramatic fluctuation in the institutional prescriptions of each ideological coalition, particularly in their rhetoric, between 1981 and 1993 than there had been during the 1966–81 years. Much fragmentation continued, however, and quite a few short-term shifts were apparent, especially in congressional voting patterns and administrative actions on federalism issues. Neither major alliance really reached across-the-board consensus on a full theory of governance to the extent that both had between 1939 and 1966.

This chapter analyzes the influences of the past on the recommendations of the 1980s and 1990s, noting the multiple continuities despite some changes. It then assesses the nature and extent of instrumentalism shaping the major new recommendations made by each camp. Finally, it takes a stab at suggesting their impact, although such an assessment must be only tentative, since insufficient time has elapsed to gauge most long-term results of the 1981–93 conservative and liberal institutional prescriptions.

## The Influence of Past Prescriptions

Past ideas of governance shaped most of the conservative and liberal rhetoric concerning institutional prescriptions during the Reagan-Bush years. Even the innovations usually had some precedents. The conservatives' enhanced support for presidential government had begun to develop strongly during the Nixon administration and, in its foreign-policy dimensions, had even earlier origins. Privatization and decentralization of public administration took some new forms while meshing well with long-term conservative hostility to the administrative state. The conservatives' rhetoric on states' rights deviated little from that of the past, although their actual behavior probably came to be more issue-focused and inconsistent than at any time since 1933. The rather dramatic innovations by a libertarian conservative minority (including those of the law and economics school) regarding judicial activism and constitutional interpretation were more consciously recognized and overtly expressed than in the 1933–37 years, but they bore considerable family resemblance to the natural-law jurisprudence and judicial activism that many observers had discerned among conservatives in that period. On the liberal side, the growing but uneasy embrace of congressionally centered checks and balances grew out of trends established in the 1960s and 1970s. Of all of the innovations seen in the 1981–93 years, the neoliberal/New Democratic endorsement of entrepreneurial public administration and of decentralized (and sometimes even dual) federalism probably represented the sharpest breaks with the past positions of the advocates' own ideological coalition.

Individual intellectuals, politicians, and activists in the Reagan-Bush period almost never made the kinds of shifts in their rhetorical position on governance prescriptions that a considerable number of them had made, primarily on presidential-congressional relations, in the late 1960s and the 1970s. When an individual switched positions in the 1980s, it was usually a short-term behavioral change, unaccompanied by an alteration of his or her rhetoric. For example, Reagan and most of the congressional conservatives who supported centralized federalism through their actions on a number of specific issues continued to proclaim loudly their devotion to states' rights and decentralized government, even as their actions suggested otherwise.

Because most individual leaders remained attached, at least in their public statements, to previous institutional prescriptions, most of the major changes in governance recommendations within each coalition derived from newcomers to the political stage. Thus the new conservative judicial activism and attempts at fusion of moral philosophy and constitutional law stemmed primarily from libertarian conservative intellectuals who had not previously been active in the conservative movement. These included Bernard Siegan, Richard Epstein, Stephen Macedo, Richard Posner, and their considerable followings. Many of the "new" conservative justifications for presidential power came from neo-Straussian political philosophers who were either new contributors or who had previously focused on subjects less specifically related to contemporary American governance ideas, including Harvey Mansfield Jr., James Ceaser, Carnes Lord, and their followers. Among liberals, similarly, most of the innovations came from neoliberals and New Democrats such as David

Osborne, Ted Gaebler, and Alice Rivlin who had been unattached publicly to previous prescriptions and modes that were being abandoned or revised. This was particularly true with regard to the administrative state and federalism spheres.[1]

Taking an overview, it can be seen that past influences outweighed stimuli for major change for most individual conservative and liberal leaders of the 1981–93 period. Usually the major advocates of change in rhetorical prescriptions concerning institutions were political novices. However, broad alterations in ideological values and substantive policy preferences (partly due to environmental changes such as the end of the Cold War and partly due to the emergence of new subgroups such as the neoliberals and the New Democrats), together with shifts in the power bases of each ideological coalition (conservative-liberal reverses from the 1939–66 pattern in the presidency and Congress, rising judicial conservatism, rising state receptiveness to centrist reform), also shaped the broad contours of each coalition's approaches to questions of governance. So, too, did the initiatives taken by the Reagan administration, (especially presidentially controlled and privatized administration, though the Reagan administration was far more closely linked to the conservative movement than the Nixon administration had been.

### Instrumental Links to Power and Programmatic Policy Ends

As before, values and policy preferences, power calculations, and responses to presidential initiatives shaped the institutional recommendations emanating from each ideological coalition. The development of the conservative and liberal prescriptions for presidential-congressional relations, which hardened into rather well-defined positions when compared with the 1966–81 period, illustrated the complex dynamics that often operated.

The substantial conservative support for presidential power in general, evident both in congressional conservatives' voting patterns (see table 19.1) and in the publicly expressed ideas of most conservative intellectuals, politicians, and activists (chapter 19), almost certainly stemmed in large part from the relative conservatism of the presidency compared with Congress during the period and the widespread perception that this represented at least a medium-term pattern. Jeffrey Hart's analysis in 1974 had set the tone in this respect. Some conservatives, uncertain how long the pattern would endure, openly expressed concerns about enhancing presidential powers in lasting ways. Senator Orrin Hatch, conservative

Republican of Utah, for instance, endorsed a statutory item veto for President Reagan in 1983 but frankly opposed a constitutional amendment on grounds that it would grant too much power to possible liberal presidents of the future. Neoconservative intellectual Jeane Kirkpatrick in 1989, while endorsing presidential government in general, cautioned: "Remembering that a future White House may adopt policies we very strongly oppose, we should not be too quick to exaggerate the dangers of immobilism from interbranch tensions—or too quick to minimize the dangers of unilateral executive action." Moreover, several of the conservative opponents of presidential government (including Samuel Francis, David Brock, and to a lesser extent Representative Mickey Edwards) displayed their power/policy-driven motivations by grounding their arguments in denials that the presidency was indeed more conservative than Congress over the long term. They, too, raised questions about the future. "How will the Republicans react when a Democrat becomes president and says, 'Let me have the line-item veto'?" asked Edwards. "What if a Democratic president reacted to the killing of priests or nuns in El Salvador by deciding to overthrow the Salvadoran government that conservatives support?"[2]

Nonetheless, most conservatives phrased their justifications for their prescriptions in terms emphasizing enduring values and public policies. A common approach was to stress certain values or public policies, link them to characteristics alleged to be inherent in institutions, and then offer the prescriptions. The problem lay in finding suitable values and policies capable of mobilizing wide conservative support.

Until the late 1980s, a very common conservative rationale for presidential government entailed the following basic argument: (1) national security values linked to the containment and ultimate destruction of Communism are of high priority (almost unanimous conservative agreement); (2) energy, unity, speed, and secrecy are much more likely to be associated with the presidency as an institution than with Congress (wide conservative and liberal agreement); (3) energy, unity, speed, and secrecy are essential to national security as previously defined; (4) the presidency is now, and is likely to be in the near future, more conservative than Congress (fairly wide conservative and liberal agreement, but some questioning of this proposition); and therefore (5) presidential power is worthy of conservative support.

Summing up this argument briefly, neoconservative intellectual Norman Podhoretz wrote in 1986 that "a body as large and diverse as Congress can never run an activist foreign policy.... [T]he less the president is able to do, the smaller the role the United States will play in the world." Neo-Straussian intellectual Judith Best concurred: "The capacity for vigorous, resolute, effective action in foreign policy resides, and must reside, in the president and not in Congress." Bruce Fein's assessment was phrased rather harshly but made a similar point: "Congress is unsuited for anything but an oversight role in foreign policy or national security. As a body, it is ignorant, supine, vacillating, and myopic."[3]

The end of the Cold War and the resultant fragmenting of conservative conceptions of national security, however, undermined the ability of these arguments to mobilize full conservative support for presidential government by late in the period. While most conservative representatives did rally behind presidential power in the Iraq-Kuwait crisis, about a fifth of the conservative senators did not; and such issues as presidential discretion on trade negotiations with Mexico caused more than a quarter of congressional conservatives to defect. Asserting "liberty" as their highest value, a number of libertarian conservatives made strong cases for congressionally centered checks and balances as more conducive than presidential government to the protection of negative freedom, especially in the absence of an international Soviet/Communist threat. Thus Mickey Edwards emphasized: "The one essential ingredient of the conservative theory of government—the very essence of our political philosophy—is that the greatest threat to man's liberty is the accrual of power by those who govern him." Checks and balances were thus preferable to energy, unity, speed, and secrecy as means of protecting liberty. Robert Higgs and Charlotte Twight noted that even Reagan as president had "declared emergencies repeatedly to impose sweeping economic restrictions on the dealings of Americans with citizens of other nations" and concluded ominously that "derogations from private property rights in a liberal democracy occur chiefly during national emergencies and. . . once restricted, private rights seldom regain their previous scope." Samuel Francis reached back to Robert Taft for an appropriate quotation: "If in the great field of foreign policy the President has the arbitrary and unlimited powers he now claims, then there is an end to freedom in the United States not only in the foreign field but in the great realm of domestic activity which necessarily follows any foreign commitments."[4]

Such conservative defenders of presidential power as Terry Eastland, Harvey Mansfield Jr., and Robert Bork tried to rally conservative and other support by stressing the need for "energy" that they believed could come only from the presidency. L. Gordon Crovitz and Jeremy Rabkin stressed "efficiency," and Eastland also employed efficiency arguments. But these seemingly neutral terms ran against the grain of most libertarian conservative values. Furthermore, the New Right and sometimes neoconservative justifications for a presidential tribune role in terms of populistic-democratic values aroused more horror than enthusiasm from most traditionalist conservatives and some others.[5]

Still another problem was the difficulty in justifying presidential government in terms of the "original intent" doctrines long cherished by most conservatives and long deployed by many of them in the cause of congressionally centered checks and balances. Despite the stretch involved, a number of conservative presidential government proponents did make the effort. In the foreign/national security sphere, they usually cited Alexander Hamilton, though some tried, without much basis, also to enlist James Madison in the cause. Sometimes they resorted to calling upon John Locke's "executive prerogative" (for emergencies) and making the argument that "the American system in effect 'constitutionalizes' it by requiring the president (and not congressmen) to swear to preserve, protect and defend the Constitution as the highest duty of his office." Douglas Jeffrey made this particular argument, but others, including Harvey Mansfield Jr., also appealed to the Lockean prerogative. To support the administrative presidency, they usually stressed the constitutional separation of powers among executive, legislative, and judicial branches and functions, as Terry Eastland, James Ceaser, L. Gordon Crovitz and Jeremy Rabkin, Nolan Clark, J. Gregory Sidak, and others did. Proposals that they justified on these grounds included not only tight presidential personnel controls over the executive branch but also expansive executive privilege, presidential excisions from statutes of points considered unconstitutional, opposition to independent prosecutors, and opposition to independent agencies and commissions dating back in some cases as far as the 1880s. Terry Eastland even sought to justify the presidential role as remolder of the judicial/legal system by citing James Madison to the effect that judges are "shoots from the executive stock." However, the tribune role was simply indefensible in original intent terms, and no major conservatives attempted such a defense. Overall, despite all of these efforts, even a number of conservatives found the conservative intellectuals' efforts to mesh presidential government with original-intent constitutional interpretations unconvincing. Thus the lack of a close fit between these two tenets, as well as a crumbling of the major values/policy foundation for conservative presidential government, left power considerations as the major basis for conservative support for presidential preeminence. Yet those, too, would undergo alteration after 1992, calling the future of the conservative presidential government model into question.[6]

Liberals' power calculations, of course, inclined them toward endorsement of congressionally centered checks and balances during this period. However, a desire to use presidential energy, unity, speed (and perhaps even secrecy) on behalf of domestic social reform and American global leadership in the future led a few, such as Stuart Eizenstat, Ted Sorensen, and Les Aspin, to continue to support the old liberal presidential government model. A somewhat larger bloc of liberals, represented by Arthur Schlesinger Jr., James MacGregor Burns, and Senator Edward Kennedy, still very supportive of egalitarian domestic socioeconomic reforms but not of foreign military entanglements, advocated strong presidential reform and administrative leadership roles—what Theodore Lowi termed the Domestic Necessity Model. Perhaps reflecting a loss of zeal for redistributive reforms, but probably motivated mainly by power and immediate policy goals, most liberals moved toward support of congressionally centered checks and balances during the period. However, many of them failed to convey a sense of genuine enthusiasm for the cause.[7]

Liberals' and conservatives' positions on other institutional issues similarly reflected a mix of short-term policy calculations, longer-term values/policy/power considerations, and reactions to Reagan administration initiatives. The domain illustrating the most evident short-term, policy-driven motivations during this period was almost certainly that of federalism. The Reagan administration, despite its vehement and frequent verbal support of states' rights, led the way. A short-term instrumentalism was apparent in the Reagan administration's willingness on a number of occasions to sacrifice decentralist principles in favor of supporting private property rights (e.g., national requirements that states permit wide trucks on highways, national product liability regulations, national offshore oil and gas leasing) and "moral" principles (e.g., national minimum drinking age standards). Asked how he could support national government threats to cut state highway aid if states did not raise the minimum drinking age, Reagan responded: "With the problem so clear-cut and the proven solution at hand, we have no misgivings about this judicious use of Federal power." States' rights were thus often jettisoned for other conservative values or policy preferences. Congressional conservatives generally followed suit. Liberals' flip-flops were just as notable as the conservatives' during the period, often reflecting short-term policy considerations rather than the pursuit of the creative new state reformist values so frequently praised by neoliberals and New Democrats. However, the fact that the state governments were no longer so clearly more conservative in their orientations than the national government (due to changes at each level) as they had been at virtually all points since the early New Deal meant that both conservatives and liberals who took medium-to-long-term perspectives could have fewer compunctions than previously in breaking, respectively, from positions of states' rights and centralized federalism.[8]

Another set of examples of short-term policy-driven behavior occurred in the realm of congressional court-curbing efforts. Many conservatives, led in particular by Senator Jesse Helms of North Carolina, continued their approach of seeking to restrict federal court jurisdiction in policy areas where they disliked judicial decisions, most notably during this period on school prayer matters. Another issue-specific conservative approach was to seek a constitutional amendment to override disliked Supreme Court decisions, a method used unsuccessfully in this period on flag-burning and abortion issues. While making no such direct attacks on the judiciary as those entailed in jurisdiction restriction, liberals took steps to overrule Supreme Court statutory interpretations in the civil rights realm with the Civil Rights Restoration Act of 1988 and the Civil Rights Act of 1991.[9]

Instrumentalism of a short-term policy-specific nature was most evident in the judicial and federalism domains between 1981 and 1993, perhaps because these two areas appeared to most observers to be the most centrist and variable in their policy effects during these years. Although the courts were becoming increasingly conservative in their personnel, many conservatives and liberals perceived institutional features that at least constrained their conservatism and, in the view of some, made the judiciary still a "liberal" force. While the structure of the fifty state governments in the aggregate retained some significant conservative policy and values biases, usually deep-seated regressivity in tax structures, because of competition among states and other factors, the states became arenas for frequent centrist reformism that was often considerably more liberal in its effects than the policies and practices of the Reagan and Bush administrations.[10]

Despite the evidence of considerable short-term, policy-specific instrumentalism, much of the instrumentalism by both liberal and conservative coalitions, as previously, focused on assessments of at least medium-term power and/or policy and values objectives. Moreover, even though most politicians and activists (and probably most intellectuals, too, though they were generally more reluctant to admit it) kept power and policy ends well in view in offering their institutional prescriptions, some intellectuals in particular appeared genuinely dedicated to their governance recommendations. Certainly a few, such as Felix Morley, who spanned the period from the 1930s to the 1980s, maintained records of great consistency over time. For Morley, constitutional immutability, states' rights, a very limited state, and congressionally centered checks and balances all reinforced one another and fostered his highest value: liberty.[11]

## The Impact of the Institutional Prescriptions

The impact of the "Reagan Revolution" on public policy probably fell short of being revolutionary, and it certainly failed to achieve that status with regard to governance patterns. In contrast to the "Roosevelt Revolution" of the 1933–45 period, which despite challenges that necessitated some compromises left a major mark on government institutions and political parties, interest groups, and popular conceptions about politics for more than a generation to come, the mark left by the conservative institutional prescriptions of the 1981–93 period will likely be unimpressive. How unimpressive, it is still too soon to judge.[12]

From the vantage point of 1996, the greatest changes produced by institutional prescriptions in the 1981–93 years appear to be those in the administrative state sphere, where the privatization drive of the Reagan administration and the conservative movement began to merge with the entrepreneurial public administration prescriptions of the New Democrats, with effects that are not yet fully evident. However, the Reagan administration/conservative prescriptions also entailed a fairly successful effort to centralize executive authority in the presidency and heighten hierarchical contols of administration by the political executives at the top, a project previously undertaken by Nixon but pursued more forcefully and consistently by Reagan. As Peter Benda and Charles Levine have demonstrated, these two administrative state prescriptions and their implementation operated to some extent at cross-purposes, thus blunting their long-term impact:

> The Reagan Administration's efforts to redeem a vision of a limited government that divests itself of functions by transferring them to the private sector, which will then drive the economy forward, has sometimes created blurred lines of control—the opposite effect of what the entire centralization thrust presumably was designed or intended to achieve.[13]

On presidential-congressional relations, neither the dominant conservative prescription for presidential government nor the calls by the majority of liberals for congressionally centered checks and balances prevailed. The abilities of Reagan and Bush to take overseas military actions in Grenada, Libya, Panama, and the Persian Gulf (the last with some congressional involvement) were partially balanced by congressional checks on military and/or diplomatic moves in Lebanon, Nicaragua, Angola, and South Africa (the last of which entailed congressional override of Reagan's veto of toughened economic sanctions against the white South

African regime). The president failed to obtain the item veto (though Clinton later partially did) or enhanced rescission authority or an end to court-appointed special prosecutors during these years. Presidential efforts to remold the judicial/legal systems already appear to have had a less-dramatic long-term impact than was commonly thought at the time.[14]

Federalism changed considerably less than Reagan and conservative rhetoric suggested that it would, in part because of moderate and liberal opposition to the "big swap," many block grants, and some other decentralist proposals, but also in part because the Reagan and Bush administrations, conservatives on the Supreme Court, and the conservative movement in general often pursued contradictory courses of action. Timothy Conlan, David Walker, Joseph Zimmerman, John Haynes, Larry Hunter, Larry Schwab, Michael Pagano and Ann Bowman, and Michael Malaby and David Webber, among others, have provided ample documentation to buttress this conclusion. Therefore, even though the rising interest among New Democrats in strengthening the states seemed likely to merge with conservatives' New Federalism ideas, the impact to this point has been somewhat less than the rhetoric on the subject would suggest; however, it appears to be increasing in such matters as welfare.[15]

Finally, on the matters of constitutional interpretation and judicial activism versus restraint, actual change was markedly less dramatic than much conservative rhetoric suggested. Many analysts, mostly liberals and independent scholars outside the conservative movement, suggested that the reasons lay in the simple impossibility of discerning original intent and implementing it on specific contemporary issues and the inordinate difficulty involved in implementing the judicial restraint prescriptions. Some conservatives, such as Gary McDowell, blamed judicial procedures. Others, following Lino Graglia's lead, centered blame on the law schools for miseducating judges and giving them "wrong" cues and on the "liberal" mass media for rewarding inappropriate jurisprudence and liberal activism with journalistic kudos. However, from within the conservative movement itself now emanated arguments for supplementing constitutional text and the original intent of the framers with moral philosophy, usually of a libertarian conservative natural law variety, and for judicial activism vis-à-vis lawmaking majorities, again most often in pursuit of libertarian conservative goals. If a new breed of libertarian conservative/ New Right judges in the mold of Bernard Siegan or Richard Posner were to gain dominance in the federal courts at some point in the future, a real "revolution," or rather a counterrevolution, would indeed result. Yet that was not the immediate outcome of the 1981–93 period.[16]

Since the impact of the conservative and liberal prescriptions of 1981–93 on the actual operations of government has thus far proved less than dramatic, it is also likely that they will have few major lasting effects on the party system, the patterns of interest-group politics, popular attitudes, or other political variables. However, in the past, the results of governance changes have often been unintended ones and have sometimes not become fully evident until considerable time has elapsed. The results of the 1981–93 prescriptions may yet provide some surprises.

## Conclusions

The institutional recommendations of the ideological coalitions during the Reagan-Bush years reflected considerable influences from the past. Probably the greatest conservative innovations were the considerable conservative coalescence for a time around a presidential government model and the emergence of conservative minorities clearly advocating the fusion of moral philosophy with constitutional law and the use of judicial activism. Among liberals, the neoliberal/New Democratic embrace of entrepreneurial administration and the state governments and the broad, if shallow, liberal support for congressionally centered checks and balances represented the sharpest breaks with the past. However, even certain innovations, such as the conservative ideas concerning natural law and judicial activism, were in some respects merely resuscitations of old prescriptions—in these instances, from the 1930s. Referring to Bernard Siegan and Richard Epstein in particular, Bernard Schwartz warned that their approach "means a return to the public law of the first part of this century, with all the abuses that accompanied it." Despite much change, the governance traditions of the past continued to exert influence.[17]

As for instrumentalism, short-term and immediate calculations of policy effects appeared to shape liberal and conservative behavior most often during the period on federalism questions and efforts to curb or overrule the judiciary, though this perception may in part have reflected greater uncertainties over policy effects of prescriptions in these two spheres than in the others. In any event, treatment of institutional prescriptions largely as means to achieve medium-to-long-term power, policy, and value ends remained quite common, as they generally had been at least since the New Deal.

Finally, the impact of the prescriptions of the Reagan-Bush years generally failed to reshape government substantially—in part because of internal contradictions (as on conservative administrative state reforms), in part because they were implemented only sporadically and inconsistently (some aspects of federalism, judicial behavior, and constitutional jurisprudence), and in part as a result of liberal-versus-conservative stalemates or necessary compromises that blunted the impact (many aspects of presidential-congressional relations). The long-term outcomes can be more accurately assessed when a few more years have passed.

## Notes

1. Bernard H. Siegan, *Economic Liberties and the Constitution* (Chicago: University of Chicago Press, 1980); Richard A. Epstein, *Takings* (Cambridge: Harvard University Press, 1985); Stephen Macedo, *The New Right v. the Constitution* (Washington: Cato Institute, 1987); Richard A. Posner, *Economic Analysis of the Law,* 3d ed. (Boston: Little, Brown, 1986). Harvey C. Mansfield Jr., *Taming the Prince* (New York: Free Press, 1989); James Ceaser, "The Theory of Governance of the Reagan Administration," in *The Reagan Presidency and the Governing of America,* ed. Lester Salamon and Michael S. Lund (Washington: Urban Institute Press, 1985); James Ceaser, "In Defense of the Separation of Powers," in *Separation of Powers,* ed. Robert Goldwin and Herbert Kaufman (Washington: American Enterprise Institute, 1987), 168–193; Carnes Lord, *The Presidency and National Security* (New York: Free Press, 1988); Carnes Lord, "Executive Power and Our Security," *The National Interest* 7 (Spring 1987), 3–13. David Osborne, *Laboratories of Democracy* (Boston: Harvard Business School Press, 1990); David Osborne and Ted Gaebler, *Reinventing Government* (Reading, MA: Addison-Wesley, 1992); Alice M. Rivlin, *Reviving the American Dream* (Washington: Brookings Institution, 1992).

2. Jeffrey Hart, "The Presidency: Shifting Conservative Perspectives?" *National Review* (22 November 1974): 1351–1355; Orrin Hatch, discussion in "The Constitution: That Delicate Balance," Public Broadcasting Service (1983); Kirkpatrick comments in L. Gordon Crovitz and Jeremy A. Rabkin, eds., *The Fettered Presidency* (Washington: American Enterprise Institute, 1989); Samuel Francis, "Imperial Conservatives?" *National Review,* 4 August 1989, 37–38; David Brock, "Mr. Symms Goes to Jamba," *Policy Review* 59 (Winter 1992): 32–39. The Edwards quote is from Robert W. Merry, "Congressional Power and Mickey Edwards," *Congressional Quarterly Weekly Report,* 3 March 1990, 714.

3. Norman Podhoretz, "The Imperial Congress," *Washington Post,* 23 December 1986, sec. A, p. 19; Judith A. Best, "Foreign Policy Is Executive Domain," *Policy Review* 60 (Spring 1992): 91; Bruce Fein, "Congress Has Not Changed Its Spots," *Policy Review* 60 (Spring 1992): 92.

4. Mickey Edwards, "A Conservative Defense of Congress," *Public Interest* 100 (Summer 1990): 81; Robert Higgs and Charlotte Twight, "National Emergency and the Erosion of Private Property Rights," *Cato Journal* 6 (Winter 1987): 761, 771; Samuel Francis, "Imperial Conservatives?" 37.

5. For energy justifications, see Eastland, *Energy in the Executive,* esp. 3, 12,

277–306; Mansfield, *Taming the Prince,* 2, 257; Robert H. Bork , foreword to *The Fettered Presidency.* For efficiency justifications, see Crovitz and Rabkin, introduction to *The Fettered Presidency,* 1–12; and Eastland, *Energy,* esp. chap. 9. Pro–tribune arguments include those from Irving Kristol, 316–317, and Michael Horowitz, 320, in *The Fettered Presidency*; and Richard Viguerie, *The Establishment vs. the People* (Chicago: Regnery Gateway, 1983), 237–238, 242. Disapproval of such arguments is found in Harvey C. Mansfield Jr., "The American Election: Towards Constitutional Democracy?" *Government and Opposition* 16 (Winter 1981): 1–18; Ceaser, "Theory of Governance," 65; Alan Crawford, *Thunder on the Right* (New York: Pantheon Books, 1980), 326–327; James B. Williams and George W. Carey, "The Founding Fathers and 'The Federalist,'" *Modern Age* (Summer/Fall 1987): 315–317; such disapproval is discussed by Robert Devigne, *Recasting Conservatism* (New Haven: Yale University Press, 1994), 73–74.

6. For attempts to claim both Hamilton and Madison, see Eastland, *Energy,* esp. 3, 9–10, 12–13, 66–68. The quotation about the executive prerogative is from Douglas Jeffrey, "Executive Authority under the Separation of Powers," in *the Imperial Congress,* ed. Gordon S. Jones and John A. Marini (New York: Pharos Books, 1988), 49; Harvey C. Mansfield Jr., "Representative Government and Executive Power," in *Economy, Diplomacy, and Statecraft,* ed. Tim Fuller (Colorado Springs: Colorado College Press, 1988), 25. For the separation of powers arguments and the noted applications, see Eastland, *Energy,* esp. 8–13, chaps. 4 and 5, and pt. 2; Crovitz and Rabkin, *The Fettered Presidency,* 1–12; Ceaser, "In Defense of the Separation of Powers," 168–193; Nolan Clark, "The Headless Fourth Branch," in *The Imperial Congress,* ed. Jones and Marini; and J. Gregory Sidak, "Spending Riders Would Unhorse the Executive," *Wall Street Journal,* 2 November 1989, sec. A, p.18. Eastland's quotation from Madison is on p. 231 of *Energy.*

7. Stuart Eizenstat is discussed by Gerald Seib, "Is the President's Authority Being Nibbled Away?" *Wall Street Journal,* 11 September 1989, sec. A, pp. 1, 12; Theodore Sorensen, "Political Perspective: Who Speaks for the National Interest?" in *The Tethered Presidency,* ed. Thomas M. Franck (New York: New York University Press, 1981), 12–15; Les Aspin, "Congress versus the Defense Department," in *The Tethered Presidency,* ed. Frank, 247–263; Arthur Schlesinger Jr., "The Imperial Temptation," *New Republic* 196 (16 March 1987): 17–18; James MacGregor Burns, *The Power to Lead* (New York: Simon & Schuster, 1984); Edward Kennedy, "Line Item Veto: Out of the Shambles," *Los Angeles Times,* 23 July 1985, sec. 2, p. 5; Theodore J. Lowi, "Presidential Power and the Ideological Struggle over Its Interpretation," in *The Constitution and the American Presidency,* ed. Martin L. Fausold and Alan Shank (Albany: State University of New York Press, 1991), 233–234.

8. The Reagan quotation is cited by Timothy J. Conlan, "Federalism and Competing Values in the Reagan Administration," *Publius* 16 (Winter 1986): 41.

9. Edward Keynes with Randall K. Miller, *The Court vs. Congress* (Durham, NC: Duke University Press, 1989).

10. For discussion of institutional factors modifying, possibly negating, conservatism in the federal courts, see Gary L. McDowell, *Curbing the Courts* (Baton Rouge: Louisiana State University Press, 1988); and Lino Graglia, "Judicial Activism: Even on the Right, It's Wrong," *Public Interest* 95 (Spring 1989): esp. 74.

For discussion of institutional factors constraining state reformism and maintaining a conservative bias in state public policy outputs, see David B. Robertson and Dennis R. Judd, *The Development of American Public Policy* (Glenview, IL: Scott, Foresman, 1989), esp. chap. 11.

11. Felix Morley, *For the Record* (South Bend, IN: Regnery Gateway, 1979), covers much of his career and political ideology, including his governance prescriptions. Numerous books and articles by Morley have been cited throughout this study.

12. Larry M. Schwab, *The Illusion of a Conservative Reagan Revolution* (New Brunswick, NJ: Transaction Publishers, 1991), esp. chap. 8, draws a similar conclusion. The book broadens the conclusion to apply to public policies as well as to governance.

13. Peter M. Benda and Charles H. Levine, "Reagan and the Bureaucracy," in *The Reagan Legacy,* ed. Charles O. Jones (Chatham, NJ: Chatham House, 1988), 137–138.

14. Eastland, *Energy,* 298–306, expresses disappointment in the impact of both the Reagan and Bush administrations. For a similar conservative assessment, see also "Taking Stock of the Presidency," *Wall Street Journal,* 8 August 1989, sec. A, p. 10.

15. Timothy J. Conlan, *New Federalism* (Washington: Brookings Institution Institution, 1988); Timothy J. Conlan, "Federalism and Competing Values in the Reagan Administration," *Publius* 16 (Winter 1986): 29–47; David B. Walker, "American Federalism from Johnson to Bush," *Publius* 21 (Winter 1991): 105–121; Joseph F. Zimmerman, "Federal Preemption under Reagan's New Federalism," *Publius* 21 (Winter 1991): 7–28; John Haynes, "U.S. House Votes in the 97th Congress on Issues with Implications for Federalism," *Publius* 13 (Spring 1983): 107–121; Larry Hunter, "U.S. Senate Votes in the 97th Congress on Federalist Issues," *Publius* 13 (Spring 1983): 123–128; Schwab, *Illusion,* 217–220; Michael A. Pagano and Ann O'M. Bowman, "The State of American Federalism," *Publius* 23 (Summer 1993): 1–22; Michael R. Malaby and David J. Webber, "Federalism in the 101st Congress," *Publius* 21 (Summer 1991): 77–92; Timothy J. Conlan, James D. Riggle, and Donna E. Schwartz, "Deregulating Federalism? The Politics of Mandate Reform in the 104th Congress," *Publius* 25 (Summer 1995): 25–39.

16. Analysts stressing the impossiblity of achieving the conservatives' stated goals include Gordon S. Wood, "The Fundamentalists and the Constitution," *New York Review of Books,* 18 February 1988, 33–40; and Arthur Selwyn Miller, *The Supreme Court: Myth and Reality* (Westport, CT: Greenwood Press, 1978), esp. 25–36; McDowell, *Curbing the Courts*; Graglia, "Judicial Activism," 57–94. See also Schwab, *Illusion,* 214–216.

17. Bernard Schwartz, *The New Right and the Constitution* (Boston: Northeastern University Press, 1990), 135.

# Conclusion

# 22

# Retrospect and Prospect

-------------------

As the United States nears the dawn of a new millennium, the conservative and liberal coalitions that have battled each other during the major part of the twentieth century are fragmented and more than a little exhausted by their struggles. Liberalism in particular has shown signs of possibly terminal illness since the late 1960s, and the end of the Cold War has recently removed a major source of unity in an increasingly divided conservative coalition. Yet despite frequent internal conflicts and predictions of crackups for each ideological coalition, the liberal-conservative struggle or one broadly similar to it under different ideological banners will likely continue into the future, given the diversity of assumptions and values, the socioeconomic and racial/ethnic cleavages, and the two-party power competition that appear to be deeply rooted in American politics and society.

This final chapter provides first a retrospective view of the conservative-liberal battles since 1933, particularly as they have related to institutional prescriptions. In doing so, it returns to the hypotheses set forth in the introduction to guide this study and seeks to address them as completely as the evidence that has been marshaled permits. It then sketches some possibly fruitful future investigations to place the 1933–93 patterns in the United States in a broad historical and comparative perspective and concludes with a brief discussion of the future prospects for ideologically based governance prescriptions in the United States.

### A Retrospective View: The Ideological Movements

The greatest continuities from 1933 to 1993 in the liberal coalition's central value system and programmatic public policies were probably the positive freedom values, backed by egalitarian and rationalistic assumptions and supportive of broad social welfare and business regulatory policies. From Franklin D. Roosevelt's 1932 Commonwealth Club address invoking socioeconomic rights through the equal rights emphases of John Rawls, Ronald Dworkin, and the new-politics liberal movements of the 1970s, 1980s, and 1990s, these values and public policies have been at the core of American liberalism. Positions almost as continuous as these have been negative freedom in realms of individual expression, especially for unpopular minorities; equal opportunity; and social security. Yet each of these has faced at least somewhat sharper internal liberal challenge than has positive freedom. Particularly in the late 1940s and the early 1950s, quite a few liberals lowered the priority of free expression, reflecting the pressures of the Joseph McCarthy era and widespread national security concerns. Moreover, a number of liberals have perceived at least some potential for contradiction between the active, positive government called for by most of their values and policy prescriptions and the limited government demanded by negative freedom of expression. Equal opportunity came under internal liberal attack, particularly in the drive for "more equality" and for "equality of group outcomes" from the late 1960s onward. And social security has been downplayed by New Democrats and neoliberals in the 1980s and 1990s, with their emphases on competition and risk-taking values.

Against the backdrop of continuing values and assumptions characteristic of liberalism, liberals have commonly aimed at curbing what they have viewed as business abuses and flaws in the marketplace and at providing social services, showing special concern for those who are less well off. Though the liberal coalition took on an increasingly middle-class, professional coloration from the 1950s onward, particularly as the influence of organized labor and old-style urban party machines waned, the liberal emphasis on those burdened by socioeconomic disadvantages continued in most respects.

The greatest continuities from 1933 to 1993 in the central value system and programmatic public policies of the conservative coalition were probably an attachment to private property rights and a preference for market mechanisms over government planning, a questioning of the egalitarian and rationalistic assumptions of liberalism, and a skepticism about the benefits of most regulatory and social welfare public policies. From the outset, libertarian and traditionalist brands of conservatism waged an internal battle for the soul of the conservative movement, a battle that has never really ended, despite varied efforts at fusion. Over time, new factions or tendencies entered the fray. For a time, from the mid-1950s to the late 1980s, national security values linked to anti-Communism also occupied the core values sphere of American conservatism and brought about considerable internal consensus on a large military budget and interventionist foreign policies aimed primarily at combating Communism. However, by the 1990s, protection of property rights and markets were again probably the main values on which almost all conservatives could agree.

While the liberal movement has generally been a coalition organized from the bottom of the socioeconomic class and status structure upward, with a focus on its leading members' perceptions of the needs of the disadvantaged (a "bottom-up" coalition, as Thomas and Mary Edsall have termed it), the conservative movement has centered its attention on the business and professional upper- and upper-middle-class members of society—those with a strong vested interest in private property rights and the wherewithal to gain distinct advantages from markets that allocate influence on the basis of one dollar, one vote (rather than the one-person, one-vote formula that the formal electoral mechanisms of government at least purport to use). As a top-down coalition, the conservatives have generally won their broadest support by employing national security and traditional values to add constituents from the less well-off sectors of the population, a technique employed quite successfully by Reagan and his allies in particular.[1]

Despite the infirmities of liberalism from the mid-1960s onward and the growing fragmentation of the conservative movement amid predictions of a conservative crackup in the late 1980s and the early 1990s, the mid-1990s found both coalitions still engaged in an active struggle for the control of American government and hegemony in American society. Centrist ideas were again an important force, threatening through the New Democratic movement to destroy liberalism or at least to remold and possibly rename it as a major political force and threatening through Ross Perot's movement to displace both liberalism and conservatism. However, the center had asserted itself on many occasions previously since 1933, particularly in the 1950s of Dwight Eisenhower's Modern Republicanism, Arthur Schlesinger Jr.'s "vital center" liberalism, and widespread commentary on the "end of ideology." The two-party system, sharp (and widening) socioeconomic cleavages in American society, and the two coalitions' long records of resilience made it unlikely that a centrist consensus would soon displace both major ideological movements.

## A Retrospective View: The Institutional Prescriptions

Just as each ideological movement retained certain core values and assumptions, so, too, did each one maintain a few key institutional prescriptions, at least in its predominant rhetoric and to some extent in its members' behavior, throughout the entire sixty-year era. Constitutional immutability, states' rights, and maintenance of at least fairly strict limits on any administrative state were the most continuous and stable prescriptions among conservatives. Constitutional flexibility, an at least moderately centralized (or cooperative) federalism, and a fairly broad-ranging administrative state were the most continuous and stable liberal recommendations throughout the era. Therefore, on three of the five major institutional continuums or sets of continuums, the *relative* positions of the liberal and conservative movements remained fairly stable.

Nevertheless, even on these dimensions, each coalition made some significant adjustments over time in its recommendations, and subgroups within each camp sometimes veered off in distinctive directions. Examples included the liberal quests of the 1970s and 1980s for a moral philosophy and/or procedural conception in which to ground the "living" Constitution, the new-politics liberals' advocacy of "radical decentralization" outside the ordinary framework of state government in the 1960s and 1970s, and the "judicialized administration" proposals of the Ralph Nader–Simon Lazarus "public-interest" liberals from the late 1960s onward. These new approaches and distinctive nuances illustrated some of the rich variations that could not be fully captured merely by consideration of general positions on a set of continuums.

In contrast to the patterns on the constitutional interpretation, administrative state, and federalism issues, conservatives and liberals nearly reversed their relative positions concerning presidential-congressional relations. The liberal presidential government model of 1933-1965, stressing the president's roles as leader of defense and foreign policy, instigator of domestic egalitarian social reform, head of the administrative state, and tribune of a national majority, gave way to rather broad but shallow liberal support for congressionally centered checks and balances by the 1980s, despite resistance from some liberal quarters to this massive shift. Meanwhile, the conservative movement, largely united in opposition to presidential "Caesarism" in the 1930s and 1940s, began to show increased receptivity to expansive presidential war and diplomatic powers in the 1950s and 1960s (though usually retaining strong rhetorical commitment to congressionally centered checks and balances during those years), and embraced by the 1980s a full-scale presidential government model stressing expansive war and diplomatic roles, chief executive roles, and roles in reshaping the judicial/legal system. Some conservatives, too, resisted the shift, and the resistance appeared to be growing by the mid-1990s. Although this set of continuums was the scene of truly major liberal and conservative shifts, some in each camp did maintain relative consistency, and the conservative and liberal models of presidential government did differ from one another in certain key respects, notably the reform instigator role, the tribune role (wider liberal support, 1933–65, than conservative support, 1969–93), and the judicial/legal system remolder role (wider conservative support in the 1980s than liberal support, with the possible exception of the late 1930s).

Liberal judicial prescriptions shifted over time from judicial restraint (1933–38), to judicial restraint in the socioeconomic sphere but civil liberties activism (1940s), to increasingly expansive judicial activism (gradually expanding from the 1950s to the 1980s). The liberals then retreated a bit, under neoliberal influence (and perhaps the growing perception of judicial conservatism) in the 1980s. Meanwhile, conservatives shifted from a judicial activism protective of private property rights (1933–38), toward judicial restraint (1940s–1980s), with some revival of advocacy for judicial activism protective of property rights among a libertarian conservative minority during the 1980s and 1990s.

In sum, then, it is evident that there was considerably more stability over time (despite significant variations and distinctive nuances among some subgroups) in the conservatives' and liberals' relative advocacy positions on three institutional continuums than on the other two. Analysis of the likely reasons for this pattern returns us to the introductory questions raised concerning the degree and nature of the instrumentalism motivating conservatives and liberals to articulate the institutional prescriptions they advanced.

### A Retrospective View: Instrumental Links to Power and Public Policy Ends

The present study began with a discussion of means-ends conceptions regarding the link between institutional prescriptions on the one hand and power, policy, and values on the other hand. Some analysts, such as William G. Andrews, have argued that, at least with regard to the presidential-congressional prescriptions, "The constitutional theory follows the party flag." At the other extreme have been those, such as C. P. Ives, who have argued that at least some institutional prescriptions constitute

for some ideological advocates "the end which would legitimate and fortify all other ends." The initial guiding hypothesis of the present study
posited a complex set of means-ends links but suggested that the ideological prescriptions for government institutions were more instrumental
means than ultimate ends. In general the evidence has confirmed that
hypothesis.[2]

What has emerged from the analysis of the 1933–93 era is a picture
suggesting that Andrews' conception was closer to the mark concerning
presidential-congressional relations and judicial roles than on the other
three institutional prescription continuums. However, even with regard
to the two on which it most accurately described the patterns, the "party
flag" conception proved to be too simplified to capture the essence of
what existed. The patterns during the Eisenhower administration, when
liberal Democrats still generally favored presidential government more
than conservative Republicans did, illustrated the limits of a purely partisan explanation. Although partisanship certainly played a part, particularly in shaping the behavior of congressional liberals and conservatives
on presidential-congressional and judicial matters, calculations of likely
medium-term coalitional power positions and consideration of perceived
inherent institutional characteristics and their relationship to long-term
policy and value preferences were also quite important. This was especially true for the intellectuals who played a large part in promulgating
and justifying institutional prescriptions for each coalition.

The long-term partial reversals that took place in liberals' and conservatives' relative positions on legislative-executive relations and Supreme
Court behavior occurred in patterns strongly suggesting the importance
of members' perceptions of where their institutional power bases lay.
Even Barry Goldwater, one of those who publicly rejected the notion of
treating institutions as means toward ends, noted in 1964 that "the state
governments and the Congress by and large stand on one side of the battle line. They face, across that battle line, the Executive Branch and, usually, the Judicial Branch, the Supreme Court." When the battle lines shifted, as with the "liberalizing" of the Supreme Court in the late 1930s or the
"conservatizing" of the presidency from 1969 onward, it is noteworthy
that the movements' relative positions concerning governance recommendations shifted accordingly and in a predictable direction.[3]

However, there was more to the broad prescriptive shifts than mere
partisanship or even assessments of the relative powers of the major ideological coalitions within each of the government institutions concerned.
Many members in each movement gave evidence, particularly in the justifications which they offered, of considering what they perceived to be

inherent traits of the institutions *qua* institutions and of relating these to their own values and public policy preferences. Therefore, when most liberals in the late 1960s and early 1970s ceased adhering to national security values that assigned primacy to a global anti-Communist crusade, they became less inclined to favor the strong presidency, which they had previously seen as providing the necessary energy, unity, speed, and secrecy to maximize that set of values and implement those policies. Cold-war liberals who remained wedded to the containment doctrine, in contrast, usually continued to support presidential government. In a similar fashion, those conservatives who most emphasized liberty as their highest value and opposed almost all public policies which they perceived to impinge on the negative freedom of the individual tended to oppose expansive presidential powers, regardless of the White House incumbent, more than did other conservatives. Felix Morley, Mickey Edwards, Robert Higgs and Charlotte Twight, Christopher Layne, Alan Crawford, Forrest McDonald, and Henry Regnery, among others, illustrated this pattern.[4]

Why did the relative positions of conservatives and liberals shift much more dramatically over time on the presidential-congressional and judicial continuums than on those concerning constitutional interpretation, federalism, and the administrative state? The reasons probably lay primarily in the fact that the long-term institutional characteristics of an immutable Constitution, state-centered federalism, and the administrative state were more stable and more biased toward fostering a fixed set of political values and public policies than were those of the presidency, the Supreme Court and (probably) Congress. In the cases of the presidency and the Supreme Court, the replacement of the occupant of the White House or enough justices to shift a High Bench majority could and did have a major impact on what values and public policies would be fostered by that institution. In Congress, the matter was considerably more complex, but even there, ideological majorities could change fairly swiftly and dramatically.

On the other hand, if the Constitution were truly immutable, its effects would be constant. That, of course, was a major reason that most conservatives throughout the sixty-year era embraced the ideas of strict construction and original intention as warmly as they did. They perceived that these ideas would be useful vehicles for protecting the core values that most united the conservative movement: private property rights and a preference for market mechanisms over government planning. In fact, the conservatives' conceptions of the framers' intentions tended to understate the proclivities toward government economic interventionism of some Founding Fathers, such as Alexander Hamilton. However, most conservatives (and most liberals, too) believed that rigid adherence to the Constitution and its framers' intentions would erect solid barriers to redistribution of wealth, expansive positive freedoms, and effective government planning of the economy. The liberal coalition, with its primary emphasis throughout the period on positive freedom and the use of government to provide social services and regulate business, saw in contrast the necessity of a living Constitution, updated for the twentieth century, and enhanced by infusing its interpretation with liberal moral philosophy and/or procedural understandings to achieve liberal ends.

State-centered federalism was, of course, not so consistent in its likely effects on values and public policies as a truly immutable Constitution, if possible, would be, but it was fairly consistent. Compulsory reapportionment of state legislatures on the basis of one-person, one-vote after the early 1960s altered some of the basic characteristics of state governments, as did new revenue sources, an end to state-imposed racial segregation in the Southern and border regions, newly professionalized state bureaucracies and legislative staffs, and in some instances new state constitutions. As has been noted, the states became more inclined over time toward "centrist reformism" than they had been in the 1930s or 1940s. Nonetheless, state-centered federalism retained throughout the era inherent characteristics of fragmentation, competition to attract business investment, artificial boundaries that often had little relationship to economic patterns, and frequently regressive state tax structures. For these reasons, the state governments were and remain unlikely vehicles for egalitarian redistribution of wealth, effective regulation of national and often global business corporations, or promotion of positive freedom on a broad and uniform scale. Liberals who favored these ends—and most favored a good portion of them—were unlikely to advocate state-centered federalism. Most of the New Democrats who did so in the 1980s and 1990s appeared to have little commitment to traditional liberal ends (one reason that so many of them shunned the label) or a different understanding of the realities. Over six decades, conservatives dedicated to private property and market mechanisms often used states' rights arguments as a means of blocking national government public policy initiatives they disliked. When state governments on occasion fell into liberal hands or for other reasons interfered with conservative values, conservatives tended to make exceptions to their general decentralized federalism rules to cope with the situation, as on trucking regulations, product liability, offshore oil and gas leases, the minimum drinking age in the 1980s and 1990s, and sitdown strikes in Michigan in the 1930s. Such interference, and the concomitant need for exceptions, occurred more frequently late in the era than it had in the early parts of the era, for the reasons noted above.

As for the administrative state, it tended in the domestic sphere to attract more liberals than conservatives to its service, and the Roosevelt administration, which vastly expanded the bureaucratic apparatus, also packed it with liberals in key positions and then locked them into place. However, as with the states and the immutable Constitution, inherent long-term characteristics—including a proclivity toward rationalism and state mastery over society—were widely seen to reside in the administrative state as an institution, largely independent of the particular mix of personnel at any point in time. The perceived inclination toward rationalism and state dominance over society and the individual, as well as the view that career bureaucrats were inexorably linked to labor unions and liberalism, fed strong conservative antipathy to the administrative state throughout the sixty-year era. When Nixon began to institute and Reagan implemented a conservative administrative presidency, the conservatives' hostility softened a little. Some conservatives, especially in big business, had long accommodated themselves to many aspects of the administrative state. Yet conservative wariness of bureaucracy and embrace of privatization ideas continued to be in evidence through the mid-1990s. Meanwhile, as liberal values became more individualistic and less collectivistic after the 1960s than they had been in the formative New Deal period, liberal enthusiasm for a hierarchical, executive-centered administrative state waned. However, even as the new-politics liberals embraced judicialized administration in the 1970s and neoliberals and New Democrats of the 1980s and 1990s called for entrepreneurial public administration, the liberal movement remained far more supportive of an expansive administrative state than the conservative coalition. Most liberals could conceive no other effective route toward guarantees of positive freedom on a broadly egalitarian basis and implementation of the services and regulatory policies that it required than through the instrument of the bureaucratic state, albeit one that they hoped to make into a restructured and revitalized version quite different in important respects from that of the New Deal.

In practice, then, there was a mingling of motivations that lay behind the basic patterns found in the liberal and conservative governance prescriptions between the early New Deal and the 1990s. These included:

1. Very short-term instrumental calculations of what would achieve immediate power or policy ends. These sometimes, but relatively infrequently, led the ideological coalitions, or important segments of them, to take actions which contradicted their major rhetorical

prescriptions of the time. Examples included liberals' eagerness to grant wage-price control authority to President Nixon in 1971 even as they railed against the "imperial" presidency and conservatives' enthusiasm for imposing national regulatory standards favoring big business and propertied interests on the states in the 1980s and 1990s in the face of their own loudly proclaimed devotion to states' rights. A number of other examples have been cited at various points in this study, but the number has been far from overwhelming. Often, of course, short-term calculations have suggested actions that comported well with longer-term considerations and have thus not been clearly visible.

2. Medium-term instrumentalism generally centered on assessment of the relative power positions of the ideological coalitions within the major institutions of government, the relating of these to broad public policy/values ends, and the adoption of institutional prescriptions and modes of implementation that appeared to "fit." The medium-term patterns and shifts in them with regard to presidential-congressional relations and the federal judiciary have been explained largely but not wholly in these terms.

3. Long-term instrumentalism generally centered on assessments of inherent (or alllegedly inherent) characteristics of institutions, the relating of these to broad public policy/values ends, and the adoption of institutional recommendations and modes of implementing them that appeared to fit. These mingled with calculations of type 1 and type 2 in shaping rhetorical prescriptions and behavior in all spheres to some extent, but appeared to offer the best explanation of the long-term relative stability in the conservative-liberal patterns concerning constitutional interpretation, federalism, and the administrative state. Complicating the picture with regard to both this approach and the previous one were changes over time in the values of the two major movements, most notably in such areas as national security values but also in other spheres.

4. Pursuit of institutional prescriptions as "ends in themselves." Difficult to identify and measure in practice, this approach was one which some advocates of institutional prescriptions, particularly among the intellectuals, perceived themselves to be following. Consistency over time, even when the prescription contradicted power, policy, or values goals, would be necessary but not sufficient to demonstrate such a pursuit. In those terms, a few advocates, such as

Felix Morley, might qualify, though even in his case there was an emphasis on the value of liberty that probably represented the "highest-level" end for him. If this approach prevailed with any broad groups, and this author remains unconvinced that it did, it would probably be among conservatives who believed themselves to be faithfully following an immutable Constitution and its framers' intentions. In the author's judgment, however, these advocates nearly always read the Constitution and the framers' intentions with twentieth-century conservative reading glasses, even if they did not recognize this fact themselves.

5. Maintenance of previous prescriptions and application of them to new situations. Frequently, in the absence of strong power, public policy, or values stimuli to break from a preexisting recommendation, liberals and conservatives adopted this approach. The tidelands oil controversy in the 1940s and 1950s, discussed extensively in chapter 11, provided but one of a number of possible examples of the processes involved here. Of course, this was one major way in which institutional prescriptions had an impact—by taking on a life of their own and helping to shape future prescriptions. Political leaders, activists, and intellectuals rarely shifted their individual public rhetorical positions (though they more readily shifted their behavioral positions) on major institutional prescriptions without compelling power or values/policy reasons for doing so. Even the members of Congress, who showed among all of the groups the greatest propensity to shift their behavior to various points on a continuum in order to achieve short-term ends, only rarely made open declarations that they were shifting their institutional recommendations.

## A Retrospective View: Impact

The other major hypothesis guiding this study and supplementing the instrumentalist one held that institutional prescriptions have had consequences, albeit sometimes unintended ones. One of these, the result of shaping future recommendations, has already been noted above. Other consequences have included those for the structures and operations of government institutions, political parties and interest groups, popular attitutudes toward government and politics, and other components of the ideologies themselves.

Unquestionably, the greatest overall effects of ideologically based institutional prescriptions in modern times have been those of the New Deal liberal theory of governance. Its conception of constitutional flexibility, rooted in pragmatism and legal realism, exerted enormous influence on political actors and public attitudes for decades to come, despite the strong resistance from defenders of an immutable Constitution and the desires of many liberals to find a solid grounding for constitutional interpretation in moral philosophy or a conception of proper procedures. Its effects, however, may well have fed a growing popular skepticism about the judicial/legal system and increasing alienation from the reshaping of consitutional law according to the personal preferences of the judges.

The New Deal liberal governance theory also left a long-term legacy in a federal system more centralized than ever before. To some extent, this also stimulated a "nationalization" of the political party and interest group system. However, compromises with conservative and moderate forces and widespread liberal fear of overcentralization led increasingly to a "cooperative" or "marble-cake" federalism that frequently blurred lines of accountability and led to ineffective public policy implementation. The results fed growing demands, even among many liberals, for decentralization and helped to generate a popular backlash against liberalism, its governance approaches, and even its substantive public policies and values by the late 1960s—a backlash that continues to plague liberalism even in the 1990s.

The administrative state prescriptions of the New Deal liberals also had a major, if mixed, impact. They vastly enlarged the traditionally small administrative state apparatus in the United States, professionalized it, and made it more hierarchical and accountable to the president than before. However, forced compromises modified the effects of the liberals' prescriptions in ways that encouraged the formation of "iron triangles" of bureaus, interest groups, and congressional committees or subcommittees; fed an advocacy explosion among interest groups; and encouraged the long-term evolution of liberalism in what Theodore Lowi termed an "interest-group liberal" direction. The administrative state itself, but particularly the liberals' linkage of it to the presidency, had the at least partially unintended long-term effect of weakening the party system, as Sidney Milkis has demonstrated.[5]

The presidential government model of the New Deal liberals evolved over time into what many came to see as an imperial presidency. Certainly both the New Deal years and Franklin D. Roosevelt's foreign/defense initiatives of 1939–41 set precedents for later expansions of presidential power, as even Arthur Schlesinger Jr. has conceded, though Schlesinger has located most of the problems of his version of the "imperial presidency" in the Cold War period. With its tribune and social reform instigator roles as well as its administrative presidency dimensions, liberal presidential government also weakened the party system. It also may have had effects, through its linkage to a growing national security policy bureaucracy, on the very content of the foreign policies and the national security values favored by both major ideological coalitions and the bulk of the American people during the years of the Cold War, as analysts such as Richard Barnet, Henry Steele Commager, and Jordan Schwarz have suggested.[6]

The New Deal liberal coalition never fully gained consensus on a set of judicial prescriptions, in large part because of the changing composition and orientation of the federal judiciary between 1933 and 1945. Nevertheless, the preferred freedoms idea, summarized by Associate Justice (later Chief Justice) Harlan Stone in the *Carolene Products* footnote of 1938, came to be embraced in the late 1930s and the 1940s by a wide array of liberal jurists, legal scholars, and other coalition participants and laid the foundation upon which much later judicial liberal activism would be built. Although its bifurcation of judicial restraint in socioeconomic matters and judicial activism on civil liberties and rights became blurred at times, it remained an important guiding principle for most liberals for more than half a century.

No other set of institutional recommendations had as much impact on government institutions and other aspects of American political life as the New Deal liberal theory of governance. However, broadened post-New Deal liberal judicial activist prescriptions were to have numerous effects (some, such as the popular antiliberal backlash of the late 1960s, quite unintended by their proponents). Another set of governance recommendations that appeared likely to have a major impact on American politics were the Reaganite conservative prescriptions for privatizing the administrative state in the 1980s and 1990s, particularly to the extent that they merged with New Democratic ideas on the subject. Though it is too soon to assess fully the nature and extent of that impact, it has already been seen that the effects partially undermined those of the Reaganite conservative administrative presidency by blurring lines of accountability, as Peter Benda and Charles Levine have stressed. Various other prescriptions, such as Nixonian conservative revenue-sharing federalism and new-politics liberal judicialized administration, had important short-term effects, often unintended, such as eroding liberal-conservative differences on the federalism dimension and adding to the national government's budget deficits in the former case and complicating effective policy making and spurring big business conservative countermobilization in the latter. Overall, it is clear that institutional ideas have had consequences, even though these have often been unintended ones and even though regular liberal-conservative conflict and frequent fragmentation within each ideological coalition has generally resulted in compromises on institutional reforms.[7]

## Historical and Comparative Perspectives

Although beyond the scope of the present study, analyses comparing the American conservative and liberal institutional prescriptions and theories of governance of 1933–93 with those of political ideologies and their movements in previous historical epochs and with those in other political systems would certainly advance our understanding of the processes by which such recommendations emerge from ideological movements and undergo change and the effects that they have had on government institutions and other aspects of politics. Leonard D. White has laid an excellent foundation with his "studies in administrative history," covering the Federalists, Jeffersonians, Jacksonians, and post-Civil War Republicans in the United States. An interesting study might build on White's to compare the staying power of Jeffersonian Republican and Hamiltonian Federalist theories of governance with the durability of the liberal and conservative institutional prescriptions of 1939–65 and explore further the impact of the early governance theories on subsequent American political developments. Another valuable inquiry could go beyond the present one in analyzing the linkages and discontinuities between the ideological prescriptions for institutions during the Progressive and New Deal eras, adding to our understanding of both. These are, of course, just a few of many possibilities for enlightening historical and comparative research on the general subject matter of this study.[8]

In comparative, crossnational political analysis, the range of interesting and fruitful possibilities is even wider than in American history. Some excellent beginnings have already been made. For example, Samuel Beer's historical and contemporary studies of British conservative, socialist, and other governance theories helped to inspire the current work and offer useful insights which could be integrated with American and other topics. Moreover, Robert Devigne's recently published *Recasting Conservatism* makes the kinds of explicit comparisons between American and British conservative institutional prescriptions which remind us that ideologies which share broadly similar values and policy preferences may, in different contexts, advocate very different ideas on governance. For instance, the decentralist rhetoric of the Reaganite and other American conservatives since the New Deal stands in sharp contrast to the central-ist proclivities of the Thatcherite conservatives in modern Britain. The French Socialists' embrace of decentralization in the 1980s after decades of centralist prescriptions is also suggestive. If the present study acts as a spur to move toward broadened historical and comparative perspectives on the subject of ideologies and institutions, it will have served a useful purpose.[9]

## Future Prospects

As for the future of American ideologies and institutions, this study has suggested that the entrenched features of the two-party system, the marked and apparently widening socioeconomic cleavage in American society, and the resilience of each ideological coalition in the face of cen-trist pressures and new ideological threats over the past sixty years point toward the distinct possiblity of continuing ideological debate between two major movements in the future. Those coalitions, especially the liber-al one, may well change labels. Almost certainly, the values, public policy preferences, and power bases of each will undergo marked alterations. Given the diversity of values and preferred policies and the crosscutting nature of sociocultural cleavages with the socioeconomic ones, of course, there may be more than two ideological coalitions contending for domi-nance. The fragmentation within each movement and the public attitudi-nal studies by such authors as William Maddox and Stuart Lilie are sug-gestive in this regard.[10]

Will the ideological coalitions of the future, whatever their names and compositions and numbers, continue to advocate distinctive institutional prescriptions? Will each be able and willing to reach clear consensus on an overarching theory of governance? Will such a theory be capable of bridg-ing the ideological movements? To these questions, there are clues but no certain answers.

Americans tend to yearn for "neutral principles," particularly in the realm of constitutional/institutional prescriptions. Arthur Schlesinger Jr. likened the conservative-liberal conflicts over presidential-congressional relations to "the two drunken men described by Lincoln who got into a fight with their greatcoats on until each fought himself out of his own coat and into the coat of the other" and called out for "Neutral principles! Neu-tral principles!" Theodore Lowi, William Andrews, Norman Ornstein, Peri Arnold and John Roos, Sotirios Barber, and numerous other analysts have expressed this yearning in various ways. On certain points—most notably in recent years the administrative state and federalism—a centrist synthesis showed some signs of emerging. However, in a society as diverse in its values as the United States in the future is likely to be, neither a centrist synthesis nor a set of "neutral" institutional principles going beyond a very high level of generality, such as Schlesinger's appeal for "shared decisions," is likely to achieve wide consensus for very long.[11]

From the Jeffersonian Republicans and Hamiltonian Federalists of the 1790s through the liberals and conservatives of 1933–93, debates over institutional prescriptions that have been treated as at least broadly instrumental means toward different political values and public policy ends have usually been a major part of the American political scene. Samuel Beer's studies suggest that the same has been true in Britain. In the continuing or perhaps increasingly diverse coalitional conflict patterns of the future in the United States, those debates are likely to continue. However, advancing party dealignment (evidenced by fluctuating patterns of institutional dominance by the partisan/ideological movements in the 1990s) as well as the rising fragmentation of both conservative and liberal ideologies, suggest the possibility that full-fledged governance theories will not soon revive. Frequent shifts in partisan/ideological control of government institutions and the lack of clarity in ideological public policy goals may at least for a time mean that institutional prescriptions will be more fleeting and less intensely pursued than during much of the era since the New Deal. Yet the legacies of the liberal-conservative struggles of 1933–93 will remain.

## Notes

1. Thomas Byrne Edsall and Mary D. Edsall, *Chain Reaction* (New York: W. W. Norton, 1991), esp. chaps. 1 and 2.

2. William G. Andrews, "The Presidency, Congress, and Constitutional Theory," in *Perspectives on the Presidecy,* ed. Aaron Wildavsky (Boston: Little, Brown, 1975), 38; C. P. Ives, "The Well–Intending Judges," *Modern Age* 13 (Summer 1969): 242.

3. Barry M. Goldwater, *Where I Stand* (New York: McGraw–Hill, 1964), 91.

4. Felix Morley, "American Republic or American Empire?" *Modern Age* 1 (Summer 1957): 20–32; Felix Morley, "Deliberate Pace in Congress Safeguards Your Rights," *Nation's Business* 51 (March 1963): 27–28; Felix Morley, *For the Record* (South Bend, IN: Regnery Gateway, 1979), 462; Mickey Edwards, "A Conservative Defense of Congress," *Public Interest,* 100 (Summer 1990): 81–88; and Mickey Edwards, "Of Conservatives and Kings," *Policy Review* 48 (Spring 1989): 24–31; Robert Higgs and Charlotte Twight, "National Emergency and the Erosion of Private Property Rights," *Cato Journal* 6 (Winter 1987): 747–773; Christopher Layne,

"The Real Conservative Agenda," *Foreign Policy* 61 (Winter 1985/86): 73–93; Alan Crawford, *Thunder on the Right* (New York: Pantheon Books, 1980); Forrest McDonald, foreword to *The Constitution and the American Presidency,* by Martin L. Fausold and Alan Shank (Albany: State University of New York Press, 1991), ix–xi; and Henry Regnery, "Emerging Conservatism: Kilpatrick, Morley, and Burnham," *Modern Age* 22 (Summer 1978): 237–245.

    5.  Theodore J. Lowi, *The End of Liberalism,* 2d ed. (New York: W. W. Norton, 1979); Sidney M. Milkis, *The President and the Parties* (New York: Oxford University Press, 1993).

    6.  Arthur M. Schlesinger Jr., *The Imperial Presidency* (New York: Popular Library, 1973), esp. chaps. 5 and 6; Richard J. Barnet, *Intervention and Revolution* (New York: New American Library, 1972); Henry Steele Commager, *The Defeat of America* (New York: Simon & Schuster, 1974); Jordan A. Schwarz, *The New Dealers* (New York: Alfred A. Knopf, 1993), esp. 337–350. Schwarz, unlike the others, emphasizes the export of New Dealish state capitalism during the Cold War era.

    7.  Peter M. Benda and Charles H. Levine, "Reagan and the Bureaucracy," in *The Reagan Legacy,* ed. Charles O. Jones (Chatham, NJ: Chatham House, 1988), esp. 137–139. On the impact of liberal judicialized administration efforts, Michael W. McCann, *Taking Reform Seriously* (Ithaca, NY: Cornell University Press, 1986), chap. 5, is particularly valuable.

    8.  Leonard D. White, *The Federalists* (New York: Macmillan, 1948); Leonard D. White, *The Jeffersonians* (New York: Macmillan, 1951); Leonard D. White, *The Jacksonians* (New York: Macmillan, 1954); and Leonard D. White, *The Republican Era* (New York: Macmillan, 1958).

    9.  Samuel H. Beer, *Britain against Itself* (London: Faber, 1982); Samuel H. Beer, *British Politics in the Collectivist Age* (New York: Random House, 1965); Robert Devigne, *Recasting Conservatism* (New Haven: Yale University Press, 1994). On the French Socialists, see Henry W. Ehrmann and Martin A. Shain, *Politics in France,* 5th ed. (New York: HarperCollins Publishers, 1992), 385–391.

    10.  William S. Maddox and Stuart A. Lilie, *Beyond Liberal and Conservative* (Washington: Cato Institute, 1984).

    11.  Schlesinger, *Imperial Presidency,* 386; Others seeking neutral principles, or believing that they have found them, include Theodore J. Lowi, "Presidential Power and the Ideological Struggle over Its Interpretation," in *The Constitution and the American Presidency,* ed. Martin L. Fausold and Alan Shank (Albany: State University of New York Press, 1991), 227–244; Andrews, "The Presidency," esp. 39–42; Norman Ornstein, "The Permanent Democratic Congress," *Public Interest* 100 (Summer 1990): 25–26; Peri E. Arnold and L. John Roos, "Toward a Theory of Congressional-Executive Relations," *Review of Politics* (July 1974): 410–429; and Sotirios A. Barber, *On What the Constitution Means* (Baltimore: Johns Hopkins University Press, 1993).

# Bibliography

Abcarian, Gilbert, and Sherman N. Stanage. "Alienation and the Radical Right." *Journal of Politics* 27 (November 1965): 776–796.

Aberbach, Joel D. "The President and the Executive Branch." In *The Bush Presidency: First Appraisals*, edited by Colin Campbell and Bert A. Rockman. Chatham, NJ: Chatham House, 1991.

Aberbach, Joel D., and Bert A. Rockman. "Clashing Beliefs within the Executive Branch: The Nixon Administration Bureaucracy." *American Political Science Review* 70 (June 1976): 456–478.

"The Abortion Decision." *Commonweal* 97 (16 February 1973): 435–436.

Abramson, Paul R., John H. Aldrich, and David W. Rohde. *Change and Continuity in the 1988 Elections.* Rev. ed. Washington: Congressional Quarterly Press, 1991.

"Adventure in Blueprints." *Nation* 144 (30 January 1937): 116–117.

Albertsworth, E. F. "The New Constitutionalism." *American Bar Association Journal* 26 (November 1940): 865–869.

"All Power to the Trade Associations?" *New Republic* 76 (15 November 1933): 4–5.

Ambrose, Stephen M. *Eisenhower: The President.* New York: Simon & Schuster, 1984.

———. *Nixon: The Triumph of a Politician, 1962–1972.* New York: Simon & Schuster, 1989.

Anderson, Paul Y. "In Defense of Congress." *Nation* 136 (28 June 1933): 722.

Andrews, William G. "The Presidency, Congress, and Constitutional Theory." In *Perspectives on the Presidency*, edited by Aaron Wildavsky. Boston: Little, Brown, 1975.

Arnold, Peri E., and L. John Roos. "Toward a Theory of Congressional-Executive Relations." *Review of Politics* 36 (July 1974): 410–429.

Arnold, Thurman. "The New Deal Is Constitutional." *New Republic* 76 (15 November 1933): 8–10.

Asher, Herbert. *Presidential Elections and American Politics: Voters, Candidates, and Campaigns Since 1952.* 5th ed. Pacific Grove, CA: Brooks/Cole, 1992.

Aspin, Les. "Congress versus the Defense Department." In *The Tethered Presidency*, edited by Thomas M. Franck. New York: New York University Press, 1981.

"Assault from Strange Quarters." *National Review* 5 (8 March 1958): 220–221.

Babbitt, Bruce. "States Rights for Liberals." *New Republic* 184 (24 January 1981): 21–23.

Bachrach, Peter. *The Theory of Democratic Elitism: A Critique.* Boston: Little, Brown, 1967.

Bailey, Stephen K. *Congress Makes a Law: The Story behind the Employment Act of 1946.* New York: Columbia University Press, 1950.

Barber, Sotirios A. *The Constitution of Judicial Power.* Baltimore: Johns Hopkins University Press, 1993.

———. *On What the Constitution Means.* Baltimore: Johns Hopkins University Press, 1984.

Barnes, Fred. "Media Realignment." *New Republic* 192 (6 May 1985): 12–15.

Barnet, Richard J. *Intervention and Revolution: The United States in the Third World.* New York: New American Library, 1972.

Barrett, Laurence I. *Gambling with History: Ronald Reagan in the White House.* New York: Penguin Books, 1984.

Bartley, Ernest R. *The Tidelands Oil Controversy: A Legal and Historical Analysis.* Austin: University of Texas Press.

Beer, Samuel H. *Britain against Itself.* London: Faber, 1982.

———. *British Politics in the Collectivist Age.* New York: Random House, 1965.

———. "The Idea of the Nation." *New Republic* 187 (19–26 July 1982): 23–29.

———. Introduction to *New Federalism: Intergovernmental Reform from Nixon to Reagan,* by Timothy J. Conlan. Washington: Brookings Institution, 1988.

Bell, Daniel, ed. *The Radical Right.* Garden City, NY: Doubleday Anchor Books, 1964.

Benda, Peter M., and Charles H. Levine. "Reagan and the Bureaucracy." In *The Reagan Legacy,* edited by Charles O. Jones. Chatham, NJ: Chatham House, 1988.

Bendiner, Robert. *Obstacle Course on Capitol Hill.* New York: McGraw-Hill, 1964.

Bennett, William. "Rebirth of a Nation." *National Review* 21 (18 March 1991): 44.

Berger, Raoul. *Government by Judiciary: The Transformation of the Fourteenth Amendment.* Cambridge: Harvard University Press, 1977.

Berger, Samuel R. *Dollar Harvest: The Story of the Farm Bureau.* Lexington, MA: D.C. Heath, 1971.

Berman, Larry, and Bruce W. Jentleson. "Bush and the Post–Cold War World: New Challenges for American Leadership." In *The Bush Presidency: First Appraisals,* edited by Colin Campbell and Bert A. Rockman. Chatham, NJ: Chatham House, 1991.

Berman, William C. *The Politics of Civil Rights in the Truman Administration.* Columbus: Ohio State University Press, 1970.

Berns, Walter. *Taking the Constitution Seriously.* New York: Simon & Schuster, 1987.

Bernstein, Marver H. *Regulating Business by Independent Commission.* Princeton: Princeton University Press, 1955.

Berry, Jeffrey M. *The Interest Group Society*. 2d ed. Glenview, IL: Scott, Foresman, 1989.

Best, Gary Dean. *The Critical Press and the New Deal: The Press versus Presidential Power, 1933–1938*. Westport, CT: Praeger, 1993.

Best, Judith A. "Foreign Policy Is Executive Domain." Letter to the Editor. *Policy Review* 60 (Spring 1992): 91.

Bickel, Alexander. *The Supreme Court and the Idea of Progress*. New York: Harper & Row, 1970.

———. *Watergate, Politics, and the Legal Process*. Washington: American Enterprise Institute, 1974.

"Big Turnabout among U.S. Liberals." *U.S. News & World Report* 80 (15 March 1976): 16–18.

Binkley, Wilfred E. "Andrew Jackson's Defiance." *New Republic* 130 (14 June 1954): 16–17.

———. "The Decline of the Executive." *New Republic* 128 (18 May 1953): 13–16.

———. *Powers of the President: Problems of American Democracy*. Garden City, NY: Doubleday, Doran, 1937.

———. *President and Congress*. Rev. ed. New York: Doubleday, 1962.

Biskupic, Joan. "Bush Boosts Bench Strength of Conservative Judges." *Congressional Quarterly Weekly Reports* (19 January 1991): 171–174.

"Blackout for the New Deal?" *New Republic* 106 (16 March 1942): 351.

Blum, John Morton. "Congress and the President." *New Republic* 144 (6 January 1961): 9–10.

———. *The Progressive Presidents: Roosevelt, Wilson, Roosevelt, Johnson*. New York: W. W. Norton, 1980.

Blumenthal, Sidney. *The Rise of the Counter-Establishment: From Conservative Ideology to Political Power*. New York: Harper & Row, 1986.

Bolling, Richard. *House Out of Order*. New York: Dutton, 1966.

Bork, Robert H. Foreword to *The Fettered Presidency*, edited by L. Gordon Crovitz and Jeremy A. Rabkin. Washington: American Enterprise Institute, 1989.

———. "Supreme Court Needs a New Philosophy." *Fortune* 78 (December 1968): 138–141.

———. *The Tempting of America: The Political Seduction of the Law*. New York: Free Press, 1990.

Bozell, L. Brent. "A Bill to Curb the Court." *National Review* 5 (1 March 1958): 200–201.

Brady, David. *In Labor's Cause: Main Themes on the History of the American Worker*. New York: Oxford University Press, 1993.

Brennan, William J. "The Constitution of the United States: Contemporary Ratification." In *Interpreting the Constitution: The Debate over Original Intent*, edited by Jack N. Rakove. Boston: Northeastern University Press, 1990.

Brest, Paul. "Berger v. Brown et al." Review of *Government by Judiciary*, by Raoul Berger. *New York Times Book Review*, 11 December 1977, 44.

Brinkley, Alan. "The New Deal and the Idea of the State." In *The Rise and Fall of the New Deal Order, 1930–1980*, edited by Steve Fraser and Gary Gerstle. Princeton: Princeton University Press, 1989.

Brock, David. "Mr. Symms Goes to Jamba: A Kind Word for Congress in Foreign Policy." *Policy Review* 59 (Winter 1992): 32–39.

Broesamle, John G. *Reform and Reaction in Twentieth-Century American Politics*. New York: Greenwood Press, 1990.

Buchanan, Patrick J. *The New Majority*. N.P.: Girard Bank, 1973.

Buckley, William F., Jr. "And Now Legislative Supremacy." *National Review* 39 (6 June 1975): 630–631.

———."Mr. Reid's Bill." *National Review* 35 (6 June 1973): 331.

———."Revenue Sharing." *National Review* 33 (6 April 1971): 390–391.

Burner, David, and Thomas L. West. *The Torch Is Passed: The Kennedy Brothers and American Liberalism*. New York: Harper & Row, 1984.

Burnham, James. *Congress and the American Tradition*. Chicago: Henry Regnery, 1959.

Burnham, Walter Dean. *Critical Elections and the Mainspring of American Politics*. New York: W. W. Norton, 1970.

———. "Party Systems and the Political Process." In *The American Party Systems*, edited by Walter Dean Burnham and William Nisbet Chambers. New York: Oxford University Press, 1967.

———."The Reagan Heritage." In *The Election of 1988: Reports and Interpretations*, edited by Gerald M. Pomper. Chatham, NJ: Chatham House, 1989.

Burns, James MacGregor. *Congress on Trial*. New York: Harper & Brothers, 1949.

———. *The Deadlock of Democracy: Four-Party Politics in America*. Englewood Cliffs, NJ: Prentice-Hall, 1963.

———. "King of the Rock." *Commonweal* 97 (9 February 1973): 415–418.

———. *The Power to Lead: The Crisis of the American Presidency*. New York: Simon & Schuster, 1984.

———. *Presidential Government: The Crucible of Leadership*. Boston: Houghton Mifflin, 1965.

———. *Roosevelt: Soldier of Freedom*. New York: Harcourt Brace Jovanovich, 1970.

———. *Uncommon Sense*. New York: Harper & Row, 1972.

Burrow, James G. *AMA: Voice of American Medicine*. Baltimore: Johns Hopkins University Press, 1963.

"Business Hops Aboard." *Nation* 136 (28 June 1933): 712–713.

Butler, Stuart M., ed. *Mandate for Leadership II: Continuing the Conservative Revolution*. Washington: Heritage Foundation, 1985.

"Caesarism." *National Review* 1 (26 November 1955): 3–4.

Califano, Joseph A., Jr. *A Presidential Nation.* New York: W. W. Norton, 1975.

Caplan, Lincoln. "The Reagan Challenge to the Rule of Law." In *The Reagan Legacy,* edited by Sidney Blumenthal and Thomas Byrne Edsall. New York: Pantheon, 1988.

Carey, George W. "Thunder on the Right, Lightning from the Left." *Modern Age* 25 (Spring 1981): 132.

Carmines, Edward G., and James A. Stimson. *Issue Evolution: Race and the Transformation of American Politics.* Princeton: Princeton University Press, 1989.

Carnoy, Martin, and Derek Shearer. *Economic Democracy: The Challenge of the 1980s.* White Plains, NY: M. E. Sharpe, 1980.

Caute, David. *The Great Fear: The Anti-Communist Purge under Truman and Eisenhower.* New York: Simon & Schuster, 1978.

Ceaser, James. "In Defense of the Separation of Powers." In *Separation of Powers: Does It Still Work?* edited by Robert Goldwin and Herbert Kaufman. Washington: American Enterprise Institute, 1987.

————. "The Theory of Governance of the Reagan Administration." In *The Reagan Presidency and the Governing of America,* edited by Lester Salamon and Michael S. Lund. Washington: Urban Institute Press, 1985.

"The Challenge to Congress." *Commonweal* 97 (26 January 1973): 363–364.

"Civil Liberties and War." *New Republic* 106 (22 June 1942): 848–849.

Clark, Joseph S. *Congress: The Sapless Branch.* New York: Harper & Row, 1965.

Clark, Nolan. "The Headless Fourth Branch." In *The Imperial Congress,* edited by Gordon S. Jones and John A. Marini. New York: Pharos Books, 1988.

Clausen, Aage R. *How Congressmen Decide: A Policy Focus.* New York: St. Martin's Press, 1973.

Cole, Richard L., and David A. Caputo. "Presidential Control of the Senior Civil Service: Addressing the Strategies of the Nixon Years." *American Political Science Review* 73 (June 1979): 399–413.

Commager, Henry Steele. "Can We Limit Presidential Power?" *New Republic* 156 (6 April 1968): 15–18.

————. *The Defeat of America: Presidential Power and National Character.* New York: Simon & Schuster, 1974.

————. "Only Two Terms for a President?" *New York Times Magazine* (27 April 1947): 48.

————. "The Perilous Folly of Senator Bricker." *Reporter* 146 (13 October 1953): 12–17.

————. "Presidential Power: The Issue Analyzed." *New York Times Magazine* (14 January 1951): 11, 23.

————. "Tocqueville's Mistake: A Defense of Strong Central Government." *Harpers* 269 (August 1984): 70–74.

"Congress Adjourns." *New Republic* 94 (28 June 1938): 200.

"Congress and the U. S. Military Commitments." *Congressional Digest* 48 (August–September 1969): 193–224.

"Congress Keep Out." *National Review* 1 (7 March 1956): 6.

Conlan, Timothy J. "Federalism and Competing Values in the Reagan Administration." *Publius* 16 (Winter 1986): 29–47.

———. *New Federalism: Intergovernmental Reform from Nixon to Reagan.* Washington: Brookings Institution, 1988.

Conlan, Timothy J., James D. Riggle, and Donna E. Schwartz. "Deregulating Federalism? The Politics of Mandate Reform in the 104th Congress." *Publius* 25 (Summer 1995): 23–39.

"Contempt for Congress." *National Review* 2 (May 30, 1956): 6.

"The Controversy in Congres over Federal 'Civil Rights' Proposals." *Congressional Digest* 25 (February 1950): 37–64.

"Controversy over the Presidential Impoundment of Appropriated Funds." *Congressional Digest* 52 (April 1973): 99–128.

Converse, Philip E. "The Nature of Belief Systems in Mass Publics." In *Ideology and Discontent,* edited by David E. Apter. New York: Free Press, 1964.

Cover, Robert M. "Books Considered." *New Republic* 198 (13 January 1978): 26–28.

Crampton, John O. *The National Farmers Union: Ideology of a Pressure Group.* Lincoln: University of Nebraska Press, 1965.

Crawford, Alan. *Thunder on the Right: The "New Right" and the Politics of Resentment.* New York: Pantheon Press, 1980.

"The Crisis of the N.R.A." *New Republic* 76 (8 November 1933): 349–350.

Crovitz, L. Gordon, and Jeremy A. Rabkin, eds. *The Fettered Presidency.* Washington: American Enterprise Institute, 1989.

Cunliffe, Marcus. *American Presidents and the Presidency.* London: Eyre & Spotteswoode, 1969.

"Curbing the Supreme Court." *New Republic* 89 (17 February 1937): 31–32.

Cutler, Lloyd N. "To Form a Government: On the Defects of Separation of Powers." *Foreign Affairs* 39 (Fall 1980): 126–143.

Dawley, Alan. *Struggles for Justice: Social Responsibility and the Liberal State.* Cambridge: Belknap Press of Harvard University Press, 1990.

De Grazia, Alfred. *Eight Bads—Eight Goods: The American Contradictions.* New York: Doubleday Anchor, 1975.

———. *Republic in Crisis.* New York: Federal Legal Publications, 1965.

Destler, I. M. "Reagan and the World: An 'Awesome Stubbornness.'" In *The Reagan Legacy: Promise and Performance,* edited by Charles O. Jones. Chatham, NJ: Chatham House, 1988.

Devigne, Robert. *Recasting Conservatism: Oakeshott, Strauss, and the Response to Postmodernism.* New Haven: Yale University Press, 1994.

Dewey, John. "The Future of Liberalism." In *Political Ideologies,* edited by James A. Gould and Willis H. Truitt. New York: Macmillan, 1973.

Diamond, Sara. *Roads to Dominion: Right-Wing Movements and Political Power in the United States.* New York: Guilford Press, 1995.

Dionne, E. J., Jr. *Why Americans Hate Politics.* New York: Simon & Schuster, 1991.

———. *They Only Look Dead: Why Progressives Will Dominate the Next Political Era.* New York: Simon & Schuster, 1996.

"Divvying Up the Dollars." *New Republic* 167 (17 October 1972): 7–8.

Dolbeare, Kenneth M., and Patricia Dolbeare. *American Ideologies: Competing Political Beliefs of the 1970s.* 2d ed. Chicago: Markham, 1973.

Dolbeare, Kenneth M., and Linda J. Medcalf. *American Ideologies Today.* 2d ed. New York: McGraw-Hill, 1993.

Dorrien, Gary. *The Neoconservative Mind.* Philadelphia: Temple University Press, 1993.

Domhoff, William. *The Higher Circles: The Governing Class in America.* New York: Vintage Books, 1970.

Donohue, William A. *The Politics of the American Civil Liberties Union.* New Brunswick, NJ: Transaction Books, 1985.

Dorsen, Norman, and John H. F. Shattuck. "Executive Privilege: The President Won't Tell." In *Resolved: That the Powers of the Presidency Should Be Curtailed,* edited by the Congressional Research Service, Library of Congress. Washington: U.S. Government Printing Office, 1974.

Dworkin, Ronald. *Taking Rights Seriously.* Cambridge: Harvard University Press, 1977.

Eastland, Terry. *Energy in the Executive: The Case for a Strong Presidency.* New York: Free Press, 1992.

"The Editors' Choice." *New Republic* 87 (23 September 1936): 207–208.

Edsall, Thomas Byrne. *The New Politics of Inequality.* New York: W. W. Norton, 1984.

Edsall, Thomas Byrne, and Mary B. Edsall. *Chain Reaction: The Impact of Race, Rights, and Taxes on American Politics.* New York: W. W. Norton, 1991.

Edwards, Mickey. "A Conservative Defense of Congress." *Public Interest* 100 (Summer 1990): 81–88.

———. "Of Conservatives and Kings." *Policy Review* 48 (Spring 1989): 24–31.

Ehrmann, Henry W., and Martin A. Shain. *Politics in France.* 5th ed. New York: HarperCollins, 1992.

"Electing a President." *National Review* 1 (28 March 1956): 6.

Ely, John Hart. *Democracy and Distrust: A Theory of Judicial Review.* Cambridge: Harvard University Press, 1980.

Epstein, Richard. *Takings: Private Prosperity and the Power of Eminent Domain.* Cambridge: Harvard University Press, 1985.

Ervin, Sam J. *The Whole Truth: The Watergate Conspiracy.* New York: Random House, 1980.

Evans, M. Stanton. "At Home." *National Review Bulletin* (11 June 1968): sec. B, p. 94.

————. *Clear and Present Dangers: A Conservative View of America's Government.* New York: Harcourt Brace Jovanovich, 1975.

————. *The Liberal Establishment.* New York: Devin-Adair, 1965.

"An Exchange of Views." *Nation* 226 (25 February 1978): 26–28.

Fallows, James. "The Passionless Presidency." *Atlantic Monthly* 243 (May 1979): 33–46.

Fausold, Martin, and Alan Shank, eds. *The Constitution and the American Presidency.* Albany: State University of New York Press, 1991.

"The Federal 'Administrative Procedure Act' Becomes Law." *American Bar Association Journal* 32 (July 1946): 377–386.

"Federalism in the 96th Congress." *Publius* 11 (Summer 1981): 155–192.

Fein, Bruce. "Congress Has Not Changed Its Spots." Letter. *Policy Review* 60 (Spring 1992): 92.

Feinman, Ronald L. *Twilight of Progressivism: The Western Republican Senators and the New Deal.* Baltimore: Johns Hopkins University Press, 1981.

Finer, Herman. *The Presidency: Crisis and Regeneration.* Chicago: University of Chicago Press, 1960.

"The First Law of Nature." *Saturday Evening Post* 207 (31 March 1934): 22.

"The First Nixon Court." *National Review* 36 (21 July 1972): 785.

Fishel, Leslie H., Jr. "A Case Study: The Negro and the New Deal." In *The New Deal: Analysis and Interpretation,* edited by Alonzo L. Hamby. 2d ed. New York: Longman, 1981.

Fisher, Louis M. *Constitutional Conflicts between Congress and the President.* Princeton: Princeton University Press, 1985.

————. "Micromanagement by Congress: Reality and Mythology." In *The Fettered Presidency,* edited by L. Gordon Crovitz and Jeremy A. Rabkin. Washington: American Enterprise Institute, 1989.

————. *Presidential Spending Power.* Princeton: Princeton University Press, 1975.

Flaherty, Francis J. "States' Rights Are Our Rights, Too," *Progressive* 46 (February 1982): 40–43.

Foley, Michael. "The President and Congress." In *The Bush Presidency: Triumphs and Adversities,* edited by Dilys M. Hill and Phil Williams. New York: St. Martin's Press, 1994.

"For a Republican Form of Government." *American Bar Association Journal* 33 (January 1947): 4–5.

Foreman, Christopher H., Jr. "Legislators, Regulators, and the OMB: The Congressional Challenge to Presidential Regulatory Relief." In *Divided Democracy,* edited by James A. Thurber. Washington: Congressional Quarterly Press, 1991.

Francis, Samuel. "Imperial Conservatives?" *National Review* 68 (4 August 1989): 37–38.

Frankel, Max. "Revenue Sharing Is a Counterrevolution." *New York Times Magazine* (25 April 1971): 28–29, 91.

Franklin, John Hope. *From Slavery to Freedom: A History of Negro Americans.* 3d ed. New York: Alfred A. Knopf, 1967.

Fredericks, W. G. "No, to Revenue Sharing." *National Review* 34 (13 July 1971): 754–757.

Freeman, J. Lieper. *The Political Process: Executive Bureau–Legislative Committee Relations.* Rev. ed. New York: Random House, 1965.

Friedman, Milton. *Capitalism and Freedom.* Chicago: University of Chicago Press, 1962.

Friedman, Milton, and Anna Schwartz. *A Monetary History of the United States, 1867–1960.* Princeton: Princeton University Press, 1963.

Fukuyama, Francis. "The End of History?" *The National Interest* 16 (Summer 1989): 3–18.

Fuller, Tim, ed. *Economy, Diplomacy, and Statecraft.* Colorado Springs: Colorado College Press, 1988.

Gans, Herbert J. *More Equality.* New York: Pantheon Books, 1973.

Garry, Patrick M. *Liberalism and American Identity.* Kent, OH: Kent State University Press, 1992.

Garson, Robert A. *The Democratic Party and the Politics of Sectionalism, 1941–1948.* Baton Rouge, LA: Louisiana State University Press, 1974.

Gerstle, Gary. "The Protean Character of American Liberalism." *American Historical Review* 99 (October 1994): 1043–1073.

Gillon, Steven M. *Politics and Vision: The A.D.A. and American Liberalism, 1947–1985.* New York: Oxford University Press, 1987.

Glad, Betty. *Jimmy Carter: In Search of the Great White House.* New York: W. W. Norton, 1980.

Goldman, Sheldon. *Constitutional Law and Supreme Court Decision-Making: Cases and Essays.* New York: Harper & Row, 1982.

Goldwater, Barry M. *The Coming Breakthrough.* New York: Macmillan, 1976.

———. *Conscience of a Conservative.* Shepherdsville, KY: Victor, 1960.

———. "My Case for the Republican Party." *Saturday Review* 47 (17 October 1964): 21–23, 49–50.

———. *Where I Stand.* New York: McGraw-Hill, 1964.

Goldwin, Robert, and Herbert Kaufman, eds. *Separation of Powers: Does It Still Work?* Washington: American Enterprise Institute, 1987.

Gottfried, Paul, and Thomas Fleming. *The Conservative Movement.* Boston: Twayne, 1988.

Gottschall, Jon. "Carter's Judicial Appointments: The Influence of Affirmative Action and Merit Selection on Voting on the U.S. Court of Appeals." *Judicature* 67 (October 1983): 165–173.

———. "Reagan's Appointments to the U.S. Courts of Appeals: The Continuation of a Judicial Revolution." *Judicature* 70 (June/July1986): 48–54.

Goulden, Joseph C. *Fit to Print: A. M. Rosenthal and His Times.* Secaucus, NJ: Lyle Stuart, 1988.

Graglia, Lino. *Disaster by Decree: The Supreme Court Decisions on Race and the Schools.* Ithaca, NY: Cornell University Press, 1976.

———. "Judicial Activism: Even on the Right, It's Wrong." *Public Interest* 95 (Spring 1989): 57–94.

Graham, Otis L., Jr. *An Encore for Reform: The Old Progressives and the New Deal.* New York: Oxford University Press, 1967.

Green, Mark, James Fallows, and David Zwick. *Who Runs Congress?* New York: Bantam/Grossman, 1972.

Green, Mark, and Frances Zwenig. "The Legislative Veto Is Bad Law." *Nation* 226 (28 October 1978): 434–436.

Green, T. H. *Works: Miscellanies and Memoir.* New York: Longmans, Green, 1906.

Greenstone, J. David. *Labor in American Politics.* New York: Alfred A. Knopf, 1969.

Greider, William. *Who Will Tell the People? The Betrayal of American Democracy.* New York: Simon & Schuster, 1992.

Grey, Thomas. "Origins of the Unwritten Constitution: Fundamental Law in American Revolutionary Thought." *Stanford Law Review* 30 (1978): 843.

Griffith, Ernest S., and Francis R. Valeo. *Congress: Its Contemporary Role.* 5th ed. New York: New York University Press, 1975.

"Gulf 'Victory' Could Lead to Entanglement, Study Says." *Cato Policy Report* 13 (January/February 1991): 10–11.

Hamby, Alonzo L. *Beyond the New Deal: Harry S. Truman and American Liberalism.* New York: Columbia University Press, 1973.

———. *Liberalism and Its Challengers: From F. D. R. to Bush.* 2d ed. New York: Oxford University Press, 1992.

Harries, Owen, ed. *America's Purpose: New Visions of U.S. Foreign Policy.* San Francisco: ICS Press, 1991.

Hart, Gary. *A New Democracy: A Democratic Vision for the 1980s and Beyond.* New York: Quill, 1983.

Hart, Jeffrey. "The Presidency: Shifting Conservative Perspectives?" *National Review* 26 (22 November 1974): 51–55.

Hayden, Tom. *The American Future: New Visions beyond Old Frontiers.* Boston: South End Press, 1980.

Hayek, Friedrich A. *The Road to Serfdom.* Chicago: University of Chicago Press, 1944.

Haynes, John E. "U.S. House Votes in the 97th Congress on Issues with Implications for Federalism." *Publius* 13 (Spring 1983): 107–121.

Hazlitt, Henry. *A New Constitution.* New York: McGraw-Hill, 1976.

Hershey, Marjorie Randon. "The Campaign and the Media." In *The Election of 1988: Reports and Interpretations,* edited by Gerald M. Pomper. Chatham, NJ: Chatham House, 1989.

Heywood, Andrew. *Political Ideologies: An Introduction.* New York: St. Martin's Press, 1992.

Higgs, Robert, and Charlotte Twight. "National Emergency and the Erosion of Private Property Rights." *Cato Journal* 6 (Winter 1987): 747–773.

Himmelfarb, Dan. "Conservative Splits." *Commentary* 85 (May 1988): 54–58.

Himmelstein, Jerome L. *To the Right: The Transformation of American Conservatism.* Berkeley and Los Angeles: University of California Press, 1990.

Hoff, Joan. *Nixon Reconsidered.* New York: Basic Books, 1994.

Hofstadter, Richard. *The Age of Reform: From Bryan to F. D. R.* New York: Alfred A. Knopf, 1972.

Hogan, Frank J. "Important Shifts in Constitutional Doctrines." *American Bar Association Journal* 25 (July 1939): 629–638.

Holt, Marjorie, ed. *The Case against the Reckless Congress.* Ottawa, IL: Green Hill Publishers, 1976.

"The Home Stretch." *New Republic* 111 (6 November 1944): 579–580.

Hoover, Herbert. *The Challenge to Liberty.* New York: Charles Scribner's Sons, 1934.

Horowitz, Donald L. "Are the Courts Going Too Far?" *Commentary* 63 (January 1977): 42–44.

Hoxie, R. Gordon. *Command Decision and the Presidency.* New York: Reader's Digest Press, 1977.

Hughes, Emmet John. *The Living Presidency.* New York: Coward, McCann & Geohegan, 1973.

———. *The Ordeal of Power: A Political Memoir of the Eisenhower Years.* New York: Atheneum, 1963.

Hunt, Franklin. "The Lawyers' War against Democracy." *Commentary* 68 (October 1979): 45–51.

Hunter, James Davison. *Culture Wars: The Struggle to Define America.* New York: Basic Books, 1991.

Hunter, Larry. "U.S. Senate Votes in the 97th Congress on Federalist Issues." *Publius* 13 (Spring 1983): 123–128.

Huntington, Samuel P. "The United States." In *The Crisis of Democracy,* edited by Michel Crozier, Samuel P. Huntington, and Joji Watanuki. New York: New York University Press, 1975.

Israel, Fred X., ed. *The State of the Union Messages of the Presidents.* Vol 3. New York: Chelsea House, 1967.

Ives, C. P. "The Well-Intending Judges." *Modern Age* 13 (Summer 1969): 233–247.

Jackson, Robert H. *The Struggle for Judicial Supremacy.* New York: Alfred A. Knopf, 1941.

Jaffa, Harry. "The Case for a Stronger National Government." In *A Nation of States: Essays on the American Federal System,* edited by Robert A. Goldwin. Chicago: Rand McNally, 1963.

Jeffrey, Douglas. "Executive Authority under the Separation of Powers." In *The Imperial Congress,* edited by Gordon S. Jones and John A. Marini. New York: Pharos Books, 1988.

Jencks, Christopher. *Inequality: A Reassessment of the Effect of Family and Schooling in America.* New York: Basic Books, 1972.

———. "Why Bail Out the States?" *New Republic* 151 (12 December 1964): 8.

Johnson, Gerald. "The President and His Power." *New Republic* 151 (28 September 1964): 19–20.

Johnson, Paul. "Wanted: A New Imperialism." *National Review* 75 (14 December 1992): 28–34.

Jones, Charles O., ed. *The Reagan Legacy: Promise and Performance.* Chatham, NJ: Chatham House, 1988.

Jones, Gordon S., and John A. Marini, eds. *The Imperial Congress.* New York: Pharos Books, 1988.

Jordan, Vernon E., Jr. "Surrender of Federal Programs to the States." *Vital Speeches* 47 (1 May 1981): 421–423.

Judis, John B. "Conservatism and the Price of Success." In *The Reagan Legacy,* edited by Sidney Blumenthal and Thomas Byrne Edsall. New York: Pantheon Press, 1988.

Kahlenberg, Richard. "Class, Not Race: An Affirmative Action That Works." *New Republic* 212 (3 April 1995): 21–27.

Kairys, David, ed. *The Politics of Law: A Progressive Critique.* New York: Pantheon Press, 1990.

Karl, Barry Dean. *Executive Reorganization and Reform in the New Deal: The Genesis of Administrative Management, 1900–1939.* Cambridge: Harvard University Press, 1963.

———. *The Uneasy State: The United States from 1915 to 1945.* Chicago: University of Chicago Press, 1983.

Kaufman, Arnold S. *The Radical Liberal; The New Politics: Theory and Practice.* New York: Atherton, 1968.

Kelman, Mark. "A Critique of Conservative Legal Thought." In *The Politics of Law,* edited by David Kairys. Rev. ed. New York: Pantheon, 1990.

Kendall, Willmoore. *The Conservative Affirmation.* Chicago: Henry Regnery, 1963.

———. "The Liberal Line." *National Review* 1 (4 January 1956): 8.

———. "Lippmann on the Rack." *National Review* 2 (18 July 1956): 11.

———. "Moon-Struck Madness." *National Review* 2 (13 June 1956): 16.

Kernell, Samuel. *Going Public: New Strategies of Presidential Leadership*. Washington: Congressional Quarterly Press, 1986.

Kesselman, Mark, et al. *European Politics in Transition*. Boston: D. C. Heath, 1987.

Key, V. O., Jr. *Politics, Parties, and Pressure Groups*. 5th ed. New York: Thomas Y. Crowell, 1964.

Keynes, Edward, with Randall K. Miller. *The Court vs. Congress: Prayer, Busing, and Abortion*. Durham, NC: Duke University Press, 1989.

Kilpatrick, James J. "The Macaroni Congresses." *Nation's Business* 62 (December 1974): 13–14.

Kinsley, Michael. "The Withering Away of the States." *New Republic* 184 (28 March 1981): 17–21.

Kirk, Russell. *A Program for Conservatives*. Rev. ed. Chicago: Henry Regnery, 1962.

Kirkpatrick, Jeane. "Why the New Right Lost." *Commentary* 63 (February 1979): 34–39.

Koenig, Louis. "Historical Perspective: The Swings and Roundabouts of Presidential Power." In *The Tethered Presidency*, edited by Thomas M. Franck. New York: New York University, 1981.

———. "More Power to the President (Not Less)." *New York Times Magazine*, 3 January 1965, 7, 42–43, 45–46.

Krauthammer, Charles. "Universal Dominion: Toward a Unipolar World." In *America's Purpose: New Visions of U.S. Foreign Policy*, edited by Owen Harries. San Francisco: ICS Press, 1991.

Krieger, Joel. *Reagan, Thatcher, and the Politics of Decline*. New York: Oxford University Press, 1986.

Kristol, Irving. "Defining Our National Interest." In *America's Purpose: New Visions of U.S. Foreign Policy*, edited by Owen Harries. San Francisco: ICS Press, 1990.

———. *Reflections of a Neoconservative*. New York: Basic Books, 1983.

———. *Two Cheers for Capitalism*. New York: Basic Books, 1978.

Kurland, Philip B. *The Constitution and the Warren Court*. Chicago: University of Chicago Press, 1970.

———. "More Power for the President?" *New York Times Book Review*, 6 September 1992, 25.

Kuttner, Robert. *The Life of the Party: Democratic Prospects in 1988 and Beyond*. New York: Viking Press, 1987.

La Follette, Charles M. "A Dangerous Method of Electoral Reform?" *ADA World*, 18 February 1950, 5.

Larson, Arthur. *A Republican Looks at His Party*. New York: Harper & Brothers, 1956.

Larson, E. Richard. "Misreading the Fourteenth Amendment." *Nation* 225 (10 December 1977): 628, 630.

Lasch, Christopher. "The Disintegration of the New Left." In *Political Ideologies,* edited by James A. Gould and Willis H. Truitt. New York: Macmillan, 1973.

Lasser, William. *The Limits of Judicial Power: The Supreme Court in American Politics.* Chapel Hill: University of North Carolina Press, 1988.

Lawrence, David. "The 'New Deal' Lives On." *U.S. News & World Report* 22 (10 January 1947): 26–27.

———. "Read Your History." In *The Editorials of David Lawrence.* Vol. 4. Washington: U.S. News, 1970.

———. "Why An 'Undeclared' War Is Constitutional." In *The Editorials of David Lawrence.* Vol. 4. Washington: U.S. News, 1970.

Layne, Christopher. "The Real Conservative Agenda." *Foreign Policy* 61 (Winter 1985/86): 73–93.

Lazarus, Simon. *The Genteel Populists.* New York: Holt, Rinehart, & Winston, 1974.

Ledeen, Michael. "Common Sense 1992." *American Spectator* 25 (June 1992): 23–26.

Lee, R. Alton. *Truman and Taft-Hartley: A Question of Mandate.* Lexington: University of Kentucky Press, 1966.

Lerner, Max. *Ideas for the Ice Age.* New York: Viking, 1941.

Leuchtenburg, William E. *Franklin D. Roosevelt and the New Deal, 1932–1940.* New York: Harper & Row, 1963.

———. *The Supreme Court Reborn: The Constitutional Revolution in the Age of Roosevelt.* New York: Oxford University Press, 1995.

Levitan, Sar A. "Budgeting States Rights." *Society* 19 (July/August 1982): 75–78.

"Liberty and War." *New Republic* 106 (15 June 1942): 815–816.

Lichtenstein, Nelson. "From Corporatism to Collective Bargaining: Organized Labor and the Eclipse of Social Democracy in the Postwar Era." In *The Rise and Fall of the New Deal Order, 1930–1980,* edited by Steve Fraser and Gary Gerstle. Princeton: Princeton University Press, 1989.

"The Lie to Mr. Eisenhower." *National Review* 3 (5 October 1957): 297–298.

Lockard, Duane. *The Perverted Priorities of American Politics.* 2d ed. New York: Macmillan, 1976.

Long, Stuart. "Thunder of Right." *Reporter* 2 (6 June 1950): 11–13.

Longley, Lawrence D., and Alan G. Braun. *The Politics of Electoral College Reform.* New Haven: Yale University Press, 1972.

Lord, Carnes. "Executive Power and Our Security." *National Interest* 7 (Spring 1987): 3–13.

———. *The Presidency and National Security.* New York: Free Press, 1988.

Lowi, Theodore J. *The End of Liberalism: The Second Republic of the United States.* 2d ed. New York: W. W. Norton, 1979.

―――. *The Personal President: Power Invested, Promise Unfulfilled.* Ithaca, NY: Cornell University Press, 1985.

―――. "Presidential Power and the Ideological Struggle over Its Interpretation." In *The Constitution and the American Presidency,* edited by Martin L. Fausold and Alan Shank. Albany: State University of New York Press, 1991.

Lubell, Samuel. *The Future of American Politics.* 2d ed. Garden City, NY: Doubleday Anchor Books, 1956.

Lyles, Kevin L. "Presidential Expectations and Judicial Performance Revisited: Law and Politics in the Federal District Courts, 1960–1992." *Presidential Studies Quarterly* 26 (Summer 1996): 447–472.

Maass, Arthur. *Muddy Waters.* Cambridge, MA: Harvard University Press, 195l.

MacDonald, Dwight. "The Constitution of the United States Needs to Be Fixed." *Esquire* 70 (October 1968): 143–146, 238–246, 252.

Macedo, Stephen. *The New Right v. the Constitution.* Washington: Cato Institute, 1987.

Maddox, William S., and Stuart A. Lilie. *Beyond Liberal and Conservative.* Washington: Cato Institute, 1984.

"The Magazine's Credenda." *National Review* 1 (19 November 1955): 6.

Mahood, H. R. *Interest Group Politics in America: A New Intensity.* Englewood Cliffs, NJ: Prentice-Hall, 1990.

Malaby, Michael R. "Federalism in the 101st Congress." *Publius* 21 (Summer 1991): 77–92.

Manion, Clarence. "The United States Should Be a Republic." In *Political Ideologies,* edited by James A. Gould and Willis H. Truitt. New York: Macmillan, 1973.

Mansfield, Harvey C., Jr. "The American Election: Toward Constitutional Democracy." *Government and Opposition* 16 (Winter 1981): 3–18.

―――. "Representative Government and Executive Power." In *Economy, Diplomacy, and Statecraft,* edited by Tim Fuller. Colorado Springs: Colorado College Press, 1988.

―――. *Taming the Prince.* New York: Free Press, 1989.

March James G., and Johan P. Olsen. "The New Institutionalism: Organization Factors in Political Life." *American Political Science Review* 78 (September 1984): 734–749.

Markmann, Charles Lam. *The Noblest Cry: A History of the American Civil Liberties Union.* New York: St. Martin's Press, 1965.

Marshall, Burke. *Federalism and Civil Rights.* New York: Columbia University Press, 1964.

Martin, John Frederick. *Civil Rights and the Crisis of Liberalism: The Democratic Party, 1945–1976.* Boulder, CO: Westview Press, 1979.

Mason, Alpheus Thomas. *The Supreme Court from Taft to Warren.* Baton Rouge: Louisiana State University Press, 1958.

Matusow, Allen J. *The Unraveling of America: A History of Liberalism in the 1960s.* New York: Harper & Row, 1984.

Maxwell, J. A. "Yes, to Revenue Sharing." *National Review* 35 (31 March 1972): 341–343.

McAuliffe, Mary Sperling. *Crises on the Left: Cold War Politics and American Liberals, 1947–1954.* Amherst: University of Massachusetts Press, 1978.

McCann, Michael W. *Taking Reform Seriously: Perspectives on Public Interest Liberalism.* Ithaca, NY: Cornell University Press, 1986.

McCarthy, Eugene J. *A Liberal Answer to the Conservative Challenge.* New York: MacFadden, 1964.

"The McClellan Investigation." *National Review* 1 (14 March 1956): 6.

McClellan, James. "State of the American Congress." *Modern Age* 21 (Summer 1977): 227–239.

McConnell, Grant. *The Decline of Agrarian Democracy.* Berkeley and Los Angeles: University of California Press, 1959.

———. *Private Power and American Democracy.* New York: Vintage Books, 1966.

McCullough, David. *Truman.* New York: Simon & Schuster, 1992.

McDonald, Forrest. Foreword to *The Constitution and the American Presidency,* edited by Martin L. Fausold and Alan Shank. Albany: State University of New York Press, 1991.

McDowell, Gary L. *Curbing the Courts: The Constitution and the Limits of Judicial Power.* Baton Rouge: Louisiana State University Press, 1988.

McFarland, Andrew. *Common Cause: Lobbying in the Public Interest.* Chatham, NJ: Chatham House, 1984.

McGill, Ralph. "The South Must Decide." *Forum* 105 (January 1946): 526–527.

McQuaid, Kim. *Big Business and Presidential Power.* New York: William Morrow, 1982.

McWilliams, Wilson Carey. "The Meaning of the Election." In *The Election of 1988: Reports and Interpretations,* edited by Gerald M. Pomper. Chatham, NJ: Chatham House, 1989.

———. "The Meaning of the Election." In *The Election of 1992: Reports and Interpretions,* edited by Gerald M. Pomper. Chatham, NJ: Chatham House, 1993.

Medcalf, Linda J., and Kenneth M. Dolbeare. *Neopolitics: American Political Ideas in the 1980s.* New York: Random House, 1985.

Meese, Edwin, III. "Interpreting the Constitution." In *Interpreting the Constitution: The Debate over Original Intent,* edited by Jack N. Rakove. Boston: Northeastern University Press, 1990.

Melone, Albert P. *Lawyers, Public Policy, and Interest Group Politics.* Washington: University Press of America, 1977.

Mensch, Elizabeth. "The History of Mainstream Legal Thought." In *The Politics of Law: A Progressive Critique,* edited by David Kairys. New York: Pantheon, 1990.

Merry, Robert W. "Congressional Power and Mickey Edwards." *Congressional Quarterly Weekly Report,* 3 March 1990, 714.

Meyer, Frank S. "The Revolt Against Congress." *National Review* 1 (March 7, 1956): 6.

Miles, Michael W. *The Odyssey of the American Right.* New York: Oxford University Press, 1980.

Milkis, Sidney M. *The President and the Parties: The Transformation of the American Party System since the New Deal.* New York: Oxford University Press, 1993.

Milkis, Sidney M., and Michael Nelson. *The American Presidency.* 2d ed. Washington: Congressional Quarterly Press, 1994.

———. *The Supreme Court: Myth and Reality.* Westport, CT: Greenwood Press, 1978.

Miroff, Bruce. *Pragmatic Illusions: The Presidential Politics of John F. Kennedy.* New York: David McKay, 1976.

Mises, Ludwig von. *Omnipotent Government.* New Haven: Yale University Press, 1944.

"Mr. Eisenhower's Third Party." *National Review* 2 (July 18, 1956): 5–6.

Mitau, G. Theodore. *Decade of Decision: The Supreme Court and the Constitutonal Revolution, 1954–1964.* New York: Charles Scribner's Sons, 1967.

Mitchell, Jonathan. "Front Fighters in Congress." *New Republic* 82 (19 June 1935): 156–157.

Moen, Matthew. "The Evolving Politics of the Christian Right." *PS: Political Science & Politics* 29 (September 1996): 461–464.

———. *The Transformation of the Christian Right.* Tuscaloosa: University of Alabama Press, 1992.

Morgan, Iwan W. *Beyond the Liberal Consensus: A Political History of the United States since 1965.* New York: St. Martin's Press, 1994.

Morgenthau, Hans. "Congress and Foreign Policy." *New Republic* 160 (14 June 1969): 17.

Morley, Felix. "American Republic or American Empire?" *Modern Age* 1 (Summer 1957): 20–32.

———. "Deliberate Pace in Congress Safeguards Your Freedom." *Nation's Business* 51 (March 1963): 27–28.

———. *Federalism and Freedom.* Chicago: Henry Regnery, 1959.

———. *For the Record.* South Bend, IN: Regnery/Gateway, 1979.

———. *State and Society.* Menlo Park, CA: Institute for Human Studies, 1976.

Moynihan, Daniel Patrick. *The Politics of a Guaranteed Income.* New York: Random House, 1973.

Mulder, Ronald A. *The Insurgent Progressives in the United States Senate and the New Deal, 1933–1939.* New York: Garland, 1979.

Muravchik, Joshua. *Exporting Democracy: Fulfilling America's Destiny.* Washington: American Enterprise Institute, 1991.

Murphy, Walter F. *Congress and the Court: A Case Study of the American Political Process.* Chicago: University of Chicago Press, 1962.

Nash, George H. *The Conservative Intellectual Movement in America Since 1945.* New York: Basic Books, 1976.

Nathan, Richard P. *The Administrative Presidency.* New York: Wiley, 1983.

————. *The Plot That Failed: Nixon and the Administrative Presidency.* New York: Wiley, 1975.

Neuberger, Richard. "Let's Limit All Terms of Office!" *New Republic* 126 (23 June 1952): 10.

"New Tools for Uncle Sam." *New Republic* 89 (27 January 1937): 371–372.

Nichols, Egbert Ray, ed. *Congress or the Supreme Court: Which Shall Rule America?* New York: Noble & Noble, 1938.

Nixon, Richard M. *RN: The Memoirs of Richard Nixon.* New York: Warner Books, 1978.

Nock, Albert Jay. *Our Enemy, The State.* New York: William Morrow, 1935.

Novak, Michael. *Choosing Our King.* New York: Macmillan, 1974.

————. *The Spirit of Democratic Capitalism.* New York: Simon & Schuster, 1982.

Nuechterlein, James A. "Watergate: Toward a Revisionist View." *Commentary* 68 (August 1979): 39.

O'Brien, David M. "The Reagan Judges: His Most Enduring Legacy? In *The Reagan Legacy,* edited by Charles O. Jones. Chatham, NJ: Chatham House, 1988.

————. *Storm Center: The Supreme Court in American Politics.* 2d ed. New York: W. W. Norton, 1990.

"One Insurance Plan—Or Forty–Eight?" *New Republic* 81 (January 2, 1935): 206–207.

O'Neill, William L. *A Better World: The Great Schism—Stalinism and the American Intellectuals.* New York: Simon & Schuster, 1982.

Orfield, Gary. *Congressional Power: Congress and Social Change.* New York: Harcourt Brace Jovanovich, 1975.

Ornstein, Norman. "The Permanent Democratic Congress." *Public Interest* 100 (Summer 1990): 24–44.

Osborne, David. *Laboratories of Democracy.* Boston: Harvard Business School Press, 1990.

Osborne, David, and Ted Gaebler. *Reinventing Government: How the Entrepreneurial Spirit Is Transforming the Public Sector.* Reading, MA: Addison-Wesley, 1992.

Padover, Saul K. "The Power of the President." *Commonweal* 89 (9 August 1968): 521–525.

Pagano, Michael A., and Ann O'M. Bowman. "The State of American Federalism, 1992–1993." *Publius* 23 (Summer 1993): 1–22.

Palmer, John L., and Isabel V. Sawhill. "Overview." In *The Reagan Record: An*

*Assessment of America's Changing Domestic Priorities,* edited by John L. Palmer and Isabel V. Sawhill. Cambridge, MA: Ballinger, 1984.

Parmet, Herbert S. *Eisenhower and the American Crusades.* New York: Macmillan, 1972.

Patterson, James T. *Congressional Conservatism and the New Deal: The Growth of the Conservative Coalition in Congress, 1933–39.* Lexington: University of Kentucky Press, 1967.

———. *Mr. Republican: A Biography of Robert A.Taft.* Boston: Houghton Mifflin, 1972.

———. *The New Deal and the States.* Westport, CT: Greenwood Press, 1969.

Pells, Richard H. *The Liberal Mind in a Conservative Age: American Intellectuals in the 1940s and 1950s.* New York: Harper & Row, 1985.

Perry, Michael J. *The Constitution, the Courts, and Human Rights: An Inquiry into the Legitimacy of Constitutional Policymaking by the Judiciary.* New Haven: Yale University Press, 1982.

Pertschuk, Michael. *Revolt against Regulation: The Rise and Pause of the Consumer Movement.* Berkeley and Los Angeles: University of California Press, 1982.

Peters, Charles. "A Neoliberal's Manifesto." *Washington Monthly* 15 (May 1983): 8–14.

Peters, Charles, and Phillip Keisling, eds. *A New Road for America.* Lanham, MD: Madison Books, 1985.

Peterson, Paul E., and Mark Rom. "Lower Taxes, More Spending, and Budget Deficits." In *The Reagan Legacy,* edited by Charles O. Jones. Chatham, NJ: Chatham House, 1988.

Pfiffner, James P. "Divided Government and the Problem of Governance." In *Divided Democracy,* edited by James A. Thurber. Washington: Congressional Quarterly Press, 1991.

Phillips, Kevin P. *The Emerging Republican Majority.* New Rochelle, NY: Arlington House, 1969.

———. *The Politics of Rich and Poor: Wealth and the American Electorate in the Reagan Aftermath.* New York: Random House, 1990.

———. *Post-Conservative America: People, Politics, and Ideology in a Time of Crisis.* New York: Random House, 1982.

Pines, Burton Yale. "A Primer for Conservatives." *The National Interest* 23 (Spring 1991): 68.

Piper, J. Richard. "Presidential-Congressional Power Prescriptions in Conservative Political Thought since 1933." *Presidential Studies Quarterly* 21 (Winter 1991): 35–54.

———. "Situational Constitutionalism and Presidential Power: The Rise and Fall of the Liberal Model of Presidential Government." *Presidential Studies Quarterly* 24 (Summer 1994): 577–594.

Plotkin, Harry. "Issues in the Campaign." In *The Election of 1984: Reports and Inter- pretations*, edited by Gerald M. Pomper. Chatham, NJ: Chatham House, 1985.

Podhoretz, Norman. "Buchanan and the Conservative Crackup." *Commentary* 93 (April 1992): 30–34.

Polenberg, Richard J. *Reorganizing Roosevelt's Government: The Controversy over Executive Reorganization, 1936–1939*. Cambridge: Harvard University Press, 1966.

Polsby, Nelson W. "Against Presidential Greatness." *Commentary* 63 (January 1977): 61–64.

Polsby, Nelson W. and Aaron Wildavsky. *Presidential Elections: Strategies of Ameri- can Electoral Politics*. 4th ed. New York: Charles Scribner's Sons, 1976.

Porter, Kirk H., and Donald B. Johnson, eds. *National Party Platforms, 1840–1968*. Urbana: University of Illinois Press, 1970.

Posner, Richard A. *Economic Analysis of the Law*. 3d ed. Boston: Little, Brown, 1986.

"The President Reports." *New Republic* 95 (6 July 1938): 237–238.

Pritchett, C. Herman. *The Roosevelt Court: A Study in Judicial Politics and Values*. Chicago: Quadrangle Books, 1948.

———. *Congress versus the Supreme Court, 1957–1960*. New York: DeCapo Press, 1973.

"A Program for Conservatives." *Nation* 143 (5 September 1936): 260–261.

"The Proposal for a Federal Compulsory Insurance System for Citizens' Medical Care." *Congressional Digest* 24 (August–September 1946), 193–224.

"Purging the Supreme Court." *Nation* 144 (13 February 1937): 173–174.

"The Question of Federal Funds for Public Schools." *Congressional Digest* 25 (Feb- ruary 1946): 35–64.

"The Question of Federal or State Control of the Employment Services." *Congres- sional Digest* 25 (April 1946): 99–128.

Quirk, Paul J. "Domestic Policy: Divided Government and Creative Presidential Leadership." In *The Bush Presidency: First Appraisals*, edited by Colin Campbell and Bert A. Rockman. Chatham, NJ: Chatham House, 1991.

Radosh, Ronald. *Prophets on the Right: Profiles of Conservative Critics of American Globalism*. New York: Simon & Schuster, 1975.

Rae, Nicol C. *The Decline and Fall of the Liberal Republicans from 1952 to the Present*. New York: Oxford University Press, 1989.

———. *Southern Democrats*. New York: Oxford University Press, 1994.

Rakove, Jack N., ed. *Interpreting the Constitution: The Debate over Original Intent*. Boston: Northeastern University Press, 1990.

Rankin, Robert Stanley. "The Presidency under the New Deal." *South Atlantic Quarterly* 33 (April 1934): 152–164.

Rawls, John. *Political Liberalism*. New York: Columbia University Press, 1993.

Rauch, Basil. *The History of the New Deal, 1933–1938.* New York: Capricorn Books, 1944.

Reagan, Ronald. "Inaugural Address, 1981." In *The Election of 1980: Reports and Interpretations,* edited by Gerald M. Pomper. Chatham, NJ: Chatham House, 1981.

Reed, Ralph. "Casting a Wider Net." *Policy Review* 65 (Summer 1993): 31–35.

"Reelect Roosevelt." *New Republic* 103 (July 22, 1940), 102–103.

Reeves, Richard. *President Kennedy.* New York: Simon & Schuster, 1993.

Regnery, Henry. "Emerging Conservatism: Kilpatrick, Morley, and Burnham." *Modern Age* 22 (Summer 1978): 242.

Rehnquist, William H. "The Notion of a Living Constitution." *Texas Law Review* 54 (May 1976): 605.

Reichard, Gary. *The Reaffirmation of Republicanism: Eisenhower and the Eighty-third Congress.* Knoxville: University of Tennessee Press, 1975.

Reichley, A. James. *Conservatives in an Age of Change: The Nixon and Ford Administrations.* Washington: Brookings Institution, 1981.

"The Revived Controversy over the Electoral College System," *Congressional Digest* 27 (April 1948), 101–128.

Riencourt, Amaury de. *The Coming Caesars.* New York: Coward-McCann.

Rieselbach, Leroy N. *The Roots of Isolationism: Congressional Voting and Presidential Leadership in Foreign Policy.* Indianapolis, IN: Bobbs-Merrill, 1966.

Riker, William H. *Federalism: Origin, Operation, Significance.* Boston: Little, Brown, 1964.

Rivlin, Alice M. *Reviving the American Dream: The Economy, the States & the Federal Government.* Washington: Brookings Institution, 1992.

Roberts, Chalmers M. *In the Shadow of Power: The Story of the Washington Post.* Washington: Seven Locks Press, 1989.

Roberts, James C. *The Conservative Decade—Emerging Leaders of the 1980s.* Westport, CT: Arlington House, 1980.

Robertson, David B., and Dennis R. Judd. *The Development of American Public Policy: The Structure of Policy Restraint.* Glenview, IL: Scott, Foresman, 1989.

Rodell, Fred. "The Case for Judicial Activism." In *Basic Issues of American Democracy,* edited by Samuel Hendel. 8th ed. Englewood Cliffs, NJ: Prentice-Hall, 1976.

Rohr, John A. *To Run a Constitution: The Legitimacy of the Administrative State.* Lawrence: University Press of Kansas, 1986.

Roosevelt, Franklin D. "Commonwealth Club Address." In *New Deal Thought,* edited by Howard Zinn. Indianapolis, IN: Bobbs-Merrill, 1966.

———. "Inaugural Address, 1944." In *The State of the Union Messages of the Presidents,* edited by Fred X. Israel. Vol. 3. New York: Chelsea, 1967.

"Roosevelt and Business: A Word of Warning." *New Republic* 75 (10 May 1933): 350–351.

Rosenthal, Alan. "Could Kennedy Budge the Congress?" *New Republic* 148 (4 May 1963): 13–15.

Ross, Irwin. *Strategy for Liberals: The Politics of the Mixed Economy.* New York: Harper & Brothers, 1949.

Ross, William G. *A Muted Fury: Populists, Progressives, and Labor Unions Confront the Courts, 1890–1937.* Princeton: Princeton University Press, 1994.

Rothbard, Murray N. "The Great Society: A Libertarian Critique." In *The Great Society Reader: The Failure of Liberalism,* edited by Marvin E. Gittleman and David Mermelstein. New York: Random House, 1967.

Rothenberg, Randall. *The Neoliberals: Creating the New American Politics.* New York: Simon & Schuster, 1984.

Rotunda, Ronald D. *The Politics of Language: Liberalism as Word and Symbol.* Iowa City: University of Iowa Press, 1986.

Russell, William F. "So Concerned and So Dedicated." *Atlantic Monthly* (May 1935): 520.

Safire, William. *Before the Fall: An Inside View of the Pre-Watergate White House.* Garden City, NY: Doubleday, 1975.

Salamon, Lester, and Michael S. Lund, eds. *The Reagan Presidency and the Governing of America.* Washington: Urban Institute Press, 1985.

Salisbury, Robert. "An Exchange Theory of Interest Groups." *Midwest Journal of Political Science* 13 (February 1969): 1–32.

Schlesinger, Arthur M., Jr. *The Coming of the New Deal.* Boston: Houghton Mifflin, 1959.

———. *The Crisis of the Old Order.* Boston: Houghton Mifflin, 1957.

———. *The Imperial Presidency.* New York: Popular Library, 1973.

———. "The Imperial Temptation." *New Republic* 196 (16 March 1987): 17–18.

———. *The Politics of Upheaval.* Boston: Houghton Mifflin, 1960.

———. "The Supreme Court: 1947." *Fortune* 35 (January 1947): 73–79, 201–202, 204, 206, 211–212.

———. *A Thousand Days: John F. Kennedy in the White House.* Greenwich, CT: Fawcett Crest, 1965.

———. *The Vital Center.* Boston: Houghton Mifflin, 1949.

Schlesinger, Arthur M., Jr., and Alfred de Grazia. *Congress and the Presidency: Their Role in Modern Times.* Washington: American Enterprise Institute, 1967.

Schneider, Jerrold. *Ideological Coalitions in Congress.* Westport, CT: Greenwood Press, 1979.

Schubert, Glendon. *The Judicial Mind: The Attitudes and Ideologies of Supreme Court Justices, 1946–1963.* Evanston, IL: Northwestern University Press, 1965.

Schwab, Larry M. *The Illusion of a Conservative Reagan Revolution.* New Brunswick, NJ: Transaction Publishers, 1991.

Schwartz, Bernard. *The Ascent of Pragmatism.* Reading, MA: Addison-Wesley, 1990.

————. "Imperial Presidential Power." *Center Magazine* 11 (January 1978): 20–21.

————. *The New Right and the Constitution: Turning Back the Legal Clock.* Boston: Northeastern University Press, 1990.

Schwartz, Herman. *Packing the Courts: The Conservative Campaign to Rewrite the Constitution.* New York: Charles Scribner's Sons, 1988.

Schwarz, Jordan A. *The New Dealers: Power Politics in the Age of Roosevelt.* New York: Alfred A. Knopf, 1993.

"Seizure—Threat Against Labor." *Nation* 174 (10 May 1952): 443–444.

Shadegg, Stephen M. *What Happened to Goldwater: The Inside Story of the 1964 Republican Campaign.* New York: Holt, Rinehart, & Winston, 1965.

"The Shape of Things." *Nation* 147 (13 September 1938): 213.

"Should Congress Give Its Approval to the President's 'Civil Rights' Program?" *Congressional Digest* 27 (April 1948).

Siegan, Bernard H. *Economic Liberties and the Constitution.* Chicago: University of Chicago Press, 1980.

Silk, Leonard. *Nixonomics: How the Dismal Science of Free Enterprise Became the Black Art of Controls.* New York: Praeger, 1972.

Simmons, David A. "Reorganization of the Federal Government." *American Bar Association Journal* 31 (February 1945): 63–66.

————. "The Supremacy of Law." *American Bar Association Journal* 32 (January 1946): 17–21.

Sitkoff, Harvard A. *A New Deal for Blacks: The Emergence of Civil Rights as a National Issue.* New York: Oxford University Press, 1978.

"The Smell of Oil." *New Republic* 115 (5 August 1946): 12.

Smith, Hedrick. *The Power Game: How Washington Works.* New York: Ballantine Books, 1988.

Smith, T. V. "Political Liberty Today: Is It Being Restricted or Enlarged by Economic Regulation?" *American Political Science Review* 31 (April 1937): 243–252.

"Social Control vs. the Constitution." *New Republic* 82 (12 June 1935): 116–118.

Sorensen, Theodore. "Political Perspective: Who Speaks for the National Interest?" In *The Tethered Presidency,* edited by Thomas M. Franck. New York: New York University Press, 1981.

"The South Girds Its Loins." *National Review* 1 (29 February 1956): 5.

Spaeth, Herbert J. *Supreme Court Policy Making: Explanation and Prediction.* San Francisco: W. H. Freeman, 1979.

Stanmeyer, William A. "Judicial Supremacy." In *The New Right Papers,* edited by Robert W. Whitaker. New York: St. Martin's Press, 1982.

"State of Disunion." *Nation* 234 (4 February 1982): 129.

"Steel and Stabilization," *Nation* 174 (10 May 1952): 360.

"Steel—What Next, Mr. President?" *New Republic* (21 April 1952): 5.

Steinfels, Peter. *The Neoconservatives: The Men Who Are Changing American Politics.* New York: Simon & Schuster, 1979.

Sundquist, James L. *The Decline and Resurgence of Congress.* Washington: Brookings Institution, 1981.

———. *Dynamics of the Party System: Alignment and Realignment of Political Parties in the United States.* Rev. ed. Washington: Brookings Institution, 1973.

———. *Politics and Policy: The Eisenhower, Kennedy, and Johnson Years.* Washington: Brookings Institution, 1968.

"Swing of the Pendulum." *New Republic* 164 (27 March 1971): 6–7.

Taft, Philip. "Political Activity of Organized Labor." In *Labor and American Politics*, edited by Charles M. Rehmus and Doris B. McLaughlin. Ann Arbor: University of Michigan Press, 1967.

Tananbaum, Duane. *The Bricker Amendment Controversy: A Test of Eisenhower's Political Leadership.* Ithaca, NY: Cornell University Press, 1988.

Taylor, Telford. "Congress vs. the President." *ADA World*, March 1954, 2.

———. *Grand Inquest: The Story of Congressional Investigations.* New York: Simon & Schuster, 1955.

Thurber, James A. "The Impact of Budget Reform on Presidential and Congressional Governance." In *Divided Democracy*, edited by James A. Thurber. Washington: Congressional Quarterly Press, 1991.

Tower, John. "Congress versus the President: The Formulation and Implementation of American Foreign Policy." *Foreign Affairs* 60 (Winter 1981/82): 229–246.

TRB. "T. R. B. from Washington." *New Republic* 144 (6 March 1961): 2.

———. "Washington Notes." *New Republic* 74 (22 March 1933): 156.

———. "Washington Notes." *New Republic* 75 (10 May): 363–364.

———. "Washington Wire." *New Republic* 130 (24 May 1954): 2.

Tribe, Laurence H. and Michael C. Dorf. *On Reading the Constitution.* Cambridge: Harvard University Press, 1991.

Tsongas, Paul. *The Road from Here: Liberalism and Realities in the 1980s.* New York: Alfred A. Knopf, 1981.

Tuccille, Jerome. *Radical Libertarianism: A Right-Wing Alternative.* Indianapolis, IN: Bobbs-Merrill, 1970.

Tugwell, Rexford G. "Address to the Federation of Bar Associations of Western New York." Reprinted in *Congressional Digest* 12 (November 1933), 268, 270, 272.

———. "The Historians and the Presidency: An Essay Review." *Political Science Quarterly* 86 (June 1971): 183–204.

Tugwell, Rexford G., and Thomas E. Cronin, eds. *The Presidency Reappraised.* New York: Praeger, 1974.

Tyrell, Emmett. "The Coming Conservative Crack-up." *American Spectator* 20 (Summer 1987): 17–19, 51.

Van Dyke, Vernon. *Ideology and Political Choice: The Search for Freedom, Justice, and Virtue.* Chatham, NJ: Chatham House, 1995.

Viguerie, Richard. *The Establishment vs. the People.* Chicago: Regnery Gateway, 1983.

Vogel, David. *Fluctuating Fortunes: The Political Power of Business in America.* New York: Basic Books, 1989.

"Voting for a Party." *New Republic* 73 (20 October 1932): 272–273.

Walker, David B. "American Federalism from Johnson to Bush." *Publius* 21 (Winter 1991): 105–119.

Walker, Thomas G., and Deborah J. Barrow. "The Diversification of the Federal Bench: Policy and Process Ramifications." *Journal of Politics* 47 (May 1985): 596–619.

Walton, Richard J. *Cold War and Counterrevolution: The Foreign Policy of John F. Kennedy.* Baltimore: Penguin Books, 1973.

———. *Henry Wallace, Harry Truman, and the Cold War.* New York: Viking Press, 1976.

"The War Powers Act Controversy." *Congressional Digest* 62 (November 1983): 257–288.

Warren, Donald I. *The Radical Center: Middle Americans and the Politics of Alienation.* South Bend, IN: Notre Dame University Press, 1976.

Wattenberg, Ben J. *The First Universal Nation: Leading Indicators and Ideas about the Surge of America in the 1990s.* New York: Free Press, 1991.

Wattenberg, Martin P. *The Rise of Candidate-Centered Politics.* Cambridge: Harvard University Press, 1991.

Weaver, Paul. "Liberals and the Presidency." *Commentary* 60 (October 1975): 48–53.

Wendt, Lloyd. *Chicago Tribune: The Rise of a Great American Newspaper.* Chicago: Rand McNally, 1979.

West, William F., and Joseph Cooper. "Legislative Influence v. Presidential Dominance: Competing Models of Bureaucratic Control." *Political Science Quarterly* 104 (Winter 1989/90): 581–606.

"What to Do with the N. R. A." *New Republic* 74 (30 March 1933): 144–146.

"What's New?" *New Republic* 164 (6 February 1971): 13.

Whitaker, Robert W., ed. *The New Right Papers.* New York: St. Martin's Press, 1982.

White, Leonard D. *The Federalists.* New York: Macmillan, 1948.

———. *The Jacksonians.* New York: Macmillan, 1954.

———. *The Jeffersonians.* New York: Macmillan, 1951.

———. *The Republican Era: 1869–1901.* New York: Macmillan, 1958.

"Why the South Must Prevail." *National Review* 3 (24 August 1957): 149.

Wicker, Tom. "The Presidency under Scrutiny." *Harper's* 239 (October 1969): 92–94.

Will, George F. *Restoration: Congressional Term Limits and the Recovery of Deliberative Democracy.* New York: Free Press, 1992.

"Will Roosevelt Go Left?" *Nation* 143 (7 November 1936): 535–536.

Williams, James B., and George W. Carey. "The Founding Fathers and 'The Federalist.'" *Modern Age* 26 (Summer/Fall 1987): 315–317.

Williamson, Richard S. "The 1982 Federalism Negotiations." *Publius* 13 (Spring 1983): 11–32.

Wills, Garry. *Nixon Agonistes: The Crisis of the Self-Made Man.* New York: New American Library, 1969.

Wilson, James Q. *The Amateur Democrat: Club Politics in Three Cities.* Chicago: University of Chicago Press, 1962.

Wolfe, Christopher. *Judicial Activism: Bulwark of Freedom or Precarious Security?* Pacific Grove, CA: Brooks/Cole, 1991.

———. *The Rise of Modern Judicial Review: From Constitutional Interpretation to Judge-Made Law.* Rev. ed. Lanham, MD: Rowman & Littlefield, 1994.

Wolfskill, George. *The Revolt of the Conservatives: A History of the American Liberty League, 1934–1940.* Boston: Houghton Mifflin, 1962.

Wood, Gordon S. "The Fundamentalists and the Constitution." *New York Review of Books* (18 February 1988): 33–40.

Yarbrough, Tinsley E. "Bush and the Courts." In *The Bush Presidency,* edited by Dilys Hill and Phil Williams. New York: St. Martin's Press, 1994.

Young, Roland. *Congressional Politics in the Second World War.* New York: Columbia University Press, 1956.

Zeigler, Harmon. *Interest Groups in American Society.* Englewood Cliffs, NJ: Prentice-Hall, 1964.

Zentner, Scot. "Liberalism and Executive Power: Woodrow Wilson and the American Founders." *Polity* 26 (Summer 1994): 577–599.

Zimmerman, Joseph F. "Federal Preemptions under Reagan's New Federalism." *Publius* 21 (Winter 1991): 7–28.

Zinn, Howard, ed. *New Deal Thought.* Indianapolis, IN: Bobbs-Merrill, 1966.

# Index

Aberbach, Joel D., 136n2, 322–23, 345
abortion, 205, 207, 272, 309, 314, 382
Abzug, Bella, 241
Adams, Brock, 222, 249
affirmative action programs: and liberalism, 108, 204, 207, 314, 363; Nixon's Philadelphia Plan, 213; Reagan-Bush attacks on, 309
Agency for Consumer Advocacy, 207, 208, 251, 275, 277, 288
Allende, Salvador, 214
America First, 23
American Association of Retired Persons, 313
American Bar Association: and the Equal Rights Amendment, 229; anti–New Deal conservatism, 38–39, 53, 68, 72, 85, 90; post–World War II conservatism, 163, 165, 170, 171, 176, 178, 185, 190, 229; roles in judicial selection, 324
American Civil Liberties Union, 19, 36, 53, 131, 147, 327
American Conservative Union, 133, 306, 347
American Enterprise Institute (formerly American Enterprise Association), 133–34
American Farm Bureau Federation (AFBF), 37–38, 133, 171, 229
American Federation of Labor (AFL), 53, 130
American Federation of Labor–Congress of Industrial Organizations (AFL-CIO): Committee on Political Education,

130; and Mondale campaign, 327; opposition to item veto, 362; roles in liberal coalition, 1955–66, 130, 147; roles in liberal coalition after 1966, 203, 208, 210, 227, 247–48
American Jewish Committee, 135
American Liberty League, 14, 37–38, 70, 88
American Medical Association (AMA), 133, 229
*American Spectator*, 230, 328
Americans for Constitutional Action (ACA), 132
Americans for Democratic Action (ADA): and Bricker amendment opposition, 362; and Cold War, 198, 145; and economic democracy, 302; and electoral college, 188; opposition to item veto, 362; and new-politics liberalism, 202, 203, 204, 327; and positive freedoms, 103; and post–World War II liberalism, 129–30; presidential power prescriptions of, 148
Anderson, John, 316
Anderson, Paul, 85
Andrews, William G., 4, 84, 395, 405
Arnall, Ellis, 32
Arnold, Peri, 405
Arnold, Thurman, 30, 50
Ascoli, Max, 135
Aspin, Les, 362, 381
Avery, Sewell, 70

Babbitt, Bruce, 325, 366
Bailey, Josiah, 21, 77, 89

435

# About the Author

J. Richard Piper is professor of political science and director of the Honors Program at the University of Tampa. He is the author of various articles in both American and British scholarly journals on political parties, ideologies, and government institutions in the United States and the United Kingdom.

# Date Due

| | | | |
|---|---|---|---|
| | | | |
| | | | |
| | | | |
| | | | |
| | | | |
| | | | |
| | | | |
| | | | |
| | | | |
| | | | |
| | | | |
| | | | |
| | | | |
| | | | |
| | | | |
| | | | |